ARTIFICIAL INTELLIGENCE A

New Tools for Law Practic

The field of artificial intelligence (AI) and the law is on the cusp of a revolution that began with text analytic programs like IBM's Watson and Debater and the open-source information management architectures on which they are based. Today, new legal applications are beginning to appear, and this book – designed to explain computational processes to non-programmers – describes how they will change the practice of law, specifically by connecting computational models of legal reasoning directly with legal text, generating arguments for and against particular outcomes, predicting outcomes, and explaining these predictions with reasons that legal professionals will be able to evaluate for themselves. These legal apps will support conceptual legal information retrieval and enable cognitive computing, enabling a collaboration between humans and computers in which each performs the kinds of intelligent activities that they can do best. Anyone interested in how AI is changing the practice of law should read this illuminating work.

Dr. Kevin D. Ashley is a Professor of Law and Intelligent Systems at the University of Pittsburgh, Senior Scientist, Learning Research and Development Center, and Adjunct Professor of Computer Science. He received a B.A. from Princeton University, a JD from Harvard Law School, and Ph.D. in computer science from the University of Massachusetts. A visiting scientist at the IBM Thomas J. Watson Research Center, NSF Presidential Young Investigator, and Fellow of the American Association for Artificial Intelligence, he is co-Editor-in-Chief of *Artificial Intelligence and Law* and teaches in the University of Bologna Erasmus Mundus doctoral program in Law, Science, and Technology.

Artificial Intelligence and Legal Analytics

NEW TOOLS FOR LAW PRACTICE IN THE DIGITAL AGE

KEVIN D. ASHLEY

University of Pittsburgh School of Law

CAMBRIDGE
UNIVERSITY PRESS

CAMBRIDGE
UNIVERSITY PRESS

University Printing House, Cambridge CB2 8BS, United Kingdom

One Liberty Plaza, 20th Floor, New York, NY 10006, USA

477 Williamstown Road, Port Melbourne, VIC 3207, Australia

314-321, 3rd Floor, Plot 3, Splendor Forum, Jasola District Centre, New Delhi – 110025, India

79 Anson Road, #06-04/06, Singapore 079906

Cambridge University Press is part of the University of Cambridge.

It furthers the University's mission by disseminating knowledge in the pursuit of education, learning, and research at the highest international levels of excellence.

www.cambridge.org
Information on this title: www.cambridge.org/9781107171503
DOI: 10.1017/9781316761380

First published 2017
Reprinted 2018

Printed in the United Kingdom by Clays, St Ives plc

A *catalogue record for this publication is available from the British Library.*

Library of Congress Cataloging-in-Publication Data

ISBN 978-1-107-17150-3 Hardback
ISBN 978-1-316-62281-0 Paperback

For Alida, forever

Contents

Illustrations

Tables

Acknowledgments

The University of Pittsburgh School of Law provided summer Dean's Scholarships that supported writing this book. Notes for and drafts of this book evolved over the course of teaching in the University of Bologna Erasmus Mundus doctoral program in Law, Science, and Technology, an opportunity for which I thank Professor Monica Palmirani. Vern Walker, Jaromir Savelka, and Thomas Gordon read prior drafts and provided helpful suggestions for which I thank them. I am especially grateful to my former Ph.D. student and continuing research colleague, Matthias Grabmair, for his careful reading and many thoughtful suggestions. Matthias's work on legal text analytics, prediction and case-based argumentation and his and Jaromir's work applying machine learning to statutes convinced me that it was time to write this book. Advising, collaborating with, and learning from Matthias have been some of the great joys of my professional life as a teacher. I would never have had a professional life as a teacher, and I would never have completed this book, without my wife Alida's constant love and support. Our daughter Alexandra, who keeps us smiling as we toil away with our research and writing, helped me select the cover art.

PART I

Computational Models of Legal Reasoning

1

Introducing AI & Law and Its Role in Future Legal Practice

1.1. INTRODUCTION

Artificial Intelligence and Law (AI & Law), a research field since the 1980s with roots in the previous decades, is about to experience a revolution. Teams of researchers in question answering (QA), information extraction (IE), and argument mining from text planted the seeds of this revolution with programs like IBM's Watson and Debater and the open-source information management architectures on which these programs are based. From these seeds, new applications for the legal domain are sure to grow. Indeed, they are growing now. This book explains how.

Programs like Watson and Debater will not perform legal reasoning. They may be able to answer legal questions in a superficial sense, but they cannot explain their answers or make legal arguments. The open-source text analysis tools on which they are based, however, will make a profound difference in the development of new legal applications. They will identify argument-related information in legal texts that can transform legal information retrieval into a new kind of conceptual information retrieval: argument retrieval (AR).

Computational models developed by AI & Law researchers will perform the legal reasoning. The newly extracted argument-related information will connect the computational models of legal reasoning (CMLRs) and argument directly with legal texts. The models can generate arguments for and against particular outcomes in problems input as texts, predict a problem's outcome, and explain their predictions with reasons that legal professionals will recognize and can evaluate for themselves. The result will be a new kind of legal app, one that enables cognitive computing, a kind of collaborative activity between humans and computers in which each performs the kinds of intelligent activities that they can do best.

This chapter introduces the subject of AI & Law and explains the role it will play in light of the new technologies for analyzing legal texts. It explains how these technologies enable new tools for legal practice using computational models of legal reasoning and argumentation developed by AI & Law researchers.

Some questions addressed in this chapter include: What is the subject of Artificial Intelligence and Law? What is a CMLR? What are the new technologies for auto-mated QA, IE, and argument mining from texts? What roles will AI & Law CMLRs and argument play given these new technologies? What are conceptual information retrieval and cognitive computing, and what kind of legal app will support them?

1.2. AI & LAW AND THE PROMISE OF TEXT ANALYTICS

The goal of much of the research in AI & Law has been to develop CMLRs that can make legal arguments and use them to predict outcomes of legal disputes. A *CMLR* is a computer program that implements a process evidencing attributes of human legal reasoning. The process may involve analyzing a situation and answering a legal question, predicting an outcome, or making a legal argument. A subset of CMLRs implements a process of legal argumentation as part of their reasoning. These are called computational models of legal argument (CMLAs).

CMLRs and CMLAs break down a complex human intellectual task, such as estimating the settlement value of a product liability suit or analyzing an offer and acceptance problem in a first-year contracts course, into a set of computational steps or *algorithm*. The models specify how a problem is input and the type of legal result to output. In between, the model builders have constructed a computational mech-anism to apply domain knowledge to perform the steps and transform the inputs to outputs.

In developing these models, researchers address such questions as how to rep-resent what a legal rule means so that a computer program can decide whether it applies to a situation, how to distinguish "hard" from "easy" legal issues, and the roles that cases and values play in interpreting legal rules. Their answers to these ques-tions are not philosophical but scientific; their computer programs not only model legal reasoning tasks but also actually perform them; and the researchers conduct experiments to evaluate how well their programs perform.

While AI & Law researchers have made great strides, a knowledge representation bottleneck has impeded their progress toward contributing to legal practice. So far, the substantive legal knowledge employed by their computational models has had to be extracted *manually* from legal sources, that is, from the cases, statutes, regulations, contracts, and other texts that legal professionals actually use. That is, human experts have had to read the legal texts and represent relevant parts of their content in a form the computational models could use. An inability to automatically connect their CMLRs directly to legal texts has limited the researchers' ability to apply their programs in real-world legal information retrieval, prediction, and decision-making.

Recent developments in computerized QA, IE from text, and argument min-ing promise to change that. "A Question-answering system searches a large text collection and finds a short phrase or sentence that precisely answers a user's question" (Prager et al., 2000). "Information extraction is the problem of summarizing the essential details particular to a given document" (Freitag, 2000). Argument mining involves automatically identifying argumentative structures within document texts, for instance, premises and conclusion, and relationships between pairs of arguments (ACL-AMW, 2016). All three technologies usually rely, at least in part, on applying machine learning (ML) to assist programs in processing semantic information in the texts.

A more general term for these techniques, *text analytics* or text mining, "refers to the discovery of knowledge that can be found in text archives ... [It] describes a set of linguistic, statistical, and machine learning techniques that model and structure the information content of textual sources for business intelligence, exploratory data analysis, research, or investigation" (Hu and Liu, 2012, pp. 387–8). When the texts to be analyzed are legal, we may refer to "legal text analytics" or more simply "legal analytics," the "deriving of substantively meaningful insight from some sort of legal data," including legal textual data (Katz and Bommarito, 2014, p. 3).

The text analytic techniques may open the knowledge acquisition bottleneck that has long hampered progress in fielding intelligent legal applications. Instead of relying solely on manual techniques to represent what legal texts mean in ways that programs can use, researchers can automate the knowledge representation process.

As a result, some CMLRs and CMLAs may soon be linked with text analysis tools to enable the construction of a new generation of legal applications and some novel legal practice tools. Specifically, CMLRs and CMLAs developed in the AI & Law field will employ information extracted automatically from legal texts such as case decisions and statutes to assist humans in answering legal questions, predicting case outcomes, providing explanations, and making arguments for and against legal conclusions more effectively than existing technologies can.

In a complementary way, the AI & Law programs can provide answers to questions that are likely on the minds of technologists in commercial laboratories and start-ups: Now that we are able to extract semantic information automatically from legal texts, what can computer programs do with it? And, exactly what kind of information should be extracted from statutes, regulations, and cases? The CMLRs demonstrate how the new text processing tools can accommodate, adapt, and use the structures of legal knowledge to assist humans in performing practical legal tasks.

Some CMLRs and CMLAs could help advanced AI programs make intelligent use of legal sources. Certainly, the extracted information will be used to improve legal information retrieval, helping to point legal professionals more quickly to relevant information, but what more can be done? Can computers reason with the legal information extracted from texts? Can they help users to pose and test legal hypotheses, make legal arguments, or predict outcomes of legal disputes?

The answers appear to be "Yes!" but a considerable amount of research remains to be done before the new legal applications can demonstrate their full potential.

Indeed, that is what this book is about: how best to perform that research. This book
will also assist practitioners and others in contributing to this research and in applying
the resulting legal apps. This includes commercial firms interested in developing
new products and services based on these models and public agencies wishing to
modernize their workflows.

1.3. NEW PARADIGMS FOR INTELLIGENT TECHNOLOGY
IN LEGAL PRACTICE

The technology of legal practice is changing rapidly. Predictive coding is transforming discovery in litigation. Start-ups like Ravel (Ravel Law, 2015a), Lex Machina
(Surdeanu et al., 2011), and the Watson-based Ross (Ross Intelligence, 2015) (see
Sections 4.7 and 12.2) are garnering attention and enlisting law firm subscribers.
These and other developments in text analytics offer new process models and tools
for delivering legal services, promising greater efficiency and, possibly, greater public
accessibility.

These changes present challenges and opportunities for young attorneys and computer scientists, but it has not been easy to predict the future of legal practice.
Declines in hiring by law firms have led to reductions in the number of law school
applicants. Prospective applicants weigh the chances of gainful employment against
the size of their student loans and look elsewhere. There is uncertainty about what
law-related tasks the technology can perform. After citing press, academic, and commercial predictions of "the imminent and widespread displacement of lawyers by
computers," Remus and Levy argue persuasively that the predictions "fail to engage
with technical details . . . critical for understanding the kinds of lawyering tasks that
computers can and cannot perform. For example, why document review in discovery
practice is more amenable to automation than in corporate due diligence work, and
why the automation of ... sports stories does not suggest the imminent automation of
legal brief-writing" (Remus and Levy, 2015, p. 2).[1]

It is also unclear what law students need to learn about technology. Law firms
have long called for law schools to graduate "practice-ready" students but even firms
seem confused about the kinds of technology the firms will require, whether to
develop the technology in house or rely on external suppliers, and the skills and
knowledge that would best prepare law students for evaluating and using the new
technologies.

William Henderson, a law professor at Indiana University's Maurer School of
Law, has argued that legal *processing engineering* has changed law practice and will

---

[1] While I agree that these predictions of displacing attorneys are overblown, Remus and Levy have largely
overlooked the AI & Law research reported in this book, research that will enable AR and cognitive
computing to assist attorneys in legal practice.

continue to do so, necessitating that law schools teach students process engineering skills.

> Because of the emphasis on process and technology now taking hold within the legal industry, the practical technical skills and domain knowledge [now taught] may be inadequate for a large proportion of law students graduating in the year 2015 ... [Students] ... are unprepared to learn that law is becoming less about jury trials and courtroom advocacy and more about process engineering, predictive coding, and the collaborative and technical skills those processes entail. (Henderson, 2013, pp. 505f)

Process engineering (or "reengineering") has been defined in the business and information management literature as a "change process,"

> the aim of [which] is quick and substantial gains in organizational performance by redesigning the core business process, [addressing] a need to speed up the process, reduce needed resources, improve productivity and efficiency, and improve competitiveness. (Attaran, 2004, p. 585)

Information Technology (IT) has been called "the most effective enabling technology" for such business process reengineering, establishing "easy communication, improving the process performance," and helping "the reengineering effort by modeling, optimizing and assessing its consequences" (Attaran, 2004, p. 595).

Henderson emphasizes the role process engineering has played in the evolution of legal work, a concept he draws from Richard Susskind's *The End of Lawyers?*, according to which legal work is evolving from bespoke (or customized) to standardized, systematized, packaged, and, ultimately, to a commoditized format:

> These changes [from legal work that is bespoke to ... commoditized] are made possible by identifying recursive patterns in legal forms and judicial opinions, which enables the use of process and technology to routinize and scale very cheap and very high quality solutions to the myriad of legal needs. [F]ormerly labor-intensive work that has traditionally been performed by entry-level United States law school graduates ... is now being done by Indian law graduates [working for Legal Process Outsourcers (LPOs)], who are learning how to design and operate processes that extract useful information from large masses of digital text. Not only are the Indian law graduates getting the employment, they are learning valuable skills that are entirely – entirely – absent from U.S. law schools. (Henderson, 2013, pp. 479, 487)

In focusing on the use of process and technology to design cost-efficient methods to deliver legal solutions, Henderson agrees with Susskind that *commoditization* is the culmination of this evolution of legal work.

> A legal commodity ... is an electronic or online legal package or offering that is ... made available for direct use by the end user, often on a DIY [Do It Yourself] basis. [T]he word "commodity" in a legal context [refers] to IT-based systems and services ... [that are] undifferentiated in the marketplace (undifferentiated in

the minds of the recipients and not the providers of the service). For any given commodity, there may be very similar competitor products. (Susskind, 2010, p. 31ff)

In other words, the result of legal commoditization is a software service or product that anyone can purchase, download, and use to solve legal problems without hiring an attorney, or, in current parlance, a kind of computerized legal application, a "legal app."

1.3.1. *Former Paradigm: Legal Expert Systems*

The two concepts, process engineering and commoditization, raise interesting questions. If process engineering of legal services is rethinking how to deliver "very cheap and very high quality" solutions, who or what will be responsible for tailoring those solutions to a client's particular problem? If, as Susskind mentions, commoditization means "Do It Yourself," does that mean the client is on its own? In other words, what kind of support does the legal app provide? In particular, can the legal app perform some level of customization?

Not so long ago, the paradigm computational model for designing a legal app would have been a legal expert system. As Susskind, the developer of a pioneering legal expert system, defined them,

> "expert systems" are computer applications that contain representations of knowledge and expertise . . . which they can apply – much as human beings do – in solving problems, offering advice, and undertaking a variety of other tasks. In law, the idea is to use computer technology to make scarce expertise and knowledge more widely available and easily accessible. (Susskind, 2010, p. 120f)

Typically, legal expert systems deal with narrow areas of law but have enough "knowledge and expertise" in the narrow domain to ask a client user pertinent questions about his/her problem, to customize its answer based on the user's responses, and to explain its reasons. Their "expertise" comprises *heuristics* that skilled practitioners use in applying legal rules to specific facts. These heuristics are "rules of thumb," frequently useful but not guaranteed to lead to a correct result (Waterman and Peterson, 1981).

The rules are represented in a declarative language specifying their conditions and conclusion. They are derived through a largely manual knowledge acquisition process: manually questioning human experts, presenting them with problem scenarios, inviting them to resolve the problems, and asking them what rules the experts applied in analyzing the problem and generating a solution (Waterman and Peterson, 1981).

Waterman's Product Liability Expert System

Don Waterman's legal expert system (let's call it W-LES) is a classic example from the 1980s of a CMLR that performed limited but automatic legal reasoning around a practical problem. It provided advice on settlement decisions of product liability

[RULE3.1: DEFINITION OF LOSS]

IF the type of the plaintiff's loss is "injury"

THEN assert the plaintiff is injured by the product.

[RULE3.2: DEFINITION OF LOSS]

IF the type of the plaintiff's loss is "decedent"

THEN assert the plaintiff does represent the decedent and the decedent is killed by the product.

[RULE3.3: DEFINITION OF LOSS]

IF the type of the plaintiff's loss is "property-damage"

THEN assert the plaintiff 's property is damaged by the product.

[RULE4: STRICT LIABILITY DEFINITION]

IF (the plaintiff is injured by the product
  or (the plaintiff does represent the decedent
    and the decedent is killed by the product)
  or the plaintiff's property is damaged by the product)
and the incidental-sale defense is not applicable
and (the product is manufactured by the defendant
  or the product is sold by the defendant
  or the product is leased by the defendant)
and the defendant is responsible for the use of the product
and (California is the jurisdiction of the case
  or the user of the product is the victim
  or the purchaser of the product is the victim)
and the product is defective at the time of the sale
and (the product is unchanged from the manufacture to the sale
  or (the defendant's expectation is "the product is unchanged
    from the manufacture to the sale"
    and the defendant's expectation is reasonable-and-proper))
THEN assert the theory of strict liability does apply to the plaintiff's loss

FIGURE 1.1. Heuristic rules defining loss and strict liability (Waterman and Peterson, 1981)

disputes (Waterman and Peterson, 1981). The inputs to W-LES were descriptions of disputes involving product liability. As outputs, W-LES recommended settlement values and explained its analyses.

The recommendations of W-LES whether to settle a legal dispute and for how much were based on heuristic rules, including claims adjusters' rules for calculating damages and "formalized statements of the California legal doctrine for product liability as stated in statutes, court opinions, and legal treatises" (Waterman and Peterson, 1981, p. 15). Figure 1.1 illustrates the program's heuristic rules defining three kinds of losses and the claim of strict liability.

W-LES mechanically processed a fact situation by applying these heuristic rules in a kind of *forward chaining*. Its inference engine cycled through the rules, testing if any could "fire," that is, if a rule's conditions were satisfied by the facts in the database representing the current problem. If so, the applicable rule did fire and its deduced consequences were added to the database. The inference engine repeatedly cycled through its rules until no more rules could apply.

Ideally, by the end of the process, the rules whose conclusions represented a solution to the problem have "fired" successfully, yielding a prediction and an assessment (or in other legal expert systems, a selection and completion of a relevant legal form). The explanation of the result consists of an "audit trail" or trace back through the rules that fired and the satisfied conditions that led to their firing (Waterman and Peterson, 1981).

Other expert systems applied rules through *backward chaining*. The inference engine begins with a set of desired goals, picks one, and cycles through its database of rules (and facts) in search of a rule whose conclusion is the desired goal. Then, it adds that rule's conditions to the set of desired goals and repeats the cycle until all of the goals are satisfied or there are no more rules (or facts) with which to satisfy remaining goals (Sowizral and Kipps, 1985, p. 3).

Waterman faced three design constraints in developing legal expert systems: legal rules vary across jurisdictions; legal rules employ ill-defined legal concepts; and inferences in the proof are uncertain.

First, different states' legal rules of product liability differ, for instance, in whether the rule of contributory or comparative negligence applies. If contributory negligence applies, the plaintiff's negligence eliminates liability. If comparative negligence, the plaintiff's negligence proportionately reduces the plaintiff's recovery. Waterman addressed this problem by representing multiple states' rules and allowing users to specify which rules to apply in order to demonstrate the differences in outcome.

Second, the legal rules employed some legal concepts without defining them (i.e., "imprecise terms" in Waterman's parlance), such as "reasonable and proper" or "foreseeable" (Waterman and Peterson, 1981, p. 18). Waterman considered a number of possible solutions. These included providing more "rules that describe how an imprecise term was used previously in particular contexts," displaying "brief descriptions of instances of prior use of the imprecise term" and letting the user decide, comparing "prior cases in which the term applied, and provid[ing] a numeric rating that indicates the certainty that the rule ... applies ... In the end, he settled on having the system ask the user if the term applied" (Waterman and Peterson, 1981, p. 26).

Third, litigators are uncertain about proving factual issues and applicable legal doctrine. Waterman's suggestions included incorporating the uncertainties as additional premises within each rule or treating uncertainties as a separate rule to be applied after other rules have been considered. Users would "consider a case independently of ... uncertainty, reach a tentative conclusion, and then adjust that conclusion by some probabilistic factor that represents their overall uncertainty about the case" (Waterman and Peterson, 1981, p. 26).

Modern Legal Expert Systems
Although no longer the paradigm, legal expert systems are still widespread in use in a number of contexts.

Neota Logic provides tools for law firms, law departments, and law school students to construct expert systems. Its website offers examples of computerized advisors concerning questions involving, for instance, the FCPA, bankruptcy risks in cross-border transactions, and the Family and Medical Leave Act (Neota Logic, 2016) (see Section 2.5.1).

CALI, the Center for Computer-Assisted Legal Instruction, and IIT Chicago-Kent College of Law's Center for Access to Justice & Technology, overseen by Professor Ron Staudt, provide a web-based tool to author expert systems. Using the tool, non-programmers with legal skills can create expert systems called A2J Guided Interviews® that lead self-represented litigants through a legal process resulting in a document to be filed in court (A2J, 2012).

As discussed in Section 2.5, firms employ management systems with expert-systems-style business rules to monitor whether their processes comply with relevant regulations.

While still widely used, legal expert systems may not be the paradigm "killer app" for the legal domain. There are at least three reasons for this. First, the techniques developed to enable expert systems to deal with uncertain and incomplete information tend to be *ad hoc* and unreliable. Second, the manual process of acquiring rules is cumbersome, time-consuming, and expensive, a knowledge acquisition bottleneck that has limited the utility of expert systems in law and many other fields (Hoekstra, 2010). Third, text analytics cannot solve this particular knowledge acquisition bottleneck. While the new text analytics can extract certain kinds of semantic legal information from text, they are not yet able to extract expert systems rules.

From time to time, we will return to expert systems, their promise, and their limitations in this book; suffice it to say here that if the legal app is to customize solutions to the particularities of the user's problem, it may be necessary to find some other paradigms.

1.3.2. *Alternative Paradigms: Argument Retrieval and Cognitive Computing*

Unlike expert systems, the two alternative paradigms, AR and cognitive computing, do not purport to solve users' legal problems on their own. Instead, computer programs extract semantic information from legal texts and use it to help humans solve their legal problems.

Conceptual information retrieval, of course, is not new. AI has long sought to identify and extract semantic elements from text such as concepts and their relationships. As defined by Sowa, "concepts represent any entity, action, or state that can be described in language, and conceptual relations show the roles that each entity plays" (Sowa, 1984, p. 8). Similarly, it has long been a goal of AI to make information retrieval smarter by using the extracted semantic information to draw inferences about the retrieved texts. Roger Schank employed the term, "conceptual information retrieval" in 1981 to describe:

> a system to deal with the organization and retrieval of facts in relatively unconstrained domains (for example, . . ., scientific abstracts). First, the system should be able to automatically understand natural-language text – both input to the database

and queries to the system . . . in such a way that the conceptual content or meaning of an item can be used for retrieval rather than simply its key words . . . If categories are specified by concepts, and if the natural-language analyzer parses text into a conceptual representation, then inferences can be made from the conceptual representations (or meanings) of new items to decide which categories they belong in. (Schank et al., 1981, pp. 98, 102)

Nor is conceptual legal information retrieval new. Pioneering efforts to achieve conceptual retrieval in the legal domain were undertaken by Hafner (1978) and Bing (1987). As discussed in Sections 7.7 and 11.2, modern legal IR services take into account the substantive legal concepts and topics of interest that users intend to target. Other recent work has focused on extending conceptual information retrieval systems so that they return legal information conceptually related not just to the query but to the problem to which the user intends to apply the targeted information (see Winkels et al., 2000).

Today, *conceptual legal information retrieval* can be defined as automatically retrieving relevant textual legal information based on matching concepts and their roles in the documents with the concepts and roles required to solve the user's legal problem. As the definition makes clear, conceptual legal information retrieval is different from ordinary legal IR. It focuses on modeling human users' needs for the information they seek in order to solve a problem, for instance in the legal argument a user seeks to make, and on the concepts and their roles in that problem-solving process.

Even focusing conceptual legal IR on helping users construct viable arguments in support of a claim or counter an opponent's best arguments is not new. Dick and Hirst (1991) explored manually representing cases in terms of schematic argument structures to support lawyers' "information seeking . . . to build an argument to answer the problem at hand." At that time, however, the authors could only assume "that in due course, . . . both language analysis and language generation by machine will be possible."

Their assumption has finally come true. For years, robust means for extracting such conceptual, argument-related information from natural language texts for purposes of conceptual legal information retrieval were not available. Today, however, language analysis tools that can *automatically* identify argument-related information in case texts are finally available, and with them a new paradigm is born: robust conceptual legal IR based on argument-related information, or AR as it is referred to in Section 10.5.

Cognitive computing is a second new paradigm for system development. Despite its name, cognitive computing is *not* about developing AI systems that "think" or perform cognitive tasks the way humans do. The operative unit of cognitive computing is neither the computer nor the human but rather the collaborating team of computer *and* human problem-solver(s).

[I]n the era of cognitive systems, humans and machines will collaborate to produce better results, each bringing their own superior skills to the partnership. The
machines will be more rational and analytic – and, of course, possess encyclopedic
memories and tremendous computational abilities. People will provide expertise,
judgment, intuition, empathy, a moral compass, and human creativity. (Kelly and
Hamm, 2013)

In a cognitive computing paradigm, human users are ultimately responsible for
customizing their own solution using a legal app, but the commoditized legal service
technology should apprise the humans of the need for customization and support
them with customized access to relevant legal information to help them construct
a solution. That is, the legal app will not only select, order, highlight, and summarize the information in a manner tailored to a human user's specific problem but
also explore the information and interact with the data in new ways not previously
possible.

In order for this approach to succeed, the technology does not need to solve the
user's problem. It will not be a legal expert system. It will, however, need to have some
"understanding" of the information at its disposal and of the information's relevance
in the human's problem-solving process and to make the information conveniently
available at the right times and in the right contexts. In this respect, AR is consistent
with cognitive computing where responsibility for finding and applying resources
to solve a user's problem is divided between intelligent tasks the computer can best
perform and those addressed to human users' expertise.

Expert systems and cognitive computing paradigms differ in the sources of their
respective "knowledge." In the former, expertise is embodied in rules that human
experts apply in solving such problems, rules that usually have been constructed
manually by engineers in the knowledge acquisition process.

In the cognitive computing paradigm, in contrast, the knowledge is embodied in
the corpus of texts from which the program extracts candidate solutions or solution
elements and ranks them in terms of their relevance to the problem. This assumes,
of course, that an available corpus of texts contains information relevant to the type
of problem. For instance, if the problem is a fact situation about which to make
arguments concerning a legal claim, a corpus of legal cases involving that type of
claim would be required.

The technology cannot read the texts in the sense that humans read, but it will
have techniques for intelligently processing the texts, identifying those elements that
are relevant to a problem, and bringing them to the user's attention in an appropriate way. Significantly, the program's knowledge for assessing relevance, that is, for
identifying, ranking, and presenting candidate solutions or elements, is acquired not
primarily manually but automatically by extracting patterns from some collection of
domain-specific data using ML.

1.3.3. *Toward the New Legal Apps*

At least, that is the goal. Although researchers in university and commercial settings recognize its extraordinary potential, at the time of writing, probably no one really knows exactly how to implement cognitive computing in the legal domain. Clearly, it will not be easy, but it does seem feasible.

AI & Law researchers and technologists are actively engaged in applying the new QA, IE, and argument mining techniques to problem-solving processes in the legal domain. They see the potential for modeling legal reasoning, argumentation, and prediction of integrating computational techniques that have been developed over the years to represent statutory rules and case decisions. The AI & Law tools illustrate the elements in legal texts that the new text processing techniques should target and the legal tasks that can then be accomplished.

They recognize, too, that AI & Law research has identified design constraints that limit, or firmly guide, what CMLRs can accomplish. Sometimes the constraints can be finessed or ignored given the task a legal app addresses, but it is good to know about them in advance. The design constraints will help technologists avoid reinventing the wheel or charging down dead ends.

The next few years will be exciting times in the development of legal practice and the history of AI & Law! The aim of this book is to present the available tools, explore how they can be integrated with the new text processing tools, and equip readers to participate in this technological revolution.

1.4. WHAT WATSON CAN AND CANNOT DO

But wait a minute! Isn't the revolution already over? IBM's Watson performs remarkable feats of QA based on IE from text. Its cousin, the Debater program already mines arguments from text. Perhaps one can simply turn Watson and Debater loose on legal texts and watch them perform legal reasoning, no?

No, as already noted, programs like Watson and Debater will not perform legal reasoning. This section addresses why not. At the same time, Watson offers a conceptual framing and text analytic tools that can be instrumental in addressing the challenge of building programs that can perform legal reasoning from text.

Highlighting Watson and Debater here is *not* meant to suggest that the future development of intelligent tools for digital age legal practice depends on IBM's proprietary techniques. In fact, Watson is based on an open-source text processing and IE tool, the Unstructured Information Management Architecture (UIMA). An alternative to UIMA, the open-source GATE annotation environment, was used in topic labeling in connection with the Debater research.

In designing and explaining the Watson technology, however, IBM researchers have framed some of the component tasks of text analytics. It is convenient to take advantage of that framing in order to suggest the tasks' potential application in the legal domain.

1.4.1. *IBM's Watson*

In February 2011, "Jeopardy!," a TV game show popular with older retirees and younger nerds, captured the imagination of the American public. The game's setup and rules are straightforward: longtime host Alex Trebek presides as three contestants face a game board with six categories. Each category has five items of increasing value. Each item comprises a small window; when opened it displays an answer. The contestants race to hit the buzzer first for a chance to state the question that goes with the answer, win the value of the item, and choose the next category and item. The cardinal rule is that the contestant's response, his or her "answer," must be in the form of a question.

The game show had been an evening TV staple since 1984, but this evening was different: one of the three contestants was not human. A team at IBM Research led by David Ferrucci had designed a computer system named "Watson" especially to participate in the "Jeopardy!" game on prime time TV against the two top human champions: Brad Rutter, whose winnings from previous appearances on "Jeopardy!" topped $3.25 million, and Ken Jennings, who, with a winning streak of 74 games, was nearly a fixture of the show, himself.

By the end of three consecutive nights of play, Watson had beaten the human champions convincingly. It was a *tour de force* for IBM Research whose Deep Blue chess-playing program had beaten Gary Kasparov, the world's reigning human chess champion, 14 years before.

Of course, Watson was fallible. Famously it flubbed in "Final Jeopardy!," the last round of the evening when the host announces the category and the show jumps to a commercial break. In the meantime each, contestant wagers an amount up to his or her current total score. When the host finally reveals the "Final Jeopardy!" answer, the contestants have 30 seconds to write their responses on an electronic display, accompanied by a now familiar jingle that has come to epitomize the tension of thinking under time pressure (i.e., "Think," composed by Merv Griffin, the true genius of the "Jeopardy!" gameshow).

On this evening, the "Final Jeopardy!" category was "U.S. Cities for $400." The answer was "Its largest airport is named for a World War II hero; its second largest for a World War II battle." "Think" jingled to its inevitable conclusion, and the host asked each contestant to reveal his, or its, question.

The audience groaned when Watson's response appeared, "What is Toronto?????" Probably, it was not because the audience was amazed that Watson had gotten it wrong. The correct response was "What is Chicago?" Anyone could see that the question was tricky. One might know that Chicago's second largest airport, Midway Airport, was named for a famous World War II naval battle in the Pacific, but hardly anyone knows that Navy flying ace, Lieutenant Commander Edward Henry "Butch" O'Hare, was a hero of that war.

Instead, the audience probably was amazed that Watson did not know a common-sense bit of trivia: *Everyone* knows that Toronto is not a U.S. city!

Although Watson's blunder was not costly (Watson wagered a mere $947), it was revealing: Watson does not have knowledge of facts and information "hard wired" in some way such as expert rules. Rather, for each question/answer (Q/A) type, Watson *learns* how to extract candidate answers to the question (or questions to the answer in "Jeopardy!" speak) from millions of texts in its database. For each Q/A type, it also learns the kinds of evidence that enable it to recognize answers to that type of question, evidence in the form of syntactic features and semantic clues in the text, where the semantic clues include references to certain concepts and relations. For each Q/A type, Watson has also learned how much confidence to have in the various types of evidence associated with the texts. As indicated by the repeated question marks, Watson had little confidence in its response (Ferrucci et al., 2010).

Watson learns from a training set of documents, for which humans marked-up or "annotated" many instances of each type of Q/A pair. The annotated training texts serve as examples of how to extract information about that type of question and answer. Watson learns the how-to-extract information from the training examples and can apply it to extract information from other texts that have not been marked up, generalizing the how-to information in the process (Ferrucci et al., 2010).

In explaining Watson's response, two IBM Watson project researchers pointed out that Chicago was a very close second on Watson's list of possible answers, but that Watson had not found much evidence to connect either of the city's airports to World War II. In addition, Watson had learned that category phrases like "U.S. Cities" are not very dispositive. If "This U.S. city's ..." had appeared in the answer, Watson would have given US cities more weight. Finally, there *are* cities named Toronto in the United States, for example, Toronto, IL, Toronto, IN, Toronto, IA, Toronto, MI, Toronto, OH, Toronto, KS, and Toronto, SD, and Toronto, Canada *does* have an American League baseball team (Schwartz, 2011).

Applying Watson in Law
It appears that IBM would like to apply Watson technology (also known as Deep QA) to the legal domain (see Beck, 2014).[2] According to IBM General Counsel, Robert C. Weber,

> Pose a question and, in milliseconds, Deep QA can analyze hundreds of millions of pages of content and mine them for facts and conclusions ... Deep QA won't ever replace attorneys; after all, the essence of good lawyering is mature and sound reasoning ... But the technology can unquestionably extend our capabilities and help us perform better ... At IBM, we're just starting to explore about how Deep QA can be harnessed by lawyers. (We're pretty sure it would do quite well in a multi-state bar exam!) But already it's becoming clear that this technology will be useful in a couple of ways: for gathering facts and identifying ideas when building

---

[2] Ross Intelligence (2015), discussed at Section 12.2, applies Watson technology in the legal domain.

legal arguments. The technology might even come in handy, near real-time, in the courtroom. If a witness says something that doesn't seem credible, you can have an associate check it for accuracy on the spot. (Weber, 2011)

Watson's mistake, however, suggests some of the challenges for applying Watson technology to the legal domain. One can but imagine the game of "LEGAL Jeopardy!" Host Alex reveals "The Category is: Sports law." Ken Jennings selects "Sports law for $1.2 Million"! The window slides open: The answer is: "American League Baseball teams that cannot legally hire replacement workers during an economic strike."

A buzzer sounds. "Watson?" Alex responds.

Watson replies, "What are the Toronto Blue Jays?"

Alex smiles. "Correct! The Toronto Blue Jays cannot hire replacement workers during an economic strike."

This time, knowing that Toronto is not a U.S. city is certainly a relevant jurisdictional consideration in legally analyzing the issue. Unlike the other American League teams, the Toronto Blue Jays are not subject to U.S. labor law, but to provincial labor law (Ontario) where the rules on hiring replacement workers differ, according to Lippner (1995), a law review article regarding the 1995 baseball strike.

Watson, however, would not necessarily need to know Toronto's location or nationality in order to answer the question correctly. Watson does not have a set of rules specifying the nation in which Toronto is located or the laws that apply to it, nor rules for reasoning about whether Canadian federal or Ontario provincial law would govern this labor law issue. But that is not how Watson would answer such questions, anyway.

As long as Watson's corpus contains the above law review article, an appropriately trained Watson could learn to identify it as relevant to this type of question, extract from it the relevant answer, and assess its confidence in the answer's responsiveness.

This is a *legal* question, however. When it comes to fielding legal questions, one expects more than just an answer. One expects an explanation of why the answer is well-founded. Presumably, Watson could not explain the answer it had extracted. Explaining the answer requires one to reason with the rules and concepts relevant to choice of law and legal subject matter, knowledge that Watson does not have and could not use.

An appropriately trained Watson could have learned types of evidence for recognizing relevant question and answer pairs, including semantic clues, for instance, concepts and relations like "legally hire," "replacement workers," "economic strike." It could also have learned how much weight to accord to this evidence in assessing its confidence that the question and answer are related.

Whether this kind of evidence is sufficient for Watson to explain the answer in a manner acceptable from a legal viewpoint is another matter. Watson's how-to-extract knowledge does not appear to extend that far, yet (but see the discussion of IBM's Debater program in Section 1.4.3).

On the other hand, the author of the law review article *does* have that legal knowledge and has summarized in his article how application of that knowledge (i.e., of the rules and cases concerning jurisdiction, legal subject matter, and choice of law) justifies his conclusion. If Watson can be trained to recognize and extract those arguments explaining legal conclusions, it would be able to point human users to the author's explanation, even if Watson could not itself construct the explanation from first principles. Even then, of course, there is an issue about whether the article and its explanation are still current.

1.4.2. *Question Answering vs. Reasoning*

This raises a question: Can a program based on Watson's technology ever really reason? Could it, for example, analyze a first-year law school problem in contract law? In the above quote, IBM's Counsel, Robert Weber emphasized "sound reasoning" and declared parenthetically that "We're pretty sure it [Watson] would do quite well in a multistate bar exam!" (Weber, 2011).

But, could the Watson technology handle the *essay* part of a state bar exam? Or could it do so only if someone (Google?) has happened to store the contents of old exam blue books (assuming computerized analysis ever manages to "read" law students' handwriting, a superhuman task if ever there was one)? Will it only(!) be a highly sophisticated technique for retrieving past answers to similar questions, and, perhaps, for highlighting the evidence (syntactic features and semantic clues in the text concerning concepts and relations) that justifies its confidence in its answer? Will it be able to adapt past arguments to a new problem? Or will it be able to solve the new problem from first principles and explain its reasoning?

In order to gain some insight into the kind of legal reasoning involved in addressing a bar exam essay question, let's briefly examine a classic CMLR by Ann Gardner (her program was unnamed but let's call it AGP) which already in the 1980s had analyzed legal issues from typical first-year law school contracts course final exam problems (Gardner, 1987).

AGP is offered here as an example of a systematic approach to computationally modeling legal reasoning about exam questions involving contract law and as a contrast to the Watson approach.

Gardner's First-Year Contracts Problem Analyzer
Anyone who has attended law school will recognize (probably with a shudder) the type of problem AGP handled: A putative buyer and seller exchange two weeks' worth of chronologically overlapping and sometimes inconsistent telegrams and purchase orders concerning a possible purchase of a carload of salt. Having sent an

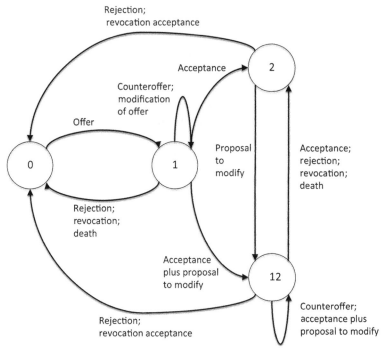

Rejection;
revocation acceptance

Acceptance

Counteroffer;
modification
of offer

Offer

Proposal
to
modify

Acceptance;
rejection;
revocation;
death

Rejection;
revocation;
death

Acceptance
plus proposal
to modify

Counteroffer;
acceptance plus
proposal to modify

Rejection;
revocation acceptance

FIGURE 1.2. ATN for offer and acceptance problems with four states: (0) no relevant legal relations; (1) offer pending; (2) contract exists; (12) contract exists and proposal to modify is pending (Gardner, 1987, p. 124)

apparent acceptance of an apparent offer, the buyer finds a cheaper source and sends a telegram purporting to reject. The question is "Has a contract been concluded?"

The inputs to AGP were descriptions of this type of offer and acceptance problem represented by a human (Gardner) in a logic language (illustrated below). AGP used an *augmented transition network* (ATN) to analyze such problems and output an analysis of the contracts issues.

An ATN is a graph structure that analyzes problems involving sequences of events as a series of states and possible transitions from one state to the next. It is "augmented" with rules that define each such possible state transition.

AGP's ATN, shown in Figure 1.2, represented *legal* states in the analysis of an offer and acceptance problem in contract law (i.e., no relevant legal relations (0), offer pending (1), contract exists (2), contract exists and proposal to modify is pending (12)). The arcs represented events or transitions from one legal state to another: from no relevant legal relation (0) to an offer pending (1) via an offer, from an offer pending (1) to contract exists (2) via an acceptance, etc.

Each arc had associated with it the rules of contract law dealing with offer and acceptance. These rules set forth the legal requirements for moving from one state to the next. For instance the offer arc from (0) to (1) has one associated rule, the definition of "offer," based on *Restatement of Contracts, Second*, section 24: "An offer is the manifestation of willingness to enter into a bargain, so made as to justify another person in understanding that his assent to that bargain is invited and will conclude it" (Gardner, 1987, p. 142).

AGP processed events in the problem in chronological order, storing its analysis in a detailed analysis tree and summarizing it in an output summary tree. The program repeats the following steps until it has processed each event in the problem:

1. Take the next event in the problem.
2. Find out the current state from the detailed analysis tree. Determine from the ATN the possible arcs out of that state.
3. For each possible arc, test if the event satisfies the rules associated with the arc and update the detailed analysis tree with the test results.
4. If the test involves a "hard" legal question (see below), that is, presents two legally defensible ways of evaluating the event, insert a branch for each interpretation into the detailed analysis tree.
5. Edit the detailed analysis tree to update an output summary tree of network states representing the different "interpretations" of the events.

For example, AGP starts with a first event:

On July 1 Buyer sent the following telegram to Seller: "Have customers for salt and need carload immediately. Will you supply carload at $2.40 per cwt?" Seller received the telegram the same day.

The events were input not in English text, but in a logic-based representation language. AGP could not read text, so a human had to manually represent that information in the logic representation (i.e., predicate logic, defined in Section 2.3.2). For instance, some excerpts of the representation are:

(send Send1) (agent Send1 Buyer) (ben Send1 Seller) (obj Send1 Telegram1)
(telegram Telegram1) (sentence S13) (text S13 "Will you supply carload at $2.40 per cwt?")
(prop-content S13 Prop13) (literal-force S13 Q13)(yes-no-question Q13)
(effective-force S13 R13) (request R13).
(Gardner, 1987, pp. 89, 105, 111)

In the above representation, Send1 is an instance of a Send with the Buyer as the Agent, the Seller as the Beneficiary, and Telegram1, an instance of a telegram, as the Object of the sending. S13 is a sentence whose text is quoted, whose propositional content is represented in Prop13 (defined elsewhere), whose literal force as a speech act is to pose a question but which also effectively presents a request (Gardner, 1987, pp. 89, 105, 111).

In step (3), testing if the event satisfies the arc, the program collects the rules associated with the arc. Like the events, all of the contracts rules were translated manually into the logical language. For instance, the rule associated with the arc from (0) to (1) defining an "offer," *Restatement of Contracts, Second,* section 24 (above), includes rule antecedents and (italicized) predicates like the following:

1. There is a *manifestation* with some symbolic *content* about an *exchange* by some agent, the prospective *offeror*.
2. The terms of the exchange are specified with *reasonable certainty*.
3. By means of the content of the manifestation, the prospective offeror has performed some *speech act* that invites acceptance by a prospective *offeree* of a proposal for the exchange.
4. The offeree is invited to furnish consideration in the exchange and the prospective offeror is apparently ready to be bound to a contract for the exchange, without doing anything more (Gardner, 1987, pp. 142).

The program checks if the rule's antecedents are satisfied given the facts of all the events processed so far plus the new event. Basically, AGP attempts to bind the artifacts of the problem to the variables in the rule guided by very limited information about what the facts and the antecedents mean.

At any step, there are multiple possible ways to bind the facts and antecedents. The program needs to search through all the possible bindings, leading to a detailed analysis tree with multiple branches. As noted, "hard" questions also lead to branches representing alternative reasonable interpretations. In order to prevent an "exponential explosion" of alternative paths, an editing function prunes the branching analysis using heuristics to focus on the most promising branches.

Incidentally, recent work on so-called "smart" contracts employs finite state automata related to the ATN in Gardner's CMLR (Flood and Goodenough, 2015, p. 42). Researchers have also applied heuristic rules to model the United Nations Convention on the International Sale of Goods and to deduce the temporal legal states of affairs as events occur in the life of a contract (see Yoshino, 1995, 1998).

Gardner's heuristics are a typical example of an AI approach to enable a computer program to handle a task that is taxing even for humans. Law students need to decide on which of the multitude of cross-communications and their contents to focus at any point in their analyses of whether there is a contract.

Gardner's Algorithm for Distinguishing Hard and Easy Legal Questions

Law students (legal practitioners and judges) also need to learn how to distinguish hard and easy questions of law, a determination that takes into account an appreciation of the facts and the substantive legal issues, as well as procedural issues concerning who has the burden of raising the question.

This is a problem that has deep roots in legal philosophy (see, for example, Fuller's critique of Hart's assertion that legal terms have core and penumbral meanings (Hart, 1958; Fuller, 1958)). It also has very practical ramifications. A clinic intake advisor,

A. For every predicate in rule, apply 3 tests:
　　1. *CommonSenseKnowledge-Answer*: Does Commonsense
　　　　knowledge rule provide an answer?
　　2. *Pos-Examples*: Does problem match positive examples of
　　　　predicate?
　　3. *Neg-Examples*: Does problem match negative examples of
　　　　predicate?
B.
　If not *CommonSenseKnowledge-Answer*
　　If not (*Pos-Examples* or *Neg-Examples*) ➜ **Question hard**
　　If (only one of *Pos-Examples / Neg-Examples*) ➜ **Question easy**
　　If (*Pos-Examples* and *Neg-Examples*) ➜ **Question hard**
　If *CommonSenseKnowledge*-Answer
　　If not (*Pos-Examples* or *Neg-Examples*) ➜ **Question easy**
　　If (only one of *Pos-Examples / Neg-Examples*)
　　　If (agrees only-one with *CommonSenseKnowledge-Answer*) ➜
　　　　Question easy
　　　else **Question hard**
　　If (*Pos-Examples* and *Neg-Examples*) ➜ **Question hard**

FIGURE 1.3. Gardner's heuristic method for distinguishing hard and easy legal questions (Gardner, 1987; Rissland, 1990)

for instance, needs a way to distinguish clients' easy and hard legal questions in order to direct them appropriately.

From the viewpoint of computational modeling, however, distinguishing hard and easy questions of law presents a conundrum. As Gardner noted, for a computer program to apply a method for distinguishing hard and easy questions, the method must itself be "easy."

AGP employed a heuristic method for distinguishing hard and easy questions of law (Gardner, 1987, pp. 160–1). Figure 1.3 depicts Edwina Rissland's algorithmic recapitulation of AGP's method for distinguishing hard and easy questions (Rissland, 1990).

For every predicate in a rule, the method involves testing whether a commonsense knowledge (CSK) rule provides an answer, or whether the problem matches positive examples of the predicate, negative examples, or both. For instance, if no commonsense rule provides an answer, but there is a match to a positive instance, the question is easy. If, however, a negative instance also matches, the question is hard.

Consider the requirement of there being a *manifestation* of willingness by the prospective offeror to enter into a bargain. As operationalized for AGP, the offeror must have performed a speech act that invites acceptance by a prospective offeree of a proposal for an exchange. Whether there is such a manifestation does not, perhaps, usually present a hard question of law, but it is litigated from time to time. In principle, AGP has a way to decide if it presents a hard question in a particular case. If there is a commonsense rule-like definition of manifestation (or of an appropriate speech act), and some instances of positive or negative examples of manifestations, AGP can apply them to the facts of the problem, and follow the heuristic in Figure 1.3.

By the time AGP completes its analysis of all of the events in an offer and acceptance problem, it has prepared a detailed analysis tree, traversals of which effectively provide a trace of its reasoning and an explanation of its answer. For instance, in AGP's analysis of event 1 above, it concludes that there is a pending offer, having found in the buyer/offeror's telegram a manifestation of an apparent and reasonably certain readiness to be bound to an exchange (see Gardner, 1987, Fig. 7.1, p. 165).

. . .

AGP illustrates some issues that a program like Watson would need to address if it were to be applied to tackle bar exam essay questions. Computationally modeling legal reasoning about contracts problems requires some model of reasoning with legal rules and concepts. It needs to distinguish between hard and easy questions of law. It also needs an ability to explain its reasoning, and that reasoning has to be intelligible to legal practitioners.

The Watson program that won the Jeopardy! game did not explain its answers. If it did explain its answers, it would probably do so in terms of the syntactic features and semantic clues in the text concerning concepts and relations that justified its confidence in its answer (Ferrucci et al., 2010, p. 73). That kind of an explanation, however, is not likely to correspond to what legal practitioners would expect.

Even if Watson could not perform the kind of reasoning AGP models, could it recognize the features of prior legal explanations and arguments, such as those in old exam blue books from past law school or bar review essay exams, and adapt them to a new problem? Would it be able to recognize when these arguments are relevant to users' queries? What level of detail could it recognize in prior explanations and arguments? Could it recognize not only the legal rules but also the application of the legal rules to the facts of a problem? Could it recognize arguments that particular rule antecedents are satisfied or not?

These are the kinds of questions discussed in detail in Part III of this book, but let us begin to explore them here.

1.4.3. *IBM's Debater Program*

Can Watson be trained to recognize and extract arguments from texts? It appears that the answer is "yes"! In Spring 2014, an IBM executive demonstrated a new program named "Debater," a descendant of Watson that employs some of the text processing technology of the Watson program to perform argument mining (see, e.g., Newman, 2014, demo at Dvorsky, 2014).

On any topic, the Debater's task is to "detect relevant claims" and return its "top predictions for pro claims and con claims." In the example of Debater's output, upon

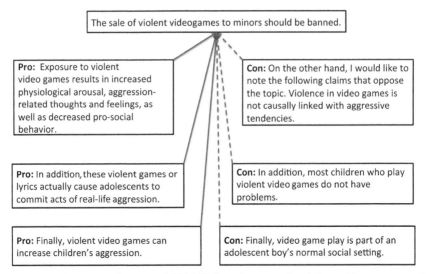

FIGURE 1.4. Argument diagram of IBM Debater's output for violent video games topic (root node) (see Dvorsky, 2014)

inputting the topic, "The sale of violent video games to minors should be banned," Debater:

1. Scanned 4 million Wikipedia articles,
2. Returned the 10 most relevant articles,
3. Scanned the 3,000 sentences in those 10 articles,
4. Detected those sentences that contained "candidate claims,"
5. "[I]dentified borders of candidate claims,"
6. "[A]ssessed pro and con polarity of candidate claims,"
7. "Constructed a demo speech with top claim predictions,"
8. Was then "ready to deliver!" (Dvorsky, 2014)

While Debater's output in the video was aural, one can present the text of its output in visual terms. Figure 1.4 shows an argument diagram constructed manually from the video recording of Debater's aural output for the example topic (available at Dvorsky, 2014). The box at the top (i.e., the "root node") contains the topic proposition. Nodes linked to it with solid-lined arrows (i.e., "arcs") support that proposition; the dashed arcs attack it. The elapsed time from inputting a topic to outputting an argument reportedly is from three to five minutes. In subsequent presentations, Debater's output has been demonstrated for other diverse topics.

Debater's argument regarding banning violent video games in Figure 1.4 invites comparison to a *legal* argument involving a similar topic shown in Figure 1.5. It concerns the constitutionality of California (CA) Civil Code sections 1746–1746.5 (the "Act"), which restricted sale or rental of "violent video games" to minors. The Court in *Video Software Dealers Assoc. v. Schwarzenegger*, 556 F. 3d 950

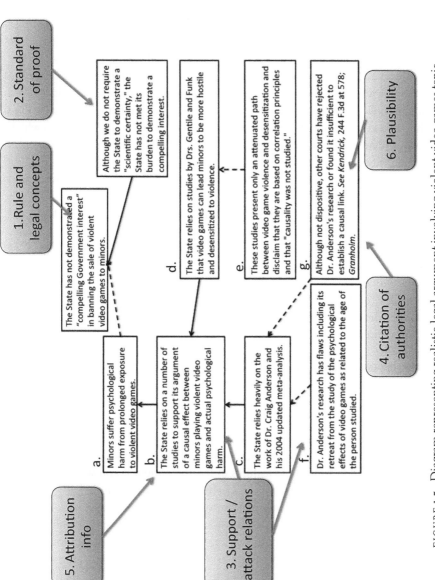

FIGURE 1.5: Diagram representing realistic legal argument involving violent video games topic

(9th Cir. 2009) addressed the issue of whether the Act was unconstitutional under the 1st and 14th Amendments of the U.S. Constitution. As a presumptively invalid content-based restriction on speech, the Court subjected the Act to the strict scrutiny standard.

The Court held the Act unconstitutional because the State had not demonstrated a compelling interest that "the sale of violent video games to minors should be banned." Figure 1.5 shows excerpts from the portion of the opinion in which the Court justified this conclusion. The nodes contain propositions from that portion and the arcs reflect the explicit or implied relations among those propositions based on a fair reading of the text. As above, the solid arrows signify that the proposition in the node at the base of the arrow supports the proposition in the node to which the arrow points; dashed arrows signify an attack relation. Thus, nodes a, b, c, and d contain propositions on which the State of CA relied to support its compelling government interest. Nodes e, f, and g contain propositions the Court employs to attack the State's propositions.

The argument diagrams in Figures 1.4 and 1.5 address nearly the same topic and share similar propositions, reflecting the fact that the Court's argument addresses some of the very same kinds of reasons and evidence as Debater's argument.

The callout boxes in Figure 1.5, however, illustrate some key features of legal argument evidenced by the Court's argument. In particular, (1) legal rules and concepts govern the Court's decision of the issue. (2) Standards of proof govern its assessment of evidence. (3) The argument has an internal structure; support and attack relations connect the various claims. (4) The Court explicitly cites authorities (e.g., cases, statutes). (5) *Attribution* information signals or affects the Court's judgments about belief in an argument (e.g., "the State relies"). (6) Candidate claims in a legal document have different degrees of plausibility.

This is not to criticize Debater's argument, which is *not* and does not purport to be a legal argument.

On the other hand, given the intention of applying Watson and, presumably, Debater to legal applications and argumentation, the comparison emphasizes the importance of addressing these features of legal argument if and when Debater *is* applied in a legal domain. It would be essential that Debater can identify the types of concepts, relationships, and argument-related information enumerated above and illustrated in Figure 1.5 in order for the system to be able to recognize and interpret legal arguments. A program so endowed could improve legal information retrieval, focusing users on cases involving concepts, concept relations, and arguments similar to the one the human user is aiming to construct. It could also highlight and summarize the relevant arguments for the user's benefit (see Section 11.3).

Finally, if the system were to perform any automated reasoning based on the retrieved texts in order to assist the user in solving his/her problem, such as by comparing arguments, predicting outcomes, or suggesting counterarguments, it would need an ability to identify concepts, concept relations, and arguments in the texts.

It is in this connection that the kinds of legal reasoning argument models and argument schemes described in Part I will likely be essential. This is the focus of Section 12.3.

1.4.4. *Text Analytic Tools for Legal Question Answering*

Watson's fundamental task was to answer questions. In the context of the "Jeopardy!" game that was enough to beat the reigning human champions.

Legal QA could be a great boon to making legal knowledge more accessible. Imagine the utility of a service that answers questions about landlord tenant law in a large metropolitan area. Of course, lawyers know that legal QA can be quite complex. An answer needs to be tailored to the questioner's circumstances. It matters, for example, if the apartment building is in Toronto, Canada, or Toronto, Kansas. Explanations and arguments need to be provided. Assumptions need to be clarified on which the answer is based and which often limit its applicability.

Many practical legal questions, however, do not require explanation and argument. At a November 2014 workshop in IBM's Chicago offices, Paul Lippe of Legal OnRamp (LOR) demonstrated an application with a large corpus of contracts involving two corporations engaged in a high volume of repeat transactions over time (Legal OnRamp, 2015). Corporate legal staffs involved in contract monitoring and maintenance would like to be able easily to answer such questions as: Which contracts include certain terms or term language such as a disclaimer of liability for consequential losses? For which contracts is a particular type of term embedded in the body of the contract as opposed to in an appendix? Such queries may be quite useful. For instance, certain terms may need to be updated frequently, and it may be easier or cheaper to do so if the terms are located in a contract's appendix. Finding the contracts in a large corpus with such a term in the body can assist the legal staff to target contracts that should be restructured.

Such queries cannot be easily and reliably answered with ordinary information retrieval tools. Using Boolean searches and keywords, one cannot easily specify locations within a contract structure or deal with the wide variety of language with which certain kinds of terms may be expressed. For instance, consider the variety of ways in which a disclaimer of liability for consequential losses can be expressed.

In answering questions, Watson analyzes the question, searches for candidate responses from a text corpus, and ranks the candidates according to its confidence that each candidate addresses the question.

Question analysis means analyzing the question text for clues "to determine what [the question] is asking about and the kind of thing it is asking for." This includes parsing the question text, which "produces a grammatical parse of a sentence[,] identifies parts of speech and syntactic roles such as subject, predicate, and object, [and identifies how some sentence segments relate to other] sentence segments." This also includes decomposing suitable questions into "useful and relevant subparts." The query analysis process does not result in one certain interpretation of what the query means. The "parsing and question analysis result in multiple interpretations of the question and . . . a variety of different queries" (Ferrucci, 2012, pp. 6, 9).

Retrieval and ranking involves searching for candidate answers for each of the query interpretations. "These queries are run against different sources to first gener-ate a broad set of candidate answers." This leads to generating multiple hypotheses about what the query means and how to answer it. "Each candidate answer com-bined with the question represents an independent hypothesis." "Each [hypothesis] becomes the root of an independent process that attempts to discover and evaluate supporting evidence in its candidate answer" (Ferrucci, 2012, p. 6).

The system uses a set of evidence scoring programs to rank the candidate answers by the likelihood that the answer addresses the question and to assess its level of confidence in the answer's correctness. "Each evidence–answer pair may be scored by 100 independent scorers. Each scoring algorithm produces a confidence. For any one candidate, there may be on the order of 10,000 confidence scores – on the order of one million in total for a single question" (Ferrucci, 2012, p. 9).

Judging the likelihood that each candidate answer is correct is a matter of combin-ing weights associated with the different evidence scores. Watson learns the weights associated with the evidence scores "using a statistical machine learning framework" (Ferrucci, 2012, p. 9).

Thus, in constructing a contracts QA facility, it is likely that the LOR team devel-oped a set of concepts and relations for distinguishing among different types of contractual terms or provisions and for identifying structural features of the contracts. Such concepts probably included *InContractBody*, *InAppendix*, *LiabilityDisclaimer*, *ConsequentialDamages*. The team probably manually annotated a subset of con-tracts (a training set) for these features. The Watson system then learned statistically to associate various syntactic and semantic information with these features and applied them to annotate the remaining contract texts (the test set).

Figure 1.6 shows a high-level architecture for analyzing texts of legal documents including contracts. Given a query, the program analyzes the question, translates it into a set of structural and conceptual feature constraints on the type of answer sought, identifies candidate documents responsive to the question, and then ranks the candidates. In the contracts application, there may be only a few evidence scorers, some more useful in answering structure-type questions, others better for answering questions regarding provision type. The weighted utilities between evi-dence scores and types of questions would not be hardwired but learned from positive and negative instances of question/answer pairs.

For semantic text analysis and conceptual information retrieval, two additional tools, shown in dashed boxes in Figure 1.6, are helpful. Relation extraction and concept expansion help to analyze questions and retrieve candidate answers from a corpus.

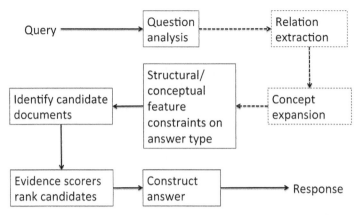

FIGURE 1.6. Architecture of text analyzer for legal documents including contracts. Dashed boxes show components for semantic analysis and conceptual information retrieval

Relation extraction attempts "to find semantic relationships (e.g., [a person may have] starred in, visited, painted, invented, [or have been] naturalized in) between concepts, although they may have been expressed with different words or with different grammatical structures" (Ferrucci, 2012, p. 7).

A system's ability to identify a conceptual relationship, for instance, a particular kind of party signing a particular kind of agreement, is essential for specifying the constraint for purposes of conceptual information retrieval and prediction (see Section 4.5.2). In the above contracts example, the concept of *LiabilityDisclaimer* may be expressed in a variety of ways, for instance, "disclaims liability for incidental or consequential damages," "assumes no responsibility for any loss," or "undertakes no liability for any loss or damage suffered as a result of the misuse of the product," all of which the program must learn are instances of *LiabilityDisclaimer*.

Another example involves claims under a federal statute for injuries caused by vaccines (see Section 10.5). One might seek to retrieve all cases involving assertions that:

<specific-vaccine> <can cause> <generic-injury>

For instance, a court may have held that "DPT vaccine can cause acute encephalopathy and death," a case that would be a useful point of reference to an attorney representing a decedent who had suffered a similar circumstance. A system's ability to identify a causal relationship between a specific vaccine and a type of injury would be essential if the system is to preferentially rank such a case and highlight its finding for the benefit of the user.

In a different legal context, one may wish to retrieve all trade secret misappropriation cases where the:

<defendant> <signed> <nondisclosure-agreement>

Some examples drawn from real trade secret cases include:

1. Newlin and Vafa had signed nondisclosure agreements prohibiting them from using ICM software and tools upon leaving ICM.
2. Ungar signed a nondisclosure agreement.
3. Defendant Hirsch was employed by plaintiff, where he executed a nondisclosure agreement (Ashley and Brüninghaus, 2009, p. 141).

Concept expansion identifies "concepts that are closely related to those given in the question," which may be key to "identifying hidden associations and implicit relationships" (Chu-Carroll et al., 2012, p. 1).

For instance, in the above legal examples of conceptual legal information retrieval, various concepts would need to be expanded:

<nondisclosure-agreement> includes: 'nondisclosure agreement', 'agreement not to disclose', 'employment contract with a nondisclosure clause'
<noncompete-agreement> includes: 'noncompete agreement', 'noncompetition agreement', 'covenant not to compete'
<varicella-vaccine> includes: 'varicella vaccine', 'Chickenpox vaccine', 'VARIVAX'

It is apparent in these examples of relation extraction that relevant concepts like "vaccine," "to sign," or "nondisclosure agreement" can be expressed in multiple ways. Concept expansion identifies semantically related concepts in a corpus, in effect, deriving a dictionary or thesaurus rather than starting with one.

1.4.5. *Sources for Text Analytic Tools*

Tools like those in Watson have become available commercially as web-based services. As noted, IBM is attempting to capitalize on its investment in the Watson system by making a selected set of Watson's functionalities available for developers in a commercially convenient form. IBM offers a variety of services under the IBM Watson Developer Cloud (also referred to as Watson Services and BlueMix) for building cognitive apps (IBM Watson Developer Cloud Watson Services, 2015). These are commercial services subject to license and to license fees. Versions are also available for academic research, such as AlchemyLanguage, a set of text analysis/natural language processing (NLP) tools (IBM Watson Developer Cloud Watson Services, 2016).

Whether or not one wishes to avoid using IBM's proprietary tools, the Watson services are an instructive example for anyone interested in the future of legal practice. Even absent an ability to directly access the services, the framing of the tools on the website is instructive. It represents a creative effort by IBM to demonstrate how the new text analytic technologies can be packaged in an accessible form. IBM's efforts provide at least one example of the kinds of IE services that are needed, how to group them, and how to present them to noncomputer programmers (IBM Watson Developer Cloud Watson Services, 2015).

Presumably, IBM will not be the only source of such tools in the future. Open-source alternatives are currently available in a rougher form that requires developers to adapt them. As noted, IBM Watson is built on the *UIMA* platform, an open-source Apache framework that has been deployed in several large-scale government-sponsored and commercial text processing applications (Epstein et al., 2012). Academic researchers in the UIMA community are developing alternative open-source versions of tools like the above. For instance, Grabmair et al. (2015), discussed in Sections 6.8, 10.5, 11.3, and 11.4, demonstrate the utility of open-source tools for extracting argument-related information from legal texts (involving the corpus of federal vaccine compensation cases mentioned above) and using it to improve a full-text legal information system's ranking of retrieved documents.

Those who wish to create legal applications based on either the Watson Developer Cloud services or UIMA tools still have to solve some challenging problems. We illustrated a few of these problems above in contrasting Watson's and Debater's outputs with what legal problem-solving demands. It is the goal of this book to frame these problems so that students and other developers can tackle them with the techniques and tools that the AI & Law field offers.

1.5. A GUIDE TO THIS BOOK

It is intriguing to imagine how a QA text-analysis program could both answer legal questions *and* provide explanations and arguments that a legal practitioner could credit. Will there be a software service for:

> *Generation of explanations and arguments in law*: assists in structuring explanations of answers and supportive legal arguments?

That has not happened yet, however, and before it does, researchers will need to answer two questions: How can text analytic tools and techniques extract the semantic information necessary for AR and how can that information be applied to achieve cognitive computing?

Readers will find answers to those questions in the three parts of this book.

Part I introduces more CMLRs developed in the AI & Law field. It illustrates research programs that model various legal processes: reasoning with legal statutes and with legal cases, predicting outcomes of legal disputes, integrating reasoning with legal rules, cases, and underlying values, and making legal arguments. These CMLRs did not deal directly with legal texts, but text analytics could change that in the near future.

Part II examines recently developed techniques for extracting conceptual information automatically from legal texts. It explains selected tools for processing some aspects of the semantics or meanings of legal texts, including: representing legal concepts in ontologies and type systems, helping legal information retrieval systems take meanings into account, applying ML to legal texts, and extracting semantic information automatically from statutes and legal decisions.

Part III explores how the new text processing tools can connect the CMLRs, and their techniques for representing legal knowledge, directly to legal texts and create a new generation of legal applications. It presents means for achieving more robust conceptual legal information retrieval that takes into account argument-related information extracted from legal texts. These techniques will enable some of the CMLRs of Part I to deal directly with legal digital document technologies and to reason directly from legal texts in order to assist humans in predicting and justifying legal outcomes.

Taken together, the three parts of this book are effectively a handbook on the science of integrating the AI & Law domain's top-down focus on representing and using semantic legal knowledge and the bottom-up, data-driven and often domain-agnostic evolution of computer technology and IT.

The recentness of the legal tech boom belies the fact that AI & Law researchers have already invested a great deal of thought in how to model legal reasoning. This book does not aim to provide a complete history of that research. Instead, it highlights selected trends in the development of CMLRs and CMLAs and explains their implications for the future given the opportunities for integrating text analytics.

Nor does this book cover all of the ways in which legal tech start-ups are harnessing data to predict legal outcomes. Instead, the focus is on how to employ and integrate semantic legal knowledge into predicting outcomes and explaining predictions. Over years of pursuing a methodology that is both empirical and scientific, AI & Law researchers have discovered what works in computationally modeling legal reasoning and what does not. By carefully attending to these lessons, constraints, and limitations, developers in the current legal tech boom interested in incorporating semantic legal knowledge may achieve AR and create a new kind of software service, a cognitive computing legal app (CCLA).

The remainder of this section summarizes the book's narrative in more detail and serves as a chapter outline.

1.5.1. *Part I: Computational Models of Legal Reasoning*

The examples in Part I of rule-based and case-based programs that can perform intelligent tasks such as legal reasoning and explanation, argumentation, and prediction, all share something in common: giving reasons.

Reasoning means "the drawing of inferences or conclusions through the use of reason." *Explanation* is "the act or process of explaining," that is, giving "the reason for or cause of" or showing "the logical development or relationships of." *Argument* involves "a reason given in proof or rebuttal" or "discourse intended to persuade." *Prediction* means "an act of predicting"; to predict means "to declare or indicate in advance; esp: foretell on the basis of observation, experience, or scientific reason"

(Merriam-Webster's Collegiate Dictionary, 2015). In law, a reason in support of an inference or conclusion usually involves asserting that a legal rule warrants the conclusion, citing an authoritative source for the rule, for example, a statute or an applicable case, and explaining or arguing that the rule applies. (Circularity can hardly be avoided in defining these fundamental inferential tasks!)

The models employ knowledge structures for representing information in the statutory or court-made rules or in the facts of the cases and schemes of inference and argument to process reasons. Heretofore, the knowledge representation structures had to be filled in manually, the source of the previously mentioned knowledge acquisition bottleneck.

Much work, discussed in Chapter 2, has addressed constructing formal logical models of statutory reasoning, a kind of model that probably is *not* yet ready to automatically connect directly to legal texts. The chapter contrasts logical models of reasoning with statutory rules and realistic statutory interpretation. It considers some computational approaches to assisting humans to find and interpret statutory rules that are alternatives to logical models and that may be able to connect with legal texts.

Models of case-based legal reasoning, discussed in Chapter 3, address analogical reasoning with legal cases or precedents, an important phenomenon in common law jurisdictions that is more likely to result in successful applications of text analytics. The chapter compares a number of case-based models in terms of: how the CMLR represents legal information in cases, the aspects of legal reasoning with cases and precedents the CMLR captures or misses, the extent to which the CMLR integrates rules, cases, and underlying values, and the compatibility of the CMLR's representational techniques with the new techniques for extracting information from texts.

Some computational models for predicting legal outcomes, described in Chapter 4, are also ripe for applying text analytics. The chapter surveys case-based and ML techniques for predicting outcomes of legal cases and assesses their compatibility with text analytics.

The culmination of all of this work in AI & Law has been the development of computational models of legal argument and legal argument schemes, described in Chapter 5, completing Part I. The chapter focuses on CMLAs that unify reasoning logically with legal rules and analogically with legal precedents. The models generate legal arguments, sometimes represented diagrammatically, for purposes of planning written arguments, instruction, or public discussion of legal issues. Some aspects of these models are also ready for applying text analytics.

1.5.2. *Part II: Legal Text Analytics*

Meanwhile, other fields of research and development, such as information retrieval, QA, IE, and argument mining, have been perfecting techniques for representing legal concepts and relations. Programs can then process the concepts and relations semantically and computational models of legal reasoning can use them intelligently. As explained in Chapter 6, this includes the development of legal ontologies and, more recently in UIMA type systems of the sort employed in Watson and Debater, and in LUIMA, an extended type system for legal domains. This part addresses how to adapt these text analytic tools to achieve conceptual legal information retrieval.

Some of the new text analytic techniques are already being integrated with commercial legal information retrieval (CLIR) tools. Chapter 7 introduces current technology for legal IR, explains these initial applications, and offers some new ones. Chapter 8 addresses how to apply ML to textual data in the contexts of e-discovery (litigation-related discovery of evidence from electronic information including texts) and legal information retrieval.

The text analytic techniques are extracting functional information from statutes and regulations and argument-related information from legal cases. As explained in Chapters 9 and 10, the techniques include rule-based extraction guided by LUIMA types and ML adapted to corpora of legal decisions.

The statutory conceptual information of interest includes not only the topics and types of statutes (e.g., regulatory domain and whether a provision is a definition or prescription) but also functional information such as the agents that a statute directs to communicate with each other. Conceptual information in cases includes argument-related information such as whether a sentence states a legal rule for deciding an issue, whether it is an evidentiary statement of fact about the case, or whether it indicates an application of the rule or elements of the rule to the facts of a case.

1.5.3. *Part III: Connecting Computational Reasoning Models and Legal Texts*

By integrating the models and tools of Parts I and II, programs can use the conceptual information extracted directly from legal texts to perform legal reasoning, explanation, argumentation, and prediction. Basically, the goal is for text analytics automatically to fill in the computational models' knowledge representation structures. In this way, the Watson services and UIMA tools can reduce the knowledge acquisition bottleneck, accomplish conceptual legal information retrieval, and address the challenges mentioned above of legal QA including the need to explain its answers. Part III explains how to make these connections and achieve CCLAs.

Chapter 11 addresses how to integrate the QA, IE, and argument mining techniques with certain CMLRs to yield new tools for conceptual legal information retrieval, including AR. Fortunately, these tools do not depend on processing *all* of a repository's documents. In designing a proposed legal app, it is not necessary that a corpus be available wholesale for text processing to identify concepts, concept roles and relations, and other argument-related information. Instead, the new text processing techniques can be applied as a kind of filter between a full-text retrieval system and human users. The filter is applied just to the documents retrieved as relevant through traditional full-text retrieval searches, promoting the documents that should be ranked higher in terms of the extent to which concepts, conceptual relationships, and other argument-related information match the user's need. Chapter 11 demonstrates this filtering approach; argument-related information extracted from legal texts improves a full-text legal information system's ranking of retrieved documents.

As explained in Chapter 12, these tools, in turn, can be integrated even more fully with some of Part I's computational models of legal reasoning and argument to create a new breed of legal apps in which computer and human user collaborate, each performing the intelligent tasks it performs best. In a complementary way, the computational models of reasoning, explanation, argument, and prediction will play significant roles in customizing commoditized legal services. They provide examples of the processes and tasks that may be adapted for the new apps and the concepts, roles, and relations that should be implemented. The new legal practice tools, based on information extracted with UIMA or other text analytic technology, can reason with legal texts, enabling practice systems to tailor their outputs to a human user's particular problem. In effect, they are the means by which a commoditized legal service, in Susskind's terms, can be customized.

Chapter 12 presents the idea that legal information queries and QA should be thought of as means for testing hypotheses about the law and how it applies. It introduces the possibility that a legal app could engage users in collaboratively posing, testing, and revising hypotheses about how an issue should be decided. Section 12.7 illustrates some practical use cases and the different kinds of legal hypotheses they involve. Readers interested in a high-level view of how legal apps could address these use cases might begin with the last chapter and then circle back to the beginning of this book.

The new apps will be subject to some limitations. While current text analytic techniques can extract much conceptual information, they cannot extract it all. Many conceptual inferences are simply too indirect and require too much background CSK to identify. Thus, it is an important empirical question how much can be accomplished with current text analytic techniques. Before concluding, Chapter 12 explores these remaining challenges.

1.6. IMPLICATIONS OF TEXT ANALYTICS FOR STUDENTS

Legal instructors, law schools, and authors have been urging legal educators to focus more on the developing technologies of legal practice. For example,

- Granat and Lauritsen (2014) identified 10 law school programs that focus students on the technology of law practice. These programs cover such topics as practice systems automating data gathering, decision-making, and document drafting, developing legal expert systems for public interest legal services and legal clinics, redesigning legal processes, applying ML to legal data and legal informatics.

- Georgetown University Law Center sponsors the Iron Tech Lawyer Competition. Law students are building legal expert systems and entering them in competition (Iron Tech Lawyer, 2015). Additional information about some of these activities may be found in Staudt and Lauritsen (2013).
- Two far-sighted authors, Lippe and Katz (2014), have urged the legal field to reckon specifically with the impact of Watson technology on the future of legal practice.

This book is intended to help law students, computer science graduate students, legal practitioners, and technologists to take up that challenge and to design and implement legal applications of a kind that has not previously been technically possible. As argued, the combination of new text analytic tools and computational models of legal reasoning provides an opportunity for those who see potential in implementing processes of legal practice computationally.

Law students and practitioners may not have computer programming expertise, but they will not necessarily need it. What they will need is an ability to think about legal practice in terms of engineering a cognitive computing process.

This book assumes readers do *not* have familiarity with computer programming. The focus is not on computer code but, more generally, on systematic descriptions of legal and computational processes. For instance, in each of the examples of CMLRs of Part I, we examine: the legal process, the program models, and the assumptions made, the inputs to and outputs from the program and how they are represented, the computational processes (at a high level of description such as via architecture diagrams, flow charts, and algorithms) with which the program transforms inputs to outputs, concrete examples of the algorithmic steps transforming specific inputs to specific outputs, how the researchers evaluated the programs, the strengths and weaknesses of the approach, and its relevance given recent developments in legal text processing.

Actually writing computer code is the last step in designing successful computer applications. Key steps inevitably precede coding. They involve specifying requirements for the ultimate program and designing a high-level software architecture to realize it. Only then do programmers attempt to implement the software. Recent models of software development may focus on a modularized process involving multiple, nested instances of these steps, but even then, specifying requirements and a high-level design of a module always precedes the coding to implement it (Gordon, 2014).

The pedagogical goal, therefore, is not to teach the reader computer programming but how to propose and design apps that assist users in performing legal processes.

If the high-level designs are sound, there will always be computer programmers to implement them.

Law students are ideally suited to engage in identifying legal processes to model, specifying requirements, and designing high-level architectures. Law students are continually introduced to legal processes that are new to them and instructed how to perform the processes step-by-step. This occurs repeatedly in the first-year curriculum, in moot court competitions, in legal clinics, in legal internships and part-time jobs with law firms, corporate legal departments, and university tech transfer departments, and in pro bono activities. Today, law students are also likely to have used computer apps from a tender age. They are intimately familiar with the new modes of communication, with the current interface conventions, and with accessing web-based resources.

Along the way, the descriptions of computational models expose readers to a variety of assumptions and uncertainties inherent in legal reasoning that affect human legal reasoning. Indeed, law students study the sources of these uncertainties throughout the law school curriculum. These assumptions and uncertainties present some design constraints that AI & Law researchers have learned to avoid, finesse, or accommodate in their CMLRs, and that will necessarily affect efforts to apply text processing tools like those in Watson and Debater. Students will also learn how, and the extent to which, the performance of these technologies can be measured experimentally, and what the measures signify.

With respect to developing cognitive computing tools for legal practice, it is a time of exploration, even for IBM. The Watson Developer Cloud is indicative of a trend to make text analytic tools convenient to use even without computer programming expertise. A well-formed proposal from a law school student, legal academic, or practicing attorney might well engage IBM's material interest. This is not as far-fetched as it may appear. Indeed, it has happened already. Law students at the University of Toronto (that's in Canada, Watson, in case you are reading this) have already engaged in building legal apps in collaboration with IBM using Watson services (Gray, 2014). They created the Silicon Valley start-up called Ross, discussed in Chapter 12. As an extra incentive, IBM has announced a "$5 million competition . . . to develop and demonstrate how humans can collaborate with powerful cognitive technologies to tackle some of the world's grand challenges" (Desatnik, 2016).

Why couldn't a law student win with a CCLA for cross-jurisdictional issues in cybercrime and security? Tutoring students' imaginations about what is possible may be all that is necessary to enable them to design and propose such an app. This book aims for that.

Cognitive computing in law will be happening soon!

2

Modeling Statutory Reasoning

The Law is a domain of rules, and many of those legal rules are embodied in statutes and regulations. Since rules can be expressed logically and computers can reason deductively, computationally modeling statutory reasoning *should* be easy. One simply inputs a fact situation to the computer program; the program identifies the relevant rules, determines whether or not the rules' conditions are satisfied, and explains the answer in terms of the rules that applied or did not apply.

Building a computational model of statutory reasoning, however, presents challenges. As explained below, statutes routinely are vague, syntactically ambiguous as well as semantically ambiguous, and subject to structural indeterminacy. If a computer program is to apply a statutory rule, which logical interpretation should it apply, how can it deal with the vagueness and open-texture of the statute's terms, or determine if there is an exception?

The chapter draws a contrast between deductively applying a statute and the complex process of statutory interpretation, which frequently involves conflicting reasonable arguments. Classical logical models may break down in dealing with legal indeterminacy, a common feature of legal reasoning: even when advocates agree on the facts in issue and the rules for deciding a matter, they can still make legally reasonable arguments for and against a proposition.

Reasoning with statutes, however, remains a pressing necessity. The chapter examines various AI & Law approaches that address or finesse these issues: a normalization process for systematically elaborating a statute's multiple logical versions, a logical implementation for applying a statute deductively, and more recent models of business process compliance and network-based statutory modeling, both potentially useful for cognitive computing.

Questions addressed in this chapter include: How can statutory rules be ambiguous, both semantically *and* syntactically? How do lawyers deal with these ambiguities, and how can computer programs cope? What are normalized legal drafting, Prolog, and a Prolog program? What is depth-first search and how does it differ from breadth-first search? What is legal indeterminacy and why is it a problem for logical models of legal reasoning? How can logic programs assess business process compliance with regulations? What problems do isomorphic knowledge representations of statutes address? What are citation networks and statutory network diagrams, and how can they support cognitive computing?

2.2. COMPLEXITIES OF MODELING STATUTORY REASONING

Statutes and regulations are complex legal texts. An often intricate maze of provisions written in legal technical jargon define what is legal and not. With their networks of cross-references and exceptions, statutes and regulations are often too complicated for the untutored citizen to understand. Even legal experts may have difficulty simply identifying all and only the provisions that are relevant to analyzing a given question, problem, or topic.

The field of AI & Law has long studied how to design computer programs that can reason logically with legal rules from statutes and regulations. It has made strides, and demonstrated some successes, but it has also developed an appreciation of just how difficult the problem is. In the process, the field has identified a number of constraints that need to be addressed or finessed in attempting to design a computer program that can apply statutory rules. As noted, these constraints include vagueness and two kinds of ambiguity in statutory rules, the complexity of statutory interpretation, the need to support conflicting but reasonable arguments about what a legal rule means, and practical problems in maintaining logical representations of statutes alongside textual ones.

Of the two kinds of ambiguity that complicate computationally modeling statutory reasoning, semantic ambiguity, and its cousin, vagueness, are familiar. The regulatory concepts and terms the legislature selects may not be sufficiently well defined to determine if or how they apply. The second kind, syntactic ambiguity, may be less familiar: the *logical* terms legislatures use, such as "if," "and," "or," and "unless," introduce multiple interpretations of even simple statutes.

2.2.1. *Semantic Ambiguity and Vagueness*

Semantic ambiguity "is uncertainty between relatively few . . . distinct alternatives" concerning a term's meaning (Allen and Engholm, 1978, p. 383). "Vagueness is a semantic uncertainty about precisely where the boundary is with respect to what a term does and does not refer to" (Allen and Engholm, 1978, p. 382).

Both are due to the fact that legislatures may employ terms that are vague or otherwise not well-defined. Waterman confronted the problem that ill-defined legal terms present for constructing legal expert system rules (Section 1.3.1), and Gardner attempted to address it with her algorithm for distinguishing hard and easy legal questions (Section 1.4.2).

Semantic ambiguity and vagueness are concessions to human, social, and political reality. The legislature cannot fashion language sufficiently detailed to anticipate all of the situations it may wish to regulate. Instead, it employs more general terminology in statutory rules and relies on the courts to interpret and apply the abstract terms and concepts in new fact situations. Intentionally rendering key provisions in a semantically ambiguous way can also facilitate legislative compromise. If the legislature attempted to use specific, detailed language, it might compound the difficulty of obtaining political consensus (Allen and Engholm, 1978, p. 384).

Semantic ambiguity and vagueness, however, are also a source of *legal indeterminacy*: opponents can agree on what legal rule applies and what the facts are and *still* generate reasonable legal arguments for opposing results (Berman and Hafner, 1988).

Even when the legislative intent is clear and the statute's language straightforward, legal adversaries routinely make reasonable but conflicting arguments about what the rule's terms mean. In their example, the case of *Johnson v. Southern Pacific Co.*,117 Fed. 462 (8th Cir. 1902) *rev'd* 196 U.S. 1 (1904), a federal statute made it "illegal for railroads to use in interstate traffic 'any car not equipped with couplers coupling automatically by impact.'" According to the statute's preamble, the act's purpose was "to promote the safety of employees ... by compelling carriers ... to equip their cars with automatic couplers ... and their locomotives with drive wheel brakes" (Berman and Hafner, 1988, p. 196).

There was no disagreement about the facts. "The plaintiff, a railroad brakeman, was injured when he attempted to couple a locomotive to a dining car, in order to move the dining car off the track." Causation was not an issue: the plaintiff's injury was caused by the fact that although the locomotive was equipped with such a coupler, it was not one that could couple automatically with this particular dining car.

Nevertheless, courts disagreed about whether the statutory rule's conditions were satisfied, and, in particular "on the meaning of all three of the predicates in the condition part of this rule: the meaning of 'car,' the meaning of 'used-in-interstate-commerce,' and the meaning of 'equipped'" (Berman and Hafner, 1988, p. 198). Are locomotives included in the "cars" required to have automatic couplers or not? Does "interstate commerce" include the time when a car is awaiting its next load or not? Were the dining car and locomotive "equipped" with automatic couplers or not? The trial and appellate courts disagreed on the answers to these questions and they certainly did not treat those answers as determined by the terms' literal meanings.

2.2.2. *Syntactic Ambiguity*

The other kind of ambiguity, syntactic ambiguity, arises from a different reality: statutory language does not always follow a single, coherent logical structure. This results in part from the properties of natural language text. Unlike mathematical and logical formalisms and computer code, text does not allow one explicitly to specify the scopes of the logical connectors, such as "if," "and," "or," and "unless." The syntax of a statute can also be unclear due to the language used in implementing exceptions and cross-references. Exceptions to a provision may be expressed explicitly but even implicitly and may appear not only within a provision but also in other provisions or even in other statutes (Allen and Engholm, 1978).

Layman Allen demonstrated that syntactic ambiguity leads to multiple possible logical interpretations of even relatively simple statutory provisions, with potentially profound consequences for those subject to regulation. He provided an example from a Louisiana statute defining a crime:

> No person shall engage in or institute a local telephone call, conversation or conference of an anonymous nature and therein use obscene, profane, vulgar, lewd, lascivious or indecent language, suggestions or proposals of an obscene nature and threats of any kind whatsoever. (Allen and Engholm, 1978)

Presumably, the legislature intentionally selected vague terms like "obscene" and "indecent" with full knowledge of their open texture.

It is much less likely that they intentionally promulgated a criminal standard with an inherent syntactic ambiguity: To be in violation of the statute, is it sufficient that a call include either obscene language OR threats, or, as the defendant in *State v. Hill*, 245 La 119 (1963) argued successfully at the District court, must it include obscene language AND threats? The Louisiana Supreme Court disagreed; it interpreted "and" as meaning "or," seemingly violating a common law maxim that criminal statutes should be strictly construed. Surely, it would have been better legislative policy to issue a syntactically unambiguous standard (Allen and Engholm, 1978).

Allen described a systematic *normalization* process for identifying such ambiguities. Given a statute, one:

1. Identifies the statute's "atomic" substantive propositions and replaces them with labels (S1, S2, . . .).
2. Uses propositional logic to clarify the syntax of the statute.
3. Restores the text of the substantive propositions.

In *propositional logic*, symbols stand for whole propositions. Using logical operators and connectives, propositions can be assembled into complex statements whose truth values depend solely on whether the component propositions are true or false. Unlike, predicate logic, defined below, propositional logic does not consider the components or structure of individual propositions (see Clement, 2016).

Applying the normalization process to the Louisiana statute yields a number of versions including the two shown in Figure 2.1. Each version is an expression in propositional logic, which renders its logical structure more clearly.

If	If
S1. a person engages in or institutes a local telephone call, conversation, or conference of an anonymous nature,	**S1.** a person engages in or institutes a local telephone call, conversation, or conference of an anonymous nature,
and	**and**
S2. that person therein uses obscene, profane, vulgar, lewd, lascivious or indecent language, suggestions or proposals of an obscene nature,	**S2.** that person therein uses obscene, profane, vulgar, lewd, lascivious or indecent language, suggestions or proposals of an obscene nature,
or	**and**
S3. that person therein uses threats of any kind whatsoever,	**S3.** that person therein uses threats of any kind whatsoever,
then	**then**
S4. that person has engaged in unlawful behavior.	**S4.** that person has engaged in unlawful behavior.
S4 :- S1, S2. S4 :- S1, S3.	S4 :- S1, S2, S3.

FIGURE 2.1. Normalized versions of two alternative interpretations of the Louisiana statute and corresponding Prolog rules (bottom) (Allen and Engholm, 1978)

2.3. APPLYING STATUTORY LEGAL RULES DEDUCTIVELY

A normalized statute in propositional logical form offers several advantages.

First, using propositional logic to clarify the syntax of the statute can make a complex statute much easier to understand. For instance, Allen contrasts a complex provision of the Internal Revenue Code (IRC section 354), which deals with the tax treatment of exchanges of securities in certain corporate reorganizations, with a normalized version as shown in Figure 2.2 on the right. The normalized version identifies the "atomic" substantive propositions and employs indentation to convey the simplified logical structure.

Allen also provided a kind of flow chart through the logic of the "propositionalized" version of the statute where every node in the graph is one of the requirements of the statute (see Figure 2.3). The labeled nodes, S1 through S9, refer to the labeled propositions in the normalized version (right) in Figure 2.2.

The flow chart can be much easier to understand than the textual or even normalized versions of the statute. It demonstrates three alternative paths through the statute from a starting point of an exchange of securities in the corporate reorganization (S2) to the desired conclusion of "no gain or loss" recognition (S1). These paths remain more or less implicit in the textual and normalized versions (although Allen combined the flow chart and the normalized version to make the paths explicit).

In the context of corporate compliance, for instance, such flow charts can help to clarify obligations of the various corporate constituents. *Corporate compliance* involves detecting and preventing violations of law by the agents, employees, officers

(a) General Rule

(1) In General. No gain or loss shall be recognized if stock ... in a corporation a party to a reorganization are, in pursuance of the plan of reorganization, exchanged solely for stock ... in such ... a party to the reorganization.

(2) Limitation. Paragraph (1) shall not apply if

(A) the principal amount of any such securities received ..., or

(B) any such securities are received and no such securities are surrendered.

(3) Cross Reference. For treatment of the exchange if any property is received which is not permitted to be received under this ... see § 356.

(b) Exception.

(1) In General. Subsection (a) shall not apply to an exchange in pursuance of a plan of reorganization within the meaning of § 368(a) (1) (D), unless

(A) the corporation to which the assets are transferred acquires substantially all of the assets of the transferor ...; and,

(B) the stock, ... received by such transferor, ..., are distributed in pursuance of the plan of reorganization.

(2) Cross Reference. For special rules for certain exchanges in pursuance of plans of reorganization within the meaning of § 368(a) (1) (D), see § 355.

(c) Certain Railroad Reorganizations. Notwithstanding any other provisions of this subchapter, subsection (a) (1) (and so much of § 356 as relates to this section) shall apply with respect to a plan of reorganization ... for a railroad approved ... under § 77 of the Bankruptcy Act, or under § 20b of the Interstate Commerce Act, as being in the public interest.

If

[S2] 1. stock or securities in a corporation a party to a reorganization are, in pursuance of the plan of reorganization, exchanged solely for stock or securities in such corporation or in another corporation a party to the reorganization, and

[S3] 2. (a) 1. the principal amount of any such securities received does not exceed the principal amount of any such securities surrendered, and

[S4] 2. (a) 2. it is not so that both (a) some such securities are received and (b) no such securities are surrendered, and

[S5] 2. (a) 3. (a) the plan of reorganization is not one within the meaning of section 368(a) (I)(D), or

[S6] 2. (a) 3. (b) 1. the corporation to which the assets are transferred acquires substantially all of the assets of the transferor of such assets, and

[S7] 2. (a) 3. (b) 2. the stock, securities, and other properties received by such transferor, as well as the other properties of such transferor, are distributed in pursuance of the plan of reorganization, or

[S8] 2. (b) 1. whether or not the plan of reorganization is one within the meaning of section 368(a), and

[S9] 2. (b) 2. the plan of reorganization is for a railroad and is approved by the Interstate Commerce Commission under section 77 of the Bankruptcy Act, or under section 20b of the Interstate Commerce Act, as being in the public interest.

then

[SI] 3. no gain or loss shall be recognized.

FIGURE 2.2. IRC section 354 and a normalized version (right) (see Allen and Engholm, 1978)

and directors of a corporation, firm, or other business. Presenting an employee's regulatory obligations in the form of a flow chart could help the employee understand what is legal and what is not legal.

2.3.1. *Running a Normalized Version on a Computer*

Second, a statutory provision in propositional logic can be run on a computer! At the bottom of Figure 2.1 are the two normalized versions of the Louisiana statute

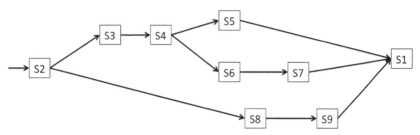

FIGURE 2.3. Flow chart for propositionalized IRC section 354 (see Allen and Engholm, 1978)

expressed in Prolog, a programming language based on so-called "Horn clause logic" associated with artificial intelligence and computational linguistics.

The normalized versions of this statute are examples of simple propositional logic. The version on the right, S_4 :- S_1, S_2, S_3, means "*If* $S_1 \wedge S_2 \wedge S_3 \Rightarrow S_4$," where $\wedge$ means "and." The version on the left uses two formulas, S_4 :- S_1, S_2 and S_4 :- S_1, S_3 to implement the disjunction (i.e., the "or") in the version.

Prolog interprets the Horn clauses, treating them as a program. For example, it treats the horn clause on the right as saying, in effect, "To show S_4, show S_1, show S_2, and show S_3."

By asking the user whether each substantive proposition S_1, S_2, and S_3 is true or false, a computer can prove the truth or falsity of S_4. In this way, the logic of the statute is automated. The logic of these normalized versions of the statute is simple enough to handle manually with truth tables. Nevertheless, a computer can also process the propositional logic of more complex statutes like that in Figure 2.2.

2.3.2. *Predicate Logic*

One would also like to express the content of a statutory provision's substantive propositions, not just its overall logical syntax. This can be done with *classical logic* (also known as predicate logic, predicate calculus, or first-order logic).

> Classical logic is the formal logic known to introductory logic students as "predicate logic" in which, among other things, (i) all sentences of the formal language have exactly one of two possible truth values (TRUE, FALSE), (ii) the rules of inference allow one to deduce any sentence from an inconsistent set of assumptions, (iii) all predicates are totally defined on the range of the variables, and (iv) the formal semantics is the one invented by Tarski that provided the first precise definition of truth for a formal language in its metalanguage. (Dowden, 2016)

Classical logic employs symbols for predicates, subjects, and quantifiers. In propositional logic, the proposition 'All men are mortal' is represented with just one symbol and has no internal structure. In contrast, in classical logic one can define a predicate $M(x)$ to express that x is mortal or employ the universal quantifier ("For all"): All x. $M(x)$ to express that all x are mortal.

Horn clause logic, the basis of Prolog, implements most (but not all) of predicate logic and allows one to express both the content of substantive propositions of a normalized version of a statutory provision as well as its logical syntax. For instance, HLA Hart's famous sample statutory provision, "Vehicles are not permitted in the park,"[1] could be expressed in Prolog (that is, Horn clause predicate logic) as:

violation(X, S) :- vehicle(X), park(S), in(X, S).

That is, "*If X is vehicle* ∧ *S is park* ∧ *X in S* ⇒ *X in S is violation.*" In Prolog, commas between predicates indicate "and"; the universal quantifier is implied.

If one inputs to the Prolog program information such as:

vehicle (X) :- motorcycle (X)
vehicle (X) :- automobile (X)

the program can prove that one may not take into the park a motorcycle, an automobile, or indeed, anything else we input as qualifying as a vehicle, by chaining the conclusion of one rule to the premise of the other.

2.3.3. *Syntactic Ambiguity as Design Constraint*

Before turning to an example of a large-scale legal logic program, let's summarize the implications of syntactic ambiguity.

Syntactic ambiguity makes the task of translating statutory texts into computationally formalized logical rules problematic (Allen and Saxon, 1987). In computationally expressed rules, syntactic ambiguity can be eliminated. The problem is that the version of a statutory rule selected for formalization into a logic programming language like Prolog is not necessarily the one that the legislature intended.

As a result of syntactic ambiguity, a knowledge engineer cannot be certain what the legislature intended. The number of syntactically possible interpretations that result from applying the normalization process to even fairly simple statutory provisions can be disconcertingly large. Section 3505, a proposed limitation of the fourth amendment exclusionary rule, stated:

> Except as specifically provided by statute, evidence which is obtained as a result of a search or seizure and which is otherwise admissible shall not be excluded in a proceeding in a court of the United States if the search or seizure was undertaken in a reasonable, good faith belief that it was in conformity with the fourth amendment to the Constitution of the United States. A showing that evidence was obtained pursuant to and within the scope of a warrant constitutes prima facie evidence of such a reasonable good faith belief, unless the warrant was obtained through intentional and material misrepresentation.

---

[1] Actually, Hart's example was "A legal rule forbids you to take a vehicle into the public park" (Hart, 1958, p. 607).

Although just two sentences long, when normalized, section 3505 yielded 48 interpretations of varying strength, as measured by their restrictiveness or inclusiveness, based simply on the syntactic ambiguities in the provision (Allen and Saxon, 1987).

As a practical matter, only a few versions may seem clearly reasonable and other versions may be clearly unreasonable. The question is who selects? If a knowledge engineer decides which normalized version to implement, it is not an authoritative choice. Legal academics or other experts in a field may express opinions about which version the legislature intended or should have intended. The only body able to make the selection authoritatively, however, is the legislature.

Unfortunately, the legislators were probably unaware of the ambiguity (Allen and Saxon, 1987). While semantic ambiguity can facilitate legislative compromise and is usually intended, syntactic ambiguity serves no legitimate function in the political process and does not facilitate political comprise. Indeed, in laying out a systematic procedure for generating normalized versions of statutory provisions, one of Layman Allen's goals was to sensitize legislators and law students to the phenomenon (Allen and Engholm, 1978; Allen and Saxon, 1987).

A law professor in Tennessee, Grayfred Gray, achieved some success in convincing a state legislative drafting committee to adopt normalization as a means of eliminating unintended syntactic ambiguity in provisions of the State's mental health law provisions concerning commitment and discharge of mental patients. The Committee was concerned "that the law be clear to the people who would have to work with it, most of whom were not lawyers" (Gray, 1985, pp. 479–80). The legislature did not seem to have a problem with normalization. The publisher of the state's statutory code, on the other hand, worried that normalization's liberal use of indentation to convey statutes' simplified logical structure would take up too much space, increasing the cost of the printed publications. Ultimately, only a few statutes were published in normalized form.

Today, on the World Wide Web, space is not an issue. Normalized versions of statutes and accompanying flowcharts could be published economically via the web, making it much easier for nonlawyers to read and understand the legal requirements. In a web-based publication, help links and dropdown menus could assist the uninitiated in using and interpreting the normalized provisions.

In the meantime, of course, the multiplicity of logical interpretations of statutes has not brought the legal profession to its knees. On the contrary, it generates employment. Attorneys and legal experts representing taxpayers or insurance companies are retained to generate and exploit alternative syntactic interpretations of complex provisions. In an adversarial context, identifying alternative logical interpretations of a statute or of a complex insurance policy provision opens the opportunity for arguing for an interpretation favorable to one's client, as in the criminal trial in *State v. Hill* above.

In a different context, such as corporate compliance, risk-averse attorneys might recommend adopting a more expansive logical interpretation of a statute to formalize in a business rules system. Selecting a safely expansive interpretation would help to reduce subsequent infractions of the legal rules.

From the viewpoint of cognitive computing, a system that could detect latent syntactic ambiguities would be a nice tool for legislative drafters. Given the input of a statutory provision in natural language, could a system automatically generate a comprehensive listing of normalized versions or partially order them in terms of their strength? In other words, can the normalization process of (Allen and Engholm, 1978) be automated? I am not aware of any research attempts to do so, but it seems worth exploring.

2.3.4. *The BNA Program*

Marek Sergot and his colleagues successfully implemented a large portion of the British Nationality Act (BNA) as a logic program written in Prolog (Sergot et al., 1986). The system ran approximately 150 rules dealing with the acquisition of British citizenship. The rules were implemented as Horn clauses in Prolog; Figure 2.4 shows a translation of three of the rules into pseudo English.

Inputs to the BNA program were descriptions of problems involving a question of citizenship. The program output an answer and an explanation. Asking a question was equivalent to stating a proposition and asking Prolog to prove it. For instance, one such proposition is:

A: Peter is a British citizen on date (16 Jan 1984) by sect. z.

Here, z is a variable standing for the number of some section of the statute that would warrant the conclusion.

> 1-(1) A person born in the United Kingdom after commencement shall be a British Citizen if at the time of birth his father or mother is:
>   (a) a British Citizen, or
>   (b) settled in the United Kingdom.
>
> This is represented in the computer as:
> *Rule1:* X acquires British citizenship on date Y
> under sec. 1.1
>   IF   X was born in the U.K.
>   AND   X was born on date Y
>   AND   Y is after or on commencement of the act
>   AND   X has a parent who qualified under 1.1 on date
>
> *Rule2:* X has a parent who qualifies under 1.1 on date Y
>   IF   X has a parent Z
>   AND   Z was a British citizen on date Y
>
> *Rule3:* X has a parent who qualifies under 1.1 on date Y
>   IF   X has a parent Z
>   AND   Z was settled in the U.K. on date Y.

FIGURE 2.4. BNA provisions as represented in rules (Sergot et al., 1986)

Prolog is both a programming language and theorem prover. Given A, Prolog attempts to construct a proof that A by reasoning backward from conclusion A to identify conditions that need to be satisfied. (Backward chaining was introduced in Section 1.3.1.) In the process, it finds all of the rules that conclude with a proposition of the form A. There may be a number of different rules with which to establish conclusion A. Prolog will try them all in the order in which the rules are written.

Let's say there is a list of n rules whose conclusions are A. If Prolog is considering a rule r_i from that list, let's call the next rule in the list r_{i+1}. Finally, when Prolog is considering rule r_j, if it finds a new rule whose conclusion is the antecedent of rule r_j, let's refer to the newly found rule as r_{j_i} and call it a "descendant" of rule r_j on a path to proving A.

Prolog will try the n rules on the list in a depth-first search order. In *depth-first search*, the program follows a path from one of the r_i on the list to its end, either success or failure, before starting a new path from r_{i+1}. In other words, if Prolog is considering rule r_i, the program always chooses to try to find a descendant r_{i_i} of rule r_i, before moving on to the next rule on the list, r_{i+1}. If and only if the path from r_i runs out without proving A will it move on to r_{i+1}.

In contrast, in a *breadth-first search*, the program tries to open a path for each of the n rules before searching for any descendants of a descendant. That is, even if a search-based program has found a descendant for rule r_i (i.e., r_{i_i}) it chooses to try to find a descendant for each of the next rules on the list $r_{i+1}, r_{i+2}, \ldots, r_n$, before trying to find a descendant of r_{i_i}.

Each rule will have conditions B1 ... Bn that need to be satisfied in order to conclude C. Remember that Prolog treats such a rule as a program: To show C, show B1, show B2, ..., and show Bn. For each of these Bn subproblems, Prolog solves it in one of four ways:

1. There may be another rule whose conclusion is of the form of Bn.
2. There may be a fact satisfying Bn.
3. The system can ask the user if Bn is true.
4. The system can ask an expert if Bn is true.

Figure 2.5 shows excerpts of the BNA program's output for the question regarding proposition A. The boldface indicates inputs from the user. Notice that the program could answer "why" and "how" questions and explain its answers. Basically, having constructed a proof of A or of an intermediate conclusion, it could fashion an explanation by reiterating the inference steps in its proof.

2.3.5. *Some Problems of Translating Statutes into Programs*

In designing and implementing the computational model of the BNA, the designers encountered four problems or constraints: Sometimes a previously formulated rule

IS Peter a British citizen on date (16 Jan 1984) by sect. Z?
Which X: Peter was born on date X ? *(3 May 1983)*

...

Is it true that Peter was born In the U.K. ? *yes*
Which X : X is father of Peter ? *why*

if X is father of Peter then X is a parent of Peter
If X is a parent of Peter and X is a British citizen on date (3 May 1983)
then Peter has a parent who qualifies under 1.1 on date (3 May 1983)
Peter was born in the U.K.
Peter was born on date (3 May 1983)
(3 May 1983) is after or on commencement, so
if Peter has a parent who qualifies under 1.1 on date (3 May 1983)
then Peter acquires British citizenship on date (3 May 1983) by sect. 1.1
Peter is alive on (16 Jan 1984), so
if Peter acquires British citizenship on date (3 May 1983) by sect. 1.1
and (16 Jan 1984) is after or on (3 May 1983)
and not[Peter ceases to be a British citizen on date Y
and Y is between (3 May 1983) and (16 Jan 1984)]
then Peter is a British citizen on date (16 Jan 1984) by sect 1.1

Which X : X is father of Peter ? *William*
Which X : William was born on date X ? *(I March 1952)*

...

Is it true that William was born in the U.K. ? *yes*

...

Is It true that William was a citizen of the U.K. and Colonies on date (31 Dec
1982) ? *yes*
IS it true that on date (31 Dec 1982) William had the right of abode in the U.K.
under the Immigration Act 1971 as then in force ? *yes*

...

Yes, I can confirm that
Peter is a British citizen on date (16 Jan 1984) by sect. 1.1 **how**
I deduced Peter is a British citizen on date (16 Jan 1984) by sect. 1.1
from the rule

FIGURE 2.5. BNA program output (excerpts) (Sergot et al., 1986, p. 376f)

or predicate needed to be *reformulated*. In addition, the statute's use of *negation,
default reasoning, counterfactual conditions,* and *open-textured terms* needed to be
addressed.

Reformulation

Formalizing an extensive statute is a process of trial and error. One frequently
encounters a new context in which a previous formulation of a rule concept is inadequate and has to be reformulated to accommodate additional constraints imposed
by subsequent rules in the act. For instance, the researchers discovered that it is
"insufficient to conclude only that an individual is a British citizen; it is also necessary to determine the section under which citizenship is acquired." Also, a newly

encountered section made evident the need for "a more explicit treatment of time" to compute constraints that enabled one not a citizen subsequently to be registered as one under certain circumstances (Sergot et al., 1986, p. 374). The researchers had to change some existing rules, conditions, or parameters or add new ones to address the new constraints.

Negation

To implement some rules in the BNA and other statutes, it would be desirable to employ rules that state a negative conclusion (i.e., not A), such as "*x* was not a British citizen at the time of *y*'s birth" or "*x* was not settled in the U.K. at the time of *y*'s birth."

Such negative conclusions require an ability to deal with ordinary or classical negation, something that Prolog does not support. Prolog can employ only "negation by failure." The theorem prover uses a rule, "infer not *P* if fail to show *P*." In other words, if there is a finite list of ways to show A, the theorem prover will check them all. If all of them fail, then it concludes not A. Negation by failure is adequate when one can make the "closed world assumption" (that is, that anything which is not known is assumed to be false).

Often, however, the closed world assumption is not reasonable. "It is notoriously difficult in law to determine all the legal provisions that might be relevant to deciding a particular case" (Sergot et al., 1986, p. 379). The researchers demonstrated some formulations in the BNA where using negation by failure would be prohibitively complex or lead the program to draw conclusions opposite from what the legislature intended. For instance, consider the difficulty of listing all of the ways that *x* can be shown to be a British citizen at the time of *y*'s birth.

A theorem prover that can handle classical negation could deal with this problem automatically, but Prolog's theorem prover would require an extended logic, which introduces other difficulties. As a result, the researchers simply resorted to having the BNA program ask the user to confirm certain negative information such as that "*x* was not a British citizen at the time of *y*'s birth" (Sergot et al., 1986, p. 381).

Default Reasoning

The authors point out that the BNA employs reasoning by default. "Conclusions made by default in the absence of information to the contrary may have to be withdrawn if new information is made available later" (Sergot et al., 1986, p. 381).

One example is section l-(2) of the BNA, the provision that deals with abandoned infants. What would happen, the authors ask, if the abandoned infant's parents, to whom citizenship had been conferred by default, suddenly turned up but were *not* British citizens? (Sergot et al., 1986, p. 381). The BNA does not seem to have a provision for that eventuality, but even if it did, there would be a problem.

Default reasoning is *non-monotonic*: propositions once proven may need to be withdrawn in light of new facts. Predicate logic (i.e., classical first-order logic as implemented in Prolog) is monotonic; it does not support withdrawing propositions that have been proven.[2]

As discussed below, a more expressive logic is required.

Counterfactual Conditionals

Statutes also commonly make use of counterfactual conditionals such as "would have [become a British Citizen] but for his having died or ceased to be a citizen . . . [by] renunciation." The legislature may employ such a formulation as a shortcut means of reference. "The drafters avoid listing a complicated set of conditions explicitly by [referring] to some other part of the legislation" from which the conditions may be inferred (Sergot et al., 1986, p. 382).

The researchers created special rules to deal with such counterfactual conditionals. They wrote "additional alternative rules; one set describing, for example, the conditions for acquisition of citizenship at commencement for individuals who were alive on that date, and another set for individuals who had died before that date, but otherwise met all the other requisite conditions before death" (Sergot et al., 1986, p. 382).

The researchers carefully analyzed the statute to hypothesize which requirements might reasonably apply in the counterfactual condition. This increased the number of rules that needed to be formalized. Presumably, the legislative drafters employed the counterfactual condition to avoid the tedious task of spelling out these conditions. On the other hand, it is always possible that the drafters meant to leave the issue open-ended.

In any event, it is another example where knowledge engineers are required to make difficult interpretive decisions without legislative authority.

Open-Textured Terms

Finally, the legislature employed open-textured predicates in the statute that they did not define. The act contains such vague phrases as "being a good character," "having reasonable excuse," and "having sufficient knowledge of English" (Sergot et al., 1986, p. 371).

The researchers adopted a straightforward approach to dealing with vague terms. The system simply asks the user whether the term is true or not in the current inquiry. Alternatively, they might have programmed it to assume that a particular vague concept always applied (or always did not apply) and to qualify its answer based on this assumption, for instance: "Peter is a citizen, if he is of good character" (Sergot et al., 1986, p. 371). The researchers note that one might also apply rules of thumb, derived from analysis of past cases where courts applied the terms, in order to reduce the terms' vagueness. Such heuristic rules, however, would not be guaranteed to cover all cases, nor would they be authoritative.

---

[2] In fact, Prolog is non-monotonic, but the implementation used for the BNA program assumed that a user had perfect information and could always answer the questions it posed (Gordon, 1987, p. 58).

The problems of resolving syntactic ambiguity, reformulation, negation, counter-factual conditions, and semantic ambiguity are problems of interpreting natural language text. Potentially, they affect any attempts to translate legislation into runnable computer code regardless of whether humans are performing the translation manually, as in the BNA program research, or programs are extracting the rules automatically from statutory texts as discussed in Chapter 9.

2.4. THE COMPLEXITY OF STATUTORY INTERPRETATION
AND THE NEED FOR ARGUMENTS

The BNA project focused on "the limited objective of implementing rules and regulations with the purpose of applying them mechanically to individual cases" (Sergot et al., 1986, p. 372). The BNA program was never intended to simulate the output of a court's reasoning about a statute, but it is interesting to compare the way it generates an answer through logical deduction as illustrated in Figure 2.5 with what a court might do.

In a landmark piece, the legal philosopher Lon Fuller demonstrated the limitations of a mechanical approach to applying legal rules. Does "a truck used in World War II" to be "mount[ed] on a pedestal in the park" and "in perfect working order" fall afoul of the no-vehicles-in-the-park regulation? (Fuller, 1958, p. 663). Or suppose that a municipal regulation states, "It shall be a misdemeanor, punishable by a fine of five dollars, to sleep in any railway station." A policeman encounters two people in the station:

> The first is a passenger who was waiting at 3 A.M. for a delayed train. When he was arrested he was sitting upright in an orderly fashion, but was heard by the arresting officer to be gently snoring. The second is a man who had brought a blanket and pillow to the station and had obviously settled himself down for the night. He was arrested, however, before he had a chance to go to sleep. (Fuller, 1958, p. 664)

According to a mechanical application of the rule, the first person violates the rule but the second does not; the former is asleep in the railway station but the latter is not. Given the likely purpose of the municipal regulation, however, this seems to be exactly the wrong result. As Fuller asks, "[I]s it really ever possible to interpret a word in a statute without knowing the aim of the statute?" (Fuller, 1958, p. 664).

The process of establishing the meaning of a statutory provision and applying it in a concrete fact situation is commonly referred to as statutory interpretation. A law court engages in *statutory interpretation* when it applies "statutes to particular cases with a view to giving authoritative and binding decisions upon the matters in dispute or under trial," "forms a view as to the proper meaning of the statutes which seem to them applicable in the case," and articulates a "view as to the way in which the statute should be understood" (MacCormick and Summers, 1991, p. 11f).

The process of statutory interpretation involves logical deduction but is quite a bit more complex. MacCormick and Summers identify a hierarchy of types of statutory interpretive *arguments*, including:

- *Linguistic*: arguments from the statute's ordinary meaning or technical meaning (i.e., legal or domain-specific technical meaning).
- *Systemic*: arguments from contextual harmonization, from precedent, and by analogy, logical-conceptual arguments, and arguments from general principles of law and from history.
- *Teleological/Evaluative*: arguments from purpose and from substantive reasons.
- *Transcategorical*: including arguments from intention (MacCormick and Summers, 1991, pp. 512–15).

An argument from the purpose of the municipal regulation banning sleeping in railway stations would be an example of a teological/evaluative argument. The list of acceptable techniques and their labels are relative to a legal system or tradition and may be subject to debate.

2.4.1. *A Stepwise Process of Statutory Interpretation*

The authors organize these argument types into a simplified, nearly algorithmic model for statutory interpretation (MacCormick and Summers, 1991, p. 531). According to the process, in interpreting a statutory provision, one considers three levels of argument in the following order: (1) linguistic arguments, (2) systemic arguments, and (3) teleological-evaluative arguments.

More specifically, the process specifies steps for making decisions based on the arguments:

Level 1: Accept as *prima facie* justified a clear interpretation at level 1 unless there is some reason to proceed to level 2;

Level 2: Where level 2 has been invoked for sufficient reason, accept as *prima facie* justified a clear interpretation at level 2 unless there is reason to move to level 3.

Level 3: If at level 3, accept as justified only the interpretation best supported by the whole range of applicable arguments (MacCormick and Summers, 1991, p. 531).

Generally, in the above series of steps, the authors recommend that arguments from intention and other transcategorical arguments (if any) be taken as grounds which may be relevant for departing from the above *prima facie* ordering.

Given this complex description of statutory interpretation, one can appreciate Ann Gardner's observation that law is a "rule-guided rather than a rule-governed activity: 'The experts can do more with the rules than just follow them . . . (they) can argue about the rules themselves'" (Gardner, 1985 quoted in Berman and Hafner, 1988, p. 208).

In order to apply the jurisprudential model of statutory interpretation in MacCormick and Summers (1991) to a concrete scenario, one might have to integrate reasoning with rules, cases, and the underlying social values and legislative purposes. Crucially, a reasoner would need to make or consider arguments for and against an interpretation. Every step of the interpretive process involves making and evaluating arguments of various types. A reasoner would need to draw analogies between a current case and past cases where courts applied the legal rule or statute and reason with the values and purposes underlying the legal rules articulated in the statutes and precedents. Even if one would apply the statutory rule deductively, he/she would need to consider whether the proposed result is consistent with the purposes and policies underlying the statute.

Although the BNA program and other programs described in Part I of this book implement computational models of legal reasoning, none of them implements a process of statutory interpretation as comprehensive as that described in MacCormick and Summers (1991).

Instead, the AI & Law field has invented components that could implement parts of the process. For instance, the BNA program constructed a proof from the plain meaning of the statute as represented by Prolog rules. Chapter 3 describes computational models of case-based legal reasoning and considers how to take underlying policies and values into account. Chapter 5 describes computational models of legal argument that provide a framework into which one could imagine implementing a computational process of statutory interpretation using the MacCormick/Summers model. See, for example, a preliminary formal framework to capture such interpretive arguments in Sartor et al. (2014).

2.4.2. *Other Sources of Legal Indeterminacy*

If the goal is to model arguments for purposes of statutory interpretation, however, there is a theoretical reason why classical logical deductive methods like those in the BNA program will not suffice. Legal adversaries frequently start with different premises. They disagree as to the facts of the case at hand or the rules of law that apply. In law, however, it is common to encounter reasonable arguments for inconsistent results where the adversaries appear to agree about the facts and about which legal rules apply. As noted, this is the phenomenon of "legal indeterminacy" (Berman and Hafner, 1988).

One source of legal indeterminacy has already been illustrated in the *Johnson* case in Section 2.2.1. Legal rules employ open-textured legal concepts about which reasonable but contradictory arguments are made.

Another source involves unstated conditions on the rule's application, such as that its result not be inconsistent with certain countervailing principles.

This is illustrated in the case of *Riggs v. Palmer*, 115 N.Y. 506 (1889) involving an heir who killed his grandfather under whose will he was to inherit. The Court stated,

"It is quite true that statutes regulating the making, proof and effect of wills, and the devolution of property, if literally construed, . . . give this property to the murderer." (Berman and Hafner, 1988).

The Court, however, refused to enforce the statutes where it would contradict "fundamental maxims of the common law," "dictated by public policy," that "[n]o one shall be permitted to profit by his own fraud, or to take advantage of his own wrong, or to found any claim upon his own iniquity, or to acquire property by his own crime" (Berman and Hafner, 1988).

Legal rules may have other unstated conditions such as: Does the rule satisfy choice of law requirements? Is the rule constitutional? Conceivably, some of these conditions can be represented as additional conditions of legal rules. Berman and Hafner point out, however, that abstract conditions like the frequently violated "fundamental maxim" above would be very difficult to formalize (Berman and Hafner, 1988).

Given the reality of legal indeterminacy, Berman and Hafner argued that classical logical models are inappropriate for modeling how lawyers reason.

> Legal indeterminacy presents a direct challenge to the concept of logical validity, by the fact that a lawyer must be able to argue for either a conclusion or its opposite.
>
> Suppose there is a theory T which has a consequence C (i.e., there is a valid logical argument whose premises are the axioms of T and whose conclusion is C). We then know that C is true in every model of T; that is, C is true in every universe where T's axioms are all true. We also know, by the law of contradiction, that if C is true, then NOT C must be false: so, NOT C is false in every model of T. . . [w]e can [also] show that no valid argument (no matter what additional assumptions we make) that begins with the axioms of T can ever conclude NOT C.
>
> [I]t is logically impossible to begin with a set of premises, and create a valid argument for both a conclusion and its opposite. This restriction certainly makes sense – but in the law, such a "logical impossibility" seems to be precisely what happens! (Berman and Hafner, 1988, p. 191).

Contradictory propositions are also problematic for classical logic models because if both propositions are true, one can prove anything (see Carnielli and Marcos, 2001). An instructive example of this "explosive" feature of classical deduction, drawn from the history of philosophy, is discussed in Ashworth *et al.* (1968, p. 184). A sixteenth-century Italian demonstrated that "anything follows from an impossible proposition, by proving that 'Socrates is and Socrates is not' entails 'Man is a horse' ":

1. "Socrates is and Socrates is not implies Socrates is not."
2. "Socrates is and Socrates is not implies Socrates is."
3. "Socrates is implies Socrates is or Man is a horse."
4. "(Socrates is or Man is a horse) and Socrates is not implies Man is a horse." Hence
5. "Socrates is and Socrates is not implies Man is a horse."

If one would like a computer to interpret statutes as a court does, by considering arguments pro and con and selecting the stronger arguments, ordinary classical logical deduction is problematic. One needs to use something else. Logicians have developed some alternative logics that can deal with inconsistency subject to various constraints. In the field of AI & Law, however, the current answer to "what else is there?" is a computational model of argument with appropriate argument schemes as explained in Chapter 5.

2.5. MANAGEMENT SYSTEMS FOR BUSINESS RULES AND PROCESSES

Not all problem-solving with statutes involves litigation to determine if a statute has been violated. Not all reasoning with legal statutes involves complex issues of interpretation and arguments pro and con. In many situations, businesses and institutions simply want to design their business processes and conduct their day-to-day operations in such a way as to avoid violating the law. Surely, one can computationally model legal rules for solving practical problems in a way that does not require modeling full-scale statutory interpretation.

Indeed, most programs modeling statutes are probably designed to assist administration of institutional compliance to avoid litigation. The BNA program, for example, was probably not designed to deal with litigation between adversaries seeking to convince a judge about the meaning of a disputed term. Instead, it would be more likely used as an administrative aid to address the run-of-the mill scenarios involving questions of citizenship. An agency charged with administering the complex BNA could use the tool to handle the large percentage of cases that are complex enough as to befuddle civil servants but that ordinarily do not give rise to litigated disputes about the meanings of the statutes or regulations.

Descendants of logical models of statutes like the BNA program and of legal expert systems like Waterman's in Section 1.3.1 still play a role in helping institutions comply with relevant regulations.

2.5.1. *Business Process Expert Systems*

Companies are obligated to ensure compliance with complex legal requirements and regulations. There is always a risk that an existing business process violates a regulatory requirement or that a proposed modification will introduce a violation at some point. Businesses also need an ability to document compliance to auditors (Scheer et al., 2006, p. 143). This requires firms to identify the applicable legal rules and regulations, to "define requirements resulting from these laws for the individual company," to identify the particular business processes that are affected and the "concrete risks which result from these requirements within [those] processes," to define measures and controls to minimize those risks, and to test whether they are being applied (Scheer et al., 2006, p. 146).

One way to implement the legal-risk-reducing measures and controls is to translate the legal requirements and regulations into *business rules*, which, if followed, reduce the risks in the affected business processes. "In general, business rules are guidelines or business practices which design or lead the conduct of an enterprise" (Wagner and Klueckmann, 2006, p. 126). Once business rules have been formulated, human managers can enforce them as policies via the company's ordinary managerial hierarchy.

The business process rules can also be implemented in software systems that assist human managers to ensure compliance (see Scheer et al., 2006, p. v). For example, the expert system can warn managers about the need to conform company policies to general regulatory requirements or warn managers of specific instances of noncompliant behavior. The rules can be represented in a logical formalism as in the BNA approach or, more likely, as heuristic rules as in Waterman's program, Section 1.3.1, and incorporated into an expert system designed to test whether a business process is compliant.

Such business compliance expert systems are being applied in the commercial sector. Today, companies like Neota Logic provide technology with which law firms and companies can easily author their own expert systems for business compliance. For instance, the Neota website reports that the law firm, Foley & Lardner LLP, has authored a number of web-based expert systems modules under the name, Global Risk Solutions, to guide clients in their efforts to ensure compliance with the Foreign Corrupt Practices Act (FCPA), a federal anti-corruption/anti-bribery statute (Neota Logic, 2016, Case Studies).

The modules collect information from a client concerning its marketing methods, location business volume, and customers and outputs visual and quantitative assessments of a client's business risks under the FCPA.

Another module provides more specific counseling based on automated information gathering. "For example, if a GRS user clicks through a variety of intake questions related to meals and entertainment, they are asked questions such as whether they are going to entertain a foreign official." Depending on the answers, a Foley attorney can follow-up with specific counseling.

Where the business rules are formulated in propositional form, they can also be organized graphically in ways that are more intelligible to business personnel. For example, propositionalized business rules can be organized in a kind of work flowchart not unlike that shown in Figure 2.3. Since humans can readily understand the flowcharts, they are an effective way to communicate the legal requirements to employees and for purposes of audits. Norm graphs are another visual tool that can assist with business compliance.

A *norm graph* embodies "an abstract model of the legal norms" (Dietrich et al., 2007, p. 187). For each legal compliance result of interest, a graph is constructed, which "enables [one] to decide whether [an] intended legal result can be reached or not ... [It] consists of legal concepts (represented by nodes) and links between them (represented by arrows)" (Oberle et al., 2012, p. 281). The "norms determine a legal consequence (LC), given one or more states of facts (SF)" (Dietrich et al., 2007, p. 187).

Norm graphs are conceptually organized to support a process of *subsumption*, a kind of taxonomic reasoning with an ontology, a lexicon of concepts organized hierarchically (Oberle et al., 2012).

> [T]he norms in the positive law do not address singular cases but rather cover general classes of real-world situations. [A decision maker] faces a specific real-world situation ... [and] must try to find the norms whose general domain covers the situation (subsumes the situation) ... [T]o mechanize subsumption the semantics must be considered ... beyond thesauri. Ontologies ... reflect semantic relationships between terms, and these relationships can particularly be defined [to] directly support the subsumption process." (Dietrich et al., 2007, p. 188)

The norm graphs in Figure 2.6 illustrate subsumption with legal norms. The figure shows norm graphs for two legal conclusions involving compliance with data protection regulations, here the German Federal Data Protection Act (FDPA) concerning the *legality* of data collection and *effective consent*:

Section 4 (1) FDPA Legality of data collection, processing, and use: The collection, processing, and use of personal data shall be lawful only if permitted or ordered by this Act or other law, or if the data subject provided consent. (Oberle et al., 2012, p. 285)

Section 4a (1) FDPA Effective Consent: Consent shall be given in writing unless special circumstances warrant any other form ... Consent shall be effective only when based on the data subject's free decision. Data subjects shall be informed of the purpose of collection, processing or use and, as necessary in the individual case, or on request, of the results of withholding consent. (Oberle et al., 2012, p. 287)

The norm graphs have associated rules or tests represented in predicate logic, which determine if the legal conclusions apply. For instance, the following formula abstracts the norms in section 4a (1) FDPA Effective Consent associated with the left side of Figure 2.6 (see Oberle et al., 2012, p. 293).

> Effectiveness(E) AND givenFor(E,C) ← (Consent(C) AND givenIn(C,F) AND
> WrittenForm(F)) OR Exception(F) AND ...

This formula means that the result E of Effectiveness is assigned to Consent C if the result F assigned to Consent C is WrittenForm or Exception and some other conditions, not shown, are satisfied. Another formula specifies when the result Exception is assigned to F.

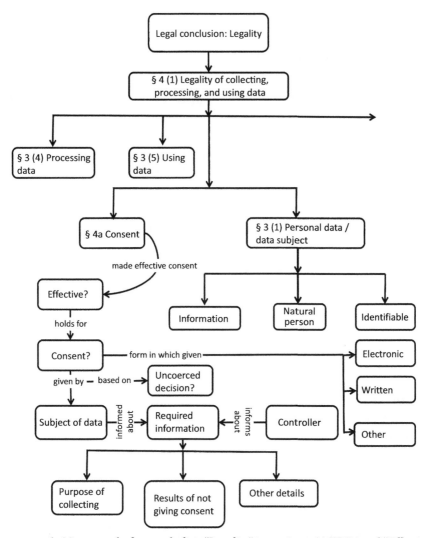

FIGURE 2.6. Norm graphs for concluding "Legality" in section 4 (1) FDPA and "Effective Consent" (see Oberle et al., 2012, pp. 305–6, Figs. 13 and 14)

With rules like these, an expert system could warn managers of the require-ments that need to be satisfied in order to conclude that a business process is in compliance. The program could apply the tests to descriptions of real-world situa-tions to determine if they are instances of the top-level norm classes representing the legal conclusions of interest, that is, whether the top-level concepts *subsume* the fact descriptions. For the subsumption to work, however, the factual scenarios must be represented in particular terms provided by a taxonomy of concepts associated with

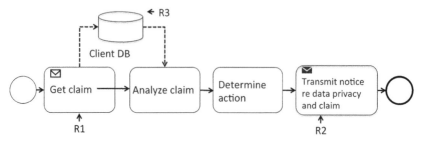

FIGURE 2.7. Sample BPMN diagram of simple insurance claim process with business rule annotations (see Table 2.1) (Koetter et al., 2014, Fig. 2, p. 220)

the regulated subject matter. In other words a subject matter ontology must also be constructed, as discussed in Section 6.5.

2.5.2. *Automating Business Process Compliance*

A goal of some research is to streamline the compliance process by enabling an expert system to analyze a model of the business process directly. The inputs to such an expert system are *business process models*, formal descriptions of proposed or operating business processes. These processes can be represented graphically in terms of schematic descriptions using the Business Process Model and Notation (BPMN), a standardized, modularized visual iconography for this purpose. The models can also be represented in a formal rule-modeling language so that expert systems can reason with them.

As noted, if an appropriate language for formalizing business rules is available and if it is compatible with the language for formalizing the descriptions of the business processes, then the business rules can be applied directly to the process model descriptions. In effect, the business rules are used to "annotate" the process models (and their graphical representations) in order to assess compliance.

For example, a BPMN diagram of a simplified insurance claim management process is shown in Figure 2.7. This insurance company happens to be subject to various requirements of the German Insurance Association (GDV) and to data protection laws in the German Federal Data Protection Act (FDPA). A human expert has translated those requirements manually into a set of three business rules, R1 through R3, shown in Table 2.1. The figure shows where each rule applies to the modeled process.

First, let's examine more closely what these three business rules are and where they came from. Human experts, knowledgeable about the business processes, need to know which regulations apply to such an insurance claim process in the relevant jurisdictions; here it happens to be a insurance company operating in Germany. For instance, according to Koetter et al. (2014), at least two regulatory provisions

TABLE 2.1. *From regulatory texts to business rules to annotations of business process (see Figure 2.7) to predicate logic forms (Koetter et al., 2014, p. 220)*

Paraphrased regulations	Business rules	As applied to business process	Predicate logic form
GDV Code of Conduct §§5–8: customer who provides personal data must be asked for agreement if this data is to be used for marketing purposes. This agreement has to be solicited within a short time span.	R1: After activity Receive claim an activity asking the claimant for agreement has to follow.	R1: Follow this by sending a data privacy notification	followedBy("Receive claim," "Send claim and data privacy notification") AND unknown
	R2: Activity asking for agreement has to be performed at most 14 days after activity Receive claim.	R2: Send at most 14 days after claim is received	followedBy("Receive claim," "Send claim and data privacy notification") AND maxTime BetweenActivities ("Receive claim," "Send claim and data privacy notification," "14 days")
German company outsourcing its data processing must ensure service providers comply with German FDPA §4b II sentence 1 BDSG re processing, storage, and exposure of personal data.	R3: Customer DB shall not be hosted outside of Germany.	R3: Do not store outside of Germany	hostingRegion ("CustomerDB," "Germany")

apply to the claims process in Figure 2.7. They are shown in the first column in Table 2.1.[3]

The human expert would need to read the actual provisions (i.e., the GDV code of conduct and the German FDPA provisions) and manually translate them into paraphrases and propositions summarizing the requirements like the three business rules shown in the second column of Table 2.1 (see Koetter et al., 2014).

---

[3] In column 1, the paraphrases of provisions in the code of conduct of the German Insurance Association (GDV) §§5–8, and in the German FDPA §4b II sentence 1 BDSG, are adapted from the authors' paraphrases in Koetter et al. (2014).

The business rules then need to be operationalized so that they can be applied to the specific business process model in question, perhaps with the assistance of a business process expert. The third column presents a simplified version as applied to the business process in Figure 2.7 (see Koetter et al., 2014).

A final step is to translate the operationalized rules, perhaps with the help of a knowledge representation specialist, into the predicate logic form shown in column 4 so that they can be applied by an expert system.

Translating the legal requirements and regulations into business rules is a complex interpretive task involving text understanding, commonsense reasoning, and business experience. For instance, German FDPA §4b II sentence 1 BDSG states:

1. The transfer of personal data to bodies

    1. in other Member States of the European Union, . . .
    shall be subject to Section 15 (1), Section 16 (1) and Sections 28 to 30a in accordance with the laws and agreements applicable to such transfer, in so far as transfer is effected in connection with activities which fall in part or in their entirety within the scope of the law of the European Communities.

2. Sub-Section 1 shall apply *mutatis mutandis* to the transfer of personal data . . . to other foreign, supranational or international bodies. Transfer shall not be effected in so far as the data subject has a legitimate interest in excluding transfer, in particular if an adequate level of data protection is not guaranteed at the bodies stated in the first sentence of this sub-section.

3. The adequacy of the afforded level of protection shall be assessed in the light of all circumstances.

4. Responsibility for the admissibility of the transfer shall rest with the body transferring the data.[4]

Formalizing this provision in its entirety would be very difficult, but a human expert would know that it is perhaps unnecessary. The expert might know from experience that the easiest way to finesse this requirement concerning the Act's protections of personal data would be to avoid transferring the personal data out of Germany. Thus, the expert would prepare a business rule (R3 in Table 2.1) as a kind of heuristic rule of thumb to ensure that the data is processed only in Germany (Koetter et al., 2014).

2.5.3. *Requirements for a Process Compliance Language*

Predicate logic alone is not adequate for the task of modeling the application of regulatory rules to business process models. A suitable language needs to support:

1. Reasoning with defeasible legal rules.
2. Isomorphic linking from the logical rules to regulatory sources.

---

4 English translation from www.gesetze-im-internet.de/englisch_bdsg/englisch_bdsg.html, last accessed August 6, 2016.

3. Expressing the kinds of obligations that statutes and regulations employ.
4. Temporal reasoning (Gordon et al., 2009).

Each of these requirements is briefly described below.

Defeasible Legal Rules
First, the language has to support defeasible legal rules. *Defeasible* rules have the property that:

> When the antecedent of a rule is satisfied by the facts of a case, the conclusion of the rule presumably holds, but is not necessarily true. (Gordon et al., 2009)

The need for defeasible legal rules arises because, "Legal rules can conflict, namely, they lead to incompatible effects" (Gordon et al., 2009). One legal rule may be an exception to the other or exclude it as inapplicable or otherwise undermine it. We have encountered this above. As Berman and Hafner observed, "the logic-based formalism breaks down when applied to cases involving the existence of conflicting rules and precedents" (Berman and Hafner, 1988, p. 1). In addition, as discussed above, reasoning with legal rules often involves reasoning by default, and such reasoning is non-monotonic. Proven propositions may have to be withdrawn, that is, reasoning with legal rules is defeasible.

When designing business processes to ensure compliance with legal regulations, we have assumed that modeling litigation-style arguments about conflicting rules could be avoided. Nevertheless, according to Guido Governatori, a veteran modeler of business process compliance, the language still needs to support "the efficient and natural treatment of exceptions, which are a common feature in normative reasoning" (Governatori and Shek, 2012).

For example, in Figure 2.2, compare the complex textual version of the IRC provision (IRC section 354) and the propositional form with its simplified logical structure on the right.

Linking to Regulatory Sources for Explanation and Maintenance
Since business management systems monitor compliance, the system's rules must be updated, maintained, and validated and its results must be explainable with reference to the regulatory texts. These functions are simplified to the extent that the linkages between the logical versions of the rules and their sources in the regulatory texts are straightforward. More specifically, the legal rule modeling language needs to support *isomorphism*:

> There should be a one-to-one correspondence between the rules in the formal model and the units of natural language text which express the rules in the original legal sources, such as sections of legislation. (Gordon et al., 2009)

Ideally, the language maintains a one-to-one correspondence between the rules in the formal model and the sections of the regulatory texts. "This entails, for example, that a general rule and separately stated exceptions, in different sections of a statute, should not be converged into a single rule in the formal model." (Gordon et al., 2009).

Maintaining isomorphism makes explanation more effective. Business rule systems can explain their analyses by recapitulating the rules that "fired," as illustrated above in the output of the BNA system. In the context of an audit, however, explaining the compliance analysis in terms of the business rules is not sufficient. An explanation must justify it in terms of the textual statutory provisions, not simply the business rules that a human expert has constructed to interpret and operationalize those provisions. For purposes of citing statutory texts and interweaving textual excerpts, an isomorphic mapping is essential.

Isomorphic mappings between statutory text and implementing rules, however, are difficult to maintain. Frequently, the mapping is complex especially where multiple, cross-referenced provisions are involved. The versions of statutes and regulations that computers can reason with logically are different from the authoritative textual versions. Statutes may be so convoluted that even a "faithful representation" remains unhelpful. As Layman Allen noted, statutes may include complex and sometimes implicit exceptions and cross-references both within and across provisions.

The fact that statutes and regulations are dynamic complicates maintaining the correspondence. The legislature may modify statutes or enact new ones, agencies may revise and update regulations, and court decisions announce new interpretations of the provisions' requirements. Even when the set of statutory provisions to be implemented is taken as static, as discussed in Section 2.3.4, the development of the BNA program was a process of trial-and-error requiring frequent revision to accommodate newly encountered rules.

When regulatory texts are amended, both the textual and corresponding logical versions need to be updated. Rule-based legal expert systems (e.g., like Waterman's program in Section 1.3.1) that use heuristic rules to summarize statutes avoid some aspects of the maintenance problem, but they still need to be updated when the statutes and regulations change. Since updating introduces modifications and additions to the rule-set, it is also important to revalidate the business rules whenever they are introduced or modified, in part by comparing them to their sources.

Some automated techniques have been developed to maintain isomorphic representations of regulations. The development environment in Bench-Capon (1991), for example, maintained a complex set of linkages between textual, logical, and intermediary representations of statutes. In such an environment, changes to the rules can be undertaken in a localized fashion. The links between the textual and logical rules can assist validation. In addition, decision aids such as textual excerpts from the statutory rules and links to commentary and cases can be linked into the program's logical explanations of a conclusion. Techniques for maintaining this faithful representation, however, require maintaining multiple representations (this development environment had three) and require complex software to keep track of them all.

Able to Express Different Types of Obligations and Reason Temporally

A language for business process compliance modeling needs to have the right "semantics" for expressing the kinds of normative concepts that statutes and regulations employ and the kinds of obligations they impose. The obligations may differ in terms of whether it:

- needs to be obeyed at all time instances in the interval in which it is in force,
- needs only to be achieved at least once while it is in force,
- could be fulfilled even before the obligation is actually in force,
- needs to be achieved immediately or else a violation is triggered,
- is such that a violation can be compensated for, or
- persists after being violated. (Hashmi et al., 2014)

A language that supports expressing these different types of obligations also needs to be able to reason temporally. Beside how long an obligation holds, legal rules have other temporal properties including "the time when the norm is in force and/or has been enacted" and "the time when the norm can produce legal effects." For a discussion of techniques for maintaining and reasoning temporally with multiple versions of statutory provisions (see Palmirani, 2011).

2.5.4. *Connecting Legal Rules and Business Processes*

The Process Compliance Language (PCL) was designed to satisfy all of the above requirements (Hashmi et al., 2014). It can represent legal rules as defeasible and avoids the problems of reasoning with contradictory rules. It also can define obligations with the above semantics and reason temporally.

A complex business process may have a lot of moving parts, however, and compliance needs to be assessed when the process is in operation. How does the model represent a process without oversimplification so that the business rules can be applied realistically?

For this to work, the model must account for the artifacts the business process produces and the changes that it makes in its environment (Hashmi et al., 2014, p. 104). The authors model a business process as a workflow-net, a kind of Petri net. *Petri nets* (introduced by the German mathematician and computer scientist C.A. Petri in 1962) are used to represent processes abstractly. Petri nets are not unlike the ATNs in Section 1.4.2, another kind of process representation. There, the process modeled was a legal one, the process of offer and acceptance in contract law. The nodes in Gardner's ATN represented states in the legal analysis; the arcs represented the possible transitions from one state to another governed by legal rules associated with each arc.

Petri nets are different from ATNs, however, in that they use two types of nodes, places and transitions, with arcs connecting one type of node to the other. In addition, the production and consumption of "tokens" are used to represent the events

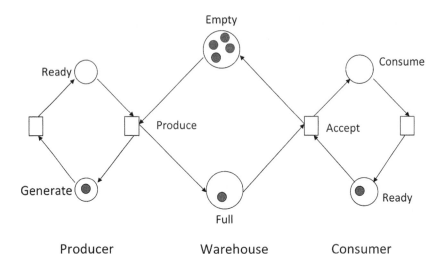

FIGURE 2.8. Petri net representing simple producer–consumer resource allocation problem (see Kafura, 2011, p. 8)

that occur in the process and the changes in the system's state that an event causes. In a Petri net, each event is modeled as a transition that consumes and produces tokens, and "the state of a system is modeled at any moment by a distribution of tokens in the net's places" (Palanque and Bastide, 1995, p. 388).

> Places and transitions are connected by directed arcs, which define when each transition is allowed to occur, and what the effect of its occurrence will be. A transition is allowed to occur when each of its input places holds at least one token; The occurrence of the transition consumes a token in each input place and sets a token in each output place. (Palanque and Bastide, 1995, p. 388)

The Petri net in Figure 2.8 represents a simple producer–consumer scenario involving resource allocation synchronization. Rectangular nodes represent transitions; circular nodes represent places. In this example, the resources are "items" that are produced and consumed. The items may be widgets, but they may also comprise information. A producer creates new items but may not generate a new item unless the number of available items is less than some maximum number. The consumer accepts one produced item at a time, but cannot accept an item unless at least one is available.

The capacity of the warehouse in the middle of the figure constrains the maximum number of available items. In this example, the maximum number is five, represented by the total number of tokens in the Full and Empty places: four in the Empty place plus one in the Full place. Thus, the figure represents a situation after the initial state where the producer has generated one item for the consumer to accept as represented by the token in the Full place. The producer then generated a new item in the Generate place and is ready to ship it to the warehouse when the item transitions to the Ready place. The production transition, however, may only occur (i.e., "fire") when there is a token in the Empty place. Similarly, the accept transition can only fire when the consumer is ready, that is, there is a token in the consumer's Ready place at the lower right, and at least one token in the Full place. Once accepted, the item may be consumed.

The Petri net model of the process can be implemented in software with rules defining the conditions for the transitions. According to the transition rules, a transition is enabled (that is, the transition can fire) "when there is at least one token on each of the transition's input places; when a transition fires it removes one token from each of its input places and produces a single token on each of its output places" (Kafura, 2011, p. 2). One could imagine variants of the transition rules that change the maximum possible number of available items or that specify the (likely different) numbers of items that can be produced or consumed at a time or the rates of production and consumption.

While admittedly very simple, the Petri net in Figure 2.8 conveys an intuition about how a complex business process can be modeled in software. Petri nets can model nondeterministic system behavior; "If there is more than one enabled transition any one of enabled transitions may be the next one to fire" (Kafura, 2011, p. 2). A Petri net extension, *labeled workflow net*, makes traces of a process's possible execution sequences; it requires each node of process model to lie on direct path between the sole source and end places, and labels some transitions as "visible" (Hashmi et al., 2014, pp. 104, 111).

The traces of the business process operation generated by the labeled workflow net can be the inputs for an expert human, or for an expert system with formalized business rules, to analyze for compliance. The business rule obligations are associated with "each task in a trace ... [and] represent the obligations in force for that combination of task and trace. These are among the obligations that the process has to fulfill to comply with a given normative framework" (Hashmi et al., 2014, p. 108). A program evaluates whether those facts, associated with the tasks and recorded in the traces, that should be true according to the business rules really are true.

The compliance analysis can be performed at various points in the life cycle of a business process:

Design-time: When the process is being designed, by analyzing the developing process model in a computerized design environment that enforces compliance with regulatory constraints *a priori*.

Run-time: While the process is running, by governing how the process unfolds to ensure execution is in compliance.

Post-execution: After execution, by analyzing a trace or history of the operations of a process to identify instances of noncompliance.

In order to make the determinations at design-time, run-time, or post-execution, a workflow net representing the business process at that point needs to be constructed and traces of its operation need to be generated for analysis (see Hashmi et al., 2014, p. 112).

2.5.5. *Example of Business Process Compliance Modeling*

Hashmi et al. (2014) applied the PCL to model regulation of a business process for complaint handling under the Australian Telecommunication Consumers Protection Code (TCPC) 2012. The code specifically mandates that every Australian entity operating in the telecommunication sector must certify that their day-to-day operations comply with the code.

Specifically, they modeled TCPC § 8, which governs the management and handling of consumer complaints (Hashmi et al., 2014, p. 113f). TCPC §8 was manually mapped into "176 PCL rules, containing 223 PCL (atomic) propositions (literals)" using all of the obligation types listed above. The authors secured the regulator's informal approval of the business rules for purposes of the exercise.

With the assistance of domain experts from an industry partner, they drew process models to capture the company's existing procedures for handling complaints and related matters under TCPC §8. This process resulted in six business process models, annotated in terms of the relevant business rules, five of which were small enough to be "checked for compliance in seconds." Evaluating compliance in the largest business process, with 41 tasks and 12 decision points, took about 40 seconds of computational time (Hashmi et al., 2014, p. 114).

The system outputs a report of traces, rules, and tasks responsible for noncompliance like that in Figure 2.9. Although the figure deals with a different business process for opening credit card accounts, it illustrates the kind of information the system can generate based on its analysis of a business process's compliance. It identifies noncompliant execution paths and cites the regulatory rule that is the source of a noncompliance issue.

In the compliance evaluation of the complaint handling process, the team identified various points at which the business processes failed to comply with TCPC §8. "Some of the compliance issues discovered by the tools were novel to the business analysts and were identified as genuine non-compliance issues that need to be resolved" (Governatori and Shek, 2012). The noncompliance issues involved ensuring that "some type of information was recorded in the databases associated [with] the processes," that customers were made "aware of documents detailing the escalation procedure," and that "a particular activity does not happen in a part of the process." Two of these noncompliance issues resulted from "new requirements in the 2012 version of the code" (Hashmi et al., 2014, p. 114).

The team employed the compliance software environment to rectify some of the noncompliance issues. The repairs included modifying the existing processes to

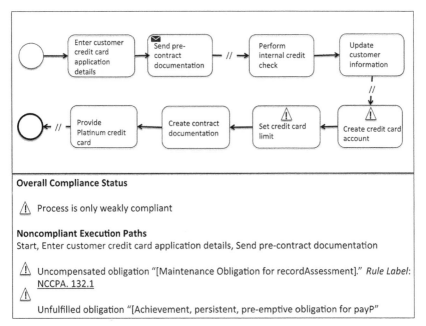

FIGURE 2.9. Compliance system report of traces, rules, and tasks responsible for noncompliance (excerpts) (see Governatori and Shek, 2012)

comply with the code or designing and adding some new business process models, such as a novel way to handle in person or by phone complaints (Governatori and Shek, 2012; Hashmi et al., 2014, p. 114).

Governatori's system performed real legal work in a realistic setting. It required extensive manual effort, however, both in developing the business rules and in representing the business process for analysis with the business rules. The formulation of the business rules from the regulatory sources was entirely a manual effort. The construction of the model of the business process as inputs for the business rules to annotate appears to have been the result of an intricate manual task as well.

Governmental agencies might benefit from automating administrative process compliance with regulations. van der Pol (2011) described a business process compliance model to be fielded by the Dutch Immigration and Naturalization Service (IND). An information system called INDiGO was to contain an expert system of business rules based on relevant laws, regulations, and policies governing the processing of IND clients' applications. The rule engine would contain a model of the process workflow including the order in which business services are to be executed, and could be consulted to provide those services relevant to a client's specific case and circumstances. The system was to analyze trace histories of the operations of the business process to identify instances of noncompliance, unsatisfactory results, or inefficiencies and provide feedback to regulators on modifying relevant statutes and regulations. The goal is to create a flexible system in which changes in law, regulation, or procedures could be implemented quickly through modifications of relevant business rules in this rule engine (van der Pol, 2011). After auspicious beginnings, however, it is not clear whether the INDiGO project has succeeded due to a lack of published information.

Expert systems and logic programming are not the only paradigms that can support computational reasoning with statutes and regulations. Regulatory systems contained in statutes can be represented as networks or graphs of the relations between objects. The connected objects can be other statutes and provisions, a *citation network*, or a set of reference concepts referred to by, and subject to, regulation across multiple statutes, a *statutory network diagram*.

For instance, in a recent project, states' systems of regulations for dealing with public health emergencies are represented as networks of nodes. The nodes represent the agents that a statute directs to communicate with other agents under specified conditions (Sweeney et al., 2014). Using expert handcrafted queries, a team of researchers retrieved candidate statutes concerning public health emergency preparedness from the LexisNexis legal databases for 11 US states. Each provision was manually coded according to a standardized codebook to identify if the provision was relevant and, if so, the provision's citation, the public health agents that are the objects of the provision, the action the provision directs and whether it is permitted or obligatory, the goal or product of the action, the purpose of the statute, the type of emergency in which the direction applies, and under what time frame and conditions (Sweeney et al., 2014).

Once different states' regulatory systems are represented as networks, the networks can be compared visually and quantitatively using network analytical measures, and tentative inferences can be drawn about a state's regulatory scheme as compared to another state's scheme. For example, Figure 2.10 compares statutorily mandated institutional interactions relating to emergency surveillance between Florida and Pennsylvania.

Comparative diagrams like these can suggest hypotheses to public health system analysts about the differences across states, which can then be studied in light of the legislative texts. For instance, based on the white links in Figure 2.10, one might ask why Community Health Centers and Home Health Agencies are linked to other public health agents in Pennsylvania but not in Florida? Investigating possible answers would involve researching the legislative texts in Pennsylvania and Florida.

The statutory network diagrams can help. They are a kind of visual interface into a state's statutes. They could enable researchers or field personnel to retrieve the provisions that direct institutional agents' interactions simply by clicking the network links representing those interactions (Sweeney et al., 2014). Thus, a researcher could,

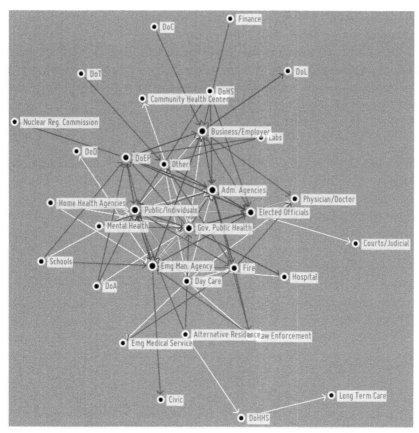

FIGURE 2.10. Statutory network diagram comparing Pennsylvania (PA) and Florida (FL) statutory schemes re public health emergency surveillance: Circles indicate public health system actors and partners in FL and PA. Grey links indicate relationships present in both states; white links indicate legal relationships present in PA but not in FL (Sweeney et al., 2014)

at least, retrieve the relevant statutes directing the linkages to Community Health Centers and Home Health Agencies in Pennsylvania. Based on those texts, one could frame queries for similar statutes in Florida using conventional legal IR tools. The queries will reveal either that Florida law contains similar directives that have been missed in constructing the statutory network, or more interestingly, that there is a gap in Florida's laws that policy-makers might conclude should be filled.

Tools like statutory network diagrams and citation network diagrams can help humans solve problems involving statutory reasoning where the computer and human share responsibility for performing the tasks most within each's capabilities. Chapter 11 on conceptual legal information retrieval examines more closely the use of citation networks and statutory network diagrams in cognitive computing. Citation information can be extracted automatically from statutory texts or retrieved from a repository of statutes and used to create citation networks. Creating a statutory network diagram is more complex, requiring extensive manual encoding of the statutes. Chapter 9 on extracting information from statutes addresses techniques to apply ML to automate or semiautomate the encoding task for constructing statutory network diagrams.

. . .

In the remainder of this book, we revisit the subject matter of representing business rules, statutes, and regulations. Section 6.5 addresses the construction of ontologies for statutes and regulations. Standardized schemes have been developed for annotating or tagging statutes and regulations with procedural and substantive semantic information that can then be used to search for relevant provisions. Chapter 9 explains how the automated approaches for extracting information from statutory and regulatory texts can support conceptual information retrieval. Other projects, discussed in Section 9.5, tackle the task of automatically extracting logical rules and constraints from regulatory texts, focusing on a small set of regulations in repetitive stereotypical forms.

3

Modeling Case-based Legal Reasoning

Since legal rules employ terms and concepts that can be vague and open-textured, a computational model of reasoning with cases would help. Courts often interpret the meaning of legal terms and concepts by drawing analogies across cases illustrating how a term or concept has been applied in the past.

This chapter presents computational models of analogical reasoning with legal cases. The models are based on three basic approaches. The first, prototypes and deformations, focuses on how to decide a case by constructing a theory based on past cases. The second, dimensions and legal factors, employs stereotypical patterns of fact that strengthen or weaken a side's argument concerning a legal claim or concept. The third, exemplar-based explanations (EBEs), represents legal concepts in terms of prior courts' explanations of why a concept did or did not apply.

The models illustrate how to represent legal cases so that a computer program can reason about whether they are analogous to a case to be decided. In particular, they illustrate ways in which a program can compare a problem and cases, select the most relevant cases, and generate legal arguments by analogy for and against a conclusion in a new case.

Legal rules and concepts are promulgated for normative purposes. Teleological arguments (i.e., arguments from the purposes or values served by a rule) play an important role in drawing legal analogies. Computational models that integrate legal rules, intermediate legal concepts (ILCs) from those rules, and cases applying the rules need to take underlying values into account. This chapter introduces techniques for computationally modeling teleological reasoning by integrating values into the measures of case relevance and models of legal analogy.

None of these systems deals directly with legal texts. Instead, they work on the basis of formal representations of case facts and legal concepts that have been manually constructed. The assumption, however, has been that one day, these case representations will be extracted automatically from natural language texts of case opinions or fact summaries. With text analytics, that day is fast approaching. The chapter contrasts how amenable the different case representations are to text analytic approaches and their implications for cognitive computing.

This chapter answers the following questions: How can legal concepts be represented computationally in a way that reflects their dialectical relationship with cases? How can cases' facts and courts' reasoning be represented computationally? What are prototypes and deformations, dimensions or factors, and EBEs? What aspects of a court's decision do they capture, and what aspects do they miss? What is a trumping counterexample? What are semantic networks and "criterial" facts? How can the legal relevance of a case to a problem be measured computationally? How can a program select relevant cases, compare them in terms of similarity, analogize them to, and distinguish them from fact situations and other cases? How can such programs be evaluated empirically? What is teleological reasoning? What roles does teleological reasoning play in drawing analogies across legal cases? What roles do hypotheticals play in teleological reasoning? How can values underlying legal rules be represented computationally, and how can a computer program integrate values into its methods for selecting relevant cases, drawing analogies, and distinguishing cases?

3.2. RELATIONSHIP OF LEGAL CONCEPTS AND CASES

Computational models of case-based legal reasoning model the interactions between legal concepts and cases. The legal concepts correspond to the open-textured terms in constitutional, statutory, or court-made legal rules. In common law and, to some extent, in civil law jurisdictions, cases play a role in elucidating the meanings of the open-textured legal concepts and in mediating the way in which those rules and meanings change.

3.2.1. *The Legal Process*

Edward Levi famously contrasted the process of legal reasoning by example with the pretense of law that it "is a system of known rules applied by a judge" (Levi, 2013, p. 1). For Levi, law involves a "moving classification scheme," where the legal concepts are the classifiers. "The kind of reasoning involved in the legal process is one in which the classification changes as the classification is made. The rules change as the rules are applied" (Levi, 2013, pp. 3–4).

In this process, courts decide whether the result of a precedent's rule should apply in a new case, in part by comparing the facts of the new case with those of the precedent. In determining whether the new case is similar to or different from a precedent, courts may elucidate but often muddy the meaning of the rule's legal concepts. When a concept's meaning becomes too incoherent, a court may introduce an exception to the rule by introducing a new legal concept, the rule is modified, and the process continues. Eventually, even the rule with exceptions becomes incoherent, and a court jettisons it in favor of a new rule (Levi, 2013).

3.2.2. *The Legal Process Illustrated*

Levi illustrated the legal process in his recounting of the development of modern product liability law. Strict product liability law, as modeled in Waterman's legal expert system (Section 1.3.1), originated in a process of case-based reasoning. Exceptions eroded the "privity" requirement limiting manufacturers' liability in a series of cases including *Thomas v. Winchester*, 6 N.Y. 397 (1852). The rule was replaced in *MacPherson v. Buick*, 217 N.Y. 382, 111 N.E. 1050 (1916) and in the later formulation of modern strict product liability law, for example, in the Restatement (Second) of Torts.

As most American law students are taught, the longstanding common law rule had been that "[a] manufacturer or supplier is never liable for negligence to a remote purchaser" (Levi, 2013, p. 25). That is, "no privity, no liability." There were some exceptional fact situations where a manufacture was held liable even to a third party despite the rule. In *Thomas v. Winchester*, a court announced a concept to name the exceptions: if an item were *imminently dangerous*, there could be liability without privity of contract. In subsequent decisions, courts classified various products as imminently dangerous, and others not, and introduced some variations on the concept, such as "inherently dangerous" or even "eminently dangerous." After all, one "concept sounds like another, and the jump to the second is made" (Levi, 2013, p. 8).

The process of classification continued with the courts seemingly enlarging the class of inherently dangerous articles but refusing to allow recovery for articles that were merely dangerous if defective:

> One who manufactures articles inherently dangerous, e.g., poisons, dynamite, gunpowder, torpedoes, bottles of aerated water under pressure, is liable in tort to third parties... On the other hand, one who manufactures articles dangerous only if defectively made, or installed, e.g., tables, chairs, pictures or mirrors hung on the walls, carriages, automobiles, and so on is not liable to third parties for injuries caused by them, except in case of willful injury or fraud. *Cadillac v. Johnson*, 221 Fed. 801, 803. (Levi, 2013, pp. 19–20)

Eventually, these example-based classifications may come to look silly and irrational, and a court throws out the rule altogether. In *MacPherson v. Buick*, the New York Court of Appeals allowed plaintiff MacPherson, a third party, to recover for injuries caused by a Buick, a type of article the Court in the previous year had classified as dangerous only if defective, denying liability in the *Cadillac* case. In Judge Cardozo's landmark opinion, the Court ruled,

> If the nature of a thing is such that it is reasonably certain to place life and limb in peril when negligently made, it is then a thing of danger... If to the element

of danger there is added knowledge that the thing will be used by persons other than the purchaser, and used without new tests, then, irrespective of contract, the manufacture of this thing of danger is under a duty to make it carefully. 217 N.Y. 389.

In 1964, the rule regarding a seller's liability for physical harm caused by defective products to third-party users or consumers was transformed into the modern product liability law that Waterman modeled. See Restatement, Second, Torts §402A. Special Liability of Seller of Products for Physical Harm to User or Consumer.

3.2.3. *Role of Legal Concepts*

To summarize, according to Levi, legal concepts play a number of roles. They are components of the rules of law. They have meanings and, to some extent at least, support deductive reasoning about whether the concept applies to a new case. The legal process is rule-guided to some extent, but it is far from just a matter of applying the rules deductively to new situations (Levi, 2013).

A primary role of concepts is to focus on particular similarities that, at any given time, society deems important in making this determination of justice. A legal concept is thus a "label" that reifies these similarities across a collection of cases. Courts reason with the similarities when they decide the new case. As Levi puts it,

> The problem for the law is: When will it be just to treat different cases as though they were the same? A working legal system must . . . be willing to pick out key similarities and to reason from them to the justice of applying a common classification. (Levi, 2013, p. 3)

In the process of deciding that certain cases are similar or different, legal rules and their concepts change. A concept expands or contracts as courts decide that it applies or not in new cases. In addition, the assessments of particular similarities as relevant or irrelevant may change as social circumstances and values change. Thus, previous analogies become suspect and lead to decisions now deemed unjust. When the facts of cases stretch the concept's meanings beyond credulity, a court may (subject to various constraints such as its place in the judicial hierarchy) replace it with a new concept in a reformulated rule. Existing legal rules and the arguments in previous cases suggest new concepts for restricting, extending, or replacing existing rules to deal with changed factual circumstances and social values (Levi, 2013) (see also Ashley and Rissland, 2003).

A closer examination of the history of product liability law in Levi's account identifies some features or factors courts applied in their example based on reasoning and argument. Courts compared cases in terms of:

- Whether the manufacturer knew about the hidden defect.
- How difficult it would be to discover the defect.
- Whether the manufacturer had fraudulently hidden the defect.

- The likelihood that the article would be used by one such as the victim.
- Who had control of the article.
- How dangerous the article was.
- Whether the danger was because of some additional act.
- The nature of the injury resulting from the defect.
- Social expectations regarding reliance on the manufacturer (e.g., pharmacist, auto manufacturer).

In the context of product liability, these are sensible criteria in terms of which to compare cases and to assess the justness of a proposed outcome based on a rule or interpretation of a legal concept (Ashley and Rissland, 2003). Changes in what society wants and what technology affords affect which criteria are deemed important. Focusing on different collections of these criteria as important leads to different orderings of cases. The legal reasoning process (and the legal forum of which it is a part) supports this dynamism with its use of rules, concepts, and case examples (Levi, 2013).

3.3. THREE COMPUTATIONAL MODELS OF LEGAL CONCEPTS AND CASES

Modeling case-based legal reasoning requires techniques to represent knowledge about case facts and to assess legally relevant similarities. Since the models must decide whether to treat cases the same way from a legal viewpoint, the similarities and differences must be represented in a form that a program can process, analyze, and manipulate.

Three types of computational models have been developed to represent case facts, define relevant similarities and differences, and relate them to legal concepts and to compare cases: prototypes and deformations, dimensions and legal factors, and EBEs. The three models vary the mix of intensional and extensional elements they employ to represent legal concepts. An *intensional* definition specifies the necessary and sufficient conditions for being an instance of the concept. For example, a "vehicle" is any instrument of conveyance used, or capable of being used, as a means of transportation. An *extensional* definition simply provides examples of what is/is not an instance of a concept. For instance, automobiles, bicycles, and a 103.1 cc Harley-Davidson Low Rider motorcycle are examples of a "vehicle" but an inoperable World War II Sherman tank is not. As explained in Chapter 5, computational models of legal argument now incorporate aspects of these case-based models in their schemes for analogical argumentation.

Computational models of legal reasoning *approximate* the process of legal reasoning with cases and concepts. Given the complex interaction of concepts and cases illustrated in Levi's examples, AI & Law researchers necessarily must simplify the process. Specifically, the models focus on a comparatively small number of cases, for example, 40 cases and hypotheticals involving workmen's compensation, fewer than

200 cases in trade secret law, or a half dozen property law cases involving hunters' rights in quarry. In addition, the models all focus on an area of the law in a less dynamic period, when the relevant concepts are more or less fixed and reasoning by example is used to classify items as in or out of the concept (Levi, 2013, p. 9). This is before the concept breaks down or is rejected because it obstructs a reclassification of the cases. For instance, the trade secrets and workmen's compensation cases involve fairly static legal concepts. (Some interesting AI & Law work by Edwina Rissland, however, does model and monitor conceptual change, Section 7.9.4).

Despite the constraints and simplifications, the developers try to ensure that the resulting models are still complex enough to perform some useful tasks. The focus has been on modeling the role of cases as exemplars of concepts and on normative values as informing the determinations of similarity and difference.

3.3.1. *Prototypes and Deformations*

Thorne McCarty's Taxman II program modeled arguments by analogy to past cases. Legal concepts in Taxman II were represented intensionally and supplemented extensionally using a technique called "prototypes and deformations."

McCarty represented three components of legal concepts: "(1) an (optional) invariant component providing necessary conditions; (2) a set of exemplars providing sufficient conditions; and (3) a set of transformations that express various relationships among the exemplars." He referred to the exemplars as *prototypes*: precedent cases and hypotheticals that were positive and negative examples of the legal concept whose meaning was being argued about. The transformations were *deformations*, mappings that allowed prototypes to be compared in terms of their constituent concepts (McCarty, 1995, p. 277, see also McCarty and Sridharan, 1981). In terms of Levi's domain, for instance, "imminently dangerous" might be thought of as a prototype concept. Groups of cases deform it into "inherently" or "eminently" dangerous, thereby preserving a quality of danger but partially altering it given the circumstances of particular cases.

The *Eisner v. Macomber* Example
The program focused on one scenario at the heart of a U.S. Supreme Court case, *Eisner v. Macomber*, 252 U.S. 189 (1920) concerning the issue of whether a pro rata stock dividend in connection with a stock split was taxable income to its shareholders under the Sixteenth Amendment to the U.S. Constitution. If not, it would fall outside the Congress's power to levy an income tax (McCarty, 1995). In the *Eisner* scenario, Mrs. Macomber owned 2,200 shares of Standard Oil. When Standard Oil declared a 50% stock dividend, she received 1,100 additional shares, part of which represented accumulated earnings by the company.

This and related cases involved subsidiary concepts such as "distribution," "shares," "bonds," "common stock," and "preferred stock." For each of these, rule-like templates represented the rights and obligations associated with the concept. For instance, the rights of corporate interest holders specified that bondholders received a fixed amount. Preferred stock holders received a fixed amount per share after bondholders. Common stock holders received a portion only of whatever is left after the bondholders and preferred stock holders were paid.

As input, Taxman II received a description of the fact situation, expressed not in natural language text but in terms of logic propositions employing the subsidiary concepts. The program output "arguments" (also in propositional form) that the dividend was or was not income, based on analogies to two prior cases and a hypothetical example.

At the time of the *Macomber* decision, these real and hypothetical cases were three available prototypes, positive and negative exemplars of *taxable income*, the main legal concept whose meaning was subject to dispute:

1. *The Lynch case*: Distribution of a corporation's cash was held to be taxable income to the shareholder.
2. *The Peabody case*: Distribution by a corporation to shareholders of the stock of another corporation was held to be taxable income.
3. *The Appreciation Hypothetical*: Appreciation in the value of a corporation's stock, held by the shareholder, without transfer of the shares was universally assumed *not* to be taxable income.

The deformations included some built-in mappings like ConstantStockRatio, which compared shareholder ownership ratios before and after a distribution.

Argument as Theory Construction
McCarty characterized legal argumentation about the meaning of a legal concept as a kind of theory construction, which he justified as follows. An arguer constructs a theory of how to decide an issue based on aligning the current facts with prototypical exemplars. McCarty focused on the arguments of the taxpayer and the Internal Revenue Service, as reflected in those of the majority and the dissent in the *Macomber* case, and designed the program to reconstruct the arguments pursuant to a template (or scheme). According to the argument template:

Taxpayer: defines taxable income so the *Eisner* facts and any negative prototypes of taxable income (the Appreciation Hypothetical) are excluded but any positive prototypes (*Lynch* and *Peabody*) are included.

Internal Revenue Service: defines taxable income so *Eisner* and any positive prototypes (*Lynch* and *Peabody*) are included but any negative prototypes of taxable income (the Appreciation Hypothetical) are excluded.

In doing so, the program, in effect, searched for a theory that links the current case with the favorable prototypes for a side (taxpayer or IRS) and excludes the unfavorable ones. Deformations or mappings across cases provided the raw material for these links. If a mapping preserves some constituent concept across the positive instances and the current case, then the *invariant property* becomes the basis of a theory that they should be decided alike.

The program employed argument strategies like looking for some continuum that could serve as an invariant property across a problem and a favorable prototype case. In linking the *Eisner* facts and the nontaxable Appreciation Hypothetical, the program found such an invariant via the built-in ConstantStockRatio mapping: before and after the "distribution," the taxpayer retained the same proportionate share of ownership of the corporation. After the dividend, Mrs. Macomber owned 3,300/750,000 of the corporation, the same ratio as before (2,200/500,000). It is as if there were no transfer.

If the program could not find an invariant property, it would search a space of options in trying to construct one, for example, by selecting and applying elementary mappings to build more complex ones. In trying to find conceptual links between prototypes, the program reasons about the meaning of their constituent components.

This appears to be similar to human argumentative reasoning. Justice Brandeis (in dissent) proposed a continuum linking distributions of equity, debt, and cash in support of his argument that the distribution was taxable income: Distributions of cash, bonds, preferred stock, and common shares all confer upon the recipient an expected return of corporate earnings. They differ only in how much return and at what risk. If one such distribution yields taxable income, so should all.

The program examined the prototypes' constituent concepts and, apparently, discovered or constructed the same continuum from the *Lynch* prototype's taxable distribution of a corporation's cash to distribution of a corporation's bonds, distribution of its preferred stock, and distribution of its common stock (i.e., the *Eisner*) scenario. Each confers on the recipient some trade-off between expected return of corporate earnings and risk.

Utility of Prototypes and Deformations for Cognitive Computing

From a legal viewpoint, Taxman II's model of arguing with concepts and cases is both sophisticated and realistic. The model focused on legal argumentation as constructing a theory by aligning selected cases in terms of a concept. Many attorneys, judges, and law clerks employ legal information retrieval systems to construct arguments like these. The challenge for cognitive computing is how to design computer programs that can assist users in constructing such arguments by formulating theories, linking them to analogous positive case examples, and distinguishing them from negative instances.

On the other hand, as a source of computational tools for achieving this goal, McCarty's approach in Taxman II may be too complex to be helpful. Searching through the intensionally defined subsidiary concepts and mappings in order to discover invariants is an intricate affair whose robustness still needs to be demonstrated in domains involving issues other than the meaning of "taxable income." Indeed, the model was implemented for only one Supreme Court argument involving one argued about legal concept and four cases.

3.3.2. *Dimensions and Legal Factors*

Dimensions and legal factors are knowledge representation techniques designed to enable comparing the similarity of cases, drawing analogies to positive case instances, and distinguishing negative ones. They provide a simpler, more extensional scheme for representing legal concepts and cases than Taxman II that may be easier to connect to case texts for purposes of cognitive computing.

Hypo's Dimensions
As introduced in the Hypo program, legal "factors are a kind of expert knowledge of the commonly observed collections of facts that tend to strengthen or weaken a plaintiff's argument in favor of a legal claim " (Ashley, 1990, p. 27). "In Hypo, [legal] factors are represented with Dimensions. A Dimension is a general framework for recording information for the program to manipulate" (Ashley, 1990, p. 28, see also Ashley, 1991).

As a note on terminology, "factor" has two meanings: (1) The term "factor" (lower case) means a legal factor, the phenomenon that a dimension represents, namely a stereotypical pattern of facts that tends to strengthen or weaken a plaintiff's argument in favor of a legal claim. (2) As we will see, the CATO program introduced Factors (initial caps), a knowledge representation technique that simplified dimensions. Like dimensions, Factors represent legal factors.

Hypo dealt with the claim of trade secret misappropriation, that is, where the plaintiff claims defendant gained an unfair competitive advantage by using plaintiff's confidential product information. It dealt with one legal concept, whether a fact situation was an instance of trade secret misappropriation. For modeling this concept, it employed 13 legal factors, represented by 13 dimensions, and used them to index 30 trade secret cases.

The legal factors underlying the 13 dimensions were identified in a number of sources including the Restatement (First) of Torts, section 757, Liability for Disclosure or Use of Another's Trade Secret, which many jurisdictions adopted as an authoritative statement of the law of trade secrets. Comment (b) identifies six factors that courts should take into account in determining if information is a trade secret. Other legal factors came from the opinions of trade secret cases, where courts identify particular factual strengths and weaknesses, and from treatises and law review articles. These secondary sources tend to group cases in footnotes that illustrate the effect on outcomes of particular factual strengths and weaknesses. They may also list

Claims: Trade Secrets Misappropriation
Prerequisites:
> There is a corporate plaintiff
> There is a corporate defendant
> Plaintiff makes a product
> Plaintiff and defendant compete
> Plaintiff has product information
> Plaintiff made some disclosures to outsiders

Focal Slot Prerequisite: Plaintiff made some disclosures to outsiders

Focal Slot: Plaintiff's Product Knowledge: Number-disclosees

Range: 0 to 10,000,000

Comparison Type: Greater-than versus Less-than

Pro Plaintiff Direction: Less-than

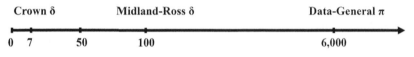

FIGURE 3.1. Secrets-Disclosed-Outsiders dimension in Ashley (1990)

counterexamples where a court reaches a conclusion in spite of a particular strength or weakness.

As illustrated in Figure 3.1, each dimension instantiated a structured template of information that defined prerequisites for the represented legal factor's application to a fact scenario. Since a case may be a more or less extreme example of a legal factor, each dimension specified a focal slot whose value in a case could vary along a range representing a stronger or weaker magnitude for the plaintiff. For instance, the focal slot value for the Secrets-Disclosed-Outsiders dimension represented the number of disclosures to outsiders in a case. The focal slot value for the Competitive-Advantage dimension captured the amount of development time and cost saved by accessing the plaintiff's information. Cases can be compared in terms of their magnitudes along a dimension, that is, in terms of their focal slot values. In the figure, the *Data-General* case is rather remarkable with disclosures to 6,000 outsiders.

A legal factor's magnitude, as represented by a dimension's focal slot value, should be distinguished from its weight. "A [legal] factor's weight is some kind of measure of the support it lends to a conclusion that the plaintiff should win a claim." Hypo did not represent a legal factor's weight quantitatively. Instead, Hypo was intended to express legal factors' weights via arguments about specific scenarios.

One reason for not representing a legal factor's weight numerically is that such weights are context-sensitive. Three cases indexed along the *Secrets-Disclosed-Outsiders* dimension in Figure 3.1 illustrate this. The *Crown* and *Midland-Ross* cases, both won by defendants, lie at the left end of the dimension; even a few disclosures to outsiders can weaken a plaintiff's claim. On the other hand, the plaintiff won in the *Data-General* case despite thousands of disclosures. Clearly, that case is inconsistent with the tenor of the dimension. The dimension indicates that this pro-plaintiff case is an exception or a counterexample by its position far to the pro-defendant end of the range. Other legal factors may counteract or "outweigh" the effect of the disclosures. In *Data-General* the disclosures were subject to confidentiality restrictions, represented in the *Outsider-Disclosures-Restricted* dimension.

Beside the fact that legal factor weights are sensitive to the particular context, Hypo did not represent weights for two other reasons. First, judges and attorneys do not argue about the weight of legal factors in quantitative terms. Second, legal domain experts do not agree what the weights are, and combining positive and negative weights numerically obscures the need for arguing about the resolution of competing legal factors. Chapter 4 presents ways to deal with legal factor weights for purposes of prediction.

Analogizing and Distinguishing Cases in Hypo's 3-Ply Arguments

The inputs to Hypo consisted of problem scenarios inputted in terms of an instantiated frame for representing facts of trade secret cases. The input problem is referred to as the current fact situation (cfs). Hypo's outputs were a three-ply argument in English that a plaintiff's trade secret misappropriation claim should [not] be successful. The three-play argument comprised:

1. An argument analogizing the cfs to a pro-plaintiff case.
2. An argument distinguishing the cited case from the cfs on behalf of defendant and citing pro-defendant counterexamples.
3. A rebuttal distinguishing the counterexample cases from the cfs and, where possible, a hypothetical suggesting facts to strengthen the plaintiff's argument in the cfs.

Hypo also made similar three-ply arguments on behalf of the defendant.

Analogizing a cfs and a cited case means stating *legally relevant* similarities that give rise to reasons why they should be decided the same way. In Hypo, such similarities are represented as shared dimensions. These dimensions represent legal factors common to the cfs and cited case. If at least one of these shared dimensions favors the side making the argument, Hypo considers the fact that the cited case was decided for that side as potential grounds for an argument for assigning the same outcome to the cfs.

Distinguishing a cited case is stating legally relevant *differences* between the cfs and the cited case, that is, reasons why they should be decided differently. In Hypo, such differences were represented as certain unshared dimensions: in an argument for the plaintiff, dimensions in the cfs, but not in the cited case, that favored plaintiff, and dimensions in the cited case, but not in the cfs, that favored the defendant. These particular unshared dimensions give rise to reasons for deciding the cases differently.

Counterexamples are cases that evidence the same or similar reasons as the cited case for deciding in favor of the side making the argument but where the opposite outcome was reached. Counterexamples make good cases for the opponent to cite in response.

Let's illustrate Hypo's arguments with the facts of a case called *Mason v. Jack Daniels Distillery*, 518 So. 2d 130 (Ala. Civ. App. 1987). In 1980 Tony Mason, a restaurant owner, developed a recipe to ease a sore throat: Jack Daniel's whiskey, Triple Sec, sweet and sour mix, and 7-Up. He promoted the drink, dubbed "Lynchburg Lemonade" for his restaurant, "Tony Mason's, Huntsville," served it in Mason jars, and sold T-shirts. Mason told the recipe only to his bartenders and instructed them not to reveal the recipe to others. The drink was only mixed out of the customers' view. The drink comprised about one-third of the sales of alcoholic drinks. Despite its extreme popularity, no other establishments had duplicated the drink, but experts claimed it could easily be duplicated. In 1982, Randle, a sales representative of the Jack Daniel's Distillery, visited Mason's restaurant and drank Lynchburg Lemonade. Mason disclosed part of the recipe to Randle in exchange, Mason claimed, for a promise that Mason and his band would be used in a sales promotion. Randle recalled having been under the impression that Mason's recipe was a "secret formula." Randle informed his superiors of the recipe and the drink's popularity. A year later, the Distillery began using the recipe to promote the drink in a national sales campaign. Mason was not invited to participate in the promotion nor did he receive any other compensation, so he sued the distillery for misappropriating his secret recipe.

An attorney with some knowledge of trade secret law would be able to identify in the *Mason* facts some legal factors that favor the plaintiff and others that favor the defendant. Plaintiff Mason adopted some security measures, F6 Security-Measures (P).[1] Mason was the only restaurant preparing the Lynchburg Lemonade drink, F15 Unique-Product (P). The defendant distillery's sales representative knew that the information Mason provided was confidential, F21 Knew-Info-Confidential (P). On the other hand, Mason disclosed the information about mixing Lynchburg Lemonade in negotiations with the distillery's agent, F1 Disclosure-in-Negotiations (D), and the recipe could be learned by reverse engineering the drink, F16 Info-Reverse-Engineerable (D).

Figure 3.2 shows an example of a 3-Ply Argument that Hypo could generate for the plaintiff in the *Mason* case. Hypo would analogize *Mason* to the pro-defendant *Yokana* case, then respond by distinguishing *Yokana* for the plaintiff and by citing a pro-plaintiff (trumping) counterexample, the *American Precision* case, and finally,

[1] The *Mason* case was introduced in Aleven (1997) as an example for the CATO program, discussed below, to analyze. CATO employed 26 Factors, numbered F1 through F27. (There is no F9.) For convenience, we will refer to Factors (and the corresponding legal factors) by number. See Table 3.1 for a complete list.

rebut by distinguishing the counterexample on behalf of the defendant. A look at Hypo's model of argument will explain how such arguments would be generated.

Hypo's Argument Model

Figure 3.3 shows the cfs (i.e., the *Mason* case), the *Yokana* case decided for the defendant (D), the *American Precision* case won by the plaintiff (P), the legal factors that apply in each case, and the overlap of legal factors across the cases. The intuition underlying Hypo's model of argument is conveyed in the Venn diagram.

As illustrated in Figure 3.3, the cfs shares pro-defendant F16 with the pro-defendant *Yokana* case. In the Hypo model, this leads to an argument that the cfs is relevantly similar to (i.e., shares a citable legal factor with) *Yokana* and should be decided the same way for defendant (see Figure 3.2, top).

The plaintiff Tony Mason could respond, however, in a number of ways. First, he could distinguish the *Yokana* case. It has a pro-defendant legal factor, F10, not shared in the cfs. In other words, there is a reason to decide *Yokana* for defendant that does not apply to the cfs. Similarly, the cfs has pro-plaintiff legal factors, F6, F15, and F21 that are not in the *Yokana* case. Those are reasons to decide the cfs for plaintiff that do not apply in the cited case (see Figure 3.2, middle).

Second, Tony Mason could cite a favorable precedent: In the *American Precision* case, the plaintiff won where pro-plaintiff F21 applied just as in the cfs.

Third, Mason could use the *American Precision* case to *trump* the defendant's argument based on *Yokana*. In *American Precision*, the plaintiff won *despite* the application of pro-defendant F16. The cfs is even more analogous to *American Precision*

→ **Point for Defendant as Side-1: (analogize case)**

> WHERE: Plaintiff's product information could be learned by reverse-engineering.
>
> DEFENDANT should win a claim for Trade Secrets Misappropriation.
>
> CITE: *Midland-Ross Corp. v. Yokana* 293 F.2d 411 (3d Cir. 1961)

← **Response for Plaintiff as Side-2: (distinguish case; cite counterexamples)**

> Yokana is distinguishable, because: in Yokana, plaintiff disclosed its product information to outsiders. Not so in Mason. In Mason, plaintiff adopted security measures. Not so in Yokana. In Mason, plaintiff was the only manufacturer making the product. Not so in Yokana. In Mason, defendant knew that plaintiff's information was confidential. Not so in Yokana.
>
> COUNTEREXAMPLES: *American Precision Vibrator Company, Jim Guy, and Shirley Breitenstein v. National Air Vibrator Company* 764 S.W.2d 274 (Tex.App.-Houston [1st Dist.] 1988) is more on point and held for PLAINTIFF where it was also the case that: defendant knew that plaintiff's information was confidential.

→ **Rebuttal for Defendant as Side-1: (distinguish counterexamples / pose hypotheticals if any) to strengthen/weaken argument)**

> American Precision is distinguishable, because: in American Precision, plaintiff's former employee brought product development information to defendant. Not so in Mason. In Mason, plaintiff disclosed its product information in negotiations with defendant. Not so in American Precision.

FIGURE 3.2. Hypo-style three-ply argument for the *Mason* case (see Ashley, 1990)

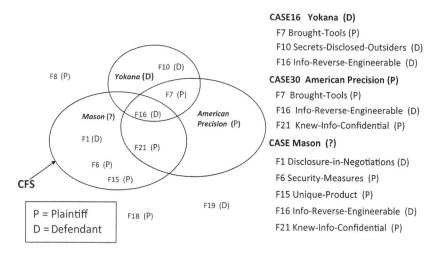

CASE16 Yokana **(D)**
F7 Brought-Tools (P)
F10 Secrets-Disclosed-Outsiders (D)
F16 Info-Reverse-Engineerable (D)

CASE30 American Precision (P)
F7 Brought-Tools (P)
F16 Info-Reverse-Engineerable (D)
F21 Knew-Info-Confidential (P)

CASE Mason (?)
F1 Disclosure-in-Negotiations (D)
F6 Security-Measures (P)
F15 Unique-Product (P)
F16 Info-Reverse-Engineerable (D)
F21 Knew-Info-Confidential (P)

FIGURE 3.3. Hypo argument model with Venn diagram (Ashley, 1990)

because they share a set of factors, F16 and F21; *Yokana* and the cfs share only a subset of that set, namely F16. In other words, *American Precision* is a trumping counterexample to *Yokana* (see Figure 3.2, middle).

More specifically, a counterexample is a case whose outcome is the opposite of the cited case and which satisfies an additional constraint as follows. If the set of legal factors a cited case shares with the cfs is a subset of the set that the counterexample shares with the cfs, the counterexample is more on point than the cited case and is called a *trumping* counterexample. If the counterexample shares the same set of legal factors with the cfs as the cited case, it is an *as-on-point* counterexample. If the counterexample shares a legal factor with the cited case and the cfs, but the magnitude of the legal factor (the corresponding dimension's magnitude) is stronger for the side favored in the cited case, it is a *boundary* counterexample. It tends to undermine a conclusion that the dimension favors that side.

Hypo could make all of these arguments. This example does not illustrate a boundary counterexample, but if the *Mason* case had involved disclosures to outsiders and defendant had relied on *Secrets-Disclosed-Outsiders*, plaintiff could cite the pro-plaintiff *Data General* case with 6,000 disclosees as a boundary counterexample. (Of course, in the rebuttal, Hypo would distinguish the *Data General* case for the defendant by pointing out that there the disclosures to outsiders were restricted.)

Case Retrieval and Ordering in Hypo

Given an input fact situation, Hypo retrieved all cases in its database that shared a dimension with the cfs. It then ordered the cases in terms of the overlaps of the sets of legal factors (as represented by dimensions) the cases shared with the cfs. Hypo organized the cases in a graph structure called a *claim lattice* by the inclusiveness

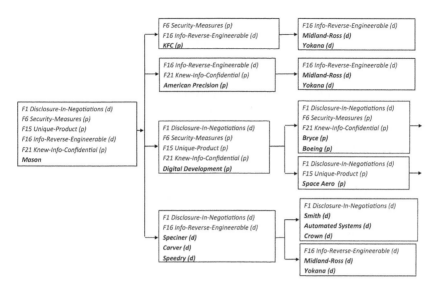

FIGURE 3.4. Hypo claim lattice (Ashley, 1990)

of the sets of dimensions they shared with the problem. Figure 3.4 shows the claim lattice Hypo could construct for the *Mason* cfs. The cfs is at the root. Each of the cfs's immediate descendants shares some subset of its applicable dimensions. Each of their descendants shares some subset of their set of dimensions shared with the cfs and so forth. Notice in the claim lattice that *American Precision* is closer to the cfs than *Yokana* reflecting the trumping counterexample relationship illustrated in Figures 3.2 and 3.3.

The Hypo model illustrates one way to computationally compare cases' similarity and relevance. Hypo does *not* compare cases in terms of the *numbers* of dimensions shared with the cfs. Rather, it compares them in terms of the inclusiveness of the sets of dimensions each case shares with the cfs. In other words, Hypo compares the *sets* of legal factors each case shares with the cfs and determines if one case's set is a subset of another case's set. If it is a subset, the former case is less on point than the latter. In Figure 3.4, for instance, the *Digital Development* case shares four dimensions with the cfs compared with *American Precision*'s two, but that does *not* make it more on point. Also, since *American Precision*'s set of dimensions shared with the cfs is not a subset of *Digital Development*'s the two cases are not comparable according to the Hypo model.

Comparing sets of dimensions makes legal sense. It approximates comparing how well a case covers the legal strengths and weaknesses in a cfs. Comparing cases in terms of the number of dimensions shared ignores the semantic differences among the legal factors.

Two programs extended the Hypo model. CABARET applied dimensions to reasoning with statutory rules and CATO implemented new argument templates for downplaying or emphasizing distinctions.

Dimensions of Legal Rule Predicates in CABARET

CABARET, a first successor to Hypo, dealt with a statutory domain, in particular, a provision of the U.S. IRC dealing with the income tax home office deduction (Rissland and Skalak, 1991). It employed dimensions to represent stereotypical fact patterns that strengthened or weakened a claim that a legal rule's predicate (e.g., "principal place of business" in the tax code provision) was satisfied.

CABARET integrated two models, one rule-based and the other case-based. The rule-based model represented legal rules from the relevant IRS provisions and their ILCs. Given a problem scenario, the rule-based model forward-chained from facts to confirm goals and backward-chained from desired goals to facts needing to be shown.

The rules were similar to those in the Waterman program (Section 1.3.1), but with one major difference. Where the rules "ran out" (i.e., no further rules defined a statutory term), the program could resort to Hypo-style case-based reasoning. Dimensions in CABARET were associated with legal factors strengthening or weakening an argument that a statutory term was satisfied. These dimensions indexed cases in which courts held that the statutory terms were satisfied or not.

Given a problem scenario and a statutory term, the case-based reasoning model determined which dimensions applied, retrieved cases indexed by those dimensions, and generated claim lattices like that illustrated in Figure 3.4 for the statutory term that was subject to argument. The claim lattice organized past cases relevant to that statutory term according to relevance as measured in the Hypo model.

CABARET integrated both computational models via an agenda mechanism: an algorithm that could reason about the current state of the analysis and call either the rule-based reasoning (RBR) or case-based reasoning (CBR) model as appropriate. The agenda mechanism employed a set of heuristic rules to reason about the current state of analysis. Examples of the control heuristics included:

- *Try other*: If CBR fails, then switch to RBR (and vice versa).
- *Sanity check*: Test conclusion of RBR with CBR (and vice versa).
- *RBR Near-miss*: If all a rule's antecedents are established but one, use CBR to broaden application of the rule with respect to the missing antecedent. For example, use CBR to show that there are cases where the conclusion was true but the rule did not fire because of the missing antecedent.
- *Match statutory concepts*: Find cases that failed or succeeded on the same statutory concepts.

Figure 3.5 shows excerpts of CABARET's analysis of a real case, *Weissman v. IRS*, involving whether a CCNY Philosophy professor's home office (two rooms and bath)

1. Taxpayer must show home office is principal place of business (p-p-b): Perform HYPO-style Dimensional Analysis on cases indexed under p-p-b concept. Conclude it's satisfied.

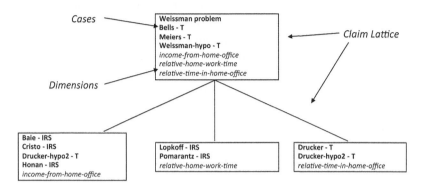

2. Apply heuristic control rule: "sanity-check-CBR-by-RBR": Backward chain on rule p-p-b: If taxpayer discharged "primary responsibility in home office" and derived "income from home office" and there is evidence as to relative time taxpayer spent in home office then home office is taxpayer's "principal place of business."

3. **Rule p-p-b is a near miss:** All antecedents satisfied but one: whether he discharges "primary responsibility in home office."

4. **Heuristic control rule matches:** If RBR near-miss then use CBR to broaden rule by finding similar cases where missing antecedent is true.

5. **Retrieve similar pro-taxpayer cases:** Case where "primary responsibility in home office" is satisfied: *Drucker* case.

6. **Generate argument analogizing *Drucker* to Weissman problem:**

   "To analogize *Drucker* and *Weissman,* consider the following factors possessed by them in common: there was evidence as to the frequency of usage of the home office by the taxpayer, the home office was necessary to perform the taxpayer's duties."

FIGURE 3.5. Example of CABARET's process for analyzing *Weissman v. IRS*, 751 F. 2d 512 (2d Cir. 1984) (Rissland and Skalak, 1991)

in his 10-room apartment qualified for a home office tax deduction under section 280A of the IRC. Professor Weissman spent only 20% of his time at the CCNY office where it was not safe to leave equipment and materials. The IRS challenged his home office deduction of $1,540 rent and expenses because, among other things, it was not his "principal place of business" (p-p-b).

Directed by the control heuristics, CABARET's analysis begins with a case-based dimensional analysis that turns up a number of most-on-point cases citable for the taxpayer. Then, a control heuristic leads to a "sanity check" with a rule-based analysis, in which the program identifies that the rule for concluding that the home office was his "principal place of business" (p-p-b) *nearly* applied: all of its antecedents were satisfied but one: whether the taxpayer discharges "primary responsibility in home office." Again, a control rule switches to CBR, finding a case where the missing antecedent is satisfied, the *Drucker* case, which it analogizes to the cfs.

CABARET demonstrated that dimensions representing legal factors were useful techniques for modeling a domain beside trade secret law, showed how to use dimensions representing legal factors in a statutory domain, and applied the dimension and legal factor-based approach to reasoning about concepts in legal rules.

Factors in CATO

CATO, Hypo's second successor, simplified the dimensional representation with Factors (Aleven, 2003). Like Hypo, CATO dealt with trade secret misappropriation in terms of legal factors, but it did so *without* using dimensions to represent them.

Instead, it replaced each dimension with a corresponding binary Factor. A Factor either applies to a scenario or it does not. It does not make use of magnitudes or ranges, nor does it have associated prerequisites to test if a Factor applied. CATO employed a more complete list of Factors, shown in Table 3.1, and modeled how to downplay or emphasize a distinguishing Factor (Aleven, 1997). CATO employed its enhanced Factors in a computerized instructional environment to help students learn skills of case-based argument such as distinguishing. As explained in Chapter 4, it also used Factors to predict case outcomes (Aleven, 2003).

CATO added a factor hierarchy, excerpts of which are illustrated in Figure 3.6, a knowledge scheme for representing reasons why the presence of a Factor mattered from a legal viewpoint (Aleven, 2003, Fig. 3, p. 192). The factor hierarchy's reasons explained why a Factor strengthened (or weakened) a trade secret claim.

Using these reasons, CATO could generate new kinds of legal arguments downplaying or emphasizing distinctions, arguments that Hypo could not. It could organize an argument citing multiple cases by issues, grouping together cases that shared common issues with the cfs even if they did not share the same Factors. In this way, CATO could draw analogies at a higher level of abstraction.

CATO could also downplay or emphasize distinctions. As illustrated in Figure 3.7, if a side's argument cites a particular distinguishing Factor in the cfs, the program could downplay it by pointing out another Factor in the cited case that mattered for the same reason. Alternatively, the program could emphasize the distinction by characterizing the difference between the cases more abstractly based on other Factors with common roots in the factor hierarchy.

Aleven's algorithms for downplaying and emphasizing interacted with the information about Factors represented in the factor hierarchy. Given a Factor-based distinction between the cfs and a cited case, it traversed the nodes of the factor hierarchy upward from the distinguishing Factor to identify a focal abstraction that could be used to draw an abstract parallel across the cases and could lead to identifying

TABLE 3.1. *Trade secret Factors (Aleven, 1997)*

Factor	Meaning	Rationale
F1 Disclosure-in-negotiations (D)	P disclosed its product information in negotiations with D.	P gave his property away.
F2 Bribe-employee (P)	D paid P's former employee to switch employment, apparently in an attempt to induce the employee to bring P's information.	D obtained P's property through improper means.
F3 Employee-sole-developer (D)	Employee D was the sole developer of P's product.	D should have property rights in his invention.
F4 Agreed-not-to-disclose (P)	D entered into a nondisclosure agreement with P.	P takes reasonable steps to protect his property.
F5 Agreement-not-specific (D)	The nondisclosure agreement did not specify which information was to be treated as confidential.	P did not specify in what he claims a property interest.
F6 Security-measures (P)	P adopted security measures.	P takes reasonable steps to protect his property.
F7 Brought-tools (P)	P's former employee brought product development information to D.	D steals P's property.
F8 Competitive-advantage (P)	D's access to P's product information saved it time or expense.	P's trade secret is valuable property.
F10 Secrets-disclosed-outsiders (D)	P disclosed its product information to outsiders.	P gave his property away.
F11 Vertical-knowledge (D)	P's information is about customers and suppliers (which means that it may be available independently from customers or even in directories).	P cannot have a property interest in its customer's business info.
F12 Outsider-disclosures- restricted (P)	P's disclosures to outsiders were subject to confidentiality restrictions.	P protects his property.
F13 Noncompetition- agreement (P)	P and D entered into a noncompetition agreement.	P protected against former employee's use of confidential information.
F14 Restricted-materials-used (P)	D used materials that were subject to confidentiality restrictions.	D used P's property despite P's protections.
F15 Unique-product (P)	P was the only manufacturer making the product.	P's trade secret is valuable property.
F16 Info-reverse-engineerable (D)	P's product information could be learned by reverse-engineering.	P's property interest is limited in time.
F17 Info-independently-generated (D)	D developed its product by independent research.	P has no property interest in information D generated independently.
F18 Identical-products (P)	D's product was identical to P's.	D copied P's trade secret property.
F19 No-security-measures (D)	P did not adopt any security measures.	P did not protect his property.
F20 Info-known-to-competitors (D)	P's information was known to competitors.	P cannot have property interest in something known.
F21 Knew-info-confidential (P)	D knew that P's information was confidential.	D knew p claimed property interest.
F22 Invasive-techniques (P)	D used invasive techniques to gain access to P's information.	D used invasive techniques to steal P's property.
F23 Waiver-of-confidentiality (D)	P entered into an agreement waiving confidentiality.	P claimed no property interest in trade secret.
F24 Info-obtainable-elsewhere (D)	The information could be obtained from publicly available sources.	P cannot have property interest in something available from public sources.
F25 Info-reverse-engineered (D)	D discovered P's information through reverse engineering.	P's property interest is limited by time.
F26 Deception (P)	D obtained P's information through deception.	P was cheated of his property
F27 Disclosure-in-public-forum (D)	P disclosed its information in a public forum.	P gave his property interest in the trade secret away.

91

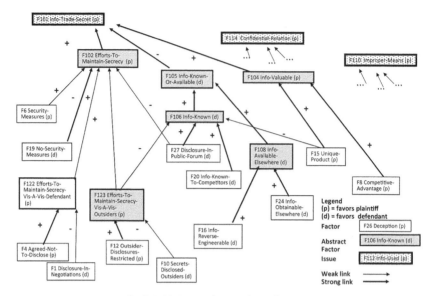

FIGURE 3.6. CATO Factor hierarchy (Aleven, 1997, 2003)

Arguments about the significance of distinction F16

⇒ **Plaintiff's argument downplaying distinction F16 in *Mason*.** In *Mason*,
     plaintiff's product information could be learned by reverse-engineering
     [F16]. This was not so in *Bryce*. However, this is not a significant
     distinction. In *Bryce*, plaintiff disclosed its product information in
     negotiations with defendant [F1], yet plaintiff won. In both cases, therefore,
     defendant obtained or could have obtained its information by legitimate
     means [F120]. But plaintiff may still win.
⇐ **Defendant's argument emphasizing distinction F16 in *Mason*.** In *Mason*,
     plaintiff's product information could be learned by reverse-engineering
     [F16]. This was not so in *Bryce*. This distinction is highly significant. It
     shows that in *Mason*, plaintiff's information was available from sources
     outside plaintiff's business [F108]. This was not so in *Bryce*.

FIGURE 3.7. CATO argument downplaying/emphasizing distinction (Aleven, 2003)

Factors in the other case that undercut the significance of the distinction. Another
algorithm could emphasize a distinction by finding a focal abstraction in the factor
hierarchy for abstractly contrasting the two cases. It could lead to identifying further
corroborating Factors in one case and contrasting Factors in the other case, with
which to support the distinction's importance (Aleven, 2003, pp. 202–8).

Aleven evaluated CATO in two ways. First, he assessed its efficacy in teaching
students basic skills of case-based legal argument, as compared to being taught the
same skills by an experienced human instructor. Second, he evaluated the argument
model in terms of how successfully it predicted outcomes of cases, as discussed in
Chapter 4.

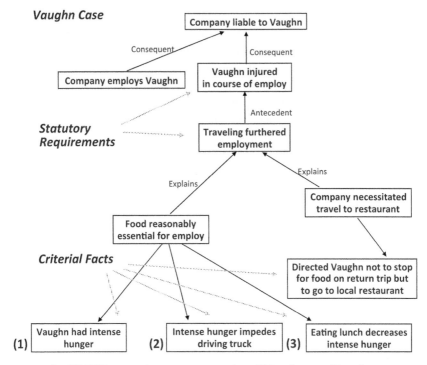

FIGURE 3.8. GREBE semantic net representation of *Vaughn* case (Branting, 1991, 1999)

3.3.3. *Exemplar-based Explanations*

Karl Branting developed a third basic knowledge representation technique, EBEs, for comparing the similarity of cases, drawing analogies to positive case instances, and distinguishing negative ones. His Generator of EBEs (GREBE) program modeled arguments by analogy to past cases using a different kind of extensional representation scheme: semantic nets (Branting, 1991, 1999).

A *semantic net* is a graph comprising nodes, which represent concepts (including both legal concepts and facts), and arcs representing relations between concepts. Using a semantic net, Branting represented a court's explanation of a case's outcome in terms of *criterial facts*, the facts the judge deemed important to support its conclusion that particular ILCs drawn from a statute were satisfied or not. Branting called these semantic net representations *EBEs*.

Figure 3.8 shows a sample EBE, the semantic net representation of the *Vaughn* case, one of the cases in GREBE's database. In the *Vaughn* case, a truck driver was injured in an accident when driving his motorcycle to a restaurant to eat before his next run. His boss had directed him to go find something to eat because of a delay in unloading his truck. The issue was whether Vaughn was injured in the course of his employ, in which case his employer would be liable (Branting, 1991, p. 810).

GREBE's knowledge sources included statutory, common law, and commonsense rules as well as 16 legal precedents, 4 paradigm cases, and 21 hypothetical test cases represented as EBEs. Each case's EBE was indexed as a positive or negative example of the open-textured statutory legal concepts as per the judge's explanation.

The inputs to GREBE were semantic nets representing the facts of workers' compensation scenarios. GREBE's output detailed textual arguments citing legal rules under the Texas workers' compensation statute and drawing analogies to precedents to justify a conclusion that an individual involved in an accident was [not] entitled to compensation.

To illustrate GREBE's process of case-based legal reasoning, here is how it handled the Jarek problem input as a semantic net. A railroad employed Jarek as a porter and one day directed him to work late. Since Jarek needed to inform his wife that he would be working late (before the age of cellphones), the Railroad permitted Jarek to make a special trip home to tell his wife. While walking home, however, Jarek slipped and was injured. The problem is represented as a semantic network of facts, most of which are listed in the right-hand column in Figure 3.9.

When input, GREBE tries to prove that Jarek is entitled to workers' compensation. Using backward chaining, it attempts to construct a proof based on its statutory rules setting forth the requirements for a successful workers' compensation claim. Those rules, however, do not define all of the statutory requirements in sufficient detail to complete such a proof. In particular, one of the requirements stipulates that the employee's travel must be in-furtherance-of-employment, but there is no rule further defining that legal concept.

An ill-defined statutory concept, however, may index multiple precedents as positive or negative examples. GREBE attempts to map the structures of the semantic

Matched criterial facts from *Vaughn* case:

Vaughn-employment	Jarek-employment
traveling-from-factory-to-restaurant2	Jarek-special-travel-home
Vaughn	Jarek
APF-Co	Railroad
Vaughn-sulfur-conveyance-activity	customary-portering-activity
APF-Co-direction1	Railroad-direction
APF-Co-direction2	Railroad-giving-permission
APF-Co-scheduling-goals	Railroad-scheduling-goals
Vaughn-modified-conveyance-back	overtime-portering-activity
Vaughn-eating-lunch	Jarek-informing-his-wife
Vaughn-food-need	Jarek-family-need
Vaughn-having-food	Jarek-being-at-home

Unmatched criterial facts from *Vaughn* case:

(reasonably-essential-for Vaughn-having-food Vaughn-sulfur-conveyance-activity)
(impedes (intensity Vaughn-food-need high) (Vaughn-sulfur-conveyance-activity))
(necessitation traveling-from-factory-to-restaurant2 APF-Co-direction1 Vaughn-having-food)
(directed-activity APF-Co.-direction1 Vaughn-having-food)

FIGURE 3.9. GREBE matches structure of *Vaughn* case to Jarek problem (Branting, 1991, 1999)

net representing the facts of the problem to the structures of each indexed precedent's EBE. For instance, in-furtherance-of-employment indexes 20 precedents. GREBE does not know in advance which of these precedents are the most relevant for a given cfs. Consequently, GREBE retrieves each one and tries to match the Jarek facts to the criterial facts in each case where the trip was held to be in-furtherance-of-employment [or not].

For instance, among other cases indexed by in-furtherance-of-employment, GREBE retrieves the *Vaughn* case whose EBE is shown in Figure 3.8. It tries to construct a justification that Jarek's special travel home was in furtherance of his employment by drawing an analogy to the similar conclusion in the *Vaughn* case. In other words, GREBE tries to prove (*in-furtherance-of Jarek-special-travel-home Jarek-employment*) by analogy to (*in-furtherance-of Vaughn-traveling-to-restaurant2 Vaughn-employment*). Operationally, that means GREBE tries to map the structure of the explanation in the *Vaughn* EBE (Figure 3.8) to the facts of the Jarek semantic net. The result of GREBE's mapping of the *Vaughn* case to the Jarek facts is shown in Figure 3.9. The criterial facts from the *Vaughn* case that were successfully matched to the Jarek facts are shown at the top. The unmatched facts are at the bottom.

In order to assess the quality of a match, GREBE employed its computational measure of similarity of two cases. Branting defined a relevant similarity as a matched criterial fact and a relevant difference as an unmatched criterial fact. GREBE computed similarity between a source case and a target case as the proportion of criterial facts matched across the two cases per the total number of criterial facts in the target case. If this ratio exceeded a threshold value, the cases were deemed to be relevantly similar.

Incidentally, from a computational viewpoint, mapping semantic net structures is complex. Think of trying to match fairly elaborate Tinker Toy structures when blinded; since one cannot see the structure, one has to try matching each node of one structure to a node of the other and "feel" if each descendant matches. The task is simplified computationally in that the links in these semantic nets are labeled. Think of matching Tinker Toy structures with multicolored rods where, at least, one can "see" what color the rods are and thus focus on matching only parts of structures involving similarly colored rods. With labeled links, a program will only proceed if the link labels match, but the task is still computationally complex.

Branting designed a variation of the A* best-first search algorithm that pursued matching the structures of case explanations in a highly selective and efficient way: Candidate mappings are pursued only in so far as they lead to a best match.

The A* search algorithm employs two parameters: $f(n)$ estimates the cost to reach the goal from the current node N and $g(n)$ represents the actual cost of reaching the current node N from the initial state. Operationally, $f(N)$ is an estimate of the number of unmatched criterial facts in the best completion of the mapping in N. $g(N)$ is defined in terms of the proportion of criterial facts in a target case that are unmatched under the mapping so far to node N. These cost estimates of available

---

Results: Three precedents for in-furtherance-of-employment:

- neg. Very strong analogy to *Coleman:* activity not in-furtherance-of-employment: part of ordinary commute home.

- pos. Strong analogy to *Vaughn*: activity is in-furtherance-of-employment: necessitated by employer APF. Co.'s instructions to Vaughn.

- pos. Weak analogy to *Janak*: activity is in-furtherance-of-employment: trip gets icewater for crew; reasonably essential for their oil drilling.

FIGURE 3.10. In-furtherance-of employment cases retrieved by GREBE for Jarek problem (Branting, 1991, 1999)

paths to the goal of structurally mapping the most similar cases guided GREBE's best-first search algorithm. Having reached some node *N* in its search, it estimated the cheapest path through *N* from the initial node to the goal node (Branting, 1991, p. 817).

As a result of matching cases indexed by the legal concept in-furtherance-of-employment, GREBE retrieves the three cases listed in Figure 3.10 and uses them to construct the arguments by analogy excerpted in Figure 3.11. As perusal of the argument indicates, GREBE produced sophisticated legal arguments in natural language text comparable to those a human might produce.

Evaluating GREBE

In order to substantiate the sufficiency of his CMLR, Branting developed a technique for empirically evaluating the quality of GREBE's arguments similar to the one in Figure 3.11.

Branting compared GREBE's analysis of a number of workers' compensation problems to those prepared by five law student volunteers. Students were asked to construct the strongest arguments they could for and against the injured person's entitlement to compensation. Students took on average 2.77 hours researching the problem and writing their analyses.

A domain expert in Texas workers' compensation law graded the students' and GREBE's responses in a blind test. GREBE's responses were made to look on the surface as though they had been prepared by a student. The expert was told that all of the analyses were prepared by law students.

The expert graded the responses for identifying issues, citing statutory rules and precedents, and the soundness and persuasiveness of the arguments. He assigned the following grades:

GREBE: 9 C's, 4 B's, 4 F's Avg. 2.0
Students: 12 C's, 1 B, 5 F's Avg. 1.78

According to the expert, none of the "students" did really well, but GREBE's arguments were better!

The stronger argument is that:
The special trip home was not an activity in furtherance of Jarek's employment.

[Draws analogy to *Coleman* case re ordinary commuting to/from work.]

However, a weaker argument can be made that:
The special trip was an activity in furtherance of Jarek's employment. This conclusion follows from the strong analogy between the given case and the facts of *Vaughn* that were relevant to the conclusion that the trip from the factory to the restaurant was an activity in furtherance of Vaughn's employment. This analogy is supported by the following inferences:
A. That Denver and Rio Grande railroad permitted the special trip home...is similar to the fact that APF Co. directed the trip from the factory to a restaurant.
B. Jarek's being at home was reasonably essential for Jarek's employment duties. This conclusion follows from the weak analogy between the given case and the facts of *Janak* that were relevant to the conclusion that icewater being at the job site was reasonably essential for oil drilling by the *Janak* crew. That Jarek had the need to inform his wife...is similar to the fact that the *Janak* crew had the need to keep cool. Relevant differences between the given case and *Janak* ...are that Jarek's employment duties were not impeded by the fact that the need to inform his wife was of high intensity. Whereas in the *Janak* case: Oil drilling by the *Janak* crew was impeded by the fact that the need for cooling was of high intensity.
C. The special trip home was necessitated by Denver and Rio Grande's instruction to work late.

[Draws analogy to *Vaughn*.]

FIGURE 3.11. Excerpts of GREBE's argument for Jarek problem (see Branting, 1991, 1999)

3.4. TELEOLOGICAL MODELS OF CASE-BASED LEGAL REASONING

Programs like Hypo, CATO, CABARET, and GREBE did not take into account the purposes and values underlying legal rules. As Don Berman and Carole Hafner pointed out in their influential critique, these early CBR models could not reason *teleologically*.

Berman and Hafner (1993) illustrated teleological reasoning with a series of cases, drawn from an American law school first-year property course, involving hunters' property rights in wild prey. This trilogy of examples, *Pierson v. Post*, 3 Caines R. (N.Y. 1805) and two English cases, *Keeble v. Hickeringill*, 103 ER 1127 (1707) and *Young v. Hitchens*, 115 ER 228 (1844), has since become a standard example in AI & Law (see Sections 5.5.2 and 6.6).

The Property Interests in Wild Animal Cases

In the *Pierson* case, plaintiff Post was hunting foxes on open land. While the plaintiff pursued a fox on horseback with hunting dogs, the defendant, "well knowing the fox was so hunted ... did, in the sight of Post, to prevent his catching the same, kill and carry it off." The Court ruled for defendant that to recover, the plaintiff had to have gained possession of the fox by capturing it or mortally wounding it. The majority reasoned that there was a need for certainty and clear guidelines in order to discourage a plague of lawsuits by disgruntled hunters. The dissenter would have ruled for the plaintiff that the pursuit is enough to convey a property interest in the fox, reasoning that the law should reward hunters for ridding the land of noxious foxes.

The plaintiff in the *Keeble* case owned a pond upon which he placed duck decoys. The defendant, intending to injure the plaintiff's livelihood, fired guns to scare away the ducks. The court found for the plaintiff, even though the plaintiff had neither wounded nor captured the ducks. The court reasoned that it should protect a man's livelihood from intentional interference, except where the interference is from a competitor acting fairly.

In the *Young* case, the plaintiff, a commercial fisherman, spread a net of 140 fathoms in length across a portion of open ocean. After the plaintiff had closed the net to a space of few fathoms the defendant went through the opening, spread the defendant's own net, and caught the fish. On appeal from a judgment for the plaintiff, the court affirmed recovery for damage to the plaintiff's net but not for the loss of the fish. The court reasoned that "it is quite certain that [plaintiff] had not possession" of the fish.

Need to Model Reasoning with Underlying Values

To illustrate the kind of reasoning with underlying values that the computational models omitted, Berman and Hafner employed a series of hypotheticals:

1. Suppose the quarry had been a quail. How would the dissenter in *Pierson* have held?

2. Suppose violence among sportsmen had resulted. How would the majority have held in *Pierson*?

3. Is the situation in *Keeble* like the case in which "one schoolmaster sets up a new school to the damage of an ancient school, thereby the scholars are allured from the old school to come to his new," a case where the action was held not to lie? Or suppose "Mr. Hickeringill should lie in the way with his guns, and fright the boy from going to school . . . sure that schoolmaster might have action" (Berman and Hafner, 1993).

Legal decision-makers pose hypothetical variations of case facts like these in order to probe the meaning of a legal rule in light of its underlying values and purposes. For example, the Justices of the U.S. Supreme Court frequently pose hypotheticals in oral arguments. The hypothetical in (1) renders inapplicable the purpose to rid the land of pests. The one in (2) affects the purpose to provide a clear and certain guideline.

A judge in *Keeble* posed the hypothetical in (3), presumably to underscore the purpose of the court's rule that it should protect an individual's livelihood from intentional interference, except where the interference is from a competitor acting fairly.

Argument I

→ *Point for defendant*: Defendant should win as in *Pierson* because the plaintiff had not yet caught the fish or mortally wounded it. The nets weren't closed.

← *Response for plaintiff*: But unlike *Pierson*, the plaintiff in *Young* is pursuing his livelihood.

Counterexample: In *Keeble*, plaintiff won even though he did not mortally wound or capture the ducks.

→ *Rebuttal for defendant*: *Keeble* is distinguishable. Plaintiff was conducting his business on his own land. Defendant was acting maliciously. In *Young*, the defendant is engaged in business competition.

Argument II

→ *Point for defendant*: You should apply the rule in *Pierson* because the uncertainty about what constitutes property rights to fish swimming in the open sea will cause endless controversy.

← *Response for plaintiff*: You should apply the rule in *Keeble* because it is important that people earn a living and the defendant has interfered with the plaintiff's right to make a living.

→ *Rebuttal for defendant*: Unlike the defendant in *Keeble* this defendant was not acting maliciously and was merely engaged in vigorous competition like the schoolmaster who merely sets up a competing school or the owner of adjoining land who also deploys decoys. Society benefits from such competition.

← *Surrebuttal for plaintiff*: Society tolerates vigorous competition but not unfair competition. The actions of the defendants will force the plaintiff to take wasteful actions to protect their catches when the defendants could be pursuing other fish which would increase the amount of fish available to consumers.

→ *Surrebuttal for defendant*: Guidelines for determining whether competition among fishermen is fair or unfair should be left to the legislature; otherwise there could be endless lawsuits attempting to establish what fishermen may or may not do.

FIGURE 3.12. Which argument better accounts for teleological concerns? (Berman and Hafner, 1993)

As Berman and Hafner put it, "Once the purpose of the rule is understood, analogous cases setting forth the rights of school masters become more relevant than cases dealing with foxes." In other words, the purpose of the rule explains why the court would decide for the plaintiff in *Keeble* even though the plaintiff had neither wounded nor captured the ducks, as would be required by the court in *Pierson*.

To illustrate their critique of the early case-based reasoning approaches, Berman and Hafner contrasted two arguments, I and II, as shown in Figure 3.12. The authors characterize arguments based on factual distinctions, like Argument I, as a kind of intellectual fencing match. They warn, however, that judges, when studying legal arguments, do not act as match referees. "[J]udges make rules that significantly affect human lives and their decisions necessarily embody their views (or prejudices) as to which rules improve the quality of life in society." It follows that advocates "in addition to arguments based on factual distinctions, [should] suggest to judges various 'policy' arguments that should affect the decision" (Berman and Hafner, 1993).

As a result, Berman and Hafner argued, computational models of case-based legal reasoning need to address the question of "Which case *should* govern and why?" as exemplified in Argument II. There, the arguers cite rules and underlying purposes of the rules.

The first-generation CBR systems did not provide a rich-enough vocabulary for representing arguments about the underlying purposes of rules. Modeling teleological reasoning requires a way to represent values and purposes underlying legal rules and a way to connect them with case facts. It also requires a way to represent the effects of decisions on underlying values and purposes in concrete fact situations.

3.5. AN APPROACH TO MODELING TELEOLOGICAL REASONING

The value-based theory construction approach in Bench-Capon and Sartor (2003) illustrates one way to take into account the values underlying legal rules.

The work builds on a formal model of legal reasoning with precedents in Prakken and Sartor (1998). According to that earlier approach, each precedent was represented as two conflicting rules:

1. *pro-plaintiff Factors* $\Rightarrow p$
2. *pro-defendant Factors* $\Rightarrow not(p)$

Here p represents the decision that plaintiff wins. The first rule states that the plaintiff wins where all of the Factors in the case favoring the plaintiff are present. The second rule states that the plaintiff loses where all of the case Factors favoring the defendant apply.

In addition, the precedent establishes a priority or *preference* relationship between the two rules. If the plaintiff actually won the case, then the first rule has priority over the second; if defendant won, then the second rule has priority over the first. This approach became the building block of many subsequent developments in logical models of case-based legal arguments.

In particular, Bench-Capon and Sartor (2003) refined and adapted it for their model of value-based theory construction. They represented cases as sets of Factors, as in CATO, but the Factors were interpreted as rules of the form, "if the Factor applies then decide for the side favored by the Factor." These rules are *defeasible*: "When we come to apply them we will typically find conflicting rules pointing to differing decisions, so we need a means of resolving such conflicts" (Bench-Capon and Sartor, 2003).

Rule conflicts are resolved by assigning preferences to the Factor-related rules. Each Factor is associated with an underlying value. As cases are decided, their outcomes give rise to more rules that assign preferences to sets of Factors and to sets of values, preferences that resolve future conflicts.

Figure 3.13 presents an example illustrating the above in the context of the property rights in wild animal cases. At the top of the figure are three values, Less litigation (Llit), More productivity (Mprod), and Enjoyment of property rights (Prop), and four Factors. Each Factor favors a side, plaintiff (P) or defendant (D), giving rise to defeasible rules including the three rules shown in the figure. In addition, each Factor serves one of the underlying values, as shown. Finally, the outcome of the *Keeble* case gives rise to the preference rule shown in the figure: "if pLiv then P > if pNposs then D," meaning that the former rule has preference over the latter.

3.5.1. *Teleology in Theory Construction*

Let us assume that the goal is to make an argument on behalf of the defendant in the *Young* case as cfs based on two precedents shown in the figure, *Pierson* and *Keeble*.

In Bench-Capon and Sartor (2003), making an argument with cases is modeled "as a process of constructing and using a theory." In this respect, the work is consistent with Thorne McCarty's approach in Section 3.3.1. The theories in Bench-Capon's and Sartor's approach are constructed from precedent cases, where the cases are represented as sets of Factors with which values have been associated and as inference rules which operationalize them as precedents.

In the Bench-Capon and Sartor model, the theory is constructed not of invariant mappings across cases but of rules defining preferences across competing Factors and preferences across the associated competing values. As depicted in Figure 3.13, to construct an argument involves completing the theory by adding rules (indicated in the figure by "ADD:"). For instance, the arguer adds a rule, "if pNposs,dLiv then D," justifies the new rule with an added rule preference: "ADD: if pNposs, dLiv then D > if pLiv then P," and justifies that by adding a value preference, "ADD: Mprod, Llit > Mprod." This last new rule means that the values of more productivity and less litigation outweigh the value of more productivity.

The authors define various theory constructors whose function is to construct explanations of existing or desired case outcomes. Theory constructors make

```
Values:  Llit      (Less Litigation)
         Mprod     (More productivity)
         Prop      (Enjoyment of property rights)
Factors:
         pNposs, D, Llit (p was not in possession of the animal, favors D b/c Llit)
         pLiv, P, Mprod (p was pursuing his livelihood, favors P b/c Mprod)
         pLand, P, Prop (p was on his own land, favoring P b/c Prop)
         dLiv, D, Mprod (d was pursuing his livelihood, favoring D)
CFS:     Young: pLiv, pNposs, dLiv; GOAL = D
Cases:   Pierson: pLiv; D
         Keeble: pLiv, pNposs, pLand; P
Rules:   if pNposs then D
         if pLiv then P
         if dLiv then D
         ADD: if pNposs,dLiv then D
Rule preferences:  if pLiv then P > if pNposs then D
                   ADD: if pNposs, dLiv then D > if pLiv then P
Value preferences:   Mprod > Llit
                   ADD: Mprod, Llit > Mprod
```

FIGURE 3.13. Theory constructed from factor and value preferences (Bench-Capon and Sartor, 2003)

the additions illustrated in Figure 3.13. The constructors include: Include-case from the case base, Include-factor, Merge-factors, Rule-broadening, Preferences-from-case, Rule-preference-from-value-preference, Arbitrary-rule-preference, and Arbitrary-value-preference.

The authors summarize the completed version of the theory in Figure 3.13 in the following way. "Now, by merging the primitive rules for pNposs and dLiv, introducing the value preference [Mprod,Llit > Mprod], and using this to derive the rule preference [if pNposs,dLiv then D > if pLiv then P], an explanation of *Young* can be obtained... According to [the theory], *Young* should be decided for D since in *Young* the rule [if pNposs,dLiv then D] is not defeated. This seems, according to Berman and Hafner, 1993, to be the theory used by the judges in *Young*" (Bench-Capon and Sartor, 2003).

Putting aside for a moment the strangeness of this legal theory and of the supporting arguments, the example in Figure 3.13 and this summary convey an intuition about how this kind of value-based theory construction works. The model takes values into account in constructing a theory and applies the theory to make legal arguments and predict outcomes of new cases. As suggested in Figure 3.14, the outcomes of past cases reveal preferences between sets of Factors present in those cases. Those preferences between sets of Factors, in turn, reveal preferences between sets of values associated with the Factors. Associated preference rules promote and demote certain sets of values organizing the values into an abstract order that is determined by past cases. When a new case is to be decided, given its Factors, theory constructors assemble an explanation which, when completed, can predict and explain the outcome of the case in a manner consistent with the cases to date.

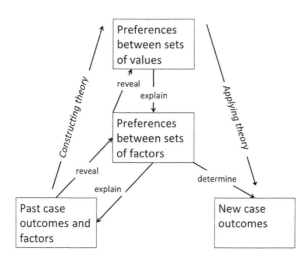

FIGURE 3.14. Argument as theory construction from factor and value preferences (see Bench-Capon and Sartor, 2003)

How Do Legal Practitioners Reason with Values?

Despite these strengths, for a number of reasons the model of legal reasoning with values in Bench-Capon and Sartor (2003) does not solve the problems raised by Berman and Hafner.

First, it is incomplete. There are some holes to be filled. Regarding the example in Figure 3.13 and the above summary, the authors note, "This explanation does rely on the introduction of a preference that is arbitrary, in the sense of not being supported by precedents" (i.e., Mprod, Llit > Mprod). The authors consider "adding a theory constructor which allows one to introduce preferences for any set of values over its own proper subsets," but allow that this may need further refinement.

Second, the model in Bench-Capon and Sartor (2003) produces multiple alternative theories. The sample theory illustrated in Figure 3.13 is only one version that the theory constructors can generate given the inputs. This means that the competing alternatives must be evaluated.

Theories can be compared in terms of consistency, explanatory power, coherence, and simplicity. Consistency and explanatory power can be measured, for instance, in terms of the number of cases the theory explains. In terms of computational implementation, however, coherence and simplicity are not very well understood and raise issues about how to make them operational (but see Section 4.6).

Third, it is not clear whether the kind of theory generated by the model in Bench-Capon and Sartor (2003) as illustrated in Figure 3.13 would make sense to judges or that judges make decisions by applying such a theory. Assessing a proposed outcome for a problem in terms of values is an ethical decision of its own. A judge needs to consider how the values apply to the problem's particular facts. It seems odd to suggest that judges determine preferences among competing values set in past cases and apply them to new cases. It is more likely that judges consider how the values apply in the particular circumstances of the problem and resolve any conflicts accordingly.

Given the model's use in Bench-Capon and Sartor (2003) of precedent-based preference rules for competing factors and values, the model does not appear to address *contextual effects* on such preferences. Even if a judge employed value preferences in past cases as a guide, he/she would still need to compare the problem to the cases in detail. A judge would want to ensure that applying a value preference is appropriate in the new factual circumstances.

McCarty's approach also did not account for how judges use values in legal reasoning about the application of a concept or how the values tie into a theory of the case. Even if the program could find, discover, or use invariants that linked cases into theories, the program appears not to know why the invariant matters, from a legal viewpoint, to the question of whether the distribution should be taxable income. Mrs. Macomber's proportionate ownership remains constant, but can the program explain why that is legally significant to the issue? Or does it know why the analogy across different types of corporate distributions, that they all involve some trade-off between risk and return, gives rise to a legal reason for treating them all as taxable income? It does not appear that Taxman II knows or can manipulate such reasons.

Realistically integrating teleological considerations into a model of legal reasoning is a challenge for all of the CBR models. Before one can tackle it adequately, however, one needs to better understand how legal practitioners take values and principles into account in reasoning about how to decide problems. Although one often hears talk of an advocate's theory of a case, it is less clear what such a theory looks like and how it is best represented by a computable data structure.

We return to these considerations in Chapter 5 on modeling legal argument.

3.6. DESIGN CONSTRAINTS FOR COGNITIVE COMPUTING WITH CASE-BASED MODELS OF LEGAL REASONING

The above examples reveal some design constraints that are relevant for cognitive computing.

First, modeling reasoning with legal rules and concepts requires modeling arguments for and against applying the rule to a fact situation.

Second, in modeling arguments about whether a legal rule's concept applies in a set of facts, cases play a significant role. The arguments focus on relevant similarities and differences among cases and the fact situation.

Third, teleological considerations including the purposes and values underlying the rules play a role in defining legally relevant similarities and differences among cases.

Fourth, in order to be a useful tool, assessing case similarity computationally requires defining a criterion for legal similarity that programs can actually compute. The computational models of case-based legal reasoning about legal concepts presented here define criteria for measuring case similarity and patterns of argument that are likely useful in retrieving cases to support human problem-solving and in highlighting how the cases have been used in the past. To some (still rather limited) extent, these criteria take into account underlying purposes and values in assessing similarity.

Fifth, the case-based models' usefulness for cognitive computing depends crucially on the extent to which their knowledge representation techniques can connect directly with case texts using techniques in Part II. In this respect, the models differ.

Aside from the importance of aligning positive and negative instances of a concept for substantiating a theory about what the concept means, the model of prototypes and deformations has not yielded tools for representing cases or computing similarities across a wider field of legal domains and cases. As illustrated in Taxman II, case-based arguments can be conceptually quite complex, but it is not currently possible to automatically identify features in cases that are only indirectly referenced or implied in their texts.

The techniques in Hypo, CATO, and CABARET are likely to be useful for cognitive computing. These include dimensions and Factors, Hypo's and CATO's techniques for comparing case similarity in terms of sets of legal factors shared with the problem and for generating arguments based on these similarity assessments. They also include CABARET's techniques for reasoning about legal rule concepts and CATO's techniques for predicting case outcomes (and IBP's, see Chapter 4).

Factors like CATO's *can* be identified automatically in texts with some success. See the IBP + SMILE program discussed in Chapter 10. As discussed in Chapter 9, progress has been made in extracting functional information associated with legal rules, which may help to automatically identify dimensions' prerequisites. Whether one can extract detailed functional information associated with a dimensional representation of a legal factor such as its focal slot value or magnitude in a case, however, is still an open question.

EBEs in GREBE would be very useful in assisting human problem-solvers in cognitive computing as would GREBE's indexing of cases as positive/negative examples of legal rule concepts. To be useful for cognitive computing, however, the explanations and facts, including criterial facts, would need to be extracted directly from texts.

GREBE's structure-mapping techniques and computational relevance measure have a limitation: they assume that facts are described similarly across cases. For example, going home to tell one's wife a message, getting ice water for a crew, or going to a restaurant for some food may all address a need that otherwise would negatively affect one's employment. If GREBE is to successfully map these facts and relations across cases, however, they must all be expressed in the program's (non-textual) case representation language in a way that is structurally and semantically compatible. If not, the structure-mapping from one case to another will not work.

This may not be a problem where one person who is sensitive to this constraint, for example, Branting, is representing a relatively small number of cases in one legal domain. Ensuring consistency of representation will be a major problem, however, where many case enterers are representing a large number of cases across a number of legal domains.

Branting employed some techniques to address the need for consistency of case representation. GREBE used a partial match improvement strategy to relax the structural mapping constraints so that criterial facts that are not identical but semantically similar can match (Branting, 1991, p. 818).

A subsequent program called SIROCCO records and reuses expert-drawn connections between abstract normative principles and narratives of case facts and events in the domain of professional engineering ethics. Its designer, Bruce McLaren, introduced an inexact match algorithm, a controlled vocabulary for representing cases and a web-based case entry tool with examples and a user's guide for helping to achieve consistency of the case representation. As a result, SIROCCO supported structure-mapping across a fairly wide range of engineering ethics cases (McLaren, 2003).

It is an empirical question, however, whether the new tools for IE can extract EBEs from text. Presumably, the need for structure-mapping across explanations in different cases' EBEs, and the premium it places on consistency of representation across cases, exacerbates the difficulties of extracting detailed, intricate explanations from legal case texts. As discussed in Chapter 10, it is feasible to extract argument-related information from case texts, including the roles played by sentences in judges' arguments about various statutory requirements. Such information is significantly more coarsely grained than the judges' detailed explanations of what facts are criterial for each statutory requirement. We return to this question in Chapter 12.

Extracting information about judges' discussions of the purposes and values underlying rules also presents challenges. To the extent that values are associated *a priori* with Factors and legal rules, the extracted Factors and rules would warrant a conclusion that the values apply. To the extent that judges reason about values underlying rules by posing hypotheticals, those might be extracted too. But it is likely to be very difficult for a program to extract and understand other aspects of what judges are saying when they consider underlying values unless the judges very explicitly explain what they mean.

4

Models for Predicting Legal Outcomes

4.1. INTRODUCTION

Using a database of cases represented as sets of features and outcomes, computer programs can predict the results of new problems. They do so usually by means of case-based reasoning (CBR) models or ML algorithms, sometimes combining the two. This chapter will explain and illustrate both.

The prediction techniques make use of different types of features represented in prior cases, ranging from names of judges deciding and law firms litigating cases of different types, to attitudinal information about judges, to historical trends in decisions, to stereotypical fact patterns that strengthen a claim or defense, that is, legal factors. Such features differ in the extent to which they capture information about the merits of a case. Judges' names, law firm names, and type of case, for instance, patent litigation or product liability, capture no information about the merits of a particular legal dispute. In contrast, legal factors, as we have seen in Chapter 3, capture quite a lot of information about the merits. Such features also differ in terms of the ease with which they can be extracted automatically from the texts of cases. Judicial and firm names are easy to extract; legal factors can be extracted but it is considerably harder to do so.

This book focuses on features that tend to capture some information about the merits of a case and that feasibly can be extracted automatically from case texts. This chapter explores alternative methods of using such features to predict case outcomes.

Machine learning techniques use feature frequency information statistically to "learn" the correspondence between case features and target outcomes. Case-based techniques are focused more on case comparison and explaining predictions. They make predictions based on the strengths of competing legal arguments. The techniques vary in the ways in which they can explain their predictions and in the extent to which their feature representations are compatible with cognitive computing.

Questions this chapter addresses include: How can computer programs learn to predict case outcomes? What is ML? What are supervised ML and decision trees? What are the advantages of random forests of decision trees? How does a CBR approach to prediction differ from ML? Will legal practitioners accept legal predictions without explanations? How can a program pose and test a prediction hypothesis? How can such prediction programs be evaluated empirically?

4.2. A NEAREST NEIGHBOR APPROACH TO AUTOMATED LEGAL PREDICTION

Predicting courts' decisions has long been a goal of AI & Law research.

As early as 1974, a computer program predicted the outcomes of tax cases involving a particular issue of capital gains tax (Mackaay and Robillard, 1974, p. 302). By that time there was already a considerable literature on legal prediction. The tax issue of interest was whether a gain was a capital gain or ordinary income under Canadian tax law, that is, was the gain "a mere enhancement of value by realizing a security, or . . . made in an operation of business in carrying out a scheme of profit making."

The predictions were based on 64 Canadian capital gains tax cases that had been represented in terms of 46 binary features (i.e., true or false). Each feature involved facts that commentators in prior studies had identified as relevant to decisions of that issue (Mackaay and Robillard, 1974). These features included, for example, that the "private party is a company," the "private party had never engaged in real estate transactions," "at the time of purchase, [the] private party had another intention than to resell at a profit," and "the present transaction is an isolated one" (Mackaay and Robillard, 1974, p. 327f).

The input to the program was a list of the feature values manually assigned to a new case. The program outputs a prediction based on the "nearest" existing cases in a two-dimensional representation of the new case in relation to the existing case (see Figure 4.1). (Actually, this was a projection down to two dimensions from a multidimensional vector space representation of the cases with one dimension per each of the 46 features. Vector space representations are introduced in Section 7.5.2.)

For the MacKaay program, the authors employed the k nearest neighbor or k-NN algorithm, which compares a problem with cases to base a prediction on those that are most similar. Basically, one measures the similarity or dissimilarity between the facts of the cases in terms of some metric. Then one predicts that a new case will have the same outcome as its closest neighbors. The metric, Hamming distance, sums the number of variables for which two cases have different values (see Mackaay and Robillard, 1974, p. 307). The authors used multidimensional scaling to project 60 of the cases onto two dimensions as shown in Figure 4.1. In the figure, the focus is on the relative positions of the points. The physical distance between any pair of points represents the dissimilarity between the corresponding cases.

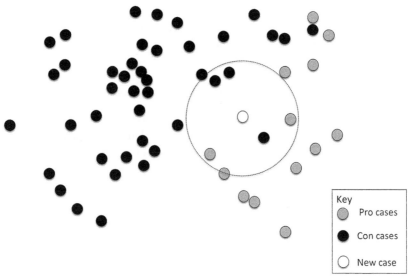

FIGURE 4.1. Projection of capital gains tax cases onto two dimensions (see Mackaay and Robillard, 1974)

The "new" case with unknown outcome (white circle) is located among its $k = 5$ nearest neighbors (dashed circle). The nearest neighbor algorithm predicts "con," the same outcome as three of the five nearest neighbors. Using such a projection for purposes of legal prediction is more equivocal. For instance, the new case is quite near a con case, but appears at the edge of a region of pro cases. One can easily imagine a counterargument that the nearby con case is an exception or a mistake and that the outcome of the new case should be "pro."

4.3. INTRODUCTION TO SUPERVISED MACHINE LEARNING

Another AI & Law approach to prediction, *ML*, employs algorithms that learn from data and use what they have learned to make predictions (see Kohavi and Provost, 1998; Bishop, 2006). They employ statistical means to induce a prediction model (or function) from a dataset that can be used to predict an outcome for a new case.

A kind of ML that has been applied to predict legal outcomes is *supervised* ML. Since it involves inferring a classification model (or function) from *labeled* training data, the ML is referred to as supervised (see Mohri et al., 2012).

The training data comprise a set of examples that have been assigned outcomes. Each example is a pair consisting of an input object (often a vector of feature values) and a desired output value. The learning algorithm needs to generalize from the training data to unseen situations.

The supervised learning algorithm analyzes the training data and infers a function or model, which ideally can be used to classify new, unseen instances. The model may, for example, be embodied in statistically computed feature weights or in a set of rules mechanically induced from the training data. Given a new instance, the model is applied to predict an outcome.

4.3.1. *Machine Learning Algorithms: Decision Trees*

A variety of algorithms have been developed for supervised learning, including decision trees, also known as classification trees (see Quinlan, 1986). For a given classifier and set of training data, a *decision tree* learns a set of questions for determining if a new instance is a positive instance of the classifier. Each question is a test: if the weight of a particular feature is less than a threshold value, branch one way, otherwise branch the other way.

The example in Figure 4.2 illustrates how to induce a tree for deciding whether to release a defendant on bail from a small set of instances of past bail decisions. The questions in this simple example are answered yes-or-no; no thresholds are employed. The rule is constructed using the C4.5 algorithm to build the decision tree (Quinlan, 2004). The algorithm chooses one attribute to divide the instances according to the outcome of the related question, such as "Involved drugs?" At C_0, the algorithm chooses drugs $=$ yes to split the instances into $\{2/n, 4/n, 5/n, 6/n\}$ at C_1 and $\{1/y, 3/y, 7/n\}$ at C_2. Since C_2 has instances with mixed results, it is split next; selecting weapon $=$ no, yields $\{1/y\}$ at C_3 and $\{3/y, 7/n\}$ at C_4. By selecting prior-record $=$ no, C_4 in turn is split into C_5 with $\{3/y\}$ and C_6 with $\{7/n\}$.

(a)

Case	Injury	Drugs	Weapon	Prior-record	Result
1	none	no	no	yes	yes
2	bad	yes	yes	serious	no
3	none	no	yes	no	yes
4	bad	yes	no	yes	no
5	slight	yes	yes	yes	no
6	none	yes	yes	serious	no
7	none	no	yes	yes	no

(b)

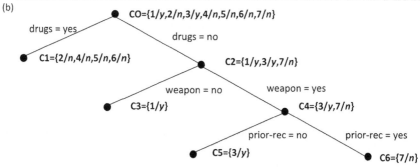

FIGURE 4.2. Bail decisions data (a) from which decision tree is constructed (b)

The algorithm stops when the C_i all have the same result or some other termination criterion such as a depth limit is met.

Decision trees make it relatively easy for humans to interpret what the C4.5 algorithm has learned. By following the root of the resulting decision tree to each leaf node, a set of rules for predicting bail decisions can be generated:

IF drugs = yes THEN bail = no

IF drugs = no AND weapon = no THEN bail = yes

IF drugs = no AND weapon = yes AND prior-record = no THEN bail = yes

IF drugs = no AND weapon = yes AND prior-record = yes THEN bail = no

Other ML models induce rules directly that humans can inspect and understand.

On the other hand, since an ML algorithm learns rules based on statistical regularities that may surprise humans, its rules may not necessarily seem reasonable to humans. ML predictions are data-driven. Sometimes the data contain features that, for spurious reasons such as coincidence or biased selection, happen to be associated with the outcomes of cases in a particular collection. Although the machine-induced rules may lead to accurate predictions, they do not refer to human expertise and may not be as intelligible to humans as an expert's manually constructed rules. Since the rules the ML algorithm infers do not necessarily reflect explicit legal knowledge or expertise, they may not correspond to a human expert's criteria of reasonableness.

One goal is for a decision tree algorithm to determine the most efficient sequences of questions for dividing the training instances into a set of positive instances and a set of negative instances. Information theoretic criteria enable the algorithm to choose the features for dividing up the instances most efficiently. C4.5 uses the criteria to minimize the expected number of questions to be asked by ordering the questions and, where the questions involve quantities, choosing the most discriminative thresholds for splitting the "yes" instances from the "no" instances.

4.4. PREDICTING SUPREME COURT OUTCOMES

Predicting the behavior of the Supreme Court of the United States has been especially prized, not only in AI & Law but also in political science research.

In Katz et al. (2014), the goal is to learn and construct a prediction function to evaluate a future case and predict its outcome, either to affirm or to reverse. The system uses vote predictions for individual justices to forecast overall Court decisions.

The inputs to the system are Supreme Court cases represented as lists of feature values, which are described later. The system outputs a binary classification: Will a justice/the whole Court affirm or reverse the lower court's judgment?

The approach is intended to mimic how a Supreme Court expert would make his/her own predictions or forecasts. The system's predictions are based on a matrix

Case Information
Admin Action [S]
Case Origin [S]
Case Origin Circuit [S]
Case Source [S]
Case Source Circuit [S]
Law Type [S]
Lower Court Disposition Direction [S]
Lower Court Disposition [S]
Lower Court Disagreement [S]
Issue [S]
Issue Area [S]
Jurisdiction Manner [S]
Month Argument [FE]
Month Decision [FE]
Petitioner [S]
Petitioner Binned [FE]
Respondent [S]
Respondent Binned [FE]
Cert Reason [S]

Justice and Court Background Information
Justice [S]
Justice Gender [FE]
Is Chief [FE]
Party President [FE]
Natural Court [S]
Segal Cover Score [SC]
Year of Birth [FE]

Trends
Overall Historic Supreme Court [FE]
Lower Court Trends [FE]
Current Supreme Court Trends [FE]
Individual Supreme Court Justice [FE]
Differences in Trends [FE]

FIGURE 4.3. Example features from Supreme Court database [S], the Segal–Cover Scores [SC], and feature engineering [FE] (Katz et al., 2014)

of observable prior data from "The Supreme Court Database" (Spaeth et al., 2013) and related sources. Each prediction is based on all previous decisions for that justice, the Court, and all previous cases.

4.4.1. *Features for Predicting Supreme Court Outcomes*

The Supreme Court Database records the features of cases, justices, and trends on which the predictions are based as summarized in Figure 4.3 (Spaeth et al., 2013). Case Information includes case source circuit, law type, lower court disagreement, issue area, and jurisdictional basis. Justice and Court Background Information consists of justice, justice gender, if the chief, and appointing president's party. Trends comprise current and overall historic Supreme Court trends, lower court trends, individual Supreme Court justice trends, and differences in trends. The authors in Katz et al. (2014) engineered some of the features from other information (marked FE).

4.4.2. *Applying Supervised Machine Learning to SCOTUS Data*

The researchers applied supervised ML methods to this feature data and, in particular, Random Forests of Decision Trees (RFDT), a more sophisticated version of the single decision tree approach illustrated in Figure 4.2 (Katz et al., 2014, pp. 3–4).

RFDT replaces a single decision tree with *ensembles* or *random forests of decision trees* in order to achieve greater diversity of sources in prediction. "Ensemble" methods generate a number of diverse trees and average across an entire forest. Random forests grow smaller trees and help to prevent the model from overfitting the data.

Overfitting occurs when an ML model has so many extra terms that it fits the random variations in data rather than real patterns (see NIST/SEMATECH, 2016). In effect, the model "memorizes" the particular training data rather than "learns" a generalization from it. Such a model will fail when making predictions about new data; it has not learned a generalized classifier from the training data that it can apply to new data.

Some ML models are especially prone to overfitting, including decision trees, which almost always overfit the data. Combining the smaller trees of a randomized forest of decision trees protects against overfitting better than a single complex tree.

Other techniques are applied to reduce the *variance* of predictive estimators. The variance is a measure of how spread out their predictions are from the mean. For example, in the nodes of extremely randomized trees (ERT) the positive and negative instances are split using a *random* subset of candidate features. Instead of selecting the most discriminative thresholds, thresholds are drawn at random for each candidate feature. The best of these thresholds is then picked as the splitting rule (Katz et al., 2014, p. 5).

In overview, the prediction method in Katz et al. (2014) works as follows: Given data up to the last case decided before the target case (the $n - 1$st case), the method applies the latest instantiation of the ERT ensemble. That is, for each justice, it passes the justice, case, and overall court level features for the current case through the set of tests in the latest set of ERT, and outputs a prediction for each justice. Then, the algorithm combines the set of justice level forecasts into a case level prediction using the majority rule.

4.4.3. *Evaluating the Machine Learning Method*

Machine learning programs are empirically evaluated to assess how well they can predict outcomes of new instances. A standard procedure for evaluating a ML program is a *k-fold cross validation* (Kohavi, 1995). The data is divided into k subsets or "folds." In each of k rounds, a different one of the k subsets is reserved as the test set. The ML model is trained using the $k - 1$ subsets as the training set. The results are averaged over the k rounds yielding a measure of the accuracy of the predictions. (Katz et al., 2014) employed 10-fold cross validation.

In k-fold cross validation, the training and test sets are disjoint, and each element in the data set is used exactly once as a test instance. The setup ensures that when an element is used as a test instance, the classifier has been retrained with a training set from which that element has been excluded.

4.4.4. Machine Learning Evaluation Measures and Results

The predictive performance of ML algorithms is often measured in terms of precision, recall, the F1-score, and accuracy. Each of these measures can be defined in terms of the concepts of true or false negative and positive instances:

True Negatives (TN): total number of negative cases that were predicted negative

True Positives (TP): total number of positive cases that were predicted positive

False Negatives (FN): total number of positive cases that were predicted negative

False Positives (FP): total number of negative cases that were predicted positive

Given the concepts of true or false negatives and positives, the primary ML evaluation measures are defined as follows:

Accuracy (A): the ratio of correct case predictions over all case predictions. $(TN + TP)/(TN + TP + FN + FP)$

Precision (P): the ratio of the number of positive case predictions that are correct over the total number of positive case predictions. $(TP)/(TP + FP)$

Recall (R): the ratio of positive case predictions that are correct over the number of cases that were positive. $(TP)/(TP + FN)$

F1-score or F1-measure: the harmonic mean of precision and recall where both measures are treated as equally important. $2 * (P * R)/(P + R)$

In their evaluation, the ML models of Katz et al. (2014, p. 10) accurately predicted 69.7% of the case outcomes and 70.9% of the individual Justice outcomes over a 60-year period. By comparison, in a contest, human legal experts accurately predicted 59% of the case outcomes and 67.9% of the Justices' votes (Katz et al., 2014, p. 4). While the model's performance level is not dramatically better than that achieved in prior research by other ML models, the Katz–Bommarito model makes accurate predictions for all of the nine Justices for any year in the time period and avoids overfitting the data.

Interestingly, the most predictive features (72% of the predictive power) comprised behavioral trends, including the voting behavior of various justices, and differences in these behavioral trends, in particular, general and issue-specific differences between individual justices and the balance of the Court and ideological differences between the Supreme Court and lower courts. Less influential predictive features included individual case features (23% of predictive power) and justice and court level background information (4.4%) (Katz et al., 2014, p. 13).

4.5. PREDICTING OUTCOMES WITH CASE-BASED ARGUMENTS

The nearest neighbor approach applied in the capital gains tax predictor is a kind of CBR; it compares cases in terms of a distance measure but does not generate explanations or consider domain arguments. In an alternative CBR approach to predicting outcomes of legal cases, comparing a current case to past cases suggests a hypothesis for predicting the same outcome as that of the most similar cases, where the prediction can be explained and justified with domain arguments and tested in light of the explanations.

4.5.1. *Prediction with CATO*

Vincent Aleven introduced argument-based prediction as a way of evaluating his CATO program (see Section 3.3.2). "How well a program predicts the outcome of cases, based on its arguments or judgments of case relevance . . . would inspire confidence that the arguments made by the program are good arguments that have some relation to the reality of legal reasoning" (Aleven, 2003, p. 212).

The program applied a simple algorithm for predicting an outcome:

1. Given a problem, retrieve cases according to a given *relevance* criterion.
2. If there are relevant cases, and all had the same outcome, predict that side will win; otherwise abstain.

CATO applied several different types of relevance criteria. Its factor hierarchy and arguments emphasizing or downplaying distinctions provided new criteria for selecting the best cases on which to base predictions (Aleven, 2003, pp. 201, 203, 208). Aleven compared seven criteria including a Hypo-type baseline (BUC) that bases the prediction on the best untrumped cases. These are the most-on-point citable cases with no trumping counterexamples. Three criteria made predictions based on certain citable or best untrumped cases that have *no distinctions* from the current case. The final three criteria made predictions based on such cases that have no *significant* distinctions from the current case.

In other words, all of these predictive criteria involved different variations of the Hypo/CATO models of case-based arguments. The latter three criteria differ from the former in that they employed knowledge represented in the CATO factor hierarchy to determine if the distinctions are significant, that is, not subject to downplaying.

In an evaluation with a database of 184 trade secrets cases, the best-performing predictive method was the one called NoSignDist/BUC: It made predictions based on citable cases, without *significant* distinctions, that are most on point and untrumped by citable cases with no significant distinctions (Aleven, 2003, p. 214). It abstained on 11% of the cases and for the remaining cases, its predictions were 88% accurate. Its use of the knowledge represented in the factor hierarchy to identify significant distinctions led to an improvement over the Hypo-type BUC baseline that was statistically significant (Aleven, 2003, p. 150). We return briefly to the evaluation of these two prediction methods below.

4.5.2. *Issue-based Prediction*

The Issue-based Prediction (IBP) program applied a hypothesis-testing algorithm that managed to improve upon CATO's prediction results while using the same

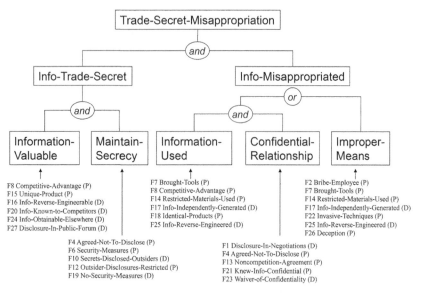

FIGURE 4.4. IBP domain model (Ashley and Brüninghaus, 2006)

Factor representation of trade secret law (Ashley and Brüninghaus, 2006). Instead of CATO's factor hierarchy, IBP employed a different domain model of why legal factors matter: a graph of trade secret law issues that semantically interconnected factors.

IBP's domain model, shown in Figure 4.4, identifies logical requirements of a claim for trade secret misappropriation (Trade-Secret-Misappropriation) in terms of the conjunction of two higher-level issues (Info-Trade-Secret and Info-Misappropriated). Each of these in turn involves sub-issues in leaf nodes, two for Info-Trade-Secret (Information-Valuable and Maintain-Secrecy) and three for Info-Misappropriated: either Info-Used and Confidential-Relationship or Improper-Means.

The IBP model is based on, and is an interpretation of, the rules laid out in the Restatement (First) of Torts, section 757 and the Uniform Trade Secrets Act, which state in part:

"Trade secret" means information . . . that:
(i) derives independent economic value . . . from not being generally known to, and not being readily ascertainable by proper means . . . and
(ii) is the subject of efforts that are reasonable under the circumstances to maintain its secrecy.

One who discloses or uses another's trade secret, without a privilege to do so, is liable to the other if
(a) he discovered the secret by improper means, or
(b) his disclosure or use constitutes a breach of confidence.

Input: Current fact situation (*cfs*)

A. Identify issues raised by *cfs* Factors
B. For each issue raised, determine the side favored for that issue:
    1. if all issue-related Factors favor the same side, then return that side,
    2. else retrieve issue-related cases in which all issue-related Factors apply
        a. if there are issue-related cases, then carry out Theory-Testing: form hypothesis that same
           side *s* will win that won majority of cases
           i. if all issue-related cases favor side *s*, then return side *s*,
           ii. else try to explain away exceptions with outcomes contrary to hypothesis
               (a) if all exceptions can be explained away, then return side *s* favored by
                  hypothesis
               (b) else, return "abstain"
        b. if no issue-related cases are found, then call Broaden-Query
           i. if query can be broadened, then call Theory-Testing for each set of retrieved cases
           ii. else return "abstain"
C. Combine prediction for each issue

Output: Predicted outcome for *cfs* and explanation

FIGURE 4.5. IBP algorithm (Ashley and Brüninghaus, 2009)

Each leaf-node sub-issue is an intermediate legal concept, an open-textured legal term. In the IBP model, each of these sub-issues is related to a set of legal factors that are semantically related to that issue and that may favor the trade-secret-claimant, plaintiff (P), or the defendant (D). As in CATO (and Hypo), these factors index cases in the database that are examples of the factors' application.

4.5.3. *IBP's Prediction Algorithm*

The input to IBP is a cfs represented as a set of CATO Factors that apply to the cfs facts. IBP's algorithm proceeds as shown in Figure 4.5. IBP identifies the issues that apply in the *cfs* based on the input Factors and the associated issues in the domain model. For each applicable issue, it determines the favored party (plaintiff trade secret claimant or defendant). If all of the issue-related Factors favor the same side, it returns that side as its prediction for that issue. Otherwise, it attempts to retrieve cases in the database indexed by all of the Factors related to that issue. If it finds such cases, it determines which side the majority of cases favors, poses the hypothesis that the majority side should win, and attempts to "explain away" any of the counterexamples. If it succeeds in explaining away the counterexamples, it predicts the majority side should win that issue. Otherwise, it abstains. If it cannot find cases indexed by all the cfs issue-related Factors, it relaxes the query incrementally by deleting Factors from the requirements and, thus, may attempt to test a more general hypothesis.

In "explaining away" counterexamples, IBP seeks to distinguish a counterexample from the cfs and find an alternative Factor-based explanation of the result in the counterexample. IBP's attempt to explain away a counterexample will fail if

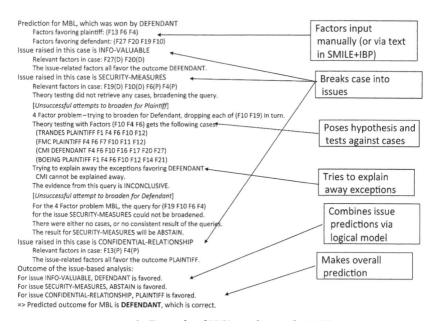

Prediction for MBL, which was won by DEFENDANT
  Factors favoring plaintiff: (F13 F6 F4)
  Factors favoring defendant: (F27 F20 F19 F10)
Issue raised in this case is INFO-VALUABLE
  Relevant factors in case: F27(D) F20(D)
  The issue-related factors all favor the outcome DEFENDANT.
Issue raised in this case is SECURITY-MEASURES
  Relevant factors in case: F19(D) F10(D) F6(P) F4(P)
  Theory testing did not retrieve any cases, broadening the query.
  [Unsuccessful attempts to broaden for Plaintiff]
  4 Factor problem—trying to broaden for Defendant, dropping each of (F10 F19) in turn.
  Theory testing with Factors (F10 F4 F6) gets the following cases
    (TRANDES PLAINTIFF F1 F4 F6 F10 F12)
    (FMC PLAINTIFF F4 F6 F7 F10 F11 F12)
    (CMI DEFENDANT F4 F6 F10 F16 F17 F20 F27)
    (BOEING PLAINTIFF F1 F4 F6 F10 F12 F14 F21)
  Trying to explain away the exceptions favoring DEFENDANT
    CMI cannot be explained away.
  The evidence from this query is INCONCLUSIVE.
  [Unsuccessful attempt to broaden for Defendant]
  For the 4 Factor problem MBL, the query for (F19 F10 F6 F4)
  for the issue SECURITY-MEASURES could not be broadened.
  There were either no cases, or no consistent result of the queries.
  The result for SECURITY-MEASURES will be ABSTAIN.
Issue raised in this case is CONFIDENTIAL-RELATIONSHIP
  Relevant factors in case: F13(P) F4(P)
  The issue-related factors all favor the outcome PLAINTIFF.
Outcome of the issue-based analysis:
For issue INFO-VALUABLE, DEFENDANT is favored.
For issue SECURITY-MEASURES, ABSTAIN is favored.
For issue CONFIDENTIAL-RELATIONSHIP, PLAINTIFF is favored.
=> Predicted outcome for MBL is **DEFENDANT**, which is correct.

Factors input manually (or via text in SMILE+IBP)

Breaks case into issues

Poses hypothesis and tests against cases

Tries to explain away exceptions

Combines issue predictions via logical model

Makes overall prediction

FIGURE 4.6. Example of IBP's prediction for MBL case

the counterexample and cfs share any "knockout Factors" (KO-Factors) favoring the result in the counterexample.

The definition of KO-Factor includes a semantic component and a statistical weight. A KO-Factor is defined as a Factor representing behavior paradigmatically proscribed or encouraged under trade secret law and for which the probability that a side wins when the Factor applies is at least 80% greater than the baseline probability of the side's winning. This probability is calculated as the ratio of the number of cases in the collection where the Factor applies and the side won divided by the number of cases in the collection where the Factor applies. The baseline probability is calculated as the number of cases where the side won divided by the number of cases in the collection. IBP's list of KO-Factors included: F8 Competitive-Advantage (P) (defendant saved development time and money by using plaintiff's information), F17 Info-Independently-Generated (D), F19 No-Security-Measures (D), F20 Info-Known-to-Competitors (D), F26 Deception (P), F27 Disclosure-In-Public-Forum (D) (Ashley and Brüninghaus, 2009).

Figure 4.6 illustrates IBP's analysis, prediction, and explanation for a real case, MBL (USA) *Corp. v. Diekman*, 112 Ill.App.3d 229, 445 N.E.2d 418 (1983). The case is input to IBP as a list of Factors. IBP breaks the case into (here three) issues based on the association of Factors and issues in the domain model, poses a prediction hypothesis, and tests it against the cases in the database that deal with that issue. Here, the initial attempts to retrieve cases with all the issue-related Factors of the Security-Measures issue failed, so the program broadened the query by dropping some Factors

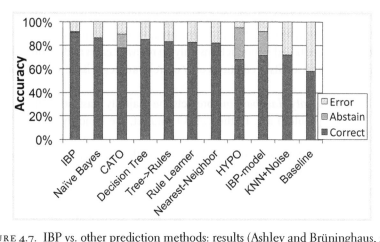

FIGURE 4.7. IBP vs. other prediction methods: results (Ashley and Brüninghaus, 2009)

until it returned some cases. On the basis of these, it posed the hypothesis that the plaintiff should win as in three of the four cases. In testing the hypothesis, it then tried to explain away the pro-defendant counterexample (the *CMI* case) but failed and had to abstain on that issue. Based on the domain model, however, the pro-defendant prediction on Info-Valuable and, thus, on the existence of a trade secret (Info-Trade-Secret) leads it to predict the defendant will win overall, which was correct.

4.5.4. *Evaluating IBP's Predictions*

IBP was evaluated in a leave-one-out (LOO) cross-validation experiment with a database of 186 trade secret decisions (including 148 cases from the CATO database). The researchers compared IBP's predictions with a variety of other algorithms, including two based on CATO, two nearest neighbor approaches, three general purpose ML models/algorithms, two versions of IBP, and a baseline.

The two CATO prediction methods were the same as in the CATO evaluation (Section 4.5.1), namely NoSignDist/BUC and the BUC baseline. (For convenience, Figure 4.7 refers to these as *CATO* and *HYPO*, respectively.) These two prediction approaches employ case-based argument-related information, legal factors, and the significance of distinctions based on the factor hierarchy.

The two nearest neighbor approaches, *Nearest Neighbor* and *KNN+Noise*, are alternative case-based algorithms that do *not* employ case-based argument-related information (see Section 4.2).

The three general purpose ML models/algorithms included *Decision Tree* (see Section 4.3.1), *Naïve Bayes* (explained in Section 10.3.3), and two supervised ML programs (*Tree→Rules* and *Rule Learner*) that induced rules from the training set of cases (see Section 4.3).

The two versions of IBP were included in order to determine the effect of "turning off" or *ablating* the IBP model's two different knowledge sources: legal issues and cases. *IBP-No-Issues* based its predictions only on relevant cases and ignored the legal issues. *IBP-Model* based its predictions only on relevant legal issues and ignored the cases.

Finally, the *majority-class baseline* predicts the majority class no matter what the facts of the new problem are. In the CATO data set, the majority of cases favored the plaintiff.

Figure 4.7 illustrates the results. IBP did best with an accuracy of 91.8%.[1] IBP's hypothesis-testing approach to prediction outperformed that of the case-based argument and nearest neighbor approaches. It also outperformed the general purpose ML models/algorithms and the baseline.

With respect to the ablation studies, using knowledge about issues to focus hypothesis-testing with precedents on the issue-related conflicts led to better prediction (*IBP* vs. *IBP-No-Issues*). Knowledge about issues, however, did not by itself lead to a strong predictive model; its role in guiding hypothesis-testing with precedents is important (*IBP* vs. *IBP-Model*). Comparing cases by using knowledge about issues, as implicit in the CATO factor hierarchy's reasons why a legal factor matters, led to better prediction (*CATO* vs. *HYPO*). Finally, using knowledge about issues to focus hypothesis-testing with precedents on the issue-related conflicts rather than to improve case comparison led to better prediction (*IBP* vs. *CATO*).

Beside achieving accurate predictions, another important aspect of prediction in the legal domain is an ability to provide a meaningful explanation of the prediction.

> [T]here is value in the explanations that lawyers give to their clients about why they are proposing the course of action they are proposing, just as there is value in judges explaining the results they reach ... [Clients and litigants] will lose this opportunity if all they are given is a computerized prediction. (Remus and Levy, 2015, p. 64)

Unlike most of the ML approaches and the nearest neighbor algorithms, IBP generates an explanation of its prediction that is intelligible to legal professionals (see Figure 4.6). Explaining a prediction in terms of testing a hypothesis is intuitively accessible to attorneys. In contrast, explaining a prediction in terms of machine-induced rules that often do not take expert legal knowledge into account or in terms of statistically induced feature weights is probably much harder for legal professionals to understand. "Like Big Data applications generally, most [prediction] programs give a user results without showing the precise combination of factors that produced those results" (Remus and Levy, 2015, p. 62).

---

[1] A recent experiment compared IBP's predictions on the subset of cases with competing Factors with those of the Value Judgment-based Argumentation Prediction (VJAP) program, whose argument model accounts for trade-offs in decisions' effects on values (see Section 5.7).

Values:
    CA: explicit confidentiality agreements should be made and enforced
    RE: a person with a secret should take reasonable efforts to protect it
    LM: a person should be allowed to develop a product using legitimate means
    QM: a person should not use morally (or legally) dubious means to obtain a secret
    MW: litigation should only take place if the secret was of some material worth

Theory Value Preferences :
    value_prefer({CA, MW}, {LM, RE})
    value_prefer({CA, QM, RE}, {LM})
    value_prefer({LM}, {RE})
    ...

Theory Rule Preferences :
    prefer(
        <{F4 *Agreed-Not-To-Disclose* (P), F18, F21 *Knew-info-confidential* (P)}, P>,
        <{F1, F16 *Info-reverse-engineerable* (D)}, D>)
        from MineralDepositsTwo

    prefer(
        <{F16 *Info-reverse-engineerable* (D)}, D>,
        <{F6 *Security-measures* (P)}, P>)
        from CMI

    prefer(
        <{F6 *Security-measures* (P), F12, F14 *Restricted-materials-used* (P), F21 *Knew-info-confidential* (P)}, P>,
        <F16 *Info-reverse-engineerable* (D) , D>)
        from Technicon
    ...

FIGURE 4.8. Excerpts from a theory learned by AGATHA with *Mason* case as cfs (Chorley and Bench-Capon, 2005a)

4.6. PREDICTION WITH UNDERLYING VALUES

Bench-Capon and his students have implemented prediction based on theories constructed with past cases whose facts are represented with expert-supplied legal factors associated with underlying values.

The AGATHA program automates the process of constructing theories from cases as described in Bench-Capon and Sartor (2003). As discussed in Section 3.5.1, these theories are induced from precedents and reflect preference rules among conflicting values and among conflicting factors. A search algorithm applies theory construction moves to branch open a tree representing a theory. The moves include countering with a contrary case, distinguishing, and analogizing.

Figure 4.8 shows excerpts of a theory that AGATHA constructed in analyzing the *Mason* case (see Section 3.3.2). At the top are the values (and their abbreviations) that, the authors posited, underlie the domain of trade secret regulation. These include values that explicit confidentiality agreements should be made and enforced (CA) and that a person should be allowed to develop a product using legitimate means (LM). AGATHA learned the value preferences shown in the middle of the figure. According to the two first value preferences, CA is preferred to LM;

the third indicates that LM is preferred over RE, a value that a person with a secret should take reasonable efforts to protect. In other words, "a confidentiality restriction is a strong point for the plaintiff [especially] when supported by some other factor." In addition, "development through legitimate means, especially when coupled with laxity on the part of the plaintiff, favours the defendant" (Chorley and Bench-Capon, 2005a, p. 53).

As suggested in Figure 3.14, these value preferences are revealed by various rule preferences that AGATHA induces from the cases. Three of the rule preferences are shown at the bottom of the figure. Each rule preference shows a set of legal factors for one side that are preferred over a set of factors for the opposing side and the precedent on which the rule preference is based. The rule preferences based on the *Mineral Deposits Two* and *Technicon* cases support the preference of CA over LM. Factors F4 Agreed-Not-To-Disclose (P), F21 Knew-info-confidential (P), and F14 Restricted-materials-used (P) are associated with the value CA, Factor F16 Info-reverse-engineerable (D) supports LM, and Factor F6 Security-measures (P) supports RE.

In Section 3.5.1, it was noted that the Bench-Capon–Sartor approach generates multiple theories. AGATHA addresses that problem to a substantial extent in an ingenious way. It uses a heuristic search algorithm to construct the best theories. The algorithm applies theory construction moves to branch open trees representing the theories. It assesses the theories in terms of their simplicity, explanatory power, depth of tree representing the theory, and degree of completion. It can then select the best trees according to these assessments.

Chorley and Bench-Capon (2005a) have operationalized these theory evaluation criteria in quantitative terms. Simplicity is measured in terms of the number of preference rules in the theory. Explanatory power is assessed by applying the theory to cases and scoring its performance in terms of the number of cases it predicts correctly, incorrectly, or for which it abstains. Explanatory power is assessed twice, once using only the factors in the theory and again with all factors. The depth of tree is the number of levels in the tree representing the theory. Finally, completeness is assessed in terms of whether there are additional theory construction moves that could be performed.

For each theory, these measures are combined into an evaluation number, which gives "a value with which to compare the theories based on how well they explain the background, [and] their structure ... They can be used to ... guide a heuristic search" (Chorley and Bench-Capon, 2005a, p. 48).

AGATHA uses the A* heuristic search algorithm to construct the best theories. Recall that GREBE also employed A* search for constructing mappings to the most analogous cases (Section 3.3.3). For $f(n)$, the estimate of the cost to reach the goal from the current node value for each theory, AGATHA made a calculation based on the theory's evaluation number. For $g(n)$, the actual cost of reaching the current node from the initial state, it employed the cost of making the next move.[2] For making this calculation, each of the theory construction moves had an associated cost reflecting its desirability. The authors ranked the moves from low to high cost as follows: counter with case, distinguish with case, distinguish problem, distinguish with arbitrary preference, analogize case (Chorley and Bench-Capon, 2005a, p. 48).

Using the theories, AGATHA generated predictions comparable in accuracy to IBP's for a subset of the CATO case base (Chorley and Bench-Capon, 2005a,b,c). Moreover, it can explain the predictions in light of the best theory that it induced from precedents taking value preferences into account.

On the other hand, although AGATHA makes use of value preferences, it is not clear that the explanations it generates with the induced rules would make sense to attorneys. The program cites precedents for preference rules, but it is not clear whether it explains its predictions in terms of arguments analogizing the facts and trade-offs contained in the precedents to the circumstances of the cfs. Nor did the program use ILCs in legal rules in a manner consistent with legal practice. The constructed theories do not refer to issues drawn from relevant statutory texts or legal rules, such as the Uniform Trade Secret Act or the Restatement (First) of Torts, section 757, the provisions of which IBP's Domain Model is an interpretation.

Finally, it is not clear if AGATHA uses values in the same way that attorneys do. See the critique in Section 3.5.1 and an alternative approach in Section 5.7 to incorporating arguments and values in predicting outcomes.

4.7. PREDICTION BASED ON LITIGATION PARTICIPANTS AND BEHAVIOR

The IBP and AGATHA approaches focus on features associated directly with the merits of a case: the legal factors that are most influential in determining the outcome of cases. In contrast, the SCOTUS prediction work described earlier focuses on features not directly associated with a claim's merits, namely issue areas, identities of justices, and historical trends.

Researchers at Lex Machina and Stanford University have adopted and extended the latter approach (Surdeanu et al., 2011). They developed techniques for predicting outcomes of patent claims based on a corpus of all intellectual property (IP) lawsuits in an eight-year period. Two IP experts annotated the cases as to their outcomes and an IP attorney reviewed the outcomes and determined the final annotations. They focused on patent infringement cases that had not been settled, that is, a court had decided either in favor of the patent owner or the alleged infringer.

Like the SCOTUS project, the researchers treated prediction as a binary classification task for a statistical learning model. Past cases were represented in terms of

---

[2] Since, in this theory construction application, it does not matter how many moves are required to produce the theory, the cost of the history of moves to reach the current node was not included in $g(n)$ as would usually be the case in A* search (Chorley and Bench-Capon, 2005a, p. 48).

"the past behavior of all the litigation entities involved in a case," including parties in the lawsuit, their attorneys and law firms, the judges assigned to the case, and the districts where the complaints were filed. For each of these participants, the behavior was modeled with four types of features:

- a unique identifier,
- past win rates of the (non-judicial or district) participant,
- judge and district bias, and
- counts of participation in past cases in any role.

Since the ways in which any given participant is identified in past cases may vary, such as different formulations of a law firm's name, the researchers developed an entity resolution component. It clusters the alternative formulations or mentions of participants' names in the texts of the various cases and resolves each cluster into a unique identifier. The win rates are the percentage of past cases won by the side of the corresponding participant. Bias is computed as the percentage of cases assigned to the judge or district that a plaintiff won. Participation counts are the number of cases in which the entity was a participant.

To generate predictions based on these features, the researchers employed statistical relational learning models (logistic regression, explained in Chapter 10, and conditional random fields, an advanced technique designed to take account of concurrent cases that share information such as the same corporate plaintiff). Their best model accurately predicted the outcomes of 64% of the cases and performed substantially better than the majority-class baseline (Surdeanu et al., 2011).

Interestingly, the model achieved this level of accuracy in predicting the outcomes of patent infringement cases even though it does not directly take into account any features concerning the legal merits of a case. For example, none of the features represents "the strength of the patents asserted" or "the similarity of the defendant's manufacturing technology to the patent's technology" (Surdeanu et al., 2011).

In *post-hoc* ablation experiments, the researchers determined that the identity of the judge and of the plaintiff's law firm made the most significant contributions to predictive accuracy, followed by significant contributions from defendant's identity, district, defendant's law firm, and defendant's attorney (in decreasing order of magnitude).

In other words, the litigation participant-and-behavior features appear to capture some aspects of the merits of a case indirectly. This is especially significant in that these features can fairly easily be extracted automatically from the cases in the corpus.

Nevertheless, text analytics are making it feasible to extract and employ features that do capture aspects of a case's merits. Employing features such as legal factors could both improve predictive performance and enable a program to explain its predictions in ways that legal professionals can understand. Moreover, employing merits-based features may act as a sanity check on predictions based on behavioral features and vice versa; a prediction that is strong in terms of one sort of features but weak on the other suggests the need for human investigation, a good example of cognitive computing.

4.8. PREDICTION IN COGNITIVE COMPUTING

Prediction is an important task in the legal field and is likely to be a focus in developing CCLAs.

As illustrated in the above examples, predictive algorithms depend on features, and the types of features vary widely across prediction approaches.

It is worth noting that, to the extent ML and case-based argumentation have been applied to the task of legal prediction, these computational methods have not *discovered* the features that influence outcomes but instead have learned the weights of such features. This is true in the Supreme Court prediction work in Katz et al. (2014), the CATO, IBP, and AGATHA programs, and the litigation participant-and-behavior approach of Surdeanu et al. (2011).

In most of the prediction programs, human legal experts have specified the features that are likely to influence prediction. Legal expert commentators identified various features in the capital gains tax program that relate to the merits of the tax issue. Similarly, a knowledgeable attorney determined the legal factors employed in CATO, IBP, and AGATHA. The task of discovering such legally significant features has not been successfully automated or, at least, has not been reported or published.

It is still possible, however, for programs automatically to annotate in case texts instances of previously discovered features. Indeed, this is a key question about the role of legal prediction in cognitive computing: to what extent can the features that predictive models employ be identified automatically in the case texts?

For some of the prediction programs, deciding whether a feature is present is a fairly direct inference from the textual assertions reported in the case opinion. This is not true for most of the features employed in the Supreme Court prediction work. Katz et al. (2014) employ features concerning the type of case, judicial attitudes, and knowledge-engineered information about historical trends in cases. These features neither represent detailed information about the facts of a case nor are they extracted directly from the text of the decision.

For other prediction methods, however, known features can be detected in case texts. For instance, the input list of legal factors in Figure 4.6 was actually based on the automated analysis of a brief textual description of the facts of the *MBL* case. A program called SMILE identified the factors in the text automatically and passed them along to IBP. SMILE learned to identify factors in the texts of such factual summaries (albeit not perfectly). The workings of the SMILE part of SMILE+IBP are explained in Section 10.4. The litigation participant-and-behavior approach of Lex Machina employs features that also can be extracted from the text of the cases, such as participation frequency and win rates of judges, parties, and attorneys, but those features do not directly address the merits of legal claims (Surdeanu et al., 2011).

Automatically annotating case texts with features that reflect a case's legal merits, along with other argument-related information, makes it feasible to apply computational models of prediction and argumentation directly to legal texts. One could retrieve case decisions from a legal information retrieval system, process their texts automatically to identify argument-related features as well as participant-and-behavior features, and use the information to rank the cases more efficiently, to make predictions more advisedly, and to enable a computer program to assist humans in legal problem-solving. This will be developed at length in Parts II and III of this book, but first we examine a final class of computational models of legal argument that combine making predictions and arguments in new ways and that take into account the effects on values of proposed decisions.

5

Computational Models of Legal Argument

5.1. INTRODUCTION

In the last decades, much of the AI & Law research community has focused on developing comprehensive computational models of legal argumentation (CMLAs). Researchers have now integrated into these CMLAs a number of the computational models of legal reasoning presented in the preceding chapters.

An argument model consists of a representation of the elements of an argument and a specification of its semantics. Argument elements include the argument itself and, possibly, statements or propositions in the argument, as well as their interrelations, for example as constituents of argument graphs. The argument semantics are specified through some well-defined process by which the status of the argument elements can be determined, for example, by inspection of the graph.

Researchers in AI have produced a variety of argument models that differ widely in the aspects of arguments they represent and in the way they specify the status of an argument.

For example, abstract argument systems, including the pioneering Dungean models, abstract away much of the structure of argumentation, simply representing arguments and attack relations between them (Dung, 1995). They specify criteria for determining the status of an argument, that is, whether an argument is acceptable, in terms of the absence of attacking arguments that are not themselves attacked. One can extend Dungean models to account for more complex argument phenomena. For instance, a widely used computational model of argument, ASPIC+, represents premises and conclusions and takes into account support as well as attack relations (Modgil and Prakken, 2014). The Value-based Argumentation Framework (VAF) (Section 5.4) also demonstrates building more complex argument phenomena, arguing about underlying values, and extending Dungean models.

Other argument models are designed to preserve structural aspects of arguments that may make them more intuitively accessible to practitioners. For example, Verheij (2009) has developed models of legal argument that employ the familiar Toulmin argument structures relating claims and evidence via warrants and backing. The Carneades model, discussed in Section 5.2, also preserves an intuitively accessible structure clearly distinguishing propositions and arguments that support a conclusion from those that attack it.

This chapter does not aim to provide a comprehensive account of the alternative argument models and their respective advantages and disadvantages in terms of such considerations as expressivity and computational efficiency. For a readable survey, see Rahwan et al. (2009).

Instead, the chapter focuses on a selection of argument models that have been applied to legal argumentation and that have been illustrated with intuitively accessible extended examples. As mentioned, the Carneades model introduced in Section 5.2 and the extended example of Carneades in action in Section 5.3 illustrate how a computational model of argument can support arguing both for a proposition and its opposite as well as how to integrate arguing with legal rules and by analogy to past cases. The VAF in Section 5.4 illustrates how to add underlying values into the argument model. An alternative model, the VJAP model (Section 5.7) takes into account the effects of proposed decisions on trade-offs among values and employs its arguments to predict outcomes. Finally, the default logic framework (DLF) of Section 5.8 models legal evidentiary arguments. Along the way the chapter addresses such issues as how some argument models compute winners and losers, the role of proof standards in certain models, and prospects for integrating probabilistic reasoning.

The chapter also answers the following questions. What is a space of legal arguments, and how does a program search it? How do computational models or frameworks of legal argument employ legal argument schemes? How does a program determine an argument's acceptability or evaluate an argument's strength? What role does logical deduction play in arguing from legal rules and facts, and what is a defeasible logic? Are computational models of legal proof standards realistic?

5.1.1. *Advantages of CMLAs*

As we have seen in Chapter 2, legal reasoning involves supporting arguments for a proposition and for its opposite even where both sides argue from the same legal rules and facts. A computer program can reason deductively with rules of law; applying classical logical deduction, it can draw conclusions by applying rules of inference like *modus ponens*. Classical logical deduction, however, cannot support arguing both for a proposition and its opposite. This makes it an inadequate tool for modeling legal argument.

Attempts to model legal reasoning must also address two other major design constraints, both of which were identified in Chapter 2:

1. Legal reasoning is *non-monotonic*; the inferences change once information is added or becomes invalid. As new evidence or authoritative sources are added, previously reasonable inferences need to be abandoned.
2. Legal reasoning is also *defeasible*. Legal claims need not be "true"; they only need to satisfy a given proof standard. The conclusion of a defeasible rule is only presumably true, even when the rule's conditions are satisfied. Arguments supporting and attacking the conclusion may contradict and defeat each other.

Computational models of legal argument address these design constraints. Some CMLAs can support arguing for a proposition and for its opposite even where both sides argue from the same legal rules and facts. Unlike classical logic, CMLAs do not employ strict inferences but instead use supporting or attacking arguments. The CMLA's argument semantics which may include acceptability criteria, proof standards, and argument schemes, defined below, enable it to resolve conflicting arguments and support inference. Together, these supply the "semantics" of an argument.

5.2. THE CARNEADES ARGUMENT MODEL

As noted, Carneades is just one of a number of models suitable for legal argument such as ASPIC+ (Modgil and Prakken, 2014), other models that extend Dungean models, or abstract dialectical frameworks (Brewka and Gordon, 2010). Indeed, although Carneades and these models use different representations and concepts they are functionally isomorphic. Nevertheless, Carneades can be illustrated in legally intuitive terms and supports "out of the box" enough concepts useful for modeling legal argumentation (such as proof standards and argument schemes) that it is worth introducing first.

Carneades computationally models the process of putting forth arguments about the acceptability of propositions. A proposition is *acceptable* if it is presumably true given the arguments up to that stage and a set of assumptions (see Gordon and Walton, 2009).

The Carneades model comprises an argumentation framework, criteria for the acceptability of arguments, proof standards, and argument schemes (Prakken, 1995; Gordon and Walton, 2006).

An *argumentation framework* defines the concept of an argument as a structure comprising a premise, a conclusion, and exceptions. The framework also specifies the aspects of argumentation that are represented and the senses in which arguments conflict for purposes of the model.

For each stage of the argumentation process, the argumentation framework defines a decision procedure to test if the proposition or argument at issue is acceptable given the acceptability criteria. The criteria provide some basis for resolving a conflict, such as preference relationships for ordering the arguments by importance. The procedure enables deciding the status of an argument, such as whether an argument has "won," "lost," or left the dispute undecided (Prakken, 1995). This determination may depend on the proof standard applicable to the issue. A *proof standard* is the level of certainty required to establish the proposition for purposes of the argument (see Weiss, 2003).

At each stage of the argumentation process, an arguer (automated or human) commonly needs to find or construct additional arguments that make an acceptable statement unacceptable or an unacceptable statement acceptable. Argument schemes aid in the search for additional arguments and counterarguments.

Argument schemes represent typical patterns of legal argument. Schemes are templates or "blueprints" for typical kinds of legal arguments whose premises can be established based on assumed facts or as conclusions of other argument schemes. Some common schemes or patterns of legal argument include arguing from legal rules, by analogy to past cases, or from underlying values. There are also argument schemes for countering such arguments, such as distinguishing a precedent or citing a trumping counterexample.

As templates, argument schemes serve a useful function in computational models. Their "components are pre-defined and can be filled with information inferred from the available knowledge" (Gordon and Walton, 2009, pp. 2, 8). In effect, these templates lay out a space of possible alternative ways in which to make or respond to an argument. Using "[h]euristic methods [a computer program can] search this space for sets of arguments in which some goal statement or argument is acceptable or rendered unacceptable" (Gordon and Walton, 2009, pp. 2, 8).

Argument schemes may include *critical questions* that help to assess if and how an argument scheme applies in a specific case. Each type of argument scheme has its own critical questions (Walton and Gordon, 2005). Some critical questions pertain to acceptability of the scheme's premises. Other questions point out exceptional circumstances in which the scheme may not apply. If the answer to a critical question reveals a failed assumption or exception, it gives rise to a possible counterargument (Prakken, 1995; Gordon and Walton, 2006; see also Grabmair and Ashley, 2010, 2011). In addition, an argument scheme may be contradicted by conflicting applications of the same or another scheme (Prakken, 2005).

Carneades constructs a legal argument incrementally as it establishes premises. At any given stage, the model evaluates if a proposition is acceptable given other propositions in the argument and a set of assumptions. In determining the status of an argument, the model may apply computational approximations of legal proof standards such as preponderance of the evidence. At each stage, the model also searches for new arguments that make unacceptable statements acceptable or acceptable statements unacceptable; the latter are counterarguments. The legal argument schemes guide this search.

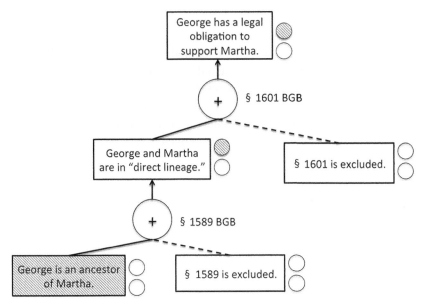

FIGURE 5.1. A Carneades argument diagram (Gordon, 2008b,c; Gordon and Walton, 2009; Walton and Gordon, 2009; see Ashley, 2012)

5.3. AN EXTENDED EXAMPLE OF A CMLA IN ACTION

One can illustrate how a computational model of legal argument can support arguing both for a proposition and its opposite in an extended example with the Carneades argument model (Gordon et al., 2007).

Carneades constructs argument diagrams (also known as argument maps) that represent the structure of a legal argument in an intuitively appealing way. The diagrams distinguish between propositions and arguments that support a proposition and those that attack the proposition. For this reason, the Carneades argument framework is called *bipartite*. In addition, arguments can be made for a proposition *p* and against the negation of *p*.

The example argument happens to involve some issues of German family law. In the Carneades diagram shown in Figure 5.1,[1] statement nodes representing propositions are boxes; argument nodes are circles (with a "+" indicating support; a dashed line indicates opposition to the argument's applicability). Statement nodes in a Carneades diagram are assigned a status of "stated," "questioned," "accepted," or "rejected." The model infers the applicability of argument nodes and the acceptability of statement nodes. (The content of the argument represented in the figure is discussed below.)

---

[1] Carneades diagramming conventions have evolved over time. See the version history at Gordon (2015b). The diagrams shown here are based on an older version that seems especially easy to understand. I am grateful to Matthias Grabmair for helping me to construct these examples.

In the Carneades framework, arguments may attack each other by rebuttal, undermining, and undercutting. *Rebuttals* are "arguments pro and con some conclusion . . . The conflict between the rebuttals is resolved by weighing the arguments and applying proof standards" (Gordon, 2015a, p. 34). When one argument contradicts (i.e., undermines) the premises of another argument, the former is called an *undermining* argument (Gordon, 2015a, p. 44). *Undercutting* arguments are those that attack another argument's applicability. In an argument diagram, an undercutter is depicted as an argument node whose conclusion is another argument node instead of a statement node (Gordon, 2015a, p. 21).

5.3.1. *Family Law Example with Carneades*

Tom Gordon and Doug Walton have provided a classic example illustrating a structured legal argument involving a set of rules roughly derived from German family law statutes (see Gordon, 2008b,c; Gordon and Walton, 2009; Walton and Gordon, 2009):

Rule §1601-BGB: x is obligated to support *y* if *x* is in direct lineage to *y*

Rule §1589-BGB: x is in direct lineage to *y* if *x* is an ancestor of *y*

Rule §91-BSHG: §1601-BGB excludes "*x* is obligated to support *y*" if "*x* is obligated to support *y*" would cause *x* undue hardship

Rule §1602-BGB: x is not obligated to support *y* under §1601-BGB unless *y* is needy.

Suppose we are given as a fact that George is an ancestor of Martha (her parent or grandparent) and we want to know, given the above set of legal rules, whether George has an obligation to support Martha.

Before we examine how the Carneades system would go about it, let's imagine how a program implementing classical logical deduction such as the BNA program of Chapter 2 would apply these legal rules to determine if George is obligated to provide Martha support.

With one application of backward chaining and two applications of deductive reasoning with *modus ponens*, the BNA program would conclude that George is in direct lineage to Martha and has an obligation to support her under rule §1601. The system cannot draw this conclusion directly from rule §1601, however, since that rule speaks only of "direct lineage." That is where backward chaining comes in (see Section 1.3.1). As illustrated in Figure 5.2, applying backward chaining, the system can find a rule, §1589, that could conclude that George is in direct lineage to Martha. Carneades then determines that the antecedent of rule §1589 is satisfied based on the fact that George is an ancestor of Martha.

Suppose one next learns that being obligated to support Martha would cause George undue hardship. As illustrated in Figure 5.3, as a matter of deductive reasoning with rules, rule §91 would then apply and George's having an obligation to

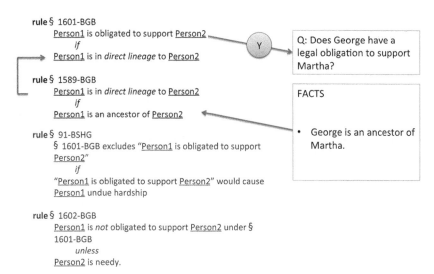

FIGURE 5.2. Classical deduction (Gordon, 2008b,c; Gordon and Walton, 2009; Walton and Gordon, 2009)

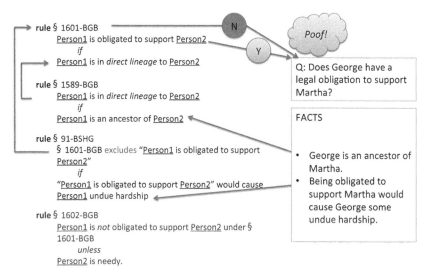

FIGURE 5.3. Classical deduction cannot prove proposition and its opposite (see Gordon, 2008b,c; Gordon and Walton, 2009; Walton and Gordon, 2009)

support Martha would be excluded. The BNA-type system has already proven, however, that George *did* have an obligation to support Martha. In other words, it would now have proven two inconsistent consequences; George is both obligated and *not* obligated to support Martha.

• **Premises**
  ○ R is a legal rule with antecedents A1, ..., An and conclusion C.
  ○ If each A*i* in A1, ..., An is *presumably* true
 	
• **Conclusion**
  ○ ... then C is *presumably* true.
 	
• **Assumptions and exceptions**
  ○ Does some **exception** to R apply?
  ○ Is some **assumption** of R not met?
  ○ Is R a **valid** legal rule?
  ○ Does some rule **excluding** R apply in this case?
  ○ Does some conflicting rule of **higher priority** than R apply in this case?
	• **Premises**
	  ○ Rule § 1601-BGB is a legal rule with antecedents: If direct-lineage(<u>Person1</u>, <u>Person2</u>)
	
	• **Conclusion**
	  ○ ... then obligated-to-support(<u>Person1</u>, <u>Person2</u>) is *presumably* true.
	
	• **Assumptions and exceptions**
	  ○ Unless **exception** to 1601 applies (i.e., rule § 1602-BGB)
	  ○ Assuming **assumptions** of 1601 are met
	  ○ Assuming 1601 is a **valid** legal rule
	  ○ Unless some rule **excluding** 1601 (i.e., rule § 91-BSHG) applies
	  ○ Unless some conflicting rule of **higher priority** than 1601 applies

FIGURE 5.4. Scheme for arguments from defeasible inference rules (see Gordon, 2008b,c; Gordon and Walton, 2009; Walton and Gordon, 2009)

This phenomenon frequently happens in legal reasoning, but, as explained in Chapter 2, it is problematic for classical logical deduction. Classical logic is monotonic; once something has been proven, it cannot be "unproven" even on the basis of new information. Moreover, in a classical model of logical deduction, an ability to prove a proposition and its opposite means that the system is inconsistent and could prove anything. (See short proof in Section 2.4.2 of this "explosive" feature of classical logic.) In other words, if one wishes a computer to make arguments pro and con from legal rules, classical logical deduction fails.

Computational models of argument like Carneades avoid this problem by using non-monotonic reasoning (also known as defeasible reasoning) and appropriate argument schemes.

5.3.2. *Arguing with Defeasible Legal Rules*

In a computational model of argument, legal rules are modeled as defeasible inference rules, and the argument schemes for drawing legal inferences from the rules are also defeasible.

As suggested in Figure 5.4 at the left, the conclusion of a *defeasible* inference rule is only *presumably* true. It is subject to a list of exceptions and assumptions to the rule's application (sometimes referred to as *critical questions*, see Section 5.2), which, if established, defeat the rule's conclusion.

For example, Rule §1601-BGB would be represented as a defeasible inference rule as shown in Figure 5.4 at the right. Its conclusion, obligated-to-support (x, y), is only *presumably* true even if the premises, direct-lineage (x, y), are satisfied. The conclusion is subject to a variety of assumptions and exceptions.

In particular, Rule §1601-BGB's assumptions and exceptions would include an exception based on rule §1602-BGB, an exclusion based on rule §91-BSHG, and more general assumptions that the rule is valid and not subject to some conflicting rule of higher priority.

Carneades can reason and construct arguments with such defeasible inference rules and diagram the arguments it makes. If one specifies a goal of showing that George does have a legal obligation to support Martha (indicated by the hashed circle at the root node in Figure 5.1), the Carneades rules engine reasons backward from that goal to find defeasible inference rules to support that goal: §§1601 and 1589. As the arguments are constructed and edited, they are visualized in the argument diagram as shown in the figure. Incidentally, Carneades' legal reasoning is an example of subsumption (see Section 2.5.1), but in determining whether a legal concept subsumes a fact situation, it employs defeasible rules and a variety of argument schemes, not just deductive inference.

Of course, so far this is pretty much the same way that the BNA program would infer a conclusion based on a statutory rule (see above). There is a subtle difference here, however. Carneades has constructed an *argument* that George is obligated to support Martha by applying an argument scheme, argument-by-deduction. As we will see, this is just one of the argument schemes that Carneades can apply.

If one then specifies a goal of defeating that argument, Carneades searches the defeasible rule's representation for exceptions, exclusions, or failures of assumptions that can prevent the argument's presumed conclusion.

Given as a fact that being obligated to support Martha would cause George undue hardship, Carneades finds an applicable rule that excludes §1601, namely §91, and modifies the diagram (Figure 5.5).

That is, with a representation of the legal rules as defeasible, the program can find failed assumptions, exceptions, or exclusions that prevent a former argument's presumed conclusion. In addition, unlike classical logical deduction, Carneades, with its defeasible legal rules and arguments, *can* support arguments pro and con a proposition (compare Figures 5.3 and 5.5).

5.3.3. *Integrating Arguing with Cases and Rules*

A second major purpose of computational argument models is to integrate into one framework the different types of arguments legal practitioners apply, including those whose models are featured in Chapters 2 through 4. Beside deductive arguments from defeasible rules, arguments by analogy to past cases or from values and purposes underlying legal rules can all be formalized with argument schemes and integrated into one argument model with critical questions.

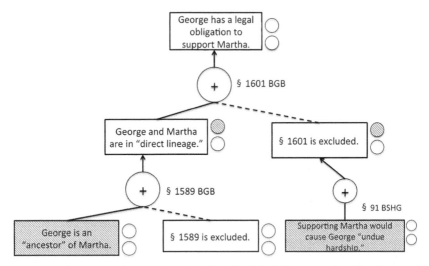

FIGURE 5.5. Arguments (pro and con) with defeasible inference rules (Gordon, 2008b, c; Gordon and Walton, 2009; Walton and Gordon, 2009; see Ashley, 2012)

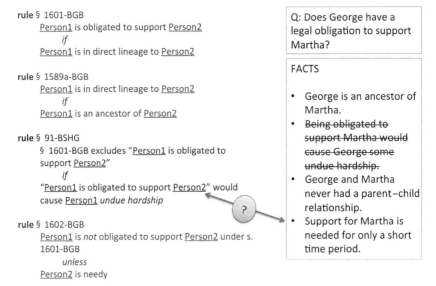

FIGURE 5.6. When the rules run out (see Gordon, 2008b, c; Gordon and Walton, 2009; Walton and Gardon, 2009)

For instance, suppose in the above example we encounter a situation, shown in Figure 5.6, where the rules "run out." We are *not* given as a fact that being obligated to support Martha would cause George undue hardship. In addition, we see that "undue hardship" is not further defined by a legal rule. A new fact has been learned, however, George and Martha never had a parent–child relationship.

TABLE 5.1. *Legal factors and precedents regarding undue hardship (see Gordon, 2008b, c; Gordon and Walton, 2009; Walton and Gordon, 2009)*

Plaintiff(P) Legal Factors (pro finding of undue hardship)	
PF1	Has-already-provided-much-support
PF2	Never-had-parent–child-relationship
PF3	Would-cause-irreparable-harm-to-family
Defendant(D) Factors (con finding of undue hardship)	
DF1	Expected-duration-of-support-is-short
DF2	Has-not-provided-care
Casebase, cb1	
Miller	P wins undue hardship issue where {PF2}
Smith	D wins undue hardship issue where {PF2, DF1}
Farmer	P wins undue hardship issue where {PF2, DF1, PF3}

Assuming the goal is still to show that George is not obligated to support Martha, can Carneades make any other arguments?

In a common law jurisdiction like the United States, attorneys would look to previously decided legal cases to determine if and how courts have determined the issue of "undue hardship." Having found such cases, attorneys would then make arguments by analogy that the current case should or should not be decided in the same way as in these prior cases.

Of course, those arguments may lead to further arguments, as well. Some analogous cases may support a conclusion that there is undue hardship and others may support the opposite conclusion; some cases will be more analogous than other cases, which may lead the arguer to distinguish them or cite counterexamples.

Chapter 3 illustrated some models of case-based reasoning that can make arguments like these. These models can be implemented as argument schemes and integrated into an overall computational model of argument like Carneades.

Let's assume that we are using a version of Carneades equipped with a CATO-style case-based argument scheme and we have available a line of precedents and legal factors (stereotypical patterns of fact that tend to strengthen or weaken a legal conclusion) related to the issue of undue hardship. In particular, assume that the legal factors and cases in Table 5.1 all deal with the concept of undue hardship.

When Carneades is instructed to argue against the proposition that George is obligated to support Martha, the program could:

1. Search the critical questions of §1601.
2. The entry "Unless some rule excluding §1601 applies" leads it to search for a rule whose consequence is that §1601 is excluded.

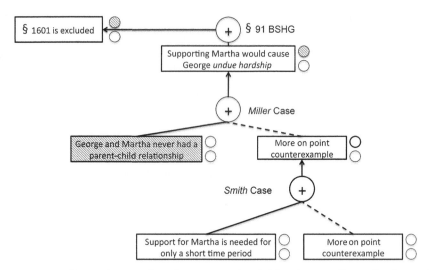

FIGURE 5.7. Carneades case-based argument (con) (Gordon, 2008b, c; Gordon and Walton, 2009; Walton and Gordon, 2009; see Ashley, 2012)

3. Finding §91, it then searches for a rule whose consequence involves "undue hardship."
4. Finding the rule of the *Miller* case (P wins undue hardship issue if {PF2}), it constructs an argument according to the case-based argument scheme that §1601 is excluded. This argument is shown in Figure 5.7.

If it were then revealed that support for Martha is needed for only a short time period, Factor DF1 would apply. If Carneades were instructed to support the proposition that George *is* obligated to support Martha, a critical question associated with the case-based argument scheme, "Unless a trumping counter-example," would lead Carneades to cite the more-on-point *Smith* case {PF2, DF1} which was decided against undue hardship (see the argument in Figure 5.8).

Carneades can construct all of these arguments. It illustrates how AI & Law work on computational models of argument can integrate the rule-based and case-based legal reasoning models we have seen in the preceding chapters.

In above example, the CATO model of case-based legal reasoning has been "plugged into" the Carneades argument model as an argument scheme. As noted, argument schemes model typical patterns of argumentation in the legal (and other) fields. This might be called the "Argument from Shared Legal Factors": If the precedent shares legal factors with the current case, then argue that the current case should be decided in the same way as the precedent.

The argument model would also be equipped with argument schemes for responding to an Argument from Shared Legal Factors including distinguishing cases, downplaying and emphasizing distinctions, and citing counterexamples

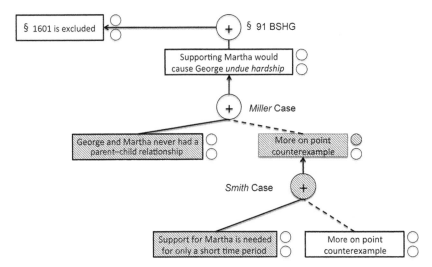

FIGURE 5.8. Carneades case-based argument (pro) (Gordon, 2008b,c; Gordon and Walton, 2009; Walton and Gordon, 2009; see Ashley, 2012)

(Aleven, 2003). One could also implement variations that pick up features and arguments based on Hypo (Ashley, 1990) or CABARET (Rissland and Skalak, 1991).

Indeed, most of the computational models of the previous chapters can be re-characterized as argument schemes and integrated in an argument model like Carneades. For example, one could implement the Argument Scheme from Theory Construction (McCarty and Sridharan, 1981; cf. Bench-Capon and Sartor, 2003): If a theory can be constructed which explains a line of precedents and hypotheticals about the same issue as the current case, then argue for applying the theory to the current case. One could also implement the Argument from Criterial Facts (GREBE, (Branting, 1991); cf. SIROCCO, (McLaren, 2003)): If an open-textured predicate in a statute was decided to have been satisfied by the criterial facts of a precedent and these criterial facts are similar to the facts of the current case, then argue that the open-textured predicate is also satisfied in this case.

5.4. COMPUTATIONAL MODEL OF ABSTRACT ARGUMENTATION

As the family law example arguments illustrate, Carneades, with its bipartite argument framework, represents a legal argument's structure: the arguments that support a proposition and those that attack it.

In contrast, an *abstract* argumentation framework, a different kind of argument framework, employs argument graphs that contain only arguments that *attack* each other. This means that the internal argument structure involving supporting and attacking arguments is abstracted away (although some structure can be reconstructed as indicated below). Invented by Phan Minh Dung, abstract argumentation

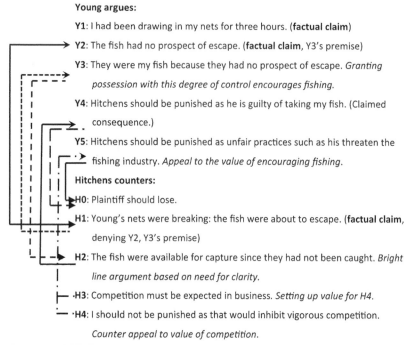

Young argues:

Y1: I had been drawing in my nets for three hours. (**factual claim**)

Y2: The fish had no prospect of escape. (**factual claim**, Y3's premise)

Y3: They were my fish because they had no prospect of escape. *Granting possession with this degree of control encourages fishing.*

Y4: Hitchens should be punished as he is guilty of taking my fish. (Claimed consequence.)

Y5: Hitchens should be punished as unfair practices such as his threaten the fishing industry. *Appeal to the value of encouraging fishing.*

Hitchens counters:

H0: Plaintiff should lose.

H1: Young's nets were breaking: the fish were about to escape. (**factual claim**, denying Y2, Y3's premise)

H2: The fish were available for capture since they had not been caught. *Bright line argument based on need for clarity.*

H3: Competition must be expected in business. *Setting up value for H4.*

H4: I should not be punished as that would inhibit vigorous competition. *Counter appeal to value of competition.*

FIGURE 5.9. Attacking arguments as per VAF (see Atkinson and Bench-Capon, 2007, p. 113)

frameworks provide certain advantages theoretically and in terms of computational efficiency (Dung, 1995).

An abstract argument framework is defined as a set of arguments A and the attack relations R between pairs of these arguments. It is modeled as a directed graph, that is, a graph whose edges are, in effect, arrows. The nodes represent arguments and the arrows indicate which arguments an argument attacks. To evaluate an argument's status in an abstract argument framework including its acceptability, one considers if the argument can be defended from attack from the other arguments in a set of arguments S that is a subset of or equal to A (Dung, 1995; Atkinson and Bench-Capon, 2007).

An argument based on one of the property-interests-in-wild-animal cases of Sections 3.4 and 3.5.1 is illustrated in Figure 5.9 as a particular kind of abstract argumentation framework, a VAF. A VAF extends the abstract argumentation framework so that arguments can be labeled by type. Some arguments involve disputes about the facts and are marked as involving factual claims or assertions. Others involve disputes about the underlying values or goals of the law and are marked according to the values promoted by the arguments if accepted (Bench-Capon, 2003; Atkinson and Bench-Capon, 2007).

For example, Figure 5.9 illustrates an argument in *Young v. Hitchens*, the dispute between the plaintiff Young, a commercial fisherman, and defendant Hitchens, who slipped through plaintiff's net and caught the fish that the plaintiff had already partially corralled.

The set of arguments A is illustrated at the right. Plaintiff Young's arguments are marked Y#; those of defendant Hitchens are marked H#. Some of the arguments are marked as involving fact claims. (Since not all of the arguments appear in the text of the decision, the authors supplied some factual arguments in order to illustrate how to model them.) Other arguments are labeled with the values they promote. The authors adopt a list of values underlying the legal regulations applicable in the property-interests-in-wild-animals domain similar to that illustrated in Figure 3.13. The arrows at the left of Figure 5.9 represent the attack relations between pairs of arguments.

Abstract argument frameworks have one major limitation: it is awkward to represent a legal argument with only attack relations. One way to deal with that in a VAF is by representing "an attacker of an attacker of the supported argument." For instance, plaintiff Young makes two arguments in support of his claim, Y4 and Y5. They are represented in the diagram as attacking the *negation* of P, where P is a claim that plaintiff should win.

The lack of structure in VAF representations of arguments is another drawback. While Figure 5.9 is my attempt to make the representation more conveniently readable, it is not as easy to interpret as a Carneades diagram. Alternative argument frameworks such as ASPIC+ combine the theoretical and efficiency benefits of abstract argument frameworks with the convenience of structured argument representations (Modgil and Prakken, 2014).

5.5. HOW CMLAS COMPUTE WINNERS AND LOSERS

The goal of the computational models of legal argument illustrated above is to combine in one model arguing about the facts of a case, the applicable law, and underlying values, and, to the extent possible, to determine the winning and losing arguments. As we will see below, the focus in some other computational models is more descriptive: to describe or model in detail, the decisions a judge makes and the justifications the judge offers as reported in the opinion.

In practical terms, arguing about case facts, applicable legal rules, underlying values, and, perhaps, procedural issues, requires a hierarchy of argumentation frameworks. Each level of argument is equipped with its own variety of argument schemes, procedures for determining the acceptability of arguments, standards of proof, and "differ[ing] notions of acceptability of arguments based on preferences between arguments, the preferences being justified at a meta-level of argumentation."

Propositions about facts, rules, and values can all appear in a value-based argument diagram as illustrated in the *Young* case argument in Figure 5.9. At this base

level, the arguments are about facts and about values. In order to resolve conflicting arguments about facts or about values, however, the program needs to "go
meta." That is, it pops up to a factual conflict-resolution level and invokes argument
schemes for resolving factual disputes, such as by asking critical questions about
witness testimony. It also pops up to a value conflict-resolution level and invokes
argument schemes for resolving disputes about values, for example with a scheme for
arguing from values as in the Bench-Capon/Sartor model (Section 3.5.1) (Atkinson
and Bench-Capon, 2007). Examples illustrating both of these conflict-resolution
levels are presented next.

5.5.1. *Resolving Conflicting Arguments about Facts*

For instance, as shown in Figure 5.9, H₁, a factual claim (i.e., "Young's nets were
breaking: the fish were about to escape.") attacks, and is attacked by another factual
claim, Y₂ (i.e., "The fish had no prospect of escape.") How would such a conflict be
resolved in a VAF?

> [E]ach conflict as to fact will need to be resolved separately through a meta-level
> argument, and the outcome of the meta-level will result in each argument being
> assigned the status justified, *arguable* or *unsupported*. [emphasis added] (Atkinson
> and Bench-Capon, 2007).

The conflict-resolution level of the argumentation framework hierarchy would be
equipped with argument schemes for reasoning about facts which include critical
questions tailored to the legal evaluation of factual assertions. These, in turn, provide
a basis for a preference ordering of competing factual claims. For example, critical
questions about factual claims probe the credibility of the witness whose testimony
supports the claim: Is the witness biased? Was the witness in a position to know?
In modern litigation contexts, expert witness testimony would be subject to critical
questions such as: Is the witness an expert in the relevant domain? Is the witness's
assertion consistent with what other experts assert? Is the expert witness's assertion
based on evidence? (see Walton and Gordon, 2005).

If answers to such critical questions can be obtained, they provide a basis for resolving a factual conflict, say, between H₁ and Y₂ in Figure 5.9, in favor of the plaintiff
Young, since the defendant is a biased witness. Then, the results of applying the preferences would be compared to the relevant proof standard. (See the right-hand side
of Table 5.2 for the Carneades definitions of the standards of proof.) The ones that
do not survive would be removed:

> Which [arguments have insufficient support] depend[s] on the proof standard appli-
> cable in the context: for beyond reasonable doubt only justified arguments will be
> retained, whereas for scintilla of evidence all arguments can be retained. (Atkinson
> and Bench-Capon, 2007)

As a result of this process, there will be a "single set of arguments accepted, which will be justified to a degree represented by its weakest member" (Atkinson and Bench-Capon, 2007).

5.5.2. *Resolving Conflicting Arguments about Values*

Also as shown in Figure 5.9, the *Young* argument involves conflicting appeals to underlying values. For instance,

Y3 (i.e., "They were my fish because they had no prospect of escape. Granting possession with this degree of control encourages fishing.")
attacks ($\longmapsto$)
H2 ("The fish were available for capture since they had not been caught. Bright line argument based on need for clarity.")

H3 ("Competition must be expected in business. Setting up value for H4.") and H4 ("I should not be punished as that would inhibit vigorous competition. Counter appeal to value of competition.")
attack ($\longmapsto$)
Y5 ("Hitchens should be punished as unfair practices such as his threaten the fishing industry. Appeal to the value of encouraging fishing.")

How does a VAF support/resolve arguments about values like Y3 vs. H2? According to Atkinson and Bench-Capon (2007), "We next need to make a value comparison: should we prefer . . . to encourage fishing or clarity?"

For purposes of making this kind of comparison, the authors need some ordering of competing values. As the authors put it in Atkinson and Bench-Capon (2007):

[W]e will need some indication of which is the right ordering of the competing values, and here precedent becomes relevant . . . [I]t is possible to cite precedents to show that a particular ordering was used in the past, authorities to give weight to adopting a particular order, or to appeal to a teleological argument to justify the order . . . Hitchens can cite *Pierson* itself, while Young can give *Keeble* as a counter example. Hitchens may distinguish *Keeble*, on the grounds that *Keeble* was on his own land, and this was the reason to grant him possession of the ducks.

These are case-based arguments similar to those we saw in the Carneades example above. In the VAF, however, they are made at the meta-level of the argumentation framework hierarchy in order to resolve the conflict in values (again applying the relevant standard of proof). The value preferences are based on the Bench-Capon/Sartor view that the cases induce a theory of preferences among values. That is, the ordering is inferred from the outcomes of precedents in which some values were preferred over others, as per the model of theory construction from factor and value preferences in Bench-Capon and Sartor (2003) as discussed in Section 3.5.1.

5.5.3. *Resolving Conflicting Arguments about Legal Rules*

Although the VAF in *Young* does not include examples of resolving conflicting arguments about legal rules, the Carneades examples above convey the following idea. In the VAF, conflicting arguments about rules would be resolved at the meta-level with the same kinds of argument schemes for reasoning with defeasible legal rules as illustrated above.

In addition, some CMLRs like Carneades supplement those argument schemes with so-called Canons of Construction or Maxims of Interpretation, more general interpretive principles to resolve conflicting arguments about legal rules, such as:

- *Lex Specialis*: More specific rules have priority over more general rules.
- *Lex Superior*: Rules backed by higher authority have priority over rules backed by a lower authority (e.g., Federal law has priority over state law).
- *Lex Posterior*: Later rules have priority over earlier rules.

In Gordon and Walton (2006), the Carneades program applied *Lex Specialis* to resolve a conflict between two rules derived from precedents concerning the meaning of "grievous bodily harm." One rule stated that "several broken ribs do not amount to grievous bodily harm" and the other rule held that "several broken ribs with complications amount to grievous bodily harm." Applying *Lex Specialis*, where the problem involved several broken ribs with complications, the program resolved conflicting arguments based on the two rules in favor of the second more specific one.

While applying a Canon of Construction conveniently resolves the rule conflict in this simple example, the approach raises some questions discussed next.

5.6. HOW PRACTICAL ARE COMPUTATIONAL MODELS OF LEGAL ARGUMENT?

Despite the important contributions of computational models of legal argument, one may reasonably ask if, when, and how CMLAs will make a practical contribution to the practice of law.

First, the above examples of legal argument are, after all, still toy examples. The fact situations are simple and few in number, and the legal resources with which to make an argument involve, at most, a half-dozen legal rules or cases. The programs illustrated so far have not been applied with hundreds of cases and certainly not cases in textual form. All of the legal resources are input and represented manually.

The argument schemes are legally realistic as far as they go, but their application can seem a bit *ad hoc*. Consider *Lex Specialis*, for example. In the above example, it is conveniently invoked to resolve a conflict between two norms derived from precedents. One could imagine, however, an argument against applying this principle of statutory or treaty interpretation to resolve a conflict between two rules elaborated in courts in different cases. Confidence in the utility of Canons of Construction may vary across civil law vs. common law legal systems. In a classic article in 1949, Karl Llewellyn famously argued that the Canons of Construction are mere makeweights. In particular, every canon had a "counter-canon" that would lead to the opposite interpretation of the statute (Llewellyn, 1949). Thus, *Lex Specialis* may apply, but its application would be subject to argument for which appropriate schemes have not been provided.

Second, the CMLAs generally have not been evaluated empirically. Of course, it is not a simple matter to evaluate a computational model of argument. We have seen, however, at least two approaches to evaluating programs that generate legal arguments. One can ask humans and the program to generate arguments about the same fact situations and invite a human expert to grade them in a blind test, as Branting did with GREBE (see Section 3.3.3). Another approach to evaluating an argumentation model is to assess how well it predicts outcomes of cases as compared to other approaches. For instance, versions of the CATO model of case-based legal argument were evaluated by comparing their outcome predictions and those of other models, such as Issue-based Prediction, as described in Chapter 4. Such an evaluation of a new CMLA, the VJAP model, is described below.

Third, although most of the proof standards have familiar legal names, the CMLA's operationalization of them do not appear to correspond closely to the legal versions of those standards. As explained below, legal standards of proof such as "preponderance of the evidence" refer to concepts that are difficult to model computationally.

5.6.1. *Role of Proof Standards in CMLAs*

Proof standards are a familiar aspect of legal arguments. For example, "beyond a reasonable doubt," the proof standard for a criminal conviction, requires proof "so convincing that a reasonable person would not hesitate to act; proof that leaves you firmly convinced . . . [no] real possibility that he is not guilty." (Weiss, 2003)

As noted, proof standards also play an important role in computational models of argument. "The acceptability of a statement depends on its proof standard." Whether a statement's proof standard is satisfied depends on whether the arguments pro and con the statement are defensible. Whether an argument is defensible depends on whether its premises hold. Whether its premises hold depends on whether the premise's statement is acceptable and so forth (Gordon et al., 2007, p. 884).

Carneades implements a number of proof standards shown in Table 5.2 (Gordon and Walton, 2006). As indicated, some of them correspond to familiar legal standards.

A comparison of the descriptions of the legal and Carneades proof standards suggests the difficulty of developing computational implementations that correspond closely to at least some of the legal standards. Beyond a reasonable doubt requires

TABLE 5.2. *Some proof standards in Carneades (Gordon and Walton, 2006) and legal counterparts (Weiss, 2003; Feller, 2015)*

Proof Standard	Legal Formulation	Carneades Version
Scintilla of evidence	A mere scintilla of evidence sufficient to justify a suspicion is not sufficient to support a finding upon which legal rights and obligations are based. That requires "such relevant evidence as a reasonable mind might accept as adequate to support a conclusion."	A statement meets this standard iff it is supported by at least one defensible pro argument.
Preponderance of the evidence (Civil Law)	This standard requires the existence of a contested fact be more probable than not.	A statement meets this standard iff it is supported by at least one defensible pro argument and its strongest defensible pro argument outweighs its strongest defensible con argument, if any. This standard balances arguments using probative weights.
Dialectical validity	Not applicable.	A statement meets this standard iff it is supported by at least one defensible pro argument and none of its con arguments are defensible.
Beyond a reasonable doubt (Criminal Law)	This standard requires proof so convincing that a reasonable person would not hesitate to act; proof that leaves you firmly convinced ... [with no] real possibility that he is not guilty.	A statement meets this standard iff it is supported by at least one defensible pro argument, all of its pro arguments are defensible, and none of the con arguments are defensible.

evidence "so convincing that a reasonable person would not hesitate to act; proof that leaves [one] firmly convinced."

Computationally implementing notions of reasonableness of human belief or conviction is not straightforward. Indeed, the authors "do not claim that the definitions of these standards, above, fully capture their legal meanings."

The Carneades versions, however, do preserve the relative degree of strictness of the legal standards (i.e., Beyond a reasonable doubt > Dialectical Validity > Preponderance of the Evidence > Scintilla of Evidence).[2] "If a statement satisfies a proof standard, it will also satisfy all weaker proof standards" (Gordon and Walton, 2006).

---

[2] As a legal standard, "scintilla of evidence" is archaic. Actually, *more* than a "scintilla of evidence" is required. For instance, the "Substantial Evidence" test in administrative law requires "such relevant evidence as a reasonable mind might accept as adequate to support a conclusion" (Feller, 2015).

5.6.2. *Integrating Probabilistic Reasoning into CMLAs*

A final critique of CMLAs might be that the argument models have tended to jumble together issues of fact, law, and underlying values, which in procedural terms are decided at different levels in a court hierarchy or different stages of a court proceeding. See, for example, the mixture of factual and value-based arguments in the VAF of the *Young* case in Figure 5.9. CMLAs also tend to oversimplify the realities of legal practice. Obtaining accurate answers to critical questions about factual assertions is not trivial. Assessing the credibility of witnesses is a job for human juries or judges. Knowing which critical questions to ask in any given context is the job for alert legal counsel. This probably goes beyond the ability of any CMLA.

This critique, however, may miss the point of a computational model of legal argument. These models with their argument schemes and pre-stored generic critical questions might best be thought of as tools to enable attorneys to model what might happen based on various assumptions about witness credibility or consistency with other testimony.

A CMLA could, thus, be seen as a tool for planning a legal argument. A litigator could use the tool to explore possible outcomes of arguments. The litigator could add all the factual, legal, normative, and procedural arguments that s/he can anticipate, observe what outcomes the model predicts, and test the sensitivity of the predictions to various changes in input arguments and assumptions made. At least, that would be the goal of legal argument modelers: to create a practical argument planning tool.

This goal might be more feasible if litigators could input their best assessments of particular arguments' likelihood of success given the uncertainties of the litigation. In most practical contexts, the propositions in a legal argument are uncertain. There is uncertainty, for instance, about whether a fact is true, or, perhaps more pertinently, whether it will be received in evidence and credited by a trier of fact. Similarly, there is uncertainty about whether a court will accept the advocate's recommendations about which legal rule to apply, how to interpret what the legal rule means, and how to apply it to a case's facts.

In planning a legal argument, it would be useful to integrate reasoning about these uncertainties into the computational argument models. For one thing, probability should come into the standards of proof. As indicated in Table 5.2, the middle column, the preponderance of the evidence standard of proof is expressed in terms of probability: the existence of a contested fact is more probable than not. As characterized in Atkinson and Bench-Capon (2007):

> [I]n an [abstract argument framework] . . . , in cases of incomplete information we may [have a] lack of knowledge as to whether or not some fact holds. We would . . . need . . . to supply some standards intermediate between beyond reasonable doubt and scintilla of evidence. One way of handling this if the information is available would be to associate arguments with probabilities.

Competing arguments could then be compared in terms of their respective probabilities of success:

> [W]hen we have to make choices ..., we could calculate the probability of [an option's being] the correct choice. This kind of approach based on probabilities for each argument, would certainly be able to give content to the notion of "balance of probabilities" ... We, however, do not believe that such information is normally available. (Atkinson and Bench-Capon, 2007)

Integrating probabilities into CMLAs raises at least two issues:

One issue is how best to organize the integration. Given the uncertainty of factual assertions, their status in the argument could best be expressed by probabilities over the alternative statuses. If the argument formalism could then compute the probabilities over the status of the inferred, nonfactual assertions but still propagate arguments according to the argument formalism, that could be an effective integration. The qualitative model of argument could thus be extended to support quantitative methods for reasoning about uncertainty.

Bayesian networks (BNs) are one such quantitative method for reasoning about uncertainty. They are commonly used to model conditional dependencies among a set of random variables. For example, the probabilities of inferred conditions such as diseases can be computed given certain observed facts or symptoms. As explained in Section 7.5.3, BNs reduce computational complexity and integrate well with ML methods. A systematic method for reducing Carneades argument graphs to BNs is presented in Grabmair et al. (2010), which also surveys other approaches to such an integration.

A second issue is "Where will the probabilities come from?" Litigators have intuitions about the uncertainties associated with various elements of their arguments. These include such things as the likelihood of getting a trier of fact to believe a given factual inference or to assign a particular value to a consequence of a proposed decision. They could estimate these uncertainties and assign them as weights to factual assertions and arguments represented in the argument diagram. The subjectivity of setting weights by intuition is ameliorated somewhat by the possibility of sensitivity testing, that is, enabling the user to assess how changes in the assumed weights affect the predictions and arguments.

Another source of probabilities could be from external data in corpora and databases. In Chapter 4, we saw probabilities derived from features summarizing information about cases, courts, judges and their backgrounds, and judicial trends (see Figure 4.3). Below, we will see probabilities derived from previous decisions' resolutions of conflicting values (although performed over a larger set of cases and in a more context sensitive manner than in the approach of Bench-Capon and Sartor (2003) in Section 3.5.1).

It is a separate question, however, whether these two approaches to using external data to supply probabilities for CMLAs can derive those probabilities directly from legal texts. The approach in the Supreme Court prediction work of Katz et al. (2014) probably cannot work directly with the texts of the cases in the corpora or databases. It depends on engineering of features such as judicial attitudes or trends; these probably cannot be extracted automatically from case texts.

Two remaining computational models of legal argument may fare better in this respect. The VJAP model discussed next (like the approach in Bench-Capon and Sartor (2003)) relies on manually assigned legal factors. The DLF (defined in Section 5.8) which models evidentiary legal argument, relies on, among other things, manually assigned evidence factors. Using the text analytic techniques explained in Parts II and III, both types of factors may come to be extracted automatically from case texts and assist in predicting outcomes.

5.7. VALUE JUDGMENT-BASED ARGUMENTATIVE PREDICTION MODEL

Grabmair has implemented the VJAP model, a model for generating arguments and predictions that take into account values underlying legal rules. He has implemented the argument schemes in a computer program that predicts case outcomes based on the resulting arguments and has tested the program in the domain of trade secret law, the same domain of application as the Hypo, CATO, and IBP programs (see Grabmair and Ashley, 2010, 2011; Grabmair, 2016).

His approach is based on an intuitively plausible assumption about legal reasoning: In making legal decisions, judges consider the effects of a decision on applicable values and assess whether they are preferable to the effects of alternative decisions. A judge must make a value judgment, that is, a determination that in a particular fact situation a decision's positive effects outweigh the negative effects.

Such value judgments are assumed to be highly context-dependent; no abstract hierarchy of values determines the value judgment in a particular case. Instead, legal reasoning involves mapping and applying value judgments from one factual context to another. This is accomplished by means of an argument that a target case's set of facts and the original factual context of the source case are both instances of an abstract concept in a legal rule which, given the effects on applicable values, justifies that they both should have a particular outcome.

In order to support these arguments, Grabmair prepared a domain model of the abstract concepts, that is, the ILCs employed in the rules for deciding a claim, a set of values and value effects underlying trade secret regulation, and competing argument schemes for the proponent of a trade secret misappropriation claim and its opponent.

ILCs are open-textured legal terms whose meanings frequently are ambiguous or vague (see Section 2.2.1) and, thus, subject to argument. An intermediate legal concept like "ownership, citizenship, guardianship, trusteeship, possession, etc." "stands as a mediating link between the requirements and the consequences." It is "intermediate" in the sense that some rule at the beginning of a chain of rules specifies

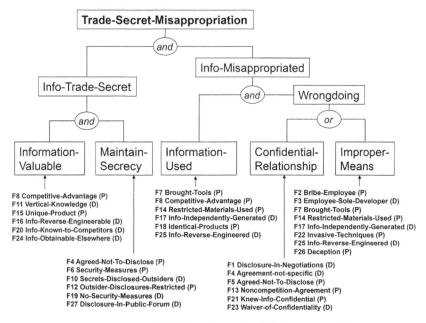

FIGURE 5.10. VJAP domain model (Grabmair, 2016)

factual requirements for preceding legal terms to apply, and those legal terms, in turn, are requirements in other rules that ultimately imply the legal or normative consequences (Lindahl, 2004; Wyner, 2008).

5.7.1. *VJAP Domain Model*

In constructing the VJAP domain model, Grabmair adapted the domain model from the IBP program (Figure 4.4). As shown in Figure 5.10, he modified the logic of the Info-Misappropriated issue, introduced a new sub-issue, *Wrongdoing*, and reorganized or added some legal factors that the original model omitted.

The issues and sub-issues and their logical connections in the VJAP domain model comprise the ILCs and legal rules for defining a claim for trade secret misappropriation:

rtsm: trade-secret-misappropriation-claim ⇐ info-trade-secret ∧ info-misappropriated

rits: info-trade-secret ⇐ info-valuable ∧ maintain-secrecy

rwd: wrongdoing ⇐ breach-of-confidentiality ∨ improper-means

rim: info-misappropriated ⇐ info-used ∧ wrongdoing

The legal factors associated with the leaf nodes represent stereotypical fact patterns that strengthen or weaken a side's argument concerning the issues/ILCs. See Table 3.1 for the complete list of trade secret law Factors.

5.7.2. *VJAP Values Underlying Trade Secret Regulation*

Grabmair has developed a new set of values or "interests" protected by trade secret law and a new way to connect the values to the Factor-based case representations of CATO and IBP (Grabmair, 2016). These values include plaintiff's interests in property and confidentiality (Figure 5.11), and the general public's interest in the usability of publicly available information and in fair competition (Figure 5.12).

Grabmair has represented in greater detail the different ways in which the legal factors affect protected values or interests. For example, certain factors may make the protected interest more or less legitimate. Others may waive the protected interest, interfere with it or not interfere with it. For each of the protected values or interests, Figures 5.11 and 5.12 indicate particular Factors' effects on the values underlying trade secret regulation. This way of representing the relationship between values and legal factors provides more semantic information for a program to apply than does the approach in Bench-Capon and Sartor (2003) or Chorley and Bench-Capon (2005a).

Consider, for example, the *Dynamics* case,[3] in which the plaintiff had developed product information and was marketing a product based on the information. Plaintiff's information was unique in that plaintiff was the only manufacturer making the product (F15 Unique-Product (P)). Plaintiff took active measures to limit access to and distribution of its information (F6 Security-Measures (P)). Plaintiff disclosed its information in a public forum (F27 Disclosure-In-Public-Forum (D)). At some point, defendant obtained the product information. Defendant entered into a nondisclosure agreement with plaintiff (F4 Agreed-Not-To-Disclose (P)). The nondisclosure agreement did not specify which information was to be treated as confidential (F5 Agreement-Not-Specific (D)). Eventually, defendant developed a competing product and commenced to sell it. Thereafter, plaintiff brought suit against defendant for trade secret misappropriation.

One can summarize strengths and weaknesses of the plaintiff's claim for trade secret misappropriation in terms of the Factors in the *Dynamics* case and based on the VJAP domain model in Figure 5.10, one can determine that there are conflicting Factors with respect to two issues under the rules, Maintain-Secrecy and Breach-confidentiality (also referred to as Confidential-Relationship) but no conflict concerning a third issue, Info-Valuable (Grabmair, 2016, p. 31). That is as much information as IBP would have about the case for purposes of prediction. AGATHA would also have information about certain values associated with those Factors and certain preference rules to resolve conflicts between Factors or between values.

VJAP, however, has additional information based on the Factors' effects on values protected under trade secret regulation (italicized below) shown in

---

[3] *Dynamics Research Corp. v. Analytic Sciences Corp.* , 9 Mass. App. 254, 400 N.E.2d 1274, 209 U.S.P.Q. 321 (1980).

Plaintiff's property interest in competitively valuable information

Interference [F21 F18 F22 F26 F7 F14 F2]

    Plaintiff's property interest was violated because of the known confidentiality of the information, the identical product, the invasive techniques, the use of deception, the former employees bringing the information, the use of restricted materials, and the payment to switch employment.

Waiver [F23 F19 F27 F1 F10]

    Plaintiff has waived his property interest because of the waiver of confidentiality, the absence of security measures, the public disclosure, the disclosure during negotiations, and the disclosure to outsiders.

More-legitimate [F15 F8]

    Plaintiff's property interest is legitimate because of the product's uniqueness and the competitive advantage.

Less-legitimate [F24 F16 F17 F11 F20]

    Plaintiff's property interest is not legitimate because of the public availability of the information, the reverse-engineerability, the independent invention, the information being about customers and suppliers, and the information being known to competitors.

Protection [F12 F6 F13 F4]

    Plaintiff has protected his property interest because of the confidentiality of outside disclosures, the security measures, the noncompetition agreement, and the nondisclosure agreement.

Non-interference [F25]

    Plaintiff's property interest was not violated because of the reverse-engineering of the information.

Plaintiff's interest in confidentiality

Less-legitimate [F24 F5 F20]

    Plaintiff's interest in confidentiality is not legitimate because of the public availability of the information, the unspecific nondisclosure agreement, and the information being known to competitors.

Waiver [F23 F19 F27 F1 F10]

    Plaintiff has waived his confidentiality interest because of the waiver of confidentiality, the absence of security measures, the public disclosure, the disclosure during negotiations, and the disclosure to outsiders.

Protection [F12 F21 F6 F13 F4]

    Plaintiff has protected his confidentiality interest because of the confidentiality of outside disclosures, the known confidentiality of the information, the security measures, the noncompetition agreement, and the nondisclosure agreement.

Interference [F14 F2]

    Plaintiff's confidentiality interest has been violated because of the use of restricted materials and the payment to switch employment.

FIGURE 5.11. Values protected by trade secret law: interests of plaintiffs in property and confidentiality (Grabmair, 2016)

Figures 5.11 and 5.12 (Grabmair, 2016, pp. 44–7). For instance, in the *Dynamics* case, arguably:

- Plaintiff's *property interest* is legitimate because (F15) plaintiff's information was unique in that plaintiff was the only manufacturer making the product.

General public's interest in the usability of publicly available information

More-legitimate [F24 F16 F25 F17 F11 F20]

The general public's interest in the usability of publicly available information applies in this case because of the public availability of the information, the reverse-engineerability, the reverse-engineering of the information, the independent invention, the information being about customers and suppliers, and the information being known to competitors .

Less-legitimate [F21 F15 F14]

The general public's interest in the usability of publicly available information does not apply in this case because of the known confidentiality of the information, the product's uniqueness, and the use of restricted materials.

General public's interest in fair competition

Interference-by-d [F21 F18 F26 F7 F14 F2]

The principle of fair competition has been violated by the defendant because of the known confidentiality of the information, the identical product, the use of deception, the former employees bringing the information, the use of restricted materials, and the payment to switch employment.

FIGURE 5.12. Values protected by trade secret law: interests of general public in the usability of publicly available information and in fair competition (Grabmair, 2016)

- Plaintiff has protected his *property interest* because (F6) plaintiff took active measures to limit access to and distribution of its information, and (F4) defendant entered into a nondisclosure agreement with plaintiff.
- Plaintiff has protected his *confidentiality interest* because (F6) plaintiff took active measures to limit access to and distribution of its information and (F4) defendant entered into a nondisclosure agreement with plaintiff.
- The *general public's interest in the usability of publicly available information* does not apply in this case because (F15) plaintiff's information was unique in that plaintiff was the only manufacturer making the product.

On the other hand, arguably, plaintiff has also compromised some of the values protected under trade secret regulation (italicized):

- Plaintiff has waived his *property interest* because (F27) plaintiff disclosed its information in a public forum.
- Plaintiff has waived his *confidentiality interest* because (F27) plaintiff disclosed its information in a public forum.
- Plaintiff's *interest in confidentiality* is not legitimate because (F5) the nondisclosure agreement did not specify which information was to be treated as confidential.
- The *general public's interest in the usability of publicly available information* applies in this case because (F27) plaintiff disclosed its information in a public forum.

The issues in the VJAP domain model in Figure 5.10 separate the full values trade-offs in a case into subsets of local and of inter-issue trade-offs. For example, the *Dynamics* case presents trade-offs in connection with effects on values protected by trade secret law. Some of these trade-offs are local in the sense that they deal with competing Factors concerning one issue. There are local conflicts in connection with Maintain-Secrecy (F6 Security-Measures (P) and F4 Agreed-Not-To-Disclose (P) vs. F27 Disclosure-In-Public-Forum (D)) and with Breach-Confidentiality (F4 Agreed-Not-To-Disclose (P) vs. F5 Agreement-Not-Specific (D)). Other value effects trade-offs are inter-issue. For instance, plaintiff's strength regarding the issue of Info-Valuable (F15 Unique-Product (P)) could arguably compensate for its weakness in the issues of Maintain-Secrecy or Breach-Confidentiality.

As explained in Section 5.7.4, the VJAP program resolves these trade-offs into confidence values in an argument graph and aggregates them quantitatively using the domain model in Figure 5.10.

5.7.3. *VJAP Argument Schemes*

VJAP models arguments that a legal rule should apply to a current case or not based on analogies to prior cases. The rules are composed of ILCs. These ILCs are the issues from the domain model of trade secret law (Figure 5.10). The analogies assert that the current case and prior cases present the same local or cross-issue trade-offs in value effects.

Employing schemes for constructing arguments by analogy based on shared value effect trade-offs, the program can retrieve cases sharing the same local or inter-issue trade-offs as a current case and use them in appropriate arguments.

For example, the argument scheme for an "Inter-Issue Trade-off from Precedent" is a rule that specifies formally the preconditions for invoking the argument on behalf of a side. Basically, a precedent case has to have been decided for that side, which shares the same inter-issue trade-off in value effects as in the current case.

Figure 5.13 shows an excerpt of the program's analysis of the *Dynamics* case constructed with this argument scheme. The underlined phrases in the text illustrate where the argument scheme introduces trade-offs in effects on values protected by trade secret law. Even though the VJAP program outputs texts that may be wordy and repetitive, a matter for future work, its arguments compare favorably with the kind of teleological argument Berman and Hafner espoused, as exemplified in Argument II of Figure 3.12.

VJAP argument schemes also support making similar arguments with precedents sharing *local* trade-offs in value effects with the current case, that is where the trade-offs pertain to the same issue.

The comparison of the *Dynamics* and *National Rejectors* cases in Figure 5.13 illustrates how, in arguing that a case does or does not satisfy a legal rule requirement

> **Example verbalization in DYNAMICS, defendant on *info-valuable*:**
> Plaintiff's product information is not sufficiently valuable because the plaintiff has taken such little efforts to maintain the secrecy of the information that despite the lack of strong evidence for the defendant, it must be assumed that plaintiff's product information is not sufficiently valuable because deciding otherwise would be inconsistent with the purposes underlying trade secret law.
>
> Specifically, regarding the maintenance of secrecy by the plaintiff, the public disclosure amounts to such a clear <u>waiver of property interest</u>, a scenario where <u>usability of public information</u> is critical and such a <u>clear waiver of confidentiality</u> interest regarding the lack of maintenance of secrecy by the plaintiff that the lack of value of the information must be deemed sufficiently established despite the lack of strong evidence for the defendant and the fact that the product information was unique.
>
> A similar inter-issue trade-off was made in NATIONAL-REJECTORS, which was decided for defendant. There, regarding the maintenance of secrecy by the plaintiff, the disclosure to outsiders amounted to such a clear <u>waiver of property interest</u> and such a clear <u>waiver of confidentiality interest</u>, the public disclosure amounted to such a clear <u>waiver of property interest</u>, a scenario where <u>usability of public information</u> is critical and such a clear <u>waiver of confidentiality</u> interest and the absence of security measures amounted to such a clear <u>waiver of property interest</u> and such a clear <u>waiver of confidentiality</u> interest that the reverse-engineerability qualified as the lack of value of the information despite the fact that the product information had been unique.

FIGURE 5.13. VJAP Program output for *Dynamics* Case (excerpts) (Grabmair, 2016, pp. 59–60)

such as Information-Valuable, the VJAP program can draw abstract analogies across cases in terms of value-effect trade-offs.

Significantly, in the VJAP model, the fact that the precedent shares the same value-effect trade-off with the current case does not necessarily mean that they share the same set of factors. A given value effect can be caused by multiple factors, as indicated in Figures 5.11 and 5.12. Consequently, VJAP is drawing analogies at a more abstract level than in previous models of legal reasoning with cases.

> VJAP retrieves potential precedents by virtue of their sharing a tradeoff with the case at bar. This involves two sets of value effects . . . , irrespective of which factors constitute these effects. This is substantially different from (and arguably 'deeper' than) the precedent candidate retrieval on the factor level as employed in HYPO, CATO and IBP. In other words, VJAP retrieves precedents that may be superficially different in terms of the factors they share yet similar on a deeper level in terms of their shared value effects. (Grabmair, 2016, p. 60)

Additional VJAP schemes enable arguments supporting or attacking an analogy. "A party may point out a favorable factor that is present in the current case and not in the precedent but still part of the [inter-issue] tradeoff argued about in the analogy. The resulting argument is an *a fortiori* argument that this favorable excess factor in the current case makes the argument even stronger" (Grabmair, 2016, p. 61). In a complementary way, the opponent may challenge the analogy "by pointing out that there exists a factor in the current case disfavoring the side arguing for the analogy that is not part of the precedent but should still be part of the tradeoff, thereby weakening the analogy" (Grabmair, 2016, p. 62).

5.7.4. *VJAP's Argument-based Predictions*

The VJAP program constructs an argument graph for each case using its set of argument schemes (Grabmair, 2016, p. iv). Given a case *c* input as a list of all applicable Factors, VJAP constructs an argument for the proposition that plaintiff's trade secret misappropriation claim in *c* will succeed.

The argument, represented in an argument graph structure, records the output of an exhaustive search using backward chaining to apply all of the argument schemes VJAP supports, including the schemes involving argument by analogy based on shared local or inter-issue trade-offs. This means that for each issue, the program checks all of the argument schemes for applicability. If a scheme applies, it is instantiated and its premises are argued in a recursive application of the same procedure. The output of each applicable instantiation of an argument scheme is an argument, which is added to the argument graph structure. The process continues until the program can find no new arguments whereupon the graph is complete (Grabmair, 2016, p. 48).

The argument graph represents *all* possible arguments about who should win the case given the program's domain knowledge. While the argument graphs are too large and complex to show here, Figure 5.14 illustrates "a pattern schema for the argument graphs that VJAP generates" in arguing about whether a plaintiff in *c* wins an issue *i* from the domain model of trade secret law (Figure 5.10). The argument graph comprises arguments, in oval-shaped nodes, related to propositions in rectangular nodes, via diamond-shaped confidence propagation nodes (discussed below). The edges connecting the nodes represent consequence and premise relations (Grabmair, 2016, pp. 48–51).

As noted, the program produces the argument graph from the top down via backward-chaining with the argument schemes represented as rules. When each argument scheme's preconditions are satisfied, the scheme adds the corresponding argument extending the graph downward. As shown in Figure 5.14, the argument graph goes "from arguments in the domain model at the top (collapsed to save space) to deep arguments about leaf issues, tradeoffs, precedents, and analogy/distinction arguments between precedent and the case at bar" (Grabmair, 2016, p. 50).

The argument graph is also bipartite. As suggested in the figure, the argument scheme search process produces legal arguments for the plaintiff and defendant on the issues in the case.

VJAP predicts the outcome of cases based on the argument graph. "It predicts case outcomes using a confidence measure computed from the argument graph and generates textual legal arguments justifying its predictions. The confidence

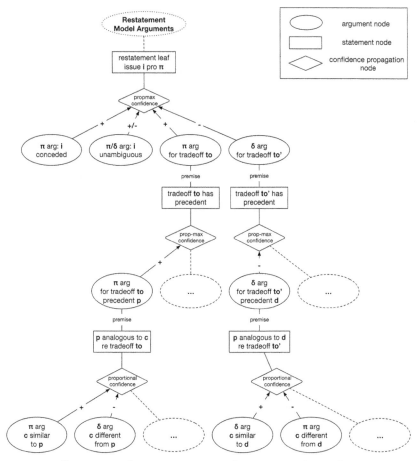

FIGURE 5.14. Statement and argument structure for reasoning about a Restatement issue with trade-offs in VJAP (Grabmair, 2016, p. 51)

propagation uses quantitative weights assigned to effects of facts on values. VJAP automatically learns these weights from past cases using an iterative optimization method" (Grabmair, 2016, p. iv).

In other words, the argument graph serves as a quantitative graphical model to predict the outcome of the case given the trade-offs in values in previous cases and contexts. "The confidence values ... represent the degree to which a statement is argumentatively established, thereby giving the system a kind of 'quantitative confidence semantics' " (Grabmair, 2016, p. 17). The values are computed based on:

1. the weights associated with the effects that each factor has on each of the values favoring either plaintiff or defendant.

2. the degree of confidence with which the premises of the argument can be established, which in turn depends on the strength of the arguments pro and con these premises.

As each argument scheme fires, extending the argument graph, it also outputs a confidence function for calculating the relative effect of the argument it has just contributed to the confidence in the overall argument. Each argument scheme has an associated function for calculating a measure of the relative persuasive force of the kind of argument it constructs. For inter-issue or local issue arguments from precedent, the confidence measure is increased in relation to the strength of the analogy between a precedent p and c and decreased to the extent they can be distinguished.

The VJAP program "predicts a case outcome by propagating confidence values across the argument graph from learned weight parameters that represent the persuasive force of the effect a certain fact has on the applicable values" (Grabmair, 2016, pp. 25–6).

> Once the graph is constructed, the system computes the confidence of [the statement that plaintiff has a winning] claim by using the factor effect weight map parameters to calculate the confidence of the leaf-nodes of the argument graph (see the bottom row in [Figure 5.14]). These initial confidence values are then propagated bottom up (or 'feed forward' in neural network terminology) using the confidence functions of the argument schemes . . . and the proportional confidence and propmax confidence functions for statements. (Grabmair, 2016, pp. 70–1)

The resulting value represents the program's degree of confidence in an outcome prediction. If greater than a threshold of 50%, it predicts that plaintiff wins, otherwise it predicts defendant wins.

5.7.5. *VJAP Program Evaluation*

For purposes of evaluating the VJAP program, Grabmair employed a database of 121 trade secret cases (74 won by plaintiff, 47 by defendant). This was a subset of the IBP dataset comprising the cases that have at least one factor for each of plaintiff and defendant. Thus, these cases supported arguments balancing trade-offs.

The database was divided into training and test sets. For training, an argument graph is constructed and a winner predicted for each case in the training set. Then, the overall prediction accuracy is determined (Grabmair, 2016, p. 71).

> In the training step, the system tries to learn optimal fact effect weight parameters to maximize prediction accuracy. To accomplish this, the construction–propagation–prediction pattern happens in a loop during which the system iteratively searches for the optimal weight map using a technique called simulated annealing. (Grabmair, 2016, p. 71)

Simulated annealing is a technique for finding a global maximum of a function such as confidence while avoiding local maxima that are not as great.

In simulated annealing . . . the training loop is run for a predefined number of iterations and the parameters (i.e. the weights of the fact effects on values) are adjusted at each iteration by replacing one random effect weight with a new random effect weight, thus generating a "neighboring" weight map to the current one. This new weight map is then evaluated through confidence propagation and overall prediction accuracy. If the neighboring weight map is better or equally good, it replaces the current weight map and the algorithm goes on into the next cycle. If the new weight map performs worse, then the system will nevertheless make it the current weight map with a small probability that is computed (using a "cooling schedule" function) from the system's "temperature," which is a function of the remaining and total number of cycles in the annealing process. The intuition is that, by occasionally taking a "bad move," the search is less likely to get stuck in local optima in the multidimensional space of possible weight map parameters. (Grabmair, 2016, p. 71)

The test step takes place after the annealing process is finished and the best weight map has been found. In the test step, the VJAP program predicts the outcomes of the test cases in "the same construction–propagation–prediction fashion by simply using the trained effect weight parameters without any more optimization" (Grabmair, 2016, p. 72). It computes accuracy as the number of correctly predicted test cases over the total number of test case predictions.

The program has predicted individual case outcomes in a LOO and a fivefold cross validation (see Section 4.4.3). Each employed the database of 121 trade secret misappropriation cases manually represented in terms of legal factors, and each case involving at least a pair of conflicting factors (Grabmair, 2016, p. 74).

In the LOO, each training and test step was executed 121 times. Each time, a different case became the test set of one case and the other 120 cases were the training set. In the fivefold cross validation, the cases were assigned at random to five sets of about equal size. On each run, a different set was the test set and the remaining four were the training set.

The VJAP program achieved an accuracy of 79.3% in the LOO evaluation and 77.9% in the fivefold cross validation. These are compared to a majority class baseline of 61.2%.

As compared with the results reported in Figure 4.7, this level of accuracy is lower than IBP's and higher than CATO's (which were assessed with a related database that included 64 cases that did not have conflicting factors). In making the comparison, however, one should take into account that the VJAP program does not abstain, takes value-related information into account, and generates more legally realistic arguments than either IBP or CATO. Moreover, it dispenses with the need in IBP to define KO-Factors.

An advantage of the VJAP program over the value-based theory construction approach of the AGATHA program (Chorley and Bench-Capon, 2005a,c), is that VJAP employs a fine-grained representation with its focus on value trade-offs within and across legal issues. That finer grain means that its arguments can achieve a better fit to the value trade-offs in past cases and better adjust for differences in the factual contexts of the past cases and current problem. Also, the VJAP program generates arguments that are intuitively acceptable to attorneys.

In generating arguments about whether rule requirements (intermediate legal concepts) are satisfied in a given case and what the outcome should be, VJAP not only applies rules and compares the problem with cases, but also reasons about the values underlying the rule in question. It argues whether the rule's requirements should be interpreted expansively, restrictively, or not at all in a given case (Grabmair, 2016). In making these arguments, the program is guided by whether an interpretation produces a decision that is coherent with value trade-offs established through prior cases. The arguments it generates also serve as the basis for predicting the case's outcome.

Finally, Grabmair also constructed a variation of the VJAP system in which arguments about a current case could only be made using precedents decided at least one year prior to the date of the current case. The goal of the so-called VJAP-timeline was "to assess the system's ability to reason with no or little precedent in some cases and many possible precedent cases in others and to examine which precedents are relied on the most by later cases" (Grabmair, 2016, p. 73).

In the evaluation, VJAP-timeline produced better prediction performance than the full VJAP model in the LOO (84.3%) and cross-validation conditions (82.1%) (Grabmair, 2016, p. 80). As far as known, VJAP timeline is the first computational model of case-based legal reasoning or argument to restrict arguments to those that are "temporally plausible given the chronology of the case dataset," a realistic constraint in legal practice.

5.8. COMPUTATIONAL MODEL OF EVIDENTIARY LEGAL ARGUMENT

Evidentiary legal argument refers to the arguments that a trier-of-fact in a trial or hearing considers in deciding whether a side has provided persuasive evidence to prove a conclusion that a legal rule's factual requirements are satisfied. This is to be distinguished from the kinds of legal arguments judges in motions or appellate practice consider in deciding what a legal rule or concept means or in resolving the legal implications of conflicting findings. The argument schemes and model in Hypo, CATO, CABARET, GREBE, Theory Construction, and the VJAP model focus on the latter.

Researchers in AI & Law have developed a number of formal models of evidentiary legal argument and related argument schemes (see, e.g., Bex, 2011; Walker et al., 2011; Verheij et al., 2015).

Walker's argument model is of particular interest here because of its descriptive focus. Walker systematically and empirically investigates evidentiary legal argumentation and judicial decision-making. His model aims to describe in detail the *actual* reasoning of triers of fact as it appears in their published decisions. Although his argument model does not (yet) include a program to analyze new cases and generate predictions and arguments, it does provide schemas of evidentiary legal arguments.

The work involves the *Vaccine/Injury Project* (V/IP) Corpus, developed by the Research Laboratory for Law, Logic and Technology (LLT Lab), Maurice A. Deane School of Law at Hofstra University. The corpus comprises Court of Federal Claims decisions as to whether claims for compensation for vaccination-related injuries comply with the requirements of the National Vaccine Injury Compensation Program (NVICP). In these cases, Special Masters decide which evidence is relevant to which issues of fact, evaluate the plausibility of evidence in the legal record, organize evidence and draw reasonable inferences, and make findings of fact (Walker et al., 2011).

Under the NVICP, a claimant is compensated only if a vaccine *caused* the injury. For policy reasons, however, the concept of causation is specially defined so as to set a lower standard than that for purely scientific causation. Under *Althen v. Secr. of Health and Human Services*, 418 F. 3d 1274 (Fed. Cir. 2005), a petitioner must establish, by a preponderance of the evidence, that:

1. a "medical theory causally connects" the type of vaccine with the type of injury;
2. there was a "logical sequence of cause and effect" between the particular vaccination and the particular injury; and
3. a "proximate temporal relationship" existed between the vaccination and the injury.

The corpus contains all decisions in the first two years of applying the *Althen* test of causation-in-fact (i.e., 35 decision texts, typically 15–40 pages per decision) (Walker et al., 2011).

Walker's model of evidentiary legal argument is called the Default Logic Framework. A DLF argument diagram represents applicable statutory and regulatory requirements as a "rule tree," that is, a tree of authoritative rule conditions, and chains of reasoning in the legal decision that connect evidentiary assertions to the Special Master's findings of fact on those rule conditions (Walker et al., 2011). The statute establishing the rule system for the NVICP exhibits a typical logical structure found in statutes in the United States (Walker et al., 2015b).

Figure 5.15 shows a partial rule tree for vaccine decisions showing the three conditions of the *Althen* rule for proving causation. Each rule tree is a graph with the root node at the top representing the overall issue that the petitioner needs to prove, namely entitlement to compensation under the NVICP. A child node represents a condition for proving the proposition in the connected parent node. Sibling child nodes are connected to their parent node by the connectors, AND, OR, UNLESS, or RULE FACTOR. The connector AND functions as a logical conjunction of necessary conditions, and OR functions as a logical disjunction of independently sufficient conditions. The connector UNLESS functions as rebuttal: if the defeating condition

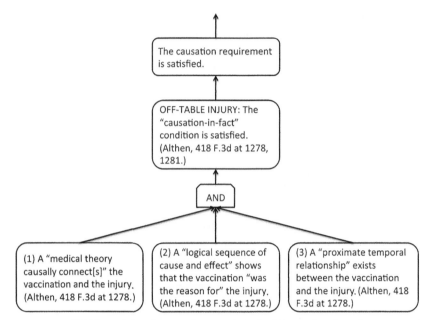

FIGURE 5.15. DLF partial rule tree for vaccine decisions, showing three causation conditions of *Althen* (see Walker et al., 2011)

is true, then the conclusion is false. The connector RULE FACTOR indicates that the truth of the condition tends to make the conclusion more or less probable. In making a finding, a fact finder should take into account the "rule factor" conditions, but the rule does not specify how to assign a truth value. A propositional node in a rule tree may be assigned a value of "true," "undecided," or "false." In a particular case, the findings of fact at the leaf nodes influence the truth value of the root node proposition (Walker et al., 2011).

Figure 5.16 illustrates a chain of reasoning extracted from the decision of the *Stewart*[4] case that connects evidence in the case to the Special Master's findings of fact for the first requirement of the causation rule in the rule tree.

In the DLF model, logical and plausibility connectives are used to connect the Special Master's findings of facts to the propositions in the rule tree. *Evidence factors* model the Special Master's stated reasons for a conclusion and assign them the plausibility value actually assigned by the fact finder (Walker et al., 2011). The DLF model for a decision captures the trier of fact's reasoning for why the evidence proves or fails to prove a legal rule's antecedents. In Figure 5.16, four evidence factors are identified, all of which support the evidentiary finding that the *Althen* rule's first of three requirements has been satisfied.

---

[4] *Stewart v. Secretary of the Department of Health and Human Services*, Office of Special Masters, No. 06-287V, March 19, 2007.

●AND [1 of 3] : (1) A "medical theory causally connect[s]" the vaccination on March 26, 2002 and cerebellar ataxia (Althen, 418 F.3d at 1278) -- that is, hepatitis A vaccine "can ... cause the type of injury alleged" (Pafford, 451 F.3d at 1355-56).

  ●"The plausible medical theory for autoimmune cerebellar ataxia is that the body, sensing a protein to which it responds, misidentifies its own cells as a target for attack." [C: 38; S: Special Master; NLS: The plausible medical theory for autoimmune cerebellar ataxia is that the body, sensing a protein to which it responds, misidentifies its own cells as a target for attack.]

  ●EVIDENCE FACTORS

    ●FACTOR [1 of 6] : "[H]epatitis A virus has been causally linked to cerebellar ataxia." [C: 38-39; S: Special Master; NLS: The logical sequence of cause and effect is that hepatitis A virus has been causally linked to cerebellar ataxia and the vaccine contains an inactivated form of the hepatitis A virus to which, in rare cases, individuals may respond with cerebellar ataxia.]

    ●EVIDENCE FACTORS

      ●FACTOR [1 of 4] : Dr. Marks testified that "medical literature shows that hepatitis A virus can cause acute cerebellar ataxia." [C: 25, S: Special Master; NLS: Secondly, medical literature shows that hepatitis A virus can cause acute cerebellar ataxia.]

        ●Very Plausible

      ...

    ●FACTOR [2 of 6] : "Medical literature links vaccines to cerebellar ataxia." [C: 39; S: Special Master; NLS: Medical literature links vaccines to cerebellar ataxia.]

    ...

    ●FACTOR [3 of 6] : "[T]he [hepatitis A] vaccine contains an inactivated form of the hepatitis A virus to which, in rare cases, individuals may respond with cerebellar ataxia." [C: 39; S: Special Master; NLS: The logical sequence of cause and effect is that hepatitis A virus has been causally linked to cerebellar ataxia and the vaccine contains an inactivated form of the hepatitis A virus to which, in rare cases, individuals may respond with cerebellar ataxia.]

      ●EVIDENCE FACTORS

        ●FACTOR [1 of 4] : "The [hepatitis A] vaccine contains inactivated hepatitis A virus." [C: 39; S: Special Master; NLS: The vaccine contains inactivated hepatitis A virus.]

          ●Very Plausible

        ...

FIGURE 5.16. DLF extracted reasoning chains (excerpts) (see Walker et al., 2011)

Walker's LLT Lab has also begun to classify the types of arguments they are finding in the V/IP Corpus (Walker and Vazirova, 2014). They can identify decisions involving, say, the first condition of *Althen* (that "a medical theory causally connects" the type of vaccine to the type of injury) and identify *all* the types of arguments employed. For instance, in a sample of 10 representative decisions, in which five were decided for the petitioner and five for the government, there appear under this *Althen* condition a total of 56 arguments based on the connective EVIDENCE FACTOR (19 arguments in decisions for the petitioner, 37 in decisions for the government) (Walker and Vazirova, 2014). The researchers suggest classifying such arguments by types of inference (deductive, probabilistic/statistical, or scientific/medical), types of evidence (legal precedent, legal policy, medical/scientific study, case report, fact testimony), and patterns based on evidentiary discrepancies (expert vs. expert, inadequate explanation).

Crucially, Walker's descriptive model addresses real (not toy) examples of evidentiary arguments, and it stays close to the texts of the decisions it models. As will be explained in Parts II and III, the argument schematization and level of detail are instrumental in enabling a novel approach to extract argument-related semantic information from case texts and use it to achieve conceptual AR and cognitive computing. Specifically, the DLF model plays important roles as a basis for identifying the argument-related information (Section 6.8), extracting findings of fact and cited legal rules (Section 10.5), eliciting users' argument-related information needs (Section 11.5.5), and formulating and testing legal hypotheses (Section 12.4.1).

5.9. COMPUTATIONAL MODELS OF LEGAL ARGUMENT AS A BRIDGE

If computational models of argument are a culmination and unifying framework of AI & Law research, what role will they play in CCLAs ? Potentially, computational argument models like the VJAP and DLF models can serve as a bridge between legal texts and the answers humans seek.

Consider, for instance, the sample queries in Table 5.3; they illustrate sensible questions humans might ask some (hypothetical) legal apps or websites covering the family law domain in the argument model examples at the beginning of this chapter. Intuitively, computational models of argument (with legal rules, legal cases, and argument schema) could play a major role in answering these questions in a realistic way.

In determining exactly what that role will be, the following questions need to be addressed:

1. Will a model enable a program to deliver answers to the questions that users can rely on? Or, will the model help systems like Watson or Debater to identify texts with relevant answers and tailor the extracted information to a user's needs? To put it another way, what kind of bridge between texts and answers will the argument model be, a direct and sufficient route in itself, or a guide for humans to construct their own answers?
2. The answers to users' queries like these lie in the legal texts of the statutes and related cases. How will information get from the texts into a computer program in a form that it can use to answer a question?
3. How will the program understand users' questions and gather background information?

TABLE 5.3. *Can CMLAs serve as a bridge between legal texts and answers humans seek?*

Asker	Askee	Question
Martha	legal-advice.com	Doesn't George have to support me?
Martha's attorney	legal-ir.com	What is the statutory argument that George has a duty to support Martha?
George's attorney	legal-ir.com	Are there any cases against the argument that George has a duty to support Martha?
Martha's attorney	eDiscovery program	Do George's and Martha's emails support that they had a parental relationship?
Judge's law clerk	legal-ir.com	What are the strongest arguments for and against the proposition that George has a duty to support Martha?
Legislative clerk	legal-ir.com	Has § 1601 been adequate to protect the state's interest in enforcing obligations of support?
Law student taking Family Law course	Intelligent tutoring system	How do I determine whether George has a duty to support Martha?

As noted in Chapter 1, the answers to legal queries often require explanation and argument. Even answering Martha's question, "Doesn't George have to support me?," may involve arguments. Although she might expect legal-advice.com to give a simple "yes" or "no" answer, realistically the system should respond in a more stereotypically lawyer-like way: "It depends." The system could then offer an explanation of at least some of the contingencies on which the answer depends, such as: "Is George an ancestor of Martha?" "Would being obligated to support Martha cause George some undue hardship?" "Did George and Martha ever have a parent–child relationship?" "How long would the support for Martha be needed?"

The relevant contingencies will need to be represented in some way so that the system can "know" to elicit the answers. There seem to be at least three ways to accomplish this. The first is the expert systems or BNA approach: The knowledge is represented manually in rules whose conditions capture the various facts that could make a difference to a conclusion that there is an obligation of support. Guided probably by backward chaining, the rule engine would inquire regarding the possible facts, as in Waterman's program of Section 1.3.1 or the BNA program of Section 2.3.4.

The second way uses a computational model of legal argument. The knowledge could be represented manually with defeasible legal rules whose critical questions identify the contingencies. Given any legal conclusion and the appropriate argument schemes, the system searches for and identifies possible counterarguments that exploit the contingencies on which the defeasible legal conclusion depends. The possible arguments drive the search via the critical questions for failed assumptions, exceptions, or exclusions that affect any conclusions. Based on these arguments, the system could offer to present the contingencies to Martha and explain why they matter.[5]

Regarding question (1), in these two approaches the model constructs the answers to the question directly. The difference lies in the way they draw inferences. The BNA program or expert system applies predicate logic using classical negation and negation by failure to attempt to prove a conclusion regarding support. In contrast, the argument system performs inferences with defeasible legal rules based on the argument model semantics. The system would, perhaps, construct a rule/argument graph, generate legal rule-, factor-, or case-based arguments as in Carneades, and aggregate the arguments qualitatively or quantitatively as in VJAP.

The third way is a Watson/Debater-type approach. Here the model does not answer the question directly, at least not at the start. Instead, types of argument-related information contained in the model guide the system in identifying texts that answer the question. The argument-related information itself is contained in a corpus of texts including, perhaps, articles from law reviews or other publications concerning the circumstances giving rise to a legal obligation of support. This means identifying texts that have not only answers but also explanations and arguments for an answer and a means to select the most relevant explanations and arguments given the problem the user is trying to solve. One might present Debater with a "topic," for instance, "Under German family law, one person (A) can have a legal obligation to support another person (B)." Debater would scan the documents in order to detect claims relevant to the topic and organize them into an argument pro or con similar to Figure 1.4. The system would order the documents in terms of its confidence in their relevance and highlight the passages that most directly address the query; the user would be left to select, read, and apply their advice to his/her own circumstances.

The third approach depends on a system's ability to understand the user's query and at least some of the legal semantics of the texts. Let's assume for the moment that the former can be addressed and focus on the latter.

The system needs to be able to identify some argument-related information in the texts, such as passages involving arguments on the topic of interest, the roles of parties in those arguments and some relevant features of the fact situation that impact the outcome of the argument such as legal factors. It would also need to identify some legal complications such as differences between the jurisdiction discussed in the article and the German family law contexts. (See the discussion of the Toronto Blue Jays jurisdictional issue in Chapter 1.) With this information, a system could conceivably construct a mapping from the retrieved texts to the current context and tailor its output to the context of the questioner, such as Martha, her attorney, or George's attorney.

---

[5] For an interesting proposed hybrid expert system with defeasible legal rules for reaching family law solutions in the best interests of children (see Araszkiewicz et al., 2013).

When the users' questions become more specific about the kinds of arguments the user seeks, more may be required than the Watson/Debater approach has provided so far. For example, Martha's or George's attorneys may seek arguments involving statutory rules or a specific rule like §1601, arguments based on cases or on a specific case like the *Mueller* case, or such arguments but where the duty of support was upheld or defeated. Users may seek arguments where the lack of a parent–child relationship defeated an obligation of support, arguments defeating such arguments, or arguments where email evidence was used successfully to show the existence of a parental relationship.

For responding to queries like these, information like that contained in computational models of legal argument would seem necessary. The kind of argument-related information associated with CMLAs could help a Debater-type system identify structural and semantic features of arguments in texts, which, in turn, can identify types of arguments, such as arguments about the meanings of statutory requirements or arguments about evidence. The system could then select the most relevant materials for constructing answers and arguments pro and con. It could recognize, retrieve, and highlight relevant arguments made previously in the cases and identify texts with contrary conclusions indicating possibly useful counterarguments.

For queries seeking the strongest arguments for and against George's duty of support or predicting the outcome, CMLAs would seem necessary to take substantive criteria into account. If legal factors like Never-had-parent–child-relationship or Has-already-provided-much-support are to be identified automatically in texts and employed in constructing arguments and making predictions, a computational model of legal argument would be instrumental. Similarly, a CMLA like the VJAP model (Section 5.7) could help the system identify and reason with legal factors in responding to the law and legislative clerks' queries concerning decisions' effects on underlying values.[6] Finally, in answering the Family Law student's question concerning how to analyze George's duty to support Martha, Debater could probably find a "how to" article, but only a CMLA could engage the student in practice arguments.

The arguments will thus be generated by combining Debater-like extraction of prior arguments from texts in a corpus with a computational model of argument making predictions, constructing arguments tailored to a problem, and exploring variations. At least, that is the goal.

With respect to question (2), how information will get from the texts into a computer program, the Watson/Debater approach has the considerable advantage over the other two of avoiding manual knowledge representation. Assuming the documents exist, it can find a document whose propositions relate to the topic pro or

---

[6] The features in the SCOTUS project (Section 4.4) probably cannot be extracted directly from the texts of decisions and require extensive feature engineering. The features employed in Lex Machina can be extracted from texts, but as far as known, they do not model substantive features of the cases.

con and its ability to do so does not depend on some knowledge engineer's having anticipated a defeasible legal rule's critical question on each and every point.

Now, as to question (3) above: How will the program understand users' questions and gather background information? This is a significant technical challenge because it involves the system understanding the problem the user hopes to solve as well as the context, including some of the considerations that can complicate a solution. This book does not offer a general solution to this problem of computer understanding. Instead, it addresses the challenge in a way that may suffice for developing legal apps that can help humans answer questions like those in Table 5.3.

This book identifies a kind of problem, helping users test legal hypotheses, that constrains the challenge of understanding users' queries but that is still a robust and useful example of cognitive computing (Section 12.4). In order to assist in understanding users' queries, it outlines the design of a user interface that employs the resources of argument models like DLF and CMLAs like VJAP (see Sections 11.5.5 and 12.5.3). These resources include the language of argument-related types and graphical representations associated with the roles sentences play in legal arguments, and semantic features of legal arguments in particular domains such as legal factors.

ML will play a number of roles. The systems will learn to extract semantic features that help it to improve relevance selection and assist humans, such as structural cues, argument roles of propositions, and substantive features like legal factors. ML will help systems learn the weights of features in assessing confidence in its understanding of a question or in its answer, explanation, or argument. Finally, the systems will also learn by associating humans' arguments with success or failure and from feedback associated with questions, answers, and arguments that users report best address their problems.

Part II continues to explain how computational models of argument will serve as a bridge between legal texts and answers focusing particularly on the DLF of Vern Walker. Chapter 6 explains how to represent concept and relation types that correspond to those in rule trees and the DLF chains of reasoning. Annotating legal texts in terms of such concepts and relations is a key to connecting the texts and computational models of argument. After introducing legal information retrieval and ML techniques, Part II explains how to annotate the texts with argument-related conceptual information. Part III explains how to use the information and ML to support conceptual retrieval of legal documents based on the arguments they contain, and how to apply argument-related information from other CMLAs potentially to predict outcomes and make new legal arguments. At each step, the goal is objectively to measure the effectiveness of the techniques, for example by comparing the conceptual information retrieval system's rankings of relevant documents with that of current legal IR systems.

PART II

Legal Text Analytics

6

Representing Legal Concepts in Ontologies and Type Systems

6.1. INTRODUCTION

As Part I indicates, knowledge representation has been a key focus of AI & Law research and a key challenge for implementing systems robust enough to serve as real-world legal practice tools.

Ontologies help to meet that challenge. An ontology specifies the fundamental types of things or concepts that exist for purposes of a system and sets out the relations among them.

After introducing some basic information about ontologies, this chapter surveys some historically influential legal ontologies and explains some modern techniques for constructing ontologies semiautomatically. It then turns to ontological supports for statutory reasoning and for legal argumentation. In connection with the latter, an extended example illustrates ontological supports for making arguments with a small collection of cases.

Finally, the chapter introduces a specialized kind of ontology, "type systems," which are a basic text analytic tool. Type systems support automatically marking-up or annotating legal texts semantically in terms of concepts and their relations. They will play key roles in conceptual legal information retrieval and in cognitive computing.

This chapter addresses the following questions. What is a legal ontology and how are legal ontologies used? What is semantic annotation? What are text annotation pipelines and what role does a type system play? What is a UIMA framework? How are legal ontologies and UIMA type systems constructed? How can developers of legal type systems take advantage of existing legal ontologies and of ontologies already developed for medicine, or for other real world domains that have legal implications?

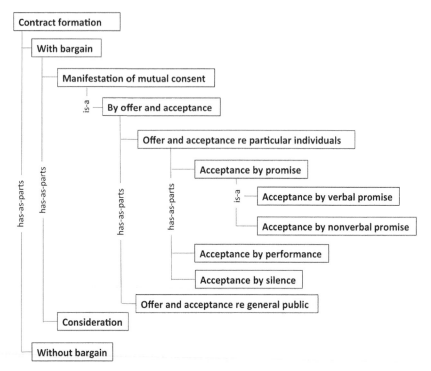

FIGURE 6.1. Sample ontology for contract formation

6.2. ONTOLOGY BASICS

Despite its metaphysical connotations, the term "ontology" is not quite so imposing in the context of computational models. An *ontology* is an "explicit, formal, and general specification of a conceptualization of the properties of and relations between objects in a given domain" (Wyner, 2008). In other words, ontologies make concepts in a domain explicit so that a program can reason with them.

For example, Figure 6.1 shows a simple ontology for the legal concept of contract formation. This kind of an ontology might have been useful for Ann Gardner's first-year contracts problem analyzer (Section 1.4.2) and captures concepts and relations described in Gardner (1987, pp. 121–3) such as "Manifestation of mutual consent" and "Acceptance by verbal promise."

Legal ontologies include some standard relations among concepts, represented by labeled links, two of which are illustrated in Figure 6.1:

- **is-a:** class membership expression, for example, an "Acceptance by verbal promise" is-a "Acceptance by promise."
- **has-as-parts:** indicating a part-whole relationship, for example, the concept of "Offer and acceptance re particular individuals" has-as-parts "Acceptance by promise," "Acceptance by performance," and "Acceptance by silence."

Other standard relations not illustrated in the figure include:

- **has-function:** indicating a functional role of the parent, for example, "an organization has social functions" (Breuker et al., 2004, p. 267).
- **has-parent, has-child:** indicating relative position in a hierarchy, for example, "Base-level Factors have Intermediate Legal Concerns as parent factors; Intermediate Legal Concerns have Intermediate Legal Concerns or Legal Issues as parent factors" (Wyner, 2008, p. 368).

The example of has-parent links would be relevant in an ontology of the conceptual components of a factor hierarchy as in CATO (Section 3.3.2).

Discussions of ontologies typically distinguish between high-level ontological frameworks and lower-level domain ontologies (Breuker et al., 2004; Breuker and Hoekstra, 2004).

An ontological framework specifies fundamental concepts. For instance, one could extend the legal ontology in Figure 6.1 to the left to provide a framework of more fundamental concepts of contract law and of law generally. In addition to "Contract formation," one might include "Contract performance" and "Contract non-performance," all as parts of a superconcept, "Contractual obligations." That concept, in turn, might have sister concepts, "Obligations in Tort," "Obligations under Criminal Law," each of which has-parent "Legal obligations."

One might also extend the ontology toward the right to create a domain ontology, that is, a specification of the objects, predicates, and relations for a given domain such as contract formation. For instance, one might identify "Exchange of telegrams," "Completion of purchase order," "Oral statement of agreement" as some of the means for performing "Acceptance by verbal promise," perhaps linking them with has-function links to the parent. Or one might specify some ways of performing "Offer and acceptance re general public" via, say, "By advertisement" or "By offering a reward."

The role of an ontology is to provide a conceptual vocabulary for representing the knowledge that a computer program can process. It "define[s] and deliver[s] the building blocks for the construction or interpretations of actual situations and histories: partial models of real or imaginary worlds" (Breuker et al., 2004). For example, if a program encounters an exchange of telegrams, based on information contained in the ontology of Figure 6.1 as extended into a domain ontology for contract formation, it has a basis for concluding that the scenario deals with "Offer and acceptance re particular individuals" rather than "Offer and acceptance re general public," a topic to which other legal rules apply.

In this way, ontologies make assumptions about concepts and relations explicit so that a program can reason with them to some extent. They also enable expanding queries to legal information retrieval systems. With respect to a query concerning offer and acceptance re particular individuals, a case involving an exchange of telegrams might be relevant to one involving an oral statement of agreement. In the world of e-commerce via the Semantic Web, ontologies also play a role in facilitating exchange of information and queries across multiple databases, perhaps helping an automated purchasing agent to align, to the extent possible, civil law and common law concepts employed in a database of international purchase orders.

6.3. SAMPLE LEGAL ONTOLOGIES

Two sample legal ontologies, the e-Court ontology and van Kralingen's frame-based ontology, illustrate the variety of roles ontologies play in knowledge representation as well as two distinction approaches to designing ontologies.

6.3.1. *The e-Court Ontology*

A team at the University of Amsterdam developed the e-Court ontology as part of a European project for semantically indexing archived legal documents, including audio/video recordings of depositions and hearings in criminal law actions. The ontology provides a structured vocabulary for describing documents and their content in the form of metadata, that is, data about data.

The metadata include non-semantic information about the documents such as author, date, authorization, type (for example, audio, video, or transcript), name, and identifier of the criminal case, as well as other structural information determined by local court procedures. The metadata also include some semantic information characterizing a document's content, for example, case descriptions, such as oral testimony in deposition or hearings, and topics from criminal procedure law, for instance, from the indictment or trial. Semantic metadata also include keywords indicating the type of crime involved, such as murder or manslaughter, or the weapon used in a particular criminal case (Breuker et al., 2004; Van Engers et al., 2008).

The metadata tags are organized in an index that users can browse to find documents. Users can also include tags as semantic constraints in queries for targeting documents. The IR system can expand user queries based on links in the ontology to subsuming or subsumed classes of semantic tags. For instance, "killing" could be expanded to "murder" and "manslaughter." "Glock 23" could be generalized to "weapon."

Figure 6.2 shows some excerpts of the e-Court ontology whose relevance to the criminal trial information retrieval task is fairly clear. The e-Court ontology was based on an ontological framework called the LRI-Core ontology (Breuker and Hoekstra, 2004). In Figure 6.2, the boldface terms are terms from LRI-Core. The non-boldface terms are part of a domain ontology for criminal procedure law in the Netherlands called CRIME.NL.

Ontologies standardize the representation of knowledge about legal concepts. This standardization includes constraints on the relations among the various types or

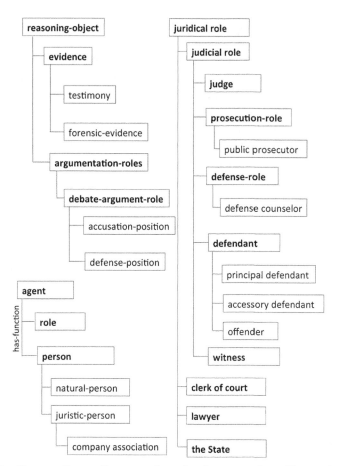

FIGURE 6.2. Excerpts from e-Court ontology showing expansion of "reasoning object," "agent," and "juridical role." Links are is-a unless otherwise noted (see Breuker and Hoekstra, 2004; Breuker et al., 2004; Van Engers et al., 2008)

concepts. For instance, in the LRI-Core ontology, "roles" are taken by "persons" who are "agents." Although Figure 6.2 does not suggest these constraints through cross links or otherwise, when constructing a knowledge base according to an ontology, formal rules embody these constraints.

Some of the above ontological relationships may support another function of ontologies: inheritance of features. Inheritance achieves a certain economy of representation. A subconcept of a concept is endowed automatically with the properties of the concept. An is-a relationship assumes that "the class of objects and the properties of the objects in the class fully and explicitly define the class. One specifies subclasses which inherit properties from the superclass while being further defined in their particular properties" (Wyner, 2008, p. 363).

For instance, in the e-Court context, by virtue of the is-a relationships in Figure 6.2, the concept of an "offender" inherits the properties of the concepts of "defendant," "judicial role," and "juridical role" (Breuker et al., 2004, p. 257). As the authors of the LRI-Core ontology put it, "properties of the concepts of the foundational ontology are inherited by the core ontology via the is-a 'backbone,' so not surprisingly a legal role has all properties of a role, etc." (Breuker and Hoekstra, 2004).

Incidentally, the LRI-Core ontology was subsequently incorporated into the Legal Knowledge Interchange Format (LKIF) (Gordon, 2008a). LKIF includes an implementation of the core ontology of basic legal concepts in the Ontology Web Language (OWL), an ontology that computer programs can read and process automatically, for instance, in conducting transactions via the Semantic Web (see Wyner, 2008, p. 363). For example, the German family law rules in the examples of argumentation with defeasible legal rules in Section 5.3 can be represented conveniently in LKIF and processed by the Carneades system.

6.3.2. *van Kralingen's Frame-based Ontology*

Some ontologies employ more elaborate facilities for representing information about concepts. They specify frames with slots to represent a concept's standard features. The frames are like templates or forms, and the slots are like the blanks in the forms to be filled in.

For example, Table 6.1 shows van Kralingen's classic frame-based ontology for representing legal entities including norms (that is, legal rules), concepts, and acts. Each frame's slots specify a place for representing the values of standard features of any given legal norm, concept, or act. The slot fillers represent particular values of those features for instantiations of legal norms, concepts, or acts (see Van Kralingen et al., 1999, pp. 1135–8, 1150–3).

It happens that the frames illustrated in the figure are to be applied to represent a college library regulation. The sample filled-in slots at the right side contain the detailed library rule information. For instance, the instantiated norm provides that the borrower shall return the book by the due date, the concept "borrowed" is defined, and the act of returning the book by the date due is described.

As knowledge representation tools, frames specify semantic constraints for a given domain, in part by defining the types of things that can serve as fillers for a particular slot. For instance, the "legal modality" slot of the norm frame in Table 6.1 specifies four types of legal modalities: ought, ought not, may, or can. The concept frame's type slot specifies four types: definition, deeming provision, factor, or meta. The "temporal aspects" slot of a legal act frame could specify constraints on the types of fillers that the slot will accept such as dates and times. If one tries to enter types of values different from those specified, the program would object.

In order to enforce the constraints, the slot values of frames can include tests with which a program can assess whether a concept applies. For example, in the

TABLE 6.1. *Three ontology frames for legal norm, concept, and legal act with slot fillers for library regulation (see Van Kralingen et al., 1999, pp. 1135–8, 1150–3)*

"Norm" element	Description	IC Library Regulations Example
Norm identifier	used as point of reference for the norm	"norm-2"
Norm type	e.g., norm of conduct or norm of competence	Norm of conduct
Promulgation	source of the norm	IC Library Regulations article 2
Scope	range of application of the norm	IC Library Regulations
Application conditions	conditions under which norm applies	Subject has borrowed a book
Subject	person to whom norm addressed	Borrower
Legal modality	ought, ought not, may, or can	Ought to
Act identifier	used as reference to a separate act description	"return-book-by-date-due"

"Concept" element	Description	IC Library Regulations Example
Concept identifier	used as point of reference for the concept	borrowed
Concept	concept described	borrowed (Person, Book)
Concept type	definition, deeming provision, factor, or meta	definition
Priority	weight assigned to a factor, if applicable	NA
Promulgation	source of concept description	{(knowledge-engineer)}
Scope	range of application of concept description	{IC Library Regulations}
Conditions	conditions under which a concept is applicable	true_from(T, registered(Person, Book)) and true_from(T, possession(Person, Book))
Instances	enumeration of instances of the concept	always_false

"Act" element	Description	IC Library Regulations Example
Act identifier	used as point of reference for the act	"return-book-by-date-due"
Promulgation	source of the act description	IC Library Regulations article 2
Scope	range of application of the act description	IC Library Regulations
Agent	individual, set of individuals, aggregate, or conglomerate	Borrower
Act type	basic acts or acts specified elsewhere	Return
Means	material objects used in the action or more specific descriptions	
Manner	way in which the action has been performed	
Temporal aspects	absolute time specification	Book should be returned by the date due
Spatial aspects	location where the action takes place	
Circumstances	situation under which the action takes place	A book has been borrowed
Cause	reasons to perform the action	
Aim	goal visualized by the agent	
Intentionality	state of mind of the agent	
Final state	results and consequences of an action	

frame shown in Table 6.1 of the concept "borrowed," the "conditions" slot includes the following tests: "true_from(T, registered(Person, Book)) and true_from(T, possession(Person, Book))." Using these tests, a program could assess the applicability of the concept "borrowed."

The instantiated frames also interrelate: the norm frame, norm-2, employs a concept, "borrowed," which is defined in the borrowed concept frame, and it refers to an act, "return-book-by-date-due" described in the action frame. In a frame-based ontology, these interrelations are implicit conceptual links enforced by ontological constraints on the type of concepts that can be used to fill the slots.

Given a legal ontology's functionality in representing knowledge in a manner a computer program can apply, as illustrated in these samples, one can appreciate its usefulness in building a legal application. The ontology defines classes of objects, specifies their possible features and attributes, enforces constraints on feature values, and specifies the relationships among objects. Using frames and slots, one can create instances of the classes and populate a knowledge base. This can support not only conceptual information retrieval, as in the e-Court ontology, but also some reasoning, as illustrated in the library regulation instantiation of van Kralingen's frame-based ontology. To enable additional reasoning, one can apply, for instance, "production rules to elements of the knowledge base to support inference" (Wyner, 2008, p. 363) or the methods of case-based argument discussed in Part I.

6.4. CONSTRUCTING LEGAL ONTOLOGIES

Legal ontologies have traditionally been constructed by hand but, increasingly, NLP and ML provide automated assistance.

Ontologies need to reflect human expert knowledge concerning which concepts and relations should be included to enable a system to perform its ultimate tasks. Automated approaches, however, can identify apparently important concepts and relations in a corpus based on statistical analysis. Automation can then flag the candidate concepts and relations for consideration by the human experts. The human experts can decide whether to include the candidates and can relabel the nodes and arcs for inclusion in the ontology.

The Drafting Legislation with Ontology base Support (DALOS) ontology (Figure 6.3) is an example of this approach (Francesconi et al., 2010). The ontology was designed to support legislative drafting across EU member states and languages focusing on the domain of consumer protection. The goal was to provide a taxonomy of types of normative provisions dealing with consumer protection but also a conceptual vocabulary for describing generic situations involving consumer protection across two languages, English and Italian.

The Ontological Layer in the top half of Figure 6.3 illustrates this conceptual vocabulary, including such terms as *Supplier* and *Consumer*, some types of

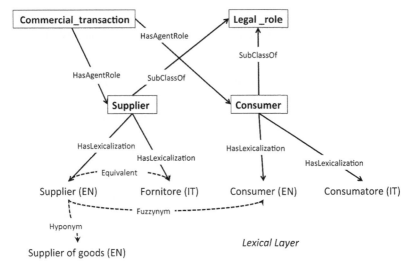

FIGURE 6.3. Ontology in the DALOS system (excerpts) (see Francesconi et al., 2010)

agents in a commercial transaction. Legal domain experts constructed the Ontological Layer manually in a top-down manner and have specified the relationships between them. For instance, *Consumer* and *Supplier* both involve being in a *Commercial_transaction*. *Commercial_transaction* HasAgentRole with *Supplier* and with *Consumer*, both of which are a SubClassOf *Legal_role*. Other relationships include HasObjectRole and HasValue.

How are such entities as commercial transactions, suppliers, and consumers referred to across the whole range of consumer transactions such as in sales contracts and credit agreements? To answer that, the researchers conducted a semiautomatic, bottom-up extraction of the terminology from corpora of domain documents in different languages using NLP technologies combined with ML techniques. The results are illustrated in the Lexical Layer in the bottom half of Figure 6.3.

In the Lexical Layer, terms are linked by a few types of linguistic relationships: hyponyms, equivalents, and fuzzynyms. A "hyponym" is word with a more specific meaning than a general term applicable to it. For instance, the English term "supplier" is linked to its hyponym, "supplier of goods," as well as to its equivalent in Italian, *fornitore*. A "fuzzynym" is a "wider associative relation linking words which may share salient features ... without being necessarily semantically similar" (Francesconi et al., 2010, p. 101). As a statistical matter, the terms "supplier" and "consumer" appear frequently together in the documents and are treated as fuzzynyms.

The Lexical Layer is constructed from a list of terms extracted automatically from a corpus of English and Italian consumer law documents, including legal and regulatory provisions as well as case law (Francesconi et al., 2010, p. 105). In the extraction process, the texts in the corpus are processed to identify parts of speech (POS) and parsed to identify certain shallow grammatical relationships of interest:

- noun (e.g., creditor, product)
- adjective–noun (e.g., current account, local government)
- noun–noun (e.g., credit agreement, product safety)
- noun–preposition–adjective–noun (e.g., purchase of immovable property, principle of legal certainty)
- noun–preposition–noun–noun (e.g., cancellation of credit agreement, settlement of consumer dispute) (Francesconi et al., 2010, p. 106).

Then, statistical measures are applied to identify the more salient terminological units. For instance, the *tf/idf*[1] measure, a measure proportional to the frequency of the term in a document and inversely related to the number of documents in the corpus in which the term is found, is computed for a term and compared to an empirically determined threshold. The term is selected for inclusion in the ontology if its *tf/idf* measure is high enough (Francesconi et al., 2010, p. 107).

The chosen terms are then collected into hyponyms or fuzzynyms based on the internal structure of the noun phrases. For instance, "time-share contract," "credit contract," and "consumer contract" were classified as co-hyponyms of the general term "contract." The terms and their relations are then added to the Lexical Layer as in the bottom half of Figure 6.3.

The final step is refining the Ontological and Lexical Layers and incrementally linking concepts between the two layers. Human experts perform this step, but they are assisted by the information now presented in the Lexical Layer. The hyponyms and fuzzynyms represent the system's best statistically based guess at which terms and "fine-grained relations … should be expertly evaluated for inclusion into the ontology, and linked to existing ontology elements by means of existing or new object properties" (Francesconi et al., 2010, p. 111).

In the Lexical Layer, the semantic relatedness of the fuzzynym relationship between, for example, the terms "supplier" and "consumer" leads the human expert to consider assigning an explicit semantic interpretation at the Ontological level, for example, an agent link, to the *Commercial_transaction* concept, and subclasses of the *Legal_role* concept (Francesconi et al., 2010, p. 102).

Interestingly, in DALOS, the documents are multilingual. Cross-language equivalences are thus semiautomatically identified with a combination of statistical analysis and human expert confirmation. For instance, as suggested in Figure 6.3, the Italian term, *fornitore* may first become associated with its English equivalent *Supplier* through a fuzzynym relationship for which a human expert then provides semantic confirmation.

---

[1] Term frequency (*tf*)/inverse document frequency (*idf*).

6.5. ONTOLOGICAL SUPPORT FOR STATUTORY REASONING

The DALOS approach aimed to support legislative drafting by helping to create a taxonomy of types of consumer protection provisions. Other ontologies assist attorneys, corporate employers, and citizens to find or apply regulatory provisions.

Today, statutes and regulations are systematically annotated with a variety of markup languages. Originally, such markups focused on enabling a document to appear the way the author intended no matter what computing platform a viewer is using.

Increasingly, however, such standards go beyond display of information and enable structural and semantic markups of documents. A structural markup is a standardized categorization of parts of a text based on their structural roles in a document (e.g., preambles, clauses, sections, subsections). A semantic markup is a standard categorization of different parts of a text according to their meaning in the document (e.g., as provisions, definitions, citations, names, dates). *XML* or Extensible Markup Language is a grammar and format for such structured data. XML files are a good choice for containing annotated documents because they are readable by humans.

Legal document markup languages, such as LegalDocML, based on Akoma Ntoso (Cervone et al., 2015), provide a systematic XML-type mechanism for representing legal documents including statutes and regulations and referencing documents based on Uniform Resource Identifiers (URIs) in some authoritative online repository. The more familiar Internet URLs are a subset of URIs that also provide a location for the resource.

For example, in Akoma Ntoso, all the documents or resources are identified by a unique name using naming conventions and an ontology of classes relating to legal documents, such as:

- Works (e.g., "act 3 of 2015"),
- Expressions (e.g., "act 3 of 2015 as in the version following the amendments entered into force on July 3rd, 2016"),
- Manifestations (e.g., "PDF representation of act 3 of 2015 as in the version …"),
- Items (e.g., "the file called act32015.pdf on my computer containing a PDF representation of act 3, 2015 as in the version …"),
- Components of the above, including expression components to represent articles, sections, etc., and
- "individuals (Person), organizations (Corporate Body), actions and occurrences (Event), locations (Place), ideas (Concept) and physical objects (Object)" (Oasis, 2016).

With statutes marked-up in LegalDocML or a similar markup language, linking between logical versions of legal rules and their statutory sources becomes easier, ameliorating some of the complexity of maintaining isomorphic representations (see Section 2.5.3). For example, the Eunomos system, a legal document and knowledge management system, based on legislative XML and ontologies,

> recognizes the need for a stricter coupling between legal knowledge and its legislative sources, associating the concepts of its legal ontology with the part of regulations defining them, structured using legislative XML...[This] ground[s] concepts of legal ontologies to their sources, making ontologies more acceptable to practitioners and synchronizing their meaning with the evolution of the text of the law across its modifications. (Boella et al., 2016)

In other words, markup languages and ontologies like that in Eunomos and Akoma Ntoso help to address the need for isomorphic representations of statutes (see Section 2.5.3). Thus, business rules can be annotated with links to their statutory sources for purposes of explanation and justification. When a statutory source is modified, links to or searches for the implementing business rules can indicate the need for possible updating.

Annotations in the statutory source texts can also maintain temporal information about amended versions of the provisions and their effective dates. In analyzing problems involving past events, a system could then determine which version of a statute was in effect at a particular time (Palmirani, 2011).

Ultimately, developers of ontologies of statutory and regulatory documents aim to support some measure of legal reasoning. The developers of Eunomos plan to associate "norms with (extended) Input/Output logic formulae whose predicates are 1:1 connected with the classes of the reference ontology, thus enabling automatic inferences on the addresses of the norms" (Boella et al., 2016). In other words, they will link the textual statutory sources of business rules with abstract representations of norms and computationally implementable logical representations of the norms via classes in the ontology.

For example, a particular directive of the EU Parliament states,

> A lawyer who wishes to practise in a Member State other than that in which he obtained his professional qualification shall register with the competent authority in that State.

A system would represent this provision with a logical formula, which states, in effect, the following: For all combinations of a lawyer (x), a Member State (y), an action in which x wants an action of practicing in y, not the Member State where x was initially qualified, there should exist a registration action by x in y. A suitable legal ontology would represent in logical terms the meaning of these concepts and their associated constraints, rather like the logically expressed conditions in the concept frame of Table 6.1 for the library regulation domain. Then, given data about an employer's roster of staff attorneys, their qualifications, and their pending assignments, a program would be triggered automatically to reason about whether the lawyers satisfied the requirement (Robaldo et al., 2015).

The work on norm graphs in Oberle et al. (2012) (Section 2.5.1) had a similar focus. The research aimed to support business compliance with statutory requirements, in particular for engineering compliant software, by integrating a statutory ontology, a subject matter ontology, and "user-guided subsumption between both" (Oberle et al., 2012, p. 312).

A *statutory ontology* contains a taxonomy of normative concepts employed in a statute, their relations to other normative concepts, as well as, their relations to concepts in the regulated domain's subject matter. In other words, it relates the statutory concepts to the concepts and relations for describing real-world situations.

The authors conceive of an ontology as employing "formal logic in order to map concept class relations from the normative rules to the subject matter to which they apply" (Oberle et al., 2012, p. 288).[2] Thus, similar to Robaldo et al. (2015) and Boella et al. (2016), a statutory ontology represents in logical terms the meaning of the statutory concepts and their associated constraints. The statutory ontology can then support subsumption of fact situations by business rule norms as described in Section 2.5.1. It also enables testing whether the normative concepts in fact subsume those situations as intended.

The envisioned program would semiautomate construction of the ontologies, focusing on a small number of legal consequences relevant to a limited regulatory domain. As the authors characterize their philosophy: "Ontologies are tedious to build. Consequently there should be more and smaller ones" (Dietrich et al., 2007, p. 189).

The authors sketch how to build such a statutory ontology, in particular a "data privacy ontology for private bodies," which formalizes elements of the German FDPA and related provisions (Oberle et al., 2012, p. 288).

The envisioned program would provide a lexicon of regulatory terms and concepts derived from an automated analysis of the statutory texts. An expert would select relevant concepts, identify taxonomic and other relationships among the concepts, and add them to the statutory ontology. By selecting particular concepts and relations, the expert could represent constraints in business rules by constructing or modifying norm graphs like those shown in Figure 2.6. If the expert wished to apply practical business information, for example, that there is a shortcut around the requirements of FDPA §4b II sentence 1 BDSG, as illustrated in Section 2.5.1, that could be represented explicitly in the norm graph as well.

The subject matter ontology also needs to be constructed. It contains schema representing information about classes and relations (italicized) such as "Web service *isa* Software *isa* Data *isa* Information object" and "Software *performs* Web Service

---

[2] Both DALOS and the FDPA ontology employed DOLCE (Gangemi et al., 2002), as a foundational ontology of concepts, entities, classes, and properties that the taxonomies extended and specialized in the direction of the particular statutes of interest (Francesconi et al., 2010, p. 103; Oberle et al., 2012, p. 289, fn. 9).

Operation Invocation, which *targets* Web Service Operation and *requests* Data *about* Entity" (see Oberle et al., 2012, p. 295).

The subject matter ontology also comprises instances of the schema to represent specific classes.

> Instances are concrete elements of classes that have relations to other instances according to the schema. For example, an instance WSOpl1 of class Web Service Operation Invocation might represent the transfer [of] data to Google Maps. (see Oberle et al., 2012, p. 296)

The goal is that, by focusing on topics such as engineering compliant software, many of the instances of concepts and relations in the subject matter ontology can be added straightforwardly from software industry sources.

Once the norm graphs, statutory ontology, and subject matter ontology are in place, the authors envision that the system could guide a software developer into designing compliant software. Various legal consequences need to be established, for instance, that the software satisfies the "legality" and "effective consent" requirements. The program attempts to subsume the targeted software design, described to the extent possible in terms of the subject matter ontology's instances. It flags norm concepts that still need to be satisfied and provides the developer with resources to try to satisfy them.

For example, consider "Electronic Form," the leaf-node concept of the norm graph at the lower right of Figure 2.6. In an interface, when a user clicks on the concept,

> The [software] developer is informed about requirements for electronic consent according to Sec. 13 (2) of the TMA [represented at the left side of the figure]. The corresponding view offers a visualisation of the legal concept as formalised in the data privacy ontology for private bodies. In addition, the view offers tabs for the concept's definition, additional commentaries, or further information all of which are part of the lexicon provided by the legal expert (Oberle et al., 2012, p. 306).

In this way, the system would provide semiautomated, user-guided subsumption enabling developers to design compliant software. At least, that is the goal.

The use of automated IE techniques from texts could make it easier to construct ontologies from statutes and build knowledge representation systems for business rules. For instance, "future research on Eunomos will include populating fields such as deontic clause, passive role, active role, crime and sanction in the extended ontology for prescriptions using information extraction (IE) techniques" (Boella et al., 2016). This topic is considered in Chapter 9.

6.6. ONTOLOGICAL SUPPORT FOR LEGAL ARGUMENTATION

What sort of legal ontology can support knowledge acquisition for the kind of argument-scheme-driven reasoning, described in Section 5.7, that involves interpreting legal rule concepts with analogical arguments taking into account underlying values? As far as I know, no off-the-shelf ontology is available for this purpose.

The following extended thought experiment illustrates the features that an ontology should provide in order to represent this kind of reasoning in a very limited domain, which nevertheless could serve as the basis for a legal educational application.

The point of the illustration is to underscore the complexity of representing knowledge to enable a computer to construct even relatively constrained but realistic legal arguments. Fortunately, for cognitive computing to work, computational models of argument do not need to generate legal arguments themselves. They do, however, inform the design of a different kind of ontology, a *type system*, explained in Section 6.7. A type system can enable a legal app to help human users find relevant arguments by identifying argument-related information in texts based on a descriptive model of legal argument like the DLF model.

6.6.1. *A Target Application for Legal Argument Ontology*

First, let's consider the targeted educational application. Suppose, one wanted a system to generate dialogues that a law professor and students might engage in about legal concepts. Table 6.2 illustrates the kind of legal classroom Socratic dialogue within the range of current argument models in AI & Law (see Ashley, 2009a, 2011).

It is a simplified version of the kind of dialogue one might hope to encounter in a first-year Property Law class as the lessons turn to the topic of property rights in wild animals and the case of *Pierson v. Post*, 3 Caines R. (N.Y. 1805), treated in legal casebooks on property law (see, e.g., Dukeminier et al., 2010). The topic deals with an issue of common (i.e., judge-made as opposed to statutory) law: Under what circumstances may "hunters" have property rights in their quarry? As noted in Section 3.4, the topic has been the focus of much discussion in AI & Law (see, for example, Berman and Hafner, 1993; Atkinson and Bench-Capon, 2007; Gordon and Walton, 2009).

An educational software developer might design a program that generates dialogues like Table 6.2 as part of an intelligent tutoring system. An online Property Law course or MOOC might incorporate such gamified versions of classroom Socratic legal dialogues, where students and instructor make and respond to arguments. Engaging students in selecting argument moves could teach both substantive law and the kinds of first-year legal argumentation skills students need to read and understand a legal casebook (see, for example, Ashley, 2000; Aleven, 2003).

TABLE 6.2. *Sample Socratic legal dialogue in a microworld with argument moves (P = Plaintiff, D = Defendant) (Ashley, 2009a, 2011)*

Transcript	Argument moves
Part 1. Teacher: What should the legal test be in the *Popov* case for determining P's property right, if any, in the baseball?	
Part 2. Student-A: The test should protect fair play such as "If P manifestly intended to gain possession of something of value, and D intentionally interfered causing P to fail, then P can recover." In *Popov*, like the *Keeble* case, P won where P manifestly closed in on its quarry, D knew P was closing in on the quarry goal, and D intentionally interfered physically with P's closing in on the quarry.	• Propose test for P • Justify test ito principles and precedents • Analogize precedent ito factors
Part 3. Teacher: Is protecting fair play the only condition? If a school master D of a competing new school frightened students on their way to the old school of the P schoolmaster, if the P recovered it would protect fair play but economic competition would be reduced.	• Pose hypo/challenge test as too broad • Justify challenge ito principles
Part 4. Student-A: The *Popov* case is different from the Competing Schoolmasters hypothetical because P and D are not in economic competition; a pro-D factor in the hypothetical does not apply in *Popov*. Nevertheless, I will restrict my test to errant "baseballs" rather than to "something of value."	• Distinguish hypo • Modify test to remove overbreadth
Part 5. Student-B: In response to Student-A, *Keeble* is different from *Popov*. In *Keeble* P pursued his livelihood on his own land, and the court protected livelihoods and landowner's rights. *Popov* is more like *Pierson* where D won even though P manifestly closed in on it quarry, D knew P was closing in on the quarry goal, and D intentionally interfered physically with P's closing in on the quarry.	• Distinguish pro-P precedent ito factors • Justify distinction ito principles • Argue principle not legally enforceable • Cite trumping counterexample ito factors
Part 6. Teacher: What test do you suggest?	• Propose test for D
Part 7. Student-B: My test is "If P did not gain possession of the baseball (e.g., by catching and securing it), then he cannot recover." This test would reduce frivolous law suits by discouraging litigants who "almost caught" the ball or "should have had it," and avoid property rights in public property. This is not a concern in *Keeble*.	• Justify test ito principles and precedents • Distinguish pro-P precedent on principle

186

Here, let's suppose the instructor introduces the scenario of the relatively recent case, *Popov v. Hayashi*, 2002 WL 31833731 (Cal. Superior, 2002). On the last day of the 2001 season, the San Francisco Giants' Barry Bonds set a new record when he hit his 73d home run. In the stands, Popov, a fan, caught the ball in his glove for an instant but then lost it when other fans immediately tackled him. Bystander Hayashi ended up grabbing the ball when it rolled out from under the scrum of fans. Plaintiff (P) Popov sued Defendant (D) Hayashi for interference with his property rights in the ball, asserting a claim of conversion.

A pedagogical goal of such a lesson is for law students to propose a defensible legal rule or test for resolving disputes between plaintiffs in pursuit of wild animals, or other quarry, and defendants who interfere with the plaintiffs' attempts to secure their quarry. A proposed test is a kind of hypothesis about how the case should be decided. Advocates (or sometimes judges) propose such a rule for deciding a case and defend it as consistent with past cases and underlying principles and policies. According to Frederick Schauer, "When we provide a reason for a particular decision, we typically provide a rule, principle, standard, norm, or maxim broader than the decision itself" (Schauer, 1995, p. 641).

Ideally, students should justify their proposed tests by making arguments that analogize or distinguish cases in the casebook text and that take underlying values or policies into account. In response, instructors will probe the students' tests and arguments in a Socratic discussion. Supreme Court Justices, opposing advocates, and law professors often propose hypotheticals in challenging a proposed decision rule. *Hypotheticals* are imagined or made-up situations that involve a hypothesis such as a proposed test, which are designed to explore a test's meaning or challenge it as too broad or too narrow. Section 3.4 illustrated hypotheticals posed by Berman and Hafner or by a judge aimed at probing how the *Pierson* and *Keeble* cases should be decided.

Figure 6.4 illustrates a general model of making legal arguments with hypotheticals, in which an interlocutor, such as a judge or instructor, poses a hypothetical to test a proponent's rule for deciding the case. In response to the instructor's hypothetical, a student may respond in a number of ways including by distinguishing the hypothetical or modifying the proposed test so that it avoids the problem the hypothetical exposes.

Let's assume further that the designer employs appropriate argument schemes to model arguments interpreting concepts in legal rules. These include schemes like those we have seen in Chapter 5 for drawing analogies to precedents and justifying them in terms of the underlying legal domain's values and policies. In addition, we assume, the designer develops schemes implementing the model in Figure 6.4 for proposing a rule or test for deciding a case, posing a hypothetical to test the rule, and responding by distinguishing the hypothetical or modifying the test. Although we have not yet encountered such argument schemes, the VJAP schemes in Section 5.7.3 come close with their focus on rule concepts and effects

→ **1. Propose test for *proponent* for deciding current fact situation (cfs):**

Construct a proposed test that leads to a favorable decision in the cfs and is consistent with applicable legal policies / values and important past cases, and give reasons.

←**2. Pose hypothetical for *interlocutor* to probe if proposed test is too *broad*:**

Construct a hypothetical example:

(a) that emphasizes some normatively relevant aspect of the cfs and

(b) to which the proposed test applies and assigns the same result as to the cfs, but

(c) where, given legal policies / values, that result is normatively wrong in the hypothetical.

→ **3. Respond for *proponent* to interlocutor's hypothetical example:**

(3.a) Justify the proposed test: Analogize the hypothetical example and the cfs and argue that they both should have the result assigned by the proposed test. *Or*

(3.b) Modify the proposed test: Distinguish the hypothetical example from the cfs, argue that they should have different results and that the proposed test yields the right result in the cfs, and add a condition or limit a concept definition so that the narrowed test still applies to the cfs but does not apply to, or leads to a different result for, the hypothetical example. *Or*

(3.c) Abandon the proposed test and return to 1.

FIGURE 6.4. Model of legal argument with hypotheticals (Ashley, 2009b)

on underlying values (Grabmair and Ashley, 2010, 2011) presented a formalism for argument schemes instantiating the model in (Ashley, 2009b), but it remains to be implemented in the VJAP program and evaluated.

One sees immediately that such a dialogue involves a lot of CSK about hunting, quarry, duck ponds, and oceans, and about the relevant similarities and differences among fish, foxes, tuition-paying students, and baseballs. An ontology that supports representing that kind of CSK would be a very complex affair. This is an example of the knowledge representation bottleneck that has impeded AI & Law research.

Suppose, however, that the game designer wants to avoid trying to represent all of that CSK in any robust way; he prefers instead to design an ontology that does little more than support the moves in the dialogue. In other words, a system could use the ontology and argument schemes for proposing a test, justifying the test in terms of principles and precedents, analogizing a problem and case in terms of factors, posing and responding to a hypothetical, or modifying a proposed test. It needs to do so, however, for only a handful of cases like those in a property law casebook.

Indeed, let's suppose that the designer is content with supporting arguments in only a "microworld" of cases. The microworld comprises just a small collection of cases (real and hypothetical), factors, policies or values, legal tests to propose, and some other ingredients for a dialogue similar to that in Table 6.2 (Ashley, 2009a, 2011). This "Property-Interests-in-Quarry" Microworld will comprise, let's say, only the cases shown in Table 6.3: *Pierson v. Post, Keeble v. Hickeringill, Young v. Hitchens, Popov v. Hayashi,* and an Escaping Boar case, as well as a hypothetical

Case Name, cite (<u>C</u>ase or <u>H</u>ypo)	Explanation (Factors – Side Favored) [Decision: <u>P</u>laintiff or <u>D</u>efendant]
Pierson v. Post, 3 Caines R. (N.Y.1805) (C)	Where *D* killed a fox, a nuisance pest, that *P* hunted for sport on open land, *P* lost claim of interference with property on issue of *P*'s possession where *P* had not killed or mortally wounded the fox. (NC-*D*, OL-*D*, MCI-*P*, KCI-*P*, N-*P*) [*D*]
Keeble v. Hickeringill 103 Eng.Rep. 1127 (K.B. 1706) (C)	Where *D* used guns to scare away ducks that *P* landowner lured to his part of the pond with decoys, *P* won claim of interference with property despite issue of *P*'s possession where *P* had not killed or mortally wounded ducks. (NC-*D*, OWL-*P*, L-*P*, MCI-*P*, ll-*P*) [*P*]
Young v. Hitchens, 6 Q.B. 606 (1844) (C)	Where *D* commercial fisherman caught fish from within the still open nets *P* commercial fisherman was closing around the fish, *D* won claim of interference with property due to issue of *P*'s possession where *P* had not captured the fish. (NC-*D*, OL-*D*, L-*P*, C-*D*, MCI-*P*, KCI-*P*, ll-*P*) [*D*]
Flushing Quail (H)	Where *D*, knowing that *P* was pursuing quail by flushing them out on open land and shooting them, intercepted the quail and killed them, *P* won?/lost? a claim for interference with a property interest where an issue involved whether *P* had a property interest in quail that *P* had not yet killed (NC-*D*, OL-*D*, L-*P*, C-*D*, MCI-*P*, KCI-*P*, ll-*P*) [?]
Competing Schoolmasters (H)	Where *D* schoolmaster scared away pupils from attending *P*'s school, *P* won?/lost? a *claim* for interference with a property interest where an issue involved whether the *P* had a property interest in students attending his school. (NC-*D*, OL-*D*, L-*P*, C-*D*, MCI-*P*, KCI-*P*, ll-*P*) [?]
Escaping Boar (C)	Where *D* possessed a wild animal nuisance pest that damaged *P*'s property, *P* won claim for negligence/strict liability on issue that animal escaped through/without *D*'s fault. (NC-*D*, OWL-*D*, L-*P*, N-*P*) [*P*]
Popov v. Hayashi, 2002 WL 31833731 (Cal. Superior, 2002) (C)	Where *D* pocketed Barry Bonds' record-breaking 73d home run baseball that *P* had caught in the upper part of his mitt, *P* partially won a claim of interference with property despite the issue of *P*'s possession where *P* had not completely secured the ball before being knocked down by other fans (not including *D*), but was awarded only half the proceeds of sale of baseball. (NC-*D*, OL-*D*, MCI-*P*, KCI-*P*, ll-*P*) [Split proceeds]

or two: the Competing Schoolmasters hypothetical mentioned in the dialogue and in Section 3.4 and a Flushing Quail hypothetical.

Let's assume that the developer also wants to model analogies that may be drawn across superficially different cases that nevertheless raise similar underlying issues, for instance in comparing the *Pierson* and the Escaping Boar cases.

Finally, the designer aims to take another shortcut : the system need not infer any of the propositions from scratch. The system will provide "canned" propositions and their components. In effect, the system (or sometimes the student/user based on a dynamically constructed menu of options) need only plug the right propositions or components into the right argument moves.

Given an argumentation model like that in Figure 6.4 and legal argument schemes like those in Chapter 5, a program could generate dialogues like the one in Table 6.2. The right-hand column recapitulates the dialogue in terms of moves associated with some of the VJAP argument schemes we have seen in Section 5.7.3, some new schemes associated with the model of arguments with hypotheticals in Figure 6.4, and selected elements of a database of argument components represented with the help of a suitable ontology (Ashley, 2009a, 2011).

More specifically, an ontological framework that represents associations among factors, legal concepts, and policies/values would help to choreograph the unfolding steps in the dialogue. Driven by the current facts of a problem and available argument schemes, a program could search the database, identify, and assemble possible arguments, select one, for instance, attacking a proposed legal rule or test as too broad, and produce the next step in the dialogue.

For example, an ontological ordering of legal terms by abstractness and legal "inclusiveness" could guide a program in responding to the teacher's Competing Schoolmasters hypothetical in Part 3 of the dialogue in Table 6.2 by making the student's proposed legal test more specific. In Part 4, the student narrows the Manifest Intent test to Manifest Intent-1, substituting "baseball" for the more general quarry, "something of value." Sometimes there may be surprises. A hypothetical that changes a fact may take a scenario out of one policy or into another. For instance, in Part 3, switching the quarry from a baseball to a tuition-paying student and applying the Manifest Intent test unexpectedly lead to a result that protects fair play but at the expense of discouraging economic competition.

The next sections present a legal argument ontology that could satisfy these design goals and support such an argument dialog.

6.6.2. *An Ontology for the Argument Microworld*

An ontology for the Property-Interests-in-Quarry Microworld needs to specify a list of concepts and relations corresponding to the types of things in the collection as well as frames specifying their components, features (slots), and slot-fillers. This includes representing cases, legal factors, legal tests and ILCs, and underlying legal policies/values.

Representing Cases and Legal Factors

Cases in the Microworld are represented with case frames. As shown in Figure 6.5, each case frame comprises slots for a name, claim (for instance, conversion, a civil wrong or tort in which one takes another's property for one's own use), result (for *P* or *D*), and a list of applicable factors.

A case frame also specifies some features whose values are important for comparing cases in terms of legal factors for the Property-Interests-in-Quarry domain. These *Comparison Features* include the starred (*) slots in the case frame from **Hunting/Catching venues** through **Interference caused**.

Depending on the factual context, it may matter, for example, in what kind of venue the hunting takes place, such as open land, ocean, or a baseball stadium, what kinds of restrictions may apply on that venue (is it privately owned or open?), or what kind of quarry was sought: noxious pest, edible game, or commercial catch. Similarly, the extent of the steps taken by plaintiff to secure the quarry, the extent to which those steps were manifested openly, and the intentionality of the defendant's interference could be important.

It requires a certain amount of legal CSK to understand that an intentional interference is worse for defendant's defense of a claimed property interference than an unintentional one, that seeking to catch a valuable baseball in the stands is like hunting a fox, that trying to divert a paying tutor to one's school is like slipping in between a competitor's nets to gather up the catch, that fans likely do not "hunt" errant baseballs in ponds or oceans, or that oceans are more open and likely free of property restrictions than ponds.

Case Frame
Name:
Short name:
Citation:
Hypothetical case?: [True | False]
Legal claim: [conversion of property | negligence | strict liability | other]
Result: [*P* | *D* | Unknown]
Applicable factors: (set of factors that apply to case)
Hunting/Catching venues:* [vacant-tract | pond | ocean | baseball-stands]
Restrictions on venues:* [open | privately-owned | subject-to-regulatory-restriction
    | by-invitation-only | plaintiff-owned]
Quarry:* [animal(wild | domestic | edible | nuisance pests | fox | quail]) | baseballs |
    students | something of value | economic goals]
Hunting/catching steps repossession:* [seeking-quarry | closing-in-on-quarry |
    catching-briefly-or-wounding-quarry |
    catching-and-securing-or-mortally-wounding-quarry]
Objective manifestation of plaintiff's quarry-seeking:* [hidden-intention |
    ambiguous-intention | clearly-manifested-intention]
Defendant Interfered with plaintiff's quarry-seeking?:* [True | False]
Intentionality of defendant's interference:* [unintentionally | negligently |
    knowingly-or-intentionally]
Interference caused:* [no-consequence |
    not(catching-and-securing-or-mortally-wounding-quarry)]

FIGURE 6.5. Case frame for Property-Interests-in-Quarry Microworld (*P* = Plaintiff, *D* = Defendant)

Factor Frame
Name:
Abbreviation:
Legal claim: conversion of property
Side favored: [P | D]
Translation into English:
Triggers: (conditions for factor to apply)
Focal slot range: (Case frame Comparison Feature whose ordered range of possible
        values represents factor's magnitude in a case)
Pro-plaintiff direction: (direction along focal slot range that favors plaintiff)
Policies / values served: (policies and values that factor affects)

FIGURE 6.6. Factor frame for Property-Interests-in-Quarry Microworld (P = Plaintiff, D = Defendant)

A program cannot understand these differences as a human does. It cannot even manipulate them in a reasonable way unless the information is represented and the program is instructed where to find relevant information at the appropriate time. If a developer wants the program to be "smart" enough to perform such comparisons or enforce such semantic constraints, he needs to build them into the system, and the ontology is a place to do so.

In this ontology, factors support comparing cases in terms both of on-pointness and of magnitudes along a factor (see Section 3.3.2). In enabling comparisons of factor magnitudes, the factors employ a case's values for the Comparison Features (the starred slots in Figure 6.5). The case frame specifies the alternative possible values for each Comparison Feature. Some of these slots involve an ordered range of possible values. For example, values of **Hunting/catching steps regarding possession** range from merely seeking-quarry to catching-and-securing-or-mortally-wounding-quarry. Values of **Intentionality of defendant's interference** range from unintentionally interfering to doing so knowingly-or-intentionally.

The ontology also needs to specify a frame for any kinds of objects the computer will be expected to "understand." For example, there will need to be a quarry frame, whose slots specify properties such as "Likely venues," "If-edible," "If-noxious-pest," "If-commercial-catch," and indeed any of the properties of quarry that are anticipated to matter in comparing the cases.

The ontology will represent legal factors with a factor frame as shown in Figure 6.6. The factor frame will specify a legal factor's name, abbreviation, legal claim, side favored and phrases for translating the factor into English. Each of the nine factors listed in Table 6.4 for the Property-Interests-in-Quarry Microworld could be represented with a new instantiation of the factor frame.

Rather than take the legal factors in a case simply as given, the factor frame could support a list of constraints to test if a factor applies to a case or hypothetical as Hypo's dimensions did (see Section 3.3.2). A triggers slot would store the tests. For example, the *Competes* and *Livelihood* factors are triggered (in Part 3 of the dialogue, Table 6.2) when the hypothetical substitutes "students" for "baseball" as quarry. The *Nuisance* factor applies if the quarry is a noxious pest (If-noxious-pest).

TABLE 6.4. Factors and policies in Property-Interests-in-Quarry Microworld
(P = Plaintiff, D = Defendant) (Ashley, 2009a, 2011)

Factors	Short Name (Abbreviation) [Side-Favored]
Quarry not caught or mortally wounded	*Not Caught (NC) [D]*
Open Land	*Open Land (OL) [D]*
Own Land	*Own Land (OWL) [P]*
P Pursuing Livelihood	*Livelihood (L) [P]*
D in Competition with P	*Competes (C) [D]*
P manifestly closes in on goal	*Manifest Closing In (MCI) [P]*
D knows P closes in on goal	*Knows Closing In (KCI) [P]*
D intentionally interferes physically with P's closing in on goal	*Intentional Interference (II) [P]*
Quarry is a nuisance pest	*Nuisance (N) [P]*

Principles or Policies	Meaning
Protect Fair Play	Discourage unsportsmanlike conduct and unfair competition
Reduce Nuisance Pests	Encourage eradication of deleterious pests
Reduce Frivolous Suits	Maximize rule's clarity of application and minimize scope so as to reduce frivolous law suits
Protect Livelihood	Protect livelihood of working parties
Avoid Property Rights in Public Property	Avoid assigning property rights in things on public property
Promote Economic Competition	Promote economic competition among businesspersons
Protect Free Enterprise	Protect free enterprise of businesspersons
Protect Landowner's Rights	Protect the rights of the landowner on his own land

The factor frame "Focal slot range" specifies the case frame Comparison Feature whose ordered range of possible values is used to represent the factor's magnitude in a case. The "Pro-plaintiff direction" indicates which end of that range favors the plaintiff. A case's magnitude along that factor is the value along the range of the associated Comparison Feature that applies in the case. For example, a program could then distinguish a case as weaker for the plaintiff in magnitude along the *Intentional Interference* factor if the defendant only unintentionally interfered with plaintiff's pursuit. If the plaintiff's intention to pursue the quarry were hidden or ambiguous, a plaintiff's case is weaker along the *Knows Closing In* factor. A case is stronger for plaintiff in magnitude along the *Own Land* factor if the hunting venue was owned by the plaintiff as in Part 5 of the dialogue (Table 6.2).

Once an ontological framework is in place, one can begin to populate a database of cases by instantiating case frames and filling slots with values.

In the *Popov* case, for example, the facts that the plaintiff did not catch and secure or mortally wound the quarry, and that the events took place on what might be considered open land (or, at least, not on a venue owned by the plaintiff) all favored the defendant Hayashi. On the other hand, the facts that the plaintiff manifestly was closing in on the quarry, defendant knew that the plaintiff intended closing in on the quarry, and the defendant intentionally interfered with plaintiff's pursuit of the quarry helped plaintiff Popov. Accordingly, as shown in Table 6.3, the *Popov* case is represented in terms of the following factors elaborated in Table 6.4: *Not Caught (NC)* [D], *Open Land (OL)* [D], *Manifest Closing In (MCI)* [P], *Knows Closing In (KCI)* [P], *Intentional Interference (II)* [P].

In this way, the ontology supports representing relevant case facts. Next, let's turn to how the ontology supports representing the relevant law.

Representing Legal Tests

In order to model the sample dialogue of Table 6.2, the ontology needs to represent the law for purposes of arguing about what the law should be. The students propose legal rules or tests and the instructor probes the proposed tests' adequacy by posing hypotheticals. The students may respond to the hypothetical by modifying the test to make it more or less restrictive. The ontology needs to support these modifications.

Let's illustrate how it will do so with the small set of proposed tests employed in the sample dialogue shown in Table 6.5. The left column lists five proposed tests. The first set of two tests deals with possession (Possession and Possession-1). The second set of three tests deals with manifest intent (Manifest Intent, Manifest Intent-1, and Manifest Intent-2). For the moment, let's put aside the right column, which shows how the tests would be represented logically.

The proposed tests employ five ILCs:

1. POSSESSION(quarry, level)
2. MANIFESTATION-OF-INTENTION-TO-POSSESS(quarry, level)
3. INTENTIONALITY-RE-INTERFERENCE(level)
4. INTERFERENCE
5. CAUSE(INTERFERENCE not(POSSESSION(quarry, level)))

The ILCs are represented with parameters that accept values. For instance, POSSESSION can specify the quarry possessed and the level of possession, that is, the hunting/catching steps that have been taken. The possible values are the same as for the Comparison Features of the case frame (the starred slots in Figure 6.5). The quarry possessed can take the values of **Quarry**: animal (wild, domestic, edible, nuisance pests, fox, or quail), baseballs, students, something of value, or economic goals. The level of possession can be the values from **Hunting/catching steps regarding possession**: seeking-quarry, closing-in-on-quarry, catching-briefly-or-wounding-quarry, or catching-and-securing-or-mortally-wounding-quarry. The ILC MANIFESTATION-OF-INTENTION-TO-POSSESS

TABLE 6.5. Proposed tests in Property-Interests-in-Quarry Microworld (*P* = Plaintiff, *D* = Defendant) (Ashley, 2009a, 2011)

Proposed Tests	Short Name	Logical rule
If *P* did not gain possession of the *baseball* by catching and securing it, then *P* cannot recover.	Possession	not(POSSESSION(baseball, mortally-wounding-or-catching-and-securing)) → not(recover)
If *P* did not gain possession of *something-of-value* by catching and securing it, then *P* cannot recover.	Possession-1	not(POSSESSION(something-of-value, mortally-wounding-or-catching-and-securing)) → not(recover)
If *P* manifestly intended to gain possession of the *fish*, and *D* intentionally interfered causing *P* to fail, then *P* can recover.	Manifest Intent-2	MANIFESTATION-OF-INTENTION-TO-POSSESS(fish, level: manifestly-intended) ∧ INTERFERENCE ∧ INTENTIONALITY-RE-INTERFERENCE (knowingly-or-intentionally) ∧ CAUSE(INTERFERENCE not(POSSESSION(fish, mortally-wounding-or-catching-and-securing))) → recover
If *P* manifestly intended to gain possession of the *baseball*, and *D* intentionally interfered causing *P* to fail, then *P* can recover.	Manifest Intent-1	MANIFESTATION-OF-INTENTION-TO-POSSESS(baseball, level: manifestly-intended) ∧ INTERFERENCE ∧ INTENTIONALITY-RE-INTERFERENCE(knowingly-or-intentionally) ∧ CAUSE(INTERFERENCE not(POSSESSION(baseball, mortally-wounding-or-catching-and-securing))) → recover
If *P* manifestly intended to gain possession of *something of value*, and *D* intentionally interfered causing *P* to fail, then *P* can recover.	Manifest Intent	MANIFESTATION-OF-INTENTION-TO-POSSESS(something-of-value level: manifestly-intended) ∧ INTERFERENCE ∧ INTENTIONALITY-RE-INTERFERENCE(knowingly-or-intentionally) ∧ CAUSE(INTERFERENCE not(POSSESSION(something-of-value, mortally-wounding-or-catching-and-securing))) → recover

Intermediate Legal Concept Frame
Name:
Short name:
Parameters: (types of values passed to the ILC)
Ranges: (Comparison Features of case frame that serve as parameters' ranges of
             restrictiveness)
Related factors: (factors which affect ILC)
Related policies / values: (policies and values underlying ILC)

FIGURE 6.7. ILC frame for Property-Interests-in-Quarry Microworld ($P =$ Plaintiff,
$D =$ Defendant)

can specify the quarry and the level of the manifestation of intention to possess,
the values of which are the value of **Objective manifestation of plaintiff's quarry-
seeking**: hidden-intention, ambiguous-intention, or clearly-manifested-intention.

Within each of the two sets of tests in Table 6.5, the tests vary in terms of their
generality. The Possession-1 test is more general, that is, more sweeping in its scope,
than the Possession test in that "something-of-value" replaces "baseball." Similarly,
the Manifest-Intent test is more general than either Manifest-Intent-1 or -2 because
it deals with "something-of-value" rather than "baseball."

Modifying the generality of a test is a way of responding to the instructor's
challenge. In the dialogue of Table 6.2, Student-A modifies his proposed test by substituting the more restrictive Manifest-Intent-1 test for the Manifest-Intent. In relying
on a more restrictive test, Student-A avoids the thrust of the instructor's hypothetical.

One can imagine other plausible ways to modify the proposed tests to make them
more or less restrictive. Three of the ILCs set standards or levels that lie on a range
of plausible levels of restrictiveness ($>$ means more restrictive than):

– Levels of POSSESSION: catching-and-securing-or-mortally-wounding $>$
  catching-briefly-or-wounding-quarry $>$ seeking
– Levels of MANIFESTATION-OF-INTENTION-TO-POSSESS: clearly-
  manifested-intention $>$ ambiguous-intention $>$ hidden-intention
– Levels of INTENTIONALITY-RE-INTERFERENCE: knowingly-or-intentionally $>$ negligently $>$ unintentionally

Each of these corresponds to a Comparison Feature of the case frame (Figure 6.5),
namely, **Hunting/catching steps re possession, Objective manifestation of plaintiff's quarry-seeking**, and **Intentionality of defendant's interference**, respectively.

The ontology will support this kind of reasoning with the meanings of ILCs and
the generality of proposed tests. Each of the ILCs would be instantiated in an ILC
frame (shown in Figure 6.7).

The ILC frame has slots for specifying which values the concept's parameters will
accept and the Comparison Features of the case frame that serve as the parameters' ranges of restrictiveness. By changing the values of these levels, the system (or
a student) could modify the proposed tests so that, for example, a version of the
Manifest-Intent test applies even if the defendant's interference were unintentional

Test Frame
Name:
Short name:
Logical rule: first order predicate logical rule
Antecedents: { Intermediate legal concepts }
Consequent: P or D
Translation:

FIGURE 6.8. Test frame for Property-Interests-in-Quarry Microworld (P = Plaintiff, D = Defendant)

Policy / Value Frame
Name:
Short name:
Translation:
Related factors: (factors that affect policy or value)
Related intermediate legal concepts: (ILCs that policy or value underlies)

FIGURE 6.9. Policy/Value frame for Property-Interests-in-Quarry Microworld (P = Plaintiff, D = Defendant)

or accidental or did not cause the plaintiff to fail to secure the quarry. That might not be good policy, but in this Microworld, ideally the system could select the appropriate argument scheme and make the counterargument that such a rule would be so general as to impinge too much on the policy to reduce frivolous law suits (see the next section).

The ontology will define proposed legal rules or tests with a frame similar to that in Figure 6.8. We will assume that each test can be expressed in the form of a first-order logical rule composed of ILCs. The Test Frame needs slots to represent these logical rules, the antecedent ILCs, and the consequent. For each of the proposed tests in the left column of Table 6.5, the right column shows the logical rule that represents it. Section 6.5 illustrated similar examples of designing an ontology to relate logical tests to legal concepts.

With these ontological components, one could represent the small set of proposed tests in Table 6.5 that will suffice for modeling the sample dialogue.

Representing Legal Policies and Argument Schemes
Finally, as suggested above, the Microworld contains policies or values that underlie the proposed tests for governing this legal domain of protecting (or not protecting) property interests in quarry. One might represent eight such policies or values as in Table 6.4.

The Policy/Value frame (Figure 6.9) provides for a name, a translation into English and, crucially, lists of factors and ILCs (the terms in proposed tests) that relate to it. Similarly, the frames for cases, factors, and ILCs also contain slots for specifying the lists of policies and values that are related to a given instantiated case, factor, or ILC.

These conceptual linkages of policies and values, cases, factors, or ILCs enable the program to operationalize analogizing, distinguishing, posing hypotheticals, and modifying proposed tests. The argument schemes that generate the dialogue in Table 6.2 make use of the linked information:

- Propose test or rule, in terms of ILCs, for deciding a case
- Draw analogies to past cases (i.e., precedents)
- Justify analogies in terms of underlying legal domain's policies/principles
- Challenge proposed test as too broad or too narrow by posing hypotheticals
- Respond to hypotheticals by modifying the proposed test, etc.

By filling in the frame representations with the appropriate information, the argument schemes will be able to follow conceptual linkages, retrieve objects, and draw inferences.

The factors are related to policies and values, and the similarities and differences are legally relevant because of the related policies and values. For example, in explaining the *Keeble* case and distinguishing *Pierson* in Part 5 of the dialogue (Table 6.2), the *Own Land* factor implicates the policy to Protect Landowner's Rights. In a complementary way, the *Open Land* factor relates to a policy to Avoid Property Rights in Public Property.

ILCs relate to factors and policies. For example, Part 7 illustrates a connection between the POSSESSION ILC, the *Not Caught* factor, and the policy to Avoid Frivolous Suits. The INTENTIONALITY-RE-INTERFERENCE ILC is related to the factor *Intentional Interference* and the policy to Protect Fair Play. If "quarry" includes non-nuisance pests, game birds, or economic goals, various factors are triggered invoking their underlying policies/values.

In sum, the microworld ontology is an attempt, in this extended thought experiment, to operationalize all and only the concepts and relations required to produce the dialogue and others like it. This includes concepts and relations of the substantive legal domain, the law of property rights in quarry, and at least some of the real-world mechanics of catching quarry. A database would instantiate the cases, factors, principles, and policies and interrelate them via the ontological framework.

6.6.3. *Limits for Automating Legal Argumentation through Ontological Support*

Such dialogues are legally realistic and have pedagogical utility. They illustrate how legal rules are subjected to interpretation, challenge, and change in the process of comparing cases. An advocate proposes a test that explains a past result, and leads to a desired result in current facts, as a matter of deductive reasoning. The proposed test, however, is subjected to a process of interpretation. Skeptics pose hypotheticals to explore the meaning of a rule's ILCs and assess its fit with past decisions and principles. The test is applied deductively to the facts of hypotheticals and precedents, but the results must be assessed in light of the domain's underlying policies and values. Precedents are revealed as authoritative sources of a rule and also as a set of facts from which advocates and judges may extract a range of rules in light of new problem's facts, other decisions, and underlying policies and values.

A microworld approach like this could serve as the basis for an impressive tutoring system. Students could try out arguments and responses involving a casebook chapter's collection of cases and hypotheticals on a particular topic like property rights in quarry. Having generated part of a dialogue, the system could assess what arguments it could reasonably make as a next step, some better, some worse, and offer students a menu of options. Students could explore the options, anticipating responses, and see if they were right.

In fact, a program to generate such dialogues has not been constructed – this is just a thought experiment after all – but the recapitulation conveys a sense of how such a program *would* work. The point of the example is to illustrate how an ontological framework for representing the associations and connections among structured objects makes possible this kind of argument-scheme-driven construction of a dialogue.

If one *were* to implement this ontology and database of structured objects and use the argument schemes of Chapter 5, the result would be general in the following sense. The dialogue in Table 6.2 would be just one of the dialogues the resulting program could generate. In principle, the program could generate the same kinds of dialogues beginning with any of the cases or hypotheticals in the microworld (see Table 6.3) (Ashley, 2009a, 2011).

On the other hand, this thought experiment illustrates some limitations in developing ontologies to support realistic legal argument.

First, how general can a legal ontology be and still be useful? The next chapter of the property law casebook involves other concepts and relations, and there are lots of other casebooks on different legal topics. There will be some overlap, and some of the ontological framework could be reused, but not all of it can be reused, and the remainder would have to be adapted manually to each new domain. For instance, compare the frames for tests and ILCs in Figures 6.7 and 6.8 with those of van Kralingen's legal norm and concept frames in Table 6.1. They both have slots for antecedents, consequents, and logical rules. The Test and ILC frames, however, have more slots specific to the Property-Interests-in-Quarry Microworld and the activities of interpreting the meanings of the ILCs in light of the value effects in concrete circumstances. Perhaps, the ontology shown for the microworld simply is not good enough or reflects flawed intuitions about ontology design and a lack of foresight concerning the phenomena for which it would need to account.

On the other hand, the comparison underscores that ontologies are designed for particular purposes. As a result, there is little agreement on what exactly should be specified in a legal ontology or with what level of detail, and assessing an ontology's adequacy or suitability depends on the purpose for which it was created

(Bench-Capon and Visser, 1997). Generally speaking, the legal ontologies developed so far have *not* focused on modeling arguments about whether a legal rule should apply to a hypothetical variation of the facts of a problem, and yet that task is essential for explaining legal advice.

Secondly, as perusal of the ontological framework plainly shows, this kind of knowledge representation is both intricate and, well, clunky. One needs to invent ungainly concepts like catch-and-secure-or-mortally-wound in anticipation of extending cases about wild animals to scenarios involving baseballs or tuition-paying students.

Representing such concepts in a manner that enables a program to "see" analogies between catching foxes, catching baseballs, and luring students is still a matter of research, a particular challenge of which is enabling a program to distinguish between analogies that are superficial from those that are analogous at a deeper level. Consider the facts of the Escaping Boar case (see Table 6.3): *D* possessed a wild animal nuisance pest, a boar, that damaged *P*'s property. On the surface, it looks rather similar to *Pierson v. Post*; both involve escaping wild animals, nuisance pests, defendants allegedly causing damage to plaintiffs' property interests.

At a deeper level, however, these cases are quite different. They involve different legal claims. The Escaping Boar case involved a claim for negligence or strict liability for keeping a (live) wild animal and allowing it to escape. *Pierson* involved conversion. Both are tort claims, but focus on different kinds of damage inflicted through different mechanisms. A simple way to handle this is to instruct the program to pay attention to the particular claims involved in a case. On the other hand, some claims, though different, are actually analogous at the deeper level of the kinds of damage or mechanisms they involve. Thus, one could imagine more sophisticated solutions as well (Ashley, 2009a, 2011).

Another aspect of the clunkiness of the representation scheme is its lack of detail. While the arguments generated by the scheme-driven search with ontological supports are sophisticated enough for a pedagogical lesson, they do not quite measure up to the test Judge McCarthy developed in the *Popov v. Hayashi* case to resolve property interests in a valuable homer baseball struck into the stands and fought over by competing fans. Judge McCarthy's three-part test is shown in Figure 6.10.

The sophistication of Judge McCarthy's test exemplifies the kind of creative legal reasoning that is characteristic of human intellectual activity. Notice how Judge McCarthy (following Professor Gray) defines "possession" in terms of the relative momenta of the ball and fan, speaks of a "pre-possessory" interest, and distinguishes "incidental" from intended contacts. Imagine refining the ontological framework and knowledge representation to support these qualifications (Ashley, 2009a, 2011).

The challenge is especially great given the fact that the process of designing such an ontology and instantiating structured objects in a database is, like my thought experiment, largely manual and requires expert foreknowledge of how the information will likely be used in the targeted kinds of argument. Ideally, an ontology would

(1) "An action for conversion may be brought where the plaintiff has title, possession or the right to possession."

(2) Professor Gray's rule: "A person who catches a baseball that enters the stands is its owner. A ball is caught if the person has achieved complete control of the ball at the point in time that the momentum of the ball and the momentum of the fan while attempting to catch the ball ceases. A baseball, which is dislodged by incidental contact with an inanimate object or another person, before momentum has ceased, is not possessed. Incidental contact with another person is contact that is not intended by the other person. The first person to pick up a loose ball and secure it becomes its possessor."

(3) "But, where an actor undertakes significant but incomplete steps to achieve possession of a piece of abandoned personal property and the effort is interrupted by the unlawful acts of others, the actor has a legally cognizable pre-possessory interest in the property."

FIGURE 6.10. Judge McCarthy's Test in *Popov v. Hayashi*

extend itself as it is being used. As discussed above, some automated techniques for assisting experts to construct and expand ontologies have been developed, but it is not clear how to apply them to this kind of ontology for legal argument (see below).

The contrast between Judge McCarthy's actual test and the tests proposed in the thought experiment raises the question of just how far argument-scheme-driven search over databases of ontologically structured objects can be extended. The field of AI & Law has produced increasingly detailed argument models and argument schemes, but its knowledge representation techniques have not kept up with the capabilities of its argument models.

Fortunately, the level of detail in Judge McCarthy's analysis would not be necessary for a satisfactory tutoring system, nor does cognitive computing require such sophisticated interpretations of ILCs or a command of commonsense reasoning at such a fine level of detail.

6.6.4. *Ontological Support for Cognitive Computing in Legal Argumentation*

As noted, for cognitive computing to work, computational models of argument would not necessarily need to generate the arguments themselves, but rather focus humans on useful argument examples found in a corpus of legal texts. Ideally, cognitive computing could help Judge McCarthy find past cases and particular passages to consider in devising a suitable test. For instance, it could help him search a corpus of past cases specifically for examples of rules for determining possession of sought-after quarry or specifically for such cases where plaintiffs (or defendants) won. It could also help him identify examples of fact findings where a trier of fact held that the requirements of such a rule were satisfied or not.

Today's legal information tools have lots of cases, but they do *not* have information about the argument roles that sentences play in those cases. If AI & Law models of argument and legal ontologies could support extracting that kind of argument-related information from case texts, they could enable conceptual information retrieval in support of human attorney's creative legal reasoning.

6.7. TYPE SYSTEMS FOR TEXT ANALYTICS

As indicated above, legal ontologies contain information for representing substantive legal concepts and rules. As discussed above, they have been focused on representing legal knowledge to improve legal information retrieval and to facilitate reasoning with statutory rules and concepts for purposes of regulatory compliance (Section 6.5) as well as for other tasks including a pedagogical application of legal argument (Section 6.6).

What is needed, however, is a legal ontology that will support a computer in identifying legal arguments and argument-related information in *texts*. A program can reason with that information to some extent and use it to find examples of past arguments in prior case texts that are relevant to human arguers' needs.

6.7.1. *Defining a Type System*

Finding such examples of legal argument requires a different kind of ontology, a "type system," and a set of software components that can identify types of information in texts and process it.

> A *type system* defines the structure for possible markup [of texts], providing the necessary data types for downstream components [in a pipeline] to make use of partially processed text, and gives upstream components a target representation for markup data. (Wu et al., 2013)

Type systems are an element of natural language text processing frameworks such as General Architecture for Text Engineering (GATE) or UIMA. As noted in Chapter 1, *UIMA* is an open-source Apache framework used in IBM's Watson QA system. In UIMA frameworks, an assemblage of software components called "annotators," organized into a text-processing pipeline, analyzes texts and extracts information corresponding to the types. Each automated annotator analyzes some region of text in a particular way, assigns semantics to it, and produces annotations or assertions about the text. Other annotators "down the line" can use the annotations to draw additional or more abstract inferences about the semantics of the text (Ferrucci et al., 2010, p. 74; Ferrucci, 2012).

The type system is organized hierarchically and coordinates communication among the annotators. In UIMA, a type system is a graph of concepts that relate to each other hierarchically in various ways as subtypes, super types, and attribute types. It supports a formalization of an annotator's analysis input and output data in a manner that the other annotators can interpret and process (Epstein et al., 2012, p. 15:1). Although the term "pipeline" suggests a linear organization of the annotators, parallel processing is also possible.

A type system functions as a kind of ontology for text analysis, defining kinds of annotations, concepts, and relations that can occur in documents (Grabmair et al., 2015). Unlike ordinary ontologies, however, type systems include textual semantic types that capture *mentions*, ways in which concepts and conceptual relations are referred to or manifested in domain texts. For instance, in writing an opinion in a vaccine injury case (Section 5.8), a judge may refer to a "vaccination for varicella." Mention types for VaccineMention and VaccinationMention provide a mechanism for annotating that text as referring to the *concepts* of vaccine and vaccination. In fact, there are a number of ways to refer to such a vaccine or vaccination, for instance, "chickenpox vaccination," "inoculation against chickenpox," "VARIVAX injection" (the commercial brand name), and so forth. All of these can be annotated as instances of mentions of the concepts of vaccine and vaccination.

Type systems have been applied in domains ranging from clinical data stored in electronic medical records (Wu et al., 2013) to paired question/answer texts in the "Jeopardy!" game.

6.7.2. *Type System Example: DeepQA*

The DeepQA system, developed with UIMA and employed in IBM's Watson, included a formal type system of both annotation types and ontology concepts.

DeepQA is based on the assumption that instances of "answer types" could be identified and extracted from the text of Jeopardy! "questions" and "answers" automatically. A Lexical Answer Type or "LAT" is "a word or noun phrase in the question that specifies the type of the answer without any attempt to understand its semantics," that is, without even knowing what the word means. If a candidate answer is also an example of the same LAT, it is some positive evidence Watson can use in ranking candidate answers by relevance (Ferrucci et al., 2010, p. 70).

For example, for a Jeopardy! category, "Oooh … Chess," and a clue, "Invented in the 1500s to speed up the game, this maneuver involves two pieces of the same color," the word "maneuver" is the LAT (Ferrucci et al., 2010, p. 70). Intuitively, one can see the utility of a LAT given the correct Jeopardy! response, "What is castling?" *Castling* is a maneuver in chess.

While LATs provide some information for assessing whether candidate answers match a question, that information is frequently insufficient. In analyzing a random sample of 20,000 Jeopardy! questions, the researchers found that "The most frequent 200 explicit LATs cover less than 50 percent of the data" (Ferrucci et al., 2010, p. 63). As a result, Watson frequently needs to generate additional information for assessing a match.

In determining if candidate answers are instances of or closely related to the clue's answer type as indicated by the LAT, Watson employs two kinds of type systems. The first type is "general-purpose NLP types, which are used to represent a linguistic analysis of the question or of a text passage" (Epstein et al., 2012, p. 15:3).

The second type is specific to DeepQA and aims at revealing more semantic information for identifying candidate texts and matching them to the LAT of the Jeopardy! question. Watson queries its text corpora and some special knowledge sources to retrieve content relevant to the question. The queries generate documents, text passages, or responses based on special knowledge. The query results are then analyzed for instances of another type, the CandidateAnswerFeature type. These are pairs of labels and scores associated with a potential answer in a search result and are used to select the best answer (see Epstein et al., 2012, p. 15:3).

For example, a Jeopardy! clue stated "He was presidentially pardoned on September 8, 1974" to which the correct Jeopardy! response was "Who was Nixon?" Of course, Watson does not know the correct response. Let's assume, however, that "Nixon" is one of the candidate answers it generated based on a retrieved passage, "Ford pardoned Nixon on Sept. 8, 1974."

Watson applies multiple passage scoring algorithms to assess the relevance of this text. One scorer "counts the number of IDF-weighted terms in common between the question and the passage." Another scorer "measures the lengths of the longest similar subsequences between the question and passage (for example 'on Sept. 8, 1974')." A third scorer "measures the alignment of the logical forms of the question and passage." A logical form is a graph of the text in which the nodes are its terms and the edges represent grammatical or semantic relationships. The logical form alignment scorer "identifies Nixon as the object of the pardoning in the passage, and that the question is asking for the object of a pardoning." Thus, "[l]ogical form alignment gives 'Nixon' a good score" (Ferrucci et al., 2010, p. 72).

In practice, DeepQA employs a large number of scoring algorithms to determine if a candidate answer is an instance of a LAT. These algorithms often employ their own type systems that focus on identifying different types of features based on relations between concepts mentioned in the answers (Ferrucci et al., 2010, p. 70).

The different types of features contribute different amounts of evidence that a question and candidate answer match depending on the type of question. "[C]ertain scores that may be crucial to identifying the correct answer for a factoid question may not be as useful on puzzle questions" (Ferrucci et al., 2010, p. 74). Watson employs ML based on a training set of many correct question/answer pairs to learn weights to assign to the different types of features according to their predictive success in different types of questions (Ferrucci et al., 2010, p. 74).

6.8. LUIMA: A LEGAL UIMA TYPE SYSTEM

As we have seen, the type system in DeepQA defines types useful for Watson's task of matching texts with candidate answers to Jeopardy! questions. AI & Law researchers have created a UIMA type system for the legal domain (*LUIMA*) focused on concepts, relations, and mentions for identifying argumentation roles of sentences in judicial decisions useful for the task of legal information retrieval (Grabmair et al., 2015). So far, they have applied LUIMA to legal decisions in the vaccine injury domain and corpus introduced in Section 5.8, but they plan to apply it to other legal domains as well.

TABLE 6.6. Hierarchical LUIMA type system: Sentence Level, Formulation, Mention, and Term Types

Level	LUIMA Types	Example
Sentence Level Types	Citation, Legal rule, Legal ruling or holding of law, Evidence-based finding of fact, Evidence-based intermediate reasoning, Evidence, Legal policy, Policy-based reasoning, Case-specific process or procedural facts	See Table 6.7
Formulation Types	ConflictingArgumentsFormulation	"at odds with"
	LegalStandardFormulation	"must be supported by"
Mention Types	DecisionBodyMention	"the court"
	TestimonyMention	"expert testimony"
	CurrentCaseContextMention	"In this case"
	ProofBurdenMention	"the burden of proof"
	VaccineMention	"Tetanus"
	VaccinationMention	"Tetanus vaccination"
Term Types	PlaintiffTerm/DefendantTerm	plaintiff, petitioner/ respondent
	CausationTerm	cause, causes, causal, causation
	DepartmentTerm	Department
	PositiveArgumentAttributeTerm	consistent, clear
	ConclusionTerm	conclude
	MustRelationTerm	must, have to
	PrescriptionTerm	may
	DecisionBodyTerm	court
	IllnessTerm	Gastroparesis, injuries
	VaccineTerm	Tetanus

As shown in Table 6.6, the hierarchical LUIMA type system comprises four levels: Sentence Level types, Formulation types, Mention types, and Term types.

The Sentence Level types at the top of the hierarchy and some examples are shown in Table 6.7. They capture nine important roles that sentences play in legal arguments such as stating a rule, a rule requirement, a finding of fact, or a conclusion that a rule requirement is satisfied given a finding of fact.

Annotating sentences in cases according to their roles in legal argumentation can improve information retrieval. Typically, relatively few sentences in a lengthy opinion capture the significant reasoning. Some of these sentences state legal rules, others report evidence in the case, and still others declare that evidence-based legal findings satisfy legal rule requirements.

Depending on a system user's goals for the information it seeks, the sentence roles may make some of those sentences more relevant than others. For instance, consider a useful kind of query in the vaccine injury context (Section 5.8). Let's assume

TABLE 6.7. Hierarchical LUIMA Type System: Sentence level types

LUIMA Sentence Level Types	Definition	Example
Citation	Sentence includes a citation to a legal authority.	"See 42 U.S.C. §300aa-12(d)(4)(B); Vaccine Rule 18(b)."
Legal rule	Sentence states a legal rule in the abstract, without applying it to particular facts.	"Under that standard, the petitioner must show that it is 'more probable than not' that the vaccination was the cause of the injury."
Legal ruling or holding of law	Sentence states a legal ruling or holding of law by the judge	"For the reasons set forth below, I conclude that she is entitled to such an award, in an amount yet to be determined."
Evidence-based finding of fact	Sentence reports the factfinder's finding on whether or not evidence in a particular case proves that a rule condition has been satisfied.	"I have found the opinion of Dr. Lacy to be more persuasive than that of Dr. Caserta, for a number of reasons."
Evidence-based intermediate reasoning	Sentence involves reasoning about whether evidence in a particular case proves that a rule condition has been satisfied.	"In this regard, I note that I have carefully considered the written report of Dr. Caserta."
Evidence	Sentence summarizes an item of evidence in the case.	"In his testimony in this case, Dr. Lacy further explained his belief that the tetanus vaccination likely caused the gastroparesis of the petitioner, Ms. Roper."
Legal policy	Sentence states a legal policy in the abstract without applying it to particular facts.	"As a matter of fundamental fairness, Mr. Popov should have had the opportunity to try to complete his catch unimpeded by unlawful activity."
Policy-based reasoning	Sentence involves reasoning about the application of a legal policy to particular facts.	"To hold otherwise would be to allow the result in this case to be dictated by violence."
Case-specific process or procedural facts	Sentence refers to the procedural setting of or a procedural issue in the case.	"The petitioner in this case contends that her condition of chronic gastroparesis was 'caused-in-fact' by the tetanus vaccination that she received on July 10, 1997."

an attorney needs cases in which a court found that varicella vaccine can cause encephalomyeloneuritis. Perhaps, the attorney has a new client presenting such facts and the attorney hopes to evaluate the chances of recovery. A suitable query might be "finding or conclusion that Varicella vaccine can cause encephalomyeloneuritis."

It happens that a case called *Casey v. Secretary of Health and Human Services*[3] presented these very facts, and yet, in an actual search using this query with a commercial IR program, the *Casey* case ranked 16th. Based on the IR program's case reports, none of the cases that the IR program ranked higher than *Casey* appeared to contain these particular facts, but more than half of the reports contained re-statements or summaries of the *Althen* rule on causation (see Section 5.8).

Given the attorney's fact-oriented purpose, it is highly unlikely that a sentence that merely re-states the legal rule on causation in vaccine cases will be helpful (Ashley and Walker, 2013, p. 36). While such a sentence contains instances of the search terms, namely "vaccine" and "cause," it is not particularly helpful because it contains no information about specific vaccinations causing injuries. In contrast, a system that had information about the user's purpose and that could identify the role of a sentence in a legal argument would prefer sentences that report relevant evidential holdings, or that state conclusions applying a legal rule to relevant facts, over sentences that simply report the legal rule. Such argument-related information could help an IR system focus on key sentences, rank cases more effectively, and improve retrieval precision generally (Ashley and Walker, 2013, p. 36).

The nine sentence types were developed by Hofstra University's LLT Lab, and are geared toward the DLF model of evidentiary legal argument described in Section 5.8. All of the examples of sentence level types in Table 6.7, except the two policy-type-related sentence level examples, come from another vaccine injury case, *Roper v. Secretary of Health and Human Services*. The policy-related sentence level examples come from *Popov v. Hayashi*, the case dealing with property interests in quarry discussed in Section 6.6.1.

The subsentence types in the LUIMA Type System hierarchy shown in Table 6.6 include Formulation types, Mention types, and Term types at the bottom level. The table provides examples of each type. The Formulation types capture common expressions in legal argument and typical ways that judges express legal standards in case documents.

The Mention types capture ways in which concepts in legal argument and the subject matter domain are referred to. They are annotated with rules that identify terminology for referring to such concepts plus additional language clues to help ensure that the terms are, in fact, being used to refer to those concepts. The subsentence Term types represent the basic terminology used in legal argumentation, as well as terms used in the particular subject matter of the legal domain.

---

[3] *Casey v. Secretary of Health and Human Services*, Office of Special Masters, No. 97-612V, December 12, 2005.

The sentence level types and the formulation types higher up in the LUIMA type system hierarchy are quite general across legal domains in cases involving legal evidentiary argumentation. The mention and term types lower down are general across legal domains too, but also contain terms and ways of mentioning concepts that are necessarily more domain-specific. In the work on LUIMA so far, quite a few terms are specific to the vaccine injury domain.

Ideally, human annotators can mark up documents in terms of these types, achieving a high level of reliability, and automated rule-based or ML-based annotators, having been trained on the human-annotated data, can automatically assign the types with a near-human level of reliability. Annotation issues are discussed further in Section 12.5.2.

Since the concepts and relations can be mentioned in candidate texts in a variety of ways, ML may help to identify these alternative expressions in an automated or semiautomated way. In the latter, ML identifies candidate expressions and human editors can approve them for inclusion (or not). In this way, techniques similar to those described above in the Dalos ontology can be applied to extend and populate an argument-related ontology and type system like LUIMA.

6.9. LUIMA ANNOTATIONS CAN SUPPORT CONCEPTUAL LEGAL INFORMATION RETRIEVAL

By combining ontologies of substantive legal concepts, legal argument-related concepts, concepts in the regulated domain, and mentions in UIMA and LUIMA type systems, conceptual information retrieval is possible. A system can use these annotated types as a guide to ranking (and reranking) retrieved documents for automatically summarizing relevant passages (see Grabmair et al., 2015).

Specifically, a system that can identify these roles of sentences in a legal argument can helpfully direct a user to the most relevant cases and passages given the user's particular need for the information, that is, how the user intends to employ the retrieved information in an argument. User queries would be augmented with specifications of the combinations of sentence types and concept relations that would be most relevant given the user's goals. Candidate documents would be retrieved that satisfy the query as augmented by the specified focal types and relations. Supporting documents would be ranked in terms of the system's confidence that the documents satisfy the constraints. Top-ranked documents would be summarized and passages would be selected to highlight portions most relevant to the argument roles of interest.

For instance, consider a judge or advocate facing a future property law dispute involving a plaintiff's hunt for an abandoned robotic deep sea probe frustrated at the last minute by a defendant hacker who intercepts the probe by overriding its computer. If the user/judge is trying to determine what test to apply, it would be useful to find sentences where judges have stated legal rulings or holdings of law, that is, sentences of type legal ruling or holding of law, such as Judge McCarthy's in Figure 6.10, concerning various types of property or quarry.

We revisit this post-*Popov* query in Section 7.4. As explained in the section, an IR system can retrieve such cases now, but these systems do not understand what the user is looking for and, even if they did, cannot determine which sentences would best satisfy such a query. IR systems do not annotate the sentences in cases by the roles they play in legal argument and thus cannot match relevant sentences by their roles to a user's needs. Even in the *Popov* case, the three parts of Judge McCarthy's test are scattered about his 6,000+ word opinion. It would also be helpful to find the judges' evidence-based findings of fact, the sentences that indicate their findings concerning whether or not their tests were satisfied.

To appreciate the significance of this shift in focus toward cognitive computing, consider three contrasting potential goals of AI & Law research in the context of Judge McCarthy's decision in the *Popov v. Hayashi* case. One could attempt to build an AI & Law system to:

1. Generate arguments like that in the *Popov* decision, culminating in Judge McCarthy's three-part test and justifying it based on analyses of prior cases.
2. Generate arguments like those illustrated in the sample Microworld dialogue of Table 6.2.
3. Help humans generate their own arguments and tests by automatically retrieving, (re)ranking, and summarizing relevant arguments and tests from past cases.

Option (1) seems to be the focus of much work in AI & Law, but it also seems to be too hard and to depend too much on hand-tooled knowledge representations that likely will not connect to natural language texts until NLP methods are greatly improved. As we have seen in Section 6.6, option (2) seems feasible given current techniques. The microworld approach, however, also depends on hand-tooled knowledge representations that will not readily connect to texts. Necessarily, the numbers and range of cases and tests will be too limited to be of much use in commercial legal settings, although they may be enough to be used in interesting tutoring systems for digital casebooks, online legal courses, or law school MOOCs.

Option (3) is the path featured in this book. Chapter 11 explains in detail how LUIMA annotations can support conceptual legal IR.

Before taking that path, however, it will be helpful for the reader to learn more about how legal IR works in Chapter 7, how to apply ML to extract information from legal texts (Chapter 8), and in particular, how to extract information from statutory and legal case texts (Chapters 9 and 10).

7

Making Legal Information Retrieval Smarter

7.1. INTRODUCTION

If computational models of legal reasoning and argument are to have a greater impact on law practice, say by enabling legal apps in the mode of cognitive computing, they will likely need to do so in conjunction with existing commercial and institutional approaches to full-text legal information retrieval and e-discovery. While the contribution of AI & Law could be substantial, the techniques may best be applied at the margins of existing commercial tools, whose processes for corpus management, indexing and index maintenance, and search are well-established, reliable, and efficient. Thus, before one anticipates the "value-added" of legal apps and cognitive computing, it is well to understand the existing technology for legal information retrieval.

This chapter explains current techniques for full-text legal information retrieval of case decisions, statutes, and other documents. These are the current tools of legal research that law students and legal professionals employ in constructing legal arguments and writing briefs. The chapter illustrates a role of legal ontologies in improving full-text legal information retrieval through query expansion and explains how some AI & Law techniques have already been harnessed to help legal information retrieval take semantic information into account for assessing relevance.

The chapter discusses the following questions: What is an inverted index? How is relevance measured in a full-text legal IR system and how does that compare with relevance measures of AI & Law models? How is the probability of a document's relevance to a query computed? What is query expansion? How can AI & Law approaches be integrated with legal IR without requiring changes to the way IR systems represent and index legal texts?

7.2. CURRENT LEGAL INFORMATION RETRIEVAL SERVICES

A viable route for realizing practical legal apps is by developing cognitive computing modules to add on to full-text legal information retrieval services. In order to understand how this might be accomplished, it is useful to understand current legal information retrieval techniques.

Full-text legal information retrieval services are well-established in certain legal markets such as in the United States. Legal practitioners know how to use the services, employ them routinely, and express confidence in them. In American law schools, students have access to Westlaw and LexisNexis as part of their legal education and tend to rely on them habitually. The students expect to use these tools in their subsequent practice, at least, if they work for firms or legal departments who can afford subscriptions. Many state and local bar associations offer, as a perquisite of membership, access to legal IR services (e.g., via Casemaker, 2015).

As mentioned in Chapter 1, law schools, international organizations, and agencies maintain extensive specialized repositories of legal texts with their own established practices for maintenance and search. (For example, Pace Law School's CISG database of cases and case annotations concerning the UN Convention on the International Sale of Goods (Kritzer, 2015), the Index of World Intellectual Property Organization (WIPO), Uniform Domain Name Dispute Resolution Policy and Rules (UDRP) Panel Decisions (WIPO, 2015). These are decisions by arbitration panels of disputes over Internet domain names.) Finally, Google Scholar Cases and Courtlistener.com offer free search capabilities over extensive case corpora.

These legal IR services comprise enormous databases of legal case, statutory, and regulatory texts. The services maintain efficient, widespread institutionalized processes for absorbing and indexing new texts as soon as they become available. The commercial services also support substantial proprietary research establishments and are constantly being improved.

Legal IR systems, however, can be improved still further. Their measures of legal relevance and similarity, though highly serviceable, do not capture aspects of legal relevance that the computational models of legal reasoning in Part I employ. Nor can the IR systems identify or make use of important information about sentences in the legal texts, such as the roles introduced in Section 6.8 that sentences play in the legal arguments reported. As a result, IR systems cannot compare cases in terms of legal relevance, make legal arguments, predict legal outcomes, or more actively assist human users to perform these tasks.

Chapters 8 through 11 present techniques for performing these tasks that could soon be appended to legal IR systems with little or no disruption to their established process. First, however, this chapter explains how full-text legal IR works, focusing on retrieving legal case decisions, and highlights some examples of how AI & Law approaches have been integrated with legal IR.

7.3. AN EXAMPLE OF USING COMMERCIAL LEGAL IR SYSTEMS

The goal of this chapter is to focus on the main conceptual ideas underlying most information retrieval systems, not to describe in detail any particular legal IR service currently available. Proprietary commercial services generally do not disclose technical information and constantly modify the way their systems are implemented. Since some readers may not have experienced using a modern legal IR system, however, here is an example of what it is like to use the two main commercial search systems for legal documents in the United States, Westlaw Next (WN), and Lexis Advance (LA).

Suppose one were an attorney in the example of Section 6.8 facing a vaccine injury problem in which a client suffered a serious condition, encephalomyeloneuritis, after receiving an injection against chicken pox, or varicella, as it is called. In seeking evidence or arguments related to proving or disproving the *Althen* Condition 1 (connecting the type of vaccine to the type of injury, see Section 5.8), an attorney might search for cases involving the same type of vaccine and the same type of injury as in the client's scenario. As noted in Section 6.8, an appropriate query might be "finding or conclusion that Varicella vaccine can cause encephalomyeloneuritis." At least one case satisfies this query exactly, the *Casey*[1] decision.

One can submit such a query in natural language to either of the above systems. As an option, one specifies the content type desired, namely "Cases," and the jurisdiction, for instance "all federal," comprising decisions of all federal courts. Upon submitting the query, in less than three seconds, each program returns an annotated list of results for the query in order of relevance (the "Results List"). Moreover, for each case in the Results List, it generates the title of the case, court, jurisdiction, date, and citation, as well as a "Case Report" summarizing information about the case and providing selected excerpts relevant to the query. In a recent attempt, each program retrieved *Casey* in its initial Results List. WN ranked the case as number 16. LA ranked it as number 1.

Each Case Report provided a brief summary citing the relevant provisions of the National Childhood Vaccine Injury Act under which the petition for compensation was brought.

The WN Report stated the name of the party who filed the petition and a partial description of an allegation. It then quoted four excerpts each concerning testimony of an expert witness on the causation issue. For instance, one stated:

> In sum, Dr. Tornatore articulated a credible and convincing theory explaining why the varicella vaccine more likely than not caused petitioner's encephalomyeloneuritis, that the varicella vaccine was a substantial factor in petitioner's encephalomyeloneuritis, and that but for the varicella vaccination, petitioner would not have developed encephalomyeloneuritis.

---

[1] *Casey v. Secretary of Health and Human Services*, Office of Special Masters, No. 97-612V, December 12, 2005.

WN offers links to the part of the text where the excerpt is located.

The LA Report stated that the petitioner "was able to prove by a preponderance of evidence that a varicella vaccine was the cause in fact of her neurological injuries." It then stated the first of a series of "Headnotes," including some general rules governing the petitioners burden:

> In order to prevail under a theory of causation in fact, a vaccine-related injury petitioner must show by a preponderance of evidence that the vaccine in question caused the injury. To meet that burden, a petitioner must establish that the vaccine can cause the injury in question, as well as show that the vaccine is in fact the cause of the injury alleged. To make the requisite showing, petitioner must offer proof of a logical sequence of cause and effect showing that the vaccination was the reason for the injury.

LA offers links to other headnotes, complete passages, and a unique visual aid, a bar linearly representing the headnotes, opinion, footnotes with colored lines indicating where query terms are located. By moving the cursor over the bar, one sees combinations of the terms that appear at that point. Clicking on the bar takes one to the corresponding portion of the text with the terms highlighted.

As a former litigator who first used a commercial legal information service on a dedicated terminal in the late 1970s, I regard the performance of WN and LA in this example as astonishingly good. Each system's output would obviously be useful. WN quotes what clearly appears to be an evidentiary conclusion of the Special Master framed as a characterization of an expert witness's testimony with which the trier-of-fact clearly agrees. On the other hand, WN ranked the *Casey* decision 16th in its results list, preferring a large number of decisions whose Case Reports recited the *Althen* rule on causation, as noted in Section 6.8. LA ranked the *Casey* decision first, but its Case Report focused on a general restatement of the rules governing how petitioner can demonstrate that the vaccine caused the injury. Using the graphical bar display, however, it is easy to locate the Special Master's findings of fact.

The question is how much do the IR systems understand about what the textual excerpts they highlight mean? If they had more semantic information about the roles of sentences in legal argument, could WN do a better job of ranking relevant information and could LA select a more relevant headnote to display in its Case Report? (See Section 11.4 for an evaluation that LUIMA annotations can improve ranking.) Moreover, are there other features of legal disputes, for example, legal factors, that an IR system could identify which would enable it to do more reasoning about the decisions in the corpus in order to assist users in predicting outcomes, making arguments, and testing hypotheses? As argued in Chapters 11 and 12, this would enable IR systems to support legal apps in conceptual legal information retrieval and cognitive computing.

First, however, let's consider how legal IR systems accomplish what they can do so well.

7.4. HOW LEGAL IR SYSTEMS WORK

A legal IR system accepts a user's query, retrieves documents from an indexed database, measures the documents' responsiveness to the query and ranks them, and outputs an ordered list of results for a user's perusal.

Users may input natural language queries expressed with sentences, keywords, case names, or citations and specify the presence or positions of required terms.

Given a query, the IR program:

1. Strips away *stop words*, common words like "the," "a," and "and," and stems, endings like "ing" or "es."
2. Identifies other remaining features beside words, such as citations to statutes, constitutional provisions or prior cases, significant phrases and special indexing concepts.
3. Counts the number of times each remaining word or other feature appears in text.
4. Uses an inverted index to retrieve candidate documents from the database, namely, all those texts indexed as containing *any* of the features in the query. (Turtle, 1995, p. 18)

The database contains documents processed in much the same way as queries and is likely to be implemented using an *inverted index* (see Büttcher et al., 2010, p. 33). The index lists certain features appearing in any texts stored in the database. For each feature, the inverted index records all documents in which it appears, its location in each document, and the number of times it appears in the document and in the text corpus as a whole (Büttcher et al., 2010, p. 48; Turtle, 1995, p. 18). Since new documents are constantly being added, various index maintenance strategies must be employed (see Büttcher et al., 2010, Ch. 7) but these will not be discussed here.

The IR system outputs a list of cases ranked according to their relevance to the query. IR systems have employed a variety of techniques and measures for assessing relevance to a query including: Boolean, vector space, and probabilistic models (see Section 7.5). All of them make use of the frequency information contained in the inverted index.

To illustrate the retrieval process, here is a sample query inspired by the post-*Popov* scenario of Section 6.9 involving the judge or advocate who faces a future property law dispute involving a plaintiff's hunt for an abandoned robotic deep sea probe frustrated at the last minute by a defendant hacker who intercepts the probe by overriding its computer. Here is one potentially useful full-text legal information query:

> action for conversion where plaintiff nearly captured an abandoned robotic deep sea probe but defendant intercepted the probe at the last minute by hacking its computer

TABLE 7.1. *Sample inverted index*

ID	TEXT	Term	Frequency	Doc. IDs
1	An action for conversion involves a serious interference.	action	3	[1][2][5]
		alone	1	[5]
2	The data conversion was completed.	certain	1	[3]
		completed	1	[2]
3	Certain actions may deceive.	conversion	2	[1][2]
4	The probing was unauthorized.	data	1	[2]
5	The action of Defendant Hack was unauthorized.	deceive	1	[3]
		defendant	1	[5]
		hack	1	[5]
		interference	1	[1]
		involves	1	[1]
		may	1	[3]
		probing	1	[1]
		serious	1	[1]
		unauthorized	2	[4][5]

The system may remove stop words and stems, transforming the query to:

action conversion where plaintiff nearly capture abandon robotic deep sea probe defendant intercept probe last minute hack computer

Table 7.1 shows how each of five sentences serves as a "document" for indexing purposes. The sentences would be indexed (after removal of stop words and stems) in the tiny inverted index at the right.

Even this small example illustrates one of the challenges of legal information retrieval: words have multiple meanings. Consider the meanings of "action" and "conversion" in three of the sentences: "An action for conversion involves a serious interference," "The data conversion was completed," and "Certain actions may deceive."

In the sample query, "action" and "conversion" are intended to communicate the user's expectation that cases involving legal actions for conversion and facts like those described would be relevant. Each term, however, has multiple meanings. Beside its legal sense of a proceeding to enforce a claim, "action" can also refer to the fact of doing something. "Conversion" denotes not only a kind of property law claim, but also a change or transformation in something. Thus, words are not ideal features for discriminating relevant from irrelevant documents. Similarly, comparing the five sentences with the query, one can see that "probe" has multiple meanings. While the query employs it as a noun, sentence [4] uses it as a verb. Also, "hack" is a proper name in [5] but the query employs it to refer to interfering with the probe's computer system.

The reader can try out the query on his or her own favorite legal IR system. In my attempt, the results generated by a commercial legal IR system for the sample query above do not obviously address cases involving property claims for conversion and presenting scenarios involving defendants thwarting plaintiff hunters' capture of their intended quarries. Perusal of the case reports of the top 20 cases reported on the IR system's results list revealed two cases involving claims for conversion among a range of other claims (e.g., federal Wiretap Act, Electronic Communications Privacy Act and Computer Fraud and Abuse Act, Copyright, trademark, trade secret, invasion of privacy, admissibility of computer evidence in criminal trials, a Bivens remedy, and three cases involving post-Civil War Abandoned and Captured Property Act claims). One can, of course, understand why the cases were retrieved given various terms in the query and their alternative senses (e.g., "conversion," "abandoned," "robotic," "intercepted," "hacking," "computer"), but none of the cases appeared to be useful.

Different models of relevance and their accompanying measures are effective to varying extents in attempting to deal with this challenge of multiple meanings of words.

7.5. IR RELEVANCE MEASURES

As noted, IR systems have employed Boolean, vector space, and probabilistic models for assessing documents' relevance to a query. Of these, the Boolean relevance measure is the simplest.

7.5.1. *Boolean Relevance Measure*

In a *Boolean* relevance measure, a query provides a set of logical criteria for the documents to be retrieved. The criteria specify the presence, and proximity, of indicated terms for documents to be responsive. The relevance measure ranks cases in terms of how completely the query's Boolean criteria are satisfied (Turtle, 1995, p. 24).

It is not easy to express the above deep sea probe example as a Boolean query, but one might try the following:

(action w/5 conversion) AND ((captur! w/5 quarry) OR (hunt! w/5 quarry)) AND ((defendant w/5 interfer!) OR (defendant w/5 intercept!))

In the above query, the exclamation marks (!) indicate that the system should include all words that begin with the indicated root, for instance, "capture," "captures," "captured," "capturing," and so forth. Perhaps anticipating the low likelihood of finding cases involving abandoned probes, the user has also substituted the broader term "quarry" in hopes that cases involving the capture of other things will be returned.

7.5.2. *Vector Space Approach to Relevance*

In a vector space approach to relevance, documents and queries can be represented as "bags of words" and compared as "term vectors" (Turtle, 1995, p. 26). A *bag of words* (BOW) representation of a document comprises a collection of terms in no particular order. Returning to the deep sea probe example, the query might be represented as a BOW as:

> sea capture action where conversion deep computer nearly hack minute robotic plaintiff abandon defendant probe intercept last

A BOW representation does not preserve the sequential order of terms as they appear in a sentence. That information about the meaning of the sentence is lost.

Since it would be hard to compare sentences represented as bags of words, one could place the terms in alphabetical order and represent them in a term vector:

> abandon action capture computer conversion deep defendant hack intercept last minute nearly plaintiff probe robotic sea where

A *term vector* represents a sentence or other document in terms of its words, citations, indexing concepts, or other features. It is an arrow from the origin $(0,0,0,\ldots,0)$ to the point representing the case text in a large dimensional space. Since each different term (i.e., a word or other feature) in the full corpus of texts corresponds to yet another dimension, the number n of dimensions is very large.

As shown in the simple, three-dimensional vector space model of Figure 7.1, a vector specifies the distance along each dimension to get to the point representing

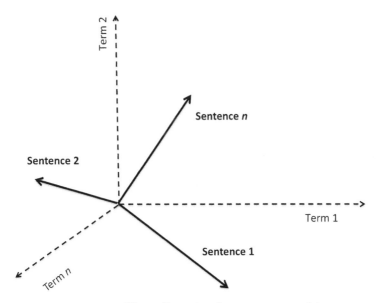

FIGURE 7.1. Three-dimensional vector space model

the whole document. Since any given document lacks many of the terms in the corpus as a whole, the distance along many dimensions will be zero (0). For the terms in the document, however, the distance along each dimension to a term will be one (1) or, in some implementations, a computed magnitude, the word's *tf/idf* weight.

The *tf/idf* weight is proportional to how many times the related term appears in the document's text (i.e., the term frequency (*tf*)) and inversely related to the number of times the term appears in the corpus (i.e., its inverse document frequency (*idf*)). Thus, a term which appears in both a query and a document adds weight to the conclusion that the query and document are similar to the extent that the term appears frequently in the document and rarely in the corpus.

One virtue of the term vector approach is the ease of computing *vector space similarity* (VSS), the similarity among documents or among queries and documents. In fact, a query is treated as a document for this purpose and is also represented as a term vector. Placing the terms in a particular (e.g., alphabetical) order, as in the above example, facilitates automatically comparing term vectors to assess their similarity. The similarity measure corresponds to the Euclidean distances between the endpoints of the term vectors in the multidimensional space. In determining similarity, a query is compared to all of the documents retrieved from the inverted index using a trigonometric calculation. One computes the cosine of the angle between their corresponding term vectors. The smaller the cosine, the smaller the angle between the corresponding term vectors, and, the full-text approach assumes, the more similar in meaning the texts represented by the vectors.

7.5.3. *Probabilistic Model of Relevance*

With a probabilistic model of relevance, IR is framed as a problem of evaluating evidence about what a user's query means, what the documents in the corpus are about, and which documents will best satisfy the query. The evidence about the content of the query and of the documents comprises the ways in which they are represented. This includes the words and phrases they contain, their definitions and synonyms in dictionaries and thesauri, other features in the documents such as citations and subject–matter indices, for instance, West digest topics and key numbers, and statistical information. It is as though the contents of the query and documents, that is, what they mean, cause the observed evidence, namely, how they are represented. Conversely, how the query and documents are represented, that is, the evidence, depends on what they mean, the cause.

Introduction to Bayesian Networks

A Bayesian network is a useful tool for modeling situations "in which causality plays a role but our understanding of what is actually going on is incomplete, so we need to describe things probabilistically" (Charniak, 1991, p. 51). In the probabilistic model of relevance implemented in the former West is Natural (WIN) system, for example, a BN automated inferences about the likelihood that a seeker's need for information, as evidenced by his or her query, is satisfied by a particular document in the database (Turtle, 1995, p. 27).

A *BN* is a graphical model of probabilistic causal relationships. Each BN node represents an "event" with a variable to indicate whether it has occurred. The arcs represent causal influences affecting the likelihood of an event's occurrence including conditional probabilities associated with those causal influences. If certain assumptions are satisfied, one can compute the probability of an event variable having a certain status given information about the status of its immediately preceding event variables in the graph. These assumptions include the independence assumption that each event is conditionally independent of its non-descendants given its parent variables (Turtle and Croft, 1990, p. 21). This independence assumption reduces the number of probabilities that need to be computed making BNs an efficient method for modeling causal reasoning.

In his article, "Bayesian Networks without Tears," Eugene Charniak provided a prosaic example of a BN, like the one shown in Figure 7.2, whose function was to help the author on his walk home to determine the likelihood that his family is out given that he hears the dog barking.

The causal interpretation of the arcs in the diagram is as follows: the prior probability of the family's being out is just 15%, but the family's being out has a direct causal connection to the dog's being out, which, in turn, is directly connected to Charniak's hearing her. The diagram, however, shows another reason why the dog would be outside having to do with the dog's digestive system. The prior probability of the dog having such a problem is just 1%, but the diagram says that the dog having a digestive problem can also cause dog-out. In addition, the diagram shows that when

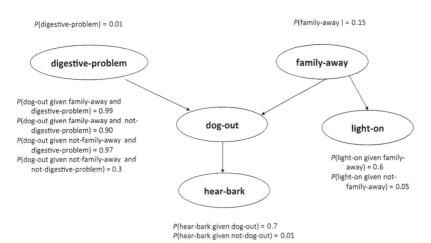

FIGURE 7.2. BN for the family-away problem (see Charniak, 1991, p. 52)

the family members leave Charniak's house, they will turn the outside light on 60% of the time, but that 5% of the time the light will be on even when they are at home, for example, if they expect a guest (Charniak, 1991, p. 52).

BNs allow one to calculate the conditional probabilities of the nodes in the network given that the values of some of the nodes have been observed. If Charniak observes that the light is on (light-on = true) but does not hear his dog (hear-bark = false), he can calculate the conditional probability of family-away given these pieces of evidence (for this case, it is about 0.5) (Charniak, 1991, p. 52). Details of the calculation may be found at Brachman and Levesque (2004, p. 248).

Using a Bayesian Network to Assess Relevance in IR

As noted, a BN is a convenient tool for evaluating evidence in a causal chain. It can deal with a legal IR system's uncertainty about what the user's query means or what the documents in its collection are about. The BN's nodes represent the probability that a user's query term correctly describes a set of documents based only on information about the concepts that represent that set of documents (Turtle and Croft, 1990; Turtle, 1995, p. 33). Using the network, an IR system can compute the likelihood that a particular document is relevant to a query.

A BN for an information retrieval system, shown in Figure 7.3, has two parts. The first part, a query network, shown at the bottom of the figure, is constructed when the user submits the query. It results from the system's processing of the query text and representing it in terms of query concepts (words, citations, etc.) The query may be expanded (see below) using an ontology or thesaurus to link a particular query concept to synonymous representation concepts.

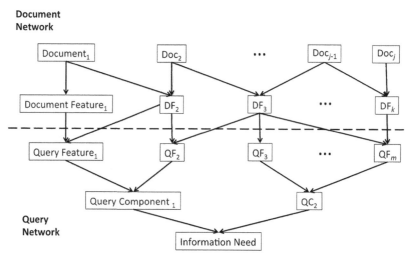

FIGURE 7.3. Inference network retrieval model (see Turtle, 1995, p. 33)

The query network is then hooked up with the document network (at the top), which has been constructed beforehand, and which does not change as the query is processed. The nodes and arcs from the query node up through the document nodes represent various conditional probability relationships. The likelihood that the user's particular information need has been met depends on the query components. The likelihood of observing a particular query component depends on the query features. The likelihood of observing a particular query feature depends on the document features. The likelihood of observing a particular document feature depends on the documents.

The prior probability that any particular document Doc_i will be observed is one over the number of documents in the corpus. In other words, before taking the query into account, the prior probability that any document will be responsive is assumed to be uniformly random (Turtle and Croft, 1990).

Tf/idf values associated with the document feature representations in the inverted index are used to estimate these conditional probabilities. By assuming each document Doc_i has been observed, in turn, the BN computes the chances that the Information Need has been met by Doc_i. The system then ranks the documents by the magnitude of the probabilities and returns to the user an ordered listing of the most likely relevant documents (Turtle, 1995).

Commercial legal IR systems have improved upon the use of BNs for relevance assessment (see, for example, Section 7.7). Nevertheless, an inference network IR approach using BNs represented an advance in effectively employing term frequency information to assess relevance. One could also use BNs to simulate the Boolean and vector space models for assessing relevance (Turtle, 1995, p. 32).

The question arose, however, just how well do full-text legal information retrieval systems work, a question that is still relevant today.

7.6. ASSESSING LEGAL IR SYSTEMS

An initial issue for assessing legal IR systems is how to measure their performance. Section 4.4.4 has already presented the classic information retrieval measures in explaining how to assess the performance of ML classifiers. In the information retrieval realm:

True Negatives (TN): the number of documents that are irrelevant and were predicted as irrelevant.

True Positives (TP): the number of documents that are relevant and were predicted as relevant.

False Negatives (FN): the number of documents that are relevant but were predicted as irrelevant.

False Positives (FP): the number of documents that are irrelevant but were predicted as relevant.

The performance of IR systems, then, is usually measured in terms of:

Precision: the ratio of the number of relevant documents retrieved over the number of all documents retrieved.

$$P = \frac{|Relevant \cap Retrieved|}{|Retrieved|} = (TP)/(TP + FP)$$

Recall: the ratio of the number of relevant documents retrieved over the number of all relevant documents in the corpus.

$$R = \frac{|Relevant \cap Retrieved|}{|Relevant|} = (TP)/(TP + FN)$$

F1 Measure: the harmonic mean of precision and recall where both measures are treated as equally important.

$$F1 = 2 * \frac{P * R}{P + R} = \frac{2 * TP}{2 * TP + FN + FP}$$

Elusion: the proportion of unretrieved documents that are relevant.

$$E = \frac{|Relevant \cap Unretrieved|}{|Unretrieved|} = (FN)/(TN + FN)$$

The elusion measure is important in assessing the effectiveness of information retrieval in e-discovery discussed in the next chapter (see Oard and Webber, 2013, pp. 152–4).

Virtually all IR systems retrieve documents and then rank them. Metrics for evaluating how well an IR system ranks retrieved documents will be defined in Section 11.4.1.

In IR systems generally, there is a trade-off between precision and recall. A less restrictive search returns more documents, but a greater fraction of them will be irrelevant (higher recall and lower precision). Conversely, a more restrictive search returns fewer documents, but a greater fraction of them will be relevant (lower recall and higher precision). Even though the trade-off cannot be avoided, there are strategies for improving both precision and recall at the same time. For instance, multistage retrieval processes that use a retrieved set of documents for a subsequent more refined search have yielded improvements in both precision and recall (see Buckland and Gey, 1994, pp. 18–19). (An example of such a strategy in IR systems is "relevance feedback" (see Section 7.9.2)).

In an early landmark study, Blair and Maron (1985) tested IBM's STAIRS full-text IR system. STAIRS applied a Boolean search model of relevance with a database of about 40,000 documents to be used in defending a large corporate law suit.

Blair and Maron employed precision and recall to evaluate the IR system. In computing precision, the lawyers who created the queries judged whether the documents retrieved were relevant. In assessing recall, random samples from sets of unretrieved documents were extracted and the attorneys determined, in a blind test, whether the documents were relevant (Blair and Maron, 1985, p. 291).

The study revealed that, while precision averaged at 75.5%, recall was very low; on average, STAIRS retrieved only 20% of relevant documents (Blair and Maron, 1985, p. 293). This level of recall contrasted sharply with what the attorneys using the system believed they were getting: namely 75% of the relevant documents. The authors attributed the low recall to the fact that so many terms have synonyms, that the documents contained oblique references, and successive search modifications to make queries more precise tended to skew searches, leaving out many relevant documents.

In the decade after the Blair and Maron's study, full-text legal IR systems like LEXIS and WIN applied the probabilistic model of relevance described above to corpora of legal cases. This development led Dan Dabney to update the Blair and Maron's study in 1993.

Dabney's study involved a large corpus of legal cases, not litigation documents. In particular, he employed LEXIS and WESTLAW to retrieve all of the state cases within the scope of 23 articles of a volume of the *American Law Reports* (ALR), a reference work that contains in-depth articles on narrow topics of the law. ALR articles, called "annotations," cite relevant cases on the topic.

Dabney, an expert legal researcher, crafted a query for each of 23 test questions, one for each ALR article. Each query aimed to retrieve the maximum number of relevant cases from LEXIS and WESTLAW without retrieving too many irrelevant cases. He then compared the final list of cases returned to the complete list of state cases that were cited by the ALR article and that were known to be contained in the corresponding database (Dabney, 1993, pp. 105–6).

Significantly, Dabney's result was not that much different from that of Blair and Maron (Dabney, 1993). Dabney's study showed that the 20% recall found by Blair and Maron could be improved, up to 40% recall, but at the sacrifice of precision. As Dabney concluded, "Most practitioners feel that the 20% recall found by Blair and Maron is alarmingly low, and many will feel that the 40% recall found here is not much better, particularly in light of the substantial loss of precision" (Dabney, 1993, pp. 126–7).

While the technology of legal IR systems for case retrieval continues to improve, there seems to have been no recent published reevaluations along the lines of these two studies.

7.7. RECENT DEVELOPMENTS IN LEGAL IR SYSTEMS

In state-of-the-art legal information retrieval systems like WN, some of the above document retrieval functionality is employed, but the ranking of documents for presentation to the user is different (Lu and Conrad, 2013).

Ranking uses evidence derived from frequency information in the documents' texts, but WN's reranking function takes additional features into consideration, including:

– Evidence from expert-generated annotations (e.g., related to West's Key Number System)
– Citation networks of citing and cited sources [2]
– Information about documents' popularity and usage given aggregate information from previous users' queries.

In addition, the ranking function "learns how to weigh the 'features' representing this evidence in a manner that will produce the best (i.e., highest precision) ranking of the documents retrieved" (Lu and Conrad, 2013). Applying ML to text is explained and illustrated in Chapter 8. Presumably, a ML model is trained with either gold standard rankings of cases retrieved for test queries or some other form of supervision such as feedback from observation of how users behave after receiving results.

Finally, WN uses information about legal issues deemed relevant to the query to recommend documents on related issues.

Recently, LexisNexis's Paul Zhang and his colleagues have developed techniques for semantically annotating legal case texts to support more intelligent, concept-based legal IR. They undertake "a rigorous semantic annotation process of legal documents, during which various text units are identified, normalized into 'standard' forms and properly indexed" (Zhang, 2015).

Similar to a hierarchical type system as described in Section 6.8, the annotations involve four layers of metadata:

1. Generic lexical level
2. Basic legal concept level
3. Legal issue level
4. Verb-predication level

At the generic lexical level, the forms of the words and phrases (i.e., their morphology) are normalized, that is, put into a standard form with respect to spelling variations and phraseology.

For the level of basic legal concepts, LexisNexis has developed a universal list of legal concepts across the entire corpus. Zhang defines "legal concept" operationally as an idea shared in common by sets of words or phrases across frequent legal discussions. Legal concepts in documents are identified and matched to concept IDs in the universal list.

---

[2] Relevance ranking in FastCase, another commercial legal IR service, also takes into account citation frequency and the relative importance of a citation (Remus and Levy, 2015, p. 24).

The process of constructing the universal concept list combines automatic and manual analysis. The process involves *n-grams*, contiguous sequences of *n* items (e.g., words) from a given text sequence. A LexisNexis team:

1. produces candidate concepts from the corpus of U.S. legal document *n*-grams (using data-mining).
2. filters the *n*-grams with linguistic rules focusing on noun phrases (NPs) and taking into account their distribution in the corpus.
3. groups the terms sharing the same meaning and, for each group, selects one term based on frequency and simple rules as the normal form to represent the concept.
4. applies manual editing to add/pair terms where necessary, to edit out unwanted terms or groups, and to select legal concepts (Zhang et al., 2014).

The resulting concepts in normal form are somewhat more abstract than surface language expressions of the concepts. These concepts range from those used in legal principles, doctrines, and jargon to factual concepts (i.e., important, frequently discussed factual terms) (Zhang et al., 2014).

LexisNexis maintains a legal issue library that contains standardized legal issues with links to case discussions of that issue. A legal issue is defined as a "statement of belief, opinion, a principle, etc. It usually contains one or more 'Concepts' to be meaningful" (Zhang et al., 2014). Legal issues are related to the reasons why one case cites another case or statute. LexisNexis has a patented process for extracting such reasons and legal issues. Texts in cases that are on the same legal issue are identified and linked to a standard entry in the legal issue library and indexed as such.

Zhang provides the following examples illustrating legal issues and concepts. Since

Statement: "Thirteen-year-olds should not own a vehicle" . . . has at least three Concepts in it: "13-year-old," "vehicle," and "to own"; . . . the author or speaker states clearly an opinion, a belief, or a piece of law . . . [and] such a statement has [a] legal implication, it is a Legal Issue. Here are examples of Legal Issues found in cases . . . [where the] Concept "vehicle," . . . is used . . .:

a. "A police officer may approach a stopped vehicle and inquire about an occupant's well-being without intruding on the Fourth Amendment."
b. "In Nebraska, a vehicle can be a tool of the debtor's trade if the debtor uses it in connection with or to commute to work."
c. "State law governs the issue of security interests in motor vehicles."
d. "In Idaho, it is a felony to purport to sell or transfer a vehicle without delivering to the purchaser or transferee a certificate of title duly assigned to the purchaser." (Zhang et al., 2014)

The predication level annotates cases in terms of verb-centered predicates (so-called "V-Triples"), which seem to be an effective way to abstract the meaning of a sentence. The sentences are parsed into syntactic trees and then converted into these predicate structures.

These four levels of metadata annotations comprise a derived representation of legal documents in terms of semantic information standardized across the whole database, which can be used for conceptual information retrieval. Reportedly, the annotation scheme has been, or will soon be, incorporated into the commercial LexisNexis system and used for semantics-based searching of documents, classification, information about reasons for citation, as well as for concept map and citation network browsing (see Zhang et al., 2014; Zhang, 2015).

7.8. COMPARING LEGAL IR AND CMLAS

Information retrieval has a significant advantage over AI & Law computational models of legal argument. Given new case texts submitted by courts in digital form, adding new cases to the inverted index is automatic. No human interpretation or intervention is required to prepare the case text for use with the IR system's measure of relevance. The system can assess the *tf/idf* measure automatically. As a result, Lexis and Westlaw process millions of case texts automatically.

On the other hand, IR relevance measures do not capture all of the elements of *legal* relevance that they could. Beyond highlighting query terms, an IR system cannot compare cases because it lacks a representation of what features are legally important. It does not even "know" which side won a case or with respect to which claims or issues. As a result, an IR system cannot infer from the retrieved cases how the problem should be decided, predict an outcome, or make arguments for and against an outcome.

The computational models of Part I do capture these aspects of legal relevance. They can compare cases in legally meaningful ways and make predictions about outcomes and arguments for and against such outcomes. These models, however, work with, at most, hundreds of cases that have been manually represented. This is the problem of the knowledge representation bottleneck. When new cases are added to a CMLA, they, too, must be represented by hand.

Ideally, these complementary strengths of full-text legal information retrieval and AI & Law approaches can be combined.

7.9. IMPROVING LEGAL IR WITH AI & LAW APPROACHES

Chapters 10 through 12 present some ways in which that may be accomplished using LUIMA and other open-source tools now available, but first it may be useful to examine some previous efforts to improve full-text legal information retrieval by adding legal knowledge through AI & Law techniques.

7.9.1. *Integrating Legal Ontologies and IR*

The first of these techniques involves using legal ontologies for the purpose of query expansion. Given the terms in a query, a program searches a legal ontology to find synonyms or related terms and expands the query accordingly.

For example, Saravanan et al. (2009) employed a legal ontology of Indian law regarding rent control, income tax, and sales tax to automatically expand user queries. Upon receiving a user query containing the term "rental arrears," the retrieval system would collect linked concept entries in the ontology including "rent in arrears," "default of payment of rent," and other related terms or phrases and use them to expand the query. Similarly, a query for "increase in rent" would be expanded to include "exorbitant rent" and "enhancement of rent."

The authors evaluated versions of the retrieval system with and without the automatic query expansion. They compared the versions' results against a gold standard set of documents relevant for each of two sets of queries. The results demonstrated improvements in both precision and recall attributable to the ontology-based query expansion (Saravanan et al., 2009).

A related use of a legal ontology is to provide a semantic markup of text components in a corpus in order to improve information retrieval. This was illustrated in Section 6.3.1. An IR system for criminal law hearings supported a measure of intelligent retrieval with indexing and search based on the e-Court ontology. Documents were annotated and tagged using terms from the legal ontology dealing with criminal procedure. Users could browse the ontology to more concretely specify conceptual requirements for documents they were seeking (Breuker et al., 2002).

The LUIMA type system (Section 6.8), is a kind of ontology used to semantically annotate legal argument roles of sentences in legal cases. As discussed in Section 11.4, LUIMA annotations have been shown to improve reranking performance in a full-text legal IR system for vaccine injury cases.

7.9.2. *Integrating Legal IR and AI & Law Relevance Measures*

Two projects have taken steps toward integrating AI & Law measures of relevance with retrieval of textual cases.

In the first one, SPIRE, a user could input a new problem as a set of legal factors. The program would then retrieve cases, from a full-text legal IR system, that shared the factors, and highlight their passages relevant to the factors of interest. Significantly, the retrieved cases were not previously in SPIRE's database. In other words, SPIRE used a CMLR like Hypo or CATO to retrieve relevant cases from a legal IR system like Lexis or Westlaw (Daniels and Rissland, 1997a,b).

SPIRE dealt with an issue in bankruptcy law of whether a debtor had submitted in "good faith" a plan to settle with the creditors. The researchers identified in the caselaw 10 factor-like features that influenced courts' decisions of good faith, such as

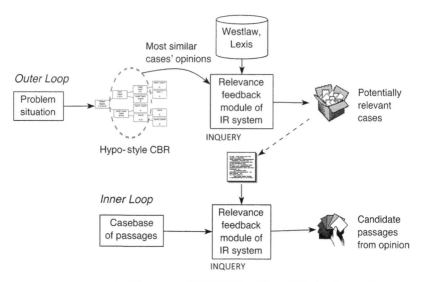

FIGURE 7.4. Architecture of SPIRE (Daniels and Rissland, 1997a)

the plan's duration, the debtor's sincerity, the debtor's prospects for future income, and any special circumstances. For each of these factors, the researchers assembled from 3 to 14 excerpts from cases where the courts indicated that or how they took the factor into account. For instance, for future income, that is, whether the debtor's income is likely to increase in the future, the excerpt might be negative or positive: "the Court cannot see any likelihood of future increases," "the prospect of a regular job with substantially increased income is not great," "her health brings into question her future ability to work," or "no evidence that raises are likely" (Daniels and Rissland, 1997a, p. 43).

SPIRE's architecture is shown in Figure 7.4. SPIRE had two loops : an outer loop, in which it retrieved case opinions from a full-text legal IR system like Lexis or Westlaw, and an inner loop, in which it identified in retrieved opinions the passages relevant to factors of interest. Each loop had a separate database. The outer loop database contained bankruptcy cases on the issue of whether debtors had submitted settlement plans in good faith. These cases were represented in terms of the 10 legal factors relevant to the good faith issue. In addition, the database stored the text of each case. The database for SPIRE's inner loop contained the short passages associated with factors. These excerpts were manually extracted from the bankruptcy cases (Daniels and Rissland, 1997a,b).

As illustrated in Figure 7.4, given a new problem input as a set of factors, SPIRE retrieved relevant cases from the case database, organized them into a claim lattice, and selected the most on point cases (see Section 3.3.2). Up to this point, the program used Hypo-style case-based reasoning.

SPIRE then passed the texts of the most on point cases to a full-text IR system called INQUERY (Callan et al., 1992). INQUERY's database comprised legal texts from an IR corpus like that of Lexis or Westlaw.

In particular, SPIRE passed these case texts to INQUERY's relevance feedback module. In effect, the case texts seeded a query instructing INQUERY's relevance feedback module to retrieve more texts from its database that were like the seed cases. A *relevance feedback* module enables users to indicate which documents, returned in response to a query, are, in fact, relevant and best represent what the user is looking for. The IR system extracts information such as additional terms from those feedback selections to augment the query and find other similarly relevant documents (Turtle, 1995, p. 40).

INQUERY retrieved these potentially relevant cases and passed them to SPIRE's inner loop for purposes of highlighting passages relevant to the factors input by the user (see dashed arrow in Figure 7.4). For each factor of interest, SPIRE extracted text excerpts from the inner loop's passage database. It assembled the passages associated with the factor of interest into a query submitted again to INQUERY's relevance feedback module. This time, however, INQUERY's database comprised the texts of just the potentially relevant cases it had previously retrieved. In effect, the passage query instructs INQUERY to retrieve from the potentially relevant cases more passages like those in the query. INQUERY returned the most relevant factor-related passages, they are highlighted in the potentially relevant cases, and the cases are returned to the user (Daniels and Rissland, 1997a).

The researchers evaluated SPIRE by the extent to which its ordering of factor-related passages, retrieved in response to queries, reduces the amount of wasted effort as users examine the retrieved passages. This is measured in terms of expected search length, the number of irrelevant items a user encounters before finding a specified number of relevant ones, here set as 1, 3, or 5 relevant passages. Using a test set of 20 documents, two sets of individual factor-focused queries prepared by the researchers, and a set of such queries generated by a human expert, the researchers found that SPIRE reduced the search by about 4, 10, or 11 items per factor (Daniels and Rissland, 1997b, p. 335).

SPIRE represented a novel way to connect an AI & Law system like Hypo or CATO with a full-text IR system. In trials, it successfully found new cases in an IR corpus that were similar to the inputted cases from SPIRE's database.

This connection also suggests how to update a factor-based case base of a CMLR or CMLA, at least in a semiautomated procedure. Periodically, using SPIRE's existing cases as inputs, one could retrieve new cases from a Lexis or Westlaw corpus that share the same factors as an input case and highlight the passages that relate to those factors. Guided by the highlighting, humans could examine the potentially relevant new cases, confirm their relevance, and enter them into SPIRE's case database (Daniels and Rissland, 1997a). From there, a CMLR like CATO, IBP, or CMLA like VJAP could use them to predict outcomes or make arguments as discussed in

Sections 4.5.2 and 5.7. The method assumes, of course, the existence of a database of cases represented as factors and a database of passages associated with factors.

7.9.3. *Augmenting Legal IR Relevance Assessment with Citation Networks*

As indicated in Section 7.7, both WN and LexisNexis make use of citation links in a network of citations to improve legal information retrieval. An early AI & Law project, SCALIR, demonstrated a way to take citation links into account to enhance relevance assessment (Rose and Belew, 1991). It comprised a networked database of nodes representing cases, statutes, and their composite terms. As its relevance measure for retrieval, it employed the spread and magnitude of a quantity called "activation" (defined below) through this network.

SCALIR presents users with an interactive graphical interface in which they can label initial nodes with terms of interest. In response, the system displayed cases and terms in the corpus to which the inputs relate with the most relevant nodes at the center and less relevant nodes toward the edges (see Figure 7.5). By clicking on displayed nodes, users can indicate nodes of special interest and a relevance feedback mechanism expands or prunes the search accordingly.

SCALIR contained the texts of cases (1,361 federal cases), statutes (87 sections of Copyright Act), and a library of terms (6,160 terms). Each of these is represented as a node (7,608 nodes) in a network interlinked with three kinds of links. C-links show that a case includes a term. S-links indicate that a statute is part of another statute or refers to it, that a term is related to another term, or that a case cites or overrules another case. H-links show that a case has some intermediate effect on another case (Rose and Belew, 1991).

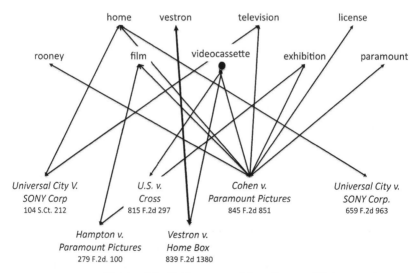

FIGURE 7.5. Retrieval for "videocassette" (see Rose and Belew, 1991)

When a user inputs a query with terms of interest, the nodes in the network corresponding to the specified terms each receive a certain amount of "activity." This begins a process of *spreading activation* in which the activated nodes associated with query terms send activation to the nodes to which they are linked. The spreading activation, however, is subject to the weight on the link and passes along the link only if the sum of the sender activations is above the certain threshold. The weight on a C-link from a term to a document depends inversely on the frequency of documents with that term. S-links are selective as to which activations they will pass along (Rose and Belew, 1991).

These linkages, weights, and thresholds determine the way in which the system discriminates among the nodes in terms of relevance to a query. After the spreading activation subsides, for any node, the system sums the inputted activations, tests if it is above a threshold, orders the nodes in terms of their activation levels, and presents them graphically as relevant. The user can refocus the search by marking the nodes for feedback (Rose and Belew, 1991).

The connectionist network approach is a step toward conceptual information retrieval (Section 1.3.2). In trials, a query for "videocassette" returned the sources shown in Figure 7.5. The search retrieved a relevant case, *Sony v. Universal*, even though the term was not literally present in the *Sony* case text. In other words, the links enabled conceptual retrieval even where the concept did not appear expressly. The links were indirect through another case that linked the concepts, that is, from "videocassette" to the *Cohen* case to "television" and "home" to the *Sony* case.

Getting the links, weights, and thresholds right can be tricky. In the instance of "videocassette," the linkage to the *Sony* case was less direct than the authors thought it could have been. As noted, the links were indirect through another case (the *Cohen* case) to television and home to the *Sony* case. Linkages did not appear for the concepts "VCR," "Betamax," and "VTR," which *were* explicitly mentioned in the *Sony* case but did not appear in the response set, as the authors had hoped they would.

Nevertheless, citation networks are a potent source of information for conceptual information retrieval. Another AI & Law program, BankXX, made use of a legal network of bankruptcy law information. The network comprised nodes for cases, representing them as sets of linked legal factors, bundles of citations, prototypical stories, and legal theories, which were also represented with legal factors. The program's goal was to construct an argument by searching the network for information corresponding to 12 types of argument building blocks, including cases for and against the arguer's goal. Three evaluation functions guided the best first search through the network, and the resulting arguments were assessed in terms of eight argument factors, including the win record of the theory used, the strength of the citations, and the strength of the best case analogies.

An empirical evaluation of how well BankXX, starting with a decided case, came up with argument elements apparent in the corresponding judicial decision, yielded positive results (Rissland et al., 1996). The work is an early example of using argument concepts to define relevance in more legal semantic terms in support of a kind of conceptual retrieval.

7.9.4. *Detecting Concept Change*

The meanings of legal concepts may change as courts apply them in new fact situations over time. Rissland and Friedman (1995) developed an ingenious approach to detecting concept change in cases stored in an information retrieval database.

The project dealt with the legal issue of whether a debtor in bankruptcy has submitted a plan in *good faith* as required in personal bankruptcy law (11 U.S. Code, chapter 13, the same domain as in SPIRE, Section 7.9.2). They created a chronologically ordered 10-year "example-stream" of 55 cases regarding the issue of good faith submission from the BankXX project (Rissland et al., 1996).

Each case was represented not as text but as a vector of 61 features, for example, debtors, debts, creditors, employment, cash flow, proposed payments, amount of debtor's surplus, percentage repayment of unsecured debt, and inaccuracies in debtor's representations. Some of these features were associated with legal factors introduced in appellate cases interpreting the good faith requirement and used in the BankXX case representation, such as percent-surplus-of-income-factor, employment-history-factor, earnings-potential-factor, plan-duration-factor, plan-accuracy-factor, relative-total-payment-amount-factor, inaccuracies-to-mislead-factor, and motivation-sincerity-factor (Rissland et al., 1996).

The researchers input each case vector in chronological order to C4.5 (see Section 4.3.1) a ML algorithm, which outputs a decision-tree representing the concept of good faith *up to that point in time*. Each decision tree node is a leaf node indicating whether good faith was satisfied (or not) or a test on an attribute. Tests focused on, for instance, whether the duration of a proposed plan or the amount of payments and surplus exceeded certain amounts, or on the debtor's motivation and sincerity.

A program compared each new decision tree's representation of the concept of good faith and the prior decision tree to detect any structural changes. In decision trees, concepts can be generalized by adding a disjunct or deleting a conjunct. Removing a disjunct or adding a conjunct narrows a concept. In addition, a concept attribute's relevance can change, for instance, the attribute can appear or disappear, or its value can be inverted. In particular, the program compared values that occur at each location in the old and new trees and measured the extent to which any attributes moved, appeared, or disappeared.

The researchers developed a *structural-instability metric* to detect concept change. It summed the changes at each level of trees and computed a weighted sum of changes over all levels. Since, given information theoretic measures used in decision tree algorithms, more predictive attributes occur higher up in a tree (closer to the root), the instability metric gave more weight to changes in attributes at higher levels.

The program averaged summations of change across each successive pair of trees and examined them for statistically significant changes in slope or trends. A negative slope indicated that conceptual instability is decreasing. A positive slope indicated increasing instability leading the system to pose a *hypothesis* that the meaning of the legal concept is drifting.

In order to test the hypothesis of concept drift, the researchers continually updated the older tree, formed a possible replacement tree, and compared their predictions over the next 12 examples. If the new tree was more predictive, it confirmed the concept's drift. The authors compared the program's detections of concept drift and confirmed its rough correspondence to the historical record of decisions.

As the authors pointed out, their "method is very general and can be used in conjunction with many incremental learning algorithms" (Rissland and Friedman, 1995). If the relevant features and legal factors can be annotated in the texts of the cases, a similar method could help a legal app autonomously to detect opportunities for posing and testing hypotheses that a legal concept has changed its meaning (see Section 12.6).

7.10. CONCLUSION

While the improvements in state-of-the-art commercial legal IR have been significant, and the efforts to integrate AI & Law techniques and legal IR systems are promising, they do not address two important areas: (1) capturing the roles that sentences play in legal arguments and (2) using those roles to support conceptual legal IR.

As illustrated in Section 6.8, the argument roles sentences play in legal decisions include citing legal authorities, stating legal rules in the abstract, reporting a decision-maker's legal rulings or holdings with respect to those rules, and recording the decision-maker's finding on whether or not evidence in a particular case proves that a rule condition has been satisfied.

If these sentence roles could be identified in the texts of cases that an IR system retrieves in response to user queries, they would provide information useful for ranking the retrieved cases and highlighting the most relevant passages given the legal researcher's intended use of the information in an argument. They could also help an IR system identify legal semantic information in case texts such as legal factors that could support legal apps in assisting humans to predict outcomes, make arguments, and test hypotheses.

These ideas will be developed in Chapters 10 through 12, but we first need to learn more about applying ML to legal texts and extracting information about legal rules from statutory and regulatory texts.

8

Machine Learning with Legal Texts

8.1. INTRODUCTION

In the examples of ML so far, a program has learned from data about judges, trends, or cases as in the Supreme Court Database, but not from the texts of cases or other legal documents. This chapter introduces applying ML algorithms to corpora of legal texts, discusses how ML models implicitly represent users' hypotheses about relevance, illustrates how ML can improve full-text legal information retrieval, and explains its role in conceptual information retrieval and in cognitive computing. The chapter also distinguishes between supervised and unsupervised ML from text and discusses techniques for automating learning of structure and semantics from legal documents.

Along the way, the chapter answers the following questions: How can ML be applied to textual data? What is the difference between supervised and unsupervised ML from texts? What is predictive coding? How well does predictive coding work? What is "information extraction" from text? How are texts represented for purposes of applying ML? What is a "support vector machine (SVM)" and why use one with textual data?

8.2. APPLYING MACHINE LEARNING TO TEXTUAL DATA

ML algorithms identify patterns in data, summarize the patterns in a model, and use the models to make predictions by identifying the same patterns in new data (see Kohavi and Provost, 1998).

A *model* is a structure that summarizes the patterns in data in some statistical or logical form in which it can be applied to new data (see Kohavi and Provost, 1998). This book has already introduced some examples of ML models, such as the decision tree for bail decisions in Figure 4.2 or the random forests of decision trees referred to in Section 4.4.

The models capture the strength of the association in the patterns between observed features and an outcome feature. For example, the decision on bail is an outcome feature, and the observed features included whether the offense involved drugs or the offender had a prior record. The Supreme Court's decision to affirm or not is an outcome feature, and the observed features included a justice's gender or the appointing president's party. The model captures the strength of the association in the patterns between observation and outcome features either statistically, logically, or in some combination of the two.

As noted, the model learned in Section 4.4, predicted outcomes of Supreme Court cases, but not based on features of their texts. This chapter (and the remainder of Part II) focuses on applications of ML where the data are primarily texts: litigation documents, legal case decisions, or statutory provisions. The features of the texts include the terms they employ and, possibly, grammatical constructs and some semantic information. The algorithms identify patterns of these features in the texts, summarize the patterns in models, and use the models to predict outcomes of, or to assign labels to, new texts.

As an introduction, we first examine a basic setup for applying ML to legal texts (Section 8.3). We then examine document retrieval in e-discovery, where ML algorithms learn users' relevance criteria. A model assigns labels to documents such as "relevant" to the claims under litigation or "not relevant" (Section 8.4).

The sample program in Section 8.5.1 deals with extracting information from a commercial IR system's corpus of legal cases. An ML system helps assign labels to cases indicating that a case is "related to the same litigation as a given prior case." The features include the similarity and distinctiveness of titles and whether history language appears that directly connects the texts. The model identifies patterns associated with these and other features and how strongly they predict that two cases are part of the same litigation.

This example lays a foundation for understanding how to learn some rhetorical structures in legal cases such as distinguishing a section that discusses the law from one that discusses case facts (Section 8.6). The models in other ML systems discussed in Chapter 10 assign labels indicating a sentence's argument role, for example as an "evidence-based finding of fact," or outcomes such as "plaintiff wins" or "plaintiff loses."

Finally, an example in Section 8.7 applies an ML approach from e-discovery to a corpus of statutory provisions. The model can assign labels of "relevant" or "not relevant" to an issue for statutory analysis. This lays a foundation for understanding other programs in Chapter 9 that apply ML and other techniques to extracting information from statutes.

Applying ML to legal texts will play key roles in a legal app for cognitive computing. One goal in cognitive computing is for ML algorithms to learn to identify patterns of textual features that are important for human problem-solving. This also involves identifying contexts and problems for which these patterns are most useful and the strengths of association between the observed and outcome features. The cognitive computing environment can then use these patterns for prediction and classification as human users solve new problems.

8.3. A BASIC SETUP FOR APPLYING ML TO LEGAL TEXTS

This section describes a basic setup for applying ML to a corpus of legal texts and evaluating it (Savelka and Grabmair, 2015). The goal of the setup is to transform a text corpus into a vector space model (see Section 7.5.2) suitable for applying an ML algorithm. While a detailed description is beyond the scope of this book, this section provides a sketch of what is involved.

The first step is to collect and process the raw data, a corpus of natural language legal texts (see Fagan, 2016, p. 34). Online services like CourtListener are a source of digital legal texts. Since downloading individual files takes too long, downloading files in bulk is preferred if not restricted by license. Although commercial licenses frequently do proscribe bulk downloading, CourtListener permits it and provides instructions[1] (Fagan, 2016, p. 35).

The next step is to transform the raw text data using some linguistic processing to tokenize, normalize, and annotate the texts.

Normalization involves converting words to lower case and stemming them to their uninflected roots in order to eliminate superficial variations (Turney and Pantel, 2010, p.154). For example, "Phelps" is converted to "phelps." "Swimming" and "swam" are converted to "swim."

Tokenizing texts involves transforming words that are hyphenated, have apostrophes, or have other punctuation, into standard forms. Tokenizing also frequently involves eliminating *stop words*, "high-frequency words with relatively low information content, such as function words (e.g., of, the, and) and pronouns (e.g., them, who, that)" (Turney and Pantel, 2010, p. 154).

Tokenization can present some subtleties. For instance, "Michael" (with a comma) is commonly transformed to "michael." "Michael's" with an apostrophe, however, may be a possessive form or a contraction. Different text processing systems employ different rules for tokenizing words like this, which may or may not preserve the semantic distinction. The choice of stop words can also have an effect on meaning. In some contexts, for example web search, frequently appearing short words like "and," "any," "not," and "or" may be treated as stop words, but in a legal context they often convey significant information content. In practice, text processing systems implement default rules for tokenization, which may need to be examined in light of the legal application.

Another aspect of tokenization involves the treatment of adjacent words. Neighboring words may be treated as *n*-grams, that is, as tokens of *n* words (Fagan, 2016,

---

[1] www.courtlistener.com/api/bulk-info/

p. 54). A bigram treats two adjacent words as a single token. For instance, "Four score and seven years ago" can be represented in five bigrams: "four score," "score and," "and seven," "seven years," "years ago." It can also be represented in four trigrams: "four score and," "score and seven," "and seven years," and "seven years ago."

Annotation involves *adding* information that may help to disambiguate similar words in a text. Useful annotations include the sense in which an ambiguous word is used in the text (sense tagging). Other annotations are words' parts of speech in the text, that is, nouns, verbs, adjectives, or adverbs (POS tagging). One can also annotate the words' grammatical roles in the parsed sentences' structures, such as direct object or object of a prepositional phrase (see Turney and Pantel, 2010, p. 155).

After a document's text is normalized, tokenized, and annotated, it is represented as a *feature vector*. This representation is similar to a term vector (see Section 7.5.2). In a feature vector, however, the features can include additional information such as bigrams or other *n*-grams as well as category information.

The feature vectors representing documents in a corpus all have the same length *n* equal to the total number of words and other features in the corpus. Each feature vector is an arrow from the origin $(0,0,0, \ldots, 0)$ to the point representing the document in an *n*-dimensional feature space. Since each different word or other feature in the full corpus of texts corresponds to yet another dimension, the number *n* of dimensions will be very large.

The magnitudes along each of the dimensions are the values of the features for that document. The magnitude may be "0" indicating that the document does not have that feature or "1" indicating that it does. Alternatively, the magnitude may indicate the frequency of the word or other feature in the document (see Fagan, 2016, p. 53), or its *tf/idf* value (see Sections 6.4 and 7.5.2) representing its frequency in the document discounted by its frequency in the corpus (see Turney and Pantel, 2010, p. 156).

The goal of ML from legal texts is to classify documents or to make predictions. In an e-discovery context, for instance, the goal is to classify a litigation-related document as "relevant" or "irrelevant." In a context involving ML from legal cases, the goal may be to classify sentences by the role they play in a legal opinion, for example, as a "Legal Ruling or Holding of Law" or an "Evidence-Based Finding" sentence. Alternatively, the goal may be to classify sentences by whether or not they support a conclusion that a legal factor applies in the case. Thus, a sentence might be classified as an instance or not of Factor F1 Disclosure-in-negotiations or F2 Bribe-employee. Conceivably, the goal of learning could be to predict outcomes for cases, based on information gleaned from cases texts that relates to litigation participant-and-behavior features of the judges or attorneys (see Section 12.2) or to the merits of the claims, such as which legal factors apply (see Section 12.4.2). In the context of ML from statutory provisions, the goal might be to classify provisions by topic such as administrative law, private law, environmental law, or criminal law.

The document vector will include a feature representing the outcome, either a classification or a prediction. Since learning models frequently can deal only with numerical features, one needs to encode categorical outcome features like the above classifications numerically, for instance with binary encoding in multiple features.

In the above sample contexts, the text unit of interest varies. In the e-discovery context, the unit of interest may be the whole document produced in discovery, or, at least, the body of the document. In the sentence classification study, the primary unit of interest is each sentence in, say, a case opinion. In the statutory topic context, the primary unit may be a provision of the statute. Each level of granularity, documents, sentences, or provisions can be represented as a feature vector. If the connections of parts of a document to the whole are important, such as each sentence's relation to the particular case opinion in which it appeared, appropriate links can be recorded.

Sets of documents can be represented for processing in a frequency matrix or *document-term matrix*. This is like a spreadsheet organized by documents in rows, and in columns by words or other features such as bigrams or other *n*-grams, one column for each such feature appearing in the corpus.

With the text data represented as feature vectors, one can divide the data into training and test sets. In order to avoid bias, one may randomly sample the vectors and assign them to the test set with some probability. The remaining vectors become the training set. An ML algorithm can then train a model on this set and apply it to make predictions or classifications about the feature vectors in the test set.

In evaluating a model's performance, especially where the data set is small, one may employ a cross-validation procedure as described in Section 4.4.3. Each feature vector in the data set would be used once as a test instance, but it would also be used to train a model to be applied to other test instances.

One can evaluate a model's performance quantitatively in terms of a metric such as accuracy, the ratio of correctly classified vectors in the test set over all of the vectors in the test set (Section 4.4.4).

A confusion matrix helps to identify the examples that the classifier got right or wrong. A *confusion matrix* is a table that contains information about a classifier's predicted and actual classifications (Kohavi and Provost, 1998). The table has as many rows and as many columns as there are classes. Table 8.1 illustrates a confusion matrix for a made-up test set of 690 sentences, each of which is treated as a document. The model classifies sentences by one of three roles, and each sentence is an instance of one of the roles. As illustrated in the table, the rows represent the instances that are actually in a class. The columns represent the instances that are predicted to be in a class.

One can inspect the confusion matrix to assess the classifier's performance. The correctly classified cases lie along the diagonal from the top left to the bottom right of the confusion matrix. These are the true positives (TPs), that is, where a feature vector was predicted to be an instance of a class and actually is an instance of the class (see Section 4.4.4). As shown in the confusion tables below the matrix, one can

TABLE 8.1. *Confusion matrix for three classes of sentence roles (top). Three confusion tables below show total true positives (TPs), true negatives (TNs), false positives (FPs), and false negatives (FNs) for each class*

		Predicted class		
$n = 690$		Legal-rule	Holding-of-law	Finding-of-fact
Actual class	Legal-rule	201	96	13
	Holding-of-law	46	87	57
	Finding-of-fact	23	64	103

TPs for L-r: 201	**FNs for L-r:** $96 + 13 = 109$
FPs for L-r: $46 + 23 = 69$	**TNs for L-r:** $87 + 57 + 64 + 103 = 311$
TPs for H-of-l: 87	**FNs for H-of-l:** $46 + 57 = 103$
FPs for H-of-l: $96 + 64 = 160$	**TNs for H-of-l:** $201 + 23 + 13 + 103 = 340$
TPs for F-of-f: 103	**FNs for F-of-f:** $23 + 64 = 87$
FPs for F-of-f: $13 + 57 = 70$	**TNs for F-of-f:** $201 + 96 + 46 + 87 = 430$

compute the number of true negatives (TNs), feature vectors predicted not to be instances of a class that actually are not instances of the class. There is one confusion table for each class.

The confusion tables also indicate the numbers of false positives (FPs), feature vectors predicted to be instances of a class that are not, and false negatives (FNs), vectors predicted not to be instances of a class that are (see Section 4.4.4). In order to understand *why* the model made mistakes, one would need to examine the examples that were false positives or false negatives and investigate which features led to the erroneous classifications.

8.4. MACHINE LEARNING FOR E-DISCOVERY

e-Discovery is the collecting, exchanging, and analyzing of electronically stored information (ESI) in pretrial discovery. *Pretrial discovery* in lawsuits involves processing parties' requests for materials in the hands of opponents and others to reveal facts and develop evidence for trial. Today, large lawsuits routinely involve millions of e-documents.

Unlike legal cases or statutes, documents produced in litigation are extremely heterogeneous, ranging from corporate memoranda and agreements to email, tweets, websites, and other Internet-based communications. The challenges in e-discovery are to extract litigators' hypotheses (or theories) about what documents are relevant to the claims and defenses in litigation and to map documents onto these hypotheses in spite of the documents' heterogeneity (Ashley and Bridewell, 2010).

8.4.1. *Litigators' Hypotheses in e-Discovery*

Hogan described e-discovery as *sensemaking*, a "process of collecting, organizing and creating representations of complex information sets, all centered around some problem the [sense makers] need to understand" (Bauer et al., 2008). In the course of this process, litigators construct a theory of relevance or a *relevance hypothesis*, a more-or-less abstract description of subject matter that, if found in a document, would make that document relevant (see Hogan et al., 2010, p. 447).

The formulation of relevance hypotheses varies in terms of the legal and other concepts relevant to a case, the level of specificity of relevant concepts of interest, the "variety of ways a concept can be expressed, whether lexically or syntactically," and the "use case." Given a request for production, a party aims not to produce too much or too little (Hogan et al., 2009, pp. 196–7, 2010, p. 447).

In the context of a lawsuit concerning tobacco advertising aimed at minors, sample relevance hypotheses might include:

– "All documents which . . . mention any 'in-store,' 'on-counter,' 'point of sale,' or other retail marketing campaigns for cigarettes."
– "Are promotional offers relevant?"
– "Is 'buy one get one free' by itself sufficient for relevance?" (Hogan et al., 2010, pp. 446–7).

Litigators' relevance hypotheses like these are based in part on the formal requests for documents filed in the case. These relate, in turn, to the complaint that elaborates the plaintiff's legal claims or the defendant's answer that denies allegations in the complaint and states defenses. As new facts and information emerge, both the complaint and defense may be modified with consequent modification of the hypotheses.

As a result, litigators' relevance hypotheses may be quite specific, expressed in terms of who communicated what to whom, when, and, to the extent possible, why. For example:

– "There are documents showing that the Vice President of Marketing knew that cigarette advertisements were targeted to children by 1989," or
– "There exist documents to or from employees of a tobacco company or tobacco organization in which a tobacco company officer refers to illegal payments to foreign officials," or
– "There are documents that are communications between Alice and her lawyer Bob between 1985 and 1989." (Ashley and Bridewell, 2010)

More generally, the latter relevance hypotheses are of the form: "There are documents of a *particular kind*, satisfying *particular time constraints*, satisfying *particular social interaction constraints*, [and referring] to *particular concepts or phrases of interest*" (Ashley and Bridewell, 2010).

As described below, when litigators apply ML techniques in e-discovery, they select documents that are positive or negative instances of what they regard as relevant. Hypotheses like the above may inform litigators' relevance selections. It does not appear, however, that the systems provide much, if any, support for litigators to explicitly formulate such hypotheses nor does it appear that the programs make any direct use of such hypotheses. In a cognitive computing paradigm, eliciting such hypotheses explicitly could be useful for guiding testing hypotheses, reformulating hypotheses and queries, and explaining results. See Section 12.4.1 for a further discussion of the role of hypothesis testing in cognitive computing, albeit against a corpus of legal cases, not of litigation documents.

8.4.2. *Predictive Coding Process*

In e-discovery, ML is often referred to as "predictive coding." Predictive coding in e-discovery typically proceeds as follows (see Privault et al., 2010; Sklar, 2011).

Using general search tools, a litigator, acting as a case manager (CM), surveys the corpus of documents produced by the opponent or to be produced by the litigator's client. To assist in the survey, the CM may use keyword, Boolean and concept search, concept grouping and filtering, or identification of near-duplicates and latest-in-thread emails.

The CM identifies documents that are instances of coding categories (e.g., relevant, responsive, privileged, issue-related). For each category, these manually selected documents become seed sets from which the ML program learns probabilistic predictive models of the category based on features the positive (or negative) instances share. With the learned model, the program can assign appropriate categories to previously unseen documents.

Once a category's seed set contains enough documents, an iterative "training" process begins:

1. The ML system abstracts from the seed instances a predictive model, a kind of profile (see Sebastiani, 2002; Privault et al., 2010) using statistical analysis and, possibly, applying shallow parsing, detecting concepts and relations, expanding with an ontology, or identifying latent semantic features.

2. The system applies the predictive model to the corpus to identify additional documents and submits some of them to the CM's team of human reviewers for confirmation. The suggested documents may come from random sampling or comprise the "examples that the classifier is most unsure about" in a process called active learning (Oard and Webber, 2013), or they may be "possibly mistagged documents or atypical outliers" (Privault et al., 2010).

3. The CM's team reviews and categorizes the program-suggested documents to ensure correctness.

4. The ML system updates its model of the category in light of the relevance feedback from the human reviewers.

5. The previous iterative steps are repeated until the unreviewed part of the corpus contains no more similar documents (Sklar, 2011).

6. Statistical sampling is applied to estimate the level of accuracy and completeness that has been achieved.

Among the ML algorithms that may be applied in generating the model or profile of a category, a "(supervised) probabilistic latent semantic analysis [may be used to infer] a generative model of words and documents from topical classes" (Oard and Webber, 2013, p. 138). In Xerox's Categorix system (Privault et al., 2010), for example, the predictive models are based on *probabilistic latent semantic analysis* (PLSA). "The basic assumption of PLSA is that there exists a set of hidden ('latent' or 'unobserved') factors which can underlie the co-occurrences among a set of observed words and documents." LSA is a

> method for extracting and representing the contextual-usage meaning of words by statistical computations applied to a large corpus of text … The underlying idea is that the aggregate of all the word contexts in which a given word does and does not appear provides a set of mutual constraints that largely determines the similarity of meaning of words and sets of words to each other. (Landauer et al., 1998)

For example, suppose an e-discovery corpus contains documents with sentences like the following:

– John-Doe, the VP-of-Marketing, resigned yesterday.
– The VP-of-Marketing approved the advertising campaign featuring a cartoon giraffe smoking a cigarette.
– This cartoon TV series entertains children while helping them discover the amazing world around them.
– What's wrong with showing kids a smoking giraffe?

While a program does not "know" who the VP of Marketing is, that cigarettes are smoked, that a giraffe can be a cartoon, or that children watch cartoons, PLSA can detect semantic connections among these terms based on the frequency of occurrence of sentences and documents that relate them. The documents are represented as term vectors in a vector space with frequency information (see Section 7.5.2). The term vector representation ignores word order, linguistic analysis, or ontological information. Thus, the PLSA is the sole basis for assessing document similarity.

Another kind of ML model applied in e-discovery, a SVM, uses statistical criteria to find boundaries between positive and negative examples of a category or class in a multidimensional feature space (see Section 8.3). An example of an SVM is given in Section 8.5.2.

Given the complex descriptions of such ML algorithms, the reader may not be surprised to learn that PLSA and SVMs "learn statistical models that are not easily interpreted or directly tunable by people" (Oard and Webber, 2013, p. 138). Other classifier designs, such as rule induction and decision trees in Section 4.3.1, can be interpreted fairly well by humans. For purposes of text classification in e-discovery, however, "the less explainable statistical text classifiers also tend to be the most effective" (Oard and Webber, 2013, p. 138).

This can be problematic in e-discovery. The absence of interpretable decision rules increases the need to rely on empirical evaluation to assess a statistical classifier's effectiveness, but these evaluation methodologies have limitations, too (Oard and Webber, 2013, p. 138).

8.4.3. *Assessing Predictive Coding Effectiveness*

From the viewpoint of a trial judge and the litigators, evaluating the effectiveness of a machine-learned classifier is a key concern. Although it would be convenient to have the full set of relevant documents in order to assess a classifier's retrieval effectiveness, often it is not feasible manually to assess the entire collection. That is exactly the problem of e-discovery; as a general rule, the collection is too large (Oard and Webber, 2013, pp. 159–60).

Even if human assessment of the completeness of document productions was possible, it is not necessarily dependable. Consider the defendants' lawyers in the Blair and Maron's study of the previous chapter who estimated that they had found 75% of the relevant documents in their client's collection. Based on a "sample of documents . . . from the unretrieved segment of the collection, and assessed for relevance by the same lawyers," their true recall was estimated at only around 20% (Oard and Webber, 2013, pp. 160).

Instead of human assessment, random sampling, statistical estimation, confidence levels, and confidence intervals are employed to estimate recall. Let's illustrate this in the context of the tobacco litigation e-discovery examples above. The following example has been adapted from Tredennick (2014a).

Let's assume that 1 million documents were produced for review. Neither party knows in advance how many of those documents are relevant, but let's suppose that one side's litigator believes it most likely that about 10,000 documents or 1% are relevant. That is his *point estimate*, the most likely value for a characteristic of the document population (Grossman and Cormack, 2014).

Since the point estimate is not certain, the litigator decides to make a *statistical estimate*. That is, he will draw a statistical sample, determine the proportion of the documents in the sample that are relevant, and apply that ratio to the whole collection. A *statistical sample* is one in which some number of documents are drawn at random from the collection. The random selection helps to ensure that the sample is representative of the entire document set so that the resulting relevance ratio can be extrapolated to the whole (Grossman and Cormack, 2014).

The size of the sample required depends on the litigator's desired confidence level. The *confidence level* is the chance that a confidence interval derived from a random sample will include the true percentage of documents that are relevant. Conversely, the *confidence interval* is a range of values estimated to contain the true value with the desired confidence level (Grossman and Cormack, 2014).

Let's assume the litigator's point estimate is that 1% of the documents are relevant, plus or minus 2%, with a target confidence level of 95%. The 95% confidence means that

> if one were to draw 100 independent Random Samples of the same size, and compute the Confidence Interval from each Sample, about 95 of the 100 Confidence Intervals would contain the true value ... it is the Probability that the method of estimation will yield a Confidence Interval that contains the true value. (Grossman and Cormack, 2014)

In the context of discussion of search protocols in litigation, 95% ± 2% is a "widely cited ... estimation goal " (Oard and Webber, 2013, pp. 161).[2]

According to the commonly used statistical method of estimation (called Gaussian), confidence intervals are calculated based on the assumption that the quantities to be measured follow a normal bell curve distribution (Grossman and Cormack, 2014).

The *margin of error* is the maximum amount by which the point estimate may likely deviate from the true value. It is frequently expressed as "plus or minus" a percentage, with a particular confidence level. In this example, the litigator's expression means that his point estimate is 1%, his desired margin of error is 2%, and the confidence level is 95%. With Gaussian estimation, the confidence interval is twice the margin of error. Here because of the floor (there cannot be negative numbers of relevant documents), the interval is 0% to 3%. In this example, with 1 million documents, the litigator's statistical estimate may be restated as "10,000 documents in the population are relevant, plus or minus 20,000 documents, with 95% confidence" or "between 0 and 30,000 documents are relevant, with 95% confidence."

With a 2% margin of error and 95% confidence level, one can calculate the required sample size as 2,396 documents.[3] The litigator draws them at random from the document set and, after reviewing them, finds that, say, 24 of the documents are relevant. Given this new information, an exact measure of the confidence interval can be calculated using a binomial confidence interval calculator.[4] Expressed as a decimal, the confidence interval can now be computed as ranging from 0.0064 (lower) to 0.0149 (upper). Multiplying these decimal values against the total number of documents in the whole set, 1 million, the litigator calculates that his exact confidence interval ranges from 6,400 to 14,900. In other words, the number of relevant documents in the set could be as high as 14,900 or as low as 6,400.

---

[2] This way of expressing an estimation effectiveness target does *not* specify what values for recall and elusion are acceptable. The goal states only the statistical precision with which the prevalence of relevant documents shall be measured (see Oard and Webber, 2013, pp. 161).

[3] See the sample size calculator at www.raosoft.com/samplesize.html

[4] See the binomial confidence interval calculator at http://statpages.info/confint.html

The litigator's review team gets to work, searches 50,000 documents (5% of the collection) with predictive coding, and finds, say, 7,500 relevant ones.

The question is what recall has the review team achieved? If the point estimate of 10,000 relevant documents were correct, the recall would be 75% (7,500/10,000). In practical terms, given the high cost of document discovery and the diminishing return on investment of further expensive search efforts, that may be regarded as a defensible recall value. On the other hand, if 14,900 documents were relevant, the upper range for the confidence interval, the recall is only 50% (7,500/14,900), which is considerably less likely to be accepted as satisfying a party's discovery obligation.

In an effort to obtain more accurate information about recall, the attorney could sample the unreviewed 950,000 documents to see what proportion of them are relevant. In other words, he could estimate the elusion. Using the same 95% confidence level and a 2% margin of error, let's assume that the litigator again reviews 2,396 documents randomly selected this time from the unreviewed documents.

Suppose that the review team finds eight relevant documents. The ratio of relevant documents in the sample of unreviewed documents is 0.33% (8/2,396) and suggests that there are 3,172 relevant documents in the unreviewed set (950,000 × (8/2,396)). Again calculating the exact binomial confidence interval yields 0.0014 to 0.0066. Applying this exact confidence interval range to the unreviewed documents, the low range is 1,330 (0.0014 × 950,000) and the high range is 6,270 (0.0066 × 950,000).

Based on this additional information, the attorney could recompute the recall his team achieved. The team found 7,508 relevant documents out of what could be a total number of relevant documents ranging as high as 13,770 (7,500 + 6,270). The recall would then be 55% (7,508/13,770), still probably not high enough to justify not continuing to search.

At this point, one could attempt to narrow the margin of error still further to 1%. In that case, the attorney would need to sample 9,508 documents from the unretrieved set. If the sample did not confirm the litigator's initial estimate of 75% recall, the review would need to continue and another sampling from the unretrieved set would be required (Tredennick, 2014a). Alternatively, the litigator could employ a direct method for measuring recall that involves picking documents at random until a required number of relevant documents are selected (384 for a 95% confidence level) and then computing the recall. If only 1% of the documents are relevant, however, that could mean reviewing another 38,400 documents (Tredennick, 2014b).

The point of this example has been to illustrate the nature of statistically estimating recall and elusion in e-discovery. It also suggests the difficulty and expense of demonstrating that an adequate level of recall has been achieved. In addition, there are theoretical issues concerning sampling to statistically estimate recall (see Oard and Webber, 2013, p. 162) as well as pragmatic ones. For instance, as noted, one can compute a required sample size for a statistical estimate. If there is a possibility, however, that one might find important "smoking gun" documents in a high-stakes litigation or that someone has rigged the distribution of documents in the collection to hide telling evidence, a larger sample size may be required than that predicted by the statistical formula (Sohn, 2013).

8.4.4. *Other Open Issues in Predictive Coding*

The e-discovery community is grappling with a number of other open issues concerning predictive coding.

In supervised learning (Section 4.3), seed sets play a vital role: their documents represent a relevant category and reflect a litigation expert's determinations. A still open question, however, is where best to start in constructing a seed set. Should one begin with:

- instances of specific concepts as selected by a subject matter expert?
- manually formulated queries identifying criteria that a relevant document must satisfy and iteratively adjusting the query as new documents are examined? (Oard and Webber, 2013, p. 137)
- a completely randomized sample regardless of specific fact issues? (Oard and Webber, 2013, p. 137)
- document clustering, that is, automatically constructed groupings of documents based on shared features? (Privault et al., 2010)
- a hybrid of the above?

According to Remus and Levy (2015, p. 17), supervising attorneys should employ keyword searches to select the initial seed set of documents and then rank them for relevance. The question of which method of generating seed sets is best, however, may depend on the detailed nature of the search and of the corpus.

A second issue deals with how best to represent texts in e-discovery. Researchers are exploring more knowledge-based techniques and enriched text representations beyond the ML staple, BOW (see Section 7.5.2). "It remains to be seen what use can be made in automated review of entity extraction, document metadata, social network analysis, the structure and patterns of email communication, the temporal and organizational locality of responsive information, and so forth" (Oard and Webber, 2013, p. 212).

For instance, previous studies have applied *social network analysis* to interpreting email in e-discovery (Henseler, 2010). This kind of analysis involves graphically representing the interactions and relations among people, groups, organizations, websites and other information-processing entities, measuring properties of these graphs, and drawing inferences from the measurements. Document senders, receivers, and owners identify themselves in email records and contents. Representing and analyzing who is communicating with whom about what topics and over what time frames can provide valuable information for selecting relevant texts for further analysis.

The complexity of predictive coding raises still other practical issues. Predictive coding in e-discovery affects litigation strategy (Sohn, 2013). At the time when keyword searches were the main e-discovery technique, counsel negotiated the terms and queries that would be used to search for documents. The query negotiations helped the parties to agree on the scope of discoverable evidence. Predictive coding, however, applies ML algorithms to text representations that involve more than just terms. Assessing the effectiveness of a search raises complex questions about measuring recall and elusion and about what levels of recall and elusion are sufficient given the costs of searching. This introduces uncertainties, may lead to disputes, and makes negotiations more complex. In addition, despite the complexities of the predictive coding process, parties need to maintain a complete audit trail documenting steps taken in order to defend one's predictive process in discovery-related hearings (Sohn, 2013).

Despite these theoretical and practical issues, evidence suggests that *technology-assisted review* is working; predictive coding and other techniques are supporting human/computer interaction in identifying documents that are relevant to production requests (see Grossman and Cormack, 2010). For example, in the TREC Legal Track series of annual contests, competing e-discovery technologists applied their methods to the same tasks and corpora. For TREC challenges from 2008 through 2011, "Every system that simultaneously achieved high precision and high recall, relative to the other participating systems, relied on . . . technology-assisted review" (Oard and Webber, 2013, p. 199). Evidence supports the conclusion "that technology-assisted production can be at least as effective as manual review, if not more so, and at a fraction of the cost" (Oard and Webber, 2013, p. 203).

8.4.5. *Unsupervised Machine Learning from Text*

Before leaving the topic of e-discovery, it is worth focusing briefly on unsupervised ML from text.

Predictive coding in e-discovery and the ML to predict case outcomes in Chapter 4 are all examples of supervised learning. That is, they illustrate "techniques used to learn the relationship between independent attributes and a designated dependent attribute (the label)" (Kohavi and Provost, 1998).

Unsupervised learning employs ML algorithms that infer categories of similar documents but without a human expert's preparing a training set of manually labeled examples (see Grossman and Cormack, 2014). Document clustering algorithms, for instance, do not use labeled training data. They group instances together without any preexisting information about what labels are correct (see Kohavi and Provost, 1998). Instead, they infer groups of documents based on their content or metadata and leave for humans the task of determining *post hoc* what the members of the group share and what labels to apply, if any (see Privault et al., 2010, p. 464; Oard and Webber, 2013, p. 139).

As noted, clustering techniques may play a role in selecting seed sets for supervised learning techniques. For example, Categorix is a system that uses unsupervised ML to group documents into clusters, which may then suggest to humans the labels that should be applied, whereupon supervised learning commences. In the unsupervised mode, the user specifies the desired number of clusters in advance but provides no information to the system as to specific categories or labels.

The system employs PLSA (see Section 8.4.2) as a similarity measure. It partitions the documents into the specified number of clusters, grouping together the documents most similar to each other (Privault et al., 2010). The system graphically displays the clusters to human experts who try to discern commonalities and assign appropriate labels. The display provides a "virtual magnet" feature that organizes documents around a "magnet" button by distances representing a document's level of similarity to a cluster of interest. Documents most similar are placed closest to the magnet button and are highlighted in red; less similar documents lie farther out and have different colors.

Once the human experts assign the labels, the system shifts to supervised learning in order to assist humans in classifying new documents according to the labels. This sequencing of unsupervised and then supervised learning helps review teams deal with the fact that document production in e-discovery frequently occurs incrementally, with new collections of documents being produced over time (Privault et al., 2010, p. 464).

8.5. APPLYING ML TO LEGAL CASE TEXTS IN THE HISTORY PROJECT

e-Discovery and predictive coding apply ML to heterogeneous texts. Since the texts are involved in litigation, they are "legal" texts in a sense, but they are not the staple texts of traditional legal research: court decisions, statutes and regulations, etc. How can ML be applied to these relatively homogeneous legal texts and what kinds of useful information can ML learn to extract? The various corpora of CLIR services like LexisNexis and Westlaw could be extensive resources for mining conceptual legal information.

The Westlaw History Project is a prototypical example of applying ML to a legal IR corpus (Al-Kofahi et al., 2001; Jackson et al., 2003). The system addressed the "history task," that is, identifying language in court opinions that affects previous cases and linking them accordingly. In particular, it addressed the Prior Cases Retrieval (PCR) problem: identifying cases that are within the appellate chain of the current or "instant" case. In a hierarchical court system, litigation commenced in a trial court may spawn decisions on motions that appear in subsequent separate opinions. The motion decisions and the trial court's "final" decision may be appealed up through the chain of appellate divisions of the same court and of higher appellate courts. Thus, a prior opinion can be from a lower court or even from the same court (Al-Kofahi et al., 2001, p. 88).

Westlaw maintains a citator database that contains known appellate chains for the 1.3 million cases of 7 million cases in the database that have appellate chains.

The History Project aimed at assisting in maintaining and augmenting the citatory database. Frequently, however, case opinions do not adequately identify prior cases. For instance, when the instant case opinion was written, a prior case may not yet have been published. Since the plan was to have Westlaw's human editors check the outputs of the system, the task application required especially high recall close to 100% and precision greater than 50% so as to avoid making too many suggestions (Jackson et al., 2003, p. 274).

8.5.1. *History Project System Architecture*

The History Project system combines IE from a text corpus, information retrieval of candidate cases based on the extracted information, and decision-making about the candidates based on ML (Al-Kofahi et al., 2001; Jackson et al., 2003). As shown in Figure 8.1, the system architecture of the History Project comprised three parts: info extraction, info retrieval, and decision-making.

In the preprocessing step in Figure 8.1, the cases in the citator database were indexed by features of their titles. Each party entity in the title gave rise to an indexing term. For instance, "the entity representing 'David E. Smith' generates the indexing terms 'Smith' and 'David+Smith' " (Al-Kofahi et al., 2001, p. 89). For each term, the number of titles in which a term appears was computed; this is the term's document frequency. The lower a term's frequency, the more discriminating the term is when

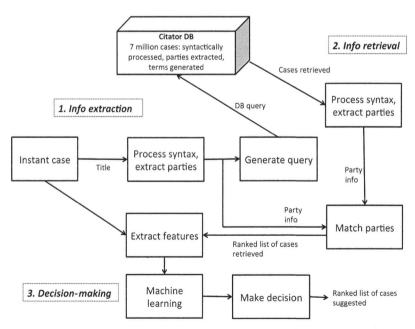

FIGURE 8.1. History Project system architecture (see Al-Kofahi et al., 2001)

it appears in a case. Each of the 7 million cases was then indexed by the up-to-eight most discriminating terms.

Given a new case, one can use the citator database to retrieve candidate cases that may be prior cases in the instant case's history. This process begins in the first stage marked 1. *Info extraction* in Figure 8.1. Given an instant case, an IE system processed the opinion and its header, pulling history language, party names, courts, dates, and docket numbers. The current case's title is processed to extract the indexing terms (as above). Then, in the information retrieval stage (Figure 8.1, 2. *Info retrieval*) given the extracted information, a retrieval system submitted queries to the citator database to retrieve candidate cases that might be part of the instant case's prior history. The most discriminating index terms are combined with information about the case's date and court information, such as jurisdiction, agency, locality, and circuit of the court, to retrieve from the citator database prior case candidates that fit the possible appellate chains for the instant court and that were decided within the past seven years of the instant case's date (Al-Kofahi et al., 2001, p. 90). The party information is extracted from each of the candidate cases, compared with that of the instant case, and a listing of the candidate cases, ranked by similarity of the parties, is returned.

In step 3. *Decision-making* (Figure 8.1), a system applies ML to decide which of the retrieved candidates are prior cases of the instant case.

As always, an initial question was how best to represent each case for purposes of ML. Here, each candidate case was represented as feature vector in terms of eight features that appeared to be relevant indications of a true, prior case (see Section 8.3). Thus, the end points associated with each candidate case feature vector are distributed across an eight-dimensional feature space. The eight features comprised:

Title Similarity: a measure of how similar the title of the instant case and that of a candidate prior case are.

History Language: a binary feature indicating if direct history language was extracted from instant case. This alone yields recall in the low 80s; precision in the 50–60% range.

Docket Match: a binary feature indicating if the instant–prior case pair has been assigned the same docket number (which is often not the case).

Check Appeal: given the instant court, an estimate of the probability, it is a successor to the prior court.

Prior Probability: an estimate of the probability that the instant case has a prior case. This is based on the ratio of cases with priors to the total number of cases in the database.

Cited Case: a binary feature indicating if the prior case candidate was cited in the instant case.

Title Weight: the estimated weight of information in the instant case title. For example, "Smith" is less informative than "Alex J. Tyrrell."

AP1 Search: a binary feature indicating if a prior case candidate was retrieved via an appeal line query in the instant case. This is a special line in the instant case's text, which may contain information about the prior case.

The problem, however, is determining which features are more important. The researchers did not know the features' relative importance *a priori*, but a ML program could learn those weights on a training set and make predictions on case texts it has not yet seen. The History Project team employed supervised learning (see Section 4.3) for this task using a SVM as the ML algorithm. SVMs are described next in greater detail.

8.5.2. *ML Algorithms: Support Vector Machines*

An SVM uses statistical criteria to discriminate between positive and negative examples of a category or class. As noted above in the discussion of predictive coding (Section 8.4.2), a statistical ML algorithm may perform more effectively than, say, a decision tree program, but, unlike a decision tree classifier, which humans can interpret intuitively, an SVM's model is not as intelligible.

An SVM identifies a boundary in a vector space between the positive and negative instances of a category or class that is maximally distant from all of the instances (Noble, 2006). Ideally, all of the candidate cases that are positive instances lie on one side of the boundary and all of the negative instances lie on the other.

The boundary is a geometrical entity, the nature of which depends on the dimensionality of the vector space. If the vector space were a line, such a boundary would be a point; if the space were a plane, it would be a line. In a three-dimensional vector space the boundary would be a plane, and in a higher dimensional space (including an eight-dimensional space as in the History Project) the boundary is called a "hyperplane." Based on the hyperplane the SVM learned, predicting the label of a previously unseen case is simply a matter of determining on which side of the boundary the new case's vector falls (see Noble, 2006, p. 1565).

Figure 8.2(1) illustrates a hyperplane separating positive and negative instances, which can be used to classify the unknown instance (white dot). Graph (2) illustrates a number of alternative hyperplanes that could separate the positive and negative instances, but an SVM algorithm picks the one shown in (3) that maximizes the margin between the boundary and all of the instances (Noble, 2006, p. 1566).

Since real data often cannot be separated cleanly using a straight line, an SVM algorithm can have a parameter that enables the hyperplane boundary to set a soft margin. The parameter determines a trade-off among the number of examples that are permitted to violate the boundary (these are the data instances that cannot be classified correctly), how much they may extend over the boundary, and the width of the margin between the boundary and positive and negative instances (Noble, 2006, p. 1566). Figure 8.2(4) illustrates a hyperplane boundary with a soft margin setup

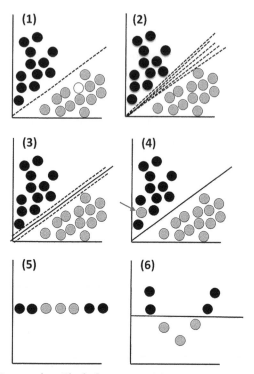

FIGURE 8.2. SVM examples. Black dots are positive instances, gray dots are negative, and the white dot is "unknown" (see Noble, 2006, p. 1566)

by the SVM algorithm despite the erroneously classified instance indicated by the arrow.

Sometimes, a boundary cannot be drawn in n-dimensions to separate the positive and negative instances. SVM algorithms can support "kernel functions" that enable the SVM to classify in $n + 1$ dimensions, a set of data originally in n dimensions. In other words, "a kernel function projects data from a low-dimensional space to a space of higher dimension" (Noble, 2006, pp. 1566–7). Figure 8.2(5) illustrates a one-dimensional data set that cannot be separated by one boundary point into positive and negative instances. On the other hand, (6) shows how the formerly non-separable data can be separated by a boundary in two dimensions. The change in location in the diagram "symbolizes" the projection into a different hyperplane by the kernel function. Selection of the right kernel function can facilitate determining such a boundary.

8.5.3. *History Project SVM*

As noted, the History Project SVM ranks prior case candidates according to the likelihood of their being truly part of the instant case history.

The researchers trained the SVM with 2,100 cases selected randomly from the database. Each of these instant cases was processed using the modules in Figure 8.1, parts 1. *Info extraction* and 2. *Info retrieval*, to retrieve candidate prior cases from the citator database. For each instant case, up to 100 prior case candidates were accumulated, the 100 prior cases with the highest title similarities.

Each prior case candidate was then represented in terms of an eight-dimensional feature vector, resulting in 113,000 training vectors. Crucially for supervised ML, the research team knew in advance from the citator whether each candidate was, in fact, a prior case of a given instant case (Jackson et al., 2003, p. 284). In other words, it was known whether the training case is a positive or negative instance of a prior case.

After training the model, the SVM was evaluated with a test set of 312 cases that had been chosen at random by the editorial staff. Of these, 123 cases turned out actually to have prior cases in the citator database.

As noted, an SVM is normally used to classify the unseen cases: it assigns positive or negative scores to each test case indicating on which side of the boundary it appears. The History Project team, however, employed the SVM for a related but different task. It reranked the prior case candidates of an instant case, based upon the distance from the learned boundary (Jackson et al., 2003, p. 285). The ranked list and corresponding distance scores were then inputted into a decision module designed to improve the system's recall.

The resulting recall was 99.2% (i.e., 122/123) and precision was 64.9% (i.e., 122/188). The average number of suggestions reported per instant case was five. That is the number of suggestions a human expert would have to consider in order to verify the system's performance.

8.6. MACHINE LEARNING OF CASE STRUCTURES

The Westlaw History Project is a paradigm example of applying ML to extract useful information from a corpus of legal cases. Although the information extracted was prior case history, in principle similar techniques can extract other kinds of information from cases that can improve legal information retrieval performance.

One such useful kind of information concerns the structure of the legal documents in the corpus. It provides clues to the meaning of their contents. For example, ML can be used to distinguish factual from legal discussions in cases based on evidence in the text. If a sentence is located in a part of the opinion where the court is discussing facts, it is likely that the sentence expresses some facts of the case.

LexisNexis, for instance, has patented a technique for generating training data for use with such ML algorithms. The algorithms learn to recognize whether a passage of a legal case contains fact, discussion, neither fact nor discussion, or both fact and discussion (Morelock et al., 2004). The method partitions texts in the documents by headings, annotates the relative location of the passage in the opinion, compares the document headings to lists of fact headings and discussion headings, and assembles training sets of the associated texts.

For purposes of the algorithm's learning to recognize and distinguish fact and discussion paragraphs, the passages are represented in terms of features including:

- Relative paragraph position, for example, the kth paragraph of total of n paragraphs in an opinion;
- Number of citations to cases or to statutes;
- Number of past-tense verbs, such as "dated," "requested," "served," "applied," "granted," "executed," and "filed";
- Number of dates, such as "Dec. 15, 1975" and "June 21, 1976";
- Number of signal words, for example, "conclude," "find," "hold," "reverse";
- Number of references to "this court" or to a lower court, such as "lower court," "the trial court," and "the trial judge";
- Number of words relating to parties, for example, "plaintiff," "appellant," "claimant," "defendants," and "respondents";
- Number of legal phrases employed, such as "criminal history," "custody dispute," or "eminent domain."

Each training instance is parsed into chunks, compared with feature values of at least five of the above features, and the relative location of the passage and the matched features are used to represent the passage for purposes of ML.

As with the History Project, the features are intuitively useful, but their *weights* are unknown. That is where ML again comes into play, to learn the weights of features in classifying the training set. A classifier informed by these weights can then predict whether unknown passages contain facts, discussion, neither, or both. The patent refers to applying two ML algorithms to learn the feature weights, naïve Bayes or logistical regression, discussed in Section 10.3.3.

8.7. APPLYING ML TO STATUTORY TEXTS

ML can also be applied to statutory texts. A recent project applied an interactive tool for predictive coding to the task of finding relevant provisions for the purpose of statutory analysis.

8.7.1. *Statutory Analysis*

Statutory analysis is the process of determining if a statute applies, how it applies, and the effect of its application (Putman, 2008, p. 61).

Before one can perform statutory analysis, one must find candidate relevant provisions to analyze. This step is well-supported by current legal IR Systems. Given a legal issue, an attorney hypothesizes that certain kinds of statutes (or specific provisions) are legally relevant to the issue and creates a search query for a legal IR system. For example, if the legal issue is "What do Pennsylvania (PA) statutes require of public health system institutions concerning preparedness for and response to public health emergencies?," an attorney might hypothesize that:

> A relevant statutory provision will direct some institution of interest such as a fire department, hospital, or health department, etc. to prepare for or respond to some emergency, disaster, or hazard.

The user may then formulate a query like the following:

> (emergency OR disaster OR hazard) AND
>
> (respond OR prepare) AND
>
> (OR fire OR hospital OR medical OR "Emergency Management Agency" OR "community health" OR "department of health" OR "environmental protection" OR ... *for each type of institution of interest*)

From the IR system's results, the attorney can pick the most promising candidate provisions.

IR systems, however, do not provide much support for determining which are the most promising candidates or for refining the hypothesis and query to capture more features that distinguish relevance. If one wanted to ensure regulatory compliance by a hospital or, in some other example, to explore the legal landscape for a business entering a new state jurisdiction such as Pennsylvania, these subsequent steps in statutory analysis are important.

8.7.2. *An Interactive ML Tool for Statutory Analysis*

For this task, some researchers have developed an iterative ML process, like predictive coding in e-discovery, but dealing with statutory texts (Savelka et al., 2015). After the provisions retrieved by the legal IR search are inputted into the interactive tool, it presents a number of candidate provisions to the user. The user provides feedback to the ML classifier, identifying positive and negative examples of the kind of statutes he or she seeks. The classifier then updates its model accordingly and the process repeats.

In this way, the relevance assessment is a kind of dialogue between the human expert and the ML statutory classification model. Users employ the tool's interactive graphical user interface (GUI), illustrated in Figure 8.3, to flag statutory provisions as relevant to the issue. The tool shows the user (a) an unprocessed statutory provision, (b) the features/terms deemed important in the current model and their weights, (c) summary statistics showing the distribution of relevant and nonrelevant provisions up to that point, and (d) a list of the labeled provisions with confidence scores. It also suggests the label for the unprocessed provision and indicates its confidence level, highlights the prominent features in the current provision at (a) and (b) in the figure, solicits the user's decision (top right), and records the user's response. Users

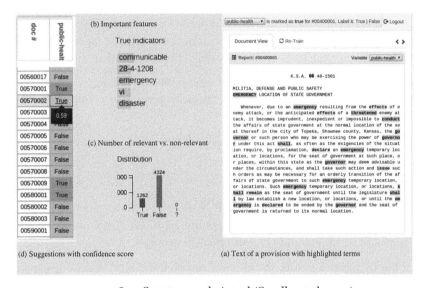

FIGURE 8.3. Statutory analysis tool (Savelka et al., 2015)

can also suggest features that could be important by highlighting a term and clicking a respective button at (a) (Savelka et al., 2015).

Upon a user's request, the classification model is retrained, learning new features and weights for each of the newly user-classified provisions. The tool employs a SVM with a linear kernel as the ML classification algorithm. SVMs are explained in Section 8.5.2.

An interesting question is whether a ML model trained on legal texts in one jurisdiction can classify similar texts from a different jurisdiction. The researchers evaluated their interactive ML approach and addressed this question in two experiments. In the first, a "cold-start" experiment, they evaluated the tool's performance on a set of Kansas statutory provisions. They compared the results of classification with the tool against two baselines involving manual assessments by expert public health system annotators. In the second, a "knowledge reuse" experiment, they evaluated the tool's performance for a similar statutory analysis involving provisions from Alaska but where the tool began by reusing the ML classifier learned on the Kansas provisions (Savelka et al., 2015).

The ML classifier's performance was evaluated in terms of precision, recall, the F1 measure (Section 7.6), and two other measures, *receiver operating characteristic* (ROC) and *area under the ROC curve* (AUC), common metrics for evaluating binary classifiers.

An ROC curve plots the true positive rate on the *y*-axis against the false positive rate on the *x*-axis for a set of different possible decision cutoffs or thresholds. The true positive rate corresponds to recall; it is the proportion of relevant documents that are correctly identified as such ($TP/(TP + FN)$) (see Section 7.6). The false positive rate is the proportion of nonrelevant documents that are incorrectly identified as relevant ($FP/(FP + TN)$). A cutoff is a threshold score on a ranked list of documents produced by, say, an ML algorithm, above which a document is deemed to be relevant and below which a document is deemed to be irrelevant. Typically, the higher a cutoff the higher the precision and lower the recall. Conversely, the lower the cutoff, the lower the precision and higher the recall (Grossman and Cormack, 2014).

The AUC represents the probability that a classifier will rank a randomly chosen positive data point higher than a randomly chosen negative one. In the context of the statutory analysis tool, the randomly chosen positive and negative data points correspond, respectively, to relevant and nonrelevant provisions. Thus, AUC is the probability that a randomly chosen relevant document is assigned a higher priority than a randomly chosen nonrelevant document. An AUC score of 100% is perfect; all relevant documents have been ranked higher than all nonrelevant ones. An AUC score of 50% indicates that it is no better than chance that a relevant document will be ranked higher than a nonrelevant one (Grossman and Cormack, 2014; Savelka et al., 2015).

The two baselines include a precision-focused baseline of a human classifier, who assumed that all of the still unprocessed documents are not relevant, and a recall-focused baseline of a human classifier, who assumed that all of the still unprocessed documents are relevant.

The interactive ML approach outperformed the baselines in both experiments, achieving good, if not excellent, classification performance. In the cold-start experiment, after labeling about 25 documents, the classifier's AUC score was above 80% (Savelka et al., 2015). Moreover, the second experiment demonstrated an interesting transfer effect. Reusing the classification model based on one state's documents gave the tool an objectively measurable advantage in classifying a new state's provisions for a similar statutory analysis. In other words, the knowledge learned from analyzing one state's statutes helped in analyzing the other's (Savelka et al., 2015).

8.8. TOWARD COGNITIVE COMPUTING LEGAL APPS

In order to solve legal problems, humans need to find documents in corpora containing materials produced in e-discovery, cases, or statutes and regulations. This chapter has demonstrated applying ML in each of these contexts in order to improve information retrieval.

In each context, a user probably has in mind a hypothesis about the kinds of documents that would be relevant to solving the problem. IR systems assist the user in expressing the hypothesis in terms of keyword searches or natural language queries, but such queries tend to retrieve only a first cut of documents that may be relevant. Beyond ranking documents and highlighting terms, the systems leave to the user the task of reading the documents, deciding which of them really is relevant, and refining the hypothesis in light of what the user finds. In e-discovery, the queries return too many documents to read. In the case of statutory provisions, determining which ones, in fact, relate to the statutory analysis is still a manual task.

The statutory analysis tool in the previous section and its interactive ML approach suggest how a CCLA might look. Predictive coding helps users, in effect, to specify what they are really looking for. The incremental interaction of the system's presenting examples and the user's flagging them as relevant or not operationalizes and refines the user's hypothesis. In the sense of cognitive computing, each is performing the kind of intelligent activity it does best; the human user exercises judgment about what is relevant and the system learns a model that embodies those judgments in a way it can apply to new documents. We have seen this approach in e-discovery and in support of statutory analysis.

Beyond flagging documents, however, a human can explain why something is relevant or not. Even before a system retrieves examples, a human can explain what would be relevant. This might be thought of as the human's explicit hypothesis about relevance and prediction about the useful materials that might be found in the corpus. In addition, the human can revise his or her relevance hypothesis in light of the examples the system produces.

Ideally the system could understand the human user's relevance hypotheses and operationalize them in retrieving documents. Given text analytic tools, this can be achieved to some extent. Section 12.4.1 describes a prototype for CCLAs that could support humans in formulating useful hypotheses explicitly that the app could test against legal texts in a corpus and that the human could modify in light of the examples produced.

In order to lay the groundwork for that, however, we need to learn more specifically how ML can extract useful information from legal texts. Chapter 9 addresses applying ML and related techniques to extract information from statutory and regulatory texts. Chapter 10 addresses applying the UIMA-related text processing tools and ML to extract argument-related information from the texts of case decisions.

9

Extracting Information from Statutory and Regulatory Texts

9.1. INTRODUCTION

Attorneys, citizens, business personnel, and policy-makers all need to access and understand regulatory texts in order to discover what the legal rules are and how to avoid violating their requirements. Thus, AI & Law has long aimed at automatically extracting information about the rules' requirements from electronically stored statutory and regulatory texts.

This chapter presents some ML and KE techniques for extracting information from statutory texts, including regulatory topics and concepts, types of norms or rules, and some functional elements of statutory provisions. We examine the relative merits of using ML and rule-based approaches to automatically classify statutory provisions and extract functional information from them.

The chapter then focuses on the more ambitious goal of extracting logical rules from statutes and regulations. Ideally, one could extract business rules from statutes automatically. The extracted rules could be applied deductively as in Section 2.3.4 or as defeasible rules in process compliance as in Section 2.5.3. Engineering design environments might, for example, help ensure that systems are designed to be compliant with rules extracted from regulations that have been formalized and integrated into the design process. That would extend even farther an approach to compliant design like the one in Section 2.5.5. Alternatively, defeasible rules, extracted from statutory texts, might be used in legal arguments as in Section 5.3.1. A QA system might use the extracted rules to answer questions about their requirements in legally sophisticated ways as suggested in Section 5.9. Unfortunately, however, the results of efforts to extract rules from regulatory texts fall far short of the ideal for automating reasoning in these ways.

Even without automating reasoning with extracted statutory rules, however, techniques for extracting information automatically from statutory texts can support cognitive computing in a variety of other ways. Automatic extraction facilitates conceptual information retrieval from corpora of statutory texts. Annotating provisions automatically in terms of semantic concepts drawn from a legal ontology such as the e-Court or Dalos ontologies of Sections 6.3.1 and 6.4 enables users to retrieve documents based on their conceptual content. A program could also automatically generate abstracts or summaries of statutory provisions in terms of the relevant concepts.

A program can even generate network analyses of systems of regulations as in Section 2.6. A statutory network can visually represent extracted information that certain provisions direct certain agents to take actions with respect to certain other agents. One such project applies ML to multi-state statutory texts, enabling the construction of statutory networks with which human analysts can compare aspects of different states' similarly purposed regulatory systems either visually or quantitatively. The networks also provide a GUI for retrieving relevant provisions from a statutory database. Applying a LUIMA type system and text annotation pipeline to process the texts may improve their representation for purposes of more effective ML.

The chapter addresses a number of questions, including: How does IE from statutory texts work? What roles do ML, NLP, and KE play? Can programs extract logical rules directly from regulatory texts? What is regulatory compliance? How can statutory network diagrams improve conceptual legal information retrieval or facilitate statutory analysis? Can a UIMA-like type-system-based text analysis pipeline assist in processing statutory texts?

9.2. RESEARCH OVERVIEW REGARDING EXTRACTING INFORMATION FROM STATUTORY TEXTS

Research on extracting information from statutory provisions has focused on extracting, or classifying provisions in terms of, the following types of information:

- Functional types of statutory provisions or norms such as definition, prohibition, obligation, and permission.
- Function-related features including elements of or arguments to functional types, such as bearer of a duty or acting agent, action, and receiving agent.
- Areas or topics of law such as administrative law, private law, environmental law, or criminal law.
- Semantic profiles that combine functional types, functional features, or topic areas.
- Regulatory concepts useful for indexing provisions, such as appear in a legal thesaurus or ontology.
- Legal rules or norms, their antecedents and consequents, including logical formulations of the rules or their components.

To extract the information, researchers have mainly employed either a KE approach with rules manually constructed by experts or supervised ML, using SVMs (see Section 8.5.2), decision trees (defined in Section 4.3.1), or naïve Bayes classifiers (explained in Section 10.3.3). In this ML work, statutory texts are usually represented as bags of words or term vectors with frequency information (see Section 7.5.2).

In order to provide a sense of the state of the art in IE from statutory texts, for each type of information above, here is a more detailed description of the research on how to extract it.

Functional types of provisions: Researchers employed ML (specifically, a multi-class SVM model and a Naïve Bayes model) to classify paragraphs of Italian statutory texts dealing with consumer protection in terms of 11 categories including "definition," "prohibition" (must not), and "obligation" (must) (see Biagioli et al., 2005; Francesconi and Passerini, 2007; Francesconi, 2009; Francesconi et al., 2010). In de Maat and Winkels (2007) and de Maat et al. (2010), the researchers categorized sentences from an assortment of Dutch statutory texts in terms of 13 classes, including labels such as "definition," "publication provision," or "change–scope." In Grabmair et al. (2011) and Savelka et al. (2014), decision tree or SVM models classified different states' statutory directives dealing with public health emergencies as obligations, permissions (for example, using "may"), or prohibitions.

Function-related features: Some functional types of statutory provisions or norms take more specific information as elements or arguments. Here "argument" means something analogous to a math function's input variables. In addition to extracting functional types, researchers employed NLP to extract arguments of statutory provisions such as the actor directed to take a specific kind of action with respect to a recipient. For instance, a data "controller" must provide "notification" to a "guarantor" (see Biagioli et al., 2005; Francesconi and Passerini, 2007; Francesconi, 2009; Francesconi et al., 2010). The ML algorithms in Grabmair et al. (2011) and Savelka et al. (2014) also identified similar elements in provisions dealing with public health emergencies, such as that a "state or local governmental public health officer" "may" "order" "isolation" of "someone who is ill" in response to "infectious disease emergency" when the person "refuses medical treatment."

Areas or topics of law: More abstract categorizations can be learned, as well, including the legal areas or topics. Naïve Bayes and multiclass SVM models learned statute labels such as environmental law, European law, and criminal law in Francesconi and Peruginelli (2008). In Opsomer et al. (2009), the authors applied an SVM to learn to classify statutory texts by categories in an index tree comprising 230 topical leaf nodes, such as principles and objectives of environmental policy, government, enforcement, procedures, and instruments of energy policy.

Other work involves identifying in a statutory document the concepts by which it should be indexed. Much work on mining statutory texts for highly specific topical and functional information has focused on automatic classification of European Union (EU) documents in terms of a conceptual ontology such as the EuroVoc thesaurus (Steinberger et al., 2013; EuroVoc, 2014). In Pouliquen et al. (2006), the authors represented statutory texts as term vectors and compared them to similar vectors associated with each of the EuroVoc vocabulary terms, such as "protection of minorities," "fishery management," and "construction and town planning." An SVM model learned to perform a similar task in Boella et al. (2012) for EuroVoc terms like "european contract," "inflation rate," or "Italy." The work in Daudaravicius (2012) functions not only in multi-jurisdictional settings but also in *multilingual* settings in the EU context.

ML models can also learn a different kind of abstract category, namely relevance to a particular problem area. In Grabmair et al. (2011), Savelka et al. (2014), and Savelka and Ashley (2015), one of the categories learned was relevance to the School of Public Health researchers' chosen problem area of regulation of public health emergencies. As noted, this work addresses multiple US states' statutes concerning public health emergencies.

Semantic profiles of statutes: Some work combines functional types, abstract categories, or conceptual indexing into a broader semantic profile of statutes or regulations. Wyner and Peters (2011) employed linguistically oriented rules to extract information from a complex, four-page U.S. Food and Drug Administration regulation concerning testing for disease agents in blood. They sought to identify in the text different types of normative rules, including obligations and permissions and their antecedents, subject agents, subject themes, and exceptions. In Winkels and Hoekstra (2012), the authors extracted concepts and definitions from statutory texts related to Dutch tax law, using semantic web technology and NLP techniques.

Legal rules or norms including logical formulations: Other work has focused on extracting legal rules or norms generally (see Bach et al., 2013; Wyner and Governatori, 2013), to ensure that business systems are designed to be compliant with relevant regulations as in Zhang and El-Gohary (2015) and Governatori and Shek (2012), to develop semiautomated techniques for improving human annotation of regulations (see Kiyavitskaya et al., 2008; Yoshida et al., 2013), or to extract functional information for comparing regulatory rules across jurisdictions (see Gordon and Breaux, 2013; Savelka et al., 2014; Savelka and Ashley, 2015).

The next few sections take a closer look at some of the mechanisms applied to extract information from the statutory texts and at the empirical evaluations of these methods. The relevant evaluation metrics are the same ones introduced in Section 4.4.4.

9.3. AUTOMATICALLY EXTRACTING FUNCTIONAL INFORMATION FROM STATUTORY PROVISIONS

Extracting functional information from statutes can be useful for conceptual information retrieval (Section 1.3.2). As noted, some systems like that in Francesconi and Passerini (2007) extract the function of individual legislative provisions from a set of

Input: provision of Italian privacy law: "A controller intending to process personal data falling within the scope of application of this act shall have to notify the 'Garante' thereof, . . ."
  Type: Obligation

Output: system extracts functional information:
  Features:

> *Addressee:* "Controller"
> *Action:* "Notification"
> *Counter-party:* "Garante"

FIGURE 9.1. Sample input/output of xmLegesExtractor (Francesconi, 2009, p. 66)

common types such as definition, obligation, liability, prohibition, duty, permission, or penalty, as well as some function-related features that go with them like the bearer of an obligation or duty and its beneficiary.

Once extracted, this conceptual information can be applied to the provision in a kind of semantic markup as metadata in an XML annotation, and compiled in a legal ontology like the Dalos ontology (see Section 6.4). As a result, the system has some information about what the concepts in the text mean and uses it to assist in conceptual retrieval.

For instance, Figure 9.1 illustrates functional information the system extracted from a provision of Italian data privacy law.

Once such information is incorporated into an ontological index of statutory provisions, human users can search for all of the provisions that assign notification obligations to "controllers" regarding a "garante" (or guarantor).

9.3.1. *Machine Learning to Extract Functional Types of Provisions*

In order to extract the functional information from statutes, the researchers in Francesconi and Passerini (2007) and Francesconi (2009) constructed two tools: (1) xmLegesClassifier and (2) xmLegesExtractor. The input to the classifier is a paragraph of text in a statutory provision; the output is the predicted functional type or class of the provision selected from a set of candidate types and classes (Francesconi and Passerini, 2007). The inputs to the extractor are the text paragraph and the predicted type. The extractor outputs fragments of text which correspond to specific semantic roles relevant for that type of provision (Francesconi, 2009, p. 66).

The project applied ML and KE in complementary ways to the statutory provisions. ML extracted more abstract functional types like "Obligation." Knowledge-engineered rules and NLP extracted more specific role-players like "Controller" to whom the obligation is addressed.

As described in Section 8.3, for purposes of ML in xmLegesClassifier, the documents were represented as a BOW with unigrams, that is, not phrases. In preprocessing, the system stemmed the words to reduce them to morphological roots, replaced digits and non-alphanumeric characters with special characters, and represented the document as a term vector with weights. They also employed feature selection thresholds to eliminate rare terms (Francesconi, 2009, p. 64).

The term vector weights are intended to capture the amount of information a term conveys about the document's meaning. The researchers tried four types of weights, including binary "weight" representing the presence or absence of a term within a document, term frequency weight representing the number of times a term occurs within the document, *tf/idf* weight, in which the weight is proportional to the frequency of a term in the document and inversely related to the frequency of the term in the corpus (see Section 6.4), and a weight combining term frequency with information gain. Distinct from *tf/idf*, information gain is a measure of how well a term discriminates across documents in different classes (Francesconi, 2009, p. 64).

The researchers applied a multiclass SVM (see Section 8.5.2) to a corpus of 582 provisions. The SVMs encountered previously in this book made binary decisions predicting whether a document is relevant or not (see Section 8.4.2) or whether a case was part of an instant case's prior history or not (Section 8.5.3). The xmLegesClassifier's decisions are not binary but multiclass: which of 11 functional types, including repeal, definition, delegation, etc., applies to the text?

In a *multiclass* SVM, the goal is to induce a hyperplane boundary separating each of the multiple classes of positive instances from the rest. Figure 9.2 conveys an intuition about how multiclass SVMs differ from binary ones. In the figure, solid lines represent these hyperplanes. The dotted lines represent hyperplanes set with a certain confidence margin to optimize the fit. The minimal distance between two dotted lines is called the multiclass margin. Darker points represent support vectors. Black points illustrate constraint violations. Points with extra borderlines

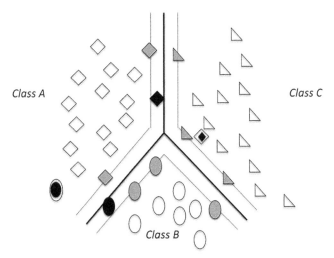

FIGURE 9.2. Multiclass SVM hyperplane example (see Francesconi and Passerini, 2007, p. 12)

indicate additional violations due to training errors (Francesconi and Passerini, 2007, pp. 11–12).

The researchers evaluated their multiclass SVM in a LOO cross-validation experiment. As explained in Section 4.4.3, a cross-validation experiment is a standard procedure for evaluating a ML algorithm. It is especially useful when there is a limited amount of data for training and testing. The training and evaluation are arranged in order to maximize usage of the limited data while ensuring that the ML algorithm is never tested on the same data on which it was trained.

In a LOO cross validation, the number of folds k equals n, the number of data points in the corpus. For n different times, the ML model is trained anew on all the data except for one point which is left out and used as the test set, and a prediction is made for that point.

The researchers measured the LOO accuracy as the fraction of correct predictions over the entire number of tests. Their SVM attained a LOO accuracy of 92.64%, using the simplest, binary scheme for weighting of the words in the feature vector (Francesconi, 2009, p. 65). As it turned out, the more complex weightings did not improve accuracy.

After the xmLegesClassifier predicts the provisions' functional types, it passes them along to the xmLegesExtractor. As noted, the xmLegesExtractor tool employed knowledge-engineered text classification rules and NLP to extract specific functional information associated with each type of provision (Francesconi and Passerini, 2007; Francesconi, 2009).

9.3.2. *Text Classification Rules to Extract Functional Information*

Given inputs of legislative raw text paragraphs and the functional types predicted by the classifier, the xmLegesExtractor outputs text fragments, called lexical units, representing entities, which play specific roles given the provision's functional type. Figure 9.1 illustrates such predefined roles including addressee, action, and counterparty, a sample input and the output of this extraction process, lexical units representing the role-players, "Controller," "Notification," and "Garante."

The extractor process comprises two steps: syntactic preprocessing and lexical unit identification. In *syntactic preprocessing*, it takes the text paragraph and breaks up the text stream into words, phrases, symbols, or other elements (tokens). It standardizes or normalizes the ways in which dates, abbreviations, and multiword forms are expressed, "lemmatizes" the text, grouping variant forms of the same words together using an Italian legal lexicon, tags POS, and conducts a shallow parse of the text into constituents or "chunks." In *lexical unit identification*, it identifies all lexical units acting as arguments or elements relevant to the specific provision type. A grammar of expert-crafted rules tailored to each specific provision type enables the system to identify the chunks corresponding to regulatory features of that type, such as those in Figure 9.1 (Francesconi, 2009, p. 66).

In order to evaluate the extractor tool, the researchers assembled a gold standard dataset of semantic roles associated with four functional types of provision: prohibition, duty, permission, and penalty. In an evaluation with 209 provisions, the rule-based classifier achieved an average precision (AP) and recall of 83% and 74%, respectively, across four types: prohibition (P 85.11%, R 92.30%), duty (P 69.23%, R 30.50%), permission (P 78.95% R 100.00%), and penalty (P 85.83% R 89.34%) (Francesconi, 2009, p. 66).

9.4. ML VS. KE FOR STATUTORY INFORMATION EXTRACTION

The xmLeges project of the preceding section illustrates a theme in automated IE from statutes and other legal texts: choosing between ML and KE approaches, or, alternatively, integrating them.

The KE approach involves identifying clear, easily observable patterns for each type of provision and manually constructing rules to identify the patterns in new texts and extract the relevant information.

The ML approach involves manually annotating training instances and using an ML algorithm automatically to generalize distinguishing features from the training set of instances.

Each approach has advantages and disadvantages (de Maat et al., 2010). The KE approach does not require manually annotated training data, but it does require manually created expert classification rules to capture the standard phrases associated with each class of provision. The ML approach is more flexible, less domain-dependent, and requires less expert knowledge. On the other hand, as noted above, certain statistical ML algorithms, like SVMs, effectively are black boxes. The reasons for classifying something as a positive or negative instance may not be easy to divine. Moreover, ML requires a sufficiently large manually annotated set of training instances.

One research group has tried both approaches on the same task, identifying the functional types of provisions in two recent pieces of Dutch legislation (de Maat et al., 2010). The 13 categories of functional types included definition, permission, obligation, delegation, various types of amending provisions, such as change–scope, change–repeal, change–renumbering, and others.

The KE classifications had been performed in earlier work. The researchers had identified a set of 88 patterns of words, extracted manually from studying 20 Dutch laws, that were associated with different functional types of provisions. The patterns included verbs or verb phrases (in Dutch) like "may," indicating a right or permission, "by x is understood y" for a definition, "is referred to as" for a citation provision, and "may create rules" for a delegation (de Maat and Winkels, 2009, pp. 32–3). The patterns were stored in a format for pattern matching against new sentences. Since provisions include multiple sentences, the classifier sought an explicit pattern in the first sentence (or list item). If it found one, the whole provision was classified

TABLE 9.1. *Problems for ML vs. KE approaches to statutory provision classification (de Maat et al., 2010)*

Problem	Description	for KE?	for ML?
Keywords in subordinate sentences	Keywords strongly linked to a class appeared in a subordinate clause that does not influence the type of the main sentence.	✓	✓
Missing standard phrases	A provision uses a phrase that was not encountered before.	✓	✓
Variations on patterns	Variations on known patterns may use the same words but different word order.	✓	X
Keywords linked to multiple classes	"May" is an indicator of a permission, but "may not" indicates an obligation.	X	✓
Insufficient data	A standard phrase present in the training set was filtered out due to a minimal required term frequency of two.	X	✓
Focus on spurious keywords	The training set may by coincidence contain many permissions, for example, that happen to involve some "advisory board." The classifier erroneously assumes that "advisory board" is an indicator of the permissions category.	X	✓
Keywords outside of standard phrase	ML may classify based on one word of a standard phrase rather than on the complete phrase.	X	✓
Skewed data	Uncommon patterns or classes may be misclassified because of their small prior chance.	X	✓

accordingly. If not, it continued to classify the subsequent sentences independently. If no sentence contained an explicit pattern, the list as a whole was classified as the default, a statement of fact (de Maat and Winkels, 2009, p. 33).

For the ML algorithm, the researchers trained a SVM classifier (Section 8.5.2) using weighted feature vectors of words (unigrams) applying three types of weighting, binary (presence or absence), term frequency, or *tf/idf* values (see Section 8.3).

The researchers compared the KE and ML approaches on two recent pieces of legislation. One made only changes in existing laws while the other included such changes and also imposed new law. The researchers found that ML scored slightly better than KE on the former, but worse on the latter. In particular, ML had problems with the classification of definitions and with the distinction between permissions and obligations. The researchers analyzed the errors and listed their causes, including those in Table 9.1.

As the table indicates, keywords appearing in subordinate sentences or missing standard phrases can be problematic for both KE and ML. Variation in pattern word order causes problems for KE, but ML is insensitive to word order (at least where a bag of words representation applies). A lack of data, spurious correlations between words and categories, or keywords that are not discriminatory are all problems for ML (de Maat et al., 2010).

Choosing between KE and ML involves a number of trade-offs. KE requires manually formulating rules to capture relevant patterns that identify instances of a classifier. ML identifies distinguishing patterns automatically although ML does not necessarily identify the same patterns as KE does and it requires the preparation of a training set of manually classified provisions. In the above experiments involving Dutch laws, KE and ML achieved roughly similar classification accuracy. In classifying provisions in a new law that was somewhat different from that of the training set, the KE rules achieved higher accuracy than the SVM classifier. It is possible, however, that a larger training set would improve the ML model's transferability (de Maat et al., 2010). When it comes to debugging, that is, inspecting the classification errors, the KE approach provides more useful information about rules that are missing, that a pattern should have triggered but did not, or that a pattern triggered but should not have. As noted previously, the SVM classifier's model is much harder to inspect, although other ML models, such as decision trees, are more readily inspectable.

Another aspect of choosing between KE and ML is the possibility of combining the two in hybrid models. For example, as discussed in Section 10.5.3, the LUIMA program employs ML for sentence role identification and KE for annotating subsentence types such as StandardLegalFormulations, for instance, "plaintiff must prove." Since such formulations present clear examples of patterns, one naturally turns to constructing rules to identify them. ML serves as an effective alternative where the distinguishing patterns are less clear or involve things like StandardLegalFormulations as components.

9.5. EXTRACTING LOGICAL RULES FROM STATUTES AND REGULATIONS

Extracting logical rules from the texts of statutes and regulations is an important goal for automating legal reasoning. Imagine the possibilities of automatically populating the BNA program (Section 2.3.4), or the Carneades program (Section 5.3.1), with rules gleaned automatically from the texts of the BNA or German family law statutes. It is an ambitious goal, but, unfortunately, a difficult one to achieve.

Natural language tools alone are probably not sufficient for the task. In Wyner and Governatori (2013), the researchers conducted a pilot study using a state-of-the-art open-source natural language translation tool, C&C/Boxer, to translate regulatory statements into semantic representations. The authors compared the output representations against manually created defeasible logical representations of five sentences from the Australian Telecommunications Consumer Protections Code (2012) on complaint management.

$< T1 >$ For the person $< /T1 >$
$< A >$ who is qualified for the ensured after s/he was disqualified, $< /A >$
$< C >$ the terms of the insured are added up together. $< /C >$

$< T2 >$ For the amount of the pension by this law, $< /T2 >$
$< A >$ when there is a remarkable change in the living standard of the nation or the other situations, $< /A >$
$< C >$ a revision of the amount of the pension must be taken action promptly to meet the situations. $< /C >$

FIGURE 9.3. Sample statutory sentences annotated for logical parts: antecedents $<A>$, consequents $<C>$, and topics $<T>$ (Bach et al., 2013)

For example, for the provision, "Suppliers must provide a means for the consumer to monitor the complaint's progress," the semantic representations identified the individuals, events, relations, and temporal relations. The tool identified the modal *must*, but it did not indicate the bearer of the obligation nor did it identify the scope of the modal operator. Finally, the representation did not capture the application of the norm to suppliers, *in general.*

In order to have any success at all in automatically extracting logical rules from statutory texts, it seems necessary to focus on a narrow area of law and to identify logical structures characteristic of that area to use as templates for rules.

For example, one project has applied ML to extract logical structures from statutory paragraphs in a corpus involving the Japanese National Pension Law. Systematic studies of multi-sentence provisions in the corpus had identified four types of relations between main and subordinate sentences, and their associated logical structures to use as templates (Takano et al., 2010). The authors of Bach et al. (2013) presented a two-stage framework for extracting from the paragraphs logical rules that impose obligations on specific agents under specific conditions. The program first learns a classifier to identify "logical parts" including antecedents (A), consequents (C), and topics (T) in the statutes. Figure 9.3 shows two examples of statutory sentences annotated for such logical parts. Based on the parts, the program then learns a classifier to select an appropriate template with which to combine the parts into logical structures and a completed rule.

Given a new legal paragraph the first classifier identifies its logical parts, the second classifier selects applicable logical templates, and the system assembles the logical rule based on the templates. The authors demonstrated some success with a subset of the logical structures identified in the Japanese National Pension Law, but the system's second phase, identifying the logical structure templates in a paragraph of law, worked considerably better with logical parts input by human experts than with those that the system identified automatically (Bach et al., 2013, p. 3:27).

Extracting rules by focusing on narrow areas of legal regulation and identifying logical structures characteristic of that area has also been applied in modeling regulations governing the design of products such as buildings.

9.6. EXTRACTING REQUIREMENTS FOR COMPLIANT PRODUCT DESIGNS

Regulatory compliance, discussed in Section 2.5.1, is an important practical concern in many industries involving the design of products, systems, or other artifacts. For example, building codes specify constraints on architectural designs such as a rule that "Courts [in the sense of open areas surrounded by building walls] shall not be less than 3 ft in width."

Regulatory codes govern product design in most areas of engineering such as civil, electrical, and environmental. The codes vary widely across regions, communities, and governmental levels. Even though regulations may constrain the product or system design, the product engineers and systems designers may not know which regulations apply. Conversely, the legal staff may not understand technical aspects of the proposed designs and, thus, fail to foresee the regulatory implications.

Considerations like these have led researchers to attempt to extract rules automatically from regulatory texts so that they can be applied more-or-less automatically to test whether proposed designs satisfy relevant legal constraints. For instance, one approach automatically extracts information from a corpus of construction regulations and transforms it into logic clauses that could be used directly for automated compliance checking (Zhang and El-Gohary, 2015).

The authors developed a multistage approach that involves:

1. *Text classification (TC)*: ML-based TC identifies sentences that contain the types of requirements relevant for automatic compliance checking (e.g., regulatory requirements in the construction industry),
2. *Information extraction*: rule-based, semantic NLP identifies in the relevant sentences the words and phrases that carry target information and labels them with predefined information tags, and
3. *Info Transformation Rules (ITr)*: semantic NLP algorithms (ITr) employ pattern-matching rules to transform extracted information into logic statements with which a logic program can reason. The rules employ syntactic and some semantic information.

For example, TC recognizes a sentence like the following as relevant for automated compliance checking of building designs: "Courts shall not be less than 3 ft in width." IE tags targeted words and phrases, such as:

Subject: Court

Compliance checking attribute: Width

Comparative relation: Not less than

Quantity value: 3

Quantity unit: Feet

Quantity reference: Not applicable.

Then, an ITr rule fires; its left-hand side identifies a rule pattern:

subject + modal verb + negation + be + comparative relation + quantity value + quantity unit + preposition + compliance checking attribute.

The right-hand side of this rule is: "Generate predicates for the 'subject' information instance, the 'attribute' information instance, and a 'has' information instance."

Once the ITr rules have generated elements, a consume-and-generate mechanism combines the elements into a logic clause:

compliant–width–of–court(Court) *if* width(Width), court(Court), has(Court,Width), greater–than–or–equal(Width,quantity(3,feet))

The ITr pattern matching rules were developed based on two chapters of the International Building Code and tested on the text of a third chapter which served as a gold standard. In that third chapter, 62 sentences containing quantitative requirements were identified automatically from which 62 logic clauses were constructed manually involving 1,901 logic clause elements.

An experiment assessed the precision and recall of the system's ITr pattern matching rules in generating those 1,901 logic clause elements based on the information tags extracted automatically from the third chapter. Two versions of the experiment were run, one with a smaller set of information tags and the other with a more inclusive set. The latter version yielded better results: precision: 98.2%, recall: 99.1%, and F1 measure: 98.6% (Zhang and El-Gohary, 2015).

The authors determined that the errors in identifying logic clause elements were caused by the IE process missing or erroneously identifying tags, errors in processing sentences with uncommon expression structures, matching errors due to morphological features, problems with certain pattern matching rules, and structural ambiguity in the regulatory texts' use of conjunctions. For example, the scope of the "and" in "shear wall segments provide lateral support to the wall piers and such segments have a total stiffness..." is not specified. It may conjoin "wall piers" and "such segments" or the preceding clause and the following clause. This is an interesting example of the challenge of dealing with syntactic ambiguity in legal statutes (Section 2.2.2).

Despite the very high performance, there are some limitations. First, the experiment focused only on processing quantitative requirements. These are important in a building code and in many similar engineering codes, but even those codes employ other sorts of requirements, not expressed in quantitative terms, which may be harder to analyze. Second, the experiment was limited to testing one chapter of the International Building Code, due in part to the difficulty of manually creating the gold standard.

9.6.1. *Implementing Compliance with Extracted Regulations*

The project of Zhang and El-Gohary (2015) concerning quantitative construction requirements is a good example of extracting complex logical rules directly from regulatory texts. Like the approach in xmLegesClassifier and Extractor (Section 9.3), it combines ML in step (1) to extract the types of regulatory requirements and KE rules in step (2) to extract the words and phrases with which to operationalize a rule. This work, however, takes the important extra step (3) of actually constructing such a rule that can be applied directly for compliance testing.

The project focuses on a fairly restricted type of regulatory provision. As yet, there is no general approach to automatically extracting logical rules from the texts of legal regulations. ML and KE take one part way, but assembling the extracted parts into logical rules requires specialized rules and templates tailored to logical patterns characteristic of specific types of regulation.

The project in Governatori and Shek (2012) dealing with telecommunications consumer complaint handling (Section 2.5.5) exemplifies reasoning with logical rules automatically to check on an institution's real-world regulatory compliance. It illustrates an ingenious way to apply the logical rules directly in a realistic business context. The authors demonstrated a technological design environment that incorporated regulatory requirements from (still) manually constructed defeasible rules governing communications systems. Human designers employing the tools can design a communication system that is guaranteed to comply with the logical rules extracted from the regulations.

It is interesting to imagine other settings in which logical rules extracted automatically from regulatory texts could be applied directly to monitoring real-world business compliance. In some compliance contexts, legal regulations govern corporate documents, suggesting another way to directly apply extracted rules. For instance, the implementing regulation of the Truth in Lending Act, Regulation Z, 12 CFR Part 226, specifies certain regulatory requirements that must be met if various "trigger words" appear in advertisements. According to the regulation, mention of an Annual Percentage Rate (APR) in a credit card advertisement triggers a requirement to make certain corresponding disclosures. In this compliance context, one could imagine extracting logical rules for monitoring these advertising requirements directly from regulatory texts and applying them directly to texts or transcripts of advertisements (Deisher-Edwards, 2015).

9.6.2. *Semiautomated Approaches to Improving*
Human Annotation for Compliance

Researchers have also devised semiautomatic techniques for extracting rights and obligations from regulatory texts, for example, from the U.S. Health Insurance Portability and Accountability Act (HIPAA). The automated techniques improve human annotators' performance (Breaux et al., 2006). In Kiyavitskaya et al. (2008), the researchers employed a semiautomatic semantic annotation tool, *Cerno* (see Zeni et al., 2013), with an extension for regulatory texts, *Gaius T*, to extract rights, obligations, or exceptions from the U.S. HIPAA Privacy Rule provision.

Cerno uses a context-free grammar, that is, rules describing how to form statements from a language's available symbols that satisfy the language's syntax, to generate the parse tree of a text whose constituents are legal language textual elements. Annotation rules then analyze the parsed texts, annotating them with tags indicating the presence or absence of certain concepts. The concepts are selected from a domain ontology. Each one has an associated vocabulary of indicators, comprising literal words and names of parsed entities which should (or should not) be present. Finally, transformation rules select certain of the annotated text fragments and output templates whose fields are filled in based on the annotations.

For extending the tool to annotate regulatory texts, the authors manually analyzed a fragment of the HIPAA Privacy Rule and generated lists of indicators for four major concepts:

1. *Right*: an action a stakeholder is conditionally permitted to perform;
2. *Obligation*: an action that a stakeholder is conditionally required to perform;
3. *Constraint*: the part of a right or obligation that describes a single pre- or post-condition; and
4. *Exceptions*: which remove elements from consideration in a domain (Kiyavitskaya et al., 2008, p. 5).

Applying the tool to other fragments of the HIPAA Privacy Rule (and to an Italian statutory provision), the researchers compared the numbers of rights, obligations, constraints, and cross-references identified by the system with those identified by a human. The results were roughly comparable. The evaluation demonstrated the need for adding more normative phrases to identify constraints. In addition, the system had some difficulty identifying the subjects and objects of constraints, as well as identifying the subjects of conjunctions and disjunctions.

Significantly, the researchers compared the outputs of nonexpert human annotators who worked with texts that Gaius T had already annotated and those who did not. The former group were about 10% more productive, worked about 12% faster, and produced annotations as accurate as those of annotators who did not work with the automatically annotated texts (Kiyavitskaya et al., 2008, p. 9).

Similarly, in Yoshida et al. (2013), the authors demonstrated that humans annotating statutes in terms of various templates performed more accurately and efficiently when supported by a tool which highlighted terms in the documents that corresponded to the templates.

The authors defined three templates for capturing information from statutory texts. A definition template is used to annotate definitions of legal terms employed in the statute. A function template identifies the types of functional processes that

Recognition of Unemployment
Article 15 (1) The basic allowance shall be **paid** with regard to the days on
which a person who has recipient qualification (**hereinafter referred to as a**
"qualified recipient" except in the following Section to Section 4 inclusive) is
unemployed

(2) A qualified recipient shall...**apply** for employment pursuant to the
provisions of an Ordinance of the Ministry of Health, Labour and Welfare.

FIGURE 9.4. Term suggestions for annotation templates (see Yoshida et al., 2013)

a statutory provision requires (or permits, etc.). A data template identifies data or
information that the statute requires a regulated party to input into the functional
process. They associated various words, concepts, and phrases with each of the three
template types. For example, the phrase "hereinafter referred to as . . .," appearing in
a parenthetical, suggests applying a definition template. Noun terms like "Notification" and verb terms like "report to" suggest using the data template to specify the
information the statute requires be submitted. Verb terms like "pay" suggest statutory
processes for annotation with a function template.

Their tool preprocesses statutory texts for human annotation, identifying the various words, concepts, and phrases that suggest the annotators apply the associated
template. As illustrated in Figure 9.4, the tool uses a single underline to suggest the
data template, a double underline for the function template, and a dotted line for
the definition template.

A human selects the template associated with the cue and manually fills in the
required information. The definition template requests the term and definition. In
the context of Figure 9.4, this would be "qualified recipient," "a person who has
recipient qualification." The function template requests the process, any modal qualification, and conditions, for example, "paid," "shall," "with regard to the days."
The data template requests the article identifier, actor, action, data and source,
modal qualifier and conditions, such as "Art. 15(2)," "public servant," "input," "data
from employment application of qualified recipient," "shall," "after separation from
employment."

In a small experiment, two groups, each comprising two civil servants and one
student, annotated multiple provisions of a Japanese statute with which they were
unfamiliar, one group with the tool and one without. The focus of the task was
annotating the statutory functions in the provisions, of which the researchers had
determined there were 22. The participants in the group using the tool completed
the annotation task more quickly (an average of 9.5 vs. 11 hours) and achieved higher
accuracy and coverage in identifying the functions.

These two projects illustrate the utility of tools that use knowledge engineered
rules and templates to partially annotate texts in support of human annotation.

Not only can these tools make human annotators' work more efficient, they can also enable nonexpert humans to annotate as well as experts. This may help meet the growing need for annotation to index statutes for conceptual retrieval (Section 6.5) and for compiling training sets for ML to automate annotation. For instance, the tool described above that helps nonexpert humans to annotate statutes in terms of actors, actions, modal qualifiers, and conditions would have helped in annotating public health statutes for ML, automated annotation, and the construction of statutory networks as described below in Section 9.7.1. Computerized support for human annotation of statutes and cases for ML, including annotation by students and via crowdsourcing, is also discussed in Sections 10.6 and 12.5.2.

9.7. EXTRACTING FUNCTIONAL INFORMATION TO COMPARE REGULATIONS

An important component of business compliance is the need to compare similarly purposed regulations across jurisdictions. Many industries and commercial institutions span multiple state and international boundaries. In areas like insurance, health care, computer security, and privacy regulation, these institutions are subject to multiple states' laws. While the overall goals of the different state and national regulatory frameworks might be similar, the regulations themselves may differ in a multitude of ways. Keeping track of the differences and factoring them into plans for regulatory compliance are constant concerns.

Travis Breaux has developed a semantic model to automate extraction of requirements from legal texts and a legal requirements specification language general enough to enable comparison of regulations across jurisdictions. He and his colleagues developed a "requirements watermarking technique" for comparing the stringency of privacy and security standards across jurisdictions (Gordon and Breaux, 2013).

The researchers studied how regulatory drafters employ "legal design patterns" in order to impose constraints on the design of industrial scale information systems. Their model demonstrates how coordinated legal definitions, requirements, and exemptions shape policy by relaxing or restricting the logical scope of legal constraints (Breaux and Gordon, 2013). An example of such a legal design pattern is a "suspension," "in which a permission ... is an exception to an obligation ...[;] satisfying the conditions of the permission causes the obligation to be suspended" (Breaux and Gordon, 2011, p. 11).

Comparison across legal instruments is also important. Breaux's privacy requirements specification language (Eddy) models legal requirements applied to complex data flows involving multiple parties (Breaux et al., 2014) and has been used to compare current corporate data privacy policies (Breaux et al., 2015).

Statutory network representations of states' laws on some topic (Section 2.6) can also be compared. The network diagrams graphically depict certain aspects of the regulations. One can compare those aspects of different states' laws both graphically (Grabmair et al., 2011) and quantitatively in terms of network analytics such as density, inclusiveness, degree, strength, reciprocity, and hub-and-authority (Ashley et al., 2014). For example, the statutory network illustrated in Figure 2.10 compares Pennsylvania's and Florida's statutes regarding public health emergency surveillance. A similar network approach could be useful in other compliance domains where multiple jurisdictions have parallel regulatory systems. In addition, employees, business system designers, field agents, or other nonlegal personnel could retrieve statutory sources substantiating a link in the diagram simply by clicking it (Ashley et al., 2014).

9.7.1. *Machine Learning for Constructing Statutory Networks*

Statutory network representations of regulatory schemes across jurisdictions require a considerable amount of data about the different jurisdictions' statutes. In the project mentioned above, School of Public Health personnel used LexisNexis queries to retrieve 12 states' statutes dealing with public health emergencies.

They manually coded the texts of the state statutory provisions for nine classifications in a kind of template that captures: the *acting agents* in the Public Health Service (PHS) that the provision directs with some level of *prescription* to perform a certain *action* with respect to some *receiving agents* under certain *conditions*, with certain *goals* and *purpose* regarding some *type of emergency disaster* in some *time frame*. The coding concepts, italicized above, are explained as follows:

Relevance: Is the provision relevant for purposes of the Public Health School analysis? If "yes":

Acting PHS agent: Whom does the provision direct to act?

Action: What action does the provision direct?

Receiving PHS agent: Whom does the provision direct to receive the action?

Prescription: With what level of prescription is the action directed: "may"? "must"?

Goal: For what goal is the action directed to be taken?

Purpose: For what purpose is the action directed to be taken?

Type of Emergency Disaster: Is the emergency disaster an epidemic, train wreck, nuclear accident, etc.?

Time frame: In what time frame can/must the action be taken?

Condition: What circumstances govern if the action is taken?

The encoding task would be more feasible if ML could extract certain information from statutory texts. From a manually encoded training set for each state, the ML system could learn to classify that state's provisions in terms of relevance as well as each of the other nine coded categories.

That is the hypothesis underlying the line of work in Grabmair et al. (2011), Savelka et al. (2014), and Savelka and Ashley (2015), mentioned in Section 9.2. In particular, the work addresses three issues that arise in extracting information from statutes using ML:

1. Representing statutory provisions in machine classifiable units or "chunks,"
2. Selecting the learning algorithm to apply, and
3. Dealing with sparse training data.

Chunking and Representing Statutory Provision Texts

The first issue is deciding how to divide statutory provisions, which can be quite long, into manageable, meaningful chunks for purposes of classification and how best to represent them.

For any sentence in a subsection of a statute, its meaning depends not only on the sentence's composition, but also on its context among the other sentences in that subsection, the other subsections in that section, the other sections in the statute, and, perhaps on other statutes, as well. In addition, some subsections may be parts of lists or other internal structures of a legal provision that, presumably, bear on the meaning of any item in the list.

The question is how to operationalize this context in a computationally reasonable way, and it turns out that there are many options.

In Savelka et al. (2014) and Savelka and Ashley (2015), each statutory document, that is, each provision of the statute, was viewed as a tree graph and divided into smaller parts or chunks that comprised the text elements on a path from the root node to each leaf node. For example, Figure 9.5 shows a provision of a Florida statute partitioned into seven subtrees, one of which is highlighted in bold face text. This is the chunk that corresponds to leaf node 5, corresponding to the fifth item of the list in subsection (b) of the provision. For purposes of ML, that is the chunk representing Fla. Stat. §101.62 (1) (b) 5.

The statutory tree graph approach has two virtues. (1) Each of the chunks can be referred to uniquely via a citation. (2) As a longitudinal slice through the tree, the chunk captures some of the statutory context of a leaf-node text. Other aspects of the statutory context such as fraternal leaf nodes are omitted. One can employ the statutory tree graph as a framework for defining variations that capture more of the statutory context, for example, by including contiguous leaf nodes in the chunk.

The next issue is how to represent each chunk or "text unit" for purposes of ML. Similarly to the basic ML setup (Section 8.3) in Savelka et al. (2014) and Savelka and Ashley (2015), stop words and particular words in titles such as "Title," "Part," or "Chapter" were removed, numerical digits were replaced with a standard token, words were put in lower case and normalized form, and the classification codes assigned by the expert human annotators were included.

Each text unit was then represented as an n-dimensional term vector with each dimension corresponding to a unique term in the document collection and with a

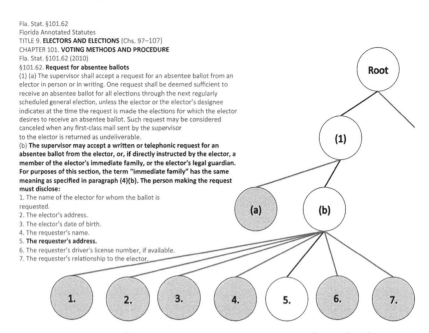

Fla. Stat. §101.62
Florida Annotated Statutes
TITLE 9. **ELECTORS AND ELECTIONS** (Chs. 97–107)
CHAPTER 101. **VOTING METHODS AND PROCEDURE**
Fla. Stat. §101.62 (2010)
§101.62. **Request for absentee ballots**
(1) (a) The supervisor shall accept a request for an absentee ballot from an elector in person or in writing. One request shall be deemed sufficient to receive an absentee ballot for all elections through the next regularly scheduled general election, unless the elector or the elector's designee indicates at the time the request is made the elections for which the elector desires to receive an absentee ballot. Such request may be considered canceled when any first-class mail sent by the supervisor to the elector is returned as undeliverable.
(b) **The supervisor may accept a written or telephonic request for an absentee ballot from the elector, or, if directly instructed by the elector, a member of the elector's immediate family, or the elector's legal guardian. For purposes of this section, the term "immediate family" has the same meaning as specified in paragraph (4)(b). The person making the request must disclose:**
1. The name of the elector for whom the ballot is requested.
2. The elector's address.
3. The elector's date of birth.
4. The requester's name.
5. **The requester's address.**
6. The requester's driver's license number, if available.
7. The requester's relationship to the elector.

FIGURE 9.5. Partitioning statutory provision into subtree chunks

magnitude corresponding to the *tf/idf* weight of that term (see Section 6.4). This is similar to the representation in Francesconi and Passerini (2007).

9.7.2. *Applying an ML Algorithm for Statutory Texts*

In working with a corpus of public health emergency statutes, the researchers have applied both an SVM (Section 8.5.2) and decision trees (Section 4.3.1) (Grabmair and Ashley, 2011; Savelka et al., 2014; Savelka and Ashley, 2015).

In terms of effectiveness in extracting information from statutory texts, there seems to be no discernible difference. As noted, however, decision trees are easier than SVM models for humans to inspect and determine which features are more important for discriminating positive and negative instances. Given the exploratory nature of the work, the interpretability of the models led the researchers to opt for using decision trees.

Let's consider in more detail the process of learning a decision tree to classify the text units of the previous section by relevance to the School of Public Health study. (The process is similar for learning decision trees for each of the other nine categories.) A text unit is represented as a feature vector of *tf/idf* value for each of an ordered set of terms. The feature vectors are very long comprising thousands of entries corresponding to all the terms present in the corpus. Most of the entries are 0, however, indicating that the corresponding term is not in the text unit.

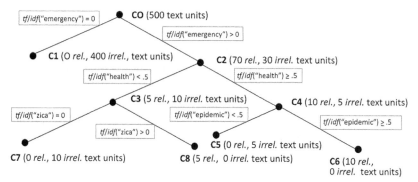

FIGURE 9.6. Decision tree for classifying statutory text units as relevant (*rel.*) or irrelevant (*irrel.*) to the School of Public Health study

In learning a decision tree from the text units in a training set, the algorithm first picks a feature on the basis of which it will split the data. Let's say that it is attempting to split the data between the text units that are relevant to a given query and those that are not. First, let's assume that the features are binary as in the decision tree for bail illustrated in Section 4.3.1. The feature values in Figure 4.2's decision tree are "yes" or "no," indicating, for instance that the offense did or did not involve drugs or that the offender had a prior record or not. Where the features are binary, an algorithm can only split the data based on equality of a feature's value and the test's conditions. The algorithm adds a decision node to the tree that tests the value of the feature: if "yes" take the right branch and if "no" go to the left.

In contrast, the feature vectors representing text units may have numerical values such as *tf/idf* values. The test at a decision node would be something like this: if the *tf/idf* of a selected feature ≥ 0.5 go right, else go left. See Figure 9.6 for a hypothetical decision tree for classifying text units representing statutory provisions as relevant or not. The tests at each branch are shown in boxes.

Beside determining the threshold, the algorithm also needs to determine which of the features is the best one to test at that given point. This requires some measure (such as entropy or Gini impurity, see Kakwani (1980)) of the homogeneity of the target classification within the subsets of data if it were split at that feature. The algorithm inspects one feature after another and determines how good a split can be effected given the data with respect to that measure. The algorithm chooses a split that maximizes the expected value of the information gained by that split as compared to the others. Once it computes the best feature available for splitting, it performs the split inserting a branch into the decision tree.

Having performed the split, the algorithm repeats the same process for the nodes that have been created on the branches but now it takes into account only the parts of the data set that belong to that node. The algorithm proceeds in this manner until a stop condition is met, for example, when some maximum depth of a tree is reached.

When one inspects the resulting decision tree (Figure 9.6), one sees just below the root node (C0) that a feature corresponding to the word "emergency" was selected as providing an opportunity for the best split. One may also see the *tf/idf* value cutoff for the split. For example, it could simply be "> 0," which means, in effect, that the word is present in the text. One may see that out of the, say, 500 documents, 400 were sent to the left as irrelevant (C1) and 100 matched the splitting condition and were sent to the right (C2). The algorithm repeats the same process at node C2 but now it takes into account only text units associated with C2, of which 70 were relevant and 30 irrelevant. From node C2, one can see that the word "health" was selected as the second opportunity for splitting. If text units have *tf/idf* values of "health" over a certain threshold, they were assigned to a right branch, otherwise to the left.

One may again follow to the right and discover that it leads ultimately to a terminal leaf node, C6, that contains text units labeled as relevant, that is, documents with *tf/idf* values surpassing the above thresholds for "emergency," "health," and "epidemic." In a similar way, one can inspect all of the paths in the tree. Note that 10 text units at node C6 all happen to be relevant. In fact, all of the terminal nodes C5 through C8 contain text units with uniform results but that would not necessarily be the case. If the terminal condition were some maximum tree depth, the leaf nodes would probably contain text units with mixed results and no classification could be made.

Once the decision trees were constructed for 10 categories (relevance, acting agent, prescription, action, goal, purpose, emergency type, receiving agent, time frame, and condition), classification of the text units proceeded in two steps. In the first step, all of the text units were classified in terms of their relevance for the public health analysis. In the second step, the relevant text units were further classified in terms of the remaining categories.

9.7.3. *Evaluating the ML Algorithm on Statutory Texts and Dealing with Sparse Training Data*

In experiments, the system has been evaluated by comparing the ML classifications and a gold standard of the classifications generated manually by the expert annotators from the School of Public Health. These evaluations have been conducted as cross validations similar to those described above (Grabmair et al., 2011; Savelka et al., 2014).

For the Pennsylvania corpus, performance across the nine categories varied considerably in Grabmair et al. (2011). For all categories except Action, ML achieved F_1 measures higher than or equal to that of the two baselines: the most frequent code (MFC) for an attribute and a keyword-enhanced MFC. The ML F_1 measures ranged from a low of 24% for goal to 86% for time frame with an average across nine categories of $F_1 = 54\%$.

One of the reasons for the relatively low performance was the problem of scarce training data. The public health experts' annotation codebook is fairly detailed and the number of codes available for a given attribute may be large. As a result, the number of instances of a given code can be very small.

In order to mitigate the problem of data sparsity and boost the classifiers' performance, the researchers explored using data from other jurisdictions. They combined one state's training data with that of other states in order to increase the amount of training data.

On the surface this idea seems appealing, but statutory texts in different jurisdictions often differ in a variety of ways even if they deal with similar subject matter. Legislators from different states may employ different terminology and structural patterns. For example, the Pennsylvania (PA) corpus of relevant statutory texts contained 1.7 times as many provisions as those of Florida (FL) but took up only 70% of the space. As a result, the relevant FL statutory texts tended to be longer than the PA statutory texts. The FL statutory texts also seemed to be more fragmented; the FL corpus generated 11,131 text units while the PA corpus had only 6,022 text units. There were 4,764 unique terms (excluding stop words) in the PA corpus and 6,569 terms in the FL corpus. Thus, it was an empirical question whether one could combine training sets across jurisdictions and improve performance.

In Savelka and Ashley (2015), the researchers described a framework for facilitating transfer of predictive models for classification of statutory texts among multiple state jurisdictions. For each of two target states, including Florida, training and test sets were created through fivefold cross validation using random sampling and repeated 20 times. That is, the program was run 100 times, each time with about 20% of the corpus used as training data and 80% as test data but randomly reassigning provisions to each on each run.

Figure 9.7 shows box plots for all of the runs in the Florida experiment. Each cluster of eight box plots shows the progression of performance in terms of the F1-measure on each of the eight tasks. The first box plot in any cluster summarizes 100 runs of the experiment in which no additional states' data set was used. The second box plot describes the 300 runs of the experiment in which an additional state's data set was used. For each 100 runs a different state's data set was used. The eighth box plot summarizes 100 runs of the experiment in which all seven extra states' data sets were used.

As can be clearly seen from the generally upward trends to the right of each cluster, for all of the tasks the classifiers' performance tends to improve as more states' data sets are used. For the FL corpus, the average F1 measures for nine categories improved from 54% using no additional state's data to 58% using data from seven additional states. The performance improved even though the additional training data came from different states whose statutory systems and language vary. The results also show that the performance is not harmed when additional data sets

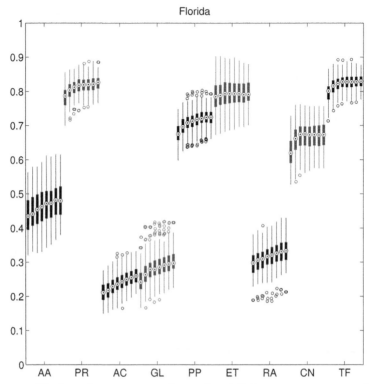

FIGURE 9.7. The box plot summarizes the results of all the experiments on each of the tasks for Florida (FL). Each box plot describes performance in terms of an F1-measure within a single experiment. The tasks included identifying: AA (acting agent), PR (prescription), AC (action), GL (goal), PP (purpose), ET (emergency type), RA (receiving agent), CN (condition), TF (time frame) (Savelka and Ashley, 2015)

are used. At worst, the performance levels off (Savelka et al., 2014; Savelka and Ashley, 2015).

9.7.4. *Applying LUIMA to Enrich Statutory Text Representation*

The projects described above (specifically Francesconi and Passerini, 2007; Francesconi, 2009; Bach et al., 2013; Zhang and El-Gohary, 2015), with their multi-staged or pipeline approaches, multilayered representations of statutory texts, and combinations of KE rules and ML, suggest the utility of applying the LUIMA approach introduced in Section 6.8 to annotating statutes.

Rule-based annotators could enrich the representation of the texts of statutory provisions with semantic subsentence- and sentence-level annotations. The LUIMA type system (Grabmair et al., 2015) could be adapted to the Public Health (PH) Emergency statutory domain including: sentence-level types for legal rules and subsentence-level types for Premise and Consequent (see Bach et al., 2013) and sub-sentence and mention types for PH agents, PH concepts, agent actions, properties of agents/concepts, regulation elements, and language clues.

The researchers plan to test the hypothesis that, by semantically annotating statutory provisions and classifying them based on the annotations, one can outperform classification systems that do not take into account such semantics. For example, the system could annotate a word "infirmary" as a mention of an agent who is playing an active role in a provision and is of the type "hospital" or a phrase "shutdown water supply" as a mention of an action, of the type "restrict," that a certain agent is required to carry out. The annotations could supplement word n-grams as features for ML classifiers.

The goal of the classifiers is to assign provisions with categories/labels for a number of prespecified attributes. For example, the system may label a specific provision as an "obligation" or as concerned with "air pollution emergencies."

If the approach were successful, labels assigned to a statutory provision could act as a kind of projection of that provision to the more general conceptual level of the type system while semantic annotations localize concepts in the text of the provision. This means that the system could substitute more abstract or more specific terminology as appropriate.

The annotators could parse queries entered by a user to determine which concepts are mentioned and, optionally, expand the queries accordingly. For example, if the query contained a word "Ebola," the system could determine that "infectious disease" is mentioned, broaden the query, and retrieve statutory provisions containing mentions of "infectious disease" even though they do not contain the exact word, "Ebola." This would help to ensure that relevant provisions are not excluded from the results simply because a user was too specific with the query.

The system could also utilize the labels and annotations to measure how semantically close each of the retrieved provisions is to the query and order them accordingly. If a user enters a query "hospital must report Ebola," the system would likely rank highly a provision containing an "obligation" for an agent of type "hospital" related to an "infectious disease" where the required action is semantically related to "reporting." This would be the case even though the provision contained few if any of the words appearing in the query.

This would also enable the system to summarize each provision as a sentence composed of the annotation labels in order to convey more succinctly what the sentence is about. This generalized summary may help a user make preliminary assessments of the relevance of retrieved provisions.

9.8. CONCLUSION

As we have seen, automated extraction of logical rules from statutory texts is not just a matter of applying NLP but poses additional challenges.

If a theme emerges from the work reported in this chapter, it is the importance of identifying recurring structures or patterns in statutes and regulations that relate to the forms and meaning of normative rules, including:

- logical structures that characterize legislation generally or specific laws,
- patterns or templates of terms, grammatical roles of words, types of concepts, modal verbs, and other elements characteristic of normative rules generally or in specific laws, or
- legal design patterns of coordinated definitions, requirements, and exemptions characteristic of particular regulated domains.

Automating programs' and humans' understanding of the normative rules will benefit from identifying such patterns, devising rules to compose elements into patterns or to decompose patterns into elements, and developing techniques for visualizing the patterns.

Enriching the representation of statutory texts with a hierarchical type system like LUIMA, that captures aspects of these patterns seems likely to be useful for ML. In the following chapters, we examine some efforts to use LUIMA annotations to extract information associated with patterns of argumentation from legal cases.

10

Extracting Argument-Related Information from Legal Case Texts

10.1. INTRODUCTION

Chapter 8 explained how ML can be applied to legal texts, and Chapter 9 explored methods for extracting information from statutory and regulatory texts. This chapter continues that discussion but focuses on using ML, NLP, and manually constructed rules to extract information from the texts of legal decisions, focusing particularly on *argument-related information*.

Information in legal cases is argument-related if it is about the roles of sentences and other information in the argument presented in a case. This includes sentence roles as, for example, statements of legal rules in the abstract or as applied to specific facts, or as case holdings and findings of fact. It also includes more general roles such as propositions in arguments, premises or conclusions, and the argument schemes (Section 5.2) that justify the conclusions given the premises, schemes such as analogizing the current facts to a prior case or distinguishing them. Finally, it comprises information that affects the strength of an argument such as legal factors, stereotypical fact patterns that strengthen a claim (Section 3.3.2), or evidence factors (Section 5.8).

At various points in this book, it has been asserted that argument-related information would support conceptual legal information retrieval *if* IR programs could identify it. The next chapter provides preliminary evidence in support of this claim. Here we discuss text analytic techniques that can extract some of this information from case texts. In particular, it describes an architecture for applying a type system and text annotation pipeline to process case texts for argument-related information about sentence roles. It continues the discussion of LUIMA (Legal UIMA), the law-specific semantic extraction toolbox based on the UIMA framework and designed to automate the conceptual markup of legal documents.

The chapter then revisits the task of manual annotation of legal texts, necessary in order to create training sets of documents for ML classification. Ostensibly a task for human annotators with some level of domain expertise, clever decomposition of the annotation tasks may make possible crowdsourced solutions for annotation.

The chapter provides answers to the following questions: How does IE extraction from legal case texts work? What roles do NLP, UIMA type systems, and ML play? How can the conceptual markup of legal documents be automated? What is manual text annotation, what tools support it, how can it be managed, and how can its reliability be evaluated? What kinds of argument-related information be extracted from legal case texts? Can annotation be crowdsourced?

10.2. ARGUMENT-RELATED INFORMATION IN LEGAL CASES

Some work in extraction of information from case texts has focused on extracting topics and subject matter. Programs have categorized legal cases by abstract West legal categories (e.g., finance and banking, bankruptcy) in (Thompson, 2001) and by general topics (e.g., exceptional services pension, retirement) in Gonçalves and Quaresma (2005). Another system retrieved documents based on queries expressing cross-references between document subject matters (e.g., "Which orders talk about abnormally annoying noise and make reference to decrees talking about soundproofing?") (Mimouni et al., 2014).

As early as 1991, researchers explored the use of argument schemes to assist in representing cases for conceptual legal information retrieval (Dick and Hirst, 1991). More recently, automatic semantic processing of argument-related information in case decision texts has been undertaken for legal IR, including automatically extracting case treatment history such as "affirmed" or "reversed in part" (Jackson et al., 2003), offenses raised and legal principles applied from criminal cases to generate summaries (Uyttendaele et al., 1998), case holdings (McCarty, 2007), and argument schemes from the Araucaria corpus such as argument from example and argument from cause to effect (Feng and Hirst, 2011). Other programs have, based on manually annotated decisions, assigned rhetorical roles to case sentences, such as identifying the case, establishing case facts, arguing the case, reporting case history, and stating arguments, ratio decidendi, or final decisions (Saravanan and Ravindran, 2010), or determined the role of a sentence in the case as describing the applicable law or the facts (Hachey and Grover, 2006).

Sometimes, of course, topic-related and argument-related information overlap. In Zhang et al. (2014) "legal issues" are mined from a case law database, each comprising a legal proposition or principle for which the case could be cited in an argument. As noted in Section 7.7, a system semantically annotates legal issues in case texts with a combination of ML and manual annotation. The result is a legal issue library of standardized legal issues and links to case discussions of the issues (Zhang, 2015).

This chapter focuses on three projects that have extracted different types of argument-related information from case texts using ML, NLP, and extraction rules:

1. Mochales and Moens's system identified sentences that played a role in an argument, labeled them as premises or conclusions, and extracted the structure of an argument from case texts (Moens et al., 2007; Mochales and Moens, 2011).
2. SMILE extracted substantive legal factors, the stereotypical patterns of fact that strengthen or weaken a side's legal claim (Ashley and Brüninghaus, 2009).
3. The LUIMA system extracts argument-related information about legal rules cited in a case and their applications to facts (Grabmair et al., 2015).

Chapters 11 and 12 will discuss how this information extracted from legal cases can improve conceptual legal information retrieval, enable AR, and perform other cognitive computing tasks.

10.3. EXTRACTING LEGAL ARGUMENT CLAIMS

In Mochales's and Moens's pioneering work on legal argument mining, the information extracted from legal texts comprised a basic unit of arguments, namely their propositions or claims (Moens et al., 2007; Mochales and Moens, 2011). According to the authors, "a claim is a proposition, an idea which is either true or false, put by somebody as true" (Mochales and Moens, 2011, p. 1). This work is a forerunner of the IBM Debater system, which, in an as yet nonlegal context, employs domain independent techniques to "detect relevant claims" on a topic (Levy et al., 2014).

Arguments involve chains of reasoning, where claims are also used as premises for deriving further claims. An argument's final claim is called its conclusion. Specifically, the authors defined *argument* as "a set of propositions, all of which are premises except, at most, one, which is a conclusion[, and which] follows an argumentation scheme" (Mochales and Moens, 2011, p. 5). As discussed in Section 5.2, argumentation schemes are templates or blueprints for different kinds of more-or-less domain-specific arguments, some of which may be implemented in a computational model of argument.

10.3.1. *Machine Learning to Classify Sentences as Propositions, Premises, and Conclusions*

The researchers applied ML automatically (1) to classify sentences as propositions in an argument (or not) and (2) to classify argumentative propositions as premises or conclusions.

They worked with two corpora. The first was the Araucaria corpus which comprised 641 documents that had been annotated according to a specific methodology as a part of a project at the University of Dundee (UK) (Reed and Rowe, 2004;

Mochales and Moens, 2011, p. 8). It included five court reports, four parliamentary records, as well as newspapers, magazine articles, and discussion boards. This corpus comprised 3,798 sentences, including an equal number of sentences that were argument propositions or nonargument propositions.

The second corpus, a set of 47 legal documents of the European Court of Human Rights (ECHR), comprised 2,571 sentences. Three annotators spent more than a year annotating the arguments in the ECHR corpus, with one judge to settle disagreements. The annotators attained a good level of agreement on the labeling (75% agreement according to Cohen's kappa coefficient, a standard measure of agreement defined in Section 10.6.1).

10.3.2. *Text Representation*

For purposes of extracting argumentation-related information, Mochales and Moens represented sentences as feature vectors. As explained in Sections 7.5.2 and 8.5.1, feature vectors and term vectors are widely used to represent texts, but here they represent sentences for purposes of detecting arguments.

For learning to identify sentences as argument propositions, the sentences were represented in terms of domain-general features based on information extracted from the sentence texts, including:

- each word, pair of words, pairs and triples of successive words,
- POS including certain adverbs, verbs, and modal auxiliaries (verbs that indicate permission or obligation such as "may," "must," "shall," and "should"),
- certain punctuation patterns,
- certain keywords indicating argumentation, for instance, "but," "consequently," and "because of,"
- depth of parse trees and number of subclauses (both measures of sentence complexity), and
- certain text statistics including sentence length, average word length, and number of punctuation marks. (Mochales and Moens, 2011)

The feature values are typically represented as binary features signaling the presence or absence of a feature in the sentence.

For classifying argumentative propositions as premises or conclusions, the authors employed an enriched set of features to represent sentences, including:

- the sentence's length relative to a threshold and position in the document (divided into seven segments),
- main verb tense and type,
- previous and successive sentences' categories,
- a preprocessing classification of the sentence as argumentative or not,
- the type of rhetorical patterns occurring in the sentence and surrounding sentences: support, against, conclusion, other, or none,

- the type of argumentative patterns in the sentence, for instance, "see," "*mutatis mutandis*," "having reached this conclusion," "by a majority,"
- whether the sentence cites an article of the law or includes a legal definition, and
- the agent type of the sentence subject, for example, the applicant, the defendant, the court, or other (Mochales and Moens, 2011).

10.3.3. *Applying Statistical Learning Algorithms*

Having represented the sentences as feature vectors, Mochales and Moens applied three statistical learning algorithms commonly used in text classification:

1. Naïve Bayes classifier,
2. Maximum entropy classifier, and
3. SVM.

The first two algorithms were applied to predict if a sentence was an argumentative proposition. Similar to systems presented in prior chapters, both algorithms predict an instance of a category Y based on the values X of the features in the feature vector. They calculate the probability of a classification Y given the feature values X and select the most likely label Y.

In the process of calculating the probabilities, both algorithms estimate parameters or weights associated with each of the features in the feature vector, but they do so in different ways.

Naïve Bayes

Naïve Bayes uses an indirect approach to estimating the feature weights. It estimates the probability of Y given X indirectly by estimating the probability of Y and the probability of X given Y and then using a formula called Bayes Rule to compute the probability of Y given X.

The Naïve Bayes classifier employs a convenient shortcut that reduces the computational complexity of the calculations. It makes a simplifying assumption that the individual features are conditionally independent of each other. This conditional independence assumption limits the number of parameters that need to be estimated when modeling the probability of X given Y (Mitchell, 2015, p. 3).

In fact, this assumption frequently is *not* satisfied, the reason why the algorithm is called naïve. If some of the features are not independent, the naïve Bayes algorithm may result in errors. For example, the two words in the phrase "Buenos Aires" rarely appear separately. Even though they are not independent, Naïve Bayes will add the evidence of each term in the phrase, in effect, double counting. Given this phenomenon, it may be preferable to use a different technique that estimates the parameters more directly from the data (Mitchell, 2015, p. 10).

Maximum Entropy Classifier

A maximum entropy classifier in language processing, also known as multinomial logistic regression, assigns a class to a document by learning what features from the input are most useful for discriminating between the different classes. It computes a probability from an exponential function of a weighted set of these observed features (Jurafsky and Martin, 2015). It is based on the principle that when nothing else is known, the probability distribution should be as uniform as possible, that is, it should have maximum entropy (Nigam et al., 1999).

In the context of text classification, a document may be represented by a set of words and the number of times each word appears in the document (see Section 8.3). The documents in the training data all have labels assigned. The maximum entropy classifier can estimate the conditional distribution of a class label. Given the labeled training data, for each class it can estimate the expected value of these word counts, that is, the weights of the features (Nigam et al., 1999).

For instance, suppose there are four classes of documents, including the "faculty" class, and one is told that 40% of documents that have the word "professor" belong to the "faculty" class. That information serves as a constraint. Without any other information, if a document has the word "professor," one would guess it has a 40% chance of being a faculty document, and a 20% chance of being each of the other classes. If the document does not have "professor," one would guess that it has a 25% chance of being each of the classes. This would be a simple maximum entropy model (Nigam et al., 1999).

The training data sets up many such constraints on the conditional distribution. Each constraint corresponds to a characteristic of the training data that should also be present in the distribution the algorithm learns. The algorithm applies an iterative technique to formulate a text classifier function that matches all of these constraints from the labeled data (Nigam et al., 1999). In effect, the model learns the weights of the features that correspond to the constraints. Intuitively, it chooses weights that make the classes of the training examples more likely in a process called conditional maximum likelihood estimation (Jurafsky and Martin, 2015).

A maximum entropy classifier does not make any assumption that features are independent. Unlike naïve Bayes, when it encounters the phrase "Buenos Aires," the use of the constraints leads it to discount the evidential weight and to avoid double counting the evidence. As a result, one can use bigrams and phrases with maximum entropy (Nigam et al., 1999). As it happened, in the experiment reported below, the maximum entropy classifier produced better results than naïve Bayes.

Support Vector Machine

For the sentences in the ECHR corpus classified as propositions in an argument, the authors applied a SVM to classify them as premises or conclusions.

As explained in Section 8.5.2 on applying ML to text, a SVM is a kind of statistical ML algorithm that identifies, in the space of feature vectors, a hyperplane boundary between positive and negative instances of a category or class (Noble, 2006). Here, the vector space is the space of feature vectors representing the sentences in terms of the enriched set of features mentioned above.

Results for Identifying Argumentative Propositions

In identifying argumentative propositions, Mochales and Moens achieved accuracies of 74% on the Araucaria corpus and 80% on the ECHR corpus. They appear to have obtained the best results by combining "word couples selected by their POS-tag, verbs and statistics on sentence length, average word length and number of punctuation marks" (Moens et al., 2007). In determining whether argumentative propositions in the ECHR corpus were premises or conclusions, they attained F1-measures of 68% for premises and 74% for conclusions (see Section 4.4.4).

The researchers examined 98 sentences that were misclassified as argumentative or non-argumentative propositions. They determined that 21% of the errors could have been classified correctly if the previous discourse content could be taken into account. Another 47% of the errors involved textual cues that can indicate arguments but turned out to be ambiguous. These included modal verbs like "should," the word "but," and the adverb "more." Some remaining errors occurred where reasoning steps were left implicit or where CSK would be needed to detect the argument.

10.3.4. *Argument Grammar for Discourse Tree Structure*

Finally, the authors experimented with whether a program could extract some of the discourse structure of an argument directly from a document. They represented argument discourse structure as a tree of argument triples. Each triple comprises a root node to which a premise leaf node and a conclusion leaf node are attached by support links. The root node of one argument triple can be attached to that of another in a chain of reasoning.

They removed 10 of the ECHR cases from the evaluation and manually constructed a set of rules for identifying and linking triples and thus constructing an argument's discourse structure. This set of rules is a kind of grammar for detecting argumentation structure and classifying propositions in the structure.

The authors evaluated the grammar by applying it to parse the texts of the remaining ECHR documents and detecting their argumentation structures. The argument trees output by the argument grammar were manually compared to the structures identified by the human annotators in terms of whether all the argumentative information is included, the individual arguments are well-formed, and the connections between arguments are correct.

Using the grammar for parsing the texts from the ECHR corpus, the authors obtained about 60% accuracy in detecting the argumentation structures. The

Conclusion: For these reasons, the Commission ... declares the
application admissible, without prejudging the merits.
> *Premise*:
>> *Conclusion*: It follows that the application cannot be dismissed
>> as manifestly ill-founded.
>>> *Premise*: It considers that the applicant's complaints raise
>>> serious issues of fact and law under the convention ...
>>> which should depend on an examination of the merits.
>>> *Premise*: The Commission has taken cognizance of the
>>> submissions of the parties.
>> *Conclusion*: In these circumstances, the Commission finds that
>> the application cannot be declared inadmissible for non-
>> exhaustion of domestic remedies.
>>> *Premise*: The Commission recalls that article Art. X of the
>>> Convention only requires the exhaustion of such
>>> remedies which relate to the breaches of the
>>> convention alleged and ... can provide ... redress.
>>> *Premise*: The Commission notes that in the context of the
>>> section powers the secretary has a very wide discretion.
>>> *Premise*: The Commission recalls that in the case of
>>> *Temple v. the United Kingdom* ... the Commission held
>>> that recourse to a purely discretionary power ... did not
>>> constitute and effective domestic remedy.

FIGURE 10.1. Excerpt of argument tree structure extracted automatically from a case (see Moens et al., 2007, Fig. 5)

structures maintained an F1-measure of about 70% in classifying premises and conclusions.

Figure 10.1 illustrates an excerpt of the tree structure extracted automatically from the text of a regulatory case by the argument grammar (Mochales and Moens, 2011, p. 19). The Commission's overall conclusion is at the top. It is supported by two arguments, each represented by a conclusion followed by premises: two premises support the first argument and three premises support the second.

Such automatically generated argument structures are useful. They can effectively summarize the arguments in a complex legal document in terms of the main issues, positions and arguments, and the supporting evidence. In order to determine if a document would be relevant and useful in making a new argument in another scenario, however, a program would need more information about what the premises and conclusions mean, and about the kinds of argument schemes that are being used.

TABLE 10.1. *Some argument schemes annotated automatically (Feng and Hirst, 2011)*

Argument scheme Argument from:	Meaning	Scheme-specific features (excerpts)	Best average accuracy of classification (%)
Example	Case *a* has property F and also property G. Therefore, generally, if *x* has property F, then it also has property G.	phrases including *for example, such as, for instance*	90.6
Cause to effect	Generally, if A occurs, then B will occur. In this case, A occurs. Therefore, in this case, B will occur.	phrases including *result, related to, lead to*	70.4
Goal to means	I have a goal G. Carrying out action A is a means to realize G. Therefore, I ought (practically speaking) to carry out this action A.	phrases including *want, aim, objective*; four modal verbs: *should, could, must, need*	90.8
Consequences	If A is (is not) brought about, good (bad) consequences will (will not) plausibly occur. Therefore, A should (should not) be brought about.	counts of positive and negative propositions in the conclusion and premises	62.9
Verbal classification	*a* has a property F. For all *x*, if *x* has property F, then *x* can be classified as having property G. Therefore, *a* has property G.	maximal similarity between the central word pairs extracted from the conclusion and the premise; counts of copula (e.g., an *a* is F), expletive (e.g., there are, it is), and negative modifier (e.g., not an F) dependency relations returned by the parser	63.2

10.3.5. *Identifying Instances of Argument Schemes*

Building on the work of Mochales and Moens (2011) and Feng and Hirst (2011) automatically identified instances of argument schemes in texts from the online AraucariaDB corpus, which, as noted above, contains some legal cases. The researchers assumed that argument components such as propositions and conclusions had been annotated successfully using the above techniques. They focused on the task of annotating five kinds of argument schemes, shown in Table 10.1.

The argument schemes in Table 10.1 are similar to those used in law. They are all related to VJAP's schemes modeling arguing from an analogous legal case (see Section 5.7.3). The cited case is used as an example that shares a property with the current problem, namely that a particular trade-off in underlying values will result or be avoided if they are decided in the same way, that is, if they are both classified as instances of a particular intermediate legal concept.

In order to annotate argument schemes, Feng and Hirst (2011) identified sets of general and scheme-specific text features. The general features include location of the conclusion in the text and relative positions and length of premises and conclusion. Some of the scheme-specific features are shown in Table 10.1 including characteristic phrases or linguistic constructions.

They employed a decision tree algorithm (Section 4.3.1) to perform the classifications based on these features, namely C4.5 (Quinlan, 2004) as implemented in the Weka package (Machine Learning Group at the University of Waikato, 2015). The last column in Table 10.1 shows a small portion of the results reported in Feng and Hirst (2011, p. 992), specifically, the best average accuracy of classifying an argument as an instance of the target scheme of interest or as other.

The authors attributed the lower performance for identifying arguments from consequences and from verbal classification to the relatively small number of training instances of these schemes and to the fact that they did not have as obvious cue phrases or patterns as the other schemes (Feng and Hirst, 2011, p. 993). In this respect, it may prove easier for ML to classify legal argument schemes. The frequent citations of cases and statements of legal rules in legal opinion texts may offer more obvious cues concerning argument schemes based on consequences illustrated in an analogous case or on classifications in terms of a legal rule concept.

For a computer program to be able to reason with arguments about cases or predict outcomes, more kinds of information need to be extracted. Beside marking up argumentative premises, conclusions, and schemes in legal case opinions, one would need to annotate substantive features such as factors that strengthen or weaken a legal argument and that can be used to predict case outcomes (Section 4.5.2). Fortunately, it is likely that programs *can* identify factors in case texts.

10.4. EXTRACTING ARGUMENT-RELATED LEGAL FACTORS

SMILE is a natural language interface to the IBP program described in Section 4.5.2 (Ashley and Brüninghaus, 2009). It serves as a "bridge" between natural language descriptions of problems and IBP's computational model for predicting case outcomes.

SMILE learns how to identify legal factors in brief textual descriptions of problems based on a training set of example sentences describing factors. As illustrated in Figure 10.2, one inputs a textual description of a problem involving trade secret law. SMILE represents it as a list of factors and inputs the list to IBP, which in turn predicts the outcome based on SMILE's input and explains the prediction.

10.4.1. *Three Representations for Learning from Text*

SMILE employed a training set of manually classified case texts. These were not the full texts of legal opinions, but *squibs*, brief narrative summaries of a case's important

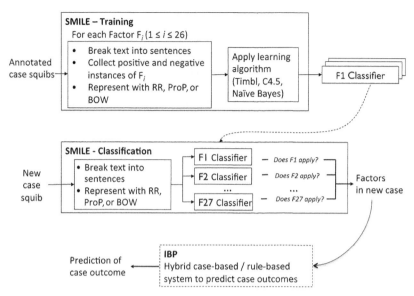

FIGURE 10.2. Overview of SMILE and IBP (see Ashley and Brüninghaus, 2009)

facts and of the court's holding, like those that first-year law students prepare in briefing cases.

In fact, law students, who were hired specially for the task, were instructed to include all facts that seemed important to the judge's decision. A guide apprised the squib writers about the 26 factors representing trade secret law problems. They were encouraged to identify and include fact descriptions in the opinions related to any applicable factors. In particular, they were asked to: (1) cut-and-paste fact descriptions in the case opinions related to particular factors, (2) incorporate them seamlessly into a readable narrative, and (3) insert delimiters into the narrative indicating the beginning and ending of the sentences associated with each factor. A researcher reviewed each squib for accuracy and reasonableness and provided feedback for revision.

In building SMILE, the researchers needed to address the important question of what makes a good representation for learning from text. For instance, take the sentence from a trade secret case that the reader has already seen in Section 1.4.4: "Newlin copied some files from ICM and brought them with him to DTI." This sentence, an example of Factor F7, Brought Tools, needs to be represented as a training instance from which a program can learn how to identify the factor.

The researchers employed three representations that incrementally take into account more semantic and syntactic information (Ashley and Brüninghaus, 2009).

The first representation is the simplest, a BOW representation, introduced in Section 7.5.2 on legal IR. The sentence is represented as a feature vector where the features are simply the words in the sentence (see Sections 7.5.2 and 8.3). A BOW representation of the above sentence is simply a list of the words in the sentence in alpha order: "and brought copied dti files from him icm newlin some them to with."

The second representation, Roles-Replaced (RR), is a feature vector similar to BOW but with an important difference. The features that are the names of the parties and instances of the product-related information are replaced with more general terms that identify their roles, like "plaintiff," "defendant," or "information." In RR, the above example of F_7 is represented as: "and brought copied defendant him information plaintiff some them to with."

The third representation, Propositional Patterns or ProP, is one in which sentences were parsed to identify "who did what." Specifically, the parsing identifies four syntactic relationships of interest: subject–verb, verb–object, verb–prepositional phrase, and verb–adjective. Then, party and product names are replaced with roles as in RR. Finally, synonyms are substituted for the nouns and verbs using a small ontology. Thus, the above sentence example of F_7 was represented as a feature vector in terms of the following features in a kind of nested alpha order:

((defendant copy) (person copy))

((copy information))

((copy_from person) (copy_from plaintiff))

((defendant bring) (person bring))

((bring them))

((bring_to defendant) (bring_to person))

(bring_with him)). (Ashley and Brüninghaus, 2009)

As explained in detail in Section 7.5.2, a program can compare sentences represented as feature vectors in BOW, RR, or ProP to determine their similarity. It computes the Euclidean distance between the end points of the vectors; the smaller the distance, the nearer, and more similar, the sentences.

In learning a classifier for each factor, the researchers applied three ML algorithms: a decision tree algorithm using C4.5 (Quinlan, 2004) (Section 4.3.1), Naïve Bayes as implemented in Rainbow (McCallum, 2004) (Section 10.3.3), and a k-nearest neighbor (k-NN) algorithm implemented in a program called Timbl (Daelemans et al., 2004) (Section 4.2).

The flow of the system is outlined in Figure 10.2. First, all texts are broken into sentences. The positive and negative instances for each factor Fi are collected. In each training case, all of the sentences from which it could be reasonably inferred that a legal factor applied in the case have been manually marked-up as positive instances of that factor. All the rest of the sentences were treated as negative instances of the factor. Then the sentences are represented as BOW, RR, or ProP to create a vector space of instances.

The first two ML algorithms, C4.5 and Naïve Bayes, learn a classifier for each factor in a training phase. In a subsequent phase, the program applies each factor's classifier to all of a problem's sentences represented as BOW, RR, or ProP.

The nearest neighbor algorithm works differently. In SMILE, the researchers chose $k = 1$. That is, each new sentence of a problem was classified in the same way as the one sentence most similar to it. Each problem sentence, represented as a feature vector with BOW, RR, or ProP, is added to each factor's vector space of positive and negative instances. The program finds the most similar sentence according to above-mentioned Euclidean similarity metric and assigns its class, as a positive or negative instance of the factor, to the new sentence. The program classifies the new case text as containing all factors for which it had at least one sentence that was a positive instance of the factor.

10.4.2. *How Well Did SMILE Work?*

In a LOO cross-validation experiment (see Section 4.4.3), the researchers determined that k-nearest neighbor with $k = 1$ worked better than the other two algorithms and used it to test which representation worked best. The RR and ProP representations achieved F1-measures averaged across factors of 26% and 28%, respectively. These F1-measures are low, but the RR and ProP representations each performed better than BOW, achieving higher average F1-measures (Section 4.4.4) and the difference was statistically significant. RR turned out better than ProP, but that difference was not significant. In other words, including background knowledge about roles and shallow NLP to identify "who did what" led to better classification-based text indexing (Ashley and Brüninghaus, 2009).

In order to assess the effect of SMILE's assignments on IBP's case-based predictions, the researchers conducted a second experiment. They compared IBP's case outcome prediction results for cases whose factors SMILE had assigned to a case text with those for the same cases but where the factors had been assigned by humans. The inputs to IBP were SMILE's outputs for the squib descriptions of cases. They also compared SMILE+IBP's predictions to a baseline of flipping a biased coin, where the probability that plaintiff wins equals the fraction of the number of cases plaintiff won over the number of cases in the collection. The accuracy of SMILE+IBP's predictions was 63%, lower than IBP's 92%, but higher than that of the biased-coin baseline, 49% (Ashley and Brüninghaus, 2009).

As far as we know, SMILE+IBP was the first AI & Law program to predict the outcomes of legal cases input as texts. SMILE analyzed textual descriptions of legal case facts and IBP predicted the outcome of the case using case-based reasoning and a logical model of legal issues. In addition, IBP then explained its analysis in terms of its hypothesis-testing approach. See Figure 4.6 for a sample of IBP's predictions.

With advances that will be described in Chapter 11, an improved version of the SMILE+IBP approach, combined with conceptual legal information retrieval, could help humans predict outcomes of problems, assess predictions, and construct arguments for and against the predictions.

10.4.3. *Annotating Factor Components*

In subsequent work, Wyner and Peters applied an annotation pipeline approach to identify information concerning trade secret legal factors in the full texts of legal decisions (Wyner and Peters, 2010, 2012). They developed a scheme for annotating fine-grained factor components with the GATE text annotation environment. These fine-grained components, sometimes called factoroids, comprised terms and phrases employed in the descriptions of trade secret legal factors in CATO (Section 3.3.2). The researchers augmented the list with synonyms of the terms drawn from Word-Net,[1] an online lexical database for English containing synonyms, definitions, and usage examples that functions as a kind of thesaurus.

For example, for the legal factor, F1 Disclosure-In-Negotiations (D), they manually identified terms including:

> plaintiff, disclose, product, information, negotiation, defendant, obtain, fair means, show, lack of interest, maintain, secrecy, joint venture, licensing agreement, sale of a business, acquire, knowledge, employment.

They expanded some of these concepts, such as "disclose" or "disclosure," with synonyms from WordNet:

> announce, betray, break, bring out, communicate, confide, disclose, discover, divulge, expose, give away, impart, inform, leak, let on, let out, make known, pass on, reveal, tell, announcement, betrayal, communication, confidence, disclosure, divulgance, exposure.

The combined lists served as a "gazetteer list" of related terms covered by a concept and useful for annotating new documents (Wyner and Peters, 2010, p. 40). Using GATE's rule-based annotation language called JAPE (like UIMA's RUTA language in Section 10.5.3), Wyners and Peters developed rules for marking up sentences according to the applicable concepts. When GATE encounters in a text words from the gazetteer list, it triggers a corresponding rule that annotates the sentence with the covering concept, for example, the type, "disclosure."

After the basic concepts of trade secret legal factors were marked up, compound rules annotated sentences in terms of more complex conceptual types such as DisclosureInformation and, ultimately, as legal factors including Disclosure-Information-Negotiation (Wyner and Peters, 2010, p. 41).

---

[1] https://wordnet.princeton.edu/

10.5. EXTRACTING FINDINGS OF FACT AND CITED LEGAL RULES

The LUIMA system extracted from legal case texts argument-related information about legal rules and their applications to facts (Grabmair et al., 2015). This was the first step in an experiment to assess the hypothesis of the LUIMA project: by semantically annotating case documents in terms of the roles propositions play in a legal argument and retrieving them based on the annotations, a program can outperform systems that rely on text matching and techniques for legal information retrieval.

This section describes how LUIMA uses rule-based and ML annotators to annotate case documents with semantic information including a sentence's roles. After that, Chapter 11 on conceptual IR explains how LUIMA uses this information to perform AR, that is, how LUIMA identifies and annotates semantic and argument-related information, and uses it to improve legal information retrieval (Ashley and Walker, 2013).

The work involves a subset of the V/IP Corpus and model of evidentiary legal argument described in Section 5.8. As explained, the DLF models the roles of propositions in a fact-finder's reasoning supporting his/her legal conclusions. For example, a proposition's role can be to state the legal rule for deciding an issue or to state a finding of fact that supports a conclusion that a condition of the legal rule is satisfied in a particular case.

10.5.1. *Applying the LUIMA Type System*

In the LUIMA project, the researchers applied their extended version of a UIMA type system to the legal domain. As introduced in Chapter 1 and elaborated in Section 6.8, a UIMA type system is a kind of ontology focused not only on the types of concepts and relations important in the domain application but also on how they are expressed in texts. LUIMA distinguishes between legal concepts and the different ways in which such concepts are mentioned (Grabmair et al., 2015).

As explained in Section 6.8, in the hierarchical LUIMA type system, higher-level types are composed from lower-level types. Specifically, a hierarchy of subsentence types supports the sentence-level annotations at the top of the hierarchy.

As shown in Table 6.6, Term type annotations, such as PlaintiffTerm, IllnessTerm, and VaccineTerm, are at the lowest level. The second level includes mention types, for example, a VaccinationMention, such as "MMR vaccination." Formulation types comprise the third level, for instance the LegalStandardFormulation, "the plaintiff bears the burden of showing that." The highest level are the legal sentence types illustrated in Table 6.7.

Three of these sentence-level annotation types will be in focus here:

1. LegalRuleSentence: states a legal rule in the abstract, without applying it to a particular case's facts.

2. EvidenceBasedFindingSentence: reports a fact-finder's finding on whether or not evidence in a particular case proves that a rule condition or conclusion has been satisfied.

3. CitationSentence: credits and refers to authoritative documents and sources, such as court decisions (cases), statutes, regulations, government documents, treaties, scholarly writing, or evidentiary documents.

Applying the LUIMA system's classification of higher levels, including sentence-level, depends on detecting the presence or absence of lower-level annotations represented as binary features. For example, an annotation rule detects the LegalStandardFormulation, "the Plaintiff bears the burden of showing that," and similar sentences by detecting a chain of specified lower level annotations: (1) a PlaintiffMention, (2) one of a class of expressions synonymous with "bear the burden," and (3) one of a class of verbs signaling evidence production (e.g., show, produce, establish, etc.) (Grabmair et al., 2015).

10.5.2. *Preparing Gold Standard Cases*

For purposes of an initial evaluation of the LUIMA hypothesis, the researchers selected 10 source cases from the V/IP Corpus introduced in Section 5.8. Referred to as the *gold standard cases*, these 10 cases had been employed in a previous study: *Cusati, Casey, Werderitsh, Stewart, Roper, Walton, Thomas, Meyers, Sawyer,* and *Wolfe* (Ashley and Walker, 2013).[2] The cases all dealt with the issue of proving, for purposes of the NVICP, that the vaccination caused the injury complained of by the petitioner, the injured party, or its representative. Petitioners won five of the cases; the respondent government won the remaining five.

The researchers adopted a systematic process for annotating the instances of LegalRuleSentences, EvidenceBasedFindingSentences, and CitationSentences in the gold standard case examples. The Research Laboratory for Law, Logic and Technology at Hofstra Law (LLT Lab) performed the annotations. Every effort was made

---

[2] *Cusati v. Secretary of Health and Human Services*, No. 99-0492V (Office of Special Masters, United States Court of Federal Claims, September 22, 2005); *Casey v. Secretary of Health and Human Services*, Office of Special Masters, No. 97-612V, December 12, 2005; *Werderitsh v. Secretary of the Department of Health and Human Services*, Office of Special Masters, No. 99-319V, May 26, 2006; *Stewart v. Secretary of the Department of Health and Human Services*, Office of Special Masters, No. 06-287V, March 19, 2007; *Roper v. Secretary of Health and Human Services*, No. 00-407V (Office of Special Masters, United States Court of Federal Claims, December 9, 2005); *Walton v. Secretary of the Department of Health and Human Services*, No. 04-503V (Office of Special Masters, United States Court of Federal Claims, April 30, 2007); *Thomas v. Secretary of the Department of Health and Human Services*, No. 01-645V (Office of Special Masters, United States Court of Federal Claims, January 23, 2007); *Meyers v. Secretary of the Department of Health and Human Services* , No. 04-1771V (Office of Special Masters, United States Court of Federal Claims, May 22, 2006); *Sawyer v. Secretary of the Department of Health and Human Services*, No. 03-2524V (Office of Special Masters, United States Court of Federal Claims, June 22, 2006); *Wolfe v. Secretary of Health and Human Services*, Office of Special Masters, No. 05-0878V, November 09, 2006.

to ensure that the process was reliable and accurate (Walker and Vazirova, 2014). A student researcher, trained in law and in the sentence-level type system, initially marked up each decision. A similarly trained law student then reviewed the initial annotations, any differences between their annotations were noted, and the first and second reviewers resolved all of those differences. Finally, a law professor (Walker) reviewed and certified them as the gold standard annotations. As described in Section 10.6.2, the LLT Lab utilizes and refines protocols to provide training and quality assurance (Walker et al., 2011).

10.5.3. *LUIMA-Annotate*

Of the LUIMA system's three modules, described in the next chapter, LUIMA-Annotate, depicted in Figure 10.3, is the module that annotates the texts of the cases employing two methods:

1. Rule-based subsentence annotation, in which a human manually constructs a grammar of annotation rules based, usually, on inspection of some examples.
2. ML, in which an ML algorithm automatically constructs, from a training set of human-annotated examples, a model that distinguishes positive and negative examples. This is similar to the predictive coding of Section 8.4.2.

When a document, say, from a CLIR service, is entered (at the left of Figure 10.3), the system must identify where one sentence ends and another begins. Sentence splitting occurs as an initial step in the Rule-Based Mention & Formulation Annotators.

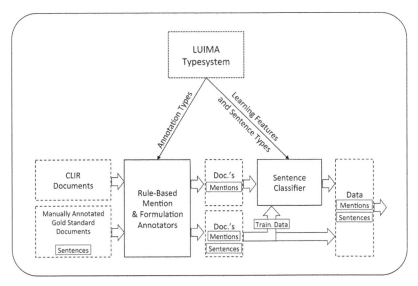

FIGURE 10.3. Schematic of LUIMA-Annotate (Grabmair et al., 2015)

Sentence splitting is an easy task for human readers but not necessarily straightforward for computers. Legal documents' ambiguous punctuation presents challenges for automated sentence splitters. For example, abbreviations and citations in legal documents employ periods (".") in ways other than to indicate the end of a sentence. A sentence splitter may interpret them erroneously as ending a sentence, and this will make subsequent ML less effective. The Lingpipe sentence splitter handles common phenomena related to the use of periods, for example, "Inc." for incorporated (Alias-i, 2008); the researchers added a module to handle law-specific uses of periods such as "v." for versus. Evaluating the module's effectiveness has been left for future work (Grabmair et al., 2015).

LUIMA-Annotate also marks up some presuppositional information. *Presuppositional information* includes factual and linguistic concepts and mentions related specifically to the regulated domain, whether it be vaccine injury, trade secret misappropriation, or some other domain (Ashley and Walker, 2013).

Specifically, LUIMA-Annotate identifies in the case texts such entities as:

— Terms: VaccineTerm, IllnessTerm, CausationTerm.
— Mentions: VaccineMention, which includes a VaccineAcronym coupled with a VaccineTerm ("MMR Vaccine"), VaccinationEventMention, Causation-Mention.
— Normalizations: VmNormalization, ImNormalization (that is, the normalized name of vaccine or illness mentioned in a sentence).

Since vaccines or illnesses may be expressed in a multitude of variations, acronyms, and abbreviations, standardized expressions or *normalizations* are included as part of the process of stemming and lemmatization (see Sections 8.3 and 9.3.2). Thus, the fact that a sentence is about "MMR vaccine" is represented in documents or queries in terms of a VaccineMention or VaccinationEvent Mention term, a normalized name for the vaccine mentioned, or the text of the mention, for example:

about:VaccineMention   or   about:VaccinationEventMention   or   vmNormalization:#mmr or content:"MMR vaccine." (Che et al., 2015)

In order to annotate citations, the researchers developed regular expressions (regex), character sequences that define search patterns for string matching patterns of different types of citations in legal documents including prior cases, statutory provisions, case files, and general references (Che et al., 2015).

Manually Constructed Subsentence Annotation Rules

The sentences are automatically annotated in terms of mentions and subsentence types. This annotation is performed by rules that have been programmed by hand in UIMA RUTA, a rule language designed especially for text matching to facilitate the rapid development of UIMA annotators.

One of the researchers who is also trained in law (Grabmair) developed some of the annotation rules based on intuitions about what would be useful across legal domains. He developed additional rules based on parts of three of the gold standard V/IP cases (*Roper, Cusati,* and *Thomas*). He manually extracted terms, mentions, and formulations from the three case texts, and constructed RUTA rules to extract them automatically. Then, he attempted to expand the scope of the rules to antic- ipate variations in wording and structure based on his intuitions. In constructing rules from the three cases, he did not consult the sentence-level annotations of the three documents prepared by the annotators of the gold standard cases. These precautions are taken so as not to "contaminate" the data or model by examin- ing data during system creation or training that will later be used in the evaluation (Grabmair et al., 2015).

As an example of a manually constructed rule of subsentence annotation, here is the rule (in RUTA) for annotating a LegalStandardFormulation:

IF (PlaintiffMention MustRelationTerm "also"? ("prove" | "show" | "establish"))
THEN
MARK(LegalStandardFormulation)

This rule means:

IF: the expression includes an instance of mentioning the plaintiff, an instance of a term expressing an obligation, an optional "also" and one of three alternative verbs THEN: annotate the expression as a LegalStandardFormulation.

For example, if the rule detects such a plaintiff mention, a term like "must," an "also" and, say, "show," it will annotate the sentence as expressing a legal standard.

At the current stage of LUIMA's development, the type system currently consists of 8 term types, 14 mention types, and 13 formulation types. The rule base com- prises 7 dictionary annotators (including vaccine abbreviations (Centers for Disease Control and Prevention, 2015)) and 49 rules for entities like StandardLegalFormu- lation, VaccineMention, ProofStandardMention, ProofStandardSatisfiedMention, and ProofStandardNotSatisfiedMention. Not all of these rules and types have been directly involved in the annotation process for the initial experiment, discussed below (Grabmair et al., 2015).

Machine Learned Sentence Annotators

LUIMA-Annotate employed ML for sentence annotations. The three classifications to be learned included whether a sentence was an instance of a (1) LegalRuleSen- tence, (2) EvidenceBasedFindingSentence, or (3) neither, that is "NotAnnotated," which was treated as a separate label for technical purposes. The dataset comprised 5,909 sentences, of which 82 were instances of EvidenceBasedFindingSentences, 227 were instances of LegalRuleSentences, and the remainder were NotAnnotated.

For purposes of ML, the texts of sentences were represented as feature vectors much as in the West History Project (Section 8.5.1) or like the Mochales and Moens work (Section 10.3) and SMILE (Section 10.4). In LUIMA, the feature vectors include *tf/idf* frequency information (see Section 6.4) for all possible word sequences up to four words in length contained in the sentence.

The researchers also tried enriching this vector representation of a sentence by adding features related to selected LUIMA subsentence types. Each added feature is a binary variable indicating if the sentence contains an expression that has been annotated as an instance of the particular type.

Here is an example of how a sample sentence has been represented for purposes of ML. The sentence is "Dr. Winston concluded that *petitioner* was suffering from *gastroparesis*, a disorder of delayed stomach emptying." Its feature vector includes *tf/idf* frequency information of all possible one-element ("Dr."), two-element ("Dr. Winston"), three-element ("Dr. Winston concluded"), and four-element sequences ("Dr. Winston concluded that"). Since the italicized terms are annotated as PlaintiffTerm and IllnessTerm, respectively, the vector also includes values of 1 for each of PlaintiffTerm and IllnessTerm (Grabmair et al., 2015).

This sentence from the *Roper* decision, one of the gold standard cases, was manually annotated as an EvidenceSentence, not as an EvidenceBasedFindingSentence, because it reported a conclusion, not of the Special Master, but of Dr. Winston, an expert witness. As such, it would be treated as NotAnnotated for purposes of this ML exercise, in which the three classifiers did not include EvidenceSentences (a task for future work).

As shown at the bottom left of Figure 10.3, the *Roper* decision and the other gold standard cases were manually annotated for the three sentence types, LegalRuleSentence, EvidenceBasedFindingSentence, and NotAnnotated, and input to LUIMA-Annotate. After subsentence mention and formulation annotation rules were applied, the cases were treated as data for training the Sentence Classifier (Grabmair et al., 2015).

10.5.4. *Evaluating LUIMA-Annotate*

The researchers evaluated how well LUIMA-Annotate performed. In particular, the experiment tested how well it assigned two sentence-level annotations, LegalRuleSentence and EvidenceBasedFindingSentence, to 10 gold standard cases.

The experiment was run as a LOO cross validation (see Section 4.4.3). In other words, there were 10 runs, one run for each gold standard case. In each run, a different annotated gold standard document's sentences served as the test set; the other nine documents' sentences were used as training data. Annotated sentences served as positive examples of their annotations; unannotated sentences were negative examples.

Values for four measures, precision, recall, accuracy, and F1-measure (defined in Section 4.4.4), were computed for every run and averaged (see Table 10.2). Three

TABLE 10.2. *Sentence classification performance measurements (best values printed in boldface) (Grabmair et al., 2015)*

ML Algorithm + additional feature	Accuracy	Precision	Recall	Macro–F
Naive Bayes	0.88	0.15	**0.75**	0.14
Naive Bayes + Type	0.89	0.16	**0.75**	0.15
Decision Tree	**0.97**	0.53	0.28	0.23
Decision Tree + Type	**0.97**	0.53	0.29	0.23
Log. Regression	0.96	**0.66**	0.38	**0.31**
Log. Regression + Type	0.96	**0.66**	0.38	**0.31**

ML algorithms, naïve Bayes (Section 10.3.3), logistic regression (Section 10.3.3), and decision trees (Section 4.3.1), were applied (using the Stanford Parser (Finkel et al., 2003-2014), and the Weka package, a repository of data-mining software tools (Machine Learning Group at the University of Waikato, 2015)).

Since logistic regression worked best of the three ML algorithms, it was selected for sentence-level annotation of a larger pool of other documents in the main system pipeline (as described in Section 11.4) (Grabmair et al., 2015).

The researchers also tested whether the addition of subsentence types to *n*-grams in the sentence representation improved performance, for example, the values of 1 for PlaintiffTerm and IllnessTerm in the above example. The additional features did not improve performance. Compare, for instance, Log. Regression and Log. Regression + Type in Table 10.2. Probably the majority of rule annotator patterns such as LegalStandardFormulation is about the same length as a four element *n*-gram, so their contribution was minimal (Grabmair et al., 2015).

As discussed in Chapter 11, LUIMA annotations can improve legal information retrieval.

10.6. ANNOTATION OF TRAINING DATA

Efforts to extract argument-related information from case texts depend on developing high-quality training sets. For this purpose, it will become increasingly important to create sets of manually annotated documents to use as a gold standard. The manually annotated documents can be used as data both for training and assessing the automated annotators.

Given the size of most corpora, humans will still need to mark up large numbers of documents even though only a fraction of the corpus needs to be annotated manually.

Ideally, there will be enough annotated data to reserve some as an untouched test set with which to assess the ML model trained on the remainder. If not, the separation between training and test sets can be enforced via a LOO or *k*-fold cross validation.

Aside from the sheer number of annotated documents required for a conclusive experiment or stable system, the annotations also need to be of sufficient quality. Obtaining good manual annotations requires assigning each text to multiple humans to annotate independently and comparing their annotations to see the extent to which they agree, that is, to measure the *reliability* of their annotations. In instances where the annotators differ, one can either account for the disagreement in the design of the experiment or resolve the conflict according to some method. If humans cannot agree on the annotations, for instance, if the meaning of the label is too ambiguous, then a ML program will not be able to learn how to apply the label, either. In this sense, human annotator reliability imposes an upper limit on the success of automated ML techniques.

A computer-supported environment can support teams of people in marking up texts. It implements a systematic procedure to guide and coordinate the annotators' efforts and monitors their reliability.

10.6.1. *Annotation in IBM Debater*

The IBM Debater team has developed a systematic approach to manually annotating training sets so that ML can extract information from texts (Levy et al., 2014).

As mentioned in Chapter 1, Debater extracts argument claims pro and con a topic from Wikipedia articles and the supporting evidence. More specifically, it detects context-dependent claims (CDC), general, concise statements that directly support or contest the given topic. It also detects context-dependent evidence (CDE), a text segment that directly supports a CDC in the context of a given topic (Aharoni et al., 2014a). In detecting claims, Debater undertakes a task similar to that of Mochales and Moens (2011), but not yet with legal texts.

Given a topic and relevant articles, a sentence component selects the 200 best sentences. A boundaries component delimits the candidate claim in each sentence. Using sentence and boundary scores, a ranking component then selects the 50 best candidate CDCs. Like LUIMA, the Debater project employs ML but Debater does so at each of the three steps: sentence selection, setting boundaries, and ranking candidates.

Debater's ML depends on human annotators' ability to perform high-quality annotation of a training set of documents. The annotators are asked to label text fragments as CDCs if and only if they satisfy the following constraints. The text fragment should:

– *Strength*: Express strong content that directly supports/contests the topic.
– *Generality*: Express general content that deals with a relatively broad idea.
– *Phrasing*: Make a grammatically correct and semantically coherent statement.
– *Text spirit*: Keep the spirit of the original text.
– *Topic unity*: Deal with one topic, or at most two related topics (Aharoni et al., 2014a).

The Debater team has developed a systematic way to organize the human annotation effort to maximize reliability. As noted, reliability in annotation refers to the level of agreement of independent (usually) human coders in assigning a label to the same piece of text.

A standard measure of labelers' agreement is Cohen's kappa (κ) coefficient (Cohen, 1960). The Cohen's kappa statistic is a value between 0 and 1 that measures the agreement actually observed among raters (P) less the agreement that would be expected if it were left strictly to chance (Pe) (see Breaux, 2009). It is expressed by the formula:

$$\kappa = (P - Pe)/(1 - Pe) \qquad (10.1)$$

The human coders, who were primarily graduate students, were paid for their work. They used an online annotation environment that enabled the team managers to monitor the labelers' performance for efficiency and accuracy of coding relative to that of their peer labelers. Team managers replaced inefficient or inaccurate coders as necessary.

Given a debate topic, five human labelers searched Wikipedia independently for articles they believe contain CDCs. Five labelers then read each of the selected articles. Working independently they detected 1,491 candidate CDCs. Five labelers then examined each of the candidate CDCs, independently deciding to confirm or reject the candidate. Candidate CDCs were accepted only if confirmed by at least three labelers.

The Debater team adapted the multi-rater agreement measure to deal with the fact that no two labelers work on all of the same tasks. They took the average measure of agreement over all of pairs of annotators for each pair who worked together on 100 or more CDCs/CDEs (Aharoni et al., 2014a, p. 67).

The team reported the following results. For 32 topics, 326 Wikipedia articles were labeled, yielding 976 CDCs. On average, the labeling process yielded 30 CDCs per Topic. (On average, only 2 out of 100 sentences include a CDC.) The average kappa agreement between pairs of labelers, a measure of the reliability of the human annotators, was 0.39. The average kappa for CDEs was 0.4. This does not suggest a high level of agreement. As noted, in natural language applications of ML, the level of human coder reliability is an upper bound on the performance of the machine-learned classifier.

Nevertheless, the levels of agreement achieved by the Debater team were remarkable given the complexity of the labeling task and the ill-definedness of the standards defining the labels, namely CDC and CDE. In particular, three of the above labeling criteria, namely strength, generality, and text spirit, are somewhat subjective. The systematic annotation process helped to ensure that the resulting CDCs correspond to claims naturally usable in discussing the topic (Aharoni et al., 2014a).

10.6.2. *Annotation Protocols*

In annotating LUIMA sentence types according to the DLF, Walker's approach at Hofstra's LLT Lab (see Sections 5.8, 6.8, and 10.5.2) is to develop and refine protocols at the same time that researchers annotate gold standard documents (Walker, 2011; Walker and Vazirova, 2014).

Protocols provide criteria and examples that specify linguistic or logical cues for human annotators to use in making annotations. They are developed empirically, as new documents are marked up, so that they will include linguistic variations discovered during the process and provide guidance for unusual patterns. They are useful both for training annotators and quality assurance. Finished protocols also provide refined definitions for the types, to the extent that they specify their proper use. They also provide insights into the construction of rule-based programming for automatic annotators.

10.6.3. *Computer-Supported Annotation Environments*

IBM's Debater annotation environment and process are as yet not available to outsiders. IBM's BlueMix services, described in Chapter 1, provide support for annotation, although subject to license. Thus, alternative open-source annotation environments are important.

The UIMA comes equipped with a developer's toolbox software including a complex annotation interface. Figure 10.4 shows the UIMA annotation environment equipped for annotating the nine LUIMA sentence types discussed above. Those annotations were performed by law students under the supervision of a computer-literate law professor with occasional technical assistance from a competent graduate

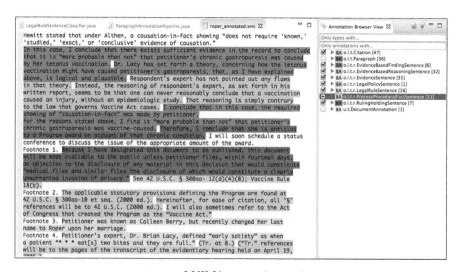

FIGURE 10.4. LUIMA annotation environment

student. Presumably, as the importance of text annotation environments grows, even more user-friendly interfaces compatible with UIMA or any successor framework will be developed.

The GATE annotation environment, a text processing pipeline architecture and alternative to UIMA, was employed in topic labeling in connection with Debater (Aharoni et al., 2014a). GATE Teamware, a web-based tool, supports the roles of annotators, editors, and managers in large-scale, multi-annotator projects. It prepares texts for manual annotation by marking up terms of lower-level types using a core type system of linguistic metadata. Expert editors can use Teamware to supervise nonspecialist annotators and to curate annotated documents. It maintains statistics about the annotation process tasks such as the amount of time annotators spend per document, the percentage of documents they complete, and other measures useful in implementing the kind of systematic process employed in IBM Debater.

Law student and attorney volunteers used GATE Teamware to annotate trade secret cases in terms of factors and factor components (Section 10.4.3) (Wyner and Peters, 2010, 2012). Figure 10.5 illustrates the markup of a case excerpt in the Teamware environment. The geographically dispersed annotators worked remotely via the Internet. The tool does not require local installation and stores data in a central repository.

Significantly, UIMA and GATE are interoperable, although it remains to be seen how effectively GATE Teamware and UIMA can be joined.

WebAnno, another browser-based tool, also supports managing multiple annotators, monitoring inter-annotator agreement, and curating data (Yimam et al., 2013). The user interface is well-organized, uncluttered, and relatively easy to use. Figure 10.6 illustrates the markup of trade secret factors in the *Mason* case (Figure 3.2) by a law student performed in an ongoing project using the WebAnno environment via a web browser. The integration of the labels and text helps to make

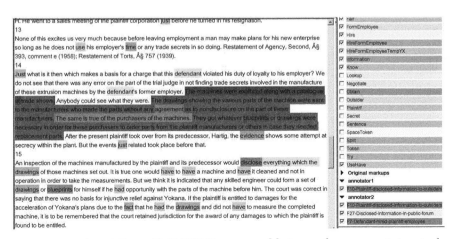

FIGURE 10.5. Annotation with GATE Teamware of factors and components in a trade secret case (Wyner and Peters, 2010)

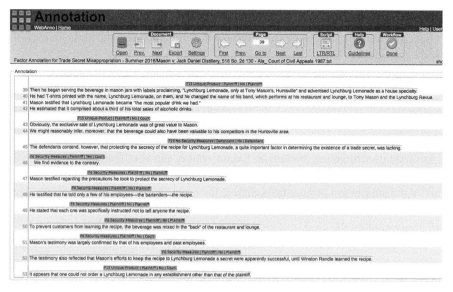

FIGURE 10.6. WebAnno annotation of trade secret factors in the *Mason* case (see Yimam et al., 2013)

the interface more intelligible to nontechnical personnel. Walker and the law students in Hofstra's LLT Lab are using WebAnno to markup Veteran disability cases in terms of the DLF and LUIMA sentence types (see Sections 5.8, 6.8, and 10.5.2).

WebAnno has been designed to connect easily to crowdsourcing platforms so that simpler annotation tasks could be handled by large numbers of unskilled annotators (Yimam et al., 2013). Some advantages and challenges of crowdsourced annotation are discussed in Section 12.5.2.

One of the main reasons for extracting information from case texts is to improve legal information retrieval, the topic of the next chapter.

PART III

Connecting Computational Reasoning Models and Legal Texts

11

Conceptual Legal Information Retrieval for
Cognitive Computing

11.1. INTRODUCTION

The LUIMA architecture, described in this chapter, takes Part II's techniques for automating conceptual markup of documents and for extracting information from legal case texts and integrates them into a prototype system for conceptual legal information retrieval. The system comprises modules for automatic subsentence level annotation, ML-based sentence annotation, basic retrieval using a full-text information retrieval system, and a ML-based reranking of the retrieved documents. The chapter explains how to evaluate such a system objectively and how to assess any contribution it makes to the full-text legal information system.

In particular, the chapter presents evidence supporting the LUIMA hypothesis, set forth in Section 10.5, that AR is feasible. By semantically annotating documents with argument role information and retrieving them based on the annotations, one *can* outperform current systems that rely on text matching and current techniques for legal information retrieval (Grabmair et al., 2015).

For example, as introduced in Section 6.8 and elaborated here in more detail, an attorney seeking cases on whether hepatitis B vaccine can cause multiple sclerosis or MS, may have two different questions in mind. He may want to know what the relevant legal rule is, as in (Q1) "What is the rule for establishing causation between a vaccine and an injury?" Alternatively, the attorney may seek cases applying the rule given particular facts, as in (Q2) "Have there been cases where it was held that hepatitis B vaccine can cause MS?" Depending on the user's reason underlying the query, different cases would be more responsive. For instance, consider the following sentences from the *Werderitsh*[1] decision:

S1: In Althen, the Federal Circuit quoted its opinion in *Grant v. Secretary of HHS*, 956 F. 2d 1144, 1148 (Fed. Cir. 1992): A persuasive medical theory is demonstrated

---

[1] *Werderitsh v. Secretary of the Department of Health and Human Services*, Office of Special Masters, No. 99-319V, May 26, 2006.

by "proof of a logical sequence of cause and effect showing that the vaccination was the reason for the injury[,]" the logical sequence being supported by "reputable medical or scientific explanation[,]" i.e., "evidence in the form of scientific studies or expert medical testimony[.]"

S2: "The undersigned holds that hepatitis B vaccine caused or significantly aggravated petitioner's MS."

S3: "The undersigned concludes that the medical theory causally connecting the vaccinations and petitioner's injury is that Mrs. Werderitsh, who is genetically predisposed to developing MS, was exposed to the environmental antigen of two hepatitis B vaccinations, producing inflammation, self antigens, and a sufficient number of T-cells to have an autoimmune reaction later diagnosed as MS."

All three deal with vaccines causing injuries, but sentences that satisfy one type of query do not necessarily satisfy the other. Sentences that play the role of stating the rule of causation will be more relevant to the first query; those that state a judge's findings of facts involving the vaccine's causing a particular injury will be more relevant to the latter.

In this example, S1 is more responsive to Q1; it states a legal rule for establishing causation between a vaccine and a subsequent injury. Given Q1, in order to recognize S1 as more relevant, a system would need to go beyond just matching words. It must recognize the *concepts* of a legal rule, namely vaccinations, causation, and injury. In S1, the vaccination is said to be "the reason for" the injury; a system would need to recognize that as another way of referring to, or *mentioning*, the concept of causation. Also, S1 mentions demonstrating a medical theory "by proof of a logical sequence of cause and effect." In the absence of a specific mention of "rule" or "standard," the system would need to recognize this formulation and the Court of Appeals citations as indicating that the sentence states a legal rule or standard. Although S1 explicitly mentions "vaccination" and "injury," a system would also need to recognize these concepts in mentions of "immunization" and "adverse medical condition," which mean the same thing and which a court might have used to paraphrase the requirement. S2 and S3, on the other hand, are responsive to Q2 in that they both refer to "hepatitis B vaccine," "cause," and "MS." They both report holdings or conclusions of the Special Master concerning the application of the legal rule to facts involving hepatitis B causing MS.

Currently, the LUIMA system *can* distinguish between sentences that present the rule and sentences that state findings of fact, that is, it can distinguish between S1 and S2 or S3. This chapter explains how the researchers integrated the LUIMA annotation approach, described in Section 10.5.3, with an information retrieval system and used this kind of argument-related information, extracted from the texts of cases retrieved by a legal IR system, to rerank the cases in a manner that improved the quality of the retrieval.

The chapter also explores how to extend the LUIMA type system to enable a range of conceptual queries not possible with current legal information systems. It discusses techniques and some remaining challenges for annotating documents in terms of the extended system of types. The chapter concludes with a discussion of alternative network-based techniques for realizing the promise of conceptual legal information retrieval.

Questions answered in this chapter include: What is AR and how can it improve legal information retrieval? Why integrate a text annotation pipeline and an information retrieval system, and how can they be integrated? What roles does ML play in the prototype for conceptual legal information retrieval? How close are we to achieving robust conceptual legal information retrieval?

11.2. STATE OF THE ART IN CONCEPTUAL LEGAL IR

Mainstream legal informational retrieval systems like LexisNexis and WN have already achieved a measure of conceptual legal information retrieval (see Section 7.7). LexisNexis provides a conceptual entree into the cases based on a network of "legal issues" mined from a case law database. Each issue corresponds to a proposition for which the case can be cited. WN's sophisticated reranking function takes into account conceptual information based on annotations and citation networks generated by experts.

Both legal IR providers report using ML for improving relevance assessment, from automatically extracted case treatment histories (Section 8.5.3) to learning legal topic-related feature weights for reranking (Section 7.7) to distinguishing fact passages from legal discussions (Section 8.6).

AI & Law researchers have tried a variety of approaches to apply argument-related information, automatically extracted from cases as described in Chapter 10, in order to improve legal IR.

Some of the work addresses conceptually indexing the cases or generating argument-focused summaries. For example, researchers applied the automatically extracted offenses raised and legal principles applied in criminal cases for indexing the cases and generating focused summaries (Uyttendaele et al., 1998). A program applied the rhetorical roles automatically assigned to case sentences based on manually annotated decisions in Saravanan and Ravindran (2010) to create structured head notes summarizing aspects of the cases.

Other work focuses more directly on using the argument-related information for retrieval. That was the goal of Dick and Hirst (1991) in using an argument scheme to represent cases. The system in Mimouni et al. (2014) retrieved documents based on queries containing conceptual descriptors and cross-references between documents. In a nonlegal context, the IBM Debater system employed the topic-relevant claims it detected to select and rank the most relevant articles with which to construct arguments (Levy et al., 2014).

11.3. LUIMA ARCHITECTURE

In order to employ argument-related information in legal information retrieval, the architecture of the LUIMA system, illustrated in Figure 11.1, links the text annotation pipeline LUIMA-Annotate with an information retrieval system, comprising two components, LUIMA-Search and LUIMA-Rerank.

LUIMA-Search consists of a search engine and case database. Given a query, it retrieves and ranks the most responsive documents and passes them along to the next component. LUIMA-Rerank reorders the documents in terms of relevance based on a model learned from true rankings in the training set and semantic features extracted from the query and search engine ranking. The evaluation described below compares the reranked list of documents with that of a CLIR system.

11.3.1. *LUIMA-Search*

Consider how a CLIR system, like those discussed in Section 7.4, would deal with the following query:

finding or conclusion that Hepatitis B vaccine can cause multiple sclerosis or MS.

Like Q2 in the Introduction (Section 11.1), this is a query for which sentences S2 and S3 would be relevant. In the experiment described below, it was 1 of 11 baseline queries given to the CLIR system, namely Q9 in Table 11.1.

An exclusively text-based search engine treats words like "finding" and "conclusion" as additional (and very common) keywords. It does not understand that the query means, in effect, "Retrieve all sentences containing a finding or conclusion that a Hepatitis B vaccination causes multiple sclerosis or MS." Even if a CLIR understood the query in the intended sense, it could not adequately address it because it does not know which sentences in the cases in its database are a court's findings or conclusions.

A legal IR system *should* be able to interpret queries in the way humans intend them, but there is as yet no general way to accomplish this feat. LUIMA-Search is a step toward enabling a legal IR system to do so. In effect, it interprets the words as legal concepts and the query as specifying constraints about the targeted roles of similar sentences in the sought-for case documents.

Figure 11.2 (top) shows the LUIMA-Search version of the above query. It includes not only the targeted text but also concept mentions and argument role information. It specifies the targeted role that some similar sentences in the cases to be retrieved should play, for instance, as a sentence stating a legal rule or, here, as one reporting an evidence-based finding of fact (Grabmair et al., 2015). This condition is specified by "type: EvidenceBasedFindingSentence." Other conditions include various constraints on what the sentence is about, as specified by mention types such as VaccineMention, VaccinationEventMention, CausationMention, or IllnessMention, or as field contents matching specified tokens including "Hepatitis B vaccine,"

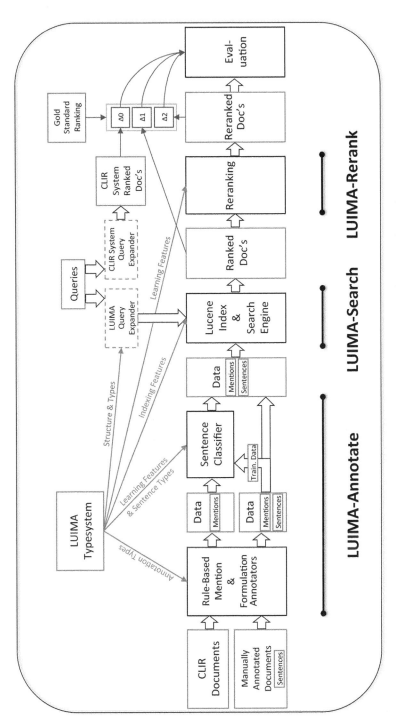

FIGURE 11.1. LUIMA pipeline architecture (Grabmair et al., 2015)

TABLE 11.1. *Eleven queries submitted to CLIR system (Grabmair et al., 2015)*

	Query	Source case name (date) Winner [Althen 1 issue]	# Cases returned by CLIR system	# Cases expert deemed relevant in CLIR system's top 30	Source case rank in CLIR system's top 30
Q1	Legal rule about vaccines causing injury	NA	157	25/30	NA
Q2	Finding or conclusion that MMR vaccine causes intractable seizure disorder	Cusati (9/22/05) Pet. [Pet.]	76	9/30	11th
Q3	Finding or conclusion that Tetanus vaccine causes chronic gastroparesis	Roper (12/9/05) Pet. [Pet.]	75	1/30	21st
Q4	Finding or conclusion that DTaP vaccine causes diabetes	Meyers (5/22/06) Govt. [Govt.]	75	1/30	9th
Q5	Finding or conclusion that Tetanus vaccine causes hand, wrist, and arm injuries	Sawyer (6/22/06) Govt. [Govt.]	75	0/30	not in top 30 (37th)
Q6	Finding or conclusion that Hepatitis A vaccine can cause cerebellar ataxia	Stewart (3/19/07) Pet. [Pet.]	75	1/30	7th
Q7	Finding or conclusion that DPT vaccine can cause acute encephalopathy and death	Thomas (1/23/07) Govt. [Govt.]	78	22/30	not in top 30
Q8	Finding or conclusion that MMR vaccine can cause myocarditis	Walton (4/30/07) Govt. [Govt.]	76	2/40	16th
Q9	Finding or conclusion that Hepatitis B vaccine can cause multiple sclerosis or MS	Werderitsh (5/26/06) Pet. [Pet.]	77	17/30	1st
Q10	Finding or conclusion that Hepatitis B vaccine can cause intractable seizure disorder	Wolfe (11/9/06) Govt. [Govt.]	75	4/30	22nd
Q11	Finding or conclusion that Varicella vaccine can cause encephalomyeloneuritis	Casey (12/12/05) Pet. [Pet.]	75	1/30	7th

Query

type:	EvidenceBasedFindingSentence *or*
about:	VaccineMention *or*
about:	VaccinationEventMention *or*
content:	"Hepatits B vaccine" *or*
about:	CausationMention *or*
about:	IllnessMention *or*
content:	"multiple sclerosis" "MS"

Sentence in database

```
<doc>
    <field name="id"> 21 Cl.Ct. 651:-210032610 </field>
    <field name="title"> Carter v. Secretary of Dept. of Health and Human Services </field>
    <field name="content"> Therefore, the petitioner was required to prove to the Special
        Master by a preponderance of the evidence that the rubella vaccine inoculation
        was the cause in-fact of her JRA. </field>
    <field name="level"> sentence </field>
    <field name="type"> LegalRuleSentence </field>
    <field name="about"> CausationTerm CausationMention PlaintiffTerm VaccineTerm
        VaccineMention </field>
</doc>
```

FIGURE 11.2. LUIMA-Search: sample query (top) and sentence entry in Lucene database index (bottom)

"multiple sclerosis," or "MS." Thus, a LUIMA-Search query appears to better capture the intended meaning of the query text.

Recall from Section 10.5.3 that LUIMA-Annotate generates semantic information about the sentence including the sentence type and other argument-related data. In the next step of an AR system, this semantic information should be used in the system's response to a query. The semantic markup of a sentence is stored in a database along with the sentence's plain text. In this way, the database can score each retrieved sentence on the basis of both a text match with the query as well as co-occurring semantic concepts. In LUIMA, this was implemented with code from the open-source Apache Lucene information retrieval software library.

The Lucene database stores the documents and indexes them in an inverted index (see Section 7.4). In particular, it stores sentences, which are identified as coming from particular legal decisions. Figure 11.2 (bottom) illustrates a sample sentence entry in the Lucene DB index. Each entry represents the text of a sentence in the entry's "content" field, as well as information about the sentence's argument role in the document, that is, the sentence-level type, the concepts mentioned, and information about its content, in terms of instances of its subsentence-level types. For instance, in the given sentence, the level is "sentence," the type is "Legal-RuleSentence," and the sentence is about "CausationTerm, CausationMention, PlaintiffTerm, VaccineTerm, VaccineMention."

The field identifiers in the LUIMA-Search query (Figure 11.2 (top)) including "type:," "about:," and "content:" correspond to the ones in the example sentence representation (Figure 11.2 (bottom)). LUIMA-Search compares the field entries in a given query with those in the database index and retrieves all sentences responsive to the query's constraints. As illustrated in Figure 11.2, a LUIMA-Search query treats all of the specified conditions as connected by logical OR terms. Ideally, given the intended meaning of the query, the connectors should be ANDs in order to identify documents that satisfy all of a user's desired specifications. Given the limited data in the corpus, however, an accommodation was necessary. By using disjunction to relax the constraints, Lucene can retrieve sentences that are only partial matches.

Having retrieved sentences, LUIMA-Search ranks them according to the number of query conditions that are satisfied using each sentence's Lucene score according to Apache Lucene's built-in scoring system. The score measures a retrieved sentence's degree of match relative to the query using term frequency vectors to assess similarity (Białecki et al., 2012). LUIMA-Search ranks documents in terms of the number of responsive sentences retrieved from each document.

11.3.2. *Reranking Documents with LUIMA-Rerank*

As shown in the LUIMA pipeline diagram (Figure 11.1), LUIMA-Search passes the documents it retrieves to the third module, LUIMA-Rerank, which learns how to *rerank* documents to maximize their responsiveness to the user's query (Grabmair et al., 2015).

In Section 7.7, we encountered reranking in state-of-the-art legal information retrieval systems like WN. A CLIR system's retrieval module alone may not produce the best ranking by itself. Reranking employs evidence derived from frequency information in the documents' texts, expert-generated annotations, citation networks, and documents' popularity in previous queries. The ranking function is optimized using ML to determine the weights to ascribe to the different features.

Here, too, the goal of reranking is to learn feature weights with which to reorder LUIMA-Search results to bring relevant results to the top. LUIMA-Rerank employs features that capture argument-related information. It learns weights for the following document features:

- *Sentence count*: the number of responsive sentences in a given document (the same number that LUIMA-Search uses to compute the initial ranking).
- *Maximum Lucene score*: Highest Lucene score of all of the sentences in the given document.
- *VSS*: Maximum cosine VSS value of the "about" fields of all sentences in a given document and the query (see Section 7.5.2).

As explained in the previous section, all of these features take into account argument-related information captured by the sentence-level and subsentence-level annotations. In particular, the Lucene score is also argument-related since the sentences are indexed with argument-related information including sentence-level type (see Figure 11.2, bottom).

LUIMA-Rerank learns the weights for this set of features from "true" rankings in a training set created by a legal expert (described below). In the learning process, the module examines each training set document's true rank with respect to a query and its reranking feature values. The module learns a logistic regression formula that assigns weights to each feature (see Section 10.3.3). The weights are set so that a global error function is minimized. The module then computes a new ranking score for the document.

The researchers assessed different versions of LUIMA-Rerank employing different subsets of the features. They employed two metrics for measuring ranking performance that will be defined in the next section.

In the evaluation of the LUIMA Rerank versions, almost all subsets of the rerank learning features performed equally well and better than the plain LUIMA-Search. Using only the maximum Lucene score feature, that is, the highest Lucene score of all of the sentences in the given document led to good performance. Adding the VSS marginally improved the ranking performance. With all three features, however, the improvement disappeared. As a result, for the final experiment (described below), LUIMA-ReRank employed only VSS and the maximum Lucene score as rerank learning features.

11.4. AN EXPERIMENT TO EVALUATE LUIMA

In experiments (as indicated at the right end of the LUIMA pipeline architecture, Figure 11.1), LUIMA-Rerank's new rankings of the LUIMA-Search outputs for 11 queries were evaluated against:

- a baseline ranking by a CLIR system,
- a true ranking established by a legal expert, and
- LUIMA-Search's original ranking (Grabmair et al., 2015).

The CLIR system generated the baseline ranking as follows. Each of the 11 queries shown in Table 11.1 was submitted to the CLIR as a baseline query. The first, Q_1, focused on the rule for establishing causation regarding vaccine injuries. The remaining 10 (Q_2 through Q_{11}) focused on findings or conclusions that particular vaccines caused particular injuries. Each of these was derived from the facts of 1 of 10 source cases, the *gold standard cases* listed in Section 10.5.2. The fact that there was only one rule-focused query (Q_1) reflects the fact that there was only one legal rule of interest, the *Althen* test of causation-in-fact. Recall that the V/IP Corpus contains all decisions in a two-year period applying that test.

The CLIR system retrieved and ranked a list of documents of which the top 30 per query were recorded as *baseline ranks*. These documents were pooled into a collection, the "document base," comprising 188 documents (11 queries * 30 cases per query − 142 duplicates).

A legal expert generated the true ranking. For each query, the expert (the author of this book, who spent five years as a litigator in a major Wall Street law firm and has been a law professor since 1989) assessed the top 30 documents as to their usefulness. The expert based the assessment (solely) on the CLIR system's case report for each of the 30 documents. The CLIR system's case report comprises a two-sentence summary of the claim involved and the court's decision, as well as four brief excerpts from the retrieved case text with the search terms highlighted. The 30 documents were then reranked to form the document's *true rank* for a given query.

For each query, Table 11.1 shows source case information, the number of cases the CLIR system returned, the number of cases in the CLIR system's top 30 cases that the expert deemed relevant, and where in its rankings the CLIR system placed the source case. Even though the CLIR system was expected to retrieve and rank highly the source case from which it was derived, this was frequently not the case.

LUIMA-Search generated its initial ordering as follows. Based on the gold standard cases, the researchers created rule-based and ML text annotators using the process explained in Section 10.5.3. The annotators were equipped to classify three of the sentence-level types, LegalRuleSentence, EvidenceBasedFindingSentence, and CitationSentence, as well as the associated subsentence-level types. These text annotators were then applied to the pool of 188 documents in the document base. The classifiers predicted the sentence-level annotations of all documents in the pool. The resulting annotated texts were stored in the LUIMA-Search database in the Lucene database format shown in Figure 11.2 (bottom).

Each of the 11 queries was translated manually into a LUIMA query like the one in Figure 11.2 (top). The 30 cases associated with each query, as represented in the Lucene database, were then ranked according to LUIMA-Search's ranking method by the number of sentences responsive to the LUIMA query (see Section 11.3.1).

LUIMA-Rerank generated its reordered rankings in a LOO cross validation with 11 runs, one for each query (see Section 4.4.3 for a description of cross validation). Each query had its associated 30 documents represented in the Lucene database format and the documents' true rankings. Each document had associated features for rerank learning, namely its VSS to the query and its maximum Lucene score (see Section 11.3.2).

In each run, a different query's documents became the test set and the remaining 10 queries' documents were the training set. The system examines each training set document's reranking features, learns a logistic regression formula that assigns weights to each reranking feature, and computes a new ranking score for the document. In the learning process, the document's true rank for a query is examined and the weights are set so that a global error function is minimized.

In each run, the completed logistic regression formula was used to predict a test query ranking. Evaluation metric values were calculated and then averaged across all the runs.

11.4.1. *Evaluation Metrics*

The systems' ranking performance was assessed in terms of two commonly employed metrics: AP and normalized discounted cumulative gain (DCG) to measure performance. These measures are normalized in the [0,1] interval, with the best score as 1.

The intuition underlying AP is the following. The program is searching for relevant documents and retrieves a ranked list of candidates, not all of which are, in fact, relevant. For each correctly returned (relevant) document, one computes the precision and then takes an average. If the returned results were 1, 1, 1, 0, 0, 1, where 1 is a relevant document and 0 is not, then the precision at every correct point is the number of correct documents that have been retrieved up to and including that point divided by the total number of documents retrieved up to that point: 1/1, 2/2, 3/3, 3/4, 3/5, 4/6. The AP of this series is 0.92.

In other words, for computing AP, one proceeds one rank at a time down the interval [1,30]. If the document at rank i is relevant, one measures the precision at i ($P@i$). $P@i$ is the proportion of retrieved documents in the top-i ranks that are relevant. Finally, one takes the average of all $P@i$ values. The number of $P@i$ values will equal the number of relevant documents. AP is expressed as a formula as follows:

$$AP = \frac{\sum_{i \in R} P@i}{|R|}$$

where R is the set of positions of the relevant documents, $|R|$ is the number of items i in the set R, and $\sum_{i \in R} P@i$ is the sum of the precisions at i for all of the items in R (Grabmair et al., 2015).

The intuition underlying normalized DCG is that each relevant document contributes to the overall quality of a ranking depending on where it is ranked relative to the ideal ranking. DCG is a weighted sum over the ranked items' relevance. The weight decreases as the rank of an item decreases. In this sense, the gain is "discounted." Usually, a logarithmic discount function is used to model the decreasing weight. *Normalized DCG* (NDCG) divides DCG by the DCG measure of the best ranking result, the ideal DCG or IDCG, and is always a number in [0, 1] (see Wang et al., 2013).[2]

To measure the performance of the whole system, the systems' ranking performance on *all* of the queries is measured in terms of mean AP (MAP) and average NDCG.

---

[2] For the more technically inclined readers, in the LUIMA experiments, NDCG was defined as follows:

$$NDCG = \frac{DCG}{IDCG} \qquad DCG_p = \sum_{i}^{p} \frac{2^{relevance_i} - 1}{\log_2(i+1)}$$

where $relevance_i \in \{0, 1\}$, p is the rank position, in our case up to 30, DCG is calculated using the predicted ranking, and IDCG, the "ideal" DCG, is calculated using the true ranking.

MAP is the average over the set of all queries of the AP for each query. It is defined as:

$$MAP(Q) = \frac{\sum_i^{|Q|} AP_i}{|Q|}$$

where Q is the set of all queries and AP_i is the average precision for each query.
   Average NDCG is defined as

$$AverageNDCG = \frac{\sum_i^{|Q|} NDCG_i}{|Q|}$$

where $NDCG_i$ is the NDCG for each query (Burges et al., 2005; Grabmair et al., 2015).

Incidentally, since the true rank was created by reranking the cases retrieved by the CLIR system, the recall (i.e., coverage of all relevant documents in response to a query) of every baseline result is 1. In addition, since LUIMA-Search appends all nonresponsive documents to the end of retrieved cases, the experimental system was not compared to the baseline in terms of recall.

11.4.2. *LUIMA vs. CLIR*

In a series of experiments, for each query in Table 11.1, using the above metrics, the researchers evaluated four configurations of LUIMA and the baseline by comparing each one's ranking of retrieved cases against the legal expert's true ranking:

1. Baseline: CLIR system's ranking for the queries in Table 11.1.
2. LUIMA-Search: Searching on full LUIMA query, ranking documents in terms of the number of retrieved sentences in each.
3. LUIMA-Search+ReRank: Searching on full LUIMA query, ranking documents in terms of number of retrieved sentences in each, reranking documents with weighted rerank features.
4. LUIMA-Search, no sentence type: Searching on LUIMA query but without the sentence type, ranking documents in terms of number of retrieved sentences in each.
5. LUIMA-Search+ReRank, no sentence type: Searching on LUIMA query but without the sentence type, ranking documents in terms of number of retrieved sentences in each, reranking them using weighted rerank features (Grabmair et al., 2015).

The researchers compared items (1) and (3) in order to assess whether LUIMA-ReRank's ranking adds value over and above the baseline CLIR system's ranking.

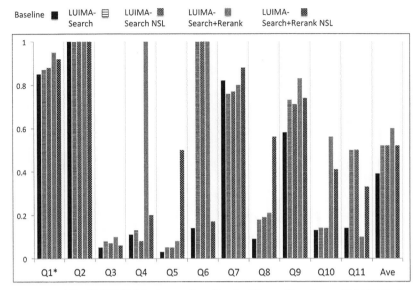

FIGURE 11.3. AP of *LUIMA Versions v. Baseline for Eleven Queries and MAP* (Grabmair et al., 2015)

Comparing items (2) and (3) will show the effect of LUIMA's reranking compared with its search. As explained in Section 10.5.3, the LUIMA-Annotate module annotated sentence levels for the documents that did not belong to the gold standard, but not as effectively as hoped. The researchers examined how the system performed without this module's sentence-level annotations in order to assess any possible negative effect on the search or rerank components' performance.

Figure 11.3 shows the AP of the baseline and the four versions on the 11 queries as well as the MAPs. Figure 11.4 shows similar results for NDCG and average NDCG.

LUIMA outperformed the CLIR system baseline in 10 of 11 queries and tied it in one, as shown in Figures 11.3 and 11.4. In Q1 (the only query involving the LegalRuleSentence type), LUIMA's improvement over the baseline was small. In Q2–Q11 (all of which dealt with the EvidenceBasedFindingSentence type), LUIMA outperformed the baseline in all queries but tied in Q2.

The fact that all versions tied with respect to Q2 indicates that they all retrieved the targeted case at the top of the list. For six queries (Q1, Q3, Q4, Q6, Q9, and Q10), LUIMA-Search+ReRank, the retrieval system that employed sentence types and reranking, performed best and obtained the highest overall average. In three other queries (Q5, Q7, and Q8), LUIMA-Search+ReRank, no sentence type, performed best; it ignored the sentence types. For one query (Q11), LUIMA-Search performed better than the LUIMA versions that performed reranking. In Q1 (the only query about the LegalRuleSentence type), the baseline performed very well, and the LUIMA versions performed only marginally better. In seven of the queries

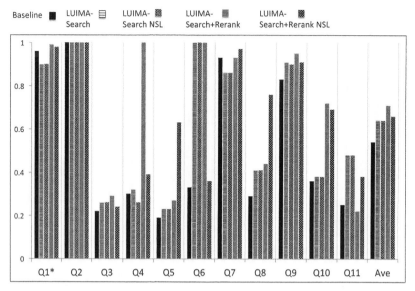

FIGURE 11.4. NDCG of *LUIMA Versions v. Baseline for Eleven Queries and Average NDCG* (Grabmair et al., 2015)

that focus on instances of EvidenceBasedFindingSentence (Q2–Q11), reranking improved retrieval performance.

In three of the queries, ignoring the sentence type actually improved performance. This reflects the weakness of the sentence classifier, which may sometimes block the beneficial effect of identifying legal concepts.

Improving LUIMA's Performance

In subsequent work, the researchers demonstrated an increase in LUIMA-Search's accuracy by expanding the structured queries with POS tagging. That is, the system automatically tagged the contents of document sentences and of query texts with the POS (noun, verb, determiner, etc.) played by each word and factored in the similarity of the POS tags across query and sentences.

They also improved the performance of LUIMA-Rerank. They modified the previous voting method based solely on the number of sentences in the top N retrieval results and added a new reranking feature based on the BM-25 (Best Match 25) metric, a refinement of *tf/idf* weighting, that better accounted for the type and location of any citations in sentences and document length (Bansal et al., 2016).

Discussion

The evaluation of LUIMA shows that automated annotation of instances of LUIMA types (Vaccines, Injuries, Causation, and Sentence Types) in documents and their use in indexing and querying led to better reranking performance than a CLIR system that did not use such information. A conceptual legal document retrieval system, focusing on argument-related information and going from natural language legal documents to retrieval results, is feasible, at least for a restricted set of documents in the domain of vaccine injury claims.

By annotating sentence role types such as Evidence-Based Finding, and soon, Legal Ruling or Holding of Law, an AR system could help a user to find "application cases." Beyond supporting a legal proposition in the abstract, such cases are examples of applying a proposition to concrete facts which may be analogous to the user's problem (see Mart, 2010, p. 222).

Since LUIMA-Annotate has marked up the retrieved cases' sentences in terms of their sentence-level roles in the argument and various subsentence annotations, in principle, the system can highlight the argument-related information for the user. In particular, retrieved cases could be summarized in a way that is tailored to the user's argumentative need. Daniel Jurafsky distinguishes between extractive and abstractive summarization:

> Extractive summarization answers the query by pulling a set of short text pieces from the documents (snippets) ... Abstractive summarization expresses the ideas [in a text] at least in part in different words. Abstractive summarization is much closer to the language one would find in a legal memo and it is currently an important research goal, but very difficult. (Remus and Levy, 2015, p. 22)

Presumably, argument-related information identified by LUIMA-Annotate, such as whether a sentence states a legal rule, draws a legal conclusion by applying a legal rule to facts, or reports a finding of fact, can help a program to perform abstractive summarization or, at least, do a better job of extractive summarization.

In sum, the LUIMA system implements general and domain-focused annotation types specific to legal textual information. It identifies subsentence annotations using manually crafted rules and sentence-level annotations using a ML sentence classifier trained on a small set of gold standard documents. By taking these annotations into account in the retrieval and reranking process, LUIMA's results on the task of ranking retrieved documents outperformed those of a commercial full-text legal retrieval system baseline. These results, however, are subject to confirmation in testing with larger, more diverse datasets. That work is currently underway.

11.5. CONTINUING TO TRANSFORM LEGAL IR INTO AR

LUIMA's designers have applied legal expertise to intelligently engineer features for argument mining, resulting in "smarter" ML and more intelligent reranking even with far smaller amounts of data than one associates with data-mining (Grabmair et al., 2015). LUIMA is a long way from transforming legal information retrieval into AR but it provides a proof of concept and an architectural foundation.

The path forward seems clear, but there are many challenges. As described below, the key is to extend the techniques for annotating argument-related, substantive legal, and propositional information in case texts.

The focus in this section is on future work; the goal is to describe the path in sufficient detail that others can follow it. This section explains how a future Legal Argument Retrieval/Cognitive Computing System, call it LARCCS, could be connected to legal information retrieval systems and illustrates new kinds of conceptual queries that it could support and that CLIR systems currently cannot. It describes some extensions to a type system that will enable new kinds of conceptual queries and addresses the prospects for automatically annotating the extended types and for eliciting users' argument needs in queries.

Although the section describes future work, it is not merely "pie in the sky." The plan for constructing a LARCCS prototype is informed by the experience of building LUIMA, by the experiences of AI & Law researchers' extracting argument-related information from case texts, described in Chapter 10, and by the goal of connecting these techniques to existing computational models of legal reasoning and argument.

11.5.1. *Connecting LARCCS and Legal IR Systems*

LUIMA provides a guide for connecting a LARCCS prototype to existing legal IR systems. LUIMA's annotation and reranking techniques can be applied to documents retrieved by a more conventional legal IR system. The top n-ranked cases retrieved by an external full-text legal information system using its normal inverted index, probabilistic models of relevance, and reranking techniques (Section 7.4) could be fed into a text annotation pipeline.

By adding an ability to perform semantic markup and reranking, the IR systems' outputs could be reordered in terms of argument-related criteria. As a result, these systems could effectively take into account more detailed information about why the user is seeking the information and how he/she intends to use it in an argument. External IR search systems such as LA, WN, or Google Scholar Cases may perform their own reranking, but as far as known, such rerankings do not include argument-related information.

Thus, in principle, it is possible that intelligent semantic analysis technology for legal documents could improve an IR system's performance *without* disrupting the IR database and indexing. The semantic annotation and argument-based reranking are applied only externally to the IR system's outputs. A caveat is whether the text annotation techniques can be applied efficiently enough to tens, hundreds, or thousands of documents output by the IR system. For purposes of discussion, let's assume that it is possible with a sufficient commitment of engineering resources. This is a big assumption, but here my goal is to motivate why such an effort could be worth the investment.

11.5.2. *Querying for Cases with Extended Argument-Related Information*

A more comprehensive argument type system for retrieving, ordering, and summarizing documents in terms of legally important concepts and relations would support users in expressing a wider range of queries with a wider range of argument-related constraints.

For example, an attorney representing a client in a vaccine-related case may wish to know what cases there have been in which special masters made evidence-based findings that a particular vaccine such as measles, mumps, and rubella (MMR) caused a particular condition like intractable seizure disorder. The attorney might want to know the kinds of evidence that the court accepted, and even more urgently, the findings and evidence there may have been in other decisions that MMR does *not* cause that condition.

Alternatively, an advocate may seek a case applying a legal rule in a situation involving particular facts. A lawyer involved in a trade secret misappropriation case may seek cases where a court has held in favor of or against a party under a legal rule defining particular elements of a trade secret misappropriation claim. The lawyer would like to find such cases where the facts of his current problem also were present, for instance that the plaintiff's product was unique, the plaintiff had taken some security measures to protect the information such as obtaining defendant's nondisclosure agreement, but where there had also been a disclosure of some of the information in a public forum.

Requests for information like these involve constraints expressed in terms of legal concepts and argument-related patterns of information. The goal of developing a cognitive computing system for legal AR is to support users in expressing their information need in terms of queries that specify argument constraints like these.

That would be the goal of a LARCCS prototype. The next two figures show examples of formulations of requests for information that enable users to express their argument needs. In Figure 11.5, those needs are formulated in terms of particular argument roles in the V/IP domain, based on the DLF computational model of legal argument (Section 5.8). For example, queries like numbers 4a, b, and c could implement the above V/IP information request concerning MMR vaccine causing seizures in terms of existing sentence-level argument-role types and legal rule requirements.

In Figure 11.6, the information need is expressed in terms of queries in the trade secret domain based on elements of the CATO, IBP, and VJAP argument models (Sections 3.3.2, 4.5.2, and 5.7). These include existing sentence-level argument-role types plus additional legal factor and value-related types (see Section 11.5.3) as well as terms representing legal rule requirements. For instance, query number 3 could implement the above trade secret rule application request.

Here, *implements* means expressing the queries in terms of constraints involving sentence argument roles, legal rules and their requirements, trade secret legal factors, and values underlying the factors.

1. What are the **Legal Rule Requirements** for proving that a particular vaccine caused a particular injury?
2. What **Legal Rulings or Holdings of Law** have there been that a particular vaccine [caused | did not cause] a particular injury?
3. What **Legal Policies or Values** have been discussed re **Legal Rule Requirements** addressing vaccines causing injury?
4. What **Evidence-Based Findings** have there been that:
    a. the measles, mumps & rubella (MMR) vaccine *causes* intractable seizure disorder?
    b. the MMR vaccine can [cannot] *cause* any type of injury?
    c. the MMR vaccine cannot *cause* a type of injury?
    d. any kind of vaccine can [cannot] *cause* myocarditis?
    e. a particular kind of vaccine cannot *cause* myocarditis?
    f. *there is [not] a logical sequence of cause and effect between* a particular MMR vaccination and a particular injury involving intractable seizure disorder?
    g. a particular vaccine *caused* a particular injury despite presence of negative **Evidence Factors**?
    h. a particular vaccine *caused* a particular injury even though onset timing (time interval between specific-vaccination and earliest Injury- onset) is greater than six months?
5. What **Evidence** has [supported | contradicted] a finding or conclusion that:
    a. the MMR vaccine *causes* intractable seizure disorder?
    b. *there is a logical sequence of cause and effect between* a particular MMR vaccination and a particular injury involving intractable seizure disorder?
6. What **Evidence Factors** have [supported | contradicted] an **Evidence-Based Finding** or **Legal Rulings or Holdings of Law** that:
    a. a particular vaccine *causes* a particular injury?
    b. *there is a logical sequence of cause and effect between* a particular vaccination and a particular injury?
7. Given the **Evidence** (e.g., regarding the injury) what **Legal Rule Requirements** does it help prove?
8. Given the **Legal Rule Requirement** (e.g., concerning causation)
    a. what **Evidence** is relevant and makes proving this condition more likely? Less likely?
    b. what arguments have been successful? Unsuccessful?
    c. what arguments relying on **citation** have been successful? Unsuccessful?

FIGURE 11.5. Queries for cases with propositions playing particular argument roles (from the *VIIP Domain*). Bold-faced terms represent existing sentence-level argument-role types. Italicized terms represent legal rule requirements

More specifically, the conditions are expressed with an expanded list of argument types including sentence-level LUIMA types (see Table 6.7) that have not yet been used extensively, such as **Legal Rulings or Holdings of Law, Evidence, Legal Policies or Values,** and some new ones like **Legal Factors** and **Applied Legal Value,** described below. The conditions also include various constraints on what the sentence is about, specified in terms of domain-specific concepts. In vaccine injury law, this includes, for example, *causes* and *logical sequence of cause and effect.* In trade secret law, it includes factor *F7 Brought-Tools (P)* and underlying value, *General Public's Interest in Fair Competition.* In principle, queries expressing constraints in these

1. What cases are there with a **Legal Ruling or Holding of Law** regarding **Legal Rule** defining *Trade-Secret-Misappropriation* where **Legal Factor: *F7 Brought-Tools (P)*?**

2. What cases are there where *defendant* won a **Legal Ruling or Holding of Law** regarding **Legal Rule** defining *Trade-Secret-Misappropriation* where **Legal Factor: *F7 Brought-Tools (P)*?**

3. What cases are there with a **Legal Ruling or Holding of Law** regarding **Legal Rule** defining *Trade-Secret-Misappropriation* where **Legal Factors: *F15 Unique-Product (P), F4 Agreed- Not-To-Disclose (P), F6 Security-measures (P), F27 Disclosure-in-public-forum (D)*?**

4. What trade secret misappropriation cases, won by plaintiff, have involved the following:
   - **Legal Rule Requirement:** *Info-Misappropriated*
   - **Legal Factor: *F14 Restricted-Materials-Used (P), F16 Info-Reverse-Engineerable (D)***
   - **Applied Legal Value:** <u>*General Public's Interest in Fair Competition*</u>

5. What cases are there where plaintiff won a **Legal Ruling or Holding of Law** regarding **Legal Rule Requirement** defining *Info-Trade-Secret* where:
   - **Legal Factor: *F10 Secrets-Disclosed-Outsiders* (D)?**
   - **Legal Factor: *F10 Secrets-Disclosed-Outsiders* (D)** and number of disclosures to outsiders is greater than 1000?

FIGURE 11.6. Queries for legal factors and argument roles (from the *trade secret domain*). Bold-faced terms represent existing sentence-level argument-role types plus additional legal factor and value-related types (see Section 11.5.3). Italicized terms represent legal rule requirements. Underlined italicized terms represent legal policies or values

terms could be implemented for purposes of retrieval in a manner like the LUIMA-Search query, shown in Figure 11.2. This specified a list of conditions including the argument role of the targeted sentence as well as conceptual constraints on what the sentence is about.

Ordinary legal IR systems can retrieve materials based on the words of queries like those in the figures, but they do not understand the argument-related concepts and constraints. An exclusively text-based search engine would treat these simply as additional, common keywords, not as legal concepts specifying argument-related information about the targeted role of similar sentences in the sought-for case documents. It may use keyword query expansion or a legal thesaurus, but even then the keyword character of the concept labels remains. Even if the legal IR system can retrieve cases relevant to the natural language queries, it could not use argument-related information to order or summarize the cases in a manner tailored to the problem the user seeks to address. If it could understand and manipulate such constraints, users would enjoy an unprecedented ability to express and find what they really are looking for.

As explained in Chapter 12, the LARCCS approach could help new commercial legal apps like Lex Machina (see Sections 12.2 and 12.3) take semantic features related to the substantive merits of a case into account for retrieval and prediction. Section 12.4.1 shows how legal apps based on LARCCS could process queries like those in Figures 11.5 and 11.6 and engage in cognitive computing, enabling human users to test legal hypotheses against corpora of cases. Before addressing these possibilities, however, at least three challenges need to be addressed:

1. Expanding a type system to support a wider range of conceptual queries across a wider range of argument, document, and domain-specific legal phenomena.
2. Annotating documents with the expanded type system.
3. Eliciting users' argument needs in a convenient and reliable manner.

11.5.3. *New Legal Annotation Types*

In order to retrieve, order, and summarize legal documents, a LARCCS semantic analysis system would need an expanded type system. The core types of Tables 6.6 and 6.7 provide a foundation, but would need to be supplemented with ones that capture additional argument-related patterns, aspects of document structure, propositional structure of legal arguments, and domain-specific information.

Additional Sentence-Level Argument-Role Types

The computational models of legal argument in Part I are associated with patterns of argument in cases which have not yet been incorporated into such an extended type system. For example, the VJAP model (Section 5.7.3) incorporates legal factors, issues based on legal rule requirements, and underlying policies and values as illustrated in its models of the trade secret misappropriation domain (Figure 5.10) and the values it protects (Figures 5.11 and 5.12). The CATO (Section 3.3.2), Bench-Capon/Sartor (Section 3.5.1), and IBP (Section 4.5.2) models all refer to some subsets of these.

In order to link these models and legal texts, the type system would need to include some new types associated with sentences discussing legal factors and underlying values in the context of a legal rule requirement.

Some kinds of queries for which it will be important to identify such sentences are illustrated in Figure 11.6. For example, query number 4 seeks pro-plaintiff trade secret misappropriation cases, some of whose sentences play the following roles: focusing on whether a particular legal rule requirement is satisfied (Info-Misappropriated), identifying applicable legal factors (F14 Restricted-Materials-Used (P) and F16 Info-Reverse-Engineerable (D)), or identifying an applicable policy or value (the General Public's Interest in Fair Competition). Such sentences relate the discussion to issues, factors, values, and their relations with which the VJAP model can make arguments and predictions, as shown in its domain model (Figure 5.10).

These argument patterns could be expressed in terms of three additional sentence types shown in Figure 11.7.

These types are intended to annotate parts of a case in which the court discusses how the legal factors and, optionally, the values underlying the factors affect the outcome of its decision whether a legal requirement is satisfied in a given case.

Legal Rule Requirement: sentence that states a requirement or element of a legal rule in the context of applying the requirement to the facts of the particular case being litigated.

Legal Factor: sentence in which a judge states as a reason why, or despite which, s/he came to a conclusion of law that a legal rule or requirement did [not] apply in a fact situation and refers to a stereotypical fact pattern that tends to strengthen or weaken the legal conclusion because of its effect on a legal policy or value.

Applied Legal Value: sentence that involves reasoning about the application of a legal policy or value to particular facts.

FIGURE 11.7. New argument-role sentence-level types

These points in an opinion text identify features with which computational models of argument such as the VJAP and DLF models can reason.

Although we have encountered these types of sentences mainly in trade secret misappropriation and vaccine injury cases, they appear in decisions involving many kinds of legal claims. In principle, all three types are general enough to apply in any legal domain in which the corresponding computational models of evidentiary or factor-based argument are appropriate.

Document Structure Types

In the preceding section and in Table 6.7, we have seen examples of sentence-level argument-role types that capture typical argumentative patterns in legal documents. As work discussed in Chapters 8 and 10 suggests, it may be both useful and feasible to add types for annotating structural elements on a wider scale, namely legal document structure and legal argument structure.

Legal Document Structure types correspond to sectional divisions in a legal opinion as indicated by headings, subheadings, and subject matter. A section may present the applicable law, state the facts of a case, or state conclusions about whether the legal standards have been satisfied given the facts. Alternatively, a section may perform some combination of these roles, effectively introducing a legal rule or requirement, related fact-finding, and application of the rule to the evidence all in one section. As discussed in Section 8.6, programs can now learn to differentiate whether passages contain facts, legal discussion, neither, or both.

An ability to distinguish sections by their primary focus may help reduce uncertainty in annotating propositions as involving legal rules, conclusions regarding legal rule requirements, or fact-finding (and vice versa). The standard section types and the LUIMA sentence types are associated: A law section often presents Legal Rule sentences or requirements. A facts section often presents Evidence, Evidence-Based Reasoning, Evidence Factors, or Evidence-Based Findings. A section applying law to facts often presents Legal Rulings or Holdings of Law based on Evidence-Based Findings for the disputed Legal Rule Requirements and Legal Rules. Of course, the way legal documents are divided into sections varies by type of document, jurisdiction, and even particular judge or author, which is a complicating factor.

Legal Argument Propositional Structure identifies propositions that serve as premises and conclusion in a court's argument. Identifying premises and conclusions was the focus of Mochales and Moens (2011), discussed in Section 10.3 and of IBM Debater, as illustrated in Chapter 1.

As recognized by Mochales and Moens (2011), premises and conclusions play a key role in the generally nested argument structure of textual legal arguments regarding issues and sub-issues. At various points in an opinion, a court introduces an issue or topic, considers arguments in connection with the issue, and draws a conclusion. For each issue, the court identifies sub-issues, considers arguments regarding the sub-issue, and draws a conclusion. Following Feng and Hirst (2011, p. 989), the nested arguments may be referred to as *argument units*. They comprise a conclusion proposition and an optional premise proposition. Each of these propositions, in turn, may comprise nested, smaller such units.

The nesting follows a court's increasingly fine-grained analysis of legal and, ultimately, factual issues. It follows the breakdown of a legal claim into the legal rules defining the requirements, findings of fact, and a determination of whether the requirements have been satisfied. Depending on the procedural posture of the case, this may continue into consideration of the evidence for and against a finding. In other words the nesting corresponds to the organization of the LUIMA sentence types above, which itself reflects the DLF rule trees and chains of reasoning presented in Section 5.8.

Beside nested argument structures, the legal argument propositional structures also include the types of legal argument schemes (Section 5.2) employed to support an inference from a proposition, the templates, or "blueprints" for typical kinds of legal argument. Such argument schemes include those for case-based argument illustrated in CATO, for example, the argument downplaying/emphasizing distinction scheme in Figure 3.7, and in the VJAP model such as the argument from inter-issue trade-off from precedent discussed in Section 5.7.3.

Additional Claim-Specific Types

While the above argument types apply generally across many legal domains (at least within a common law judicial system), other necessary additions to the type system would be geared to particular ones: claim-specific concepts, relations, and mentions and presuppositional information.

Claim-specific concepts, relations, and mentions are those typical of a specific kind of legal claim, its associated rules, and factors. Within a claim for vaccine injury or trade secret misappropriation, certain concepts, relations, and mentions recur frequently across cases. These include the claim's legal rules and requirements whose application given the facts are disputed issues. Claim-specific concepts in trade secret misappropriation include the name of the claim and its elements or issues, such as that the information was a trade secret (Info-Trade-Secret), or that it was used in breach of a confidential relationship (Confidential-Relationship) as per the IBP or VJAP models (see Figures 4.4 and 5.10).

Claim-specific concepts also include instances of general semantic types that are specific to that kind of claim. Trade secret misappropriation has its own legal factors, for example, F7 Brought-Tools (P), and its own applied legal values such as the General Public's Interest in Fair Competition. Within a particular legal domain like trade secret law, the fact patterns associated with legal factors are stereotypes. They are all instances of the sentence-level type, Legal Factor, but it makes sense to associate a subtype with each one.

Each of a claim's legal factors also needs to be associated with the various ways in which it may be expressed linguistically. For example, the trade secret factor, F4 Agreed-Not-To-Disclose (P), applies to each of the sentences illustrated in Section 1.4.4 drawn from real cases, such as "Newlin and Vafa had signed nondisclosure agreements prohibiting them from using ICM software and tools upon leaving ICM" and "Ungar signed a nondisclosure agreement."

Other types of claims will have their own legal factors. This includes property interests in wild animals (see Section 3.4) or trademark law claims, where factors are employed in determining such issues as the likelihood of confusion, an element of trademark infringement.

Presuppositional information includes subsentence types associated with factual or linguistic concepts and relations important in discourse about a regulated domain. While it is not feasible to represent all of the knowledge about the domain, one could represent certain aspects given the legal issues that typically arise.

Table 11.2 shows some of that presuppositional information for the vaccine injury domain and for trade secret misappropriation. In the former domain, the *Althen* rules for causation focus on such facts as the time interval between a specific vaccination with a vaccine covered by the statute and the onset of injury. In the latter, the magnitude of certain legal factors (see Section 3.3.2) depends on particular values, such as the number of disclosures to outsiders plaintiff made or the amount of product development time and expense defendant saved by accessing plaintiff's information. These kinds of facts (associated with focal slot prerequisites in Hypo dimensions (Section 3.3.2), or base factor-related concepts in Wyner and Peters (2010)) are semantic information which can be annotated in opinion texts and used to facilitate AR and case comparison.

Much of this part of the type system would not be of general applicability across legal domains. On the other hand, some of the concepts and relations such as reasoning about temporal durations are general in nature, whether they refer to time saved in product development, the elapsed time between injection and the onset of an injury, or the time it takes for a fisherman's nets to close. Research should explore applying state-of-the-art temporal annotators like SUTime or HeidelTime to markup dates, times, and durations in the case texts (see Strötgen and Gertz, 2013). An event calculus could then reason with temporal constraints, for example, as illustrated in

TABLE 11.2. *Presuppositional information in two legal claim domains*

Legal claim domain	Semantic relations	Meaning (objects or event referents)
Vaccine injury	1. Covered-vaccine	a vaccine covered by the VICP
	2. Specific-date	a specific month, day, year
	3. Specific-vaccination	a vaccination on a Specific-date
	4. Generic-injury	a type of injury, adverse condition, or disease
	5. Injury-onset	a symptom, sign, or test result associated with the onset of a Generic-injury
	6. Onset-timing-expected	expected time interval between time of vaccination with a Covered-vaccine and the earliest Injury-onset
	7. Onset-timing	time interval between Specific-vaccination and the earliest Injury-onset
Trade Secret Misappropriation	1. Number-disclosures-outsiders	number of disclosures to outsiders plaintiff made
	2. Tools-brought	product development tools defendant employee brought from plaintiff employer
	3. Time-to-reverse-engineer	amount of time it would reasonably take to reverse engineer information
	4. Security-measure-types	types of security measures plaintiff took
	5. Product-development-savings	amount of product development time and expense defendant saved by accessing plaintiff's information
	6. Improper-means-types	types of improper means defendant engaged in to obtain plaintiff's information
	7. Employee-inducements	value of inducements defendant offered to plaintiff's former employee

query 4h in Figure 11.5 concerning onset times of an injury after a vaccination (see Zhou and Hripcsak, 2007; Thielscher, 2011).

11.5.4. *Prospects for Annotating Expanded Legal Types*

Assuming that one has expanded a type system to support conceptual queries over a wider range of argument patterns, document structure, and claim-specific types, the second challenge for developing a LARCCS prototype involves the prospects for automatically annotating legal documents in terms of these new types.

The expanded type system captures different argument-related aspects of a text. For instance, Figure 11.8 illustrates an excerpt from the trade secret opinion in

Tony MASON v. JACK DANIEL DISTILLERY
518 So.2d 130 (1987) Court of Civil Appeals of Alabama.
August 5, 1987.

DEFENDANTS' CROSS APPEAL ...

Applying these factors to the evidence in this case, we find that some of the factors support and some negate the conclusion that Lynchburg Lemonade was **Mason's** trade secret. ...

Mason testified regarding the precautions he took to protect the secrecy of Lynchburg Lemonade. He testified that he told only a few of his employees—the bartenders—the recipe. He stated that each one was specifically instructed not to tell anyone the recipe. To prevent customers from learning the recipe, the beverage was mixed in the "back" of the restaurant and lounge. Mason's testimony was largely confirmed by that of his employees and past employees.

The testimony also reflected that Mason's efforts to keep the recipe to Lynchburg Lemonade a secret were apparently successful, until Winston Randle learned the recipe. It appears that one could not order a Lynchburg Lemonade in any establishment other than that of the plaintiff.

We note that absolute secrecy is not required for the recipe for Lynchburg Lemonade to constitute a trade secret—"a substantial element of secrecy is all that is necessary to provide trade secret protection." *Drill Parts*, 439 So.2d at 49.

The defendants also contend that Mason's recipe was not a trade secret because it could be easily duplicated by others. The defendants put on the testimony of at least two individuals as experts in the field of bartending, or mixing alcoholic beverages. This testimony characterized Lynchburg Lemonade as a member of the Collins family of drinks, of which "there [are] dozens ..., if not hundreds [with] [e]ssentially the same elements." At least one witness testified that he could duplicate the recipe after tasting a Lynchburg Lemonade.

Certainly, this testimony is a strong factor against the conclusion that **Mason's** recipe to Lynchburg Lemonade was a trade secret. We do not think, however, that this evidence in and of itself could prevent such a conclusion. Rather, this evidence should be weighed and considered along with the evidence tending to show the existence of a trade secret.

...

Our review of the record indicates that the plaintiff did present a scintilla of evidence that his recipe, or formula, for Lynchburg Lemonade was a trade secret. The trial court, therefore, did not err in denying the defendants' motion for a directed verdict based upon the non-existence of a trade secret.

...

This case is reversed and remanded to the trial court for proceedings not inconsistent with this opinion.

Comment [1]: 1. EvidenceBasedFindingOfFact 2. Proposition / premise

Comment [2]: 1. Evidence 2. F6 Security-Measures p 3. Proposition / premise

Comment [3]: 1. EvidenceBasedFindingOfFact 2. F15 Unique-Product p 3. Proposition / premise

Comment [4]: 1. LegalRule 2. Proposition / premise 3. ARGUMENT FROM EXAMPLE

Comment [5]: Proposition / premise

Comment [6]: 1. Evidence 2. F16 Info-Reverse-Engineerable d 3. Proposition / premise

Comment [7]: 1. EvidenceBasedFindingOfFact 2. Proposition / premise

Comment [8]: 1. LegalRulingOrHoldingOfLaw 2. Case-specific process or procedural facts. 3. Proposition / premise

Comment [9]: 1. LegalRulingOrHoldingOfLaw 2. Case-specific process or procedural facts.

Comment [10]: 1. LegalRulingOrHoldingOfLaw 2. Proposition / conclusion

Comment [11]: CaseSpecificProcessOrProceduralFacts

FIGURE 11.8. Argument mining for the *Mason* case opinion. Annotations (with WebAnno) are: trade secret misappropriation legal factors, core LUIMA sentence types, proposition/premise or proposition/conclusion, and ARGUMENT SCHEMES

the *Mason* case, whose facts are summarized in Figure 3.2. The sentences have been annotated manually in terms of four different types using WebAnno (Yimam et al., 2013):

– various trade secret misappropriation legal factors.
– various core LUIMA sentence types.
– proposition/premise or conclusion as in Mochales and Moens (2011).
– various argument schemes as in Feng and Hirst (2011).

While it is still an empirical question how reliably humans, and how successfully computers, can mark up these types in legal cases, annotation techniques have been developed and evaluated for many of them. Trade secret factors such as F6 Security-Measures, F15 Unique-Product, and F16 Info-Reverse-Engineerable have been marked up automatically (see Section 10.4) and computer environments have supported manually annotating such factors (see Section 10.4.3 and Figure 10.5). Techniques have been applied and evaluated for annotating three core LUIMA sentence types including LegalRule and EvidenceBasedFinding (see Section 10.5.3). Premises, conclusions, and argument schemes including argument from example (see Section 10.3.5) have been automatically identified based on manual annotations (see Section 10.3).

Analyzing all of these types in one project has not yet been attempted. An undertaking of that scope presents some special challenges discussed below in Section 12.5.1. It also presents some opportunities.

In semantic retrieval of argument-related information, the sentences of interest often are instances of multiple types. Almost all of the annotated sentences in Figure 11.8 were marked-up in terms of more than one type. For example, consider the following sentences from the second paragraph of the *Mason* text in the figure:

> He testified that he told only a few of his employees – the bartenders – the recipe. He stated that each one was specifically instructed not to tell anyone the recipe. To prevent customers from learning the recipe, the beverage was mixed in the "back" of the restaurant and lounge.

A human has marked up that excerpt as instances of the sentence-type, Evidence, the legal factor, F6 Security-Measures p, and argument structure type, Proposition/premise.

It seems plausible that sentences signaling trade-secret-specific legal factors will also tend to be evidence or evidence-based findings of fact and premise propositions in a judicial argument. Factors abstractly summarize patterns of facts in evidence and capture their impact as premises in an argument that an issue has or has not been satisfied. Moreover, the terms and phrases, "told only a few of his employees," "recipe," and "instructed not to tell anyone the recipe" may, given training instances, suffice for a ML algorithm to associate this kind of evidence with the particular legal factor, F6 Security-Measures.

In addition, the excerpt appears in a section that deals with the application of law to facts (see the proximity in the section of legal rule sentences, legal rulings or holdings of law, and evidence-based findings of fact). As noted in Section 11.5.3, a program can learn such document structure types and automatically identify them in legal documents to some useful extent.

The excerpt also appears in a progression of arguments leading to a conclusion, namely a legal ruling and holding of law, that plaintiff Mason had met the standard of providing some evidence that his cocktail recipe was a trade secret. As to this kind of argument structure, Mochales and Moens (2011), Levy et al. (2014) (in Debater), and Feng and Hirst (2011) have shown some success in annotating nested argument units and argument schemes in legal argument (see Sections 10.3.3, 10.3.5, and 10.6.1).

Thus, the sentences of interest in conceptual legal information retrieval may be annotated by multiple argument-related and document-structure types. A ML algorithm could probably detect the significance of the conjunctions of these telltale signs, but the challenge remains.

At a lower level of the type system, annotating certain presuppositional information could enable more focused case comparisons. In Figure 11.8, for instance, the evidence concerning factor F16 Info-Reverse-Engineerable is significant. Trade secret protection lasts only as long as it would reasonably take to reverse engineer the secret. If this information is available in a case, it is worth recording (see Time-to-reverse-engineer in the list of presuppositional information in Table 11.2). The testimony that Lynchburg Lemonade could be readily duplicated after just one tasting is, therefore, potentially quite damaging. The fact that plaintiff Mason won despite this limitation makes the *Mason* case a useful counterexample to the effect of factor F16. Ideally, a conceptual legal information retrieval system could enable users to retrieve such counterexamples, but this needs to be demonstrated.

To the extent that the presuppositional information in Table 11.2 can be annotated, the conceptual IR queries could specify constraints in more detail. See, for example, query 4h in Figure 11.5 seeking evidence-based findings of causation despite onset timing (the time interval between specific vaccination and earliest injury onset) greater than six months. Similarly, query 5 in Figure 11.6 seeks a legal ruling or holding of law favoring plaintiff despite more than 1,000 disclosures to outsiders. The former involves some simple temporal reasoning. The latter is like reasoning with the magnitude of a dimension, Secrets-Disclosed-Outsiders, in Hypo (Section 3.3.2). Both queries would be beyond the capacity of current legal information retrieval tools, but annotating this kind of presuppositional information could enable users to express more exactly the kinds of cases they need for their arguments.

The issues of who would manually annotate texts like that in Figure 11.8 for use as training instances and how they would do so are discussed in Section 12.5.2.

11.5.5. *Eliciting Users' Argument Needs*

The third challenge for developing a LARCCS prototype to support conceptual legal information retrieval is designing a methodology for eliciting users' argument needs in a convenient and reliable manner. A legal app would need to provide an easy-to-use interface for specifying more complex queries that it could then expand into the kind of structured queries specifying argument-related constraints. This will be a difficult challenge to meet.

In order for a conceptual information retrieval system to process a query, it needs to be in a form that can match the way that documents are indexed in a database such as Lucene. Table 11.3 illustrates what such a structured query looks like for a simple natural language query. It contains specifications of the fields and their contents and had to be constructed manually.

While natural language text would be the most convenient way for users to frame queries, relying on NLP of more complex queries expressed in plain English is not yet a feasible option.

Leading users to express their retrieval requirements in terms of argument-related constraints will likely require a human–computer interface that can integrate a number of techniques. Intuitively, a graphical interface could help.

TABLE 11.3. *Structured query translated from "Finding or conclusion that MMR vaccine causes intractable seizure disorder"*

Feature	Meaning	Structured Query Entry
Sentence type:	Annotated sentence type such as Evidence Based Finding Sentence or Legal Rule Sentence.	EvidenceBasedFindingSentence
About:	What sentence is about in terms of annotated mention or terms, such as VaccineTerm, IllnessTerm, or CausationTerm.	(OR VaccineMention VaccineTerm CausationMention Causation–Term AdverseMedical ConditionMention IllnessMention IllnessTerm)
VmNormalization:	Normalized name of vaccine mentioned in sentence.	"mmr"
ImNormalization:	Normalized name of illness mentioned in sentence.	"null"
Content:	Plain text of sentence.	(OR "MMR vaccine" "causes" "seizure" "disorder")
POS–tag:	Tags indicating part of speech of each component of sentence content.	(OR "Finding VBG" "or CC" "conclusion NN" "that IN" "MMR NN" "vaccine NN" "causes VBZ" "intractable JJ" "seizure NN" "disorder NN")
Citation:	Whether sentence, preceding sentence, or succeeding sentence is a citation.	NA

In particular, argument diagrams may assist users to specify information about the propositions and argument roles in which they are interested. The diagrams would be based on elements of a computational model of argument such as the DLF model (Section 5.8) or the VJAP model (Section 5.7). Consider, for example, Figure 5.15, which presented a DLF argument diagram representing applicable statutory requirements, including a rule tree of conditions. Figure 5.16 illustrated a chain of reasoning in the legal decision that connected evidentiary assertions to the special master's findings of fact on those conditions (Walker et al., 2011).

One can imagine a user submitting a query to the legal app by means of an input data scheme based on a more abstract version of such a DLF argument diagram. The scheme would present input structures based on rule trees and reasoning chains about which the legal app has information. Users would select an input structure for the legal rule of interest. Figure 11.9, for example, illustrates an input scheme concerning the *Althen* rule of causation.

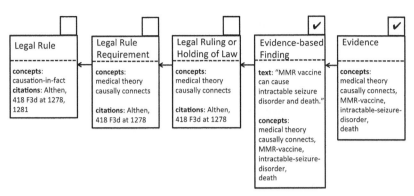

FIGURE 11.9. Query input data scheme. Nodes represent successive levels of a DLF-style rule tree and reasoning chain. Here user seeks cases with evidence and an evidence-based finding that "MMR vaccine can cause intractable seizure disorder and death," in connection with a legal ruling on the "medical theory causally connects" requirement of the *Althen* rule on causation-in-fact

The structure includes nodes abstractly representing various successive levels of the rule tree and reasoning chain, from the legal rule at the left down to the evidence level at the right. In other words, each node refers to an argument role associated with the sentence-level type of the corresponding node in the tree or chain. Here, the nodes refer to a Legal Rule (the *Althen* rule of causation-in-fact), a Legal Rule Requirement ("medical theory causally connects"), an Evidence-based Finding, and so on. The system would fill in the "citation" and "concept" information from the rule tree.

The user indicates (with check marks) the level[s] of the rule tree and chain for which he/she seeks information and fills in the "text" field of the targeted node with the specific proposition of interest. In effect, a check mark indicates the argument role the proposition should play in the cases retrieved. Here the user seeks cases with evidence and an evidence-based finding of causation in connection with a legal ruling on the "medical theory causally connects" requirement of the *Althen* rule on causation-in-fact. He/she has specified that the evidence-based finding should be that "MMR vaccine can cause intractable seizure disorder and death." Conceivably, the system could associate concepts with those mentioned in the proposition, for example, a normalized MMR-vaccine concept.

In effect, the filled-in data scheme would guide the IR system in retrieving and ranking cases for relevance given user-indicated argument-related constraints. One could imagine similar input schemes based on legal factor-based models of a claim, such as the VJAP domain model of Figure 5.10. Such a structure could aid a user in specifying the issues and factors for which they seek legal holdings or evidence-based findings. The system would offer a list of input schemes corresponding to the paths through the model for which it has information.

One could also develop input forms with items specifying argument-related query constraints similar to the above. Users would indicate that they seek documents that have sentence(s) playing particular argument roles whose content they specify with propositions. Menus of concepts and citations would help users in completing the forms. Where targeted information is spread across multiple sentences, a form-based approach could change the granularity of entry from sentences to passages or paragraphs. This approach could be used in place of a graphical interface or as a supplement.

Conceivably, natural language versions of input queries may serve as a complementary medium for confirming the user's intention. The system could translate a query that the user entered with an input scheme or form into an equivalent natural language version. The interface could offer menu options with which the user could refine or modify the query and observe the effects on the natural language version. For example, the system could translate the query represented in Figure 11.9 as "Retrieve all sentences, in the context of the *Althen* causation-in-fact rule's requirement of a medical theory causal connection, that contain a finding of fact and evidence that the MMR vaccine can cause intractable seizure disorder and death." Then, it would ask the user to confirm the translation or modify the query.

11.6. CONCEPTUAL INFORMATION RETRIEVAL FROM STATUTES

So far the discussion has focused primarily on conceptual legal information retrieval of argument-related information from a corpus of legal cases. To what extent can conceptual legal information retrieval be applied to statutes and regulations? As with AR, the answer depends on developing a type system to capture concepts that are: (1) important to users' queries and the problems they are trying to solve and (2) capable of automatic annotation in statutory and regulatory texts and other documents that refer to them.

For example, medical personnel in the public health emergency domain introduced in Chapter 2 might face a situation involving a patient with a rare but contagious disease. Ideally a conceptual legal information retrieval system could help them easily find answers to questions like "What regulations establish reporting relationships between government public health agencies and hospitals concerning contagious diseases?"

A CLIR program would most likely misinterpret such a query submitted as text because it could not understand the concepts to which it refers or the network of relationships among instances of the concepts established by regulations.

This section first addresses a type system approach to representing the regulatory concepts, describes a network-based technique for representing legally mandated relationships between instances of the concepts, and then illustrates how the networks are useful for conceptual legal information retrieval.

11.6.1. *A Type System for Statutes*

Although legal ontologies have been developed for statutory domains (Section 6.5), as far as known, efforts are just beginning to apply a type system and pipeline approach to representing the semantics of regulatory texts for purposes of enabling conceptual information retrieval (see, e.g., Wyner and Governatori, 2013, discussed in Section 9.5).

A suitable system of general statutory types would include structural elements of statutes, types of legal rule statements, and elements of legal rules, as well as concepts and relations more specific to a regulatory domain. Some useful general statutory types are shown in Figure 11.10 in the left column. At the top is an incomplete listing of the structural elements commonly encountered in statutory texts such as numbered elements like titles, sections, paragraphs, chunks of text that are separated typographically but not numbered, kinds of sections, and kinds of cross-references.

The figure lists types of "statements," a basic component of a statutory provision, including definitions and rule statements. A statement can be either a whole sentence or a part of the sentence. There are also types of rule statements, for example, rule statements that impose an obligation, confer a permission, etc. Three

- Structural Elements
  - Numbered elements: titles, sections, subsections, paragraphs
  - Unnumbered elements
  - Section types preamble, definitions, appendix
  - Regulatory Cross-references: internal ref., external ref.
- Statements
  - DefinitionStatement
  - RuleStatement
    - ObligationStatement
    - PermissionStatement
    - ProhibitionStatement
    - LiabilityStatement
    - PurposeStatement
  - RuleStatementParts
    - Antecedent
    - Consequent
    - Exception
  - Statutory Statement Variables: action, acting, receiving agents
    - Acting Agent: whom does the statement direct to act?
    - Receiving Agent: whom does the statement direct to receive the action?
    - Action: what action does the statement direct?
    - Prescription: with what level of prescription does the statement direct the action: ``may"? ``must"?
    - Goal: for what goal does the statement direct the action?
    - Purpose: for what purpose does the statement direct the action?
    - Time frame: in what time frame can/must the action be taken?
    - Condition: what circumstances govern if the action is taken?

Regulatory Domain Concepts and Relations

- Regulatory Topic (e.g., environmental, criminal, intellectual property, public health emergency preparation and response)
- Agents
  - PublicHealthSystemActor
    - GovernmentalPublicHealthAgency
    - Hospital
    - HealthCareProvider
    - BusinessEmployer
    - ElectedOfficial
- Actions
  - PublicHealthSystemActions
    - ReportingAction
    - SurveillanceAction
    - QuarantineAction
- Concepts
  - InfectiousDisease
  - PublicHealthEmergency: epidemic, train wreck, nuclear accident
  - Time: intervals, dates
- Mentions
  - AgentMentions
    - GovernmentalPublicHealthAgencyMention
    - HospitalMention
  - ActionMentions
    - ReportingMention
  - TimeMentions: IntervalMention, DateMention

FIGURE 11.10. General (left) and domain-specific (right) statutory types

1. What provisions have a RuleStatement with GovernmentalPublicHealthAgency, Hospital, and ReportingAction(InfectiousDisease)?

2. What provisions have a RuleStatement with GovernmentalPublicHealthAgency, BusinessEmployer, and ReportingAction(InfectiousDisease)?

3. What provisions have an ObligationStatement involving PublicHealthEmergency and HospitalAgent?

4. What PublicHealthSystemActors are linked in an ObligationAssertion in Pennsylvania provisions but in no other states?

5. What provisions have a RuleStatement with an ObligationStatement with Hospital and RegulatoryTopic(Criminal) and RegulatoryTopic(PublicHealthEmergencyPreparation-Response)?

FIGURE 11.11. Statutory conceptual queries from the *Public Health Emergency* domain

common parts of a rule statement are also listed: the antecedent "if" part, the consequent "then" part, and exceptions.

The lower half lists a class of statutory statement variables that seem of general applicability for statutory rules including the *action* that a statutory provision indicates with a certain level of *prescription* an *acting agent* should or may perform with respect to a *receiving agent* given a certain *condition* within a particular *time frame* in order to achieve a particular *goal* and legislative *purpose* (see Sweeney et al., 2014).

Statutes also have regulatory topics and regulate domains that involve certain concepts that are useful for representing the semantics of what a rule statement is about. Some additional types for concepts in a particular regulated domain, public health emergency preparation and response, are shown in the right column of Figure 11.10. Our public health colleagues at the University of Pittsburgh have identified these concepts, for example, public health system actors, kinds of emergencies, and the associated actions such as surveillance, reporting, and quarantine. As discussed in Section 9.7.1, they have used these concepts in manually annotating 12 states' public health emergency statutes, and we have applied ML to identify the concepts automatically in statutory texts.

With a system of statutory types like these, one could compose conceptual queries like the ones shown in Figure 11.11 with which to retrieve statutory information. For instance, query number 2 expresses the above example about regulations that establish reporting relationships between government public health agencies and hospitals concerning contagious diseases.

Ideally, a program would use a type system and text mining techniques automatically to identify these semantic types in both texts and queries. It would use this conceptual legal information to rank texts in response to user queries, leading users more quickly to the answers they seek, and to highlight and abstract the retrieved texts so that users understand what they have retrieved and how it addresses their queries.

A conceptual information retrieval system like the one envisioned would "know" that the semantic features captured in the type system and annotated in the texts are important, but it would not know from the start how important the features are to the different types of queries users submit. As users process queries, however, the system could learn how important the features were to successful queries using ML techniques like those in Section 11.3.2. Based on users' feedback as to which queries achieved their goals, the system would update its weights for assessing confidence in the responsiveness of documents to past queries and thus refine its method for assessing its confidence in its ranking of documents given a new query. Thus, in a sense the users would "teach" the conceptual retrieval system how to measure relevance in this regulatory context.

11.6.2. *Network Techniques for Conceptual Legal IR*

A number of projects employ *network analysis*, that is, drawing inferences about relevance based on linkages and their weights in a network, to implement conceptual legal information retrieval. As mentioned in Section 7.7, LA extracts, from its full-text case law corpus, a network of special legal issues, which can assist users in retrieving other cases for the same issue. WN's reranking function takes into account citation networks. The system in Mimouni et al. (2014) retrieved documents based on queries containing semantic descriptors and indicators of cross-referential relations between documents in a citation network (e.g., "Which orders talk about abnormally annoying noise . . . and make reference to decrees talking about soundproofing?").

In a statutory legal information retrieval application, Winkels and Boer (2014) have developed a method for automatically determining a context of laws relevant to the particular legal article a user has retrieved from an online hyperlinked legislative database. The small corpus comprises two articles of the Dutch "foreigners law." For each article, a "context network" was developed comprising a selection of all incoming references to, and all outgoing references from, the article in focus. The contexts were based on a weighting scheme, which favored references that are outgoing, are not internal references, refer to definitions in prior articles, were recently changed, or have a high degree of network centrality.

Network analysis has supported corpus-based inferences about legal regulations. The system in Hoekstra and Boer (2014) helps answer questions such as "What is the most important or influential regulation in the Netherlands?" by analyzing the network of co-citations between the interconnected web resources associated with the legal regulations in the MetaLex Document Server. Szoke et al. (2014) also employed citation network analysis in order to determine the most influential regulations in a corpus of hundreds of legislative documents represented in HTML format from which citation information was extracted automatically. In a network of legal sources, Gultemen and van Engers (2014) employed a fine-grained interlinking of statutory law at the paragraph–article level.

Most of the above network-based approaches relied on citation linkages, but one can also employ statutory networks to represent semantic aspects of the laws.

11.6.3. *Conceptual Legal IR with Statutory Network Diagrams*

The LENA project at the University of Pittsburgh School of Public Health employs a statutory network for conceptual legal information retrieval. As noted in Section 2.6, links in such a network represent relationships between participants mandated by statute. Specifically, LENA network diagrams graphically represent which agencies and actors in a states' public health system are directed by statute to interact with one another in order to deal with public health emergencies (Ashley et al., 2014).

The system could help users, such as public health agents working in field offices, to answer questions such as "What regulations establish the relationships between government public health agencies and hospitals?" A statutory network diagram like the one in Figure 11.12 serves as a visual index into the legal information database. When a user clicks on a link, the system could retrieve the specific statutory provisions that establish the relationship between participants and that justify the link between the nodes. In this way, LENA statutory network diagrams act as a conceptual interface into an Emergency Law Database of the statutory texts that direct these interactions. Since public health agents in the field may *not* be attorneys familiar with full-text legal IR tools, it can be more intuitive to retrieve provisions relevant to their responsibilities by clicking on a link in the diagram (Ashley et al., 2014).

For example, LENA statutory networks could have assisted humans in drawing legal inferences in the aftermath of the situation in 2014 when a patient, Timothy Allen Duncan, arrived at the Emergency Department of Texas Presbyterian Hospital complaining of nausea and headache following a trip to Africa. He was examined and released, but he returned to the hospital and soon after died of hemorrhagic fever caused by the Ebola virus. According to a subsequent report of the U.S. House of Representative's Energy and Commerce Committee, it was "unclear when and how the Texas Department State Health Services was notified that Mr. Duncan's symptoms were consistent with Ebola." In light of apparent communication lapses, it appears that the hospital emergency department staff had not been sufficiently alerted to the possibility of seeing an Ebola-exposed patient (Ashley et al., 2014).

In order to demonstrate the utility of LENA and the Emergency Law Database, researchers at the School of Public Health used them to answer the question "What Texas laws require interaction between hospitals and governmental public health

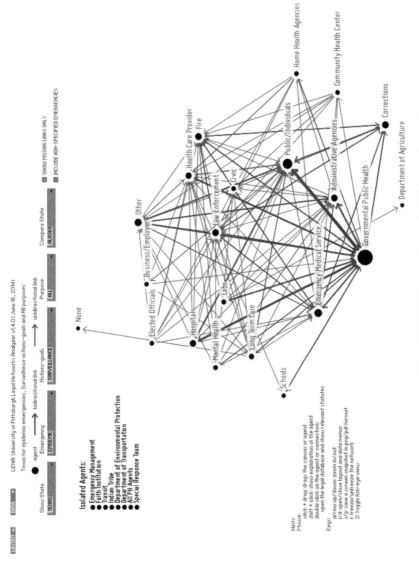

FIGURE 11.12. Texas LENA Statutory Network (Ashley et al., 2014)

entities?" Answering such a question is straightforward for legally trained personnel using commercial legal IR systems, but it would be problematic for nonlegally
trained people to find the answer *quickly*.

The screenshot of LENA in Figure 11.12 shows the legally directed network of
agents named by Texas law concerning epidemic emergencies involving infectious
diseases. Circular nodes represent agents in the public health system. A line (or
"edge") connecting agents shows that a law or group of laws directs action between
two agents. Its thickness represents the number of legal directives requiring such
interaction. Governmental Public Health is the largest node, representing state and
local boards of health and health departments. The size of a node corresponds to
the agent's centrality in the network; the larger the node, the more central the role
the agent plays. It is proportional to the number of incoming directives from, and
outgoing directives to, other agents. The darker link between Governmental Public Health and Hospitals is bidirectional; some of the functions between the two
agents are instigated by Governmental Public Health, and others are initiated by
Hospitals.

When a user selects the link between these two agents, the LENA Emergency
Law Database returns 119 laws that direct some kind of interaction between these
agents. In order to narrow the search, a user can enter terms like "reportable" and
"diseases" as key words. This yields 24 citations, 3 of which relate to the question
of interest. These laws require hospitals in Texas to notify the local or regional
health department by phone immediately after identifying a case of viral hemorrhagic fever. There do not appear to be any Texas statutory requirements mandating
that health-care providers share information concerning a patient's travel history or
that require hospitals to delve into a patient's point of origin. Nor did any of the 24
cited laws direct communication from governmental public health agencies to hospitals concerning an ongoing health alert (such as Ebola was at the time) (Ashley et al.,
2014). Thus, the LENA tool and the Emergency Law Database could assist policy-
makers to identify gaps in a state's regulatory scheme for dealing with public health
emergencies.

The statutory network diagrams and database could also help policy-makers and
legislators draw comparisons with other states. Researchers can conduct similar
searches to discover and compare different states' disease reporting requirements.
Searches with the LENA database revealed that epidemic emergency reporting
requirements can be quite different from that in Texas. For example, Kansas and
Wisconsin both require hospitals to report such disease-related events to a government agency within hours (Ashley et al., 2014).

The results provided with LENA tools are based on a snapshot of the states'
infectious disease response networks. The statutes and regulations undergo frequent
revision and the Emergency Law Database and LENA resources would need to be
updated regularly to be reliable. Of course, that is where automated extraction of
information from statutory texts would be especially useful (see Section 9.7.1).

11.7. CONCLUSION

This chapter has presented programs that employ text annotation for conceptual legal information retrieval and that can assist human users in finding relevant materials with which to draw legal inferences. The next chapter considers tools that enable computational models of legal reasoning to assist humans by drawing certain kinds of legal inferences.

12

Cognitive Computing Legal Apps

12.1. INTRODUCTION

The prototype proposed in Section 11.5 would transform legal information retrieval into AR. If, as argued there, some of the legal knowledge representation frameworks of Part I's computational models of legal reasoning, argument, and prediction can be annotated automatically in case texts, then a legal app could accomplish more than conceptual legal information retrieval. It could support cognitive computing. This chapter describes a cognitive computing environment tailored to the legal domain in terms of tasks, interface, inputs, and outputs and explains how type systems and annotations based on the computational models will help humans frame hypotheses about legal arguments, make predictions, and test them against the documents in a corpus.

A hypothesis predicts how a legal issue should be decided, such as:

- The plaintiff should win the issue of trade secret misappropriation where defendant deceived it into disclosing its confidential product data even though the information could have easily been reverse engineered.
- The plaintiff can still show causation even though more than six months elapsed between the vaccination and the onset of the injury.
- Plaintiff's claim for conversion should fail where she had not actually caught the baseball, even though the defendant intentionally interfered with her attempt.

Posing and testing legal hypotheses like these is a paradigmatic cognitive computing activity in which humans and computers can collaborate, each performing the intelligent activities that they do best. Humans know the hypotheses that matter legally; the computer helps them to frame and test these hypotheses based on arguments citing cases and counterexamples. The type system annotations will enable a conceptual legal information system to retrieve case examples relevant to the hypotheses, generate summaries tailored to the users' needs, construct arguments, and explain predictions.

The chapter discusses challenges that still need to be addressed in order to construct these new CCLAs. How can the computational models of case-based, rule-based, and value-based legal reasoning and argumentation be integrated with conceptual legal information retrieval? What roles do the type system and pipelined text annotators play in this integration? What kind of manual conceptual annotation of training sets of documents will be required? What will CCLAs look like? How will they help humans to frame and test legal hypotheses?

After explaining some general limitations of the approach, the chapter explores how far one can progress in realizing computational models of arguments based on legal texts. One can extract instances of argument schemes, use them to direct users' attention to relevant texts and passages, and suggest arguments and counter-arguments. But can a system suggest novel arguments? Pose new legal hypotheses that it has reason to believe would be interesting and test them? What lies on the legal horizon, and where should a would-be developer begin?

12.2. NEW LEGAL APPS ON THE MARKET

In the last year, *Legaltech News* (Legaltech News, 2016) reports new developments in legal apps almost every week.

12.2.1. *Ross*

Perhaps the most intriguing of the newer legal apps, *Ross*, a cloud-based legal QA service based on IBM Watson (Ross Intelligence, 2015), accepts questions in plain English and returns answers based on legislation, case law, and other sources. Based on its understanding of users' questions in natural language, such as "Can a bankrupt company still conduct business?," Ross provides an answer along with citations, suggests readings relevant to the topic, and also monitors the law for changes that can affect a user's "case" (Cutler, 2015).

A team of law students at the University of Toronto created Ross, taking second place in an IBM-hosted contest, and with IBM support created a Silicon Valley start-up (Jackson, 2015). Their demo video lists sample questions the program can handle, including:

1. What corporate records does a Canadian company need to keep?
2. How much can directors of Canadian corporations add to the state capital account of a class of shares?
3. Can an employee start a competing business?
4. If an employee has not been meeting sales targets and has not been able to complete the essentials of their employment can they be terminated without notice? (Jackson, 2015).

In response to the last question, the Ross screen cites *Regina v. Arthurs*, [1967] 2 O.R. 49, 62 D.L.R. (2D) 342, 67 C.L.L.C. 14,024 (C.A.) along with excerpts and text. Ross reports 94% confidence in the case's responsiveness and summarizes the decision: "If an employee has been guilty of serious misconduct, habitual neglect of duty, incompetence, or conduct incompatible with his duties, or prejudicial to the employer's business, or if he has been guilty of willful disobedience to the employer's orders in a matter of substance, the law recognizes the employer's right summarily to dismiss the delinquent employee." Ross suggests additional readings from legislation, case law, legal memoranda regarding "just cause terminations," and other sources. It also monitors new materials added to the corpus that may be relevant to a user's previous queries (Cutler, 2015).

Remus and Levy characterize the approach of "IBM Watson and similar question-answering systems" as requiring experts to

> attach to each paragraph [of each document in an assembled project database] a set of natural language [legal] practice questions such that the paragraph is the correct answer for each of the attached questions. (Remus and Levy, 2015, pp. 24f)

For example, a question might be "When can a debtor reject a collective bargaining agreement?" (Remus and Levy, 2015, pp. 25).

Since questions like this can be phrased in multiple ways, the system needs to recognize that a user has asked a version of a question that the system knows how to answer. For instance, a user may phrase the question more specifically:

> Can a debtor reject a collective bargaining agreement where debtor is a city that filed for Chapter 9 bankruptcy and previously attempted to negotiate with a private union before rejecting its collective bargaining agreement?" (Remus and Levy, 2015, pp. 26)

The challenge is whether a system can learn to recognize the variations based on a training set of versions of each question provided by experts. The system will learn weights associated with features of the training instances that distinguish the positive from the negative instances of the question. These features comprise word or n-gram frequencies (Section 8.3), their synonyms and hyponyms in word networks (Section 6.3), concepts mentioned and their relationships (Section 6.7) (see Remus and Levy, 2015, pp. 26). The learned weights, in turn, inform the system's level of certainty that it "understands" the user's question.

As users submit new versions of a question, the system forms new links between them and its pre-stored answer (see Remus and Levy, 2015, p. 27). In this way, Ross learns from user feedback. For instance, the *Regina v. Arthurs* case is followed by a query inviting users to "press thumbs up" to save the response to their "case" "if the response is accurate" or to "press thumbs down for another response." The feedback is intended to inform and update Ross's confidence in the responsiveness of the answer to the user's version of a question (Cutler, 2015).

While Ross improves in responding to questions, its responses are pointers to relevant passages in legal texts. It does not appear that Ross can more actively assist users in making arguments or predicting outcomes.

12.2.2. *Lex Machina*

LexisNexis has recently acquired *Lex Machina*, the service that makes legal predictions regarding patent and other intellectual property cases. As discussed in Section 4.7, its legal predictions are based on, among other things, analysis of litigation participant-and-behavior features extracted from an extensive corpus of IP cases.

Apparently, the creators of Lex Machina intended to incorporate more semantic information about the cases' merits. According to Surdeanu et al. (2011), the authors "would like to combine both merits of the case as well as prior factors [i.e., participant-and-behavior features] into a single model." Whether, and the extent to which, features directly related to the substantive merits of a case have been included in the current version is not clear.

12.2.3. *Ravel*

Ravel (Ravel Law, 2015a), founded by Stanford Law School graduates, and the library of Harvard Law School are engaged in a joint effort to scan a large portion of U.S. caselaw and make the case texts accessible in a digital format along with Ravel's visual maps graphically depicting how one case cites another in connection with a legal concept (Eckholm, 2015).

> On Ravel sites currently available to the public, for example, a lawyer planning to challenge the 2010 *Citizens United* decision, which permitted corporations to make independent political expenditures, can enter "campaign finance" and see in schematic form the major cases at the district, appellate and Supreme Court levels that led up to the 2010 decision and the subsequent cases that cite it. (Eckholm, 2015)

The output includes a list of n cases relevant to "campaign finance," where a "case is 'Relevant' when it's important in the context of your specific search terms" (Ravel Law, 2015d). Each case is represented with excerpts from the opinion in which the search terms are highlighted. The accompanying visual map, a kind of structured citation network (see Section 2.6), represents as circles cases dealing with "campaign finance" such as the *Citizens United* case. The circles' sizes indicate how often the case was cited. The lines represent citations with the lines' thickness indicating the "depth of treatment," perhaps a measure of the extent to which a case is cited or discussed in the citing opinion. The citation network is structured along the x-axis to show a chronology in years and along the y-axis broken into a court system hierarchy: state courts, district courts, courts of appeals, and the U.S. Supreme Court for this particular query. Alternatively, the *y*-axis can show cases by relevance with more relevant cases at the top.

With the graphic display, one can trace citations from a seminal case such as *Buckley v. Valeo* to more recent cases. As one clicks on a case, it appears at the top of the case list (Ravel Law, 2015c).

Ravel also provides fee-based analytical services focusing on judicial history and past cases. Given a query, for instance regarding certain kinds of motions, the program reports "how a particular judge has responded to [those kinds] of motions in the past," "the cases, circuits, and judges [a] judge finds most persuasive," "the rules and specific language [a] judge favors and commonly cites," and "distinctions that set [a] judge apart." Case analytics include information about specific paragraphs or sentences and how they have been referred to in subsequent decisions (Ravel Law, 2015b).

12.3. BRIDGING LEGAL TEXTS AND COMPUTATIONAL MODELS

The new legal apps on the market introduce innovative tools and user interfaces that will be important for cognitive computing. For example, Ravel's graphical interface, structuring citation networks in terms of chronology and court hierarchy, introduces legal researchers to the virtues of citation networks on a large scale. Ravel's plan to include statutes in its citation networks will make the networks even more useful. Incidentally, Ravel's citation networks deliver on the promise of the SCALIR project (Rose and Belew, 1991), as discussed in Section 7.9.3, and of the statutory citation networks discussed in Sections 2.6 and 11.6.3.

The new legal apps also incorporate ML and legal outcome prediction. Ross employs ML to update confidence levels in the relevance of materials returned in answering questions. Lex Machina predicts outcomes of legal problems based on features extracted directly from the texts of decisions. Both Ross and Lex Machina exploit histories of judicial decision-making to assist users in anticipating how a judge will react to an argument. It appears, however, that the features Lex Machina employs for prediction do not directly take into account substantive aspects of cases.

If and when a legal app can take into account substantive features extracted from case texts in making arguments or predicting legal outcomes, the field will have taken a big step forward. With their assembled corpora and techniques for extracting information from texts, Lex Machina, Ross, and Ravel are well-positioned to take this step, but it does not appear that they have done so yet. As explained below, computational models of legal reasoning can help.

12.4. COGNITIVE COMPUTING APPS FOR TESTING LEGAL HYPOTHESES

This section explores how to achieve a new kind of CCLA by linking some of Part I's computational models of legal reasoning (CMLRs) and Part II's techniques for extracting argument-related information from legal texts and using it for conceptual information retrieval.

In these new legal apps, computational models of legal reasoning will serve as a bridge between corpora of legal texts and human users solving realistic legal problems. The Apps probably will not be able to annotate logical rules or semantic networks in sufficient detail to enable all of the CMLRs described in Part I to run directly from texts. Probably, however, they will be able to identify the portions of texts that contain the legal rules, legal holdings and findings of fact, arguments justifying conclusions, and explanations of reasons, as well as particular legal factors and evidence factors, to support a cognitive computing collaboration with users.

Equipped with CMLRs, CCLAs will employ this information extracted from legal texts to assist humans to investigate and answer legal questions, predict case outcomes, provide explanations, and make arguments for and against legal conclusions more effectively than is currently feasible with existing technologies.

12.4.1. *A Paradigm for CCLAs: Legal Hypothesis-Testing*

As explained in Chapter 1, cognitive computing should support collaborative intelligent activity between humans and computers in which each does what it can do best. In introducing the commoditization of legal services, the last stage in Susskind's evolution of legal work, that chapter left an open question: "If process engineering of legal services is rethinking how to deliver 'very cheap and very high quality' solutions, who or what will be responsible for tailoring those solutions to a client's particular problem?"

Formerly, it was a goal of expert systems development in AI to generate rules embodying a firm's expertise and ways of solving problems. As in Waterman's expert system of Section 1.3.1, one would attempt to extract heuristic rules from manual analysis of legal texts. Equipped with such rules, given a new problem, the system could apply the rules to tailor a solution to that problem. Or at least that was the intention. The effort proved largely intractable, however; the knowledge representation bottleneck stymied the expert systems approach.

Cognitive computing has a similar goal, to achieve a kind of mass customization of legal advice, but shifts the focus to the human user by striving for an intelligent computer–human collaboration. That approach raises a similar question, however: what kind of collaboration and how will it be achieved?

Here is one answer. Instead of extracting production rules, the aim is to annotate patterns of analysis and argument that can guide human's problem-solving efforts. In particular, the annotated patterns of analysis and argument can help humans to frame, test, and evaluate legal hypotheses relevant to solving their problems. Here, *hypothesis* means a prediction, in the form of a rule-like generalization based on substantive legal considerations, of how a legal issue should or may reasonably be decided given certain conditions. By "test" and "evaluate" legal hypotheses, I mean not only to assess whether the prediction is correct but also to retrieve examples and counterexamples of the hypothesis for consideration and to consider arguments pro and con. These arguments may lead the human to revise and reevaluate the hypothesis. They could also help the human to fashion the strongest arguments in favor of a position that an advocate must take in support of a client's position while fully apprising him of the counterarguments.

In helping humans to frame, test, and evaluate substantive legal hypotheses, the envisioned CCLAs would engage humans in a paradigmatic collaborative activity. Humans are better at conceiving of interesting hypotheses, which, if confirmed, will have strategic or tactical ramifications for the legal positions they take and the manner in which they will justify them. Computers will quickly analyze huge text corpora in search of evidence relevant to a human's hypothesis.

The legal apps could engage users in an iterative process of reformulating a hypothesis both in express terms and via selecting case examples that confirm or contradict the current hypothesis. The CCLA will not output "the answer" but output tentative conclusions, summarizing the evidence supporting or contradicting the hypothesis in its current form. It will construct arguments about the hypothesis based on the evidence, including listing examples that appear to satisfy the query and confirm the hypothesis, and also point out apparent counterexamples that disconfirm the hypothesis, and near misses, examples that nearly satisfy the antecedents of the rule-like hypothesis.

Ultimately, human users will have to read the selected examples, counterexamples, or near misses. The legal app, however, will frame its presentation around the hypothesis. This would focus the reader on documents selected as substantively most relevant to the hypothesis. In addition, the App would abstract and summarize the relevant documents in a way that made clear their relationship to the query or hypothesis.

The remainder of this section explains how a new CCLA could help humans to formulate a variety of substantive legal hypotheses and to test and evaluate them against a corpus of legal documents. The targeted types of legal hypotheses are explained and illustrated. We sketch how a CCLA could operationalize the hypotheses into subsidiary queries and interpret the results.

Extended examples in two domains illustrate the process of translating hypotheses into queries for conceptually relevant cases and applying an appropriate computational model of legal argument to the retrieved information in order to assess the hypothesis and explain it with arguments and counters.

The next section presents a critique of the sketch, identifying research challenges that still need to be solved, and underscoring some general limitations of the approach.

12.4.2. *Targeted Legal Hypotheses*

When attorneys consider the various legal issues a factual scenario raises, they likely consider potential arguments and counters for each issue and frame hypotheses about which side should succeed. Instinctively attorneys consider both the reasons in support of reaching a particular outcome and the reasons against it. These reasons include favorable facts that an attorney has proved or believes s/he can prove, as well as unfavorable facts the opponent has proved or may prove.

An attorney may thus hypothesize that a side should prevail on an issue where certain conditions favor that conclusion even though other conditions favor a contrary conclusion. The basic form of such a hypotheses is shown in Figure 12.1.

In these formulations, [*side*] is a generic party, say plaintiff or defendant. The issue [*x*] can be a legal claim, element of the claim, or the application of a legal rule or rule requirement. Conditions [*y*] and [*z*] can refer quite generally to a holding of law, finding of fact, legal factor, evidence factor, type of evidence, or statement of fact.

In either formulation, the hypothesis is a prediction about the decision of a legal issue, that is, about the outcome of a legal claim, element, legal rule, or requirement given the conditions specified in the hypothesis, including holdings of law, findings of fact, evidence factors, types of evidence, statements of fact, or combinations thereof, that favor that side and despite the conditions that favor the opposing side.

The proposed legal app is intended to assist human users in testing the two types of hypotheses against a corpus of cases. We are not attempting to model analyzing the legal problem based on first principles or on statutory texts independently of case decisions applying them. Thus, the predictions should be seen as relative to and limited by the information in a given set of legal case texts.

In this sense, the two formulations involve predictions that are partly empirical and partly normative. Formulation [1], a *should-hypothesis*, is a prediction that the outcome of the decision *should* be as specified, given the information contained in a given a set of legal cases. This means that, in terms of some underlying computational model of legal argument and the cases in that set, it determines if the prediction can be confirmed given the strength of the case-based legal arguments pro and con. Formulation [2], a *can-hypothesis*, predicts merely that the outcome of the decision *can* be as specified given a set of legal cases. It is a much weaker prediction than a should-hypothesis and can be satisfied by even a single case that satisfies the condition and has the specified outcome.

With the envisioned legal app, users will be able to frame and test hypotheses in the above formats, like the ones illustrated in Figures 12.2 and 12.3. These hypotheses

[1] *Should-hypothesis*: The issue of [*x*] *should* be decided for [*side*] where condition [*y*] even though condition [*z*].

[2] *Can-hypothesis*: The issue of [*x*] *can* be decided for [*side*] where condition [*y*] even though condition [*z*].

FIGURE 12.1. Two templates for targeted legal hypotheses

The issue of *trade secret misappropriation* <u>should</u> be decided for:

(a) Plaintiff where *plaintiff's former employee brought product development information to defendant.*

(b) Plaintiff where *defendant deceived plaintiff into disclosing confidential information*

(c) Plaintiff where *defendant deceived plaintiff into disclosing confidential information* even though *plaintiff's information was able to be reverse engineered.*

(d) Plaintiff where *plaintiff took security measures to protect the confidential information, plaintiff's product was unique in the market,* and *defendant agreed not to disclose the information,* even though *plaintiff disclosed the information in a public forum.*

(e) Plaintiff where plaintiff *has protected his property interest* and *his confidentiality interest because of the security measures and the nondisclosure agreement* even though *plaintiff has waived his property interest because of the public disclosure* and *plaintiff has waived his confidentiality interest because of the public disclosure.*

(f) Defendant where plaintiff *disclosed the information in a public forum* even though plaintiff has *taken efforts to maintain the secrecy of the information* and *plaintiff took measures to protect the information* and *defendant entered into a nondisclosure agreement.*

The issue of *trade secret misappropriation* <u>can</u> be decided for:

(g) Defendant where *plaintiff's former employee brought product development information to defendant.*

FIGURE 12.2. Sample legal hypotheses CCLAs should target (from the *trade secret misappropriation domain*)

Plaintiff can succeed on the issue of:

(a) a *vaccine injury claim for compensation* where the vaccine was MMR vaccine and the injury was intractable seizure disorder.

(b) the *Althen test of causation* where the vaccine was MMR vaccine and the injury was intractable seizure disorder.

(c) a *logical sequence of cause and effect between vaccination and injury* where the vaccine was MMR vaccine and the injury was intractable seizure disorder.

(d) the *Althen test of causation* where any vaccine was involved and the injury was myocarditis.

(e) a *vaccine injury claim for compensation* even though the court held for defendant on the issue of *causation under the Althen test.*

(f) a *logical sequence of cause and effect between vaccination and injury* where the vaccine was MMR vaccine and the injury was intractable seizure disorder even though some evidence factors favored defendant.

(g) a *logical sequence of cause and effect between vaccination and injury* where the vaccine was MMR vaccine and the injury was intractable seizure disorder even though the onset timing was greater than 6 months.

(h) the *Althen test of causation* where the vaccine was MMR vaccine and the injury was intractable seizure disorder and some evidence factors favored plaintiff even though other evidence factors favored defendant.

FIGURE 12.3. Sample legal hypotheses CCLAs should target (from the V/IP domain). *Issues* in italics.

are drawn from two of the legal domains previously discussed: trade secret law, introduced in Section 3.3.2, and the V/IP domain, introduced in Section 5.8.

The figures suggest how computational models of legal reasoning could be applied to evaluate hypotheses. In Figure 12.2, the hypotheses are almost all should-hypotheses (formulation [1]). In order to evaluate them, one could apply a model of legal-factor-based argument and prediction, functionally similar to the VJAP model (Section 5.7). As discussed in Section 12.4.4, such a model can evaluate should-hypotheses predicting what an outcome should be as well as can-hypotheses (formulation [2]) predicting what the outcome can be. For example, hypothesis (a) will yield an argument that plaintiff should win while (g) will focus on an argument, if any, that a defendant could win. An argument for (g) would be a counterargument to that in (a). In generating the argument for (a), the App would consider and respond to counterarguments like that of (g).

In Figure 12.3, in contrast, all of the hypotheses are can-hypotheses. One could apply a computational model of evidentiary legal reasoning to evaluate these hypotheses, for example, one like the DLF (Section 5.8). For reasons discussed in Section 12.4.4, such a descriptive model of argument would not be able to evaluate should-hypotheses without more information.

As described next, hypotheses like those in Figures 12.2 and 12.3 will be operationalized by translating them into queries employing conceptual legal criteria like those illustrated in Section 11.5.2. As we saw there, the conceptual criteria are expressed in terms of type systems and annotation methods comparable to the ones described in Part II and Chapter 11.

There are, of course, many other forms of substantive legal hypotheses that humans may wish to evaluate against corpora of legal documents. For instance, an empirical legal scholar may seek to confirm a hypothesis that fraud plays a central role as an instrumental rationale and substantive claim in cases in which courts pierce the corporate veil to hold shareholders liable (see Oh, 2010). The new App cannot assist with confirming that kind of hypothesis unless and until one can develop a way to operationalize such a hypothesis for testing against a corpus of cases.

12.4.3. *Operationalizing Hypotheses*

Given a hypothesis of the form shown in Figure 12.1, retrieving cases relevant to the hypothesis is the kind of conceptual AR that a system like the LARCCS prototype of Section 11.5 would be designed to handle.

First, there is the challenge of helping human users to formulate a hypothesis to test. Eliciting such hypotheses from users presents similar challenges to those discussed in Section 11.5.5 for eliciting users' argument needs in conceptual information retrieval. A well-designed user interface will need to apprise humans about the targeted kinds of hypotheses it can process. The system will present templates for the two hypothesis formulations above and provide example hypotheses of each type. It will support human users in formulating similar hypotheses using a combination of visual aids, text processing, tools for editing sample hypotheses, and dynamically generated menus presenting the system's version of a user's inputs for confirmation.

Given a hypothesis, the legal app will construct subsidiary queries for cases where courts have held for *side* on issue x where conditions y even though conditions z. Operationalizing hypotheses like those in Figures 12.2 and 12.3 by translating them into subsidiary queries is a key step.

The targeted subsidiary queries are very like the conceptual queries of Section 11.5.2. They seek cases with propositions playing particular argument or legal roles. The kinds of argument-related and legal-related information available for expressing the conditions y and z include the expanded list of types in Section 11.5.3, namely propositions stating:

- legal rules or conclusions about whether legal rules' requirements are satisfied,
- factual findings, evidence factors, evidence or evidential reasoning,
- applicable legal factors or related policies, values, and reasoning, or
- case procedures.

In particular, hypotheses about trade secret law like those in Figure 12.2 would be translated into conceptual queries for legal factors and argument roles like those in Figure 11.6. For example, hypothesis (a):

The issue of trade secret misappropriation should be decided for plaintiff where plaintiff's former employee brought product development information to defendant.

could be operationalized, in part, with a conceptual query like:

What cases are there with a **Legal Ruling or Holding of Law** re **Legal Rule** re *Trade-Secret-Misappropriation* where **Legal Factor:** F7 *Brought-Tools (P)*?

As another example, hypothesis (g):

The issue of trade secret misappropriation can be decided for defendant where plaintiff's former employee brought product development information to defendant.

would involve a more specific query like:

What cases are there where defendant won a **Legal Ruling or Holding of Law** re **Legal Rule** re *Trade-Secret-Misappropriation* where **Legal Factor:** F7 *Brought-Tools (P)*?

These are conceptual queries 1 and 2, respectively, in Figure 11.6.

Hypotheses about the V/IP domain like those in Figure 12.3 would be translated automatically into conceptual queries for cases with propositions playing particular argument roles like the ones in Figure 11.5. For example, the condition in hypothesis (a) in Figure 12.3:

> Plaintiff can succeed on the issue of a vaccine injury claim for compensation where the vaccine was MMR vaccine and the injury was intractable seizure disorder.

could be expressed with query 4a in Figure 11.5:

> What **Evidence-Based Findings** have there been that: measles, mumps & rubella (MMR) vaccine *causes* intractable seizure disorder?

A module like LUIMA-Search would translate formulated hypotheses like the above into subsidiary conceptual queries as in Section 11.5.2 and translate the queries, in turn, into sets of constraints like that in Figure 11.2 using the argument types of Section 11.5.3. The search and rerank modules would then retrieve and rank cases as described in Sections 11.3.1 and 11.3.2. This presupposes the same kind of connection to a legal IR system as described in Section 11.5.1 in which argument-related information will have been annotated automatically in the cases in a corpus of texts retrieved from the CLIR system.

12.4.4. *Interpreting Hypotheses*

The process described thus far is a kind of legal hypothesis-driven conceptual information retrieval. The legal app will assess the results of the queries to determine whether instances of the targeted hypothesis have been retrieved, which sides the instances favor, that is, whether the retrieved cases are positive, negative, or mixed instances of the hypothesis, and thus, whether or not the results appear to confirm the hypothesis. The App may be able to accomplish more than that, however.

Where a computational model of argument from Part I applies to the annotated features of cases, identifying legal factors or other argument-related information, the App may construct legal arguments in support of or against the hypothesis and evaluate the hypothesis in light of the competing legal arguments. In doing so, the App will apply argument schemes with defeasible legal rules and cases, legal factors, and underlying values.

The App will confirm or question the user's hypothesis and explain why in terms of the arguments. Based on its analysis, the App will offer the human user various options including modifying the hypothesis. In effect, the App will assist the user in exploring a space of plausible hypotheses concerning a legal claim or issue and in collaboratively testing and revising the hypotheses. The next section illustrates this collaborative hypothesis-testing, first with the VJAP model and then with the DLF model.

Collaborative Hypothesis-testing with a Predictive Argument Model
As an example of collaborative hypothesis-testing with a computational legal argument model like VJAP (Section 5.7), consider hypothesis (d) of Figure 12.2, a should-hypothesis:

> The issue of a claim of trade secret misappropriation should be decided for plaintiff where plaintiff took security measures concerning his/her unique product and the defendant agreed not to disclose the information even though the plaintiff had disclosed the information in a public forum.

Using a legal app interface that offered menu-support and accepted natural language inputs, a user could input a legal hypothesis like this as a query and flag it as a hypothesis to test. The program would annotate the text of the query in terms of the expanded list of argument types in Section 11.5.3, including the type for Legal Factors. The program would translate the natural language formulation annotated with instances of Legal Factor types into a list of specific legal factors. Where there is uncertainty about the interpretation of the hypothesis, the App could offer menu choices indicating its top n interpretations of the terms of the user's hypothesis for the user's confirmation.

Having confirmed a specific interpretation of the user's hypothesis, the program would begin a process to test it. First, the program would decompose the hypothesis into queries for cases with the specified trade secret domain legal factors and argument roles such as query 3 in Figure 11.6:

> 3. What cases are there with a legal ruling or holding of law re claim of Trade-Secret-Misappropriation where legal factors: F15 Unique-Product (P), F4 Agreed-Not-To-Disclose (P), F6 Security-measures (P), F27 Disclosure-in-public-forum (D)?

The legal app would access a database of cases against which to apply these queries. Conceivably, the database could be assembled at run-time from a legal IR program's general corpus using a generalization of query 3 such as:

> trade secret misappropriation claims where plaintiff took security measures to protect the confidential information, plaintiff's product was unique in the market, and defendant agreed not to disclose the information, but plaintiff disclosed the information in a public forum.

The legal app would annotate the output of the legal IR program for the query at run-time in terms of Legal Factors and the other argument types from the expanded list. Depending on the efficiency of annotation, it might focus on a subset of types apparently relevant to the hypothesis and related queries. Alternatively, it would employ a previously assembled and annotated corpus of trade secret misappropriation case opinions, perhaps supplemented at run-time with updating queries to a legal IR program. Conceivably, users could specify jurisdictions and time frames to target the database.

The annotation would result in a database of sentences and related cases indexed by sentence-level types, including the general Legal Factor type and the trade-secret-claim-specific legal factors. We assume that the system can interpret sentences that express legal rulings or holdings and/or evidence-based findings well enough to know which side is favored by the ruling, holding, or finding. Phrases involving plaintiff or defendant terms and indicating that a side "won," "prevailed," "has succeeded," and others will probably be treated as standard legal formulations (Section 6.8). Interpreting more complex instances of these sentence types may raise issues of attribution and polarity discussed in Section 12.5.1.

The Legal App would apply query 3 to the annotated database, retrieve cases that satisfy the queries, and analyze the results. Initially, the analysis might simply compare the numbers of cases responsive to each query. While there may be no cases in which plaintiff won a claim for trade secret misappropriation despite the presence of a disclosure in a public forum (Factor F27 Disclosure-in-public-forum (D)) more likely, there is a mix of cases, some won by plaintiff and some won by defendant.

The legal app could issue a preliminary report of the numerical comparison: n pro-plaintiff instances consistent with the hypothesis and m pro-defendant ones contrary to the hypothesis. The report would include a proviso that it is based only on the current database of n trade secret cases (within a particular jurisdiction or time frame).

At that point, the App could offer the user some options including:

1. *Modify database (App/User)*: Expand or change the database to search for additional instances relevant to the hypothesis.
2. *Modify hypothesis (App/User)*: Change the hypothesis and rerun the searches.
3. *Make legal argument (App/User)*: Construct a legal argument in support of or against the hypothesis.
4. *Evaluate hypothesis (App/User)*: Evaluate hypothesis in light of the legal arguments.

The *Modify database* option assumes that there are available options concerning the database. For instance, one could specify jurisdictions or time ranges that restrict the database. Perhaps the search could include additional textual corpora or the IR query could be revised. The parenthetical "(App/User)" indicates that either the App or the user can suggest modifications to the database.

Regarding the *Modify hypothesis* option, typical changes would be to make the hypothesis more general or more specific by subtracting or adding legal factors or, possibly other facts, to the query constraints. In this way, the user's hypothesis becomes a hypothesis about the legal significance of a disclosure in a public forum in a more or less fully specified factual scenario, for instance:

(d') The issue of claim of trade secret misappropriation should be decided for plaintiff where defendant agreed not to disclose the information, even though plaintiff disclosed the information in a public forum.

Hypothesis (d′) is less specific than hypothesis (d) in that it involves only legal factors F4 Agreed-Not-To-Disclose (P) and F27 Disclosure-in-public-forum (D).

Another typical modification is to focus the hypothesis on particular legal issues relevant to the claim. For instance, given the VJAP model of a trade secret misappropriation claim (Figure 5.10), and a scenario involving F4 and F27, a natural focus is on the issues of whether the information is a trade secret and whether the information was misappropriated, or more specifically, was there a confidential relationship and did the plaintiff maintain secrecy as in hypothesis (d″) :

> (d″) The issue of *maintain secrecy* in a claim of trade secret misappropriation should be decided for plaintiff where defendant agreed not to disclose the information, even though plaintiff disclosed the information in a public forum.

The *Make legal argument* option would invite the App (or the user) to make legal arguments in support of and against the current hypothesis. Using a computational model of argument like VJAP (or the CATO or IBP models), the App could make legal-factor-based or value-based arguments for and against the hypothesis given the fact situation.

For instance, in a scenario associated with hypothesis (d), plaintiff took security measures concerning its unique product and the defendant agreed not to disclose the information even though the plaintiff had disclosed the information in a public forum. That is, the applicable factors include F4 Agreed-Not-To-Disclose (P), F6 Security-measures (P), F15 Unique-Product (P), and F27 Disclosure-in-public-forum (D). By inputting these factors to a model like VJAP, the App could construct arguments similar to that shown in Figure 5.13 illustrating an argument for the *Dynamics* case, which is an instance of hypothesis *d*.

If the *user* specifies an argument, the program would attempt to respond to it, but the inputted argument would have to be in a form the system could understand in terms of the applicable CMLR or argument. For instance, the user could specify a case or fact situation as a counterexample to which the App would try to respond with a distinction.

The *Evaluate hypothesis* option is related to the previous one. Basically, the App could evaluate the hypothesis, that is, predict the outcome of the related factual scenario, in light of the applicable legal arguments pro and con. Using the VJAP model (or CATO or IBP) the App would predict an outcome for the fact situation and justify it in terms of the arguments. The user option allows the user to change the predicted outcome and direct the App to evaluate it.

The legal arguments for these last two options, *Make legal argument* and *Evaluate hypothesis*, employ the argument schemes supported in the computational model of argument. That would include arguments by analogy to past cases consistent with the hypothesis, distinguishing cases that are contrary to the hypothesis (i.e., counterexamples), and considering effects on underlying values of cases that are positive or negative instances of the hypothesis. As illustrated in the *Dynamics* argument in Figure 5.13, the justification identifies cases and arguments in support of the prediction, but also counterexamples. It attempts to distinguish them or otherwise downplay their significance based on legal factors, underlying values, and the deleterious effects on values of an opposite conclusion in the current scenario. Based on the counterexamples, the App could also identify near miss hypothetical variations of the hypothesis that could affect the outcome given slightly different facts as in Ashley (1990).

Collaborative Hypothesis-Testing with a Descriptive Evidentiary Argument Model

In an evidentiary legal argument domain like the V/IP domain, a legal app could also process hypotheses like those in Figure 12.3, for instance:

> a) Plaintiff can succeed on the issue of a vaccine injury claim for compensation where the vaccine was MMR vaccine and the injury was intractable seizure disorder.

As noted, these can-hypotheses, patterned after form [2] in Figure 12.1, are different from the should-hypotheses in Figure 12.2 dealing with legal factors. Instead of "An issue *should* be decided for plaintiff" or "a plaintiff *should* succeed," they are phrased as "a plaintiff *can* succeed" given the condition described in the hypothesis, in the sense of "some plaintiffs have succeeded." The differences reflect differences in the underlying computational models of argument and the scope of legal arguments they model.

A descriptive computational model of evidentiary legal argument accurately represents a court's factual holdings, supporting and contradicting reasons, and legal decisions about whether legal rules' requirements have been satisfied. The model does not support arguing about the meaning of the legal rule requirements.

Conceivably, a descriptive model of evidentiary legal argument could provide a basis for prediction. "[T]he Corpus supplies data for . . . [using] logical structure to predict outcomes in similar cases or to formulate arguments for use in similar cases" (Walker et al., 2011, pp. 303, 329). An extensive corpus of cases annotated in terms of such a model would provide a database of successful and unsuccessful paths through a rule tree along with the associated arguments. These paths can be aligned across cases based on the particular rules and requirements. In this respect, they are similar to the EBEs of GREBE (see Section 3.3.3), another model that traces the reasoning of a judge in determining whether a legal rule's requirements have been satisfied.

Given such a corpus, a program could trace a path from the assumed facts and sub-issue conclusions of the hypothesis to a desired conclusion. The rule tree indicates the rule requirements that remain to be satisfied. The cases indicate known successful and unsuccessful paths that have been tried and could provide frequencies with which a particular path or segment in an elaborated rule tree has been tried or been successful.

The corpus would also provide a detailed track record of how particular triers of fact, that is, particular judges or special masters, have decided specific issues in the past. It records the judge's reasons in selecting and interpreting evidence and resolving conflicting evidence. For an attorney facing a similar problem scenario, the judge's reasoning is instructive as an example of the kind of evidence the attorney will need to produce and the kind of argument the attorney will need to construct. It is also instructive as an example of how this particular trier of fact, for instance, the Special Master in the *Casey* decision, has dealt with certain issues, evidence, and even expert witnesses. Thus, applying the DLF-like model to legal decision texts could potentially enable the *Lex Machina* project to find and apply fine-grained information for predicting how a particular judge would decide a particular issue.

Based on this information in the corpus, given a hypothesis, a legal app could confirm or disconfirm the hypothesis and summarize the statistics. If the hypothesis is confirmed, the legal app could point to the successful paths and arguments consistent with the hypothesis. It could suggest arguments based on those positive instances and caution the user about any exceptions and unsuccessful arguments. If it disconfirms the hypothesis, the App could point to the exclusively negative paths.

An interesting question is whether, using a descriptive argument model, the legal app can predict that the plaintiff *should* win an issue given the facts posed in the hypothesis. Here, "should" is used in the combined normative and empirical sense of a form [1] should-hypothesis. While it makes sense to pose a normative hypothesis for confirmation with such a model, the subsidiary queries would be, in essence, whether the findings of fact satisfy the requirements of the relevant legal rules defining a claim or issue. It would be difficult in such a model to evaluate the normative hypotheses in the absence of arguments by analogy to cases about the meaning of legal rule requirements.

Descriptive models are aimed at capturing another kind of normative information underlying the fact trier's evidentiary reasoning. As noted, such a model records whether a decision in a case is a conclusion of law or a finding of fact, and how it relates to other decisions in the case. The model also records the decision-maker's reasons in the decision-maker's own language with a representation of how they affect the decision, that is, whether they support it, contradict it, and how strongly. For instance, Table 12.1 shows examples of evidentiary reasons in Special Masters' decisions annotated in the DLF representations of three cases, the *Casey* (n. 1), *Howard* (nn. 2–5), and *Stewart* (n. 6) cases.[1]

As the table illustrates, the reasons are each instances of patterns of a kind of policy-informed "commonsense" inference about evidence or disease causation that one would expect to see across multiple evidentiary decisions. At the right of each reason,

---

[1] *Casey v. Secretary of Health and Human Services*, Office of Special Masters, No. 97-612V, December 12, 2005; *Howard v. Secretary of the Department of Health and Human Services*, Office of Special Masters, No. 03-550V March 22, 2006; *Stewart v. Secretary of the Department of Health and Human Services*, Office of Special Masters, No. 06-287V, March 19, 2007.

TABLE 12.1. *Examples of DLF evidentiary reasons in Special Masters' decisions (left)*
and possible underlying policies or principles (right)

Evidentiary reason of trier of fact	Possible underlying principle or policy
1. "[B]ecause ataxia, encephalitis, and certain other symptoms characteristic of a natural varicella infection were also seen after the vaccination with the attenuated varicella virus, it is plausible that the varicella vaccine caused those symptoms."	*Observing symptoms characteristic of a natural infection after a vaccination with the attenuated virus increases the plausibility that the vaccine caused those symptoms.*
2. "Dr. Katz' comments concerning Exs. 43 and 44 at the hearing . . . were so brief as to be completely unenlightening."	*An expert's analysis should be commensurate with the complexity of the topic.*
3. "Dr. Katz 'declined the opportunity to respond to Dr. Berger's critique.' "	*If a speaker has an opportunity to respond to a contradictory comment but declines to do so, a listener may assume that the speaker has no reasonable response to make.*
4. "[I]t seems unlikely that Sierra could really have been 'withdrawn' or 'depressed' for six weeks, and had 'puffy' hands and feet for more than three weeks, and yet petitioner did not take the infant to the doctor during that time period."	*If an infant had really presented troublesome symptoms over a period of weeks, a parent would have likely sought medical help.*
5. "[T]he petitioner's descriptions of Sierra's symptom history have changed more than once."	*If a child had really presented symptoms, one would expect that the description of the symptoms would remain constant.*
6. "The appropriate temporal framework for causation between viruses and cerebellar ataxia runs from 1 to 21 days."	*As the time interval increases between vaccination and injury (i.e., the onset interval) beyond the expected, the likelihood of demonstrating causation may decrease.*

the figure shows an expression of the possible principle or policy underlying the reason.

If claim-specific instances of such reasons and evidence factors are sufficiently stereotypical across cases in that domain or if they are instances of more general policies or values underlying evidential reasoning that are made explicit, then cases may be annotated as such, compared automatically, and the comparisons could be factored into the predictions as a kind of combined normative and empirical gloss.

12.5. CHALLENGES FOR COGNITIVE COMPUTING LEGAL APPS

A legal app that collaborates with humans to frame, test, and evaluate legal hypotheses should be possible soon. As the above sketch suggests, *if* argument-related information can be successfully annotated automatically, existing computational models of legal argument could work with textual descriptions of hypotheses and cases, predicting outcomes and supporting them with arguments.

That *if* is the first of three substantial research challenges to address before the goal of collaborative hypothesis-based querying and testing can be realized. To what extent can legal argument-related information be extracted from texts, including legal factors, evidence factors, and sentence roles in legal argument? A second major challenge is whether there will be enough manually annotated training data for ML and automatic annotation. Third, it will be a challenge to design an interface in which users can specify hypotheses as well as queries. Aspects of these challenges have already been discussed in the preceding chapter but will be revisited here in light of the goal to support hypothesis-testing.

12.5.1. *Challenges: Automatically Annotating Legal Argument-Related Information*

The work reported in Chapters 9 through 11 provides reason for optimism that argument-related information can be annotated automatically sufficiently well to support hypothesis-testing.

We have already seen a number of examples. As described in Section 10.3, Mochales and Moens have applied ML to automatically identify propositions in a legal corpus as argument premises and conclusions, with F_1-measures of 68% for premises and 74% for conclusions. Using knowledge-engineered rules, they identified nested argument structures with 60% accuracy. Feng and Hirst have automatically annotated argument schemes such as argument by example with accuracies ranging from 63% to 91% (Section 10.3.5). In an evaluation described in Section 10.5.4, the LUIMA team has annotated automatically two legal argument roles that sentences play, LegalRuleSentence and Evidence-BasedFindingSentence, with F_1-measures of 68% and 48% (Bansal et al., 2016). The SMILE program has identified legal factors automatically in trade secrets misappropriation cases with lower F_1-measures averaged across factors of 26% to 28%, but well enough to improve IBP's predictions over an informed baseline by 15% (Section 10.4). In addition, the SPIRE program reduced expected search length by reordering cases using a corpus of factor texts (Section 7.9.2).

Although not aimed at annotating cases, the techniques for classifying statutory provisions and extracting functional information in the Dalos project (Section 9.3), and from quantitative construction regulations (Section 9.6), or learning from training data based on multiple states' statutes (Section 9.7.3), also suggest that annotating legal factors can work. Even automated annotation and extraction of logical rules has had some success (Section 9.5). Legal factors should be easier than logical rules to annotate automatically. Factors are like the antecedents of rules and thus simpler than rules. On the other hand, the case texts in which factors are to be annotated may be more varied than statutory texts.

While promising, given the range of these results, clearly more work is required. There are four pressing needs, namely a need to deal with certain issues of attribution, to distinguish the polarity of certain propositions, to acquire certain domain-specific concepts and relations, and, crucially, to generate more manually annotated training instances.

Attribution

When justifying a hypothesis based on cases, it is important that a legal app be able to distinguish among a judge's conclusions and statements a judge attributes to the parties or witnesses. "Attribution . . . is the problem of determining who believes a stated proposition to be true" (Walker et al., 2015a). A given sentence in a decision may report a party's allegation, an expert witness's testimony, a document exhibit's text, a judge's legal conclusion or finding of fact, or any of the above but from a cited case.

The CCLA will need to determine whether in expressing a proposition, a judge accepts it as true (Walker et al., 2015a). Parties' statements are often just assertions they would like to support. The fact that a judge attributes to a party a statement that looks like a legal factor demonstrates that the topic was discussed, but it does not show that the judge determined the factor to be present. A judge may quote witness assertions as evidence, but the judge may cite competing evidence before indicating his/her decision.

Here is an example illustrating the kind of distinction based on attribution that LUIMA cannot yet draw but needs to. Consider the same two sentences, S2 and S3 from the *Werderitsh* decision, used at the beginning of Chapter 11 to illustrate sentences responsive to query Q2, "Have there been cases where it was held that hepatitis B vaccine can cause MS?," and a new sentence, S4:

S2: "The undersigned holds that hepatitis B vaccine caused or significantly aggravated petitioner's MS."

S3: "The undersigned concludes that the medical theory causally connecting the vaccinations and petitioner's injury is that Mrs. Werderitsh, who is genetically predisposed to developing MS, was exposed to the environmental antigen of two hepatitis B vaccinations, producing inflammation, self antigens, and a sufficient number of T-cells to have an autoimmune reaction later diagnosed as MS."

S4: (*New*) "Dr. Leist's conclusion that hepatitis B vaccine, since it failed to produce antibodies in Mrs. Werderitsh, could not have caused or exacerbated her MS ignores the other three types of MS that Dr. Martin described for which antibodies are irrelevant."

A program that understands to whom to attribute an assertion could make use of such information in reranking. If a user sought prior cases with *holdings* regarding particular assertions, sentences like S2 and S3 would be preferred over S4. They are all responsive to Q2. They all refer to "hepatitis B vaccine" "cause" and "MS." S4 would be less useful a response to Q2, however, because it reports a conclusion of Dr. Leist, an expert witness, rather than of the special master (as indicated in S2 and S3 by "The undersigned holds" or "concludes"). If the LUIMA system could recognize the *attribution* of the statement to an expert witness in S4 and infer that S4 is not an evidence-based conclusion by the special master (Walker et al., 2015a), it could distinguish between S2 and S3, on the one hand, and S4 on the other.

As illustrated in Walker et al. (2015a), attribution also involves a range of subtler issues with implications for reranking. In the example, the special master criticizes Dr. Leist's conclusion in S2 as "ignoring" information of another expert, Dr. Martin.

Conceivably, a system should not only recognize the attribution of the statement to an expert witness but also the negative polarity of the assertion. These inferences, however, can be quite subtle. Dr. Martin, like Dr. Leist, is the losing respondent government's witness. In other words, the special master is positively disposed to some conclusions of an expert witness of the losing side. One cannot assume that just because an expert witness testified for the side of the loser, the special master accepted none of his/her assertions.

In order to identify speakers and reason about their beliefs in statements attributed to them, a program will need to apply a discourse model, a data structure representing the actors in the decision, that is, the named entities and types of actors, and their "properties, actor relations (including possible actions), and other information" (Walker et al., 2015a). For instance, the discourse model would include information that a "'petitioner' is the person who files the petition for compensation and the 'special master' is the person who decides the facts" (Walker et al., 2015a).

In dealing with attribution, it is important to annotate intra-sentence attribution relations indicating that someone asserted something, that is, the relation among *attribution subject, attribution cue,* and *attribution object*. For instance, a sentence may indicate a more or less complex relation among terms as in "The Special Master determined that the vaccination caused the injury." A similar need applies in other areas, for example, indicating the conditions and conclusions of a particular rule.

Walker (2016) has argued that annotating such intra-sentence attribution relations presents special challenges for achieving human annotator reliability and is creating protocols to guide the annotation. Annotating intra-sentence relations also presents some technical challenges in terms of annotation interface design and in representing the relations. It is considerably harder for humans to annotate such relations correctly and coherently than it is to mark up spans of text and assign a type.

Developing and evaluating a discourse model for the LUIMA approach is a focus of current research. Computational linguistics provides some useful tools, such as discourse parsing to generate some information about the structure of a coherent discussion. First, the parser segments the text (e.g., a paragraph) into clauses or other basic units of discourse. Based on a framework for analyzing discourse such as Rhetorical Structure Theory (RST) (Mann and Thompson, 1987, pp. 87–190),

Cognitive Computing Legal Apps   371

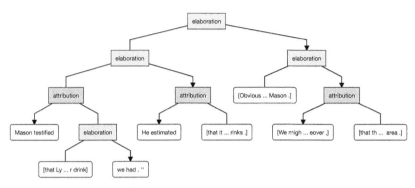

FIGURE 12.4. RST-Tree for *Mason* excerpt showing some attribution information

it then classifies the relationships between the segments and outputs an RST-Tree. Among other things, the RST-Tree shows information about attribution.

For example, Figure 12.4 shows the RST-Tree of a textual excerpt from the *Mason* case of Section 3.3.2:

> Mason testified that Lynchburg Lemonade became "the most popular drink we had." He estimated that it comprised about a third of his total sales of alcoholic drinks. Obviously, the exclusive sale of Lynchburg Lemonade was of great value to Mason. We might reasonably infer, moreover, that the beverage could also have been valuable to his competitors in the Huntsville area.

The discourse parse shows an attribution to the plaintiff Mason as a witness, followed by an elaboration, another attribution to Mason, followed by an attribution to "We," which, based on information not shared by the parser, means the judges (i.e., the court).

Conceivably, a discourse parser[2] could be incorporated into the annotation pipeline of the previous chapter. It could generate RST-Trees for targeted portions of text, and use the segmented units, their relations, and the related attribution information as a feature in the next step of the pipeline (Falakmasir, 2016). In addition, the discourse model will need information about how judges refer to themselves in indicating their conclusions.

Of course, the paragraph in Figure 12.4 is not a particularly complex example of judicial writing. Recall Judge McCarthy's three-part test in *Popov v. Hayashi* for determining who owns a baseball hit into the stands (see Figure 6.10). Judicial prose will test the limits of natural language parsing for years to come.

Distinguishing Polarity

In annotating legal texts for purposes of assessing hypotheses, the legal app needs to distinguish the polarity of rulings of law, holdings on issues, findings of fact,

[2] See, e.g., the open-source tool at http://agathon.sista.arizona.edu:8080/discp/

and proffered evidence. This means, for example, that in a vaccine injury case, the system needs to determine whether, regarding the holding on the first *Althen* requirement, the Special Master decided that MMR vaccine could cause intractable seizure disorder or not. Did the Special Master regard the Government's expert witness's testimony as supporting a finding of causation or as contradicting it? In a trade secret case, concerning the legal rule requirement that the alleged trade secret information must have been misappropriated, did the judge hold in favor of the plaintiff or the defendant?

In argument mining generally, identifying the polarity of the propositions in the conclusion and premises is important, that is, whether a proposition supports the conclusion or is against it. This also helps to distinguish arguments and counterarguments.

Although polarity in argument mining presents some "unique challenges" (Aharoni et al., 2014b), some researchers are successfully using rule-based or ML approaches to distinguish it in annotations within or even across domains.

Perhaps the simplest approach is to implement a rule that identifies linguistic evidence of negation and annotates the polarity of the proposition accordingly. For example, in a type system for clinical NLP, ' "cancer has not spread to the lymph nodes' would yield a negative 'locationOf' relationship" (Wu et al., 2013, p. 9).

In another nonlegal context, the Debater team addresses polarity with ML. As we saw in Chapter 1, IBM's Debater program identified the polarity of propositions relative to a topic, that is, whether the proposition was pro or con the topic. In Debater, the researchers applied a supervised ML approach to train a classifier to annotate polarity (Slonim, 2014). They:

1. Defined the concept of a "Pro/Con polarity" and provided examples,
2. Trained humans to detect polarity, providing ground-truth data,
3. Applied ML to develop a classifier that captures the "statistical signature" of polarity,
4. Assessed the classifier over ground-truth data in new instances.

The Debater team's systematic approach to ML based on manual annotation of training sets is discussed in Section 10.6.1.

It is still an empirical question whether the means for expressing negation in rulings of law, holdings on issues, findings of fact, and decisions regarding evidence present patterns and constraints sufficient for a similar annotation rule or ML approach to succeed.

Acquiring Domain-Specific Concepts and Relations

The expanded type system of Section 11.5.3 aims to be comprehensive in defining roles of propositions in legal arguments generally across legal domains. As a paradigm of cognitive computing, collaborative hypothesis-testing could be useful across legal domains where legal or evidence factors can be identified.

Legal domains, however, necessarily involve concepts and relations drawn from the regulated subject matter. For instance, in the vaccine injury domain introduced in Chapter 5, issues of legal causation are related to those of medical causation.

For any particular legal domain, the legal app will need to acquire and represent domain-specific knowledge. This includes claim-specific concepts, relations, and mentions, the kind of presuppositional information illustrated in Table 11.2, and basic vocabulary, such as the names of illnesses and vaccines in the vaccine injury domain. Some techniques for annotating this information have been discussed in Sections 10.5.3, 11.5.3, and 11.5.4.

Regulated domains are dynamic, however. New terminology is introduced, such as new commercial vaccines or newly discovered links between vaccines and injuries. Consequently, there is a need to maintain and update aspects of the regulated domain-specific information including the specialized vocabulary.

Nonlegal institutions are engaged in the activities of developing type systems and ontologies as they seek to improve conceptual information retrieval in their specialized domains. Since this is particularly true in medicine and public health, it would be efficient to connect a legal type system with medical ontological resources and type systems. Online medical ontologies extensively cover vaccines and the injuries they may cause and provide dictionaries for normalizing vaccine and injury names with all their abbreviations or commercial names.

An active area of research is how to make different ontologies, developed in different domains, interoperable:

> Direct interoperability among different UIMA NLP modules requires them to be based on the same type system [or to construct] annotators ... to serve as wrappers to translate among different type systems. (Liu et al., 2012)

Research on techniques to enable cross-domain use of medical ontologies and type systems is presented in Liu et al. (2012) and Wu et al. (2013).

Although the methods for achieving interoperability of legal type systems and those of other domains lie beyond the scope of this book, there may be low-hanging fruit. Even simple vocabulary listings of terms and variations in a standardized form with some semantic information would be useful in dealing with the need to normalize terminology such as illnesses, vaccines, their abbreviations, and their commercial names.

12.5.2. *Challenges: Manual Annotation of Training Instances*

A recurring theme since Chapter 9 has been the growing need for humans to annotate statutes, cases, and other legal documents. If the hypothesis-testing paradigm is useful across legal domains even more manual annotation will be required. As noted in Section 10.6, while not all of the texts in a corpus will need to be analyzed and annotated, one still needs valid training sets, and this will require a sizable investment of resources in manual annotation of texts, but by whom?

Here, we explore two answers to that question. First, crowdsourcing is an intriguing possibility for annotating texts, even legal texts. *Crowdsourcing* involves enlisting large numbers of people to perform tasks requiring human intelligence that computers can currently not perform such as marking up a training set of texts. Employers can use websites such as Amazon Mechanical Turk to post tasks to be performed in parallel by large, paid crowds of workers called providers or *Turkers*. Second, it is possible that instead of relatively inexpert Turkers, law students and trainees could perform the annotations as part of their studies. In either case, the humans would employ an online annotation environment such as those illustrated in Section 10.6.3.

Crowd-Sourced Annotation Environments
Researchers demonstrated the feasibility of a crowdsourcing approach to annotating requirements in legal privacy policies in Breaux and Schaub (2014). One task involved extracting from privacy policies descriptions of requirements for data collection, sharing, and usage.

The researchers addressed the question of whether a "crowd" of annotators with no legal training can reliably annotate legal texts. The key seems to be carefully breaking down the annotation task into smaller subtasks, each simple and well-defined enough to be undertaken by nonspecialist annotators. Breaux and Schaub (2014) decomposed the annotation task into four identification subtasks, each focusing on a different target: action verbs, types of information, sources and targets, and purposes. Where feasible, other identification tasks were performed automatically, such as using NLP to identify modal verbs.

An online interface developed by the researchers presents crowdsource annotators with text excerpts from privacy policies, such as

> We may collect or receive information from other sources including (i) other Zynga users who choose to upload their email contacts; and (ii) third party information providers.

The annotators select and highlight relevant phrases and press "concept" keys to encode the phrase as an instance of a particular concept. In the above extract, for example, an annotator may highlight "collect," "receive," and "upload" and relate them to the appropriate concepts on a list of concepts of interest (Breaux and Schaub, 2014, p. 169).

Their experiments demonstrated that crowds could perform sentence-level and phrase-level coding. Their decomposition workflow involving coding simpler components resulted in "an acceptable aggregate response at a reduced overall cost" (Breaux and Schaub, 2014, p. 171).

Breaking the overall annotation problem into simpler coding tasks was feasible with the kinds of texts employed in Breaux and Schaub (2014), regarding consumer-oriented data privacy policies. Presumably, the tasks were well-defined ones that could be performed without the need to consider the whole document.

It is harder to imagine how to decompose the activity of annotating legal cases into component tasks simple enough to be applied by human annotators without some level of legal expertise or training. Those annotators would need to access a case's overall factual and legal context in order to make intelligent annotation decisions.

Annotation for Students

Certainly, students can annotate texts effectively and many have done so. The IBM Debater team employed graduate students to identify (nonlegal) topics and evidence (Section 10.6.1). In a legal context, the LUIMA group used vaccine decisions annotated by law students. Students at Hofstra's LLT Lab marked up sentences for types including LegalRuleSentences or EvidenceBasedFindingSentences (Section 10.5). Students have annotated legal factors in trade secret cases at the University of Pittsburgh (Section 10.6) and in the work of Wyner and Peters (2012) (Section 10.4.3 and Figure 10.5).

Annotation has been applied as a teaching tool in other domains of argumentation. It can help learners "engage in scientific argumentation" (Zywica and Gomez, 2008), another domain where researchers apply argumentation mining with human-annotated ML training sets (Teufel et al., 2009). In high-school subjects such as social studies, literature, and science, annotations may be applied "to highlight important information like main ideas (argument or claim), supporting ideas (evidence), key content vocabulary words," "important facts or main ideas," "definitions provided in the text," and "major conclusions drawn" (Zywica and Gomez, 2008). These types correspond roughly with the annotation types for legal argument, as well.

The question is, can annotation become an integral part of legal education and training? There is mounting evidence that it can. A current movement in legal education toward online open-source casebooks includes facilities for students and others to mark up texts and to make the annotations publicly available (see Berkman Center for Internet and Society, Harvard Law School Library, and Harvard Library Lab, 2016).

Annotation has been used to help train law students in close reading of legal materials. Classroom Salon, a web-based tool that allows "students to read together, annotate the passage, and answer questions," supports annotations in the form of written comments to which students can assign tags (Blecking, 2014). In a law school intervention that included annotation with "Classroom Salon," researchers demonstrated "measurable gains in reading" (Herring and Lynch, 2014).

A computer-supported environment for highlighting and annotating argument-related information in legal texts could help students learn structures of legal reasoning and better interpret argumentative texts. The concepts and relations to be annotated involve substantive law and the structure of legal decisions and arguments. First-year law students encounter them as part of learning to read cases and statutes. Legal instructors attempt to teach first-year law students to recognize propositions in legal decisions that state a legal rule, express a judge's holding that a rule requirement is satisfied or not, or express a finding of fact. It would be educationally valuable for students to annotate the texts with these argument roles because it would draw their attention to key aspects of a case.

Similarly, annotation may assist new employees of law firms to learn their employer's particular approach to writing legal memoranda and briefs. As law students, junior associates and new employees in legal departments, and beginning judicial clerks perform annotations to learn, they could generate annotated texts for use in argument mining as a byproduct.

The author and his students have been developing and pilot-testing a convenient web-based annotation environment, suitable for use with tablet computers, on which law students can identify and annotate sentences that play key roles in legal argument. A mock-up of the annotation environment is shown in Figure 12.5. A student has selected the case of *NEW JERSEY v. T.L.O.* from the "Documents" list on the left, containing for purposes of illustration, landmark U.S. Supreme Court cases. This case deals with the constitutionality of a high-school vice principal's search of a student's purse for cigarettes that led to discovering evidence of the student dealing marijuana.

Law students habitually highlight text in reading their assignments. With a little extra support, they could annotate the highlighted excerpts. Here a student

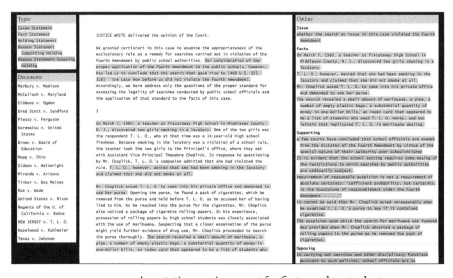

FIGURE 12.5. Annotation environment for first-year law students

has marked up a variety of statements, six of which appear in the middle screen. After marking each statement, the student selected a color-coded annotation type at the top left under "Type" and the system highlights the statement accordingly. The sentence types have been selected for pedagogical relevance, but correspond closely to sentence-level argumentation types:

Issue-Statement: Statement of issue regarding which court is asked to make a decision or "holding"

Reason-Statement-Supporting-Holding: Statement of a reason supporting a particular holding

Reason-Statement-Opposing-Holding: Statement of a reason opposing a particular holding

Fact-Statement: Statement of a fact on which a reason is based

Holding-Statement: Statement in which court reports its conclusion regarding the issue

As the student annotates the statements, the system automatically constructs an outline at the right, organizing the highlighted sentences into an argument summary identifying the issue, presenting the facts the Court deemed related to the issue, and presenting the statements supporting (or opposing) the Court's holding or conclusion. Clicking a statement in the outline moves the text in the middle screen to that statement in its original context. In this markup environment, students can observe the utility of framing issues, developing supporting reasons, considering contrary reasons, and coming to a conclusion or holding.

With a bit of additional support, students could add commentary to the entries in the outline (e.g., "This is strongest reason pro," "I disagree with this holding," "I don't understand this reason con"). The system could also provide feedback to a student about the reliability of his/her annotations given peers' markups of the same material. It might also engage students in competition based on their reliability information.

Intuitively, as law students and legal employees become more reliable annotators, the annotation quality will benefit from their expertise. Of course, for this kind of annotation to succeed, an online annotation environment needs to make it as effortless as feasible to read and to annotate as one reads (Section 10.6). The environment also needs to support computing the reliability of multiple annotations of the same texts, similar to that of the Debater project (Aharoni et al., 2014a) (Section 10.6.1).

Limits on Semantic Annotation

Although a legal app can accomplish a great deal with argument-related information annotated in case texts, the kinds of semantic information that can be annotated are limited.

A general limitation is that information such as a proposition has to be expressed fairly directly in the texts for humans to able to annotate it reliably or for the pipeline techniques to annotate automatically. Whether manual or automatic, annotation techniques are generally not effective if information must be inferred indirectly from the text or from multiple passages scattered across the text. As noted in Section 10.6, the reliability of human annotators is an upper limit on the success of ML from text. The more indirect the inferences or scattered the textual sources, the harder it is for humans to agree in their annotations and the lower their reliability.

Some indirect inferences could be supplemented via ontological associations (Chapter 6). For instance, the teleological reasoning methods (Chapters 3 and 5) use value-based reasoning. Judges may not refer explicitly in the text to particular values. Where the values are associated with legal factors as in Figures 5.11 and 5.12, however, a program that can identify legal factors can still reason with its built-in knowledge of the values associated with particular legal factors.

Other annotation limits concern patterns in legal texts that are too fine-grained, too general, too rare, or too complex for text analytic techniques to identify them well enough for a CMLA to apply. For example, the extent to which one may extract logical rules directly from complex statutory and regulatory texts is still an open question. As discussed in Section 11.6.1, we are attempting to identify the if/then structure of regulatory provisions to assist in identifying domain entities for statutory network representations of the provisions. Others, notably Zhang and El-Gohary (2015), have had some success with extracting logical rules for a limited range of provisions. The extent to which one can detect fine-grained logical structures with methods that can scale across regulatory domains is an important empirical question for the future of the field.

As discussed in Section 10.3.4, programs can identify some general argument features in textual arguments, such as nested argument trees of claims and conclusions, but an open question is to what extent programs can understand and reason with them. Where the reasons for the conclusion have been elaborated in semantic network representations as in GREBE (Section 3.3.3) or SIROCCO (Section 3.6), a program can use them to assess relevance and to compare and reason with explanations and arguments. The semantic network representation scheme is quite general, however. It can be applied across a wide range of fact situations, and that makes it difficult for ML to be effective, especially when propositions with similar meanings can be expressed in so many different ways. With a controlled vocabulary and representation scheme, as in SIROCCO, and sentence types acting as signposts, as in the DLF framework, it may become more feasible to manually annotate semantic networks. Automated annotation of the networks, however, remains to be demonstrated.

Something similar can be said of argument schemes. As we have seen, argument schemes play a major role in AI & Law efforts to model legal argumentation (Chapter 5). Some argument schemes can be annotated (see Table 10.1), and some elements of argument schemes identified, such as, arguing by case analogy in terms of legal factors.

Having identified an argument scheme, however, the extent to which a program can also fill-in the scheme's slots with detailed information is an open question. It can be done well enough to assist with conceptual information retrieval. For instance, a program can identify where in an opinion an argument by analogy appears to have been made with respect to a legal concept in dispute. But whether it can be done well enough for a program then to apply a burden of proof and draw a legal inference directly from text, as some modelers seem to hope, has not yet been established.

Finally, certain information used by existing prediction models may not be extractable from texts. This includes engineered features based on behavioral trends in decisions of individual justices, the Court, and lower courts (see Section 4.4).

In sum, the new techniques may not be sufficient to support all of the automated reasoning performed by the computational models of Part I. The new legal apps may not make use of certain features for which there are computational models of legal reasoning. In that sense, some automated legal reasoning tasks are still "a bridge too far" for text analytic techniques to elicit in detail.

Conversely, commercial legal apps, including some of those mentioned at the beginning of this chapter, are extracting information from text that computational models of legal reasoning in AI & Law are not able to use. This includes, for example, histories of a particular judges' decision-making. This kind of information, however, can be integrated with the methods described in Part III.

12.5.3. *Challenges: Query-Interface Design*

A second challenge concerns the need for an innovative query-interface design that enables users to relatively easily specify their hypotheses and argument needs. A similar issue was discussed in Section 11.5.5 on conceptual information retrieval. As noted there, the goal is for users to input their queries with a combination of menu selections and natural language. The App could present its interpretation of the user's query either in natural language or as a structured query, and invite the user to confirm or to modify using menu options. The App would then translate the query into conceptual constraints.

A similar approach could enable users to enter their hypotheses. As the templates in Section 12.4.2 indicate, even though the hypotheses can be quite general in scope, they are constrained in form. The interface could illustrate the kinds of hypotheses it can support as in the natural language hypotheses in Figures 12.2 or 12.3 or their structured equivalents. It could invite the user to select a hypothesis and modify it to suit.

An online form with templates could help users fill in issues and conditions in a hypothesis that an "issue of [x] should [or can] be decided for [side] where condition [y] even though condition [z]." Pull-down menus would provide lists of the types of legal claims, claim elements, legal rules, or rule requirements that a user can specify as an issue. The lists would be determined by the claims and legal rules for which the system provides coverage. Based on the user's selection of issue, the interface would provide menus for filling in the conditions. The user could select from a list of legal factors or components for specifying legal holdings, findings of fact, evidence factors, types of evidence, or statements of fact.

For example, the hypothesis in Section 12.1 concerning a baseball property conversion claim could be expressed as:

> Issue of [property conversion] should be decided for [defendant] where condition [Not Caught (D)] even though condition [Intentional Interference (P)].

Using menus, the user could select the issue (property conversion), the side (defendant), and the conditions, two factors from the Property-Interests-in-Quarry Microworld (Table 6.4), one for the defendant and the other for the plaintiff.

Conceivably, users could also enter simple texts for the conditions, which the system could translate into plausible structured entries which it would confirm with the user. The system could translate the resulting structured hypothesis back into a natural language version for confirmation or modification.

Once the user's hypothesis is expressed in a form that can be processed, the legal app would operationalize it by translating it into subsidiary queries as described in Section 12.4.3. At that point, the interface would need to support the collaborative hypothesis-testing interactions with the user as described in Section 12.4.4. This involves enabling the App and user collaboratively to modify the database or hypothesis based on the preliminary report, to make legal arguments, or to evaluate the hypothesis.

Supporting this level of collaboration between App and user will present its own challenges, but they are characteristic of the kind of interactions cognitive computing requires. The interaction is not unlike the incremental process in which predictive coding in e-discovery (Section 8.4.1) or in statutory analysis (Section 8.7.1) supports users in refining their hypotheses about relevance and operationalizing them in queries.

Today's predictive coding systems for e-discovery are good examples of cognitive computing. Predictive coding is a collaborative intelligent activity between humans and a computer system to model the relevance of texts in a corpus for solving particular legal problems in which each partner does what it can do best. Humans select positive and negative instances of what they regard as relevant to the legal problem they are facing. The computer system generates a statistical model of the training set thus far, and retrieves and classifies additional documents. Together human and system refine the model of relevance. As noted in Section 8.4, litigators have hypotheses in mind when they search for documents in e-discovery, for example, hypotheses that the opponent's files contain documents related to the various legal issues raised in the pleadings, including the plaintiff's complaint, the defendant's answer, and the parties' document requests. With respect to litigators' hypotheses, however, current predictive coding for e-discovery does not make hypotheses explicit; the hypothesis is represented only implicitly as a ML model.

The CCLA proposed here must take the extra step of helping the user express a hypothesis about a substantive legal and evidentiary issue. This seems to be a step in the right direction. Ultimately, the relevance hypotheses in e-discovery and statutory analysis are informed by the potential implications of the retrieved documents for substantive legal and evidentiary issues. Making explicit the user's hypotheses about the latter should someday help to explain and guide the iterative reformulation of hypotheses and queries regarding the former.

12.6. DETECTING OPPORTUNITIES FOR NEW HYPOTHESES AND ARGUMENTS

This chapter and Chapter 11 have explained how semantic annotation could enable a cognitive computing model to help humans to find and use relevant materials in arguments and to frame, test, and evaluate hypotheses against a corpus of legal texts. Achieving this goal is subject to addressing the above challenges, which are substantial but nevertheless seem feasible to accomplish in the next few years.

Text analytics and semantic annotation will *not* enable systems to read texts in the sense that humans do, at least, not anytime soon. While a program may intelligently process argument-related information, it does not understand the arguments in a deeper sense.

On the other hand, a program may not need a deep understanding to detect an opportunity for posing a new legal hypothesis or argument. A program may be able to identify such opportunities by detecting violations of expectations that suggest new hypotheses or analogies across legal domains that may lead to new arguments.

Violations of Expectations. Predictive methods generate expectations that a prediction will be correct. When a prediction turns out to be wrong, it violates the expectation and invites one to reason why (see Schank, 1996).

Guided by expectation failures, a system may be able to explore legal text corpora autonomously searching for "interesting" hypotheses to pose and test novel argument features or even novel arguments. Where a system annotates claims, issues, winning and losing sides, arguments, and legal factors, in principle, it can explore a corpus looking for cases whose outcomes violate expectations.

For example, the argument-related features in a case may predict an outcome inconsistent with the case's actual outcome. If a claim has pro-defendant legal factors, the VJAP or IBP models are more likely to predict that defendant would win. If the plaintiff wins, and the win cannot be explained in terms of known pro-plaintiff factors, it suggests a hypothesis that the text contains as yet unannotated countervailing features, perhaps a pro-plaintiff legal factor in the court's discussion of the claim that the system does not know exists or how to identify. This could lead it to "notice" that text and enlist the human expert collaborators in a kind of sensemaking activity. The system would present the hypothesis and assist them to analyze the text more closely for factors to explain the anomaly.

Changes in the meaning of a legal concept over time can also lead to violations of expectations. Section 7.9.4 presented a technique for monitoring the outcomes of decisions applying a particular legal concept. Measurable changes in the decision trees implementing the concept provided a clue for hypothesizing that the concept was drifting and to a technique for confirming the hypothesis.

Incidently, any type of case outcome prediction can raise expectations, including predictions based on historical trends, as in the U.S. Supreme Court predictions (Section 4.4), or on analogies to value trade-offs in past cases, as, for example, in the VJAP model (Section 5.7). Expectations raised by litigation participant-and-behavior features in Lex Machina, case analytics in Ross, or citation network trends in Ravel (Section 12.2) that are inconsistent with a given case's outcome can also indicate the need for assessing a hypothesis about undetected argument features.

Cross-Domain Analogies. The text annotation techniques described in this book identify argument-related reasons in prior cases that computational models of legal argument can employ. These argument models primarily reuse arguments and reasons from similar prior cases involving the same legal claim and adapt them to argument needs and facts of a new case in the same domain. The retrieved cases and their arguments may be novel to a particular human user but they have been used before in cases.

This begs the question whether a system can assist humans to construct and assess truly novel arguments, that is reasonable legal arguments that are not drawn from prior cases within the same legal domain. "As lawyers recognize, creativity and novelty in legal argument generally comes from importing legal concepts from one area of law into another, and by combining existing arguments in new and persuasive ways" (Remus and Levy, 2015, p. 62). Presumably, constructing reasonable arguments that are also novel requires a deeper semantic understanding of the texts than the annotation techniques discussed here will provide. Consider the analogy in Section 3.4 of the gun-toting schoolmaster who frightens students from attending the school of his competitor.

These text annotation techniques and computational models of legal argument represent the meaning of a legal reason in a variety of ways. The text excerpt associated with the reason is annotated as a type of legal reason, for example, a legal factor, an evidence factor, or a holding that a rule requirement has or has not been satisfied. The type annotation indicates the way the text excerpt has been used as a proposition in an argument, such as a reason for or against a finding of fact or conclusion that a legal rule requirement has been satisfied. The computational model's knowledge representation structures also provide information about the reason. For instance, CATO's factor hierarchy, IBP's or VJAP's domain models associate the reason with particular legal issues, including rule requirements, and with other reasons. The VJAP model (Section 5.7) also associates the reasons with underlying values or legal policies. In addition, selected concepts and relations expressed in those text excerpts are annotated as subsentence types including as a standard legal formulation (Section 6.8).

Where this kind of argument-related information about reasons can be annotated, human users can retrieve cases that presented analogous situations for decision, where the analogy is conceived both in terms of shared factual concepts and relations, *but also* similarities in the structures of arguments in the retrieved case and in the arguments the user seeks to make. See the discussion in Section 11.5.3 of different types of argument structure that annotations of propositions can reveal.

Given this information, a legal app could help human users find examples of past decisions that address problems conceptually and structurally similar to a current problem, illustrate the general structure of such analyses or arguments, illustrate specific resolutions with similar evaluations or trade-offs, or exemplify successful and unsuccessful arguments in similar prior cases. Even if this falls short of a deep understanding of what the reasons mean and why they matter from a legal viewpoint, it could provide the system with more of conceptual basis for making smarter relevance assessments than is available with current full-text legal IR systems.

It is an open empirical question whether a corpus of cases annotated with this kind of argument-related information can enable a program to learn more about what the reasons mean, their range of application, and the extent to which they can be generalized and applied outside of a particular legal claim. According to Wittgenstein, meaning lies in use (Wittgenstein, 1958, nos. 30, 43). The argumentation schemes and text annotation provide more information about how the reasons have been used. For example, one of Vern Walker's goals in developing the DLF model was to systematically study judicial evidentiary reasoning (Walker, 2007). The expectation is that some, perhaps much, of the commonsense reasoning about evidence in the vaccine injury domain illustrated in Section 12.4.4 could apply in other legal contexts.

Annotation of domain-specific legal factors in cases involving different kinds of claims may also reveal cross-domain patterns in the relationships between factors and underlying values and principles. These patterns include the ones identified for trade secret law in Figures 5.11 and 5.12, namely, interfering with or waiving an underlying value, making its application more or less legitimate, not interfering with it or affirmatively protecting it. Presumably, analogous relationships between factors and values apply in other domains of intellectual property such as trademark and copyright. As text annotation techniques make explicit more of the argument structure of legal decisions and identify the argument schemes applied, it should become feasible to recognize similarly purposed legal arguments in a different legal domain where similar underlying policies and values have been at stake.

A question for future research then is whether the concept of "similar prior cases" may be generalized to take argument structure into account across legal domains. Given annotation of argument-related reasons, can a program identify patterns that suggest the likelihood of cross-domain substantive analogies? If so, a legal app could offer to focus users on prior case arguments from another domain that may appear to be peripheral but that at a deeper level are actually analogous and would be novel in the users' legal domain of application.

12.7. WHAT TO DO NEXT?

Let's assume that a law student or legal practitioner, having made it this far in this book, is motivated to create a cognitive computing app for the legal profession, but does not know where to begin. This potential developer, we will assume, is a bit unsure exactly what the legal app will do. How should he/she proceed?

The short answer is to identify potential use cases for a cognitive computing app. A *use case* can be thought of as a series of anticipated interactions between a user and a system to be designed that would enable the user to achieve a goal (see Shrivathsan, 2009).

In the course of this book, we have encountered a number of use cases. In e-discovery, one use case is helping attorneys find relevant documents in a corpus of ESI in pretrial discovery (Section 8.4). Another use case is assisting attorneys in finding and analyzing relevant statutory provisions (Section 8.7.1). A third is assisting attorneys in posing and testing substantive legal hypotheses against a corpus of case texts (Section 12.4).

While the third use case involves making substantive legal hypotheses explicit, the previous two also involve hypotheses. When attorneys search for relevant documents or statutes, they have hypotheses in mind concerning the kinds of texts that will be relevant and how they relate to substantive legal issues. It is just that the predictive coding process does not usually involve making these hypotheses explicit.

One can identify use cases by observing legal practice in whatever venue or context one engages it, identifying systemic problems of practitioners in accessing and using texts to solve legal problems, and considering the kinds of legal hypotheses they pose and how new text analysis tools can help them evaluate the hypotheses in ways that were not possible before.

The venues and contexts include the traditional ones of legal practice such as a law firm, legal department, or legal clinic. They also include legal research and study in law school classrooms, libraries, bar exam prep courses, or at home. Less traditional venues lie at the interface with members of the lay public who need to understand and interact with some aspect of the legal system. The latter include services aimed at consumers, for example, an online dispute resolution website, a portal to public interest legal services, or sources of free online legal resources. Government-sponsored legal QA systems aim to help citizens with problems in tax, zoning, or landlord–tenant law. Other services such as in-house corporate advisory systems about ethical or regulatory compliance assist employees to avoid committing foreign corrupt practices.

Here are some use case examples involving legal processes and corpora that are ripe for developing CCLAs.

Contracts Use Case. Corporations and their legal advisors have realized that even when no litigation is pending or threatened, the corpora of digital materials that accumulate in the course of doing business, including contracts and other legal records, are a potential resource for improving corporate operations and governance, *but only if* the texts can be analyzed and understood.

Contracts are relatively well-structured texts, and many companies maintain repositories of contracts in electronic form including licensing agreements, leases, and employment-related agreements. As a result, semantic analysis of contract texts is both feasible and economically important. Indeed, semantic retrieval from a contracts corpus with tools able to understand contract structure and to characterize provisions in substantive terms already exists and is rapidly improving.

LegalSifter, a Pittsburgh start-up, has identified a variety of use cases involving annotating repositories of contracts, including for purposes of due diligence, lease accounting, and financial services regulatory compliance. Regarding due diligence, programs can probably annotate terms and conditions in repositories of contracts including "assignment and change of control clauses ... effective dates, parties, people to whom notices are sent, [and] notice addresses." For lease accounting, automatic annotation could identify significant event times such as lease commencement, expiration, or assessment dates, as well as option clauses for renewal, termination, purchase, or payment. For financial services, it could keep track of provisions dealing with "governing law" and "termination rights" (LegalSifter, 2016; see also Remus and Levy, 2015, pp. 14, 18), which mentions a commercial service using data-driven techniques advertised as able to induce basic templates for a firm's contracts and to flag discrepancies between proposed new contracts and the templates.

An interesting use case involves tracking changes in contracts and contract administration over periods of time. Annotations of contracts over months or years could help management determine longer-term changes and trends in "payment terms," "master agreements," or exposure to "consequential damages." Conceivably, temporal relationships would emerge, for instance, whether sales contract terms are still complying with a company's strategic guidelines or trends in revenue yields in different contract types (LegalSifter, 2016).

A key for automated analysis is identifying features for comparing selected types of contract provisions in terms, say, of how restrictive they are on a licensee or lessee, or the extent to which they limit certain risks. This, in turn, means identifying those features' semantic components such as temporal spans, rates of return, or limitations on liability, and determining how to find or infer them automatically. A type system can reify the important structural components of contracts, the useful features for comparison, and their underlying semantic components. Through some combination of manual marking up training sets of contract texts, ML, and manually constructed annotation rules, it should be possible to automatically annotate the corpus and support conceptual retrieval. Human users who are conducting due diligence or planning business strategies could then iteratively formulate, refine, and test hypotheses, at least manually, through conceptual retrieval based on the annotations.

Extending e-Discovery Use Case. A use case extending e-discovery also involves tracking information over time and across multiple clients' matters.

As explained in Section 8.4, the text corpora generated by e-discovery in litigation include quite diverse texts of parties and their opponents. Since most of the texts are relatively unstructured, from the viewpoint of semantic legal annotation, there are few obvious concepts and relations to grab onto. The connection between relevant documents and legal issues is almost entirely implicit.

In a variation of an e-discovery use case, a collaborative computing legal app could help users to partially formulate some relevance hypotheses explicitly without over-burdening users' already onerous task. In the process, the links between relevant documents and legal issues could become more explicit.

In litigation discovery, the parties' pleadings govern which documents will be relevant to the litigation. Generally, a document is legally relevant only in so far as it relates to a legal issue in the plaintiff's complaint, the defendant's answer, or in the related pleadings that frame the lawsuit. In drafting the pleadings, the parties have identified the legal claims and defenses they are prepared to assert. They have thereby made explicit many of the legal issues that will be raised.

It should be possible, therefore, for litigators to link documents to the legal issues to which they are relevant. A dropdown menu tool could list the issues raised in the pleadings. At some point in the predictive coding process, litigators could use the menu to associate documents with the corresponding issues. The linking activity would direct litigators' attention to the claims and defenses raised in the lawsuit, a good discipline in conducting discovery. These linkages represent, in effect, at least part of a litigator's hypothesis about why the documents are relevant to the lawsuit, and they could be helpful in explaining that relevance in court.

The conceptual links may not have much impact on automating the e-discovery task in a given case, at least not initially. As noted, the detailed way in which a particular document relates to a legal claim, for instance, an alleged fraud, is likely to be entirely implicit.

Over time, however, across corpora of anonymized documents produced in multiple cases litigated by a firm, the associations between documents and issues may be useful. ML could develop profiles associating issues with types of documents, terminology, patterns of usage, types of senders and receivers, or patterns of distribution. This learned information, in turn, could help to improve automated clustering of documents (see Section 8.4.5) and provide additional filters for selecting documents relevant to the particular issues in a new case.

Before this kind of cross-client and cross-matter activity is feasible, of course, it will be necessary to develop techniques for anonymizing documents in e-discovery automatically. Tools for automating anonymization, an important use case in its own right, are currently under development in a number of firms.

Use Cases Extending Legal Hypotheses and Corpora. The queries and predictive hypotheses illustrated above are only a few examples of useful legal hypotheses. Anyone who has studied or practiced law has likely developed intuitions about other kinds of hypotheses people want to test against a corpus of legal texts. These vary across legal domains, audiences, tasks, and the kinds of underlying conceptual relationships of interest. The techniques described here are still emerging from academic and commercial research groups and need to be adapted to other legal corpora, tasks, hypotheses, and user communities.

One feature makes the LARCCS approach especially appropriate for applying to a variety of legal corpora. It would analyze and rerank the *output* of more traditional legal IR systems. As a result, it would not require changing the manner in which cases are represented, indexed, and retrieved in those IR systems.

This expands the opportunities for constructing novel use cases for the wide range of text corpora involved in modern legal research. These include proprietary commercial repositories like Westlaw, LexisNexis, or Bloomberg, access to which is subject to subscription agreements, or Google Scholar Cases and Court Listener, which offer free search capabilities. Interestingly, some of the commercial repositories of legal texts, or portions thereof, have become available subject to license directly through the Watson Developer Cloud.

Today, however, there are also many alternative sources of useful legal text corpora. A comprehensive, indexed list of free sources of potential data may be found at Library (2015). The open access to law movement, including AustLII, the Australian Legal Information Institute and other LIIs worldwide, provides a wide array of legal documents as do a number of courts, legislatures, regulatory agencies, and treaty organizations. Many of the free sources are subject to less-restrictive open-source licenses of various types.

Some law schools, organizations, and agencies also sponsor specialized repositories of legal texts such as Pace Law School's CISG database of cases and scholarly materials concerning the UN Convention on the International Sale of Goods (Kritzer, 2015), or the Index of WIPO UDRP Panel Decisions (WIPO, 2015). Law schools may also collect student essays and student exam answers. Organizations sponsoring moot court competitions amass corpora of participants' arguments and may make them available to some extent for reference. Finally, law firms, corporate legal departments, and legal clinics have private repositories of legal arguments in the form of legal memoranda and briefs.[3]

These diverse sources share a need to support conceptual information retrieval and cognitive computing. Across the legal communities and domain tasks served by these diverse sources, the nature of the hypotheses people want to test will likely vary, as will the kinds of patterns that are useful for drawing inferences in cognitive computing. Hypotheses may focus on substantive differences across jurisdictions. For example, how does the kind of "personal data" subject to legal requirements vary across jurisdictions subject to EU Data Protection Directives and those subject to U.S. federal and state law? Do the concepts of "reasonable measures," "value," or "public" in the definition of "trade secret" in the Economic Espionage Act, 18 U.S. Code §1839(3), have the same meanings as in state trade secret law? Alternatively, the hypotheses may focus on concept evolution over time. For example, are courts addressing the concept of "treatment" in the HIPAA Privacy Rule in the same manner as in the Congressional hearings? What trends have there been in the meaning of the requirement of "good faith" in submitting a bankruptcy plan under 11 U.S. Code chapter 13?

The form and nature of the legal sources will also vary. A law firm's legal memoranda and briefs record how the firm has addressed particular problems or types of problems in the past. Briefs present the interesting possibility of a corpus of triples: a firm's brief pro an issue, an opponent's brief con, and a court's actual decision resolving the dispute. The expanded argument types above could identify nested argument structures concerning competing conclusions about legal rule requirements. Additional techniques would be needed, however, to compare the competing argument structures, identify their salient differences, and capture the resolution in a manner from which tentative strategic lessons could be drawn.

As one moves from legal case opinions, briefs, and legal memoranda to law review articles and treatises, one will need to expand the argument-related type system to encompass the argumentation patterns of these media. Law review authors' claims tend to be more general; they hypothesize about changes in the law and their implications for policy. The kinds of arguments these authors employ to substantiate their claims will be more general, as well, necessitating greater reliance on the nested argument structures of claims and conclusions.

Finally, for some venues of public interest, the processes and tasks, hypotheses, relevant concepts and relations, and levels of expertise of human users will vary. A resource for advising veterans about legal issues of proving service-connected posttraumatic stress disorder will focus on different aspects of past case arguments than one aimed at supporting their pro bono legal counsel. Adapting to these more general kinds of queries and hypotheses will require imagination and a

[3] These repositories are subject to a variety of legal and technical constraints that must be taken into account in designing a proposed legal app. They also vary as to their technical accessibility and the extent of preprocessing required (see Section 8.3).

willingness to observe how real consumers, employees, and citizens engage in the processes.

Common Tasks across Use Cases. Whatever the use case, the approach will involve some basic inquiries. One needs to establish how a program could *help* practitioners to apply semantic information annotated in the legal texts to answer questions, test hypotheses, make predictions, explain answers or predictions, or argue for and against conclusions. The emphasis on "help" underscores the cognitive computing focus on supporting a collaboration between computer system and human users. The system has access to a great deal of textual information, but needs to organize that information to assist humans.

A developer should investigate the kinds of hypotheses that users are interested in testing, the kinds of textual information that will help them do so, and the kinds of explanations and arguments they expect in support of or against the conclusions. Answers to the following questions should help in designing an appropriate type system, annotation process, and collaborative interaction:

1. What concepts in the textual documents are most important for these tasks, and what kinds of textual references or mentions indicate the presence of a concept? (see Sections 6.7, 6.8, and 11.6.1)
2. How can a program automatically annotate the concepts? (see Chapters 9 and 10)
3. How can a program learn to rank its candidate texts in terms of importance of annotated concepts? (Section 11.3)
4. How can a program support users in employing targeted concepts in framing conceptual queries or hypotheses? (Sections 11.5 and 12.4)
5. How can a program employ the retrieved texts to evaluate the hypothesis? (Section 12.4)

A developer may still wonder where to begin with question (1). What kinds of types are important for posing and evaluating legal hypotheses? What aspects of the substantive law need to be annotated?

The answer involves another question: What aspects of the documents and the situations they represent do humans compare in terms of substantive legal features? Such comparisons often lie at the base of evaluating hypotheses that predict legal outcomes, limits, and trends. To the extent that the elements for these comparisons can conceivably be annotated in text, they need to be represented in the type system.

Most of the argument structures we have seen in this book enable substantive comparison of cases in terms of measures of their fact situations' strengths relative to a particular type of claim. The cases can be compared in terms of:

- Models of legal factors and issues (IBP, Section 4.5.2) augmented with value trade-offs of decisions (VJAP, Section 5.7),
- Coverage of requirements in DLF rule trees and evidence factors (Section 5.8),

- Roles of sentences in legal arguments and component LUIMA types (Section 6.8),
- Structural matches of criterial facts (GREBE [Section 3.3.3] and SIROCCO [Section 3.6]),
- Citation network centrality (BankXX, Section 7.9.3).

Comparing the restrictiveness of regulatory standards has been modeled with:

- Norm graphs (Section 2.5.1),
- Requirements watermarking (Section 9.7),
- Network analysis of statutorily mandated interactions (see Sections 2.6 and 11.6.3),
- Restrictiveness of rule trees or decision trees implementing the concepts (see Section 5.8) and concept change (Sections 7.9.4 and 12.6),
- Some combination of the above to compare the outcomes and relative strengths of cases decided under the regulatory standards.

It may be that the concepts for comparison cannot be readily annotated automatically (question 2) such as the semantic networks of criterial facts in GREBE or SIROCCO. Alternatively, perhaps the hypotheses are not of a type the program can process directly, but it can still help the human user frame conceptual queries for documents or cases to compare (question 4). For instance, programs can assist humans in analyzing the statutory or citation networks with network analytics or heat map summarizations, but a human has to pose the hypothesis and interpret the evaluation.

To the extent that the intended collaboration involves the system in reasoning with the annotated information for purposes of evaluating a hypothesis through prediction and argumentation (question 5), a computational model of legal argument would most likely need to be in place. At this point, only some of the above case comparison types connect to such a model and can be extracted automatically in texts to some extent. As we have seen in Chapter 5, argument models developed in the AI & Law community can perform some level of prediction, argumentation, and reasoning based on legal factors. When supplemented with coverage of rule tree requirements, evidence factors, and sentence roles in legal argument and their components, a legal app could assist humans in posing and evaluating legal hypotheses directly from case texts.

Success in this endeavor would represent a paradigm of cognitive computing and a pinnacle of AI & Law.

12.8. CONCLUSION

In helping human users to make their hypotheses explicit and to test them against a corpus by specifying queries in terms of conceptual constraints, CCLAs will engage humans and computers in a fruitful collaboration.

Many challenges remain, including the need for human annotation and for designing new interfaces that can elicit and process users' legal hypotheses and help them to evaluate the results. Annotation requires an investment in interface design, process engineering, and human labor, and it is an open question how widely one can reasonably scale such resource intensive work across legal domains.

It seems realistic, however, to hope that enterprises such as law firms, database providers, corporate legal departments, government agencies, or legal clinics would support this work. Together one could tailor type systems to capture concepts and relations relevant to their particular argument-related information retrieval requirements, corpora, and legal practice issues, enlist human annotators using the most convenient computer-supported annotation environments available, train the ML models on the annotated data, and apply them to the corpora in order to support the enterprise's operations through customized legal AR, analysis, and prediction.

Glossary

Ablation	"Turning off" a model's knowledge source to determine the contribution it makes to the model's efficacy.
Abstract argumentation framework	An argumentation framework whose argument graphs contain only arguments that attack each other.
Acceptable	A proposition in an argument that is presumably true given the arguments up to that stage and a set of assumptions.
Accuracy	(A) The ratio of correct case predictions over all case predictions.
Algorithm	A set of computational steps for solving a problem.
Area under the ROC curve	(AUC) A ML metric for evaluating a binary classifier, AUC relates to the probability that a classifier will rank a randomly chosen positive data point (e.g., relevant provision) higher than a randomly chosen negative one (nonrelevant provision).
Argument mining	Automated analysis of corpora to identify argument structures in documents such as premises, conclusions, argumentation schemes, and argument–subargument and argument–counterargument relationships between pairs of arguments.
Argument retrieval	(AR) Enabling an information retrieval system to use information about the roles that propositions play in legal arguments and other argument-related information to improve retrieval performance.

Argument scheme	A template with predefined components for constructing a typical type of argument.
Argument-related information	Information in legal cases about the roles of propositions, and other text elements, in the argument presented in a case. Useful for argument retrieval, it includes sentences' roles in arguments as propositions, premises, or conclusions, statements of rules in the abstract or as applied to specific facts, or as case holdings and findings of fact, legal factors, and evidence factors.
Argumentation framework	Defines an argument as a structure comprising a premise, a conclusion, and exceptions.
Attribution	In a legal decision, information signaling or affecting the court's judgments about belief in an argument.
Augmented Transition Network	(ATN) Graph structure that analyzes problems involving sequences of events as a series of states and rule-defined possible transitions from one state to the next.
Average precision	(AP) A measure of ranking performance equal to the average of the proportions of retrieved documents that are relevant in the top-i ranks of retrieved documents.
Backward chaining	Testing if any rule's conclusion is a desired goal and adding that rule's conditions to the set of desired goals.
Bag of words	(BOW) A representation of a document as a collection of terms that ignores the sequential order of the terms in the document.
Bayesian network	(BN) A graphical model of probabilistic causal relationships. Each node represents an event with a variable to indicate whether it has occurred. The arcs represent causal influences affecting the likelihood of an event's occurrence including conditional probabilities associated with those causal influences.
Bipartite	An argument diagram that distinguishes between propositions and arguments that support a proposition and those that attack the proposition.
Boolean relevance measure	In an information retrieval system, a set of logical criteria for the documents to be retrieved.

Breadth-first search	Given a list of rules to try with a given conclusion, the program tries to prove a descendant rule for each of the rules on the list before trying to prove a descendant of any of the rules' descendants.
cfs	This stands for the "current fact situation", that is, the case at hand, about which arguments are being made.
Citation network diagram	System of statutes, regulatory provisions, or cases represented as a network or graph of the reference relations among them.
Cognitive computing	Collaborative problem-solving by human and computer working together, each performing the intelligent activity that each does best.
Computational model of legal reasoning	(CMLR) A computer program that implements a process evidencing attributes of human legal reasoning. The CMLRs that implement a process of legal argumentation are called computational models of legal argument (CMLAs).
Conceptual legal information retrieval	Automatically retrieving textual legal information relevant to answering a user's question based on matching documents' concepts and roles with those required by a solution to the user's legal problem.
Confidence interval	In a statistical estimate, range of values estimated to contain the true value regarding a characteristic of interest in a population, with the desired confidence level.
Confidence level	In a statistical estimate, the chance that a confidence interval derived from a random sample will include the true percentage of elements in a population that have a characteristic of interest.
Critical question	Component of argument scheme that addresses acceptability of the scheme's premises and points out exceptional circumstances in which the scheme may not apply.
Cross validation or *k*-fold cross validation	A standard procedure for evaluating a ML program in which the data is divided into k subsets or "folds." In each of k rounds, a different one of the k subsets is reserved as the test set. The ML model is trained using the $k-1$ subsets as the training set.

Decision tree	A ML technique that learns a tree-like set of questions or tests for determining if a new instance is a positive instance of a classifier. Each question is a test: for example, if the weight of a particular feature is less than a threshold value, branch one way, otherwise branch the other way.
Defeasible rule	A rule whose conclusion presumably holds when the rule's condition is satisfied, but is not necessarily true.
Depth-first search	Given a list of rules to try with a given conclusion, the program tries to prove the descendant of the current rule and, if successful, makes the descendant the current rule before trying any of the other rules on the list.
Dimension	In the Hypo program, a general framework for representing legal factors.
Document-term matrix	In ML from text, a spreadsheet representing documents in rows and by words. Each row is a vector representing a document in terms of the words/features it contains from all of the words/features in the corpus.
e-Discovery	The collecting, exchanging, and analyzing of electronically stored information (ESI) in pretrial discovery.
Elusion	In information retrieval, the proportion of unretrieved documents that are relevant.
Evidence factor	Indication of fact trier's stated reasons for a conclusion and assignment of plausibility. Shows why evidence tends to be sufficient to prove a legal rules' antecedents (or not).
Extensible Markup Language	(XML) A standardized set of rules for annotating (i.e., marking up) documents in a human-readable and computer-readable format.
Extensional definition	Provides examples of what is/is not an instance of a concept.
F1-score or F1-measure	The harmonic mean of precision and recall where both measures are treated as equally important.
Factor	(initial caps) In the CATO program, a knowledge representation technique for representing legal factors that simplified Dimensions.

Feature vector	Text representation where the value for each feature is the magnitude of the feature in a text along a feature dimension. Similar to a term vector but uses features other than terms and term frequencies.
Forward chaining	Testing if any rule's conditions are satisfied by the current facts in the database and adding that rule's conclusion to the database.
Heuristics	Frequently useful "rules of thumb" that are not guaranteed to lead to a correct result.
Horn clause logic	An implementation of most of predicate logic and the basis of the Prolog programming language.
Hypothesis	A prediction, in the form of a rule-like generalization based on substantive legal considerations, of how a legal issue should or may reasonably be decided given certain conditions.
Hypothetical	An imagined or made-up situation that involves a hypothesis such as a proposed test, and which is designed to explore a test's meaning or challenge it as too broad or too narrow.
Intensional definition	Specifies the necessary and sufficient conditions for being an instance of the concept.
Intermediate legal concept	(ILC) A rule's open-textured legal term whose meaning is subject to argument.
Inverted index	A common information retrieval system data structure that lists features appearing in any texts stored in the database and for each feature, a record of all documents in which the feature appears, their locations, and frequency.
Isomorphism	When there is a one-to-one correspondence between the rules in a formal model and the sections of legislation modeled.
Legal factor	A kind of expert knowledge of the commonly observed collections, or stereotypical patterns, of facts that tend to strengthen or weaken a plaintiff's argument in favor of a legal claim.
Legal text analytics	Also known as legal text mining: Automated discovery of knowledge in archives of legal text data using linguistic, statistical, and ML techniques.

Lex Specialis	Maxim of interpretation according to which more specific legal rules have priority over more general rules.
Logistic regression	A statistical learning algorithm that predicts the odds of being an instance of a category based on the values of independent variables (predictors). It employs an iterative statistical procedure to estimate weights for the predictors.
Lucene	An Apache open-source text search engine library that supports implementing document-term matrices, as well as indexing, retrieval, and ranking functions.
LUIMA	A UIMA-based type system adapted to the legal domain. It focuses on concepts, relations, and mentions for identifying argumentation roles of sentences in judicial decisions useful for the task of legal information retrieval.
Machine learning	(ML) Computer programs that can learn to make predictions based on data.
Majority-class baseline	Baseline that predicts the majority class no matter what the facts of the new problem.
Mean average precision	(MAP) The average over the set of all queries of the AP for each query.
Mentions	In a type system, a type capturing ways in which concepts and conceptual relations are referred to or manifested in domain texts.
Model	In ML a structure that generalizes a set of data for description or prediction and that can be used as a classifier.
Monotonic reasoning	Logic in which a proposition once proven can never be withdrawn.
n-grams	A contiguous sequence of n items (e.g., words) from a given text sequence.
Network analysis	In information retrieval, drawing inferences about relevance of a document based on links and link weights of a document or its concepts in a network.
Non-monotonic reasoning	Logic in which inferences may change as information is added or becomes invalid. A proposition once proven may be withdrawn.

Normalized discounted cumulative gain	(NDCG) A measure of ranking performance by cumulating each relevant document's contribution to the overall quality of a ranking depending on where it is ranked relative to the ideal ranking.
Ontology	A general, formal specification of the concepts corresponding to the objects in a domain, their relations, and properties.
Overfitting	When a ML model is too flexible so that it fits random variation in data as if it were a structural feature.
Point estimate	In a statistical estimate, the most likely value for a characteristic of the population.
Precision	(P) The ratio of the number of positive instance predictions that are correct over the total number of positive instance predictions.
Predicate logic	Logic, also known as predicate calculus or first-order logic, employing logical connectives and separate symbols for predicates, subjects, and quantifiers. Extends propositional logic by representing structure of propositions.
Presuppositional Information	In LUIMA, includes factual and linguistic concepts, relations, and mentions related specifically to the regulated domain.
Pretrial discovery	Processing law suit parties' requests for materials in the hands of opponents and others to reveal facts and develop evidence for trial.
Probabilistic latent semantic analysis	(PLSA) A statistical method for extracting and representing words' contextual-usage meanings based on a large corpus of text. Contexts in which words appear or not in the corpus determine the similarity of their meanings.
Proof standard	The level of certainty required to establish a proposition for purposes of an argument.
Propositional logic	Logic employing logical connectives and symbols that stand for whole propositions.
Protocols	Provide criteria and examples that specify linguistic or logical cues for human annotators to use in annotating texts.

Random forests of decision trees — (RFDT) A ML technique replaces a single decision tree by averaging over an ensemble of decision trees in order to achieve greater diversity of sources in prediction.

Rebuttals — Arguments that are pro and con a particular conclusion. Weighing the arguments and applying proof standards resolve the conflict.

Recall — (R) The ratio of positive case predictions that are correct over the number of cases that were positive.

Receiver operating characteristic — (ROC) A ML metric for evaluating a binary classifier, an ROC curve is a plot of the true positive rate against the false positive rate for the different possible decision thresholds.

Relevance feedback — In information retrieval, a functionality that enables users to indicate which of the documents returned in response to a query are relevant and best represent what the user seeks.

Relevance hypothesis — In e-discovery, a litigator's theory or abstract description of subject matter which, if found in a document, makes the document relevant.

Reliability — Reliability in annotation refers to the level of agreement of independent (usually) human coders in assigning a label to the same piece of text.

Reranking — Functionality in information retrieval system to reorder documents to maximize their responsiveness to a user's query.

Semantic net — Graph comprising nodes, which represent concepts (including both legal concepts and facts) and arcs representing relations between concepts.

Sensemaking — Organizing and representing complex information sets to address the sense maker's problem.

Simulated annealing — A computational technique for finding a global maximum of a function such as confidence while avoiding local maxima that are not as great.

Spreading activation — In information retrieval with a citation network, a process in which the activated nodes associated with query terms send activation to the nodes to which they are linked.

Statistical estimate	Estimating a characteristic of population by drawing a statistical sample, determining the proportion of the elements in the sample that have the characteristic, and applying that ratio to the whole population.
Statistical sample	Sample in which some number of elements are drawn at random from the population.
Statutory analysis	Process of determining if a statute applies, how it applies, and the effect of this application.
Statutory network diagram	System of statutes represented as a network or graph of the relations between reference concepts referred to by, and subject to, regulation across multiple statutes.
Statutory ontology	A taxonomy of the classes of normative concepts employed in a statute, their relations to other normative classes, as well as their relations to classes of concepts of the regulated domain's subject matter.
Subsumption	Taxonomic reasoning that something is a member of a more general class using an ontology of concepts organized hierarchically.
Supervised machine learning	ML methods that infer a classification model from labeled training data. The training data comprise a set of examples that have been assigned outcomes.
Support vector machine	(SVM) A ML technique that applies statistical criteria to find boundaries between positive and negative examples of a category or class.
Teleological reasoning	Reasoning that takes into account the purposes and values underlying legal rules.
Term vector	A representation of a document in terms of its words, citations, indexing concepts, or other features. The term vector is an arrow from the origin to the point representing the document in a large dimensional space with a dimension corresponding to each feature in the corpus.
tf/idf	In information retrieval systems, a weight proportional to how many times a related term appears in a document's text (i.e., the term frequency (*tf*)) and inversely related to the number of times the term appears in the corpus (i.e., its inverse document frequency (*idf*)).

Type system	An ontology for annotating (marking up) texts in terms of a hierarchy of concepts and relations so that an annotation pipeline can automatically assign semantics to regions of text.
UIMA	(Unstructured Information Management Architecture) An open-source Apache framework for question answering systems in which text annotators are organized into a text-processing pipeline that assigns semantics to regions of text.
Undercutting argument	An argument that questions another argument's applicability.
Undermining argument	An argument that contradicts the premises of another argument.
Unsupervised machine learning	ML techniques such as clustering algorithms that infer groupings of unlabeled instances based on their content.
Use case	In system design, a series of expected interactions between a user and the system that would enable the user to achieve a goal or solve a type of problem.
Vaccine/Injury Project	(V/IP) Project and corpus, developed by the Research Laboratory for Law, Logic and Technology (LLT Lab), Maurice A. Deane School of Law at Hofstra University, comprising Court of Federal Claims decisions whether claims for compensation for vaccination-related injuries comply with the requirements of the National Vaccine Injury Compensation Program.
Vector space similarity	(VSS) The similarity among documents or queries in a vector space as measured by the Euclidean distance between the endpoints of the term vectors (or by the cosine of the angle between the term vectors).

Bibliography

A2J. 2012. *A2J Author*. www.kentlaw.iit.edu/institutes-centers/center-for-access-to-justice-and-technology/a2j-author (accessed January 30, 2015).

ACL-AMW. 2016. *3d Workshop on Argument Mining at the Association of Computational Linguistics (ACL 2016)*. http://argmining2016.arg.tech/ (accessed May 12, 2016).

Aharoni, Ehud, Alzate, Carlos, Bar-Haim, Roy, Bilu, Yonatan, Dankin, Lena, Eiron, Iris, Hershcovich, Daniel, and Hummel, Shay. 2014b. Claims on demand – an initial demonstration of a system for automatic detection and polarity identification of context dependent claims in massive corpora. *COLING 2014*, 6.

Aharoni, Ehud, Polnarov, Anatoly, Lavee, Tamar, Hershcovich, Daniel, Levy, Ran, Rinott, Ruty, Gutfreund, Dan, and Slonim, Noam. 2014a. A benchmark dataset for automatic detection of claims and evidence in the context of controversial topics. *ACL 2014*, 64–8.

Al-Kofahi, Khalid, Tyrrell, Alex, Vachher, Arun, and Jackson, Peter. 2001. A machine learning approach to prior case retrieval. Pages 88–93 of: *Proceedings of the 8th International Conference on Artificial Intelligence and Law*. ICAIL '01. New York, NY: ACM.

Aleven, Vincent. 1997. *Teaching Case-based Argumentation through a Model and Examples*. Ph.D. thesis, University of Pittsburgh, Pittsburgh, PA.

Aleven, Vincent. 2003. Using background knowledge in case-based legal reasoning: a computational model and an intelligent learning environment. *Artificial Intelligence*, 150(1–2), 183–237.

Alias-i. 2008. *Alias-i. Lingpipe 4.1.0.* http://alias-i.com/lingpipe (accessed July 22, 2015).

Allen, Layman E. and Engholm, C. Rudy. 1978. Normalized legal drafting and the query method. *Journal of Legal Education*, 29, 380–412.

Allen, Layman E. and Saxon, Charles. 1987. Some problems in designing expert systems to aid legal reasoning. Pages 94–103 of: *Proceedings of the 1st International Conference on Artificial Intelligence and Law*. New York, NY: ACM.

Araszkiewicz, Michał, Łopatkiewicz, Agata, and Zienkiewicz, Adam. 2013. Factor-based parent plan support system. Pages 171–5 of: *Proceedings of the Fourteenth International Conference on Artificial Intelligence and Law*. New York, NY: ACM.

Ashley, Kevin D. 1990. *Modeling Legal Arguments: Reasoning with Cases and Hypotheticals*. Cambridge, MA: MIT Press.

Ashley, Kevin D. 1991. Reasoning with cases and hypotheticals in HYPO. *International Journal of Man–Machine Studies*, 34(6), 753–96.

Ashley, Kevin D. 2000. Designing electronic casebooks that talk back: the cato program. *Jurimetrics*, 40, 275–319.

Ashley, Kevin D. 2009a. Ontological requirements for analogical, teleological, and hypothetical legal reasoning. Pages 1–10 of: *Proceedings of the 12th International Conference on Artificial Intelligence and Law*. New York, NY: ACM.

Ashley, Kevin D. 2009b. Teaching a process model of legal argument with hypotheticals. *Artificial Intelligence and Law*, 17(4), 321–70.

Ashley, Kevin D. 2011. The case-based reasoning approach: ontologies for analogical legal argument. Pages 99–115 of: *Approaches to Legal Ontologies*. Dordrecht: Springer.

Ashley, Kevin D. 2012. Teaching law and digital age legal practice with an AI and Law seminar. *Chicago.-Kent Law Review*, 88, 783.

Ashley, Kevin D., Bjerke Ferrell, Elizabeth, Potter et al. 2014. Statutory network analysis plus information retrieval. Pages 1–7 of: *Second Workshop on Network Analysis in Law, 27th Annual Conference on Legal Knowledge and Information Systems (JURIX 2014)*. Krakow, December 2014.

Ashley, Kevin D. and Bridewell, Will. 2010. Emerging AI & Law approaches to automating analysis and retrieval of electronically stored information in discovery proceedings. *Artificial Intelligence and Law*, 18(4), 311–20.

Ashley, Kevin D. and Brüninghaus, Stefanie. 2006. Computer models for legal prediction. *Jurimetrics*, 46(3), 309–52.

Ashley, Kevin D. and Brüninghaus, Stefanie. 2009. Automatically classifying case texts and predicting outcomes. *Artificial Intelligence and Law*, 17(2), 125–65.

Ashley, Kevin D. and Rissland, Edwina L. 2003. Law, learning and representation. *Artificial Intelligence*, 150(1–2), 17–58.

Ashley, Kevin D. and Walker, Vern. 2013. From information retrieval (IR) to argument retrieval (AR) for legal cases: report on a baseline study. Pages 29–38 of: *Proceedings of the 26th Annual Conference on Legal Knowledge and Information Systems (JURIX 2013)*. IOS Press: Amsterdam.

Ashworth, Earline Jennifer. 1968. Propositional logic in the sixteenth and early seventeenth centuries. *Notre Dame Journal of Formal Logic*, 9(2), 179–92.

Atkinson, Katie and Bench-Capon, Trevor. 2007. Argumentation and standards of proof. Pages 107–16 of: *Proceedings of the 11th International Conference on Artificial Intelligence and Law*. New York, NY: ACM.

Attaran, Mohsen. 2004. Exploring the relationship between information technology and business process reengineering. *Information and Management*, 41(5) 585–96.

Bach, Ngo Xuan, Minh, Nguyen Le, Oanh, Tran Thi, and Shimazu, Akira. 2013. A two-phase framework for learning logical structures of paragraphs in legal articles. *ACM Transactions on Asian Language Information Processing (TALIP)*, 12(1), 3:1–3:32.

Bansal, Apoorva, Bu, Zheyuan, Mishra, Biswajeet, Wang, Silun, Ashley, Kevin, and Grabmair, Matthias. 2016. Document Ranking with Citation Information and Oversampling Sentence Classification in the LUIMA Framework. Pages 33–42 of: Floris Bex and Serena Villata (eds.), *Legal Knowledge and Information Systems: JURIX 2016: The Twenty-Ninth Annual Conference*. Amsterdam: IOS Press.

Bauer, Robert S., Jade, Teresa, Hedin, Bruce, and Hogan, Chris. 2008. Automated legal sensemaking: the centrality of relevance and intentionality. In: *Proceedings of the Second International Workshop on Supporting Search and Sensemaking for Electronically Stored Information in Discovery Proceedings (DESI II)*. http://discovery.ucl.ac.uk/9131/ (accessed June 12, 2016).

Beck, S. 2014. *Emerging Technology Shapes Future of Law*. www.americanlawyer.com/id=
1202664266769/Emerging-Technology-Shapes-Future-of-Law (accessed September 9,
2014).

Bench-Capon, Trevor. 1991. Exploiting isomorphism: development of a KBS to support British
coal insurance claims. Pages 62–68 of: *Proceedings of the 3rd International Conference on
Artificial Intelligence and Law*. New York, NY: ACM.

Bench-Capon, Trevor 2003. Persuasion in practical argument using value-based argumentation frameworks. *Journal of Logic and Computation*, **13**(3), 429–48.

Bench-Capon, Trevor and Sartor, Giovanni. 2003. A model of legal reasoning with cases
incorporating theories and values. *Artificial Intelligence*, **150**(1), 97–143.

Bench-Capon, Trevor and Visser, Pepijn. 1997. Ontologies in legal information systems: the
need for explicit specifications of domain conceptualisations. Pages 132–41 of: *Proceedings
of the 6th International Conference on Artificial Intelligence and Law*. ICAIL '97. New
York, NY: ACM.

Berkman Center for Internet and Society, Harvard Law School Library, and Harvard Library
Lab. 2016. *H2O Guide: Overview*. https://h2o.law.harvard.edu/p/overview_help (accessed
February 18, 2016).

Berman, Donald H. and Hafner, Carole D. 1988. Obstacles to the development of logic-based
models of legal reasoning. Pages 183–214 of: Walter, Charles (ed.), *Computer Power and
Legal Language*. Westport, CT: Greenwood Press.

Berman, Donald H. and Hafner, Carole D. 1993. Representing teleological structure in case-
based legal reasoning: the missing link. Pages 50–9 of: *Proceedings of the 4th International
Conference on Artificial Intelligence and Law*. New York, NY: ACM.

Bex, Floris J. 2011. *Arguments, Stories and Criminal Evidence: A Formal Hybrid Theory*, vol.
92. Dordrecht: Springer Science & Business Media.

Biagioli, Carlo, Francesconi, Enrico, Passerini, Andrea, Montemagni, Simonetta, and Soria,
Claudia. 2005. Automatic semantics extraction in law documents. In: *ICAIL '05: 7th
International Conference on AI and Law*. New York, NY: ACM.

Białecki, Andrzej, Muir, Robert, and Ingersoll, Grant. 2012. Apache lucene 4. Pages 17–24 of:
SIGIR 2012 Workshop on Open Source Information Retrieval.

Bing, Jon. 1987. Designing text retrieval systems for conceptual searching. Pages 43–51 of:
Proceedings of the 1st International Conference on Artificial Intelligence and Law. ICAIL
'87. New York, NY: ACM.

Bishop, Christopher M. 2006. *Pattern Recognition and Machine Learning*. New York:
Springer.

Blair, David C. and Maron, M. E. 1985. An evaluation of retrieval effectiveness for a full-text
document-retrieval system. *Communications of the ACM*, **28**(3), 289–99.

Blecking, Anja. 2014. Classroom salon – an innovative method for investigating student
learning. In: Kendhammer, Lisa K. and Murphy, Kristen L. (eds.), *Innovative Uses of
Assessments for Teaching and Research*. Washington, DC: American Chemical Society.

Boella, Guido, Di Caro, Luigi, Lesmo, Leonardo, Rispoli, Daniele, and Robaldo, Livio. 2012.
Multi-label classification of legislative text into EuroVoc. In: Schäfer, Burkhard (ed.),
JURIX 2012. Amsterdam: IOS Press.

Boella, Guido, Di Caro, Luigi, Humphreys et al. 2016. Eunomos, a legal document and
knowledge management system for the web to provide relevant, reliable and up-to-date
information on the law. *Artificial Intelligence and Law*, **24**(3), 245–83.

Brachman, Ronald and Levesque, Hector. 2004. *Knowledge Representation and Reasoning*.
Amsterdam: Elsevier.

Branting, L. Karl. 1991. Building explanations from rules and structured cases. *International Journal of Man–Machine Studies*, **34**(6), 797–837.

Branting, L. Karl. 1999. *Reasoning with Rules and Precedents.* Dordrecht, Holland: Kluwer, pp. 8–28.

Breaux, Travis D. 2009. *Legal Requirements Acquisition for the Specification of Legally Compliant Information Systems.* Ann Arbor, MI: ProQuest.

Breaux, Travis D. and Gordon, David G. 2011. Regulatory requirements as open systems: structures, patterns and metrics for the design of formal requirements specifications. *Carnegie Mellon University Technical Report CMU-ISR-11-100.*

Breaux, Travis D. and Gordon, David G. 2013. Regulatory requirements traceability and analysis using semi-formal specifications. Pages 141–57 of: *Requirements Engineering: Foundation for Software Quality.* Dordrecht: Springer.

Breaux, Travis D., Hibshi, Hanan, and Rao, Ashwini. 2014. Eddy, a formal language for specifying and analyzing data flow specifications for conflicting privacy requirements. *Requirements Engineering,* **19**(3), 281–307.

Breaux, Travis D. and Schaub, Florian. 2014. Scaling requirements extraction to the crowd: experiments with privacy policies. Pages 163–72 of: *Requirements Engineering Conference (RE), 2014 IEEE 22nd International.* IEEE.

Breaux, Travis D., Smullen, Daniel, and Hibshi, Hanan. 2015. Detecting repurposing and over-collection in multi-party privacy requirements specifications. Pages 166–75 of: *Requirements Engineering Conference (RE), 2015 IEEE 23rd International.* New York, NY: IEEE.

Breaux, Travis D., Vail, Matthew, and Anton, Annie. 2006. Towards regulatory compliance: extracting rights and obligations to align requirements with regulations. Pages 46–55 of: *Proceedings of RE06.* Washington, DC: IEEE Computer Society.

Breuker, Joost, Elhag, Abdullatif, Petkov, Emil, and Winkels, Radboud. 2002. Ontologies for legal information serving and knowledge management. Pages 1–10 of: *Legal Knowledge and Information Systems, Jurix 2002: The Fifteenth Annual Conference.* Amsterdam: IOS Press.

Breuker, Joost and Hoekstra, Rinke. 2004. Epistemology and Ontology in Core Ontologies: FOLaw and LRI-Core, two core ontologies for law. Pages 15–27 of: *Proceedings of the EKAW04 Workshop on Core Ontologies in Ontology Engineering.* Northamptonshire, UK.

Breuker, Joost, Valente, André, and Winkels, Radboud. 2004. Legal ontologies in knowledge engineering and information management. *Artificial Intelligence and Law,* **12**(4), 241–77.

Brewka, Gerhard and Gordon, Thomas F. 2010. Carneades and abstract dialectical frameworks: a reconstruction. Pages 3–12 of: *Proceedings of the 2010 Conference on Computational Models of Argument: Proceedings of COMMA 2010.* Amsterdam: IOS Press.

Buckland, Michael K. and Gey, Fredric C. 1994. The relationship between recall and precision. *JASIS,* **45**(1), 12–19.

Burges, Chris, Shaked, Tal, Renshaw, Erin et al. 2005. Learning to rank using gradient descent. Pages 89–96 of: *Proceedings of the 22nd International Conference on Machine Learning.* ICML '05. New York, NY: ACM.

Büttcher, Stefan, Clarke, Charles L. A., and Cormack, Gordon V. 2010. *Information Retrieval: Implementing and Evaluating Search Engines.* Cambridge, MA: MIT Press.

Callan, James, Croft, Bruce W., and Harding, Stephen M. 1992. The INQUERY retrieval system. Pages 78–83 of: *In Proceedings of the Third International Conference on Database and Expert Systems Applications.* Dordrecht: Springer-Verlag.

Carnielli, Walter A. and Marcos, Joao. 2001. Ex contradictione non sequitur quodlibet. Pages 89–109 of: *Proceedings of the Advanced Reasoning Forum Conference*, vol. 1. Berkeley and Monte Rio, California, USA.

Casemaker. 2015. *Casemaker.* www.casemaker.us/ProductsStateBarConsortium.aspx (accessed August 12, 2015).

Centers for Disease Control and Prevention. 2015. *Vaccine Acronyms & Abbreviations.* www.cdc.gov/vaccines/about/terms/vacc-abbrev.htm (accessed July 22, 2015).

Cervone, Luca, Di Iorio, Angelo, Palmirani, Monica, and Vitali, Fabio. 2015. *Akoma Ntoso.* www.akomantoso.org/akoma-ntoso-in-detail/what-is-it/ (accessed October 8, 2015).

Charniak, Eugene. 1991. Bayesian networks without tears. *AI Magazine*, **12**(4), 50–63.

Che, Bingqing, Qiang, Meng, and Yichi, Yepeng. 2015. *Capstone Project Report: LUIMA.*

Chorley, Alison and Bench-Capon, Trevor. 2005a. AGATHA: automated construction of case law theories through heuristic search. Pages 45–54 of: *Proceedings of the 10th International Conference on Artificial Intelligence and Law*. New York, NY: ACM.

Chorley, Alison and Bench-Capon, Trevor. 2005b. AGATHA: using heuristic search to automate the construction of case law theories. *Artificial Intelligence and Law*, **13**(1), 9–51.

Chorley, Alison and Bench-Capon, Trevor. 2005c. An empirical investigation of reasoning with legal cases through theory construction and application. *Artificial Intelligence and Law*, **13**(3–4), 323–71.

Chu-Carroll, Jennifer, Brown, Eric W., Lally, Adam, and Murdock, J. William. 2012. Identifying implicit relationships. *IBM Journal of Research and Development*, **56**(3.4), 12:1–12:10.

Clement, Kevin. 2016. Propositional logic. In: *The Internet Encyclopedia of Philosophy*. IEP. www.iep.utm.edu/ (accessed August 4, 2016).

Cohen, Jacob 1960. A coefficient of agreement for nominal scales. *Educational and Psychological Measurement*, **20**(1), 37–46.

Cutler, Kim-Mai. 2015. *YC's ROSS Intelligence Leverages IBM's Watson to Make Sense of Legal Knowledge.* http://techcrunch.com/2015/07/27/ross-intelligence/ (accessed December 31, 2015).

Dabney, Daniel P. 1993. *Statistical Modeling of Relevance Judgments for Probabilistic Retrieval of American Case Law.* Berkeley, CA: University of California.

Daelemans, Walter, Zavrel, Jakub, van der Sloot, Ko, and van den Bosch, Anton. 2004. *TiMBL: Tilburg Memory based Learner*, Version 5.02 (now 6.3). http://ilk.uvt.nl/timbl/ (accessed July 19, 2015).

Daniels, Jody J. and Rissland, Edwina L. 1997a. Finding legally relevant passages in case opinions. Pages 39–46 of: *Proceedings of the 6th International Conference on Artificial Intelligence and Law*. ICAIL '97. New York, NY: ACM.

Daniels, Jody J. and Rissland, Edwina L. 1997b. What you saw is what you want: using cases to seed information retrieval. Pages 325–36 of: *Proceedings of the Second International Conference on Case-Based Reasoning*. Providence, RI: Springer.

Daudaravicius, Vidas. 2012. Automatic multilingual annotation of EU legislation with EuroVoc descriptors. Pp. 14–20 of: *EEOP2012: Exploring and Exploiting Official Publications Workshop Programme*. Istanbul, Turkey.

de Maat, Emile, Krabben, Kai, and Winkels, Radboud. 2010. Machine learning versus knowledge based classification of legal texts. In: Winkels, R. (ed.), *JURIX 2010*. Amsterdam: IOS Press.

de Maat, Emile and Winkels, Radboud. 2007. Categorisation of norms. Pages 79–88 of: *JURIX 2007*. Amsterdam: IOS Press.

de Maat, Emile and Winkels, Radboud. 2009. A next step towards automated modelling of sources of law. Pages 31–9 of: *Proceedings of the 12th International Conference on Artificial Intelligence and Law*. ICAIL '09. New York, NY: ACM.

Deisher-Edwards, Julie. 2015. *TILABuddy: An Automated Approach to Corporate Compliance*. Unpublished student course paper on file with author.

Desatnik, Eric. 2016. *The IBM Watson AI XPRIZE, a Cognitive Computing Competition*. www.xprize.org/AI (accessed May 21, 2016).

Dick, Judith and Hirst, Graeme. 1991. A case-based representation of legal text for conceptual retrieval. In: *Workshop on Language and Information Processing, American Society for Information Science*. Washington, DC.

Dietrich, Antje, Lockemann, Peter C., and Raabe, Oliver. 2007. Agent approach to online legal trade. Pages 177–94 of: *Conceptual Modelling in Information Systems Engineering*. Dordrecht: Springer.

Dowden, Bradley. 2016. Liar's paradox. In: *The Internet Encyclopedia of Philosophy*. IEP. www.iep.utm.edu/ (accessed August 4, 2016).

Dukeminier, Jesse, Krier, James, Alexander, Gregory, and Shill, Michael. 2010. *Property*. New York: Aspen.

Dung, Phan Minh. 1995. On the acceptability of arguments and its fundamental role in non-monotonic reasoning, logic programming and n-person games. *Artificial Intelligence*, 77(2), 321–57.

Dvorsky, George. 2014. *IBM's Watson Can Now Debate Its Opponents (Demo at 45.47 Minute Mark)*. http://io9.com/ibms-watson-can-now-debate-its-opponents-1571837847 (accessed February 1, 2015).

Eckholm, Erik. 2015. *Harvard Law Library Readies Trove of Decisions for Digital Age*. www.nytimes.com/2015/10/29/us/harvard-law-library-sacrifices-a-trove-for-the-sake-of-a-free-database.html?_r=0 (accessed December 30, 2015).

Epstein, Edward, Schor, Marshall, Iyer, Bhavani, et al. 2012. Making Watson fast. *IBM Journal of Research and Development*, 56(3.4), 15:1–15:12.

EuroVoc. 2014. *EuroVoc*. http://eurovoc.europa.eu/drupal/ (accessed August 27, 2014).

Fagan, Frank. 2016. Big data legal scholarship: toward a research program and practitioners guide. *Virginia Journal of Law and Technology*, 20, 1–81.

Falakmasir, Mohammad. 2016. *Comprehensive Exam Answer: Argument Mining (Revised)*. University of Pittsburgh Intelligent Systems Program.

Feller, Robert. 2015. Judicial review of administrative decisions and procedure. In: Philip Weinberg and William R. Ginsberg (eds.), *Environmental Law and Regulation in New York* 3:48 (2nd edn.). 9 N.Y.Prac.: New York Practice Series – Environmental Law and Regulation in New York.

Feng, Vanessa Wei and Hirst, Graeme. 2011. Classifying arguments by scheme. Pages 987–96 of: *Proceedings of the 49th Annual Meeting of the Association for Computational Linguistics: Human Language Technologies – Volume 1*. Association for Computational Linguistics.

Ferrucci, David A. 2012. Introduction to "This is Watson." *IBM Journal of Research and Development*, 56(3/4), 1:1–1:15.

Ferrucci, David A., Brown, Eric W., Chu-Carroll, Jennifer et al. 2010. Building Watson: an overview of the DeepQA Project. *AI Magazine*, 31(3), 59–79.

Finkel, Jenny, Rafferty, Anna, Kleeman, Alex, and Manning, Christopher. 2003–14. *Stanford Classifier*. http://nlp.stanford.edu/software/classifier.shtml (accessed July 22, 2015).

Flood, Mark D. and Goodenough, Oliver R. 2015. Contract as automation: the computational representation of financial agreements. Office of Financial Research Working Paper,

15-04. https://financialresearch.gov/working-papers/files/OFRwp-2015-04_Contract-as-Automaton-The-Computational-Representation-of-Financial-Agreements.pdf (accessed July 29, 2016).

Francesconi, Enrico. 2009. An approach to legal rules modelling and automatic learning. Pages 59–68 of: *Proceedings of the 2009 Conference on Legal Knowledge and Information Systems: JURIX 2009: The Twenty-Second Annual Conference*. Amsterdam, The Netherlands : IOS Press.

Francesconi, Enrico, Montemagni, Simonetta, Peters, Wim, and Tiscornia, Daniela. 2010. Integrating a bottom-up and top-down methodology for building semantic resources for the multilingual legal domain. Pages 95–121 of: Francesconi, Enrico, Montemagni, Simonetta, Peters, Wim, and Tiscornia, Daniela (eds.), *Semantic Processing of Legal Texts*. Berlin, Heidelberg: Springer-Verlag.

Francesconi, Enrico and Passerini, Andrea. 2007. Automatic classification of provisions in legislative texts. *Artificial Intelligence and Law*, **15**, 1–17.

Francesconi, Enrico and Peruginelli, Ginevra. 2008. Integrated access to legal literature through automated semantic classification. *AI and Law*, **17**, 31–49.

Freitag, Dayne. 2000. Machine learning for information extraction in informal domains. *Machine learning*, **39**(2–3), 169–202.

Fuller, Lon L. 1958. Positivism and fidelity to law: a reply to Professor Hart. *Harvard Law Review*, 630–72.

Gangemi, Aldo, Guarino, Nicola, Masolo, Claudio, Oltramari, Alessandro, and Schneider, Luc. 2002. Sweetening ontologies with DOLCE. Pages 166–81 of: *Knowledge Engineering and Knowledge Management: Ontologies and the Semantic Web*. Dordrecht: Springer.

Gardner, Anne vdL. 1985. Overview of an artificial intelligence approach to legal reasoning. Pages 247–74 of: *Computer Power and Legal Reasoning*. St. Paul, MN: West Publishing Co.

Gardner, Anne vdL. 1987. *An Artificial Intelligence Approach to Legal Reasoning*. Cambridge, MA: MIT Press.

Gonçalves, Teresa and Quaresma, Paulo. 2005. Is linguistic information relevant for the classification of legal texts? Pages 168–76 of: *Proceedings of the 10th International Conference on Artificial Intelligence and Law*. New York, NY: ACM.

Gordon, David G. and Breaux, Travis D. 2013. A cross-domain empirical study and legal evaluation of the requirements water marking method. *Requirements Engineering*, **18**(2), 147–73.

Gordon, Thomas F. 1987. Some problems with prolog as a knowledge representation language for legal expert systems. *International Review of Law, Computers & Technology*, **3**(1), 52–67.

Gordon, Thomas F. 2008a. The legal knowledge interchange format (LKIF). *Estrella deliverable d4*, 1–28 (accessed March 22, 2017).

Gordon, Thomas F. 2008b. Constructing legal arguments with rules in the legal knowledge interchange format (LKIF). Pages 162–84 of: *Computable Models of the Law*. Dordrecht: Springer.

Gordon, Thomas F. 2008c. Hybrid reasoning with argumentation schemes. Pages 543 of: *Proceedings of the 2008 Conference on Knowledge-based Software Engineering: Proceedings of the Eighth Joint Conference on Knowledge-based Software Engineering*. Amsterdam: IOS Press.

Gordon, Thomas F. 2014. Software engineering for research on legal argumentation. In: *Proceedings of the 1st International Workshop for Methodologies for Research on Legal Argumentation (MET-ARG)*. (On file with author.)

Gordon, Thomas F. 2015a. *Carneades 3.7 User Manual*. https://carneades.github.io/manuals/ Carneades3.7/carneades-3.7-manual.pdf (accessed November 16, 2015).

Gordon, Thomas F. 2015b. *Carneades Tools for Argument (Re)construction, Evaluation, Mapping and Interchange*. http://carneades.github.io/Carneades/ (accessed November 23, 2015).

Gordon, Thomas F., Governatori, Guido, and Rotolo, Antonino. 2009. Rules and norms: requirements for rule interchange languages in the legal domain. Pages 282–96 of: *Rule Interchange and Applications*. Dordrecht; Springer.

Gordon, Thomas F., Prakken, Henry, and Walton, Douglas. 2007. The Carneades model of argument and burden of proof. *Artificial Intelligence*, 171(10–5), 875–96. Argumentation in Artificial Intelligence.

Gordon, Thomas F. and Walton, Douglas. 2006. The Carneades argumentation framework-using presumptions and exceptions to model critical questions. Pages 5–13 of: *6th Computational Models of Natural Argument Workshop (CMNA), European Conference on Artificial Intelligence (ECAI)*, Italy.

Gordon, Thomas F. and Walton, Douglas. 2009. Legal reasoning with argumentation schemes. Pages 137–46 of: *Proceedings of the 12th International Conference on Artificial Intelligence and Law*. New York, NY: ACM.

Governatori, Guido and Shek, Sidney. 2012 (August). Rule based business process compliance. Pages 1–8 of: *6th International Rule Challenge @ RuleML 2012. CEUR Workshop Proceedings*. Volume 874. Paper 5.

Grabmair, Matthias. 2016. *Modeling Purposive Legal Argumentation and Case Outcome Prediction using Argument Schemes in the Value Judgment Formalism*. Ph.D. thesis, University of Pittsburgh, Pittsburgh, PA.

Grabmair, Matthias and Ashley, Kevin D. 2010. Argumentation with value judgments: an example of hypothetical reasoning. Pages 67–76 of: *Proceedings of the 2010 Conference on Legal Knowledge and Information Systems: JURIX 2010: The Twenty-Third Annual Conference*. Amsterdam: IOS Press.

Grabmair, Matthias and Ashley, Kevin D. 2011. Facilitating case comparison using value judgments and intermediate legal concepts. Pages 161–70 of: *Proceedings of the 13th International Conference on Artificial intelligence and Law*. New York, NY: ACM.

Grabmair, Matthias, Ashley, Kevin, Chen, Ran. et al. 2015. Introducing LUIMA: an experiment in legal conceptual retrieval of vaccine injury decisions using a UIMA type system and tools. Pages 1–10 of: *Proceedings of the 15th International Conference on Artificial Intelligence and Law*. ICAIL 2015. New York, NY: ACM.

Grabmair, Matthias, Ashley, Kevin D., Hwa, Rebecca, and Sweeney, P. M. 2011. Towards extracting information from public health statutes using text classification and machine learning. In: Atkinson, Katie M. (ed.), *JURIX 2011: Proceedings of the Twenty-Fourth Conference on Legal Knowledge and Information Systems*. Amsterdam: IOS Press.

Grabmair, Matthias, Gordon, Thomas F., and Walton, Douglas. 2010. Probabilistic semantics for the Carneades argument model using Bayesian networks. Pages 255–66 of: *Proceedings of the 2010 Conference on Computational Models of Argument: Proceedings of COMMA 2010*. Amsterdam: IOS Press.

Granat, Richard and Lauritsen, Marc. 2014. Teaching the technology of practice: the 10 top schools. *Law Practice Magazine*, 40(4) www.americanbar.org/publications/ law_practice_magazine/2014/july-august/teaching-the-technology-of-practice-the-10-top-schools.html (accessed February 2, 2015).

Gray, Grayfred B. 1985. Statutes enacted in normalized form: the legislative experience in Tennessee. Pages 467–93 of: *Computer Power and Legal Reasoning*. St. Paul, MN: West Publishing.

Gray, Jeff. 2014. University of Toronto's next lawyer: a computer program named Ross. *The Globe and Mail* www.theglobeandmail.com/report-on-business/industry-news/the-law-page/university-of-torontos-next-lawyer-a-computer-program-named-ross/article22054688/ (accessed February 3, 2015).

Grossman, Maura R. and Cormack, Gordon V. 2010. Technology-assisted review in e-discovery can be more effective and more efficient than exhaustive manual review. *Richmond Journal of Law & Technology*, **17**, 1–48.

Grossman, Maura R. and Cormack, Gordon V. 2014. Grossman–Cormack glossary of technology-assisted review. *Federal Courts Law Review*, **7**, 85–112.

Gultemen, Dincer and van Engers, Thomas. 2014. Graph-based linking and visualization for legislation documents (GLVD). Pages 67–80 of: Winkels, Radboud, Lettieri, Nicola, and Faro, Sebastiano. (eds.), *Network Analysis in Law*. Collana: Diritto Scienza Tecnologia/Law Science Technology Temi, 3. Napoli: Edizioni Scientifiche Italiane.

Hachey, Ben and Grover, Claire. 2006. Extractive summarisation of legal texts. *Artificial Intelligence and Law*, **14**(4), 305–45.

Hafner, Carole. 1978. An information retrieval system based on a computer model of legal knowledge. Ph.D. thesis, University of Michigan, Ann Arbor, MI. AAI7807057.

Hart, Herbert Lionel Adolphus. 1958. Positivism and the separation of law and morals. *Harvard Law Review*, **71**, 593–629.

Hashmi, Mustafa, Governatori, Guido, and Wynn, Moe Thandar. 2014. Normative requirements for business process compliance. Pages 100–16 of: *Service Research and Innovation*. Dordrecht: Springer.

Henderson, William D. 2013. A blueprint for change. *Pepperdine Law Review*, **40**(2), 461–507.

Henseler, Hans. 2010. Network-based filtering for large email collections in e-discovery. *Artificial Intelligence and Law*, **18**(4), 413–30.

Herring, David J. and Lynch, Collin. 2014. Measuring law student learning outcomes: 2013 lawyering class. UNM School of Law Research Paper.

Hoekstra, Rinke. 2010. The knowledge reengineering bottleneck. *Semantic Web*, **1**(1,2), 111–15.

Hoekstra, Rinke and Boer, Alexander. 2014. A network analysis of Dutch regulations – using the MetaLex Document Server. Pages 47–58 of: Winkels, Radboud, Lettieri, Nicola, and Faro, Sebastiano (eds.), *Network Analysis in Law*. Collana: Diritto Scienza Tecnologia/Law Science Technology Temi, 3. Napoli: Edizioni Scientifiche Italiane.

Hogan, Christopher, Bauer, Robert, and Brassil, Dan. 2009. Human-aided computer cognition for e-discovery. Pages 194–201 of: *Proceedings of the 12th International Conference on Artificial Intelligence and Law*. New York, NY: ACM.

Hogan, Christopher, Bauer, Robert S., and Brassil, Dan. 2010. Automation of legal sensemaking in e-discovery. *Artificial Intelligence and Law*, **18**(4), 431–57.

Hu, Xia and Liu, Huan. 2012. *Mining Text Data*. Boston, MA: Springer US.

IBM Watson Developer Cloud Watson Services. 2015. *IBM Watson Developer Cloud Watson Services*. www.ibm.com/smarterplanet/us/en/ibmwatson/developercloud/services-catalog.html (accessed February 1, 2015).

IBM Watson Developer Cloud Watson Services. 2016. *Alchemy Language*. www.ibm.com/smarterplanet/us/en/ibmwatson/developercloud/alchemy-language.html (accessed May 22, 2016).

Iron Tech Lawyer. 2015. *The Program in Legal Technologies, Georgetown Law, Iron Tech Lawyer*. Georgetown Law School. www.law.georgetown.edu/academics/centers-institutes/legal-profession/legal-technologies/iron-tech/index.cfm (accessed February 3, 2015).

Jackson, Brian. 2015. *Meet Ross, the Watson-Powered "Super Intelligent" Attorney*. www.itbusiness.ca/news/meet-ross-the-watson-powered-super-intelligent-attorney/53376 (accessed December 31, 2015).

Jackson, Peter, Al-Kofahi, Khalid, Tyrrell, Alex, and Vachher, Arun. 2003. Information extraction from case law and retrieval of prior cases. *Artificial Intelligence*, 150(1–2), 239–90. *Artificial Intelligence and Law*.

Jurafsky, Daniel and Martin, James. 2015. Classification: naive Bayes, logistic regression, sentiment. Chapter 7, pages 1–28 of: Jurafsky, Daniel and Martin, James (eds.), *Speech and Language Processing*. Stanford University. Draft of August 24, 2015, https://web.stanford.edu/~jurafsky/slp3/7.pdf (accessed September 29, 2016).

Kafura, Dennis. 2011. *Notes on Petri Nets*. http://people.cs.vt.edu/~kafura/Computational Thinking/Class-Notes/Petri-Net-Notes-Expanded.pdf (accessed August 9, 2016).

Kakwani, Nanak. 1980. On a class of poverty measures. *Econometrica: Journal of the Econometric Society*, 437–46.

Katz, Daniel M. and Bommarito, Michael. 2014. *Legal Analytics – Introduction to the Course*. www.slideshare.net/Danielkatz/legal-analytics-introduction-to-the-course-professor-daniel-martin-katz-professor-michael-j-bommartio-ii-31350591 (accessed May 12, 2016).

Katz, Daniel M., Bommarito, Michael, and Blackman, Josh. 2014. *Predicting the Behavior of the United States Supreme Court: A General Approach* (July 21, 2014). http://ssrn.com/abstract=2463244 (accessed May 26, 2015).

Kelly, John E. and Hamm, Steve. 2013. *Smart Machines: IBM's Watson and the Era of Cognitive Computing*. New York, NY: Columbia University Press.

Kiyavitskaya, Nadzeya, Zeni, Nicola, Breaux, Travis D. et al. 2008. Automating the extraction of rights and obligations for regulatory compliance. Pages 154–68 of: *Conceptual Modeling – ER 2008*. Dordrecht: Springer.

Koetter, Falko, Kochanowski, Monika, Weisbecker, Anette, Fehling, Christoph, and Leymann, Frank. 2014. Integrating compliance requirements across business and IT. Pages 218–25 of: *Enterprise Distributed Object Computing Conference (EDOC), 2014 IEEE 18th International*. New York, NY: IEEE.

Kohavi, Ron. 1995. A study of cross-validation and bootstrap for accuracy estimation and model selection. Pages 1137–43 of: *Proceedings of the 14th International Joint Conference on Artificial Intelligence – Volume 2*. IJCAI'95. San Francisco, CA: Morgan Kaufmann Publishers Inc.

Kohavi, Ron and Provost, Foster. 1998. Glossary of terms. *Machine Learning*, 30(2–3), 271–4.

Kritzer, Albert H. 2015. *CISG Database*. Institute of International Commercial Law, Pace Law School. www.cisg.law.pace.edu/ (accessed February 4, 2015).

Landauer, Thomas K, Foltz, Peter W., and Laham, Darrell. 1998. An introduction to latent semantic analysis. *Discourse Processes*, 25(2–3), 259–84.

Legal OnRamp. 2015. *Legal OnRamp*. www.legalonramp.com/ (accessed February 1, 2015).

LegalSifter. 2016. *LegalSifter Use Cases*. www.legalsifter.com/use-cases (accessed May 3, 2016).

Legaltech News. 2016. *Legaltech News*. www.legaltechnews.com/ (accessed September 19, 2016).

Levi, Edward H. 2013. *An Introduction to Legal Reasoning*. Chicago: University of Chicago Press.

Levy, Ran, Bilu, Yonatan, Hershcovich, Daniel, Aharoni, Ehud, and Slonim, Noam. 2014. Context dependent claim detection. Pages 1489–500 of: *Proceedings of COLING 2014*, the 25th International Conference on Computational Linguistics: Technical Papers. Dublin, Ireland.

Library, Harvard Law School. 2015. *Free Legal Research Resources.* http://guides.library .harvard.edu/c.php?g=310432&p=2072006 (accessed February 3, 2015).

Lindahl, Lars. 2004. Deduction and justification in the law: the role of legal terms and concepts. *Ratio Juris*, **17**(2), 182–202.

Lippe, Paul and Katz, Dan. 2014. 10 Predictions about how IBM's Watson will impact the legal profession. ABA Journal www.abajournal.com/legalrebels/article/10_predictions_ about_how_ibms_watson_will_impact (accessed February 2, 2015).

Lippner, Jordan. 1995. Replacement players for the Toronto Blue Jays? Striking the appropriate balance between replacement worker law in Ontario, Canada, and the United States. *Fordham International Law Journal*, **38**, 2026–94.

Liu, Hongfang, Wu, Stephen, Tao, Cui, and Chute, Christopher. 2012. Modeling UIMA type system using web ontology language: towards interoperability among UIMA-based NLP tools. Pages 31–6 of: *Proceedings of the 2nd International Workshop on Managing Interoperability and CompleXity in Health Systems.* New York, NY: ACM.

Llewellyn, Karl N. 1949. Remarks on the theory of appellate decision and the rules or canons about how statutes are to be construed. *Vanderbilt Law Review*, **3**, 395–408.

Lu, Qiang and Conrad, Jack. 2013. *Next Generation Legal Search – It's Already Here* https:// blog.law.cornell.edu/voxpop/2013/03/28/next-generation-legal-search-itsalready-here (accessed May 22, 2015).

MacCormick, Neil and Summers, Robert S. 1991. *Interpreting Statutes: A Comparative Study.* Dartmouth Aldershot.

Machine Learning Group at the University of Waikato. 2015. *Weka 3: Data Mining Software in Java* www.cs.waikato.ac.nz/ml/weka/ (accessed July 22, 2015).

Mackaay, Ejan and Robillard, Pierre. 1974. Predicting judicial decisions: the nearest neighbour rule and visual representation of case patterns. *Datenverarbeitung im Recht*, **3**, 302–31.

Mann, William C. and Thompson, Sandra A. 1987. *Rhetorical Structure Theory: A Theory of Text Organization.* University of Southern California, Information Sciences Institute.

Mart, Susan Nevelow. 2010. Relevance of results generated by human indexing and computer algorithms: a study of West's headnotes and key numbers and LexisNexis's headnotes and topics, *The Law Library Journal*, **102**, 221–49.

McCallum, Andrew. 2004. *Bow: A Toolkit for Statistical Language Modeling, Text Retrieval, Classification and Clustering* www.cs.cmu.edu/~mccallum/bow/ (accessed July 19, 2015).

McCarty, L. Thorne. 1995. An implementation of Eisner v. Macomber. Pages 276–86 of: *Proceedings of the 5th International Conference on Artificial Intelligence and Law.* New York, NY: ACM.

McCarty, L. Thorne. 2007. Deep semantic interpretations of legal texts. Pages 217–24 of: *Proceedings of the 11th International Conference on Artificial Intelligence and Law.* New York, NY: ACM.

McCarty, L. Thorne and Sridharan, Natesa. 1981. The representation of an evolving system of legal concepts: II. Prototypes and deformations. Pages 246–53 of: *Proceedings of the 7th International Joint Conference on Artificial Intelligence – Volume 1.* San Francisco, CA: Morgan Kaufmann Publishers Inc.

McLaren, Bruce M. 2003. Extensionally defining principles and cases in ethics: an AI model. *Artificial Intelligence*, **150**(1), 145–81.

Merriam-Webster's Collegiate Dictionary. 2015. *Merriam-Webster's Collegiate Dictionary.* Springfield, MA: Merriam-Webster. http://search.credoreference.com/content/entry/mwcollegiate/explanation/0 (accessed February 5, 2015).

Mimouni, Nada, Fernandez, Meritxell, Nazarenko, Adeline, Bourcier, Daniele, and Salotti, Sylvie. 2014. A relational approach for information retrieval on XML legal sources. Pages 169–92 of: Winkels, Radboud, Lettieri, Nicola, and Faro, Sebastiano (eds.) *Network Analysis in Law.* Collana: Diritto Scienza Tecnologia/Law Science Technology Temi, 3. Napoli: Edizioni Scientifiche Italiane.

Mitchell, Thomas. 2015. *Generative and Discriminative Classifiers: Naive Bayes and Logistic Regression* www.cs.cmu.edu/~tom/mlbook/NBayesLogReg.pdf (accessed July 14, 2015).

Mochales, Raquel and Moens, Marie-Francine. 2011. Argumentation mining. *Artificial Intelligence and Law,* 19(1), 1–22.

Modgil, Sanjay and Prakken, Henry. 2014. The ASPIC+ framework for structured argumentation: a tutorial. *Argument & Computation,* 5(1), 31–62.

Moens, Marie-Francine, Boiy, Erik, Palau, Raquel Mochales, and Reed, Chris. 2007. Automatic detection of arguments in legal texts. Pages 225–30 of: *Proceedings of the 11th International Conference on Artificial Intelligence and Law.* ICAIL '07. New York, NY: ACM.

Mohri, Mehryar, Rostamizadeh, Afshin, and Talwalkar, Ameet. 2012. *Foundations of Machine Learning.* Cambridge, MA: MIT Press.

Morelock, John T., Wiltshire, James S., Ahmed, Salahuddin, Humphrey, Timothy L., and Lu, X. Allen. 2004 (August 3). System and method for identifying facts and legal discussion in court case law documents. US Patent 6,772,149.

Neota Logic. 2016. *Neota Logic.* www.neotalogic.com/ (accessed August 9, 2016).

Newman, Rick. 2014. *IBM Unveils a Computer that can Argue.* The Exchange. http://finance.yahoo.com/blogs/the-exchange/ibm-unveils-a-computer-than-can-argue-181228620.htm (accessed February 1, 2015).

Nigam, Kamal, Lafferty, John, and McCallum, Andrew. 1999. Using maximum entropy for text classification. Pages 61–7 of: *IJCAI-99 Workshop on Machine Learning for Information Filtering,* vol. 1. Stockholm, Sweden.

NIST/SEMATECH. 2016. *NIST/SEMATECH e-Handbook of Statistical Methods* www.itl.nist.gov/div898/handbook/ (accessed May 30, 2016).

Noble, William S. 2006. What is a support vector machine? *Nature Biotechnology,* 24(12), 1565–7.

Oard, Douglas W. and Webber, William. 2013. Information retrieval for e-discovery. *Information Retrieval,* 7(2–3), 99–237.

Oasis. 2016. *Akoma Ntoso Naming Convention Version 1.0,* Committee Specification Draft 02/Public Review Draft 02, 04 May 2016 www.akomantoso.org/akoma-ntoso-in-detail/what-is-it/ (accessed June 12, 2016).

Oberle, Daniel, Drefs, Felix, Wacker, Richard, Baumann, Christian, and Raabe, Oliver. 2012. Engineering compliant software: advising developers by automating legal reasoning. *SCRIPTed,* 9(2), 280–313.

Oh, Peter B. 2010. Veil-piercing. *Texas Law Review,* 89, 81–145.

Opsomer, Rob, Meyer, Geert De, Cornelis, Chris, and van Eetvelde, Greet. 2009. Exploiting properties of legislative texts to improve classification accuracy. In: Governatori, Guido (ed.), *JURIX 2009: Proceedings of the Twenty-Second Conference on Legal Knowledge and Information Systems.* Amsterdam: IOS Press.

Palanque, Philippe A. and Bastide, Remi. 1995. Petri net based design of user-driven interfaces using the interactive cooperative objects formalism. Pages 383–400 of: *Interactive Systems: Design, Specification, and Verification.* Dordrecht: Springer.

Palmirani, Monica. 2011. Legislative change management with Akoma-Ntoso. Pages 101–30 of: Sartor, Giovanni, Palmirani, Monica, Francesconi, Enrico, and Biasiotti, Maria Angela (eds.), *Legislative XML for the Semantic Web*. Law, Governance and Technology Series, vol. 4. Dordrecht: Springer.

Pouliquen, Bruno, Steinberger, Raif, and Ignat, Camelia. 2006. *Automatic Annotation of Multi-lingual Text Collections with a Conceptual Thesaurus*. arXiv preprint cs/0609059.

Prager, John, Brown, Eric, Coden, Anni, and Radev, Dragomir. 2000. Question-answering by predictive annotation. Pages 184–91 of: *Proceedings of the 23rd Annual International ACM SIGIR Conference on Research and Development in Information Retrieval*. New York, NY: ACM.

Prakken, Henry. 1995. From logic to dialectics in legal argument. Pages 165–74 of: *Proceedings of the 5th International Conference on Artificial Intelligence and Law*. New York, NY: ACM.

Prakken, Henry. 2005. AI & Law, logic and argument schemes. *Argumentation*, 19(3), 303–20.

Prakken, Henry and Sartor, Giovanni. 1998. Modelling reasoning with precedents in a formal dialogue game. *Artificial Intelligence and Law*, 6, 231–87.

Privault, Caroline, O'Neill, Jacki, Ciriza, Victor, and Renders, Jean-Michel. 2010. A new tangible user interface for machine learning document review. *Artificial Intelligence and Law*, 18(4), 459–79.

Putman, William H. 2008 *Legal Analysis and Writing for Paralegals*. Boston, MA: Cengage Learning.

Quinlan, J. Ross. 1986. Induction of decision trees. *Machine Learning*, 1(1), 81–106.

Quinlan, J. Ross. 2004. *C4.5 Release 8* www.rulequest.com/Personal/ (accessed July 19, 2015).

Rahwan, Iyad, Simari, Guillermo R., and van Benthem, Johan. 2009. *Argumentation in Artificial Intelligence*, vol. 47. Dordrecht: Springer.

Ravel Law. 2015a. *Ravel: Data Driven Research* www.ravellaw.com (accessed December 30, 2015).

Ravel Law. 2015b. *Ravel Judge Analytics* (accessed December 31, 2015).

Ravel Law. 2015c. *Ravel QuickStart Guide*. https://d2xkkp2ofm9wy8.cloudfront.net/downloads/Ravel_QuickStart_Guide.pdf (accessed December 31, 2015).

Ravel Law. 2015d. *What Determines Relevance*. https://ravellaw.zendesk.com/hc/en-us/articles/213290777-What-determines-Relevance- (accessed December 31, 2015).

Reed, Chris and Rowe, Glenn. 2004. Araucaria: software for argument analysis, diagramming and representation. *International Journal on Artificial Intelligence Tools*, 13(04), 961–79.

Remus, Dana and Levy, Frank S. 2015. *Can Robots be Lawyers? Computers, Lawyers, and the Practice of Law* (December 30, 2015) http://ssrn.com/abstract=2701092 (accessed July 24, 2016).

Rissland, Edwina L. 1990. Artificial intelligence and law: stepping stones to a model of legal reasoning. *Yale Law Journal*, 1957–81.

Rissland, Edwina L. and Friedman, M. Timur. 1995. Detecting change in legal concepts. Pages 127–36 of: *Proceedings of the 5th International Conference on Artificial Intelligence and Law*. New York, NY: ACM.

Rissland, Edwina L. and Skalak, David B. 1991. CABARET: statutory interpretation in a hybrid architecture. *International Journal of Man–Machine Studies*, 34, 839–87.

Rissland, Edwina L., Skalak, David B., and Friedman M. Timur. 1996. BankXX: supporting legal arguments through heuristic retrieval. *Artificial Intelligence and Law*, 4(1), 1–71.

Robaldo, Livio, Humphreys, Llio, Sun, Xin et al. 2015. Combining input/output logic and reification for representing real-world obligations. In: *Proceedings of the Ninth International Workshop on Juris-Informatics*. JURISIN 2015. Kanagawa, Japan.

Rose, Daniel E. and Belew, Richard K. 1991. A connectionist and symbolic hybrid for improving legal research. *International Journal of Man–Machine Studies*, 35(1), 1–33.

Ross Intelligence. 2015. *Ross: Your Brand New Super Intelligent Attorney* www .rossintelligence.com/ (accessed December 30, 2015).

Saravanan, Manimaran and Ravindran, Balaraman. 2010. Identification of rhetorical roles for segmentation and summarization of a legal judgment. *Artificial Intelligence and Law*, 18(1), 45–76.

Saravanan, Manimaran, Ravindran, Balaraman, and Raman, Subramanian. 2009. Improving legal information retrieval using an ontological framework. *Artificial Intelligence and Law*, 17(2), 101–24.

Sartor, Giovanni, Walton, Doug, Macagno, Fabrizio, and Rotolo, Antonino. 2014. Argumentation schemes for statutory interpretation: a logical analysis. Page 11 of: *Legal Knowledge and Information Systems: JURIX 2014: The Twenty-Seventh Annual Conference*, vol. 271. Amsterdam: IOS Press.

Savelka, Jaromír and Ashley, Kevin D. 2015. Transfer of predictive models for classification of statutory texts in multi-jurisdictional settings. Pages 216–20 of: *Proceedings of the 15th International Conference on Artificial Intelligence and Law*. New York, NY: ACM.

Savelka, Jaromir, Ashley, Kevin, and Grabmair, Matthias. 2014. Mining information from statutory texts in multi-jurisdictional settings. Pages 133–42 of: *Legal Knowledge and Information Systems: JURIX 2014: The Twenty-Seventh Annual Conference*, vol. 271. Amsterdam: IOS Press.

Savelka, Jaromir and Grabmair, Matthias. 2015. *(Brief) Introduction to (Selected Aspects of) Natural Language Processing and Machine Learning, Tutorial at Workshop on Automated Detection, Extraction and Analysis of Semantic Information in Legal Texts*. http://people.cs.pitt.edu/~jsavelka/docs/20150612ASAILTutorial.pdf (accessed July 1, 2016).

Savelka, Jaromır, Trivedi, Gaurav, and Ashley, Kevin D. 2015. Applying an interactive machine learning approach to statutory analysis. Pages 101–10 of: *Legal Knowledge and Information Systems: JURIX 2015: The Twenty-Eighth Annual Conference*. Amsterdam: IOS Press.

Schank, Roger C. 1996. Goal-based scenarios: Case-based reasoning meets learning by doing. Pp. 295–347 of: David Leake (ed.), *Case-based Reasoning: Experiences, Lessons & Future Directions*. Menlo Park, CA: AAAI Press/The MIT Press.

Schank, Roger C., Kolodner, Janet L., and DeJong, Gerald. 1981. Conceptual information retrieval. Pages 94–116 of: *Proceedings of the 3rd Annual ACM Conference on Research and Development in Information Retrieval*. SIGIR '80. Kent, UK: Butterworth & Co.

Schauer, Frederick. 1995. Giving reasons. *Stanford Law Review*, 47, 633–59.

Scheer, August-Wilhelm, Kruppke, Helmut, Jost, Wolfram, and Kindermann, Herbert. 2006. *Agility by ARIS Business Process Management: Yearbook Business Process Excellence 2006/2007*, vol. 243. Springer Science & Business Media.

Schwartz, Ariel. 2011. *Why Watson Wagered $947, and Other Intel on the Jeopardy Supercomputer* www.fastcompany.com/1728740/why-watson-wagered-947-and-other-intel-jeopardy-supercompute (accessed February 1, 2015).

Sebastiani, Fabrizio. 2002. Machine learning in automated text categorization. *ACM Computing Surveys (CSUR)*, 34(1), 1–47.

Sergot, Marek J., Sadri, Fariba, Kowalski, Robert A. et al. 1986. The British Nationality Act as a logic program. *Communications of the ACM*, **29**(5), 370–86.

Shrivathsan, Michael. 2009. *Use Cases Definition (Requirements Management Basics)*. http://pmblog.accompa.com/2009/09/19/use-cases-definition-requirements-management-basics/ (accessed July 1, 2016).

Sklar, Howard. 2011. Using built-in sampling to overcome defensibility concerns with computer-expedited review. Pages 155–61 of: *Proceedings of the Fourth DESI Workshop on Setting Standards for Electronically Stored Information in Discovery Proceedings*. Pittsburgh, PA.

Slonim, Noam. 2014. *IBM Debating Technologies How Persuasive Can a Computer Be?* Presentation at Frontiers and Connections between Argumentation Theory and Natural Language Processing Workshop (July 22, 2014). Bertinoro, Italy.

Sohn, Edward. 2013. *Top Ten Concepts to Understand about Predictive Coding*. www.acc.com/legalresources/publications/topten/ttctuapc.cfm (accessed May 27, 2015).

Sowa, John F. 1984. *Conceptual Structures: Information Processing in Mind and Machine*. Boston, MA: Addison-Wesley Longman Publishing Co., Inc.

Sowizral, Henry A. and Kipps, James R. 1985. *Rosie: A Programming Environment for Expert Systems*. Technical Report. DTIC Document.

Spaeth, Harold J., Benesh, Sara, Epstein, Lee et al. 2013. *Supreme Court Database, Version 2013 Release 01* http://supremecourtdatabase.org (accessed August 30, 2015).

Staudt, Ronald and Lauritsen, Marc. 2013. Symposium on justice, lawyering, and legal education in the digital age. *Chicago-Kent Law Review*, **88**(3) http://studentorgs.kentlaw.iit.edu/cklawreview/issues/vol-88-issue-3/ (accessed February 3, 2015).

Steinberger, Raif, Ebrahim, Mohamed, and Ignat, Camelia. 2013. *JRC EuroVoc Indexer JEX-A Freely Available Multi-label Categorisation Tool*. arXiv preprint.

Strötgen, Jannik and Gertz, Michael. 2013. Multilingual and cross-domain temporal tagging. *Language Resources and Evaluation*, **47**(2), 269–98.

Surdeanu, Mihai, Nallapati, Ramesh, Gregory, George, Walker, Joshua, and Manning, Christopher D. 2011. Risk analysis for intellectual property litigation. Pages 116–20 of: *Proceedings of the 13th International Conference on Artificial Intelligence and Law*. New York, NY: ACM.

Susskind, Richard. 2010. *The End of Lawyers?: Rethinking the Nature of Legal Services*. Oxford: Oxford University Press.

Sweeney, Patricia M., Bjerke, Elisabeth E., Potter, Margaret A. et al. 2014. Network analysis of manually-encoded state laws and prospects for automation. In: Winkels, Radboud (ed.), *Network Analysis in Law*. Diritto Scienza Technologia.

Szoke, Akos, Macsar, Krisztian, and Strausz, Gyorgy. 2014. A text analysis framework for automatic semantic knowledge representation of legal documents. Pages 59–66 of: Winkels, Radboud, Lettieri, Nicola, and Faro, Sebastiano (eds.), *Network Analysis in Law*. Collana: Diritto Scienza Tecnologia/Law Science Technology Temi, 3. Napoli: Edizioni Scientifiche Italiane.

Takano, Kenji, Nakamura, Makoto, Oyama, Yoshiko, and Shimazu, Akira. 2010. Semantic analysis of paragraphs consisting of multiple sentences: towards development of a logical formulation system. Pages 117–26 of: *Proceedings of the 2010 Conference on Legal Knowledge and Information Systems: JURIX 2010: The Twenty-Third Annual Conference*. Amsterdam, The Netherlands : IOS Press.

Teufel, Simone, Siddharthan, Advaith, and Batchelor, Colin. 2009. Towards discipline-independent argumentative zoning: evidence from chemistry and computational linguistics. Pages 1493–502 of: *Proceedings of the 2009 Conference on Empirical Methods in Natural Language Processing: Volume 3.* EMNLP '09. Stroudsburg, PA: Association for Computational Linguistics.

Thielscher, Michael. 2011. A unifying action calculus. *Artificial Intelligence*, **175**(1), 120–41.

Thompson, Paul. 2001. Automatic categorization of case law. Pages 70–7 of: *Proceedings of the 8th International Conference on Artificial Intelligence and Law.* New York, NY: ACM.

Tredennick, John. 2014a. *Measuring Recall in E-Discovery Review: A Tougher Problem than You might Realize, Part 1* www.catalystsecure.com/blog/2014/10/measuring-recall-in-e-discovery-review-a-tougher-problem-than-you-might-realize-part-1/ (accessed September 1, 2016).

Tredennick, John. 2014b. *Measuring Recall in E-Discovery Review: A Tougher Problem than You might Realize, Part 2* https://pdfs.semanticscholar.org/4465/8cef0355aa63279f6dc 2657eb1326dac8229.pdf (accessed September 1, 2016).

Turney, Peter D.and Pantel, Patrick. 2010. From frequency to meaning: vector space models of semantics. *Journal of Artificial Intelligence Research*, **37**(1), 141–88.

Turtle, Howard. 1995. Text retrieval in the legal world. *Artificial Intelligence and Law*, **3**(1–2), 5–54.

Turtle, Howard and Croft, W. Bruce. 1990. Inference networks for document retrieval. Pages 1–24 of: *Proceedings of the 13th Annual International ACM SIGIR Conference on Research and Development in Information Retrieval. SIGIR '90.* New York, NY: ACM.

Uyttendaele, Caroline, Moens, Marie-Francine, and Dumortier, Jos. 1998. SALOMON: automatic abstracting of legal cases for effective access to court decisions. *Artificial Intelligence and Law*, **6**(1), 59–79.

van der Pol, Jorke. 2011. *Rules-Driven Business Services: Flexibility with the Boundaries of the Law.* Invited talk of Jorke van der Pol, Senior advisor, Ministry of the Interior and Kingdom Relations, Immigration and Naturalisation Service, The Netherlands at the *Thirteenth International Conference on Artificial Intelligence and Law*, University of Pittsburgh School of Law.

Van Engers, Tom, Boer, Alexander, Breuker, Joost, Valente, André, and Winkels, Radboud. 2008. Ontologies in the legal domain. Pages 233–61 of: *Digital Government.* Dordrecht: Springer.

Van Kralingen, Robert W., Visser, Pepijn R. S., Bench-Capon, Trevor J. M., and Van Den Herik, H. Jaap. 1999. A principled approach to developing legal knowledge systems. *International Journal of Human–Computer Studies*, **51**(6), 1127–54.

Verheij, Bart. 2009. The Toulmin argument model in artificial intelligence. Pages 219–38 of: *Argumentation in Artificial Intelligence.* Dordrecht: Springer.

Verheij, Bart, Bex, Floris, Timmer, Sjoerd T. et al. 2015. Arguments, scenarios and probabilities: connections between three normative frameworks for evidential reasoning. *Law, Probability and Risk*, **15**, 35–70.

Wagner, Karl and Klueckmann, Joerg. 2006. Business process design as the basis for compliance management, enterprise architecture and business rules. Pages 117–27 of: Scheer, August-Wilhelm, Kruppke, Helmut, Jost, Wolfram, and Kindermann, Herbert (eds.), *AGILITY by ARIS Business Process Management.* Berlin Heidelberg: Springer.

Walker, Vern R. 2007. A default-logic paradigm for legal fact-finding. *Jurimetrics*, **47**, 193–243.

Walker, Vern R. 2011. Empirically quantifying evidence assessment in legal decisions. Presentation at the *Second International Conference on Quantitative Aspects of Justice and Fairness* (February 25–6, 2011). Fiesole, Italy.

Walker, Vern R. 2016. The need for annotated corpora from legal documents, and for (human) protocols for creating them: the attribution problem. In: Cabrio, Elena, Hirst, Graeme, Villata, Serena, and Wyner, Adam (eds.), *Natural Language Argumentation:*

Mining, Processing, and Reasoning over Textual Arguments (Dagstuhl Seminar 16161). http://drops.dagstuhl.de/opus/volltexte/2016/6692/pdf/dagrep_v006_i004_p080_s16161.pdf (accessed March 2, 2017).

Walker, Vern R., Bagheri, Parisa, and Lauria, Andrew J. 2015a. *Argumentation Mining from Judicial Decisions: The Attribution Problem and the Need for Legal Discourse Models.* ICAIL 2015 Workshop on Automated Detection, Extraction and Analysis of Semantic Information in Legal Texts (June 12, 2015). San Diego, CA.

Walker, Vern R., Carie, Nathaniel, DeWitt, Courtney C., and Lesh, Eric. 2011. A framework for the extraction and modeling of fact-finding reasoning from legal decisions: lessons from the Vaccine/Injury Project Corpus. *Artificial Intelligence and Law*, 19(4), 291–331.

Walker, Vern R., Lopez, Bernadette C., Rutchik, Matthew T., and Agris, Julie L. 2015b. Representing the logic of statutory rules in the United States. Pages 357–81 of: *Logic in the Theory and Practice of Lawmaking*. Dordrecht: Springer.

Walker, Vern R. and Vazirova, Karina. 2014. Annotating patterns of reasoning about medical theories of causation in vaccine cases: toward a type system for arguments. In *Proceedings of the First Workshop on Argumentation Mining, at the 52nd Annual Meeting of the Association for Computational Linguistics, ACL 2014*, vol. 1. Baltimore, MD.

Walton, Doug and Gordon, Thomas F. 2009. *Legal Reasoning with Argumentation Schemes.* www.dougwalton.ca/talks/09GordonWaltonICAIL.pdf (accessed June 6, 2015).

Walton, Douglas and Gordon, Thomas F. 2005. Critical questions in computational models of legal argument. Pages 103–11 of: Dunne, Paul and Bench-Capon, Trevor (eds.), *Argumentation in Artificial Intelligence and Law*. IAAIL Workshop Series. Nijmegen, The Netherlands: Wolf Legal Publishers.

Wang, Yining, Wang, Liwei, Li, Yuanzhi et al. 2013. A theoretical analysis of NDCG ranking measures. In: *Proceedings of the 26th Annual Conference on Learning Theory (COLT 2013)*. Princeton, NJ.

Waterman, Donald A. and Peterson, Mark A. 1981. *Models of Legal Decision Making: Research Design and Methods*. Rand Corporation, The Institute for Civil Justice.

Weber, Robert C. 2011. Why 'Watson" matters to lawyers. *The National Law Journal.* www.nationallawjournal.com/id=1202481662966/Why-Watson-matters-to-lawyers?slreturn=20150424173345 (accessed May 24, 2015).

Weiss, Charles. 2003. Expressing scientific uncertainty. *Law, Probability and Risk*, 2(1), 25–46.

Winkels, Radboud and Boer, Alexander. 2014. Finding and visualizing context in Dutch legislation. Pages 23–9 of: Winkels, Radboud, Lettieri, Nicola, and Faro, Sebastiano (eds.), *Network Analysis in Law*. Collana: Diritto Scienza Tecnologia/Law Science Technology Temi, 3. Napoli: Edizioni Scientifiche Italiane.

Winkels, Radboud, Bosscher, Doeko, Boer, Alexander, and Hoekstra, Rinke. 2000. Extended conceptual retrieval. Pages 85–97 of: *Legal Knowledge and Information Systems: JURIX 2000: The Thirteenth Annual Conference*. Amsterdam: IOS Press.

Winkels, Radboud and Hoekstra, Rinke. 2012. Automatic extraction of legal concepts and definitions. In: *JURIX 2012: Proceedings of the Twenty-Fifth Conference on Legal Knowledge and Information Systems*. Amsterdam: IOS Press.

WIPO. 2015. *Index of WIPO UDRP Panel Decisions.* www.wipo.int/amc/en/domains/search/legalindex.jsp (accessed February 4, 2015).

Wittgenstein, Ludwig. 1958. *Philosophical Investigations* (3rd edn.). New York: The Macmillan Company.

Wu, Stephen Tze-Inn, Kaggal, Vinod, Dligach, Dmitriy et al. 2013. A common type system for clinical natural language processing. *Journal of Biomedical Semantics*, 4, 1–12.

Wyner, Adam. 2008. An ontology in OWL for legal case-based reasoning. *Artificial Intelligence and Law*, 16(4), 361–87.

Wyner, Adam and Governatori, Guido. 2013. A study on translating regulatory rules from natural language to defeasible logic. In: *Proceedings of RuleML*. Seattle, WA.

Wyner, Adam and Peters, Wim. 2010. Towards annotating and extracting textual legal case factors. Pages 36–45 of: *Proceedings of the Language Resources and Evaluation Conference (LREC 2010), Workshop on Semantic Processing of Legal Texts (SPLeT 2010)*. Valletta, Malta.

Wyner, Adam and Peters, Wim. 2011. On rule extraction from regulations. In: *JURIX 2011: Proceedings of the Twenty-Fourth Conference on Legal Knowledge and Information Systems*. Amsterdam: IOS Press.

Wyner, Adam and Peters, Wim. 2012. Semantic annotations for legal text processing using GATE teamware. Pages 34–6 of: *LREC 2012 Conference Proceedings: Semantic Processing of Legal Texts (SPLeT-2012) Workshop*. Istanbul, Turkey.

Yimam, Seid Muhie, Gurevych, Iryna, de Castilho, Richard Eckart, and Biemann, Chris. 2013. WebAnno: a flexible, web-based and visually supported system for distributed annotations. Pages 1–6 of: *ACL (Conference System Demonstrations)*. Sofia, Bulgaria.

Yoshida, Yutaka, Honda, Kozo, Sei, Yuichi et al. 2013. Towards semi-automatic identification of functional requirements in legal texts for public administration. Pages 175–84 of: *JURIX. Proceedings of the Twenty-Sixth Conference on Legal Knowledge and Information Systems*. Amsterdam: IOS Press.

Yoshino, Hajime. 1995. The systematization of legal meta-inference. Pages 266–75 of: *Proceedings of the 5th International Conference on Artificial Intelligence and Law*. New York, NY: ACM.

Yoshino, Hajime. 1998. Logical structure of contract law system – for constructing a knowledge base of the United Nations Convention on contracts for the international sale of goods. *Journal of Advanced Computational Intelligence*, 2(1), 2–11.

Zeni, Nicola, Kiyavitskaya, Nadzeya, Mich, Luisa, Cordy, James R., and Mylopoulos, John. 2013. GaiusT: supporting the extraction of rights and obligations for regulatory compliance. *Requirements Engineering*, 20, 1–22.

Zhang, Jiansong and El-Gohary, Nora M. 2015. Automated information transformation for automated regulatory compliance checking in construction. *Journal of Computing in Civil Engineering*, 29, B4015001.

Zhang, Paul. 2015. *Semantic Annotation of Legal Texts*. Invited Talk, ICAIL 2015 Workshop on Automated Detection, Extraction and Analysis of Semantic Information in Legal Texts.

Zhang, Paul, Silver, Harry, Wasson, Mark, Steiner, David, and Sharma, Sanjay. 2014. Knowledge network based on legal issues. Pages 21–49 of: Winkels, Radboud, Lettieri, Nicola, and Faro, Sebastiano (eds.), *Network Analysis in Law*. Collana: Diritto Scienza Tecnologia/Law Science Technology Temi, 3. Napoli: Edizioni Scientifiche Italiane.

Zhou, Li and Hripcsak, George. 2007. Temporal reasoning with medical data: a review with emphasis on medical natural language processing. *Journal of Biomedical Informatics*, 40(2), 183–202.

Zywica, Jolene and Gomez, Kimberley. 2008. Annotating to support learning in the content areas: teaching and learning science. *Journal of Adolescent & Adult Literacy*, 52(2), 155–65.

Index

ablation experiments, 120, 124
abstract argumentation framework, 139–141, 147
acceptability, 128–131, 140–141, 145
accuracy, 113–115, 120, 124, 158–159, 239, 242, 262, 265, 291, 292, 294, 297, 305, 326
AGATHA, 121, 151, 160
Aharoni, E., 306, 307, 372, 377
Akoma Ntoso, 181, 182
Al-Kofahi, K., 248–253
Aleven, V., 81, 85, 90–92, 115, 139, 185, 298
algorithm, 4, 22, 36, 40, 53, 88, 92, 96, 108–111, 113–116, 125, 158, 204, 234, 238, 242, 247, 251
  A* best-first search, 96
  answer-typing, 204
  CATO prediction, 115
  clustering, 247
  downplaying/emphasizing distinctions, 92
  hard/easy questions of law, 22, 40
  IBP hypothesis-testing, 116–120
  k nearest neighbor, *k*-NN, 108, 115, 296, 297
  logistic regression, 305
  machine learning, 114, 125, 234–239, 242, 247, 251–252, 254, 255, 264, 266, 275, 278, 289, 297, 301, 305
    decision tree, 110–112, 232, 239, 251, 261, 278, 294, 296, 297, 305
    metrics, 114
    naïve Bayes, 261, 289, 297, 305
    support vector machine, SVM, 242, 251–253, 256, 261, 264, 266, 278, 291
  NLP, 270
  simulated annealing, 158
  statutory interpretation, 53
Allen, L., 40–47, 57, 63
Araszkiewicz, M., 166
Araucaria, 286, 288, 291, 293, 294

argument, 287
argument mining, 5, 23–27, 293, 328, 372, 376
argument retrieval, 11, 164, 299, 316–320, 328, 335, 339, 350, 359
argument scheme, 129, 130, 134–139, 141–145, 147, 149–158, 160, 166, 188, 190, 196–199, 201, 286, 292, 294, 315, 334, 336, 338, 361, 365, 379
argument-related information, 26, 31, 34, 35, 106, 167, 185, 201, 285–294, 299–310, 315, 316, 321, 327–334, 342, 359, 361, 368, 376, 377, 381, 383, 391
argumentation framework, 129, 131, 141, 143
  abstract, 140–141, 148
  Carneades, 131, 139
Ashley, K., 30, 76, 81–87, 116–120, 131, 135, 137–139, 185–201, 239–241, 261, 276, 280, 287, 294–298, 300, 302, 365
Atkinson, K., 140–143, 148, 185
attribution, 26, 363, 369–371
augmented transition network, ATN, 19, 65

Bach, N. X., 262, 269, 282
backward chaining, 10, 48, 94, 132, 156, 165
BankXX, 232
Bauer, R., 240
Bayes rule, 289
Bayesian network, 148, 218–221
Belew, R., 230, 231, 354
Bench-Capon, T., 64, 100–103, 121, 139–143, 148, 151, 200, 333
Berman, D., 40, 53–56, 63, 97–100, 102, 154, 185, 187
Bex, F., 160
Biagioli, C., 261
Bing, J., 12

—